WESTERN CIVILIZATION

A Brief Introduction

WESTERN CIVILIZATION

A Brief Introduction

F. ROY WILLIS

University of California, Davis

Macmillan Publishing Company

New York

Macmillan Publishing Company
866 Third Avenue, New York, New York 10022

Collier Macmillan Canada, Inc.

Library of Congress Cataloging-in-Publication Data

Willis, F. Roy (Frank Roy),
  Western civilization.

  Includes bibliographies and index.
  1. Civilization, Occidental—History. I. Title.
CB245.W55 1987   909'.09821   86-12469
ISBN 0-02-428110-7

Printing: 5 6 7   Year: 0 1 2 3

ISBN 0-02-428110-7

Preface

This book is approximately half the length of the volumes that form the staple intellectual diet for the students in Western Civilization courses. It was written in the firm belief that a book that achieves full, balanced coverage of the course of Western Civilization without indulgence in intricate detail and plethora of issues would be a valid alternative for professors and students alike. For the past fourteen years, I have taught a one-quarter course at the University of California, Davis, that surveys in ten weeks the development of Western Civilization from the Persian Wars in the fifth century B.C. to the First World War twenty-four centuries later. I was therefore acquainted with both the challenges and the opportunities of presenting a brief introduction to the variety of the history and culture of the West, and I could approach the writing of this book with a pragmatic awareness of the potential pitfalls and satisfactions in what I was undertaking. The French philosopher Blaise Pascal put his finger on an important truth when he apologized to a friend, "I have made this letter longer than usual because I lack the time to make it shorter."

For the professor, a brief history of Western Civilization like this one can be used in several different ways. If assigned as the principal reading matter, it makes it possible to teach a survey of the whole evolution of Western Civilization in a one-semester or even a one-quarter course without imposing excessive reading assignments on the student. Second, it can be used to provide the essential background material needed by the student in courses where the professor chooses to assign substantial readings in primary sources, either by use of an anthology or by selection of individual texts. Chapter 2, on the Greeks, for example, provides the information on Greek religion and drama necessary for informed reading of such a play as Sophocles's *Antigone*. Reading the *Communist Manifesto* becomes more meaningful after the study in Chapter 14 of the emergence of class antagonism in the factory cities of northern England. Third, a short but comprehensive text permits the professor to expand in lectures upon selected themes or to make use of audiovisual materials without fear that the student will be missing necessary coverage.

For the student, a short book has a number of advantages. Since excessive detail has been pruned away, the most important topics stand out more clearly. The sequence of events appears more logical. The interrelationship of different aspects of society and culture becomes more evident. For example, in seeking to explain the changing status of women in Western society, to which great attention is given in this book, I have shown how status was affected by the nature of the legal codes, whether Hammurabi's in the eighteenth century B.C. or the Emperor Augustus's in the first century A.D.

To achieve brevity without sacrificing comprehensiveness, I have used a number of methods. A framework of analysis, described in the Introduction, is followed in approaching each society studied, enabling the student to make increasingly valid comparisons between societies. The economic base of the society of Greece in the fifth century B.C., for example, can be compared with those of the Roman empire in the first century A.D. and of the Byzantine empire of the sixth century A.D. Quotations have been chosen not merely to introduce a specific author but to provide source material on a particular society. For example, the chaotic conditions of life in imperial Rome are described in quotations from the poems of Ovid and Juvenal, the sufferings of soldiers in the First World War in the verse of Wilfred Owen. Photographs have been closely integrated with the text and are themselves an important teaching device. Timelines provide a guide to the interrelationship of events. The maps have been designed for clarity of reference and to provide graphic illustration of themes discussed in the text, such as the threat of fragmentation posed to the Austrian empire in the nineteenth century by its incorporation of many non-German nationalities. Suggested readings at the end of each chapter direct the student to the most significant recent scholarship.

The book combines three basic forms of coverage. First, there is a clear chronological coverage, emphasizing political and economic events. Second, there is a full exploration of the cultural achievements of the West, in philosophy, literature, arts, and music. Third, I have paid great attention to the advances in social history during the past two decades. The book therefore includes study of (a) the role of women and minorities; (b) the nature of the popular culture of the illiterate as compared with the so-called "high" culture of the educated classes; and (c) details of social life, such as health, diet, working conditions, and social disturbances. Fourth, although the book is not a history of world civilization, the relationship of the West to the rest of the world's peoples and cultures is described. The rise of Islam, for example, is shown to have important repercussions on the society of medieval Europe.

I am grateful to a number of colleagues, whose invaluable suggestions greatly helped in preparation of the manuscript: Ted Bogacz, U.S. Naval Academy; Louise E. Hoffman, The Pennsylvania State University at Harrisburg; Hans Kellner, Michigan State University; John A. Mears, Southern Methodist University; Robert J. Moore, Columbia College; Perry M. Rogers, The Ohio State University; Don Thomas Sine, U.S. Naval Academy; John L. Tevebaugh, Grand Valley State College; William A. Vincent, Michigan State University; Charles W. Weber, Wheaton College; and Richard Wires, Ball State University. I am also indebted to Sidney Zimmerman, a developmental editor of extraordinary abilities, who has also prepared the *Instructor's Manual* to accompany this text.

Finally, I hope that both professor and student will find the book enjoyable. As an inveterate traveler, I have always found great pleasure both in teaching and writing about the history of civilization. I can only wish that this enthusiasm proves infectious.

F. R. W.

Contents

part II   The Middle Ages

8 The Two Reformations   232

9 The Overseas Discoveries and the New Empires   256

part *IV*   The Age of Absolutism

10   Power and Glory in the Seventeenth Century   287

part **V**   **Revolution and Reaction**

13   The Atlantic Revolution, 1776–1815   375

14   The Industrial Revolution   399

15   The Conservative Reaction, 1815–1848   *421*

part *VI*   The Age of Nationalism and Imperialism

16   The Zenith of the European Nation-State, 1848–1914   *444*

part *VII* The Contemporary Age

19 The Age of Dictators, 1919–1945   *519*

List of Maps
and Timelines

Maps

Timelines

WESTERN CIVILIZATION

A Brief Introduction

Introduction: The Study of Civilization

Civilized life began about 10,000 years ago when human beings in various parts of the world began to change from hunters and food gatherers, and started to develop settled agriculture, metallurgy, specialization by occupation, writing, and urban communities. From that time on, human beings lived in complex, structured societies. The purpose of this book is to study the history of that part of those societies which is known as "Western." The Greek word for *west* was used to refer to the place where the sun sets, while their word for *east* was where it rises. As a result, for Greeks the continent of Europe was Western, and Asia was Eastern. We have inherited their distinction. Western civilization is then, quite simply, the civilization that developed on the continent of Europe and was carried to, and further developed in, areas in other parts of the globe that were colonized by people from Europe.

How is one to study civilization, if one conceives it in the broadest sense as a whole gamut of activities and experiences of human beings living together in complex societies? The approach adopted in this book is quite consciously to separate the interconnecting relationships that form the structure of each society studied, to examine what we can of each facet of that society, and then to attempt to reintegrate them into a whole.

First, each of the societies we shall study has its own economic structure, which means its method of producing and distributing the commodities necessary for its everyday life and for the support of noneconomic activities such as religion or art. For each society, therefore, we must ask what was the form of this society's agriculture, its artisan or industrial production, and the services it provided.

Second, upon this economic base and frequently as a result of the nature of that base, a system of social relationships was created. We shall be interested in knowing how the wealth created by the economic system was shared by the different groups within the society. We shall also want to look at the relationships among these groups—whether there is social and economic movement within this system, either upward or downward—and at the characteristic ways of life of these social groups.

Third, each of these societies has a political superstructure, or government. We shall want to know how power was distributed among the social groups we have previously identified, and what provisions were made for changing that distribution. It will be important to know the political theory underlying this distribution of power, and whether there existed in the society other forms of political theory that seemed to the inhabitants of the society to offer a more desirable method of government than that currently in force. In such a case, we shall be searching for the origins of revolution.

Fourth, every society assigns its available resources, both human and material, to uses established either by public authorities or by private groups and individuals. How the society uses its resources tells us a great deal about the character of that society. Public expenditure determines to an important degree the quality of life of a society. For example, it establishes the proportion of the society's resources that are used for military purposes or for public health. Private expenditures not only are an indication of the distribution of wealth within the society, but give an insight into individual goals. The turning point— for the worse—in Dutch society of the seventeenth century came when the Calvinist middle classes gave up their subdued dark clothing and began to ape their French enemies by wearing extravagant silks and satins.

Fifth, each society develops its distinctive culture, which, in the broadest sense, can be defined as a world of ideas, beliefs, and patterns of behavior. Until recently, in the study of civilization, "culture" was defined as the achievements of leading thinkers and artists. Now their creative work is often referred to as "higher culture" or "formal culture." These achievements have been one of the most important elements in shaping Western ways of thought, and they receive significant attention in this book. But the study of Western civilization has been greatly changed in the past two decades or so, because researchers in social history and in such related fields of the social sciences as anthropology and sociology have made it possible to understand a good deal of the mental world, the so-called popular culture, of the less educated and less articulate classes of the society—the peasants, the urban workers, and the underprivileged. We shall therefore also be interested in the thoughts and experience of the groups who throughout history have formed the majority of the population.

Finally, the members of every society formulate their values. They define the relationship of human beings to a god or gods, and thus develop their religion; they determine how human beings should treat each other and thus shape their ethical concepts; they also decide their society's concept of the beautiful, or rather its many concepts, and thus lay down their view of the aesthetically desirable. We shall therefore also look at the value systems developed over time in the West.

This, then, is the framework of analysis that will be employed in this book, although we shall try hard not to apply it in a mechanical way. There are, however, two warnings that should be made.

The first concerns the concept of time. This book is organized in time spans to help us make sense of the many events, lives, and movements that form an indispensable factual basis for understanding Western civilization. But time is very different in character depending on what we are dealing with. Change can be long-term, as with changes in the methods of premodern agricultural production or in the ways of preliterate thought. Changes that are "medium-term" might take place over a century or more before being established, as in the coming of Protestantism in the sixteenth century or the development of modern scientific concepts in the seventeenth. Short-term change is just what the phrase implies, the rapid bustle of events on a daily or yearly basis, which may or may not form part of a lasting pattern within a given society. We should, in short, ask ourselves, when we turn to analyze the many sides of Western society described here, in what time frame we are working.

Second, there is a danger in studying Western civilization, and in particular in looking for certain traits that set Western human beings apart from those in other civilizations. By narrowing our focus, we risk missing the interconnections that exist between Western and other civilizations. The evolution of Western civilization was affected at every stage by its relationship with other civilizations; and, increasingly from the time of the Greeks on, Western civilization affected other civilizations. These connections have been pointed out throughout the book. Medieval Europe, for example, is incomprehensible without some understanding of the rise of Islam.

Nevertheless, while bearing the previous warning in mind, it is justifiable for us to concentrate for a while on understanding the evolution of our own society in order to understand ourselves. Western society today is heir to, and in fact the result of, what has happened in the West in the past 10,000 years. We possess religious traditions, forms of state, class structures, economic systems, cultural inheritances, and ways of thought and behavior that have been formed by the course of our history. The story is not an unalloyed source of self-congratulation. There is destruction as well as creativity, exploitation as well as self-sacrifice, conflict as well as cooperation. But without knowledge of our past in all its diversity, our lives will lack an essential dimension.

part I
The Ancient World

The Discus Thrower, by Myron (late fifth century B.C.) *The classical vision of the consummate athlete.* (Alinari/Art Resource.)

THE ANCIENT WORLD

Dates	Political & Military Events	Social, Economic, & Demographic Events	Religion & Philosophy	Art, Architecture, Literature, & Music	Science & Technology
B.C. DATES					
c. 4 million		Humanlike creatures appear			
c. 3 million		Homosapiens appear			Old Stone Age: stone tools, fire
c. 100,000					
c. 14,000			Magical rites, fertility goddesses	Cave paintings; sculpture; engravings on bone	New Stone Age: sophisticated stone tools
c. 8,000		Plant cultivation, domestication of animals, farming villages		Rock paintings; sculpture	Copper tools, weapons; flood control; irrigation; textile weaving; pottery
c. 3,500	Sumerian city-states	Rule of priests	Creation and flood myths; belief in afterlife; polytheism	Invention of writing: cuneiform	
c. 3,000		Advanced agriculture in Nile Valley		Hieroglyphics	Bronze
c. 2,700	Old Kingdom, Egypt		Worship of Re, Osiris; pharaoh as god (Egypt)	Sumer: Gilgamesh epic; pyramids (Egypt); ziggurats (Sumer)	Early mathematics; potter's wheel
c. 2,200		Semitic peoples in Fertile Crescent			
c. 2,000	Minoan Kingdom, Crete	Seaborne trade in Eastern Mediterranean	Worship of female deities; bull leaping ritual (Crete)	Palace of Knossos; syllabic writing	
c. 1,900	Abraham, Hebrew patriarch	Wanderings of Hebrews from Mesopotamia to Canaan	Hebrew covenant with god Yahweh		
c. 1,750	Hammurabi, Babylon	Barley, silver as currency in trade; written law-code	Worship of Marduk (Babylon)		
c. 1,700	Indo-Europeans in Fertile Crescent			Indo-European languages develop	Mathematical advances

c. 1,600	Mycenae founded				Iron-smelting; medical diagnosis of illness
c. 1,550				Temple of Karnak (Egypt)	
c. 1,500				Temple of Queen Hatshepsut (Egypt)	
c. 1,400				Temple of Luxor (Egypt)	
c. 1,350	Akhenaton, Egypt	Phoenician colonists in Mediterranean	Monotheism—worship of Aton (Egypt)	Phoenician alphabet	
c. 1,300	Moses	Exodus from Egypt	Ten Commandments to Hebrews		
c. 1,225	d. Ramses II, Egypt			Temple of Abu Simbel (Egypt)	Use of iron spreads to Europe
c. 1,200	Indo-Europeans enter Europe. Assyrian Empire. Dark Age in Greece; Dorian invasions	Agricultural settlements at Sparta, formation Greek city-states			
c. 1,000	Hebrew Kingdom David Solomon			Psalms	
c. 800		Overpopulation in Greece; overseas colonization	Hebrew prophets Greek polytheism	Greece: Olympic games; Greek epics—Homer, Hesiod; vase painting begins	
c. 750	City of Rome founded				
c. 722	Assyrians conquer Israel				
c. 604	Nebuchadnezzar, Babylon (604–562)				
c. 594	Solon, Athens	Reforms of constitution, laws (Athens)			
c. 586			Babylonian Captivity of Jews		
c. 522	Darius I, Persia (c. 522–486)			Sappho (Greece)	Discovery of new planets

(continued)

THE ANCIENT WORLD (continued)

Dates	Political & Military Events	Social, Economic, & Demographic Events	Religion & Philosophy	Art, Architecture, Literature, & Music	Science & Technology
c.					
507			d. Pythagoras		
500	Roman republic formed		Sophists (Athens) Polytheism in Rome		
490	Persian Wars (490–79)				
461	Pericles' rule, Athens (461–29)			Temples on Acropolis; sculpture; drama; history (Greece)	
456				d. Aeschylus	
431	Peloponnesian War (431–404)				
406				d. Sophocles d. Euripides	
400				d. Thucydides	
399			d. Socrates		
370					d. Hippocrates
347			d. Plato		
336	Alexander the Great (336–323)	Alexandria founded			
323	Division of Alexander's Empire				
322			d. Aristotle		
264	First Punic War (264–41)	Expansion of slavery in Rome; small farmers dispossessed; great estates formed			
218	Second Punic War (218–12)				
149	Third Punic War (149–46); destruction of Carthage				Astrolabe invented (mid-2nd century)

Dates					
73		Slave revolt: Spartacus			
54				d. Catullus	Julian Calendar
46					
44	d. Julius Caesar				
43			d. Cicero		
27	Augustus, Emperor (27 B.C.–A.D. 14)			Augustan Age of Literature	
19				d. Virgil	
8				d. Horace	
A.D. DATES			Birth of Christ (? 8–4)		
14	Julio-Claudian emperors (14–68)				
18				d. Ovid	
29			Crucifixion of Christ		
67			Execution St. Peter, St. Paul	Nero's Golden House	
69	Flavian Dynasty (69–96)				
70			Sack of Jerusalem	Imperial Forums, Colosseum, Rome	
117	Hadrian, Emperor (117–38)				Ptolemy
123				d. Tacitus	
161	Marcus Aurelius, Emperor (161–80)		Marcus Aurelius, *Meditations*		
200					d. Galen
211	Caracalla, Emperor (211–17)		Christian catacombs, Rome		Imperial baths
235	Breakdown of imperial government (235–84)	Gothic raids across Danube			
284	Diocletian, Emperor (284–305)				

1

The Ancient Near East

THE BEGINNINGS: PRE-HISTORY

Civilized life developed very late in the history of our planet, and even in the history of the human species. The earth is now thought to be about 5 billion years old. Life in its most primitive form of a one-celled organism may have originated about 2 billion years ago. The earliest creature resembling a human being, and hence known as "hominid" or "humanlike," lived between 3 and 4 million years ago, and probably, from the evidence of the oldest fossils found, originated in Africa. But the ancestor of the human beings who live on the planet today, the species called *homo sapiens*, cannot be dated back before 100,000 years ago and was not widely spread around the world until 40,000 years ago.[1] And only about 10,000 years ago did *homo sapiens*, by then the only surviving form of human being, begin to cultivate food and domesticate animals, the two skills essential to the development of settled, civilized communities.

The Old Stone Age

The earliest period of human history is known as the Stone Age, because the majority of the tools and weapons discovered by archeologists are made of

---

[1] All early dates are approximate, and are rounded off as an average of the earliest and latest estimates. The dates in pre-history refer to those areas where change first occurred, and do not imply simultaneous advance in all parts of the world. The Neolithic Age, for example, ended in Mesopotamia in 4000 B.C. but continued in Britain until the first century B.C.

Paleolithic Cave Paintings, Lascaux, France (c. 14,000 B.C.) These realistic depictions of bison, antelope, and deer probably evoked religious blessings upon the hunt. (Caisse Nationale des Monuments Historiques et des Sites. © Arch. Phot., Paris/SPADEM/VAGA, New York, 1986.)

stone, although early human beings also used wood and bone. Beginning about 3 or 4 million years ago, during what is called the Paleolithic or Old Stone Age, human beings developed tools, learned the use of fire, and communicated by use of language. For subsistence, they hunted and gathered food such as berries, fruits, and wild grains, and so the age is also referred to as the "hunter-gatherer" period.

The polar ice cap advanced four times between 600,000 and 10,000 B.C. and covered large parts of Asia, Europe, and North America. In spite of huge climatic and ecological changes, however, human beings showed their adaptability by surviving. Life for most was, however, harsh in the extreme. They lived in small family or tribal groups in which the men could collaborate in hunting savage animals or in fishing. The women stayed behind to look after the children, to gather the seeds and wild berries, and to make clothing for the families by stitching animal skins with bone needles and by weaving primitive cloth from rough fibers.

The New Stone Age

During the Neolithic or New Stone Age (8000–4000 B.C.), advances were made almost simultaneously in several parts of the world. Seeds were selected and planted so that they would reproduce, and settled farming villages were created in the center of the fields of wheat, barley, and millet. While women were probably responsible for the development of agriculture, since they were the ones who chose and planted the seeds, men, as the hunters, were responsible for the herding of wild animals, such as sheep, goats and cattle, into fenced enclosures, and thus for the eventual establishment of domesticated herds that would provide a ready supply of milk, cheese, and meat. Thus, during the New

11

Stone Age, the food supply was more secure and ample, as well as more appetizing than during the Old Stone Age. Not only did Neolithic people have baked meat and fish, but bread, porridge, barley cakes, squash, yams, and, as early as 8000 B.C., beer made from fermented cereals.

The change from food gathering to food producing was probably most advanced in the upland plateau that stretches from the eastern edge of Asia Minor across the upper reaches of the Tigris and Euphrates rivers as far as Iran, as well as in the oases farther south in Palestine. In this area are some of the oldest cities yet excavated. The earliest was Jericho, which was founded about 8000 B.C.

One of the most fascinating prehistoric cities is Catal Hüyük in southern Anatolia or modern Turkey. Founded about 6000 B.C., Catal Hüyük covered 24 acres. Its inhabitants lived in one-story houses with flat roofs, built around inner courtyards. With the wealth made from trade in obsidian, a volcanic glass that can be used for jewelry, mirrors, or knives, life had become more luxurious. The food supply now included honey for sweetening, wine from blackberries, vegetable oil, nuts, and fruits. Religion had entered the home. One room in five was devoted to a shrine to a female goddess of fertility who was served by female priests. Women seem to have dominated the household as well. Permanent, spacious platforms were provided for them in the living rooms where the elders' councils met, while men had only tiny, movable platforms. (The discovery of many sculpted heads of bulls suggests that they worshipped the bull as well.) Some scholars, in fact, have concluded that the normal society in the New Stone Age was a matriarchy.

The Age of Copper, c. 4000–2500 B.C.

About 4000 B.C. human beings in the Near East turned to the next crucial task in the development of civilization, the formation of a technology that would enable them to gain greater control over their environment. Within a thousand years they had created a series of inventions that were to transform not only their material existence, but their forms of government, ways of religion, social structure, and their intellectual capacity.

The working of metals, first copper in about 4000 B.C. and then bronze, the harder alloy of copper and tin, in about 3000 B.C., provided far more reliable and versatile tools and weapons than could have been made with stone. The wheel came into wide use for many purposes. Solid disks of wood and later spoked wheels were added to carts, making it possible to transport people and goods far more effectively than on the sleds used previously. And the wheel was also adapted to the making of pottery, thus enabling the potter to increase production and to achieve symmetry and variety of design. Invention of the plow in the rain-watered lands at the north of the Tigris and Euphrates valleys a little before 3000 B.C., and the harnessing of oxen to the plow, vastly increased the productivity of the land and of the people working it. Advances in carpentry

Cuneiform Writing from Babylon (c. 2300 B.C.) *In cuneiform, or wedge-shaped, writing, the symbols were made by pressing a stylus into a wet clay tablet. This tablet is a record of salary payment made in return for temple services.* (The Metropolitan Museum of Art; acquired in exchange with J. Pierpont Morgan Library, 1911.)

and in <u>use of sails made it possible to employ far larger boats on the Nile and the Tigris and Euphrates, and thus enhanced long-distance trade.</u>

Perhaps most important of all in the long run was the invention in Mesopotamia of writing, in order to record the spoken word. This achievement was first carried out in Sumeria, the area at the mouth of the Tigris and Euphrates rivers. Here priests, wishing originally to have an accurate record of the deposits of grain in the temple warehouses, invented cuneiform, or "wedge-shaped" writing. Using a reed shaped like a wedge that they jabbed into a tablet of wet clay, which was later baked, they devised about 2000 signs by which all sounds employed in human speech could be written down.

These inventions were the technological foundations for what the archeologist V. Gordon Childe has called the "Urban Revolution." They made possible the feeding of an increasing population in cities, differentiation of occupations, expansion of trade, development of law and judicial administration, provision of a surplus for support of intellectual, artistic, and religious life, and an enormous advance in the organizational and coercive powers of government. The expansion of agricultural villages into great cities created a vitally new form of human community, which was henceforth to be the major instrument of change in our civilization. In the ancient Near East, two areas proved especially receptive to this new way of life—the Nile Valley of Egypt and the Fertile Crescent, the vast arc of fertile land that stretched from Palestine on the eastern Mediterranean to the valleys of the Tigris and Euphrates rivers in Mesopotamia.

THE CIVILIZATION OF MESOPOTAMIA

The valleys of the Tigris and Euphrates rivers are known as Mesopotamia, from the Greek words meaning "between the rivers." This area was divided into three clearly marked regions. The marshy delta, where annually the swollen waters of the rivers deposited a rich coating of silt over the low-lying land, was Sumer or Sumeria. The plains on the middle reaches of the rivers, with adequate rainfall but little flooding, was first known as Akkad, but later came to be known as Babylonia, after the city of Babylon. The third region, in the north at the headwaters of the rivers, was conquered by the Assyrians between the eleventh and seventh century B.C. and became known as Assyria. Thus, the history of early Mesopotamia can be envisaged as a periodic shift northward of the center of political power. The city states of Sumeria, which developed between 3500 and 3000 B.C., were dominant for the following millenium. Preeminence was taken by Akkad-Babylonia about 2400 B.C., at first under King Sargon I of Akkad and later under the kingdom known as Old Babylonia. Assyria continually expanded from about 1200 B.C. until it was crushed in 612 B.C. by the combined forces of Medes and Chaldeans, after which there was a brief revival of Babylonia under the Chaldeans or New Babylonians.

The City-States of Sumeria, c. 3500–2400 B.C.

The Sumerian people, who settled in the delta of the Tigris and Euphrates rivers from about 4000 B.C. and began to form city-states there about 500 years later, probably originated in Iran or even farther to the East. They spoke a language totally distinct from those of the other peoples who settled in the Tigris and Euphrates valleys, and almost nothing is known about them before they settled in small agricultural villages among the delta swamps. Between 3500 and 3000 B.C., however, they had formed a complex society of city-states of which we possess rich material and written records.

The basis of the Sumerian economic system lay in control of the waters of the delta of the Tigris and Euphrates rivers. Each year, the melting snows of the northern mountains caused the two rivers to deposit a thick layer of fertile silt among the swamps of the delta. The silt could only be worked, however, after fields had been either drained or irrigated by means of elaborate canals and embankments, which required the coordinated work of thousands of laborers. The grains, fruits, and animals raised on these fields supported a heavy density of population.

The society that evolved on this agricultural foundation was hierarchical. At its base was a class of slaves, captured in wars with other cities, or citizens sold into slavery for debt. The greater part of the population were free peasants who were, however, required to participate in the communal works of water engineering. Above them were the groups involved in the administration and protection of this society. The needs of defense, which grew greater as cities

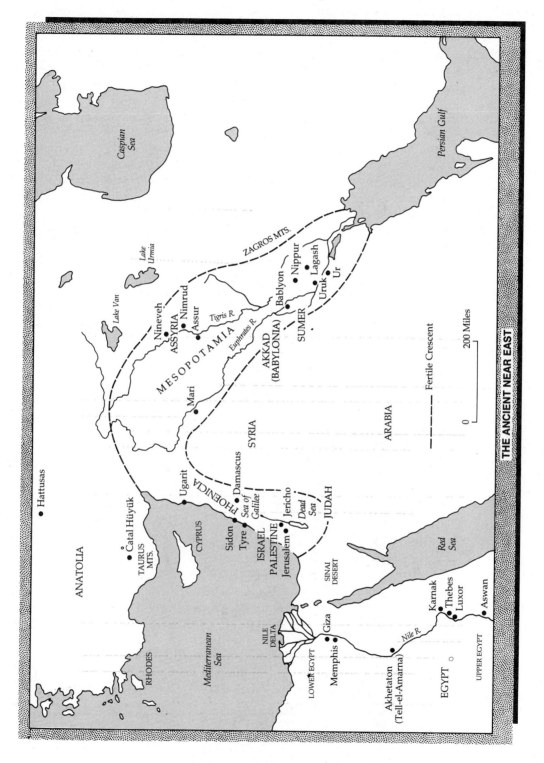

THE ANCIENT NEAR EAST

15

fought over water rights or over the extension of their agricultural land, were the responsibility of military aristocrats, who were also large landowners, commanded by a king. Administrative tasks were closely allied to religious functions, since planting and harvests required anticipation of the annual floods and planning was dependent on an understanding of natural forces regarded as expressions of the will of the gods. The administration was carried out by priestly bureaucrats living in a separate section of the city, in a temple community. A large class of scribes carried out basic judicial functions and supervised the purchase of agricultural produce, recorded its price, and oversaw its sale. Priests not only acted as intermediaries of the citizens with their gods, but also supervised the calendar, predicted the floods, and planned the harvests.

Political leadership at first lay in the hands of the priestly class, who were considered to have been delegated the right of rule by the gods. By about 3000 B.C., however, as wars became more frequent, the kings became preeminent, taking for themselves positions of the priestly and warrior classes.

Priority in the use of the society's resources thus lay with the kings, priests, and nobles. The peasants lived in villages of mudbricks in the fields, while the city laborers and traders lived and worked in cramped homes and workshops

King Gudea of Lagash (c. 2100 B.C.) Gudea built fifteen large temples in honor of the god Ningirsu. He is shown here in the clothing and posture of a Sumerian priest-king. (The Metropolitan Museum of Art, purchase, Dick Fund 1959.)

in narrow alleyways between the temple compound and the riverfront. Within the temple compound itself were workshops for the hundreds of specialized artisans serving the needs of the temple, such as jewelers and carpenters, as well as elaborate homes for the priests. The two most elaborate buildings of the city were the palace of the king and the temple of the city god, built in a terraced foundation and known as a ziggurat. The extent to which the kings had succeeded in taking for themselves a large share of the city's surplus was demonstrated when the English archeologist Leonard Woolley excavated a royal tomb at Ur. With growing horror, his party uncovered not only a splendid array of golden daggers and headdresses, carvings in carnelian and lapis lazuli, and elaborate chariots, but row after row of skeletons in rich costumes. At the king's death, many of his courtiers and soldiers had died with him, probably after taking a drug that made them lie unconscious while the grave was filled in over them.

The intellectual achievements of the priestly class were of lasting importance. They had, as we saw, developed cuneiform writing. In order to plan the farming year, they studied the cycles of the sun and moon, and produced a calendar with twelve lunar months, to which they added an extra month every third year to agree with the solar year. They based part of their numerical system on the number 60, and hence from them we have taken our 60-minute hour and the division of the circle into 360 degrees. To survey the fields and to restore the boundaries after the floods, they created very accurate methods of measurement, such as the calculation of the area of a rectangle. Their most important function, however, was to administer the religion.

The Sumerians were polytheistic; that is, they worshipped many gods. Some of them were common to all the Sumerian cities. Inana was the goddess of love, war, and fertility; Anu was the god of the sky. Many lesser gods were believed to interfere in human activities, bringing either evil or good, and thus making essential the mediation of the priests. Each city believed that one particular god was its patron and owner, and that the agent of that god, probably originally one of the priests and later the military leader, ruled the city on behalf of that god.

The priests elaborated a complicated system of religious beliefs and customs, and drew up a mythology whose purpose was to explain the nature of the gods and the character of life on earth. A rich epic literature was passed on orally before being written down, of which the most important poems that have survived were a description of the creation of the earth and the *Epic of Gilgamesh*, a being one-third man who, after the death of his best friend, demands that the gods reveal to him the secret of immortality.

Gilgamesh sets off in search of Utnapishtim, who has been given eternal life as a reward for saving human beings and animals from destruction during a great flood. In a superb telling of the story of the flood, which parallels in many ways the tale of Noah in the Old Testament of the Bible, Utnapishtim graphically describes the storm that had overwhelmed the earth:

For six days and six nights the winds blew, torrent and tempest and flood overwhelmed the world, tempest and flood raged together like warring hosts. When the seventh day dawned the storm from the south subsided, the sea grew calm, and the flood was stilled; I looked at the face of the world and there was silence, mankind was turned to clay.[2]

Utnapishtim at first scorns Gilgamesh, who has fallen asleep when told as a test to stay awake for six days and seven nights. "Look at him," says Utnapishtim, "the strong man who would have everlasting life, even now the mists of sleep are drifting over him." Finally, however, he takes pity on Gilgamesh and tells him where to find a plant that gives eternal life. But even then Gilgamesh allows a serpent to eat it; and the poem ends with his people's lament for his entry into eternal darkness. "Fate has spoken; like a hooked fish he lies stretched on the bed, like a gazelle that is caught in a noose."

Sargon I of Akkad

The Sumerians were conquered in the twenty-fourth century B.C. by Sargon I (reigned c. 2370–2315), the king of the region of Akkad. The Akkadians were among the earliest of the many peoples to move into the Fertile Crescent from the Arabian peninsula and the Syrian desert who are known as Semitic. The name Semitic implied that they were all considered to be descended from Shem, the eldest son of Noah, but it is used today to indicate that they all spoke languages with a similar root. The Semitic peoples include, in addition to the Akkadians, the Amorites, the Canaanites, the Arameans, the Hebrews, and the Arabs.

The Akkadians restricted the use of the Sumerian language to religious texts and services, and used their own Semitic language for everyday life; but they took over most of the Sumerian cultural achievements as well as their economic system. Sargon was reputed to have governed justly and to have used his armies to extend the trade of the cities. His successors were faced with numerous revolts of the peoples they had conquered, however, and the empire collapsed in the middle of the twenty-second century B.C. Sumerian power revived briefly, but about 2000 B.C. the Sumerians were conquered by Elamite invaders, from Iran, while at roughly the same time Akkad was taken over by a Semitic people called Amorites. The destruction carried out by the Elamites in the delta was devastating. The city of Ur was burned down and many of its inhabitants slaughtered, as one of their poets recalled two centuries later when they finally were able to rebuild the city:

Ur—its weak and its strong perished through hunger;
Mothers and fathers who did not leave their houses were overcome by fire;
The young, lying on their mothers' laps, like fish were carried off by the waters;

[2] *The Epic of Gilgamesh,* translated by N. K. Sanders (Harmondsworth, England: Penguin Books, 1972), pp. 111, 114, 119.

In the city the wife was abandoned, the son was abandoned, the possessions were
scattered about . . .
O Nanna, Ur has been destroyed, its people have been dispersed.[3]

Hammurabi and the Old Babylonian Kingdom

The Amorites conquered the whole of Mesopotamia during the following century. They established their capital at the village of Babylon (from an old Semitic
word, "babili," meaning "gates of the gods"), and hence the Amorites' kingdom
is called Old Babylonia. (A kingdom we call New Babylonia was established in
the same area about 1400 years later.) The Old Babylonians did little to develop
the civilization they had inherited from Sumeria. They accepted Sumerian religion and merely revised the myths to insert their own god Marduk as the
creator of all things. Some advances were made in mathematics, such as the
use of quadratic equations. Trade was facilitated by a more reliable system of
pricing expressed in barley or later in silver. Bureaucrats were well trained to
administer the provinces of the empire.

The most important Babylonian ruler, Hammurabi (c. 1792–1750 B.C.), is
best remembered for his law code, which was written in cuneiform on a stone
shaft set up in a public place. Although Hammurabi increased the severity of
punishment, especially for those guilty of crimes against the state, using whip-
ping, mutilation, or execution, he did regard himself as the protector of the
weak and in particular of women and children.

Nevertheless, many earlier laws that discriminated against women remained in force. A woman could still be divorced for not having children and
could be drowned for adultery. She could even be thrown into the Euphrates
for gossiping, and could be sold into slavery for three years to cover her husband's debts. Hammurabi's laws were stringent and his punishments brutal,
but at least a king had given notice that he would not change the law capriciously.

The Indo-European Invasions

New invaders known as Indo-Europeans swept into the Fertile Crescent in the
seventeenth century B.C. They were nomads, whose original home has not been
established, who had moved into the region to the north of the Black and
Caspian Seas by about 2500 B.C. They spoke languages that were derived from
one common language, known as Indo-European because the languages based
on it are now spread from northern Europe to northern India. Language, not
race, was therefore the common characteristic of the Indo-European peoples.

---

[3] "Sumerian Lamentation," translated by S. N. Kramer, in James B. Pritchard, ed., *Ancient
Near Eastern Texts Relating to the Old Testament*, 3rd ed. (Princeton, N.J.: Princeton University Press,
1969), p. 460.

From the common original language, in a process of differentiation lasting millennia, are derived the Celtic languages (Welsh, Cornish); the Germanic languages (German, Danish, Dutch, English); the Romance or Italic languages (French, Italian, Spanish, Portuguese); the Greek language; the Slavic languages (Russian, Polish); and the Indo-Iranian (Sanskrit, Persian). During the first wave of invasions, which lasted from about 1700 to 1400 B.C., Indo-European peoples spread into northern India, north Africa, the Fertile Crescent, and Greece. A later wave, from about 1200 to 900 B.C., carried them into Western Europe.

Babylon was sacked in 1600 B.C. by a raiding party of an Indo-European people called the Hittites, who founded an empire that lasted in Asia Minor and the Near East for almost 500 years. Although the Hittites carried on the cultural traditions in literature, law, and religion of the early Mesopotamian states, they are remembered for having carried through the important technological advance of smelting iron, which they used to make iron weapons and horse-drawn chariots. The Hittites did not incorporate Babylon into their empire, but left it in the hands of another Indo-European people, the Kassites, who maintained a conservative and largely uncreative regime until about 1200 B.C. The simultaneous collapse of the Hittite and Kassite states left the Fertile Crescent open to attack from the most powerful military machine the region had ever seen, the army of the Assyrians.

The Empire of the Assyrians

The Assyrians were a Semitic people who had settled in the north of the Fertile Crescent in the third millenium B.C. Exposed to attack from the nomadic peoples to the north and from the more prosperous empires to the south, they had become disciplined militarists in their long struggle to win security. At the end of the twelfth century B.C., they embarked upon an aggressive drive that took them across Syria to the eastern Mediterranean.

Their military technique, backed as it was by frightening threats that were invariably carried out, proved irresistible, as the superb friezes they erected in the palaces of their three successive capital cities of Assur, Nimrud, and Nineveh show. They opened a battle by launching hails of arrows, and destroyed their discomfited opponents by charges of cavalry and pikemen. If the enemy retreated behind his city walls, the Assyrians smashed the gates with battering rams or scaled the walls with assault ladders, and even floated on inflated animal skins to mount assault from the less defended river side. The population of the defeated city was tortured and slaughtered or removed hundreds of miles into slavery. These techniques were perfected by King Sennacherib (705–681 B.C.) and King Assurbanipal (reigned 669–633 B.C.), under whom the Assyrians conquered the whole of the Fertile Crescent and even for a time took possession of Egypt. Sennacherib's boast of how he destroyed Babylon was an open warning to other cities that might dare to resist Assyrian might:

Assurbanipal Hunting Lion *Assyrian rulers, such as Assurbanipal (reigned 669–633 B.C.), decorated their palaces with low relief sculptures depicting siege warfare, plunder, or the hunt. (Hirmer Fotoarchiv.)*

The city and its houses, from its foundation to its top, I destroyed, I devastated, I burned with fire, the wall and the outer wall, temples, and gods, temple towers of brick and earth, as many as they were, I razed and dumped them into the Arakhtu Canal. Through the midst of the city I dug canals, I flooded its site with water, and the very foundations thereof I destroyed. I made its destruction more complete than that by a flood.[4]

It is hard to see much benefit to civilization from the exploits of the Assyrians, although their terrifying sculptures are proof of the artistic instinct that was harnessed to the cause of military expansion. Their subject peoples felt only overwhelming joy when the Medes swept out of Iran and joined with the Babylonians in burning Nineveh to the ground in 612 B.C.

The New Babylonian Revival, 612–539 B.C.

The Medes left control of Mesopotamia to their allies, the Chaldeans, another Semitic people who had moved into the area of the Old Babylonian kingdom about 1000 B.C. The restored city of Babylon became a byword in the Near East for the opulence of its court and the magnificence of its buildings. Nebuchadnezzar (reigned 604–562 B.C.) constructed a palace with beautiful terraces overlooking the Euphrates River and on the roof, by means of subterranean waterpipes, he created a park full of trees and flowers known, according to a description of a later Alexandrian historian, as the Hanging Gardens, one of the seven wonders of the ancient world.[5]

[4] Cited in Lewis Mumford, *The City in History* (New York: Harcourt Brace and World, 1961), p. 68.

[5] The other six were the lighthouse at Alexandria; the statue of Zeus at Olympia, Greece; the Colossus, a statue of the god Helios, at Rhodes; the temple of the god Artemis at Ephesus; the tomb of Mausolus (the "mausoleum") at Halicarnassus; the Great Pyramid of Khufu at Giza, Egypt.

Like earlier Sumerian rulers, Nebuchadnezzar prided himself on his patronage of literature and science, especially of astronomy. His astronomers discovered several new planets and invented the twelve signs of the zodiac, each of which was used to designate one part of the sky. But like the Assyrians, however, Nebuchadnezzar believed in the forcible removal and bondage of defeated peoples, as when, after capturing the Hebrew capital of Jerusalem in 586 B.C., he brought thousands of Jews into "Babylonian Captivity," which they protested in Psalm 137: "By the rivers of Babylon, there we sat down, yea, we wept, when we remembered Zion." They not only lamented, however. They called for revenge: "O daughter of Babylon, who are to be destroyed: happy shall he be, that rewarded thee as thou hast served us. Happy shall he be, that taketh and dasheth thy little ones against the stones." In 539 B.C., Babylon was captured by Cyrus the Great, emperor of Persia, and laid waste.

The Legacy of Mesopotamia

The people of the Tigris and Euphrates valleys had made vitally important advances in civilized life, many of which were to be diffused by other peoples into the lands of the eastern Mediterranean and into Iran and the Indus Valley of India. They had demonstrated how intensive agriculture can be created by water engineering and by improvements in animal breeding and plant selection. Their cities permitted specialization of occupation and vastly improved productivity; and they used well-developed business techniques including receipts, letters of credit, and a commonly accepted system of weights and measures. They had made significant scientific advances in mathematics, astronomy, physics, and medicine. While in government their principal effort resulted in the elaboration of authoritarian rule, they had recognized the need for written law as the basis of an orderly society. Their architects knew the use of the column, the arch, and even the dome, but, working mainly with clay bricks, were compelled to show their ingenuity in the design of terraced ziggurats and the open courtyards of enormous palaces. Sculpture advanced from the stylized forms of the Sumerians to the extraordinary vivacity of the Assyrian *bas reliefs*. Finally, religion not only led to fruitful speculation on the nature of the universe and of human beings in their relation to gods and to each other, it also stimulated the composition of some of the most powerful epic poems of the ancient world.

SMALLER POWERS OF THE WESTERN FERTILE CRESCENT

The Mediterranean lands of the Fertile Crescent did not advance as rapidly as those of the Tigris and Euphrates valleys. Jagged mountain ranges ran north–south, which interrupted communcations. The vast distances of the Syrian desert had to be crossed by difficult caravan journeys to reach the prosperous cities of Mesopotamia. Rainfall was infrequent and unreliable. Only in the few inland oases and the Mediterranean coast was the land easily cultivable. The area appeared inviting, nevertheless, to the Semitic peoples seeking a better livelihood than that offered in the forbidding wastes of the Arabian desert. By 1800 B.C. three of these migratory peoples had settled along the coastal plain—the Canaanites, the Arameans, and the Hebrews.

Apart from scattered references to the Canaanites in the Bible, nothing was known about the early history of these peoples until the twentieth century, when archeologists discovered the ruins of one of their principal cities, Ugarit, on the coast of Syria. Ugarit was at its height between 1400 and 1200 B.C., when a vast royal palace was constructed covering 9000 square yards. The archives in Ugaritic have been deciphered and reveal that these early Canaanites had extensive contacts with the Hittites and with the Egyptians.

The Phoenicians, a people of Canaanite origin, became, after 1300 B.C., some of the world's greatest sailors and traders. Their ships roamed the whole Mediterranean sea and penetrated along the Atlantic shores of Europe as far as southern Britain. They exchanged cedar wood from the forests of Lebanon, glass, and a dyed purple cloth, for such raw materials as copper and silver from Spain and tin from Britain. They were the most ambitious colonists before the Greeks, sending out settlements to Sicily, Spain, and North Africa.

The most lasting contribution of the Phoenicians was, however, the invention of the alphabet. Whereas Babylonian cuneiform writing, which was in wide use throughout the Near East, used hundreds of signs, each of which represented a word or syllable, the Phoenicians used twenty-nine (and later twenty-two) signs for consonants, leaving the reader to add the vowel sounds. The Greeks perfected the alphabet by using as vowels five signs that had originally denoted consonants. The invention of the alphabet must be regarded as one of the crucial contributions to human freedom, because it broke the monopoly of learning possessed by a class of priests or scribes, as in Mesopotamia and Egypt, and made available to a far larger number of people access to the stores of accumulated human knowledge.

Where the Canaanites were traders by sea, the Arameans were traders by land. From their capital city of Damascus in Syria, they created commercial ties with all the cities of Mesopotamia, with the more southerly lands of the Fertile Crescent, and with Egypt; and they even sent expeditions as far as India. Their alphabet, which was similar to the Phoenicians', was widely used throughout the Near East by the seventh century B.C.

Early History of the Hebrews

Around 2000 B.C. the Semitic tribes of Hebrews, who would later be called Jews, were widely scattered around the northern edges of the Arabian Desert and in Mesopotamia. The origin of the name *Hebrew* is believed to be an ancient Semitic word, *abar*, "to cross or pass over," and may refer to the passage across the great Syrian desert by the followers of Abraham. Possibly around 1900 B.C., the

Hebrew patriarch Abraham led his family or clan from Ur in Sumeria into northern Mesopotamia and from there across Syria into the land of Canaan, or Palestine. The covenant that Abraham made with God, whom the Hebrews called Yahweh, established the relationship of God with the Hebrew people:

> I will make of thee a great nation, and I will bless thee, and make thy name great, and be thou a blessing; and I will bless them that bless thee, and him that curseth thee I will curse (Genesis 12:2–3).

Possibly in the thirteenth century B.C., the Hebrew leader Moses led the escape, or "Exodus," from Egypt of Hebrew tribes claiming descent from the twelve sons of Jacob, also known as Israel. These tribes had been enslaved by the Egyptians. In the Sinai desert, the Bible tells us, Yahweh made a new covenant with the Israelites by giving Moses stone tablets containing the Ten Commandments. Moses died just before the Hebrews reentered Canaan.

After fighting successfully to reestablish themselves in Canaan, the Hebrews formed a loose confederation that eventually won control of the land. To hold off new invaders known as Philistines (after whom Palestine was named by the Romans), the jealously independent Hebrews agreed to unite under a king, Saul (reigned c. 1010–1005 B.C.). Saul was killed in battle with the Philistines, but his successor David (reigned 1005–965 B.C.) proved to be a skillful military commander, a sly diplomat, and a charismatic ruler.

David, as portrayed in the Old Testament, was a person of driving human passions—amorous, compassionate, ambitious, and reckless. He saw that the quarreling Hebrew tribes needed a capital city of great beauty that would be a physical symbol of their religious and political unity. He chose the small, rough village of Jerusalem to be this bond, the site of their Temple to which their hopes would turn in any future tribulations. The Temple was constructed by his son Solomon (reigned 965–925 B.C.) on a vast stone platform on the northeast edge of the city. No expense was spared to bring in the finest cedars from Lebanon, brass, copper, and gold.

In spite of his reputation for wisdom, Solomon's exactions bore so heavily on the poorer farmers that revolt broke out shortly after his death, and the kingdom was split into two parts, the northern kingdom of Israel with its capital at Samaria, and the smaller, southern kingdom of Judah, with its capital at Jerusalem. Dissension between the tribes left the Hebrews prey to outside attack. Israel fell to the Assyrians in 721 B.C. and Judah to the Babylonians under Nebuchadnezzar in 586 B.C. The Temple and the city walls were razed and the Jews (which originally meant "the people of Judah") were taken into captivity in Babylon.

When the Jews were permitted to return to Jerusalem and to rebuild the Temple in 538 B.C., they were unable to establish an independent political power. After being governed first by Persia and then by Macedon, Palestine became part of the Roman Empire in 63 B.C. In A.D. 66, the Jews rose against their Roman rulers and massacred the garrison in Jerusalem. The city was besieged by the future emperor Titus, who, in A.D. 70, broke Jewish resistance, burned the Temple, and carried its sacred candelabra and other furnishings back to Rome for display in his victory triumph. After the Jews revolted again in A.D. 135, the Romans decided to end any possibility of the revival of Jerusalem as a Hebrew religious center, by creating a completely new Roman city on the site. The involuntary and voluntary migration of Jews out of Palestine during the 700 year period between the Babylonian Captivity and the revolt against Hadrian began what is known as the dispersion, or *diaspora*, of the Jewish people.

Hebrew Religion

The early Hebrews contributed very little to the scientific, literary, political, or economic development of the Near East. Their religious ideas, however, gave the Jewish people a bond they were never to lose, and laid the groundwork for both Christianity and Islam, two religions of infinitely greater expansive power than Judaism.

At first, as nomadic wanderers, the Hebrews probably thought that holy spirits existed in the various forms of nature, such as rocks and streams, but at least from the time when Moses was supposed to have received the Ten Commandments, they distinguished themselves from all the other peoples of the Near East by an uncompromising monotheism, belief in their one god Yahweh, who had chosen them as his people. In the first five books of the Bible, which are known as the Torah or Pentateuch, it is clear that the preservation of the family and of the Jewish people as a whole was the primary purpose of their interpretation of Yahweh's commands. In what was called levirate marriage, for example, a widow married her brother-in-law if she did not have a child by her deceased husband. A wife who had borne no children could be divorced. A husband could have several wives in order to assure numerous offspring. Ritual festivals were also established, which commemorated events in the history of the Jews and at the same time served to remind them of their common bonds. Passover, for example, when Jews ate unleavened bread and sacrificed lambs, was a reminder of the exodus from Egypt under the leadership of Moses.

In the eighth and seventh centuries B.C., prophets like Isaiah rejected the emphasis on ritual observance and demanded instead a moral regeneration. God, they preached, was using the Assyrians and the Babylonians to punish the Jews for their moral failing. But they also held out hope that at some time in the future God would send a savior, or Messiah, from the family of David to bring once again an era of peace and prosperity for the Jewish people. This promise was to be taken up by the Christians, who saw Christ as the promised Messiah:

> And the spirit of the Lord shall rest upon him, the spirit of wisdom and understanding, the spirit of counsel and might, the spirit of knowledge and the fear of the Lord. . . . And he shall set up an ensign for the nations, and shall assemble the outcasts of Israel, and gather together the dispersed of Judah from the four corners of the earth (Isaiah 11:2, 12).

The Legacy of the Phoenicians, Arameans, and Hebrews

The importance of the Phoenicians and Arameans for Western civilization is complex and varied. Both peoples were great traders, and their merchants learned from the cultural achievements of the advanced states with which they traded, notably the Egyptians and Mesopotamians, transmitting the knowledge of those states to their less advanced trading partners. The original contribution of both peoples was, however, to make written language a more accessible tool. The Aramean spoken language was widely used for communication by merchants and government officials in the Near East by 1000 B.C., and their version of the Phoenician alphabet became the international script of the region. The Phoenician alphabet itself proved the most suitable for writing of several alphabets being developed along the shores of the eastern Mediterranean. It possessed a far simpler form and far fewer symbols than either the Mesopotamian cuneiform or the Egyptian hieroglyphics, and thus was much easier to use. The alphabet was eventually adopted by the ancient Greeks and through them influenced all Indo-European writing.

While the Hebrews had participated in the material advances of the Fertile Crescent, their principal legacy to Western civilization lay in their religious thought. While their religion rather than their political cohesion bound them as a nation, that religion developed characteristics that were incorporated into newer religions. These later religions, however, felt no sense of belonging to a Jewish nation, and at different times felt a direct resentment at that nation for its supposed exclusiveness. The Jews offered to Christianity and to Islam the belief in monotheism, a conception of the duality of good and evil struggling in this world, belief in the responsibility of the individual in achieving righteousness in the sight of God, and a moral code that demands ethical conduct from individuals and governments.

EGYPT: THE GIFT OF THE NILE

If one approaches Cairo by air across the vast wastes of the Libyan desert, one sees with incredulity, laid out across the brown sands, the tiny green ribbon of the Nile River, which was responsible for the development of 5000 years of civilization in this unpromising land. Rising 4000 miles to the south in Central Africa, the world's longest river drained the waters of one-tenth of the second largest continent. It spread them with completely predictable regularity every spring over a narrow strip of land, never more than 13 miles wide, which stretched the 600 miles from the first cataract at Aswan to beyond present-day Cairo and over the triangular delta, where the river split into several branches before reaching the Mediterranean Sea. The silt deposited by these floods was extremely fertile, but as in the delta of the Tigris and Euphrates, engineering works were needed to make full use of the waters. By about 4000 B.C., the delta region in the north, known as Lower Egypt, and the long valley to the south, known as Upper Egypt, had made the Neolithic transition from food gathering and hunting to settled farming.

The Archaic Period and the Old Kingdom, c. 3000–2200 B.C.

The two parts of Egypt were united about 3000 B.C. by Menes, the ruler of Upper Egypt. This union was symbolized in the headdress worn by the kings (who are known only as Pharaoh, or "Great House," from the fifteenth century B.C. on), which was a double crown, combining the concave, red crown of Lower Egypt and the white, bulbous crown of Upper Egypt. Historians count thirty-one dynasties in Egyptian history, from the foundation of the first dynasty by Menes until the abolition of the last dynasty when Rome annexed Egypt in 30 B.C. Little is known about the first two dynasties, and hence the period is known as the Archaic Period (3000–2700 B.C.). The Old Kingdom, which extends from the Third to the Sixth Dynasties (c. 2700–2200 B.C.), was the first great period of Egyptian civilization, during which were formed the characteristics of the country's economy, society, religion, and art, which were to endure with remarkable stability for 3000 years.

The Egyptian economy was dependent on drainage works in the delta of the Nile and a combination of irrigation ditches and embankments in the upper stretches of the river. Once these engineering works were built and maintained, the land was enormously fertile. It produced cereal crops of barley and wheat; vegetables such as beans, lentils, and onions; a wide variety of fruits, including grapes, figs, and dates; and raw materials for textiles, such as cotton and flax. Domesticated animals included cattle, sheep, pigs, and goats, while the skies were filled with geese and ducks, which the Egyptians hunted both for pleasure and for food. Its mines produced gold, silver, and copper, as well as every type of stone from limestone to alabaster. While agriculture was the basic occupation, artisans worked to manufacture metal goods, textiles, pottery, glass, and jewelry, and a large trading class was engaged in exchange of goods within Egypt and, to a lesser degree, the export of Egyptian products for the few imported items Egypt required, such as timber.

The slave population, which became far more numerous in the later centuries of Egyptian history than under the Old Kingdom, was employed primarily in such public works as the construction of pyramids and temples and in the mines. The majority of the population were peasants, who lived in tiny brick homes amid the irrigated fields. They shared the crops they produced with the officials of the pharaoh, who was considered to be the original owner of all land, or with the landlords to whom the pharaoh assigned a major portion of the cultivated land. Even in the most prosperous times, life for the laboring classes was hard; but at times of invasion or of governmental breakdown, it became even more precarious. As in Mesopotamia, there was an intermediate class of merchants who, however, did not become very numerous until after 2000 B.C.; of scribes, employed in temple and governmental administration; and of craftspeople. The nobility, who had been granted their lands by the pharoah, carried out local government and revenue collection and fought in the armies. In the many wars after 1500 B.C., however, a separate class of full-time soldiers was created. The class of priests was numerous and rich, justifying its share of the country's revenues by not only fulfilling its many religious duties but by its contribution to philosophic speculation, to literature, and to art. The royal family of the pharaoh constituted a class apart, with the undisputed right to draw upon the country's riches and labor, especially in preparation of the pyramids, in which the pharaoh's embalmed body was to wait through eternity for the periodic returns of his *ka*, or soul.

The pyramids were constructed on the very edge of the Libyan desert overlooking the valley of the Nile. Sited above the level of the floodwaters of the Nile, they were nevertheless close enough to be accessible by boat from the new capital city of Memphis (near modern Cairo). The pattern of the pyramids, surrounded by funeral temples and smaller tombs for the pharaoh's wives and courtiers, was set in the Step Pyramid of Saqqara of King Zoser, which was designed by Imhotep, his chief minister, architect, and doctor. This pyramid,

The Great Sphinx and Pyramid of Pharaoh Khufu, Giza, Egypt
The 481-foot high pyramid, completed about 2600 B.C., is the largest in Egypt. The Sphinx has the body of a lion, symbolizing kingship, and a human head, representing intelligence. (Hirmer Fotoarchiv.)

erected about 2700 B.C., was 240 feet high, but the pharaohs of the fourth dynasty were determined to outdo Zoser's achievement. The most imposing pyramid ever erected was that of Khufu, sometimes called Cheops, at nearby Giza, which when finished about 2600 B.C. was 480 feet high. As many as 100,000 Egyptian workers and slaves may have been conscripted in its construction. The pyramid consists of 2 million blocks of limestone, some of which weigh up to 15 tons, which were probably dragged on sledges up an earthen rampart to be placed on the upper part of the pyramid. Napoleon Bonaparte, during his campaign in Egypt in 1798, surprised his officers with a rapid calculation that the stone from the three pyramids at Giza was sufficient to build a wall 10 feet high around the whole frontier of France.

The pharaoh's body was carefully embalmed, or mummified, in ceremonies that lasted seventy days, and it was placed inside several interlocking coffins. It was then carried to a funeral chamber deep in the heart of the pyramid, in which had been placed all the things the pharaoh would need in the afterlife, such as chairs, tables, beds, clothing, jewelry, food, wine, cosmetics, and weapons. In the early days servants were actually sacrificed and placed in the tomb, but later small models of slaves, servants, boatmen, overseers, and courtiers were used instead. Within the tombs and over the walls of the many surrounding temples and vestibules, skilled artists depicted with amazing liveliness and charm the life of the pharaoh and the scenes of war and peace of his reign. In the tombs of the aristocrats in particular, the everyday life of the river and of the farming estates comes to life. Geese flutter from the reeds along the Nile. A herdsman carries new-born calves on his back. Boatmen battle each other with poles. Musicians and acrobats perform. Thus, within the tombs the atmosphere is not that of morbid solemnity, but rather of a riotous and colorful joy in which the pleasures of this life are enhanced in the afterlife.

Egyptian Religion

Egyptian religion is the explanation of the extravagant expenditures on pyramids and tombs that characterize Egyptian civilization throughout its history, and of the joyful celebration of death that so astounds a visitor to the tombs. Egyptian religion was already well developed by the time of the Old Kingdom. In part, their gods were connected with the natural objects around them, especially with animals, who play a significant role in the later development of the presentation of the gods. Gods are often portrayed as birds or animals, or as human beings with the head of an animal. Hathor, the goddess of love and childbirth, was shown with a human body but a pair of cow's horns. Anubis, god of the dead, had a human body but the head of a jackal. Eventually animals themselves were worshipped. At Saqqara, for example, a series of extraordinary, huge black granite sarcophagi have been found that contain the mummified remains of bulls of the cult of Apis.

More important were the natural features that influenced Egyptian life, notably the all-powerful sun and the river Nile. The sun god, Re, the most important deity of the Old Kingdom, was regarded as having embodied in himself all the local guardian gods who had been worshipped in the different provinces of Egypt. Re was believed to ride a boat out of the east each morning, bringing light and happiness, and to sail in another boat in the west in the evening, where he could float along another river Nile, which passed beneath the earth through a nether world, in order to reappear the next morning in the east. Boats recently discovered at the base of the Pyramid of Khufu may have been a representation of Re's solar boat. Re's journey was not the only Egyptian description of the heavens. They sometimes explained that a huge cow, with a star-studded belly, formed the arch of heaven, and at other times that a female, with her feet in the east and her arms in the west, was bending over the earth.

Osiris was the god of the Nile, and the legend of Osiris became central to Egyptian religion. Osiris, the legend held, had taken the place of the sun god as ruler on earth, and had governed wisely with the help of his loving wife Isis, who was also his sister. Osiris was murdered by his brother Set, who cut him into a million pieces, which he scattered throughout Egypt. Isis finally pieced Osiris together again, and he was brought back to life to rule as king of the nether world, in which the living dead would have their virtures and sins weighed. A feather was placed on one pan of a balance, and the heart of the person being judged in the other pan. If the heart was heavier than the feather, the person was condemned to live in eternal gloom in the nether world, and not to know the pleasures that waited for the righteous of luxurious ease in the landscape of flowers. Horus, the son of Isis and Osiris, avenged his father by killing Set, and became king on earth in his place.

Egyptians came to believe that their ruling pharaoh was Horus, and that on his death the pharaoh descended to the nether world and became Osiris. He was, however, also believed to rise into heaven as Re, the sun god, whose symbol was the pyramid in which the pharaoh was buried. The overlapping and even contradictory religious beliefs did not bother the Egyptians, who had no sacred book like the Bible or the Koran as a sole source of authority, and perhaps the vitality of their religion was due in part to its ability to change over the centuries with no sense of inconsistency.

The position of the pharaoh remained central in this religious evolution. He was the only person who could act as intermediary between human beings and gods, and he alone, for that reason, could be represented in the tombs face to face with the gods. He was therefore regarded as responsible for *maat*, justice and truth, the principle that the Egyptians believed permeated the universe and which the pharaoh was to enforce in his administration of the state. As priest, judge, and political ruler, the pharaoh could thus justify his enormous share of the country's physical resources, which was poured into the construction of his dwelling for the afterlife, where his *ka*, or soul, on its periodic returns to his mummified body, could enjoy again the pleasures of material life.

The Middle Kingdom, c. 2000–1800 B.C.

At the end of the Old Kingdom, the power of the pharaohs dwindled. The excessive expenditures on tombs had reduced the royal revenues. Local power had fallen into the hands of aristocrats, who were themselves claiming immortality and hence the right to build ever more expensive tombs. Even the priests were refusing their support unless rewarded with vast land grants. During the so-called First Intermediate Period (c. 2200–2000 B.C.), Egypt was in chaos, as one contemporary text shows:

> Why, really! Laughter has disappeared, and is no longer made. It is wailing that pervades the land, mixed with lamentation . . .
> Why, really! The ways are not guarded roads. Men sit in the bushes until the benighted traveler comes, to take away his burden and steal what is on him . . .
> Ah, would that it were the end of men, no conception, no birth! Then the earth would cease from noise, without wrangling![6]

Unity and prosperity were restored by rulers from Thebes in Upper Egypt, which was made the new capital. Amun, the local god of Thebes, became the principal deity of Egypt, and both his attributes and name were eventually joined with those of Re, to become the god Amun-Re. The pharaohs of the Middle Kingdom were expansionist military leaders who secured their southern frontier by leading expeditions up the Nile into Nubia, and even crossed Sinai to wage campaigns in Palestine. But they were also concerned with the country's economic development, especially in the oasis region of Fayyum, where they embarked upon large-scale irrigation works and built another capital city called Lisht.

The Middle Kingdom was invaded and conquered in the eighteenth century B.C. by Asian invaders called Hyksos, or "Shepherd Kings," whose military superiority was due to their use of the horse, the war chariot, and long-range bows made of wood and horn. Eventually, however, the local Egyptian nobles acquired mastery of these weapons and drove the Hyksos out of Egypt. Their New Kingdom was to last for almost 500 years, and marked the greatest variety and luxury of all Egyptian civilization.

The New Kingdom, c. 1570–1100 B.C.

The pharaohs of the New Kingdom used their new military power to win themselves an empire that could be exploited. In the south they extended their power to what is now Sudan, and in the northeast they conquered Palestine and Syria and even reached as far as the Euphrates River. As a result of the payment of tribute and of the encouragement of long-distance trade, luxuries

---

[6] "Oracles and Prophecies," translated by John A. Wilson, in James B. Pritchard, ed., *Ancient Near Eastern Texts Relating to the Old Testament*, 3rd ed. (Princeton, N.J.: Princeton University Press, 1969), pp. 141–142.

Funeral Temple of Queen Hatshepsut, Thebes, Egypt (c. 1500 B.C.) *Tombs and funerary temples of the new Kingdom were constructed in the hills of the left bank of the Nile. Hatshepsut's temple is decorated throughout with wall paintings and reliefs extolling the glories of her ancestors and herself. (Hirmer Fotoarchiv.)*

poured into Egypt, and especially into their expanding capital city of Thebes, the home of their god Amun. For them, Thebes was "the mistress of every city," the pattern that all should hope to achieve. To beautify their city, they enlarged the temple of Amun at Karnak into what became the largest temple in the world. Spread over 227 acres, the central hall alone is more than 100 yards in length. Meanwhile, on the opposite bank of the river, deep in the cliffs overlooking the Nile Valley, they dug out, and embellished with elaborate wall paintings, tombs for their mummified bodies.

Three remarkable rulers of this eighteenth dynasty stand out as the great builders of Thebes. Queen Hatshepsut was one of the most fascinatingly ambitious women in Egyptian history. About 1500 B.C., after being named regent, she seized the throne for herself, claiming that she was not figuratively but actually the daughter of Amun-Re. Dissatisfied with being merely queen, she took the title of king, dressed as a man, and omitted the female endings from her name and titles. On the left bank of the Nile she erected a vast funeral temple, which, in two stepped terraces, cut deeply into the cliffs to provide large areas of wall space, which her artists embellished with scenes glorifying her exploits.

Her stepson, Thutmose III, so hated her that after her death in about 1470 B.C. he had her name effaced from all the temples, and even walled in the huge obelisks of red granite that she had erected in the center of the Karnak temple. Thutmose III himself proved to be one of the greatest generals of Egypt, and it was he who was most responsible for the extension of Egyptian power into the

Sudan and into the Fertile Crescent, where he personally led the armies. To celebrate these victories, he erected two obelisks of his own at Karnak, which were later reerected in Rome and Constantinople.

Amunhotep III, who became pharaoh about 1410 B.C., used the income from the provinces acquired by Thutmose III to embark on a building spree of his own. He tried to rival the temple complex at Karnak with another a mile farther up the Nile, at Luxor, which he joined to that of Karnak by a road lined with statues of rams between whose legs the king is standing. But his taste for the grandiose took Egyptian art into the search for the colossal that was to reach its extravagant finale two centuries later in the buildings and statues of Ramses II. Amunhotep III erected two statues outside his funeral temple on the left bank, which are known as the Colossi of Memnon, whose fingers alone are 4 feet long. At the same time, however, the carving and painting in the tombs reached its most elegant refinement, especially in the tombs of nobles such as Ramose.

It is doubtful, however, whether the peasantry of Egypt profited from the prosperity of the New Kingdom, even though the tombs depicted them as happily helping in the hunt or working the fields. A more accurate glimpse of their problems is presented in a letter from one scribe, serving as a royal tax collector, warning his friend not to go back to work on the land:

> The mice abound in the fields. The locusts descend. The cattle devour. The sparrows bring disaster upon the cultivator . . . the yoke of oxen has died while threshing and plowing. And now the scribe lands on the river-bank and is about to register the harvest-tax. The janitors carry staves and the Nubians rods of palm, and they say "Hand over the corn" though there is none. The cultivator is beaten all over, he is bound and thrown into the well, soused and dipped head downwards. His wife has been bound in his presence, his children are in fetters. His neighbors abandon them and are fled. So their corn flies away.[7]

The Religious Revolution of Akhenaton

In the mid-fourteenth century B.C., Pharaoh Amunhotep IV decided that Egypt was more threatened by priestly power and corruption than by external military danger. Probably out of personal religious conviction, he challenged directly the most entrenched interest group in Egyptian society. He abandoned polytheism, had the names of the gods chiseled off their monuments, and disbanded their priests. He declared that there was only one god, Aton, whose power was not merely in Egypt, but was universal. Aton was not to be represented like previous Egyptian gods in human or animal form, but only by the solar disk. He changed his own name to Akhenaton, "Pleasing to Aton," whose glory he celebrated in a lovely hymn:

---

[7] Alan Gardiner, *Egypt of the Pharaohs* (New York: Oxford University Press, 1961), pp. 32, 33.

Thou appearest beautifully on the horizon of heaven,
Thou living Aton, the beginning of life! . . .
At daybreak, when thou arisest on the horizon,
When thou shinest as the Aton by day,
Thou drivest away the darkness and givest thy rays . . .
Trees and plants are flourishing . . .
The ships are sailing north and south as well,
For every way is open at thy appearance,
The fish in the river dart before thy face;
Thy rays are in the midst of the great green sea . . .
O sole god, like whom there is no other.[8]

Akhenaton founded a new capital city farther north, which he named Akhetaton, "the horizon of Aton." There he and his wife Nefertiti engaged in theological speculation and patronized an engaging, almost impressionistic form of art. Vassal states in Palestine and Syria became rebellious, however, and the local princes in Egypt joined with the priests in opposition to a ruler they believed sacriligious. Akhenaton's brother, the nine-year-old Tutankhamen, was brought back to Thebes as his successor, and restored the worship of the traditional gods. He died only nine years later, however, and is known today primarily for the treasures discovered in 1922 in his unlooted tomb.

Ramses II

The break-up of the empire was temporarily halted by the great general, Pharaoh Ramses II, in the thirteenth century B.C. He and the Hittites fought each other to a standstill in Syria and finally made a peace treaty dividing the area between them. His overwhelming egoism is seen in the vast monuments that he erected from one end of Egypt to the other. In the south was the temple of Abu Simbel, now reerected after being saved from flooding in the waters of the Aswan High Dam, in which four colossal statues of Ramses sit facing the Nubians in silent warning not to advance into Egypt. In Karnak, he completed the hypostyle hall, with columns 12 feet in diameter, and constructed a huge funeral temple for himself on the opposite bank of the Nile. He placed cartouches containing his own names on virtually every major building already existing.

Egypt in Decline

Ramses II was the last of the great pharaohs. When a new wave of Indo-European invaders pushed into the Near East (about 1200–900 B.C.), the Egyptians were expelled from the Fertile Crescent. The kingdom broke apart once again about 1100 B.C., and then became prey to one foreign conqueror after

[8] Egyptian Hymns and Prayers," translated by John A. Wilson, in James B. Pritchard, ed., *Ancient Near Eastern Texts Relating to the Old Testament*, 3rd ed. (Princeton, N.J.: Princeton University Press, 1969), p. 370.

Girl Musicians, Tomb of Nakht, Thebes, Egypt (fourteenth century B.C.) In Egyptian tombs, colorful wall paintings indicate that the joys of this life will continue in the afterlife. Nakht was scribe of the granaries. (Photograph by Egyptian Expedition, The Metropolitan Museum of Art.)

another. In the eighth century, Egypt was invaded from the south by Nubians from the kingdom of Kush; the Nubians were driven out of Egypt by the Assyrians a century later. Back in Kush, they founded a new capital city of Meroë on the Nile, where they showed how Egyptianized they had become by erecting there temples in the style of Karnak and miniature pyramids like those of Giza. The Persians conquered Egypt in the sixth century. The Greeks under Alexander of Macedon invaded in the fourth century, and it was then governed by the Ptolemies, the descendents of one of Alexander's generals. Octavian, the future Roman emperor Augustus, defeated the navy and army of Queen Cleopatra and her Roman lover Mark Antony in 31 B.C. The following year Egypt became one of the provinces of the Roman Empire.

The Legacy of Egyptian Civilization

In many ways, the achievements of the Egyptians were less adaptable to the needs of their neighbors than those of the countries of the Fertile Crescent. Their very conservatism and sense of superiority within a jealously guarded isolation made it difficult for others to learn from them. Their art, too, seemed to function only within the confines of Egypt's own religious system. The disciplined exploitation of the peasantry by the state in vast irrigation projects or road building and as nearly slave labor on the great agricultural estates seemed peculiar to the geographic conditions of the Egyptian land and economy. Even their mathematics appeared to serve only Egyptian purposes. Their geometry was highly advanced where useful for surveying flooded fields or constructing pyramids, but they were less concerned with abstract mathematics. Although their hieroglyphic writing advanced from the use of pictures of objects (pictograms) to development of symbols for spoken sounds, once again their conservatism—and especially their desire to use the language for decorative purposes on religious buildings—prevented them from using alphabetic writing alone.[9]

Yet one must not underestimate the extent to which later peoples of the Mediterranean world learned from the Egyptians. In religion, the Egyptians had advanced from nature worship to the concepts of personal immortality, accountability at death for behavior in this life, and responsibility of the state and its citizens to maintain justice and morality. They had briefly, under Akhenaton, accepted monotheism.

Their artistic achievements could also be emulated by others. Early Greek statues of the seventh and sixth centuries B.C. are clearly derived from the static style of the conventional Egyptian statues, while the Greek temples such as the Parthenon developed from "post-and-lintel" architecture (the laying of a beam of stone horizontally across two vertical columns), which had been used in Karnak a thousand years earlier. The colorful decoration of the tombs as preparation for the afterlife reappears in the tombs of the Etruscans in central Italy, perhaps as a result of their commercial contacts with the Egyptians.

In medicine the Egyptians were probably the most advanced of the ancient world. A specialized class of doctors and dentists had developed a scientific approach to the diagnosis of illness and its treatment, perhaps because the process of mummification gave them the opportunity to engage in dissection of the corpse of the deceased.

Socially too, the Egyptians taught their neighbors a lesson. They believed in the concept of a harmonious society, in which all groups have not only duties but rights. They believed especially in the harmony of family life, and the statues and paintings portray affection and trust between man and wife as well as delight in their children. Even though women were inferior in law and a man could have many wives and concubines, the rights of a woman, and especially of a Chief Wife, were guaranteed by law. The many surviving love poems are testimony to the gentleness and joy of human relationships in ancient Egyptian society. Indeed, Egyptian life possesses a certain charm, which may explain in part its fascination for later peoples of the West; much of this charm is tinged

---

[9] After the use of hieroglyphics was abandoned in the fifth century A.D., the ability to read it was lost until the French scholar Jean-François Champollion in the early nineteenth century again worked out its meaning by a comparison of hieroglyphic, Greek, and a later form of Egyptian writing on the Rosetta stone, discovered by the armies of Napoleon in the expedition of 1798.

by melancholy, as in the "Song of the Blind Harper" from the walls of the tomb of Prince Nakht at Thebes:

> Spend a happy day. Rejoice in the sweetest perfumes. Adorn the neck and arms of your wife with the lotus flowers and keep your loved one seated always at your side. Call no halt to music and the dance, but bid all care be gone. Spare a thought for nothing but pleasure: for soon your turn will come to journey to the land of silence.[10]

SUGGESTED READINGS

The Stone Age

The discovery of the earliest hominids in East Africa is described in Richard E. Leakey and Roger Lewin, *Origins* (1977). Two fine introductions to human development before the invention of writing are Robert J. Braidwood, *Prehistoric Men*, 8th ed. (1975) and Grahame Clark, *World Prehistory in New Perspective* (1977). The Neolithic development of agriculture and the urban revolution that followed are analyzed by V. Gordon Childe, *What Happened in History?* (1954).

Mesopotamia

C. W. Ceram, *Gods, Graves, and Scholars: The Story of Archaeology* (1951) is a popular, reliable survey of the great archeological discoveries of the nineteenth and twentieth centuries throughout the Near East. The Sumerians come alive through their writings in Samuel N. Kramer, *History Begins at Sumer* (1959). The origins of Mesopotamian civilization are explained in the short, classic study of Henri Frankfort, *The Birth of Civilization in the Near East* (1951). All Mesopotamian history is covered, with an emphasis on social and economic development in the scholarly H. W. F. Saggs, *The Greatness That Was Babylon* (1962). The Assyrians receive a surprisingly sympathetic treatment in Jorgen Laessoe, *People of Ancient Assyria* (1963). The New Babylonians under Nebuchadnezzar are shown as fine city builders in two well-illustrated books, Albert Champdor, *Babylon* (1958), and John Oates, *Babylon* (1979). For the great empire that destroyed Babylon, a good recent survey is J. M. Cook, *The Persian Empire* (1983).

The Mediterranean Lands of the Fertile Crescent

The Hittites are seen as driven by economic necessity rather than the search for power in J. G. McQueen, *The Hittites and Their Contemporaries in Asia Minor* (1976). For the creators of one of the world's first trading empires, see Sabatino Moscati, *The World of the Phoenicians* (1968). Harry Orlinsky, *Ancient Israel* (1954), and John Bright, *A History of Israel* (1972), are straightforward narrative, and should be accompanied by a more detailed survey of the development of Hebrew religious thought such as J. A. Bewer, *The Literature of the Old Testament in Its Historical Development* (1962). Colin Thubron's illustrated history, *Jerusalem* (1976), enables one to appreciate the beauty of the Hebrew capital.

---

[10] Jon Manchip White, *Everyday Life in Ancient Egypt* (New York: Capricorn Books, 1967), p. 189.

Egypt of the Pharaohs

Color illustrations are essential for an appreciation of the subtlety of Egyptian art, as in the early development described in Cyril Aldred, *Egypt to the End of the Old Kingdom* (1965). For the pyramids alone, see the excellent unravelling of their mysteries in I. E. S. Edwards, *The Pyramids of Egypt* (1975), while more details on the religious beliefs are presented in Henri Frankfort, *Ancient Egyptian Religion* (1961), and Rosalie A. David, *The Ancient Egyptians* (1982). Donald B. Redford presents Akhenaton's religious reforms against a broad political setting, in *Akhenaten: The Heretic King* (1984). T. G. H. James, *Pharaoh's People: Scenes from Life in Imperial Egypt* (1984), includes studies of the life of the farmer, the scribe, and the craftsman. A fine synthesis of Egyptian culture is J. A. Wilson, *The Culture of Ancient Egypt* (1956).

2

The Greeks

The influence of the Near East on Western civilization, although vitally important, was indirect. The achievements of the Fertile Crescent and the Nile Valley had to be absorbed by other peoples before they could become formative elements in the new civilization that began in the eastern Mediterranean in the second millenium B.C. and reached its first cultural climax in the city-states of Greece in the fifth century B.C.

Neolithic agriculture was developed in Europe between 6000 and 3000 B.C., partly under the influence of migrating peoples from western Asia. The use of copper and bronze had spread to eastern Europe by 2500 B.C., and the use of iron by about 1200 B.C. The scientific and mathematical advances of Mesopotamia as well as commercial expertise were learned by trading peoples like the Phoenicians and Arameans, and diffused along their commercial routes, while empires like the Hittite and the Persian spread the intellectual heritage of the Fertile Crescent by more warlike means. Moreover, peoples from outside the first areas of civilization broke in not only to take for themselves the material luxuries but frequently to adopt for themselves the heritage of art and learning of the lands they conquered. The greatest of these waves of invasions occurred between 1700 and 1400 B.C., when Indo-European peoples swept westward and southward, possibly from near the Black Sea, into a region stretching from northern Greece to northern India and, simultaneously, Semitic peoples continued to push northward and westward from the edges of the Arabian desert into the Fertile Crescent and Egypt. A second wave of invasions by Indo-Europeans followed between 1200 and 900 B.C., this time moving farther west along the Mediterranean littoral.

THE ORIGINS OF GREEK CIVILIZATION, 2000–800 B.C.

The Minoan Civilization of Crete, c. 2000–1400 B.C.

The area of Europe where the civilization of the Near East was most easily diffused was the islands and shores of the Aegean sea, where between 6000 and 2000 B.C. settlers, who may have come from North Africa and Asia Minor but who were definitely not Greeks, had established small farming communities organized around kinship ties. The first of these communities to achieve a high level of culture were on Crete, the largest of the Greek islands, which was also the best located for sea-borne contact with the trading cities of Phoenicia and Egypt. By about 2000 B.C. the Minoans, whose name is derived from the word Minos, which was either the name of an early king or a title like pharaoh, were trading throughout the eastern Mediterranean, exchanging timber, textiles, olive oil, and pottery for copper, silver, and gold, for foodstuffs, and for the luxuries of the Near East. Their merchants probably also profited from supplying the metals of the western Mediterranean, such as copper, to the Near East. Excavation in the vast Minoan palace at Knossos has revealed a joyful, peaceful civilization. Wall paintings, reminiscent in some ways of the tomb paintings of Egypt, show brightly dressed courtiers enjoying music and festivals in gardens filled with flowers, birds, and animals. The deity most frequently presented was the Great Mother, the snake goddess who protected fertility and was guardian of both human beings and animals. The favorite sport, probably also a rite at a religious festival, was bull leaping, in which boys and girls seized the horns of a bull and launched themselves backward into a somersault to land behind the bull. In the palace cellars were vast containers for storage of wine, oil, and wheat, while running water supplied a surprisingly modern system of sanitation. There were even schools within the palace, where slates containing painfully copied student texts have been found.

Archeologists excavating in Crete have found three types of script inscribed mainly on baked clay tablets. The earliest was hieroglyphic. The second, which was syllabic, is known as Linear A. Neither has been deciphered. However, another form of syllabic script, known as Linear B, was discovered on tablets at Knossos and at many sites on the mainland of Greece. This script was deciphered by an English architect named Michael Ventris in 1953. The language proved to be archaic Greek, although written in Minoan script, and to have been developed by the invading people known as the Mycenaeans, who captured Knossos about 1450 B.C.

Mycenaean Civilization, c. 1600–1100 B.C.

The Mycenaeans were descendants of the Achaeans, the first Greeks who had penetrated the peninsula from the north about 2000 B.C. These Greeks were an Indo-European people, organized into clans governed by kings. They already rode horses into war and carried battle axes, thus possessing the power quite

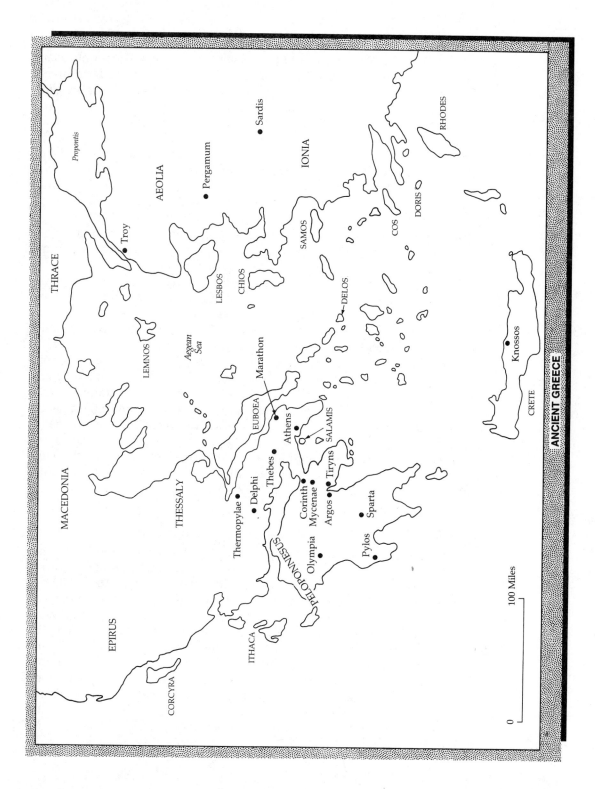

ANCIENT GREECE

THRACE

MACEDONIA

EPIRUS

THESSALY

Propontis

Troy

AEOLIA

IONIA

Sardis

Pergamum

RHODES

DORIS

COS

SAMOS

CHIOS

LESBOS

Aegean
Sea

LEMNOS

DELOS

CORCYRA

ITHACA

Thermopylae

Delphi

EUBOEA

Marathon

Athens

SALAMIS

Thebes

PELOPONNESUS

Corinth

Mycenae

Tiryns

Argos

Olympia

Sparta

Pylos

Knossos

CRETE

100 Miles

0

easily to subdue the Neolithic peasantry of mainland Greece, whose only weapons were sharpened sticks and bones. The earliest settlements of these Greeks were in the forbidding plain of Argos on a peninsula called the Peloponnesus. Here they compelled their newly conquered subjects, now made slaves, to erect vast citadels at Mycenae and Tiryns, with walls so thick that later Greeks called them Cyclopean, thinking they had been built by a giant named Cyclops. The Mycenaeans, as modern historians refer to these Achaeans after the founding of Mycenae, were predatory warriors, who used their military strength to seize spoils in gold and silver and prisoners as slaves and concubines. Their most memorable feat was in fact a military expedition, their campaign to capture and destroy the rich city of Troy on the coast of Asia Minor (about 1260 B.C.). This adventure provided later Greeks with the subject matter of the two great epic poems, the *Iliad* and the *Odyssey*, which were probably written down, if not composed by, a poet called Homer in the eighth century B.C.

Excavations have shown, however, that the Mycenaeans were far more than savage warriors. They rebuilt the palace of Knossos, which had probably been destroyed by fire (perhaps following a great tidal wave caused by a volcanic eruption) at about the time of their invasion. But the rebuilt palace may not have survived beyond 1380 B.C. before being once again destroyed by earthquake and fire. The Mycenaeans became superb sailors, who used piracy as well as peaceful commerce to supply their cities. They exported olive oil and wine, and, like the Minoans, probably were intermediaries in trade between Western Europe and the Near East. When in the nineteenth century the amateur German archeologist Heinrich Schliemann, who had already made a name for himself by discovering the ruins of Troy, began excavations at Mycenae, he unearthed treasures from all over the Mediterranean—gold death masks, cups of silver and bronze, and elaborate jewelry that had been buried with the bodies of the warrior aristocracy.

The Dark Age, 1200–800 B.C.

In the two centuries following the Trojan War, Mycenaean civilization collapsed. Its fall was traditionally assumed to have been caused by the sudden invasion of the Dorians, one of several Greek tribes who entered Greece about 1200 B.C. It is now believed that internal conflict had already reduced the Mycenaean cities to a state of military weakness, economic breakdown, and depopulation. Leaders returning from the Trojan War had found their positions usurped. The Mycenaean cities were at war with each other. Refugees were on the move, not only within Greece but to safety and new lives around the coasts of the Aegean Sea. Disorder had made it impossible for peasants to plant or gather their harvests as before. Trade had dwindled. Thus, when the Dorians arrived, armed with weapons of iron, they did not have to wage war against a flourishing civilization but simply to complete a destruction that the Mycenaeans had inflicted upon themselves.

The Dorians were content to lead first a nomadic life and later a settled, isolated agricultural life in the more fertile valleys of the Peloponnesus. Here they founded the villages of Sparta and Argos, which were later to develop into strong city-states. Some Dorians continued to move southward to capture Crete, and others moved on again to Rhodes and the other islands of the eastern Aegean and eventually to the coast of Asia Minor. Northern Greece and the northern shores of Asia Minor were settled by Greeks speaking the Aeolic dialect. Other migrants from central Greece, who spoke the Ionic dialect, settled the central part of the Asia Minor coast, which was called Ionia.

The four centuries following the invasions are known in Greek history as the Dark Age. It was a period of chaos about which little is known, partly because civilized city life, with its written records, had virtually ceased. When we again have knowledge of the history of the Greeks, about 800 B.C., it is clear that during the Dark Age several vitally important changes had occurred in Greek society.

In the first place, the Greeks had invented the institution of the *polis*, which we usually translate as a "city-state." Probably the first to do so were the Greek refugees in Ionia, who were established in coastal valleys or on peninsulas jutting into the sea and isolated among a hostile population. They had formed rules of government to which they all subscribed and had recognized that they were linked by bonds transcending those of family or clan. They had, in short, formed political bonds of citizenship. Meetings of the citizens for worship or commerce were followed, almost instinctively, by community discussion of property matters or disputes or common problems of the community, which became institutionalized as a council, or *boulê*, in which all community members were free to participate.

Second, however, in the countryside a very sharp differentiation had occurred between a land-owning aristocracy and the poor peasantry. One of the earliest Greek poems, *The Works and Days* of Hesiod, depicts the "gift-hungry" nobility as a hawk holding a nightingale in its claws:

> This is what the hawk said when he had caught a nightingale
> With spangled neck in his claws and carried her high among the clouds. . . .
> "What is the matter with you? Why scream? Your master has you.
> You shall go wherever I take you, for all your singing.
> If I like, I can let you go. If I like, I can eat you for dinner.
> He is a fool who tries to match his strength with the stronger. . . ."
> So spoke the hawk, the bird who flies so fast on his long wings.[1]

Only profound social reform could end this class antagonism.

Third, a major change had occurred in the relationships between the sexes. In the poems of Homer, which probably depict the values of the Mycenaean age, women enjoy a certain equality with men and some freedom of action. For

---

[1] Hesiod, *The Works and Days*, translated by Richmond Lattimore (Ann Arbor: University of Michigan Press, 1962), p. 43.

example, Penelope, who is waiting for the return of her husband Odysseus from the Trojan Wars, refused to pick a new husband from a crowd of suitors, telling them that they must wait until she has woven the shroud of her father-in-law, a shroud that she unravels every night. Women at least had a choice of husband and a significant role in running not only their households but outside commercial activity as well. By the eighth century, however, perhaps because of the military preoccupations of the Dorians, society had become male-dominated. Women were increasingly segregated in the back rooms of the home in a separate area while men sought, both for business and pleasure, the company of other men.

Fourth, as a result of the pressure of population growth on the relatively few fertile areas of mainland Greece, there was a large landless population restless to find new opportunities. When the period of chaos of the Dark Age was over, thousands of dispossessed Greek farmers and their families, often under the leadership of the younger sons or the illegitimate children of the great aristocrats, embarked on a vast wave of colonization that, lasting 200 years, from 750 to 550 B.C., was to plant more than 600 colonies along the shores of the Mediterranean and Black Seas.

The Greek Epic Poems

One of the lasting legacies of the Dark Age was the Greek epic poem. Legends about the Gods and about the past of the Greek people had been sung by wandering poets, or bards, for hundreds of years. They were memorized with the help of repetitive rhythms in the verse, and passed on from generation to generation. Some of the favorite stories and myths were written down at the end of the Dark Age by Homer, who perhaps lived between about 850 and 750 B.C., and Hesiod, who may have lived a little later. The poems of Hesiod gave the Greeks the basis of their mythology, while the poems of Homer, studied by every Greek school child throughout antiquity (and by many non-Greek students ever since) were a formative influence on Greek language and literature and to some extent on the Greek concept of themselves.

Hesiod was a wealthy farmer who wrote a book, *The Works and Days*, describing for his brother how to run a farm, with special attention to the days that would be propitious according to the stars. His misogynism, which went through all his writings, was evident in his advice to the young farmer to get a slave girl to work in the fields, but to postpone marrying until he was thirty, since women were born deceivers. When Zeus created the first mortal woman, Pandora, Hesiod warned, she disobeyed him by opening a box that let loose in the world all the troubles that have afflicted mankind ever since. In the *Theogony*, he systematically described the creation of the earth from chaos and the origins of the gods.

Homer's *Iliad* was the story of the siege of Troy by the forces of the My-

Ajax and Achilles Playing Dice. Amphora by Exekias The military equipment shown was only developed in the eighth century B.C. The warriors are holding the hoplite's long, thrusting spears, and wearing greaves to protect their legs. Their round shields rest against the wall. (Alinari/Art Resource.)

cenaeans. It focused on the quarrel between the Greek hero Achilles and the chief king of the Greeks, Agamemnon, who has taken from him a slave girl he loved. While Achilles sulks in his tent, the Trojan leader Hector kills Achilles' best friend, Patroclus. Only then does Achilles set out to do battle. After he has killed Hector, he unwillingly agrees to the plea of Hector's old father, Priam, for the return of the body of his son. The *Odyssey*, which was probably written slightly later than the *Iliad*, is the story of the return to Greece from Troy of Odysseus and his men, who have innumerable adventures, both terrifying and humorous, during the ten years it takes them to get back. The poems were insightful in their presentation of human character under stress. They laid down for the Greeks an ideal of heroism, of courage in the face of challenge and of tragedy, that became one of the enduring themes of Greek literature and art. They taught that the Gods were somewhat like human beings, with their foibles, their jealousies, and their passions, but also their striving for a better world. Knowledge and love of the Homeric epics acted as a cement uniting Greeks over time and place.

THE ARCHAIC AGE, 800–500 B.C.

Economic and Military Change

After 800 B.C., the Greek world underwent rapid economic change. The establishment of a far-flung network of trade was furthered by the movement of colonization. By the middle of the sixth century, independent Greek city-states had been founded at some of the finest trading locations of the ancient world—at the mouth of the river Don, through which the wheat of the Ukraine was shipped; at Byzantium, the site of the future city of Constantinople, which controlled the outlet of the Black Sea; in the Nile Delta, near the site of the future city of Alexandria; along the southern shore of Sicily, commanding the narrow straits between the eastern and western Mediterranean; on the Bay of Naples, with access to the products of southern Italy; at the mouth of the river Rhône in France; on the eastern coast of Spain; and on both the Spanish and Moroccan shores, controlling the outlet of the Mediterranean to the Atlantic Ocean. These cities maintained good relations with their mother city on the Greek mainland, worshipped the same gods and usually adopted the same constitution; but they also had close cultural and commercial ties with the other Greek cities whose language they shared and with whom they participated in such "Pan-Hellenic" festivals as the Olympic Games.

Commerce among the Greek cities stimulated change in both the country-side and the cities of mainland Greece. Farmers began to specialize in production of goods that could be sold for export, such as wine and olive oil, in addition to raising the food needed to feed their families. A growing class of artisans in the cities produced a wide variety of manufactured goods, including cloth,

Temple of Poseidon, Paestum, Italy (early sixth century B.C.) *Paestum was founded by Greek colonists from Sybaris about 600 B.C. Its Doric temples are some of the best preserved in existence. (Alinari/Art Resource.)*

pottery, weapons, decorated metalwork, and perfumes made of oil. The merchant class expanded to handle the sale of these products overseas and to import into mainland Greece foodstuffs for the cities, such as the grain of southern Russia and Asia Minor, and raw materials such as the iron ore of western Italy.

The increase of prosperity of the merchant, artisan, and farming classes made possible changes in military technique, which undermined the predominance of the aristocracy. In the Dark Age, cavalry had been the principal fighting force, and thus the aristocracy, which owned horses and chariots, had been the main fighting force. In the Archaic Age, the cavalry was replaced by hoplites, soldiers drawn largely from the independent farmers who armed themselves with breastplates and helmets, and carried shields that covered them from cheekbone to thigh. Their main weapon was an iron-tipped spear, 9 feet long. These infantry forces became invincible when they were organized into a phalanx, a mass formation eight ranks deep that charged at the battle cry, or paean, of their leader like a moving wall of iron. An army composed of these citizen-soldiers was far more democratic than the cavalry, since far larger numbers could afford the equipment needed and since participation in the phalanx required a sense of equality and mutual trust among the hoplites.

The combination of economic and military change produced great tension between the aristocrats and the other classes, and threatened to bring about a new age of chaos. Occasionally, conflict was avoided by agreement among the quarreling groups by bringing in an arbiter, or "lawgiver," who would impose legal and political solutions. More frequently, the newly prosperous merchant groups joined with the peasantry to throw off the controls of the landed aristocracy, and in its place accepted one-man rule, or "tyranny." Between 650 and 500 B.C., most Greek cities were governed by "tyrants," who, far from being oppressive as the word "tyrant" later came to imply, received popular support in their program of reforms.

The Society of Sparta

Sparta is the outstanding example of a city-state that turned to lawgivers rather than tyrants. The Spartans were the descendants of Dorians who had invaded the Peloponnesus about 1100 B.C. About 720 B.C., finding their own region of Laconia too small and infertile to support their increasing population, they conquered the richer lands of Messenia to the west and made its inhabitants into state slaves called helots, like the original inhabitants of Laconia whom they had conquered.

Ruling the largest state in Greece, in which they were outnumbered ten to one by the people they had subjugated, the Spartans concluded that only by harsh self-discipline could they maintain their dominance. After a dangerous slave revolt about 650–620 B.C., the Spartans rewrote their constitution, attributing it to a mythical lawgiver named Lycurgus, who had supposedly lived in

the ninth century B.C. The new constitution froze Spartan society into a disciplined, militaristic mold that was to stunt their intellectual growth and dehu-
manize both them and their subjects for the rest of their history. Spartan society
was divided into three classes: state slaves, who were 90 percent of the population; free noncitizens, called "dwellers around," people who originally lived
in the frontier region but became the main commercial-artisan group and constituted 7 percent of the population; and the Spartans themselves, a mere 3
percent of the population.

Only male Spartans were citizens. For them, an austere, disciplined life
was prescribed. Male babies were inspected at birth by state officials, and the
sickly were ordered to die by exposure. At the age of seven, the boy was taken
from his mother, and, living in barracks under harsh instructors, was taught
the military arts. At twenty, he became a front-line soldier, and only at thirty
was he permitted to return to live with his wife. He continued to do military
service until the age of sixty, and to take meals at communal tables in the
barracks. In this way Spartans were inculcated with the ideals of obedience,
self-denial, courage, and contempt for both commerce and culture. Their meals
were rough and unpalatable, and included a black broth famous among other
cities for its forbidding aroma. After sharing one meal in the barracks, a visitor
remarked that now he understood why the Spartans were not afraid to die! The
institution of government carried on the equality of the barracks. The Spartans
had two kings, with equal powers, to avoid the danger of one-man rule. Legislation was prepared by a council of twenty-eight "elders," all over the age of
sixty. The kings were supervised by five *ephors* or guardians, who also ran
foreign policy, presided over the assembly, and in fact ran the state if the kings
were weak. All citizens met in an assembly to vote on laws, but not to debate
them.

This society rather surprisingly gave greater freedom and equality to
women than any other in Greece. Household work was done by slaves. The
Spartan women were expected to keep healthy through gymnastics and to eat
well, in order to bear strong children. With the men constantly absent in the
barracks or on campaign, they ran the household and farm. Adultery was rarely
punished because Spartans were in need of youths for the army. Since, however, as a result of the constant wars, there were usually more women than
men in Sparta, families had to give a large dowry to arrange the marriage of a
daughter to one of the few eligible male citizens; and a wife was regarded as
worthy of esteem only when she had given birth to male children.

Spartan society fascinated, and often repelled, the citizens of the other
Greek states, although they grudgingly admired their rigid morality. According
to one story, an old man who was looking for a seat at the Olympic games was
being cheered by the crowd. When he reached the Spartan section of the amphitheater, every young Spartan, and most of the older ones, offered him their
seats, whereupon the crowd applauded. The old man commented: "All Greeks
know what is right; only the Spartans *do* it."

Athens Under Solon, Pisistratus, and Cleisthenes

By contrast, the city-state of Athens was fortunate in that its constitution was remodeled first by a lawgiver named Solon and then by the tyrant Pisastratus and the reforming archon (chief magistrate) Cleisthenes. The original city of Athens was a Mycenaean settlement on a high rock, the Acropolis, which offered an ideal defensive position overlooking the plains of the region called Attica, a peninsula shaped like a horse's head, which protruded southward into the Aegean Sea from the Greek mainland. The soil was poor and the streams unreliable. Attica did possess a few natural advantages. The clay soil could be made into pottery of extreme fineness. It had rich deposits of silver and lead. A circle of mountains protected it from invasion from the north; and it had easy access to the fishing grounds and the shipping lanes of the Mediterranean.

By the eighth century B.C., Athens passed from monarchy to rule by aristocracy, while the peasantry had been reduced to share-croppers. Many had even been sold into slavery for personal debts. Hence there was a widespread demand for the redistribution of the land, the end of sharecropping, the abolition of debt slavery, and the freeing of debt-slaves. These reforms would have implied the drastic reduction of the power of the aristocracy. In 594 B.C., the aristocrats, fearing bloodshed, called in Solon, the most trusted of their citizens, to carry out a program of reforms. Solon modified the harsh legislation of an earlier lawgiver, Draco, who in 621 B.C. had codified the laws for the first time and had, according to later commentators, imposed the death penalty for very trivial offenses. Solon canceled all mortgages on land, freed those in slavery for debt, and even bought back those sold into debt slavery abroad. His reforms permitted all citizens to take part in an assembly, which chose a Council of Four Hundred or *Boulê* that was given power to check the older assembly of aristocrats called the *Areopogus*. Solon did, however, recognize the class basis of Athenian society by dividing the citizens into four groups according to income, with only the two wealthier groups being permitted to share in executive power. He also attempted to restore the moral fiber of Athens, by ordering fathers to teach a trade to their sons, punishing the lazy, and forbidding women to wear extravagant clothes or cosmetics. His puritanical rules for women's conduct may, indeed, have given legal sanction to the segregation of women within their own quarters of the home, and certainly encouraged men to stay away from home as much as possible.

The institutions of Solon were made more efficient by Pisistratus between 546 and 527 and by Cleisthenes after 508 B.C. Pisistratus tackled the continuing economic problems by giving state land and loans to poor farmers and by planting colonies on the Dardanelles to safeguard the wheat supply from Russia. To stimulate civic pride, he laid great emphasis on worship of the goddess Athena, the patron of Athens, for whom he expanded the temple on the Acropolis. The four-yearly festival in her honor, called the Panathenaic Festival, was made a great public celebration, second only to the Dionysian Festival, in honor of Dionysus, the god of wine, music, and fertility.

Cleisthenes was responsible for the final remodeling of the Athenian constitution. He divided the state into territorial units called *demes*, which were about the size of a village or a city ward, and then formed ten completely new tribes from combinations of the demes. In this way, territorial rather than family or clan loyalty became the basis of political allegiance. Each of the ten tribes picked by lot one-tenth of the 500 members of the Council, or *Boulê*, the main executive body. The assembly, which included all citizens and met about forty times a year, was the legislative body. Citizens were also eligible to volunteer for choice by lot for service on the large juries, which numbered between 101 and 1001. To prevent any individual from becoming dangerously powerful, from about 500 B.C. a majority of the members of the assembly could banish a person for ten years by writing his name on a broken piece of pottery, called an *ostrakon*; the custom was known as ostracism. The only position where competence was required and leadership could be perpetuated was as one of the ten generals, chosen annually by the assembly. Cleisthenes had thus institutionalized a system of participatory democracy. Not only were the 30,000 to 50,000 citizens eligible to make laws personally, but many would have served in both executive and judicial positions in the council and on juries.

Athenian Society

We should not, however, conclude that this was an egalitarian society. At the base of Greek society was the class of slaves. In Athens, which had a population of between 200,000 and 250,000, they comprised one-third of the population. Every city had a slave market, and only the poorer families among the citizens managed without owning at least one slave. Slaves were available from many parts of Europe, Asia, and Africa. Only a few black African slaves were put on sale, and they fetched a high price, primarily because of their scarcity. They served mainly to display the wealth of the person who had purchased them. Slaves from the Eastern Mediterranean countries and the Near East were usually regarded as obedient and skilled in commercial matters. Greek slaves, who had either been captured in war or who had been sold by their parents, often became domestic workers, as cooks or housemaids. Slaves from such northern areas as Thrace or Scythia, whom the Greeks tended to regard as savage but strong, were usually assigned to the hardest work in the fields or to almost certain death by overwork in the mines. Good-looking girls of whatever nationality were often purchased for prostitution.

Greek slaves never became a class so resentful at its exploitation that their owners lived in fear, as the Romans did, of the ever-present danger of a slave uprising. Except for those in the mines, slaves worked side by side with their owners, whether as farmers in the fields or carrying out such household chores as meal preparation or cloth weaving in the home. They were encouraged to have families, partly to keep them contented and partly to make more laborers available. Those in commerce were able to acquire skills, and could often put aside money with which they might eventually buy their freedom. In old age, the family who owned them was expected to provide support. Nevertheless, the abuses were great. Children in particular were subject to all kinds of abuse. Families could be broken up for sale. Individual owners were free to use cruel punishments, so long as they did not actually kill their slaves. Conditions in the mines were inhuman.

All cities permitted aliens to reside within their boundaries, primarily for the purpose of carrying on commerce or other economic activities. Resident aliens composed one-tenth of the population of Athens, which welcomed those with capital and skill in banking or those who would undertake menial manufacturing jobs. Most cities regarded resident aliens with suspicion, avoiding giving them citizenship, and taxed them at a higher rate than their own citizens.

The major part of the population were independent free farmers, who were regarded as the 'bulwark of a democratic polis by philosophers like Aristotle. Usually working with two or three slaves, they would grow olives, grapes, figs, and occasionally some wheat. They clustered in small villages scattered across the landscape, rather than living alone in the middle of their own fields. Here they enjoyed companionship, security, and the possibility of taking part in the politics of their own locality or deme. From the time of the hoplites in the eighth century B.C., this class of free farmers had been the basis of the Greek armed

Greek Women Working Wool
The vase, in black-figure style of c. 560 B.C., shows women folding coverlets or twirling a weighted spindle to spin thread from the raw wool (The Metropolitan Museum of Art, Fletcher Fund, 1931.)

forces, and they normally remained loyal to their city through the most dangerous crises, even when their urban leaders vacillated.

Within the cities, a male elite dominated political, economic, and intellectual life. Some were descendants of the old land-owning aristocracy; others were of an upper middle class that had arisen through commerce, banking, manufacturing, or even agriculture. For this group, who did not number more than a few thousand, Athens provided the pleasures and the opportunities of the agora, the gymnasium, and the stadium, and from this group came the aristocrat Pericles, who was able to turn perennial reelection as general into a system of one-man rule that lasted from 461 to 429 B.C.

The separation of women from the lives of the men of their family was most obvious in this upper social group. Slave girls and farming women worked more closely with men in the fields or the household. But when a family was wealthy enough, women were segregated in separate quarters, usually upstairs, where their only visitors were close relatives. There they devoted themselves to spinning, weaving, and other tasks necessary for the house. A wife had little possibility of intellectual comradeship with her family, since she was not educated in the liberal arts as boys were. Moreover, she was usually fifteen years or more younger than her husband. Partly for that reason, the law laid down that she was to be under the guardianship of her father until marriage, of her husband after marriage, and of her male children if widowed.

There is, however, some evidence that not all women lived the dull life of intellectual deprivation. Many men expected their courtesans to be their intellectual equals, and to provide the stimulation that their poorly educated wives could not. Aspasia, the courtesan of Pericles, was widely admired for her philosophical accomplishments. Some philosophers welcomed women to their academies. Further evidence of the independence of Greek women can be found in the plays of Aristophanes where some women are portrayed as assuming the right to run the government, which was a direct challenge to the status quo of their society. It is doubtful whether a woman like Aristophanes's Lysistrata would have followed the advice Pericles gave to women in his Funeral Oration: "Your great glory is not to be inferior to what God has made you, and the greatest glory of a woman is to be least talked about by men, whether they are praising you or criticizing you."[2] Pericles' view of women's behavior, however, is much closer to the classical norm than Aristophanes.

GREECE: FROM THE PERSIAN INVASIONS TO THE PELOPONNESIAN WAR

Many of the greatest achievements of the Greek genius were created in the brief half-century between the end of the Persian wars in 479 B.C. and the beginning

[2] Thucydides, *The Peloponnesian War*, translated by Rex Warner (Harmondsworth, England: Penguin Books, 1972), p. 151.

of the civil struggles known as the Peloponnesian War in 431 B.C. Victory over the Persians seemed to give the Greeks the confidence as well as the security to embark upon daring experiments in extending the range and goals of almost every human intellectual activity. The self-inflicted destruction of the Peloponnesian War brought a cowing of the Greek spirit. Much of what we think of as the Greek heritage to civilization is the product of this golden half-century between the two periods of war.

The Persians had been expanding constantly since Cyrus the Great (reigned 550–529 B.C.) had defeated the Chaldeans and freed the Jews from Babylon. In the east, Cyrus had expanded Persian borders into India. In the west, he had conquered the kingdom of Lydia in Asia Minor, which included the coastal Greek cities of Ionia. Egypt fell to his son Cambyses (reigned 529–522 B.C.). And Darius I (reigned 522–486 B.C.) had taken the Punjab in India and Thrace in Europe.

Faced by hard-fought revolt by the Ionian cities, Darius determined to punish them and to destroy Athens, their principal ally on the mainland. In 490 B.C., expecting little opposition, he dispatched a force of only 100 ships and 20,000 men. The Persian army was, however, twice the size of the force that Athens raised to oppose it at the plain of Marathon. The Athenian general Miltiades, however, ordered the center of his army to retreat and then fell on the advancing Persians with the two wings of his force. More than 6000 Persians were killed, and Athens was temporarily saved.

To the Greek historian Herodotus, it was proof of the value of freedom, which the Athenians had achieved with the reforms of Cleisthenes:

> Thus Athens went from strength to strength and proved, if proof were needed, how noble a thing freedom is, not in one respect only but in all; for while they were oppressed under a despotic government, they had no better success in war than any of their neighbors, yet, once the yoke was flung off, they proved the finest fighters in the world.[3]

Ten years later, under the emperor Xerxes (reigned 486–465 B.C.), the Persians returned in force with an army of at least 150,000 soldiers. They were delayed briefly by a heroic resistance of 300 Spartans, all of whom were killed at the pass of Thermopylae, but soon had burned Athens itself, whose inhabitants had been transferred at the orders of their leader Themistocles to the nearby island of Salamis. Following the strategy of Themistocles, who had persuaded the Athenians to spend the silver from newly opened mines to build a fleet, the Athenians lured the unwieldy Persian ships into the straits of Salamis, where they sank them before the eyes of a horrified Xerxes, who sat enthroned and impotent on the shore. The next year a large Spartan army defeated the Persians in central Greece at the battle of Plataea, thereby ending the invasion threat.

The Athenian contribution of leadership and military power to the defeat

---

[3] *Herodotus: The Histories*, translated by Aubrey de Selincourt (Harmondsworth, England: Penguin Books, 1954), p. 339.

of the Persians was recognized by most Greeks as the decisive factor in victory, and the majority of the Greek cities agreed at the end of the war to form the Delian League to continue the attacks on Persia under the leadership of Athens. The Spartans refused to join, and withdrew to their homeland on the Peloponnesus. At first the Athenians behaved with restraint. The treasury of the league was kept on the island of Delos. The independence of the members was respected. Athens contributed most of the ships used by the league in attacks on the Persians in Asia Minor. Moreover, it appeared that Athens was becoming more democratic at home. The powers of the Areopagus were further reduced. Poorer citizens were encouraged to take a fuller share in the life of the city by payment for service on juries, in the Council, and in the army and navy. Pericles, during the long period when he controlled the policy of Athens (461–429 B.C.), remained the spokesman of the poorer classes. Far from being a closed society like that of the Spartans, Athens threw itself open to the world. Its assemblies, its theaters, its schools, its athletic grounds, its temples, were open to the inspection of the world, because the Athenians believed, as Pericles said, that they were "the school of Hellas."

But the Athenians deluded themselves when they failed to see that their empire was slowly changing their character, and that from liberators in the eyes of their allies they were becoming oppressors. No city was permitted to secede from the Delian League after 470 B.C. The treasury was moved from Delos to the Acropolis of Athens in 454 B.C. The Athenian fleet was used against recalcitrant allies for the collection of tribute, and Athens intervened in local political quarrels to help the democratic groups crush the aristocratic factions. Members of the League were compelled to use the Athenian coinage, and Athens even established colonies on the territory of some of its allies.

In 431 B.C. Sparta and Corinth came to the aid of the discontented members of the Delian League in an attack on Athens that opened the Peloponnesian War (431–404 B.C.) Pericles persuaded the Athenians to withdraw within their walls, abandoning the fields of Attica to the Spartans and waiting for their navy to win a decisive sea battle. Plague broke out within the city, however, killing one-third of the Athenian population, including Pericles himself. Afterwards, the poorer classes of Athens found leaders from their own group, and often attempted to use their control of the assembly and even the juries for punitive action against the aristocrats.

As the fighting dragged on indecisively, the Athenians resorted to greater brutality. On one occasion, they murdered all the adult males of a neutral island and sold the women and children into slavery. A vainglorious expedition sent against the Greek cities of Sicily was a total failure and caused great loss of money and lives. In the last years of the war, the Spartans even succeeded in defeating the Athenian fleet. In 404 B.C., starving and rent by internal dissension, the Athenians made a humiliating peace with Sparta. They were forced to destroy their own walls and almost all of their ships, and to submit to an aristocratic government known as the Thirty Tyrants. Their empire was dissolved.

The Peloponnesian War destroyed the power of Athens, but no other city took its position of leadership. The victors quarreled among themselves, and for the next century there was constant fighting among changing coalitions established by Sparta, Thebes, and Corinth, with Athens itself occasionally intervening on one side or the other. The outcome of all this fighting, the historian Xenophon (c. 430–355 B.C.) commented, was "the opposite of what all men believed would happen. . . . While each party claimed to be victorious, neither was found to be any better off, as regards either additional territory, or city, or sway, than before the battle took place; but there was even more confusion and disorder in Greece after the battle than before."[4]

The Greek cities were to fall easy prey to the armies of Macedon, a tribal state in northern Greece, whose people, although partly of Greek blood and influenced by Greek culture, were a tougher breed of peasants and mountaineers than the city dwellers who had openly despised them for centuries.

THE GOLDEN AGE OF HELLENIC CULTURE

Although Athens was the incubator of the highest achievements of the culture of the golden age—which we call Hellenic after Hellas, the Greek word for their own country—the whole Greek world shared in this great intellectual boom. The philosophers who developed scientific speculation into the nature of matter lived in Ionia. The Hippocratic school of medicine was founded on the Aegean island of Cos. The scientist Empedocles was born in Agrigento in Sicily. Aristotle came from Stagia, in northern Greece. Even the Spartans shared—though less fully than other Greek states—in a remarkably homogeneous Greek intellectual world.

The most outstanding characteristics of this Greek attitude of mind were, first, an interest in human beings and the achievement of their full potential; second, a spirit of inquiry, employing the most sophisticated processes of human reason; third, a fascination with the working of, and respect for, the demands of human community, most specifically in the form of political community represented by the *polis* or city-state; fourth, a fascination with philosophy, notably with metaphysical explanation (the questioning as to why the universe operates as it does) and ethics (the influence on individual conduct of the concepts of right and wrong); and fifth, the pursuit of beauty, as an abstract idea that can be embodied physically in a temple, a statue, or a poem.

Greek Religion

At first sight, Greek religion may appear to be in complete contrast to the pursuit of rationality and humanism, but to appeal instead to the irrational in human

---

[4] Xenophon, Hellenica VII. 26–27, translated by Carleton L. Brownson, in Loeb edition, vol. II (London: W. Heinemann, 1921), p. 227.

beings. The Greeks were polytheistic. In addition to certain abstract forces, such as love, which were deified, by the time of the Dark Age they had created a whole panoply of gods who, though immortal and more powerful than human beings, showed all the passions and foibles of Greeks themselves. The more important gods were believed to live on the northern mountain Olympus, where Zeus, the god of the sky, behaved like a patriarchal father of a typical aristocratic family. Demeter was the earth goddess, who safeguarded fertility and the harvest. Aphrodite was the goddess of love and Poseidon the god of the sea. Apollo, the sun god, brought light and was the many-sided god of arts, prophecy, archery, flocks, and herds. Certain gods or goddesses were patrons of individual cities. Gray-eyed Athena was patron of Athens, but also goddess of wisdom—perhaps an oblique indication of how the Athenians rated themselves. These gods could be pleased by ritual prayers and sacrifices, as well as by the construction of lavish temples for their statues and by festivals in their honor. This form of communal worship, or even appeasement, of the gods, reached its climax when all the Greek cities joined together every four years from 776 B.C. on at Olympia for the Olympic Games, which honored Zeus. Games were also held at Delphi to honor Apollo and near Corinth for Poseidon.

Perhaps the most seemingly irrational action of the Greeks was to appeal to oracles, who were priests or priestesses or later persons in trances, who interpreted the answers of the gods to specific questions asked by petitioners. The answers, usually in verse, were frequently so difficult to interpret that it was hard to prove that the gods had failed to respond correctly. (The most famous response was probably that of the Delphic oracle, which told the Athenians to rely on their "wooden walls" for defense against the Persians. Their leader Themistocles argued that the oracle meant their new wooden ships; and, sure enough, they sank the Persian fleet off Salamis as the oracle had predicted.)

Yet Hellenic religion was not out of harmony with the rest of Greek life. The Greeks had humanized the gods because they did not wish to fear abstract forces with which they could not come to terms on a personal level. The Greeks refused to believe that human beings were born evil and required penance to purge themselves of some primordial sin. They imposed no set of required beliefs, and demanded no specific ritual of worship for acceptance into the favor of the gods. In a subtle way, Greek religion led the Greeks to ask questions rather than to pronounce final truths about fate, morality, and retribution, and they turned to specialists, literally, to dramatize those questions. Modern theater was born in the plays written for presentation at the religious festivals of Greece.

Greek Lyric and Drama

Greek drama of the fifth century B.C. was in a direct sense the continuation of the Greek poetic tradition begun by the epic poets of the Dark Age. The legends contained in Homer's poems had been sung for audiences to the accompaniment of stringed instruments even before they were written down; and in their final form they became the most popular public entertainment. Between 800 and 500 B.C., in what is called the Lyric Age of literature, a number of poets wrote deeply personal verses that were performed in public, usually to the accompaniment of a lyre. One of the most admired writers was Sappho (who lived on the island of Lesbos in the early sixth century B.C.). Sappho wrote *monody*, verse to be performed by one individual with accompaniment. She described her delight in natural scenery, in festivals and the weddings of her friends, and especially her love for the many people, male and female, who entered her life. One charming little poem recommends the perfect headdress:

> My mother always said
> that in her youth she was
> exceedingly in fashion
>
> wearing a purple ribbon
> looped in her hair. But
> the girl whose hair is yellower
>
> than torchlight should wear no
> colorful ribbons from Sardis—
> but a garland of fresh flowers.[5]

The choral lyric, performed by a group, was perfected by Pindar (518?– c. 438 B.C.), in odes he wrote for processions celebrating athletes who had been victorious in the Olympic or other games. In the sixth century B.C., at the festival dedicated to Dionysus, the recitation of poetry to music was brought to the stage, with the presentation of the story of Dionysus by a leader and a chorus.

The first plays were little more than rhetorical displays on religious themes by the leader and the chorus, but in the last half of the sixth century Athenian playwrights began to present their own versions of the myths of the god with imagined conversations. With the addition of a second, and later, of a third actor, each of whom could take several roles by changing costumes and masks, a complex form of dialogue was developed. Writers of both tragedy and comedy competed for the right to present their plays each spring at the five-day festival. After an opening-day devoted to processions and poetry recitations, the second day was given over to five comedies. On each of the last three days, the dramatists who had won the competition were each permitted to present three tragedies. Unfortunately, only forty-seven plays have survived out of the 1200 written at this time. Fortunately, thirty-three of these are by the greatest dramatists of Athens—Aeschylus, Sophocles, and Euripides.

Aeschylus (525–456 B.C.) terrified his audiences by presenting *nemesis*, the vengeance of the gods on guilty human beings. In his play *The Persians*, written

---

[5] *Greek Lyric Poetry*, translated by Willis Barnstone (New York: Bantam Books, 1962), p. 64.

only seven years after the Persian invasions, the Greeks have been used by the gods to punish the Persians for their overweening pride:

> And corpses, piled up like sand, shall witness,
> Mute, even to the century to come,
> Before the eyes of men, that never, being
> Mortal, ought we cast our thoughts too high. . . ,
> Behold, the punishment of these! remember
> Greece and Athens! lest you disdain
> Your present fortune, and lust after more,
> Squandering great prosperity.[6]

In the cycle of three plays called *The Oresteia*, he probed the question of human responsibility for their own destruction. Overwhelming punishment, he showed, can come as a result of the mixture of evil and good in a human being, or, even more frighteningly, from one small flaw in an otherwise admirable human being. His example is Agamemnon, who is murdered by his wife Clytemnestra and her lover upon his return from the Trojan Wars. The first play ends with Clytemnestra standing with one foot on the corpse of her husband, sneering at the warning of the chorus that her son Orestes will avenge the death of his father. But Aeschylus has also carefully shown that Agamemnon was not blameless. He has attacked Troy for his own ambition. He has ignored the warnings of the gods. He has committed sacrilege. He has, in short, caused his own doom through *hubris*, the offense of affronting the gods by overweening ambition.

The second play focuses on Orestes, who, in order to avenge his father, must kill his own mother, a crime for which he himself must inevitably be punished by the Furies, three old hags with dog's heads and snakes for hair. He is only rescued from this retribution, which has driven him mad in the third play, by the intervention of Athena herself. The praise of Athena, which ends the play, might well have pleased the Athenian audience; but it is clear that Aeschylus burned with rage at the injustice of the gods. For him, there was only one redeeming feature of this inequity of overwhelming punishment for minor, or even justifiable, crimes—that the human being is purified and grows stronger through suffering.

Sophocles (496–406 B.C.) refused to blame the suffering of his characters on the capriciousness, or the injustice, of the gods. His characters operate in a world of moral certainty, where each action invokes an inevitable consequence. But he demonstrates to his audience that every decision is many-sided, and that there are no simple answers to moral questions. He used his play *Antigone* to present the dilemma of a woman torn between obeying her own conscience, that is, the dictates of a universal moral or natural law, and the command of the state. At one superficial level the play can be interpreted as a plea for placing

---

[6] David Grene and Richmond Lattimore, eds., *The Complete Greek Tragedies* (Chicago: University of Chicago Press, 1959), I, 232–33.

individual moral duty above the immoral demands of the state. Creon, the dictator of Thebes, has forbidden anyone to bury the body of Antigone's brother, who had rebelled, so that his spirit will roam endlessly in torment. Antigone chooses death by giving her brother ceremonial burial. But Sophocles is not satisfied with so simple a choice. He shows that Creon also has a moral dilemma. He believes the well-being of the state is dependent on exemplary punishment of rebels, but his own son loves, and is about to marry, Antigone. He also hints that Antigone is far from the paragon of virtue she at first appears to be. How, Sophocles asks his audience, can she cause such suffering to the man who loves her by sacrificing herself for her brother? She is, he hints, a "rigid spirit," with a sort of lovelessness that seeks martyrdom. In a world of conflicting moral absolutes, Sophocles shows, only the rigid can operate with complete self-assurance.

Euripides (c. 480–406 B.C.) made no pretense that the gods were just or that society was humane. He raged at the immorality of the ancient myths, at the bloodletting provoked by governments, at the oppression by society of women and slaves. His main interest was in the psychology of human beings, and especially at the impact on imperfect character of the disruptive passions of love, hate, and jealousy. In his play *Medea*, we are at first sorry for the barbarian princess Medea, who has been abandoned by Jason for another woman upon their return to Greece, even though she has helped him find the Golden Fleece. In a famous lament on the sufferings of women, Medea seems to indulge self-pity:

> Of all things upon earth that bleed and grow
> A herb most bruised is woman. We must pay
> Our store of gold hoarded for that one day,
> To buy us some man's love; and lo, they bring
> A master of our flesh! . . .[7]

But Medea will not submit to such ignominy. She sends a magic wedding gown as a gift to Jason's new favorite, who burns to death when she puts it on. And, in a dreadful punishment of Jason, she resolves to murder her own two sons by Jason. The Greek audiences found the plays of Euripides almost too hard to bear, and rarely awarded him the festival prize. Only after the misery of the Peloponnesian War did the Athenians understand his message, and after his death he became the favorite playwright of Athens.

Far fewer of the Greek comedies have survived than tragedies; but we are fortunate in possessing eleven of the plays of Aristophanes (c. 446–388 B.C.). The Greek comic playwrights often satirized the politicians or philosophers or even the other playwrights of the city. Aristophanes, for example, presented Aeschylus and Sophocles quarrelling as to which is the better writer. Dionysus

---

[7] Euripides, *The Medea*, translated by Gilbert Murray (London: George Allen and Unwin, 1910), p. 15.

himself decides that it is Aeschylus, after he has weighed their verses on a huge
scale on the stage. But Aristophanes could also be daringly contemporary in
his political satire. Disapproving of the Peloponnesian War, he wrote *Lysistrata*
in 411 B.C. to suggest a solution. Led by the Athenian Lysistrata, the women
of Athens and Sparta barricade themselves on the Acropolis, and refuse to have
anything to do with their husbands until they make peace. With the treasury
of Athens in their hands, Lysistrata says, they will run the country. After all,
they run their household budgets. Moreover, the main state expense will be
ended, since they intend to abolish war. Eventually the soldiers, made penitent
by enforced sexual abstinence, make peace, and are welcomed back by their
wives.

Greek Science and Philosophy

In philosophy, a Greek word meaning "love of wisdom," the Greeks were
concerned as early as the sixth century B.C. with finding a reasonable or logical
explanation of the working of the physical world. As a result, the earliest philosophers were also scientists, who combined an interest in experiment with a
search for an intellectual theory. For example, many ingenious theories as to
the nature of matter were suggested. Thales of Miletus (early sixth century B.C.)
argued that water is the basic element, since it is present throughout the world
and changes its nature depending on temperature. Empedocles, a Sicilian philosopher, taught that all matter is composed of four different kinds of material
particles (fire, water, earth, and air,), and that all motion is the movement of
particles caused by the alternating action of two forces, harmony and disharmony. By far the most radical theory was that of Democritus of Abdera in
Thrace, who claimed that all matter is composed of tiny, invisible particles that
differ in weight and size, which he called atoms, and which he believed are in
constant motion and indestructible. What our senses perceive is due solely to
the arrangement of atoms, and hence our knowledge derived from our senses
must always be inexact. Pythagoras (c. 582–507 B.C.) of Samos argued that
ultimate reality was not to be found in material things but in numbers. Pitch in
music, he demonstrated, by study of the relationship between the length of a
chord and its pitch, is a mathematical proportion. He then expanded the theory
to the proposition that numbers are at the basis not only of all material phenomena in the universe but even of such nonmaterial concepts as justice.

Both theory and experiment were used to advance the knowledge of medicine. Empedocles, for example, found that the blood flows into and out of the
heart. Hippocrates of Cos, who is considered to be the father of medicine,
emphasized diet and rest, and studied the influence of heredity by following
the recurrence of specific disease in specific families. He taught that illness is
caused by an imbalance in the body of four humors—yellow bile, black bile,
phlegm, and blood, which can be remedied by bleeding the sick. He founded
a school of medicine, from which the modern Hippocratic oath is taken.

In Athens itself, the first philosophers to gain prominence were the sophists, "teachers of wisdom," who for money taught young Athenians the art of rhetoric, by which they could win arguments in the assembly or elsewhere. They were, however, frequently criticized for impiety, for teaching that the gods are unknowable. One sophist argued: "Man is the measure of all things, of things that are what they are, and of things that are not what they are not." Another argued the impossibility of knowledge: "There is nothing: even if there is anything, we cannot know it; even if we could know it, we could not communicate our knowledge to anyone else."

It was Socrates (469–399 B.C.) who provoked the most skeptical thinking in Athens, and who eventually paid with his life for stimulating the independence of thought that governments can rarely tolerate in the aftermath of unpopular wars.

Details of the life of Socrates are sparse. He was the son of a stonemason and a midwife, and claimed later that he had followed the profession of both his parents. After working for a while as a stonecutter, he said, he had become a midwife—but for men, and not for women. His art was to examine whether "the thought which the mind of the young man is bringing to birth is a false idol, or a noble and true creation." He felt himself to be a "gadfly," whose sting would startle human beings into the self-questioning from which self-knowledge would emerge. Although pot-bellied and pug-nosed, he exerted enormous personal magnetism over the many people to whom he talked in the streets, the marketplace, or the assembly. His approach, as related and perhaps idealized in the writings of his student Plato (427–347 B.C.), was misleadingly humble. He disarmed the person with whom he was speaking by claiming that he knew nothing, only how to ask questions. But the questions he asked were always so phrased as to elicit the answer he wanted, an answer that Socrates believed already lay in the mind of the person he was questioning.

His method went through three steps. First he destroyed preconceptions, by making clear through his questions that the ideas the other person held had a false basis. Second, he used inductive inquiry, reasoning from the particular to the general. For example, if he wished to find out what was beauty, he took a number of examples of things that were regarded as beautiful, and asked what those objects had in common. He then took the third step, definition. What those objects had in common he defined as beauty. He always sought the awareness of moral reality, such as truth and justice, which he believed were ideas with which human beings were born. In fact, he believed that human nature was essentially good, and that the purpose of society and the state should be to enable them to achieve that goodness.

In 399 B.C., the Athenian population, obsessed with material goals in the aftermath of the sufferings of the Peloponnesian War, interpreted his call for justice as an attack on themselves. He was accused of corrupting the youth and of impiety toward the gods, found guilty by a jury, and condemned to death. He accepted the verdict with equanimity, gathered his friends around him for a last conversation on the nature of immortality, and died before them by drinking hemlock.

Plato was disgusted with Athens for its treatment of Socrates, which he blamed on Periclean democracy run wild. Far more admirable, he decided, were the tyrannies in the Greek cities of Sicily and the self-denying military oligarchy of Sparta. In his greatest book, *The Republic*, he attempted to design a city-state that would achieve the justice for which Socrates had lived. The book is organized around a theory of knowledge, which Plato attempted to explain in the famous allegory of the cave. Human beings, he wrote, are like prisoners chained by the legs and neck in an underground cave, so that the only thing visible to them is the shadows cast on the back wall of the cave of objects behind them that are being moved in front of fires. They believe that the shadow of the object is the real object itself. When some of the prisoners are freed to go outside, where they can see the objects themselves, they are at first dazed and want to return to the shadows. But eventually they realize what are the real objects and what are only shadows. Education, Plato wrote, is for human beings the method by which they are able to distinguish the real objects from the shadows.

But what did he mean by the real objects? They are, said Plato, "ideas." What is it that a writing table, a dining table, and a card table have in common? They all resemble the "idea" of a perfect table, Plato would reply. If we did not have an idea of a table, then we would not know that each of these objects is a table. Far more important, however, we also have an idea of justice, and goodness, and beauty, and even of the perfect state. Plato, however, was quite realistic about the extent to which human beings could grasp these ideas. Everybody, he noted, knows what a table is, but only a few can grasp the nature of justice. Therefore, when he described his perfect state, he divided the citizens into three classes. The rulers were those who could grasp the ultimate ideas. They would naturally have to be philosophers. "Unless philosophers bear kingly rule in cities, or those who are now called kings and princes become genuine and adequate philosophers . . . there will be no respite in evil for cities or for humanity."

A second class, the guardians, would be similar to the Spartan warriors in training and way of life, and the philosopher-kings would be chosen from among them. Women and men would have absolute equality. They would receive the same education in war, music, and gymnastics, and would have the same duties.

> No calling in the life of the city belongs to woman as woman or to man as man; by nature the woman has a share in all practices, and so has the man. For a woman to hold the guardianship, she will not need special education. We will be dealing with the same nature in woman as in man and the same education will be required for both.[8]

[8] Plato, *The Republic*, translated by W. D. H. Rouse (New York: New American Library, 1956), p. 253.

The third class was the workers, for whom Plato prescribed a kind of communal living. Property was to be owned in common. Children were to be taken from their parents and educated by the state, and recognized as the common offspring of all the parents.

Plato thus concluded by laying the foundations for a political theory that Socrates, the admirer of Athenian democracy, would probably have abhorred— a state in which the rulers believe they have a moral duty to force people to lead good lives for their own sake.

Plato founded a school in Athens known as the Academy, which continued to influence the Greek world for 900 years. His most famous pupil was Aristotle (384–322 B.C.), who founded a school of his own called the Lyceum. Although Aristotle theorized on the nature of ideas, he was also interested in the physical form in which the ideas are embodied and which could only be known by meticulous research and classification. He believed in experiment. For example, to study the development of the chicken embryo, he broke open fertile eggs at fixed intervals. He collected facts of every kind. To write his book on the ideal state, he studied 158 constitutions. To write on biology, he adopted a form of classification of living things into species and genera that is similar to the one still in use. To organize his voluminous data, he developed rules for logical thought, especially a series of arguments called syllogisms. One of the most frequently quoted is

All men are mortal.
Socrates is a man.
Therefore, Socrates is mortal.

In politics Aristotle taught the need of a far more moderate form of state than Plato. In *The Politics*, he classified the constitutions he had studied into three forms, each of which could be either good or bad. Rule by one person was monarchy if good, tyranny if bad; rule by the few was aristocracy if good, oligarchy if bad; rule by the many was polity if good, democracy (by which he usually meant rule by a mob or by the poor) if bad. He did not argue for the existence of an ideal state, but rather believed that different peoples in different places require different forms of constitution. Even so, he felt in general that a state was best run by a large middle class of "moderate and adequate property," who would pursue in politiccs what he regarded as the ideal in individual life, the golden mean.

Greek Architecture and Sculpture

Greek architecture and sculpture reached their most perfect form in the temples that Pericles erected on the Acropolis of Athens, with the aid of the money he had forcibly acquired from the Delian League.

During their occupation of Athens, the Persians had ruined the temples on the Acropolis and burned down the houses of the city. In the haste to rebuild,

The Temples of the Acropolis, Athens, Greece   *The reconstruction of the temples on the Acropolis ordered by Pericles was begun in 447 B.C. and completed, in spite of the Peloponnesian War, in 395 B.C. The centerpiece of the carefully sited temples was the Doric Parthenon, the temple to the goddess Athena. (Greek Government Tourist Organization.)*

the Athenian had thrown up the same small, cramped unsanitary houses on the narrow, winding streets that they had had before; and even the walls of the city were a hodge-podge of broken stones grabbed hither and thither from the ruined buildings and even from cemeteries. Domestic life for the Athenian was thus simple and somewhat distasteful. They had little furniture. Heat was from small, smoky, charcoal braziers. Rats and mosquitos abounded. Whenever possible, Athenians slept outdoors on the roof. The Athenian men were thus given an incentive to seek the distractions of the gymnasium or the stadium outside the city wall or the vivacity of social life in the marketplace. For well-to-do Athenian women, segregated in the home, the only release was to attend religious festivals, where their emotional outpourings may have been more occasioned by release from the boredom of the home than by piety.

The Greeks believed, however, that no matter how drab their homes might be, the public buildings of their cities should be the most splendid possible. Around the marketplace, or *agora*, they would erect beautiful colonnaded porches called *stoas*, with shops at the back and apartments on the upper floor. Here too, the principal government buildings were erected. In Athens, the *bouleterion* housed the Council of Five Hundred, and the *strategeion* the generals. Even more impressive were the city's religious buildings. Pericles ordered constructed on the Acropolis a group of buildings that would make full use of the natural advantages of the site, an anvil-shaped rock 300 feet high above the city's houses. The temple of the goddess Athena, the Parthenon, was the first new building to be constructed, in the amazingly short time of eleven years. Then, where the path from the lower city that formed the route of the Panathenaic procession entered the floor of the Acropolis itself, a massive gateway called the Propylaeon was erected to dramatize the first glimpse of the magnificent west facade of the Parthenon. Finally, two contrasting buildings, the tiny temple of Athena Nike and the more elaborate Erectheion, a temple to the mythical king Erectheus of Athens, who was believed to have begun the worship of Athena, were started. Work was finally completed in 395 B.C.

The Parthenon and Propylaeon were built in Doric style, which appears deceptively simple but was one of the most harmonious building styles ever invented. The Greeks took the post-and-lintel style of architecture (a cross-beam laid on two upright columns) and developed it into a distinctive style that was later imitated by the Romans and other Western societies. To protect the inner brick wall of the sanctuary, the Greeks erected a colonnade around the outside of the building, which was then covered with a sloping roof. Each of these simple features was elegantly refined. The column, or shaft, sat on a platform of three steps. The columns were fluted with sharp edges, and bulged slightly to avoid an appearance of rigidity. Two simple round stones called the capital were placed on the top of the column, and a line of flat stones called the architrave was laid on the capitals. The triangular pediment formed by the roof and the spaces above the architrave were used for insertion of sculptures. Finally, a wonderful frieze representing the Panathenaic procession was placed on the four inner walls of the temple. The architectural features are thus similar

Aphrodite of Cnidus, by Praxiteles (mid-fourth century B.C.) *Praxiteles was unsurpassed in portrayal of the beauty of the human form and especially of the female figure. (Alinari/Art Resource.)*

in some ways to those of the Egyptian temples. But the Egyptian temple is turned inward, a secret place for priests and godlike rulers; the Greek temple turns outward, open without secrets to the inspection and possessive admiration of the people whose god it houses. The strength of the Doric temple was emphasized by the use of the contrasting style known as Ionic for the temple of Athena Nike and the Erechtheum. The Ionic column is softer in appearance. Its capital is composed of two swirls of stone called volutes, and the base of the columns is formed of moulded circles. Although modern visitors are astounded by the beauty of the pink and green marble of these buildings, the Greeks painted them in bright colors, creating a liveliness of effect we can only guess at.

By the fifth century B.C. Greek sculptors had achieved great technical virtuosity. Only a century earlier, they had been working largely in the formalized style they had inherited from Egypt and the Near East, showing people standing or perhaps walking forward in rather rigid postures and with a highly conventionalized facial expression called the "archaic smile." Toward the end of the sixth century, however, sculptors began to portray men nude, and thus to show the structure and muscles of the human body, while the drapery over female bodies had become an equally subtle method of suggesting the human form while disguising it. In the first half of the fifth century, free-standing sculptures, often made in bronze like the Charioteer found at Delphi as well as in marble like the Caryatides of the Erechtheum, showed total mastery of the presentation of the human body. Far from the white marble we are accustomed to today, the Greeks painted their stone figures with "natural" if rather bright colors, while bronze figures had eyes made of colored stones and mouths and eyelids decorated with gilt. At the same time, the human form was idealized, which means that the imperfections of particular, individual models were removed so as to represent "men better than the average," to quote Aristotle. Western civilization has inherited the fifth-century Greek conception of the perfect human form as its classical ideal.

Relief sculpture also advanced, as the sculptors solved the problem not only of using human figures in an abstract design but of presenting the human figure accurately in any position or motion as required by the design. When the Parthenon was begun, this art was at its height. Thus, sculptures that Phidias designed for the frieze of the Parthenon are not only representations of surging lines of horses with the citizens of Athens watching them pass by, they are an idealization of Athena's festival. Phidias has set out to represent not one Panathenaic procession but all, and by doing so to show the unity of the Athenian people through all time. In just the same way, the sculptor Myron, in the statue of the *Discus Thrower* originally sculpted about 450 B.C., is not depicting one discus thrower but a representation of the motion of discus throwing. Among the greatest sculptors this idealism in representation lasted until the middle of the fourth century, and found its final expression in the works of Praxiteles (c. 370–c. 330 B.C.), such as his *Aphrodite of Cnidus*, which are noted for their elegance of design and for their perfection of surface.

Vase Painting

While the sculpture of the Greeks served principally to adorn temples and thus had at least a sacred association, their painting remains to us chiefly on pots that were produced for commerce. Of mural or other large scale painting we know nothing directly, but, because so many of the pots have survived, we now possess a fair amount of knowledge about vase painting among the Greeks. We can date painted pots back to the Mycenaean age, but for the most part we trace this art form from about the eighth century B.C., and the highest achievements we generally connect with Athens.

In the eighth century B.C. its potters enriched an inherited geometric style by introducing human figures and increasing the number of decorative bands around their pots. The geometric style was followed about the middle of the seventh century by what is called the "black-figure" style, which was a technique of incising figures on the orange-brown clay body of a vase and then painting the figure in black. Toward the end of the sixth century, black-figure pots began to give way to what is called the "red-figure" technique, in which the figure is outlined, the background painted black, and details are drawn in line. During the red-figure period, greater attention was paid to human anatomy, naturalistic positioning of the figures, and a limited rendering of three dimensions. At the beginning of the fifth century, a technique that had been experimented with since the beginning of the sixth century finally came into its own as a major painting style along with the red-figure and the remains of the black-figure styles. In this latest style, a white coating was painted on the vase and onto this coating figures were drawn with brush and painted in several hues. These paintings have at times an extraordinary grace and subtlety not previously achieved in Greek vase painting. By the middle of the fourth century, vase painting declined in quality as the wealth of the city-states was exhausted by continuous warfare.

ALEXANDER THE GREAT AND THE HELLENISTIC AGE

The incessant quarreling among the Greek city-states that continued in the half-century following the Peloponnesian War so disgusted many Greeks that they began to look for a savior in the strong, efficient state of Macedon to the north. When the Macedonian king Philip, who had seized the throne in 359 B.C., decided to bring the Greek cities under his control, he found that a substantial minority were prepared to welcome him in spite of the impassioned pleas by the great Athenian orator Demosthenes to oppose the military autocracy of Macedon and instead to find salvation in a confederation under a rejuvenated Athens. Philip easily defeated the armies of Athens and Thebes at the battle of Chaeronea in 338 B.C. and immediately pleased his Greek supporters by unifying the Greek cities in a new league and by promising to lead them in an invasion of the declining Persian empire.

Philip, however, was assassinated in 336 B.C., just as he was preparing to set off for Persia. His son Alexander (reigned 336–323 B.C.) immediately took over his father's position and ambitions. Alexander had been well trained for his new role. His tutor from the age of thirteen was Aristotle, who had thoroughly grounded him in the philosophy, ethics, politics, and science of Greece. He had commanded a wing of the army at Chaeronea, and had governed Macedon in Philip's absence. With the powerful Macedonian army, consisting of a cavalry of nobles and infantry of peasants and supported by troops of the Greek league, he crossed into Asia Minor to recapture the Ionian cities. The Persians failed to halt him, first at the battle of the river Granicus (334 B.C.) and later on the borders of Syria at Issus (333 B.C.). Within two years he had completed the conquest of Syria and Egypt, where he founded a new city called Alexandria in the Nile Delta. He then struck out for the heart of the Persian empire, driving down the Tigris and Euphrates valleys to capture Nineveh, Babylon, and Susa, and into Persia itself to take Persepolis and Ecbatana. Although by then his army was rebellious, he was far from satiated with conquest. He struck even farther east into Central Asia to Afghanistan, descended the Khyber Pass into India, and followed the Indus Valley to the Arabian Sea. He caught fever in Babylon in 323 B.C. and died, at a time when he was planning another dual expedition by sea, with one expedition to capture India and another to sail around Arabia from the Persian Gulf to Egypt.

Alexander was one of the world's great conquerors. He had led his armies on a 20,000-mile march over a period of thirteen years, and had never been defeated. In that time he had created an empire stretching from the eastern Mediterranean to the Indus Valley. But he was far more than a conqueror. He had far-reaching goals for his empire. He believed that he would be able to fuse the civilizations of the West and the East. In his own person he tried to use religion as the element of unity. He sought to be recognized as a god in Greece. In Egypt he claimed to be the son of the God, Amun-Re. In Persia, the nobles recognized that their god Ahura Mazda had made him their Great King. In Babylon, he worshipped the god Marduk and restored his temple. He associated Greeks and Persians equally in government, and attempted to solve the racial animosities between them by intermarriage. In one dramatic ceremony he had eighty Macedonian officers marry Persian noblewomen. To integrate his vast empire, he built roads, opened new sea routes and ports, and issued a common imperial coinage. Perhaps most important of all, wherever he conquered he founded new cities (usually naming them Alexandria), in which a Greek population was settled to spread knowledge of Greek language, art, law, and commercial practices. The most important of these cities was his original Alexandria in Egypt, which became within a century the most important city of the ancient world.

Within a generation of his death, his empire had been divided among three of his generals and their successors. Macedon and Greece were governed by the Antigonid dynasty, although at times the Greek cities were able to break away for temporary periods and resume their internal fighting. Persia and most of the Fertile Crescent were governed by the Seleucid dynasty, and here the rulers gave special emphasis to founding even more Greek cities, of which the most important were Antioch in Syria and Seleucia in Mesopotamia. Egypt and Palestine were taken by the Ptolemies. All three empires were governed as absolute monarchies, like those of the Egyptian and Mesopotamian empires. The ruler was worshipped as a god or as a representative of god on earth, and he governed through his bureaucracy and mercenary army. Political participation of the citizens as known in the Greek *polis* virtually ceased.

In these three empires and in the smaller kingdoms on their borders, Greek culture was predominant. But it was not the Hellenic culture, the classical culture, of the age of Pericles. It was a more superficial, emotional, and yet appealing culture, which we call Hellenistic, or "Greeklike," which was the product in part of the different values of the Greeks after the Peloponnesian War, and in part of the influence of the Near Eastern cultures on the Greek culture brought by Alexander.

Hellenistic culture was the product of an age of great material prosperity. Long-distance commerce was booming between Europe, Asia, and Africa. Sea routes were opened up across the Indian Ocean to bring back the products of the flourishing cities of the Mauryan empire in India, which itself had been linked to the newly unified Han empire in China from the second century B.C. By the first century B.C., Europe was linked overland by the silk route across Central Asia to China. Alexandria in Egypt controlled the export of the wheat surplus of the Nile, as well as such African products as ivory and ebony. Its artisans produced many coveted products, such as jewelry in gold and silver, elegant glassware, and furniture and textiles. The caravans of Arabia passed through the pink city of Petra, from where their goods were shipped to the ports of the eastern Mediterranean. The wealth created a city-building boom. Fine new *stoas* (colonnaded promenades) were built, one of the most impressive being that of Attalos in the marketplace of Athens. The middle class built themselves luxurious homes and bequeathed to the cities temples, bridges, and theaters. The absolute monarchs possessed such vast incomes that they built aqueducts, theaters, stadiums, baths, and harbors, on a scale that dwarfed Pericles' constructions in Athens.

The sculpture favored by these new patrons was more realistic and emotional than the Greek sculpture of a century earlier. The sculptors excelled in the presentation of old age, of violent suffering, and sometimes of cloying sentimentality. Portrait busts were popular because they were accurate—or exaggerated—presentations of the subject. In architecture, the uncompromising Doric style was far less popular than the softer Ionic or the highly elaborate new type called Corinthian, with its capitals of carved stone foliage.

Quality declined in literature. Drama was either rough slapstick or cheap sentimentality. Poetry was often rarefied attempts by an urban elite to idealize the simple life of the countryside. In science, however, which profited from the

fascination with the material world, great advances were made. The foremost scientific center of the Hellenistic world was the so-called Museum of Alexandria, which was a kind of research university supported by the Ptolemies and staffed by highly paid professors from throughout the Hellenistic region, who had been attracted by access to the finest library of the ancient world, with its collection of 700,000 works. Euclid (c. 323–258 B.C.) dominated the world of mathematics with his famous synthesis of plain and solid geometry known as *Elements of Geometry*. Mathematical advances made possible progress in astronomy. Aristarchus (c. 310–230 B.C.) even suggested—without documentation—that the earth revolved around a motionless sun and rotated on its own axis. His theory was dismissed, however, because it was counter to the more plausible theory supported by Aristotle that the planets and sun move around a stationary earth. Although Archimedes (c. 287–212 B.C.) developed the theory of hydrostatics, the science of the mechanics of fluids at rest, and showed that for a body to float it must displace its own weight of water, his contemporaries were more impressed by his inventions, which included a pulley for moving ships across land and a screw that could pump water out of mines. His friend Eratosthenes (c. 275–195 B.C.) calculated the circumference of the earth as well as its distance from the sun, and drew a map of the known world divided into squares by lines of latitude and longitude.

As frequently happens in a materialistic society, the philosophers rejected it. The so-called Cynics made a display of their rejection of materialism by wearing rags, asking impertinent questions calculated to disturb the complacent, and annoying the authorities by imaginative forms of antisocial behavior. The Skeptics argued that since our knowledge derives from our senses, nothing can be known with certainty.

Two important philosophers started schools that attempted to permit those alienated from this materialistic world to find mental repose. Epicurus (342–270 B.C.) told his followers to avoid the main causes of mental suffering, such as making money or getting married. The less they sought, the less they had to fear. Fear of death was the least necessary of all, since after death the body decomposes into its constituent atoms. The ideal of life was to live like Epicurus, in a calm vegetable garden surrounded by a group of friends engaged in quiet conversation. Epicurus differed from most Greek philosophers in admitting women equally on a basis with men, and his own companion Leontia was reputed a fine philosopher herself. The philosophy of the Stoics, founded by Zeno (336–263 B.C.), was more demanding and in some ways perhaps more noble. Zeno held that the universe is governed by a law of nature, and that human beings must accommodate to that law, which is shared by all human beings and therefore unites them in an ongoing community. The goals of a wise person are bravery, justice, and moderation, but the Stoics also argued that the universe is controlled by a divine will and that the Stoic must achieve tranquillity by accepting unquestioningly whatever misfortune the divine will imposes.

It was the culture of this Hellenistic world, this mixture of the achievements of all the civilizations of the Near East with those of Hellenic Greece, which was to be absorbed by the rising new power of Rome, and made the essential foundation of Western civilization. Fifth-century Greece had remained the inspiration for Hellenistic culture, just as it was to remain an ideal to be rediscovered again and again in different periods of cultural revival in the West. But it is perhaps fortunate that it was Hellenistic rather than Hellenic culture that was taken up by the Romans. Hellenic culture was in many ways a rarefied product, hard to export and difficult for foreigners to accept. Hellenistic culture, more broadly based, more materialistic, less demanding for its appreciation, could more easily be accepted as the common culture of empires embracing many peoples of vastly varied background. Just such an empire, which was to prove infinitely more durable than the empire of Alexander, was about to be created by the upstart city of Rome.

SUGGESTED READINGS

General Introduction

Greek political development is succinctly presented in Anthony Andrewes, *The Greeks* (1967), and Moses I. Finley, *The Ancient Greeks* (1977). H. D. F. Kitto, *The Greeks*

(1963), is readable and idiosyncratic. Satisfactory narratives accompany superb photographs in Horizon, *The Horizon Book of Ancient Greece* (1965), and Peter Green, *Ancient Greece: An Illustrated History* (1979).

Early Greece

The Minoan civilization on Crete is reviewed in R. W. Hutchinson, *Prehistoric Crete* (1962). For the Mycenaean age, begin with the poems of Homer, especially the *Iliad* in the translation by E. V. Rieu (1946). Recent reinterpretations as a result of new excavations and decipherment of the Linear B Script are amusingly presented in Emily Vermeule, *Greece in the Bronze Age* (1964); while John Chadwick explains how Michael Ventris was able to unravel the script, in *The Decipherment of Linear B* (1960). Chester G. Starr brings light to the Dark Age and later in *The Origins of Greek Civilization, 1100–650* B.C. (1961). For a recent interpretation, see A. M. Snodgrass, *Archaic Greece* (1983). The rise of the *polis* is described in W. G. Forrest, *The Emergence of Greek Democracy, 800–400* B.C. (1966). Raphael Sealey, *A History of the Greek City States, 700–388* B.C. (1976), prefers interpretation to narrative.

Greece in the Fifth Century B.C.

For the economic underpinnings of Greek civilization, see M. M. Austin and P. Vidal-Naquet, *Economic and Social History of Ancient Greece* (1979). Maurice Pope, *The Ancient Greeks: How They Lived and Worked* (1976), and Robert Flacelière, *Daily Life in the Athens of Pericles* (1964), are good introductions to social life, but, for the role of women, should be supplemented with the sparkling study of Sarah B. Pomeroy, *Goddesses, Whores, Wives, and Slaves: Women in Classical Antiquity* (1975). The best studies of Sparta are K. M. T. Chrimes, *Ancient Sparta* (1949), and W. G. Forrest, *A History of Sparta, 950–192* B.C. (1969).

Greek Religion and Culture

William K. C. Guthrie, *The Greeks and Their Gods* (1950), covers both the myths and the Greek religious practices, while his *Greek Philosophers: From Thales to Aristotle* (1950) is a comprehensive survey of the development of philosophy. Marshall Clagett, *Greek Science in Antiquity* (1971), is the best introduction. Greek drama is best approached through the plays themselves, in the fine translations by David Grene and Richmond Lattimore, edited for the University of Chicago Press, especially perhaps beginning with Aeschylus, *Agamemnon*, Sophocles, *Antigone*, and Euripides, *Medea*, before relaxing with Aristophanes, *Lysistrata*.

Well-illustrated histories of art include A. W. Lawrence, *Greek Architecture* (1975); J. Boardman, *Greek Art* (1973); and Rhys Carpenter, *Greek Sculpture* (1960). R. E. Wycherley explains the appearance of Athens in *How the Greeks Built Cities* (1962).

The Hellenistic Age

Alexander the Great continues to fascinate writers, most recently N. G. L. Hammond, *Alexander the Great: King, Commander, and Statesman* (1981), Robin Lane Fox, *Alexander the Great* (1974), and Peter Green, *Alexander the Great* (1974); but George Cawkwell, *Philip of Macedon* (1978), reminds us that his father's achievements should not be neglected.

For the civilization of his empire and its successor states, see Michael Grant, *The Ancient Mediterranean* (1969), and his *From Alexander to Cleopatra: The Hellenistic World* (1982); and W. W. Tarn and G. T. Griffith, *Hellenistic Civilization* (1961). The economic foundations of the prosperity are analyzed in the classic study of M. I. Rostovtzeff, *Social and Economic History of the Hellenistic World* (1953), and, less comprehensively, in C. Bradford Welles, *Alexander and the Hellenistic World* (1970). J. Onians, *Art and Thought in the Hellenistic Age: The Greek World View, 350–50 B.C.* (1982), is a reliable introduction.

3

The Romans

Although the Romans seized enthusiastically upon the whole cultural inheritance of the Hellenistic world, they brought to Western civilization gifts that were essentially different from those of the Greeks. The Romans were pragmatists, whose turn of mind was essentially unfriendly to the abstract theorizing of the Greeks. Their genius lay in the manipulation of the material world, as in the movement of water over aqueducts or of soldiers along vast, stone-paved highways. They rarely theorized over the nature of society. Instead they organized it. Their laws, commonsensical and functional, became the basis of the legal system of the majority of the countries of the Western world. They admired stability, and sought to achieve it by amassing unassailable strength. Their powerful armies and later their great navies were used for 500 years to suppress all potential rivals within the boundaries of an empire that eventually stretched from Spain to the Fertile Crescent, and they spent the following 500 years maintaining within their empire a Roman peace, a *Pax Romana*. The Romans thus turned their practical genius to the unification of the West. For the first time the western Mediterranean, and indeed large parts of Western Europe, were unified with the eastern Mediterranean and most parts of the Near East. Goods, people, and ideas moved with relative freedom through the integrated empire of Rome, leaving a legacy that was to survive in spite of the political fragmentation that followed the break-up of the Roman empire in the fifth century A.D.

THE RISE OF ROME

Origins of Rome

The Romans were descendants of an Indo-European people who had moved into Italy between 1500 and 1000 B.C. and intermingled with the indigenous inhabitants. The dialect that they spoke eventually became the Latin language. They probably settled on two tiny hills, later known as the Capitol and Palatine hills, sometime during the eighth century B.C. There is, however, very little proof that the legend of the founding of Rome, which was immortalized in Virgil's great poem *The Aeneid*, has any basis in fact. It was, however, a useful stimulant to Roman patriotism. As Virgil narrated it, Aeneas led the defeated Trojans from their city after its destruction by the Greeks to find a new home in the western Mediterranean. Ilia, one of his descendants, had twin sons by the god Mars, and named them Romulus and Remus. Their great-uncle threw them into the Tiber River, from which they were washed up on the Palatine Hill where a she-wolf took care of them. The twins founded a new city, and then quarelled as to which had been the first founder. Romulus killed Remus, and hence the city was called, in his honor, Rome. Romulus, the orator Cicero concluded later, "must at the very beginning have had a divine intimation that the city would one day be the seat and hearthstone of a mighty empire, for scarcely could a city placed upon any other site in Italy have more easily maintained our own present widespread dominion."

The site of the new city was a group of seven small hills overlooking the river Tiber at a ford about 14 milies from its mouth. The Capitol and Palatine hills were easily defensible, like the Acropolis in Athens, and on their summits the Roman herders erected rough huts of mud and wattle. During the next 250 years, the city developed rapidly, especially after the draining of the level valley between the two hills, which became known as the Roman Forum. Under the rule of kings, a 6-mile wall of stone and earth was built for defense. Substantial temples of dressed stone and terra cotta were raised on the Capitol Hill. A strong army of legions was formed, with phalanxes similar to those in Greece.

These early Romans greatly admired the Greek cities that had been founded on the coasts of southern Italy and Sicily in the seventh and sixth centuries B.C., and they took from them their early alphabet and many of the myths of the Greek gods. They were even more influenced by the mysterious people called the Etruscans, who lived in the areas to the north between the Tiber and the Arno rivers, especially as Rome was governed by Etruscan kings during the sixth century B.C.

The Etruscan cities, such as Tarquinia and Cerveteri, had grown rich from their advanced agriculture in wheat, grapes, and olives, their control of the mineral deposits of Italy, and especially the trade and occasionally the marauding of their powerful fleet. Like the Egyptians, they poured much of their wealth into creating cities of the dead, vast necropolises that stood on hilltops parallel

Etruscan Tomb Sculpture, Cerveteri, Italy (sixth century B.C.) Husbands and wives were portrayed in reclining but lifelike postures on the top of their tombs. For the Etruscans, like the Egyptians, the afterlife was regarded as a continuance of the pleasures of life on earth. (Alinari/Art Resource.)

to the cities of the living. Here, in tombs dug out of solid rock, the Etruscans decorated the walls with vibrant paintings of dancers, musicians, and banqueters, while statues of the dead were laid on funeral couches surrounded by the vases, bowls, jewels, and foods that they might need in a luxurious afterlife. As in the Egyptain tombs, no trace of somberness darkens the expectation of enhanced pleasure in an afterlife of music and feasting, and the married couples faced the future with a mutually trusting tranquility that seems the finest testimony to the quality of Etruscan life in this world. From this highly civilized people, whose greatness lasted barely three centuries, the Romans learned much. Their architectural style, especially their use of the arch, their urban planning, their early literature, their religious beliefs, and their military techniques, all had Etruscan origins.

About 500 B.C., the Romans, led by the aristocrats, or patricians, drove out their Etruscan king, and set up a republican form of government. The patricians preserved some of the institutions of the period of kingly rule, notably the Senate, a council of landowning elders, and the Assembly formed of all the arms-bearing male citizens. In place of the kings, they instituted two consuls, selected annually by the Senate, who could veto each other's decisions. In times of crisis, the consuls could, with the Senate's agreement, appoint a dictator as head of the army for six months. Other official executive positions were created as needed. Two magistrates supervised the administration of justice. Officers attached to the tribunes (elected officials representing the common people) were placed in charge of markets, roads, the food supply, and some religious ceremonies. The censors organized the military draft and checked on the moral fitness of citizens running for public office.

The power of the patricians, who were composed mainly of wealthy landowners descended from the early clans that had first settled Rome, was challenged by the nonpatrician majority, who were known as plebeians. The plebeians, who were the artisans, tradesmen, small farmers, and laborers, had social and economic grievances against the patricians, which they proposed to remedy by political means or if necessary by violence. Relations between the patricians and plebeians were troubled throughout the Roman Republic; but the plebeians slowly won a greater share in the government of Rome. On five separate occasions between 494 and 287 B.C., they engaged in a *secessio*, the equivalent of a general strike, in which they withdrew their services by actually leaving Rome; and in the first *secessio* won the right to elect officials of their own called "tribunes," who could protect them from unjust application of the laws. In reaction a patrician named Coriolanus was reputed to have refused food to the starving plebeians until they agreed to give up their tribunes, but Coriolanus was himself driven from the city. The plebeians then created their own assembly, which chose four tribunes who gained the right to veto the laws of the other assemblies and actions of the magistrates. In 367 B.C. the plebeians won the right to pick one of the two consuls. Finally, the plebeian assembly was reorganized to include both patricians and plebeians, with one vote for each person regardless of status, and the Tribal Assembly, as it was now called, was able to pass laws binding on the whole state, known as *plebiscites*. In addition, the plebeians were instrumental in forcing the erection in the town center of the Twelve Tables, bronze plaques inscribed with the public and private law of the city. They thus compelled the magistrates, who were largely patrician, to respect the legal rights of the plebeians, and at the same time began the formulation of Roman law that was to develop over the centuries into one of the most rational and comprehensive legal codes ever written. It took them more than two centuries, however, before they could abolish slavery for debt, a practice the patricians had used not only to take over the lands of a farmer who owed them money, but to make him their slave as well.

The Conquest of Italy, c. 500–275 B.C.

During the five centuries of republican rule, the Romans were rarely at peace. Like many later conquerors, they persuaded themselves that all their wars were fought in self-defense. Their first campaigns brought the warlike tribes in the hills surrounding Rome under control. At the beginning of the fourth century B.C., they drove north against the Etruscan cities, which were defeated one by one. They then turned south, reorganizing their legions to give them greater maneuverability in hill fighting, and arming them with javelins that could be hurled long distances. These harshly disciplined troops formed the heavy infantry that became the most successful military force of the Mediterranean world. By 282 B.C. the Bay of Naples had been captured, and fifteen years later the rest of the peninsula had been taken.

Roman rule proved lasting because of the brilliant organization that the Romans immediately imposed. The tribes near Rome were given full Roman citizenship. Many cities farther away were granted partial citizenship, with the right to control many of their own internal affairs. About half of the people in

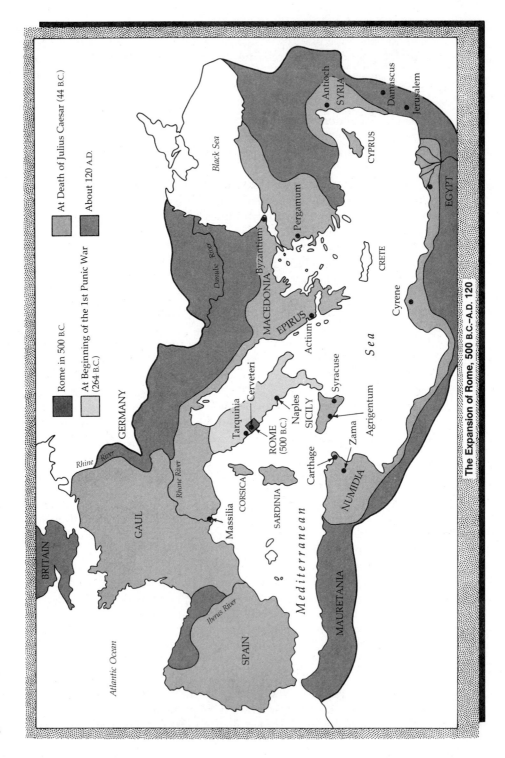

The Expansion of Rome, 500 B.C.–A.D. 120

Legend:
- Rome in 500 B.C.
- At Beginning of the 1st Punic War (264 B.C.)
- At Death of Julius Caesar (44 B.C.)
- About 120 A.D.

BRITAIN

Atlantic Ocean

GERMANY

GAUL

Rhine River

Rhone River

SPAIN

Iberus River

Massilia

CORSICA

SARDINIA

Mediterranean Sea

MAURETANIA

Carthage

NUMIDIA

Zama

ROME (500 B.C.)

Tarquinia
Cerveteri

Naples

SICILY

Agrigentum

Syracuse

Danube River

MACEDONIA

EPIRUS

Actium

Byzantium

Pergamum

Black Sea

CRETE

Cyrene

Sea

CYPRUS

EGYPT

SYRIA

Antioch

Damascus

Jerusalem

Italy were known as "allies" and were theoretically independent, except that their foreign policy was controlled by Rome and they were liable for military service. The Romans normally confiscated about one-third of the land of the peoples they conquered, and they ensured obedience by planting new cities, called "colonies," which were usually settled by Roman soldiers rewarded for service with land in the vicinity. The first of the colonies was Ostia, the port of Rome. Others were located at strategic points at fords, mountain passes, or crossroads. These cities were joined by a network of roads so superbly engineered that some have lasted to this day.

The Punic Wars

Control of the Italian peninsula brought Rome into conflict for control of the western Mediterranean with the great Phoenician colony of Carthage, near present-day Tunis on the North African coast. The Carthaginians held Sardinia and western Sicily, from which the Romans hoped to obtain wheat, and controlled the western Mediterranean with a fleet operating out of colonies on the European and African coasts. To drive the Carthaginians from Sicily, the Romans built themselves a fleet, supposedly copied from a grounded Carthaginian ship, but changed the Carthaginian design by adding a spiked gangplank with which they could grapple enemy ships to put on board a force of legionaries. This First Punic War (264–241 B.C.) dragged on for twenty-three exhausting years before the Carthaginians gave up Sicily. Several years later the Romans took over Sardinia and Corsica. To govern these overseas possessions the Romans made these islands into overseas provinces, and compelled them to pay tribute of one-tenth of their wheat harvest. They thus established a system of imperial rule that could easily be extended to any future possessions.

Carthage attempted to recoup its strength by taking possession of Spain, in order to use its precious metals and its soldiers in a new war against Rome. When forces under their general Hannibal captured a Spanish city allied to Rome, the Romans declared war. The Second Punic War (218–202 B.C.) proved far longer and more perilous than they had expected. Hannibal showed himself to be one of the world's great commanders. He brought an army of 90,000 infantry and 12,000 cavalry and even a detachment of elephants across the Alps into Italy. He fought his way to the hills near Rome where, at Lake Trasimene, he defeated a large Roman force. The Romans then employed delaying tactics, hoping to wear out Hannibal in many costly skirmishes; but they were forced into a major battle at Cannae in 216 B.C., where almost their entire army was destroyed. Hannibal still did not possess the strength to breach the walls of Rome itself, and for ten years he roamed across Italy, unable to strike the decisive blow.

The Romans finally tried a new strategy by dispatching a young general named Scipio to Africa to attack Carthage itself. Hannibal was forced to return, and was defeated at the battle of Zama in 202 B.C. by Scipio, who was henceforth known as Scipio Africanus. The Romans then annexed Spain. Carthage was defeated a third and last time by Rome in the Third Punic War (149–146 B.C.), the city was laid in ruins, and salt was sowed in its fields. The Carthaginian territories in Africa were made into the Roman province of Africa.

The Punic wars, as the Greek historian Polybius (c. 203–120 B.C.) noted, had brought Rome into the eastern Mediterranean, thus for the first time linking the Near East with the Mediterranean basin. "Previously the doings of the world had been, so to say, dispersed. . . . But ever since this date history has been an organic whole, and the affairs of Italy and [Africa] have been interlinked with those of Greece and Asia. . . . The Romans, feeling that the chief and most essential step in their scheme of universal aggression had now been taken, were first emboldened to reach out their hands to grasp the rest and to cross with an army to Greece and Asia."[1]

Completion of the Conquest of the Mediterranean

Posing as the defender of the purported independence of Greek city-states, Rome fought several wars with Macedon, which it finally annexed in 148 B.C. Rebellious Greek cities, cowed by the ruthless destruction of Corinth in 146 B.C., were placed under pro-Roman governors. And the smaller Greek states in Asia Minor were terrified into submission. The Seleucid kingdom had been conquered by the middle of the first century B.C.; and Egypt, the last great Hellenistic kingdom, fell to the armies and navy of the future emperor Augustus, in 30 B.C. In the two centuries since the beginning of the Punic wars, Rome had increased its possessions a hundredfold. As Polybius remarked, "The Romans had subjected to their rule not portions, but nearly the whole world, and possess an empire which is not only immeasurably greater than any which preceded it, but need not fear rivalry in the future."[2]

THE ECONOMICS OF EMPIRE BUILDING

The character of Roman society was completely transformed by the acquisition of an empire. Rome's economy at the beginning of the republic had been based on small-scale agriculture, and even the inhabitants of the city of Rome itself owned their small plots with which they could feed their families. These tough, hard-working families, with a stern morality of self-denial, had been the backbone of the armies that conquered the Italian peninsula, and their virtues were regarded throughout Roman history as the ideal that should be inculcated in every new generation. The historian Livy (59 B.C.–A.D. 17), looking back at the time of social upheaval at the end of the first century B.C., asked his readers to

[1] Polybius, *The Histories*, in the Loeb edition (London: W. Heinemann, 1922–1927), I, 3. 3–6, pp. 7–9.
[2] Polybius, *The Histories*, I, 1. 7–8, p. 7.

remember "the brave days of old," and "how, with the gradual relaxation of discipline, morals first gave way, as it were, then sank lower and lower, and finally began the downward plunge which has brought us to the present time, when we can endure neither our vices nor their cure."[3]

During the wars with Carthage, the economic position of the small farmer was undermined. Rome obtained its wheat as tribute from Sardinia, North Africa, and Spain, and the government sold it below the current price or gave it away free. It was thus more profitable to raise animals or to grow olives and grapes in cental Italy on large, well-capitalized estates than to produce wheat as earlier on small farms. Some small farmers went bankrupt. Others were dispossessed by being drafted into the army. Many fled to Rome to escape the ravaging armies of Hannibal. Their lands were acquired by the senatorial oligarchy or by a class of newly enriched capitalists who had done well as army suppliers during the wars. Most important of all, these vast estates were worked by slaves.

Rome had very few slaves before the First Punic War, perhaps as few as 20,000, but the victories over Carthage and the Eastern empires brought into Rome slaves from all the Mediterranean basin and the Near East. These slaves, as well as captives sold by pirates and children sold by penurious peasants, were put on sale in vast market centers, such as the city of Capua and the island of Delos. Although many educated slaves were bought to be household servants or to work in private business or the government bureaucracy, the majority were used for hard labor in the mines and the great estates. Prices were low. A rich Roman would buy 400 to 500 slaves. Most of the slaveowners chose to live in Rome, and to leave the task of exploiting the slaves to overseers who were free to torture and even to kill them. As a result, all Romans lived with a constant fear of a slave uprising. A favorite saying was, "Every slave we own is an enemy we harbor." In the city of Rome itself, where two-fifths of the population of 1 million were slaves, slaves were permitted to wear the same clothes as Romans so that they would not be aware of the vastness of their numbers. When slave uprisings broke out, such as that led by Spartacus in 73 B.C., in which an army of 70,000 slaves held a Roman army at bay for months, terrifying punishment was exacted. Six thousand slaves were crucified, and their bodies left hanging at intervals for hundreds of miles along the Appian Way as a terrible warning to other slaves.

In Rome, slavery destroyed the economic foundation of the city. The dispossessed farmers found that most of the laboring jobs and many of the skilled jobs in manufacturing and government were done by slaves. They did all the household work, from tutoring the children to cooking the meals. The principal jobs available to the Roman worker were in the service trades, running shops, bars, and bakeries, and acting as artisans in small workshops producing cloth, pottery, or shoes. The Roman middle class, if it had some capital, engaged

---

[3] Livy, *History*, in the Loeb edition (London: W. Heinemann, 1919), preface, 5, 9–10, pp. 5–7.

mainly in commerce and banking. Private business people called *publicans* received contracts from the state to import the wheat collected as tribute and to
redistribute it in the city, as well as to collect taxes and construct public works.
A class of capitalists or traders called *equestrians*, occupying the social position
immediately below the patricians, made fortunes in banking, although they
were also permitted to take up less important administrative positions in the
provinces. At the summit of this society was an oligarchy of family clans, whose
power was expressed through the Senate.

Although the size of the Senate was increased to 600, the state was in fact
run by about twenty great families, most of whom traced their origins back to
the early days of the republic or beyond. They exercised influence through
personal contacts with those for whom they had done and from whom they
expected favors. They renewed their finances and their blood by occasionally
admitting into their ranks a "new man," and they frequently struck lucrative
deals with the wealthier members of the equestrians, to whom they would
grant such concessions as tax-farming rights. The families also employed large
numbers of freedmen to scatter bribes during elections and to organize mobs
for the intimidation of their opponents. Hundreds of thousands of unemployed
attached themselves to one or other of these great families. They would appear
in crowds in the morning at the homes of the aristocrats for handouts of food
or money, and they were an organized if unofficial force on which the aristocratic family could call in their frequent and increasingly violent confrontations
with other families.

By the end of the second century B.C. the great families were divided into
two groups, the *Optimates* ("Elites"), usually called the "aristocratic" party, and
the *Populares*, translated as the "popular" party. Although it might seem at first
sight that these groups represented the rich and the less well off, in fact they
indicated a division within the oligarchy itself. The aristocratic faction consisted
of wealthy families that sought to avoid far-reaching social and economic change.
The popular party was composed of equally well-to-do families that saw, however, that their position could be maintained only by reforms that would better
the condition of the lower classes, above all of the dispossessed farming class.
The Senate became the stronghold of the aristocrats. The populists turned, as
a result, to the popular assemblies and the tribunate. Unfortunately, not all
leaders of the popular faction were sincere reformers. Many manipulated the
passions of the mob for their own political or material advancement.

Rome thus developed an economy and society whose existence depended
on possession and exploitation of an empire. In theory and in practice, Rome
justified its existence by the services it rendered to its empire—the maintenance
of peace, the provision of law, the expansion of commerce, the encouragement
of culture. It made no claim, and little effort, to pay through exports of manufactured or agricultural goods for the vast imports not only of foodstuffs and
raw materials but of every luxury of the known world with which its fleets
supplied it.

THE DESTRUCTION OF THE REPUBLIC

The struggle between the aristocratic and the popular parties, which eventually destroyed the republic itself, was initiated in 133 B.C. by a wealthy reformer named Tiberius Gracchus. Tiberius in many ways represented what was best in the Roman oligarchy. His mother was Cornelia, the daughter of Scipio Africanus, who had defeated Hannibal. She was not only the mother of twelve children and an efficient household administrator, but also a highly educated writer with a deep sense of the moral duties of families like her own, the Cornelii, to work for the improvement of conditions of the Roman poor. Tiberius was obsessed by the depopulation of central Italy caused by the expulsion of the small Roman farmers from their lands, and, once elected tribune, he demanded that private owners be compelled to give back public lands they had acquired for redistribution among the poor in 20-acre farms. Tiberius was also, in the eyes of the Senate, a rabble rouser. "The wild beasts that roam over Italy," he told the Roman crowd, "have every one of them a cave or lair to lurk in; but the men who fight and die for Italy enjoy the common air and light, indeed, but nothing else. . . . They fight and die to support others in wealth and luxury."[4] He and several hundred of his supporters were beaten to death by a group of senators and their gangs when he stood for reelection. Ten years later, his younger brother Gaius Gracchus was chosen tribune, and he revived the proposals of Tiberius. He was besieged on the summit of one of Rome's hills by a private army sent by some of the senators, and, fearing defeat, he asked his slave to behead him. His head was brought to the Senate for a reward, its weight in gold!

After the reorganization of the Roman army by Marius, a victorious general, consul, and leader of the popular party, in 106 B.C., the social conflicts took a more ominous turn. Marius enlisted volunteers, mostly from the poorest classes, in ten-cohort legions, composed of 5000 men each. The soldiers received good pay and grants of land, and were expected to give total loyalty, not to the Roman government but to the general who paid them. Other generals followed the example of Marius, and as a result the stage was set for a series of attacks on the city of Rome by sections of its own army.

To prevent Marius' followers from forcing the Senate to name him military commander in Asia Minor and Greece, the aristocratic party welcomed into the city the army of a rival general named Sulla. In 88 B.C., Sulla seized the city. When Sulla's army withdrew, Marius brought his forces into Rome, and engaged in a demented blood lust against his senatorial opponents, many of whom were murdered in the Roman Forum. Five years later, Sulla, who had made himself dictator, carried out a similar massacre in an effort to destroy the popular party totally, even to the extent of hounding the young Julius Caesar, who was a nephew of Marius. Sulla then restored the power of the aristocrats and,

---

[4] *Plutarch's Lives* (London: W. Heinemann, 1914–1954), IX, 5, pp. 165–167.

satisfied that he had brought constitutional order, retired to private life in 79 B.C.

New leaders almost at once aspired to power. Pompey (106–48 B.C.), one of Sulla's lieutenants, had made his name by the suppression of a slave uprising, by fighting piracy in the Mediterranean, and by conquests in the Euphrates region. Crassus, a rich general and senator, was joined by Pompey in the battle against the slaves, but by 63 B.C. had become suspicious of Pompey's ambitions and allied himself instead with a rising young soldier and would-be leader of what remained of the popular party, Julius Caesar (102–44 B.C.). The plans of Crassus and Caesar for having their own nominees picked as consuls were temporarily thwarted by the great orator Cicero (106–43 B.C.); and Pompey's return in triumph the following year seemed to set back their plans for personal power even more. The Senate, however, foolishly refused to grant Pompey's demand for allotments of land for his soldiers or to approve the settlement he had imposed in the Near East. As a result, Pompey agreed to join with Crassus and Caesar in an informal agreement known as the Triumvirate, to enforce their demands on the Senate.

Caesar was elected consul in 59 B.C., and the following year was sent as proconsul to Gaul, where he subdued hostile peoples over a nine-year period. Pompey's veterans were rewarded, and Crassus won tax-collecting privileges

Julius Caesar (102–44 B.C.) Caesar's successes were due to his superb military skills, his administrative genius, and his capacity for self-promotion. He was assassinated by senators, who feared he was about to destroy the republican constitution. (Alinari/Art Resource.)

for his supporters. The Triumvirate soon quarreled, especially as Caesar had not only built up a powerful military force in Gaul but had won immense popularity in Rome by the complete defeat of the Gallic tribes. (He had also skillfully dramatized his own achievements with his book, *The Gallic Wars*.)

Threatened with a trial for alleged misconduct as consul, in 49 B.C. Caesar crossed the river Rubicon from Gaul into Italy with part of his army, thus violating Roman law and starting the second Civil War in Roman history. Pompey, appointed by the Senate to defend the Roman republic against Caesar, was caught by surprise, and fled with many senators and other supporters to the east. First overcoming Pompey's lieutenants in Italy and Spain, Caesar then followed him to Greece, where he defeated his superior forces. Pompey himself took refuge in Egypt, where King Ptolemy XIII sought Caesar's favor by having him beheaded. When Caesar learned of this he declared war on Egypt, had Ptolemy executed, and set Cleopatra and her young brother on the Egyptian throne. By 45 B.C., Caesar controlled the Roman state.

Caesar showed that he had far-reaching plans for the solution of Rome's problems. To solve the constitutional impasse, he took for himself many of the important offices, becoming head priest, consul, tribune, and dictator. The Senate was increased in size to 900 by inclusion of his supporters, but was treated mainly as an advisory body. He tackled the problem of the dispossessed peasantry by founding overseas colonies and by redistributing part of the state lands in Italy. In Rome he provided work in the construction of public buildings. And he organized elaborate entertainments to amuse the crowds and a strong police force to keep them cowed. He attempted to cut down corruption among office holders.

About sixty senators, resenting Caesar's accumulation of power and fearing the end of the republican constitution, joined in a conspiracy against him. They were led by two prominent members of the aristocratic party: one was Gaius Cassius (d. 42 B.C.), one of Pompey's commanders in Greece who had been pardoned by Caesar after the defeat of Pompey's forces; the other was Marcus Brutus (85–42 B.C.), a descendant of an earlier Brutus who was considered the Father of the Republic. When Caesar attended the Senate unarmed on March 15, 44 B.C., the senators, led by Cassius and Brutus, fell upon him and stabbed him to death.

The conspirators had expected the traditional Roman republic, under senatorial dominance, to be restored, but the murder of Caesar set off thirteen years of civil war. Caesar's grandnephew Octavian (63 B.C.–A.D. 14), whom he had adopted and to whom he had bequeathed most of his fortune, demanded that the Senate make him consul; and when they refused he seized Rome with his own army. Mark Antony, one of Caesar's closest collaborators who had inflamed the Roman mob against the conspirators and had himself expected to become Caesar's successor, then joined with Octavian and another ambitious political leader named Lepidus, in forming a second Triumvirate, which was given dictatorial power by the Senate. The Triumvirate's armies defeated the

forces that Brutus and Cassius had assembled in the eastern provinces, at Phi-
lippi in Greece in 42 B.C., and Brutus and Cassius committed suicide. The
Triumvirate broke apart. Lepidus was forced out in 36 B.C. Antony took control
of the eastern provinces, including Egypt, where he became the new lover of
Queen Cleopatra; and Octavian took Rome and the western provinces. Octavian's navy destroyed the fleet of Antony and Cleopatra at the Battle of Actium
(31 B.C.), off the coast of Greece, and their army in Egypt the following year.
Antony and Cleopatra committed suicide, and Octavian returned to Rome to
take up again the work of remodeling the state that Caesar had begun.

THE EMPIRE FROM AUGUSTUS TO MARCUS AURELIUS

The Augustan Constitution

Julius Caesar had considered restoring monarchy to Rome, and had been murdered. Octavian was wiser. He decided to take personal power within the
framework of the old institutions, and thus profit from the sanctity with which
500 years of operation had endowed the republican institutions. Roman political
theory held that, when Romulus founded Rome, he received authority (*imperium*) from the gods, and specifically from Jupiter, who was regarded as the
guarantor of the city. The imperium had been passed from Romulus to the
assembly of family elders, who in turn had shared it, temporarily, with the
officials they appointed, such as the consuls. But it was felt very early that the
imperium was legally conferred only when the mass of the people, acting through
their assemblies, concurred.

The notion of state authority as vested in certain officials for specific periods, originally of fairly short duration, remained basic to the whole conception
of republican government as it grew enormously complex over time. This view
of legitimate authority differentiated the Roman system from the Greek search
for the ideal state. The Romans believed that states were practical institutions
existing for the purpose of assuring stability, confidence, and prosperity, all of
which were interconnected and of supreme value. They had little patience for
a book such as Plato's *Republic*, or for the revolutionary remodeling of existing
states.

Romans were therefore delighted when Octavian, in 27 B.C., handed back
his authority to the Senate and the assemblies, and restored the authority of
the magistrates. It was in fact a gesture to the crowd, because Augustus had
stage-managed what was to follow. Immediately the Senate expressed its gratitude by appointing him tribune for life, consul, censor, head priest, and dictator, and begged him to accept the titles of *Imperator* (commander of the army),
Princeps (First Citizen), and *Augustus* ("highly revered"). With real power in his
hands, Augustus ensured that the Senate would enjoy the appearance of authority. He even attended debates in the Senate house, in spite of the forbidding

Augustus as Commander-in-Chief *The breastplate depicts, at the top, the chariot of dawn, which implies a new beginning; in the center, the surrender of the barbarians; and at the bottom, Mother Earth bringing new prosperity.* (Museo Vaticano/Alinari-Art Resource.)

precedent of Caesar's last appearance there, and allowed the senators to criticize his policies. According to the somewhat salacious but also sagacious historian Suetonius:

> Augustus' speeches in the House [Senate] would often be interrupted by such remarks as, "I don't understand you" or "I'd dispute your point if I got the chance." And it happened more than once that, exasperated by recriminations which lowered the tone of the debates, he left the House in angry haste, and was followed by shouts of: "You ought to let senators say exactly what they think about matters of public importance."[5]

Augustus also ensured that senators were indebted to him directly. He gave provincial administrative positions to more than a hundred senators every year and permitted the Senate to control eight of the richest provinces directly. The Senate became increasingly sycophantic, and even begged him to put the title *Pater Patriae* ("Father of His Country") above the door of his house on the Palatine Hill.

Augustus made constructive use of his powers. To prevent the interference of the military in politics, he cut the army in half, paid the remainder well, enlisted them for long terms, and stationed them on the frontiers away from

[5] Suetonius, *The Twelve Caesars*, translated by Robert Graves (Harmondsworth, England: Penguin, 1969), p. 81. Original source—Suetonius, *Aug.* 54.1.

their home provinces. In Rome he maintained only a personal Praetorian Guard of 4500 men. After several short campaigns along the northern borders of the empire, he abandoned any further attempt to expand the empire, and assigned the armies a purely defensive role. The main theme of his empire became the maintenance of peace, which he celebrated by erecting a beautiful altar, the *Ara Pacis* or Altar of Peace.

With internal peace assured, he encouraged freedom of economic enterprise by the capitalist class. Roads were well maintained and pirates suppressed. The currency remained firm in value. The great estates in Italy became profitable exporters of wine and oil. The population in Rome itself received work in newly founded manufacturing enterprises for pottery, bronze, glass, and woolen cloth. To appease the provinces, Augustus gradually abandoned the system of using provincial governorships as rewards for loyalty, which had implied that the provinces could be stripped for the enrichment of the appointee. Instead he appointed provincial bureaucrats called legates, and assured more equitable tax collection by sending closely supervised officials called procurators to run the tax collection. He also decentralized power as much as he dared, even involving the native aristocracies in local administration. He also made sure that his actions would have a religious sanction. He himself headed the state religion. He ordered the erection of a temple to the deified Julius Caesar in the center of the Roman Forum, and permitted the eastern provinces to erect temples to his own cult as a god. The western provinces soon followed this example.

Augustus deliberately adopted a modest demeanor, living frugally with his own family, wearing clothes woven by the women of his household, and eating and drinking moderately. He insisted on a return in the general population to the virtues of an earlier Rome, forbidding ostentatious display and strictly controlling sexual mores. In particular, he exhorted women to marry young, have many children, and preserve the harmonious home life that had been the basis of the early republic.

Exhortation was soon turned into law. Women were permitted to marry at the age of twelve and boys at fourteen. Women not married by twenty and men by twenty-five were punished by the censors. Widows who failed to remarry were also penalized. Women were also rewarded for bearing children. A free woman who had had three children and a freedwoman with four were made exempt from the legal guardianship of a male. This exemption gave her the right to administer her own property.

There were many reasons for this legislation. Augustus was undoubtedly influenced by his own wife, Livia, a rather severe Roman spouse who ran his home in austere dignity, offered him advice on state matters, and was his lifelong companion. But there were also reasons of state. The child-bearing years of women in imperial Rome were very short. Many died in childbirth, as the numerous tombstones of women who died between the ages of fifteen and twenty-nine show. Whereas the median age for men in Rome was forty-six, for women it was only thirty-four. In addition there was a shortage of women

because parents engaged in infanticide, particularly of unwanted girls. Finally, Augustus's emphasis on the nuclear family, of parents and children, rather than the extended family composed of several generations and even the remotest kin was a blow at the great senatorial lineages that had dominated the politics of the late Republic.

The Rebuilding of Rome

Augustus was also determined that by the time of his death the city of Rome should be a physical reflection of the great changes he had brought about in the way Romans felt about themselves. He began a magnificent rebuilding of the city, at the end of which he was reputed to have boasted that he had found Rome made of brick and left it made of marble. He completed the great colonnaded law court, the Basilica Julia, which had been begun by Caesar. Overlooking the Tiber, he built an enormous circular mausoleum for his own burial. And on the Palatine Hill, next to his simple home, he erected an overpowering temple in colored Numidian marble, dedicated to Apollo, the "restorer of Peace."

His reforms did not, however, win the approval of all Romans. The savage proscriptions he had instigated following the murder of Julius Caesar, in which hundreds of his opponents, including Cicero, had died, were not forgotten. Admirers of the republic were bitterly resentful of the manner in which he placed hand-picked nominees in the principal administrative offices, and thus undermined the institutions he claimed to have restored. The great historian Tacitus (c. A.D. 56–123), looking back a century later, decided that Augustus had begun the corruption of power that led to the savagery and chaos of the four Julio-Claudian emperors who followed him:

When [Augustus] had seduced the army by gifts, the common people by the provision of cheap food, and everyone by the blandishments of peace, then little by little he began to enlarge his powers, to encroach upon the proper functions of the Senate, the magistrates and the laws. No one opposed him. Men of spirit had died on the battlefield or in the proscriptions. The remainder of the aristocracy were rewarded by wealth and position in proportion to their readiness to accept servitude.[6]

The Julio-Claudian Emperors, A.D. 14–68

The one weakness of Augustus's maintenance of the semblance of senatorial power was that he could not secure the hereditary right of his family to succeed him. He did, however, persuade the Senate to recognize his adopted son Tiberius, whom he had married to his only child Julia, as princeps upon his death. Tiberius ruled firmly and efficiently, although he squirmed under the interference of his mother, Livia; and he retired whenever possible to his palace on the island of Capri, where, Roman gossip mongers related, he engaged in every form of illicit lust. He was finally smothered in his own bedclothes by the prefect of his guard. Caligula (reigned A.D. 37–41) was demented. He thought he could talk to the gods through their statues, and was on occasion heard giving them orders. He executed leading aristocrats for treason and confiscated their possessions. He was murdered by the Praetorian Guard. His uncle Claudius (reigned A.D. 41–54) was a kindly, scholarly man, who could have governed well had he been able to control the excesses of the women in his court. He was murdered with poisoned mushrooms prepared for him by his wife, Agrippina. Nero (reigned A.D. 54–68) was a cruel profligate, who considered himself a person of supreme artistic genius. Among the many he murdered were his mother and two wives. Most of the Roman population thought that he was personally responsible for the great fire in A.D. 64, which burned most of the central part of the city, especially when he took the opportunity to build a vast palace for himself on the ruins. Eventually, the army marched on Rome to overthrow him, and he was helped to commit suicide.

Although the crimes and follies of the Julio-Claudian emperors dominate the writings of such Roman historians as Suetonius and Tacitus, the achievements of the Augustan age were continued and consolidated. A larger imperial bureaucracy ensured administrative stability. Roman jurisprudence was further refined. The army remained effective in protecting the frontiers, and even under Claudius extended imperial rule over Britain and Mauretania (northwestern Africa). In literature, the period began the so-called Silver Age, which lasted until the death of Emperor Marcus Aurelius in A.D. 180. The philosopher Seneca popularized Stoicism; his nephew Lucan wrote epic poems, in one of which Caesar is portrayed as an evil genius who destroyed the republic; Persius wrote satirical poems in which the virtues of Stoicism are contrasted to the corruption

---

[6] Cited in Donald R. Dudley, *The World of Tacitus* (London: Secker and Warburg, 1968), p. 77. Original source—Tacitus Ann. I. 2.2.

of the Rome of his own day. Finally, in architecture, one of the most grandiose buildings of the whole imperial age was Nero's Golden House, a palace covering 125 acres in the heart of Rome surrounded by landscape gardens where both tame and wild animals roamed. It was, however, torn down after Nero's death; the great amphitheater called the Colosseum was erected on its ruins by the Flavian emperors.

The Flavian Dynasty, A.D. 69–96

Order was restored after the chaos of Nero's reign by the three emperors of the Flavian dynasty, Vespasian (reigned A.D. 69–79), Titus (reigned A.D. 79–81), and Domitian (reigned A.D. 81–96). Generals themselves, they satisfied the army with the spoils of campaigns in the Near East and the north, including the sack of Jerusalem by Titus in A.D. 70. Financial stability was assured with the coming of internal order. Provincial families were brought in to restore the vigor of the Senate. Vast programs of public works were undertaken, not only in Rome itself but throughout the empire. Rome's crowds were particularly impressed by the spectacles the Flavians staged in their new Colosseum, in which audiences of up to 50,000 could watch battles of gladiators and animals and elaborate naval battles in the flooded amphitheater.

The Five Good Emperors, A.D. 96–180

The century from A.D. 96 to A.D. 180, under the so-called Five Good Emperors, was possibly the most prosperous period in all Roman history. Each ruler picked his successor before his death and associated him in the exercise of power, so that struggles over the transition of authority were avoided. Wars such as those fought by Emperor Trajan (reigned A.D. 98–117) in Dacia (Rumania) and in the Fertile Crescent were almost invariably successful, and brought new spoils to Rome. Hadrian (reigned A.D. 117–138) ensured stability on the northern frontier by building his famous wall across northern England, as well as an earthen rampart across the whole length of Germany. The character of Roman government changed for the better as the influence of the provinces grew. Two of the emperors were Spanish, and all believed that citizenship should be more widely extended. Local self-government was extended in the empire. Hadrian was responsible for the codification of the laws of the magistrates in a form that could be used throughout the empire. The philosopher-emperor Marcus Aurelius (reigned A.D. 161–180) was perhaps the most striking of these emperors, a man who wrote his *Meditations*, a classic piece of Stoic philosophy, while on campaign in Germany. After his death, however, the imperial order decayed. A century of chaos began again, with the appointment by Marcus Aurelius of his sadistic son Commodus (reigned A.D. 180–192) as emperor. The greatest intellectual achievements of the Roman empire were the product of these first two centuries following the takeover of power by Augustus.

THE CULTURE OF REPUBLICAN AND IMPERIAL ROME

Roman Religion

Religion was the most powerful force unifying the Roman state, and yet Roman religion was surprisingly open to all innovation regarded as not directly threatening to the Roman state. The Romans inherited from the earliest days a belief in the presence of spirits in every daily action. The most important of these were Janus, who guarded the doorway; the Lares, beneficent spirits of ancestors; the Penates, who protected the storeroom; and especially Vesta, who looked after the hearth and therefore the home. In every family the daughter had the duty of guarding the fire of Vesta, kept permanently burning in the hearth of every house as a symbolic link of all generations of the family with each other and with the gods. When the Roman state adopted an official religion, it was therefore natural that it too should have a sacred fire of Vesta burning in her temple in the Forum and guarded by six virgins, the famous Vestal Virgins, whose purity was itself a guarantee of the goodness of the Roman people. (Vestal Virgins who betrayed that trust were buried alive! But the Romans, practical in all things, pensioned those who remained true to their vows for thirty years, and permitted them to marry.) Yet the Romans incorporated the religious beliefs of almost every people, except the Jews and the Christians, with whom they came into contact. They took their central triad of gods—Jupiter, Juno, and Minerva—from the Etruscans and erected the most prominent temple on the Capitol Hill for these deities. All the Greek gods were eventually given a Roman name and form. The Greek goddess of fertility, Aphrodite, for example, became the Roman Venus. And the Greek god Zeus, father of the Greek gods, was assumed to be the same as Jupiter.

When the Roman troops penetrated Asia Minor, they brought back some extraordinary religions, such as the worship of Cybele, a goddess whose priests were eunuchs who slashed themselves with knives. From Iran came the cult of Mithras, a harsh, soldiers' religion to which only men were admitted, which worshipped the god Mithras, who had killed a bull in combat and thereby released all the life on earth by its sacrifice. From Egypt they brought the cult of the goddess Isis, a nobly dignified worship, which was the most popular of all in Rome in the first and second centuries A.D. Women in particular loved the worship of Isis, a goddess who shared her blessings equally among all classes, who pardoned sinners, who was supreme over male gods, and who above all was receptive to the appeals of her worshippers. Her most famous portrayal in literature was in the novel, *The Golden Ass*, by Apuleius, in the second century. The novel tells of the adventures of Lucius, a young man who is turned into as ass after unwisely using ointment from a witch. After many difficult trials, Lucius despairs of ever being restored to human form when suddenly, while lying on the shore by moonlight:

> I had scarcely closed my eyes before the apparition of a woman began to rise from the
> middle of the sea, with so lovely a face that the gods themselves would have fallen

down in adoration of it. . . . Her long thick hair fell in tapering ringlets on her lovely neck, and was crowned with an intricate chaplet in which was woven every kind of flower. Just above her brow shone a round disc, like a mirror, or like the bright face of the moon, which told me who she was. . . . All the perfumes of Arabia floated into my nostrils as the Goddess [Isis] deigned to address me: "You see me here, Lucius, in answer to your prayer. I am Nature, the universal mother, mistress of all elements. . . .Weep no more, lament no longer; the hour of deliverance, shone over by my watchful light, is at hand."[7]

A huge priesthood administered the state religion, and was headed by the pontifex maximus, who, after Julius Caesar, was usually the emperor. Large numbers of colleges of priests specialized in such functions as the safeguard of foreign relations. The most sought after of the priests were the augurs, who claimed to be able to tell from such evidence as the liver of a sacrificed animal whether the immediate future was favorable for any particular action. Even nonbelievers in the aristocracy welcomed the apparatus of the state religion as a sure method of maintaining the obedience and trust of the population. Augustus in particular turned it to his own purposes by erecting temples and by insisting on the worship of Julius Caesar. He himself was officially deified after his death, and it became a test of civic loyalty to require worship at the shrines of the deified emperors. Any sect, such as the Christians, who refused to do so were then regarded as guilty of undermining the state rather than of undermining the religion, and could be punished for the crime of treason.

Roman Philosophy

Many aristocratic Romans regarded the state religion as a convenient superstition, and personally practiced philosophy. The two most popular schools of philosophy were Epicureanism and Stoicism, which, as we saw in Chapter 2, had both been founded by Greeks during the Hellenistic Age. Perhaps the greatest formulation of Epicureanism was *The Nature of Things* by Lucretius (96–55 B.C.). Lucretius argued that human existence is bounded by nature, and that nature is nothing more than a flow of atoms. The only source of knowledge is sense experience. The purpose of life is the avoidance of distress, especially that caused by fear of the gods or of death. Like Epicurus himself, he thought relaxation in a quiet garden by a running stream surrounded by friends was the ideal life.

Whereas many who claimed to follow Epicureanism used it merely as an excuse for a life of self-indulgence, the aristocrats who followed Stoicism were a sterner breed. Seneca (2 B.C.–A.D. 65) was the writer most responsible for making Stoicism the predominant belief of the Roman upper classes in the first two centuries A.D. In his own life he had ample opportunity to display his capacity for Stoicism. Serious illness had interrupted a promising literary career,

[7] Apuleius, *The Golden Ass*, translated by Robert Graves (Harmondsworth, England: Penguin, 1950), pp. 268–270. Original source—Apuleius, *Golden Ass* 1.3-4.

and led to a long convalescence in the intellectual stimulus of Alexandria. His first incursion into politics was interrupted by banishment to Corsica. As tutor and advisor to Nero, he ran the Roman empire wisely for the first five years of that unstable emperor's reign, only to be dismissed and ordered to commit suicide. Having faced the worst himself, Seneca was able with some credentials to argue the Stoic message of hope. Life's troubles—the loss of wealth or position—were passing problems, but one possessed, regardless of the actions of others, control of one's own mind and one's relationship to universal nature, a kind of cosmic providence in which justice reigned and all people were equal. Before the coming of Christianity, Stoicism more than any other creed had ennobled the life of individuals in an increasingly crass and egotistical age.

Roman Law

Roman law became deeply influenced by Stoic belief in the existence of a "natural law" derived from human reason and therefore applicable to all nations. But even from its origin Roman law was influenced by the belief that law should correspond to something fixed and unchanging in the world of human beings. In the early republic, it was believed that the law had always existed, and that it was the duty of magistrates simply to apply the law to specific instances. The Twelve Tables erected in the Forum in the fifth century B.C. were merely an attempt to write down these preexisting laws. However, the interpretation became increasingly more complex. Each magistrate or judge was allowed at the beginning of his term to state his interpretation of the law; and later experts, called jurisconsults, gave commentaries on the decisions of the magistrates and on the laws. An important attempt was made to formalize these laws, judgments, and interpretations in the second century B.C., and an even more ambitious effort was made by Hadrian in the second century A.D. The final formulation was not completed until the emperor Justinian in Constantinople in the sixth century.

Roman law was very different from contemporary law. The Romans believed that status determined one's treatment under the law. Different treatment was accorded to citizens, those born free, the freed, resident aliens, women, and so on. Slaves possessed no legal rights, since they were not believed to be people. Power of the *pater familias* (the father of the family) was the binding force in society. Children were under the control of their fathers theoretically for their whole lives, and in the early centuries could even be put to death by them. Roman law had, however, made a number of important advances. It guaranteed equality of treatment to people of equal status, and, by the beginning of the third century, was beginning to accept the Stoic notion that all free people within the empire, regardless of nationality, enjoyed equal rights. Punishment was to some extent in proportion to the seriousness of the crime. Protection was given to the weaker members of society and even to slaves. And the law of private property, by far the most developed section of Roman law, had made possible the harmonious economic development of an empire of 70 million people.

Roman Literature

The great writers of Rome are traditionally divided into those who wrote during a "golden age," which extended from about 80 B.C. to the death of Augustus in A.D. 14, and a "silver age" of slightly lesser quality, which lasted from A.D. 14 to the death of the Emperor Marcus Aurelius in A.D. 180. Moreover, the golden age is subdivided between the period of the late republic, known as Ciceronian because dominated by the writer, orator, and statesman Cicero, and the period of the reign of Augustus, which is known as Augustan not merely because it coincided with the years of his rule but because the influence of Augustus is visible in much that was written.

Cicero believed on principle that intellectuals had the duty to involve themselves in the political life of their country and should not use their creative activity as an excuse for avoiding civic participation. He himself took many of the elected offices of the Roman republic, from aedile to consul. His speeches in the Senate, especially those in which he denounced the conspirator Catiline for planning to seize Rome by force and his later denunciations of Mark Antony, were masterpieces of Latin prose turned to his own political ends, but they led to his execution in the proscriptions of 43 B.C. During his eventful life Cicero wrote constantly on rhetoric, ethics, and especially on politics. His treatise *On the Republic* was the only book of political philosophy written by a Roman that can compare with the great books on political theory of Athens; but, unlike the Greeks, who passionately sought to understand how a perfect state could be created, Cicero argued in favor of continuity, of a state that develops and maintains its traditions over time.

The outstanding poets of the late republic were the philosopher Lucretius, who claimed that he wrote in verse solely to make the philosophy of Epicureanism less forbidding to the average Roman, and the lyric poet Catullus (c. 84–c. 54 B.C.). Most of Catullus' surviving poems are addressed to Lesbia, a woman who over the years drove him from wild passion to deepest hatred. "Let us live, my Lesbia, and let us love," one poem begins. "Suns may rise and set again. But once our brief light fails, our night is one never-ending sleep."[8]

The great poets of the Augustan age were aware that they were expected to echo the morality of the new emperor and to express the optimism of the new age, not least in their adulation of the emperor himself. Horace (65–8 B.C.) set the standard in *Odes* he dedicated directly to Augustus and in the lines, only too frequently quoted on the gravestones of soldiers: *"Dulce et decorum est pro patria mori"* ("How seemly and sweet it is to die for one's country.") But he

---

[8] Author's translation.

could also be a scathing satirist. In another ode, Horace directs a blast against Rome and its feckless population:

> The fickle crowd, the false swearing courtesan.
> They all move back, these friends, when our casks are drained
> Of wine, and only dregs are left; too
> Crafty are they to share our misfortunes . . .
> Alas, for shame, these wounds and these brother's woes!
> From what have we refrained, this our hardened age?
> What crime is left untried? From what, through
> Fear of the gods, has our youth held back or
> Restrained its hand?[9]

It was Virgil (70–19 B.C.), perhaps the finest of all Latin poets, who most harmoniously expressed the ethic that Augustus championed. In his early poems, the *Georgics*, he wrote about the problems and joys of farming, and looked back in elegant nostalgia at the simple rural life of the original Romans:

> This was the life which once the ancient Sabines led,
> and Remus and his brother; this made Etruria strong.
> Through this, Rome became the fairest thing on earth.[10]

Virgil devoted the rest of his life to writing the twelve long books of the epic poem, *The Aeneid*. In telling the story of the flight of Aeaneas from Troy, his adventures on his way to Italy, and his establishment of the first Roman state, Virgil succeeded in his goal of writing an epic that would focus the patriotism and enhance the virtues of the Roman people. Although coming at times close to hero worship of Augustus, Virgil transcended this goal by presenting in human form in the actions of his characters devotion to the values, the *pietas*, he admired—the devotion to family, to country, and to the gods. Hampered constantly by ill health and dead himself before completing his poem, Virgil could see beyond the pursuit of military glory to the sadness and human suffering that such wars entail:

> Yes, Aeneas drove his strong sword
> Right through the young man's body, and buried it there to the hilt.
> It penetrated his light shield, frail armor for so aggressive
> A lad, and the tunic his mother had woven of pliant gold,
> And soaked it with blood from his breast.
> Then the soul left the body.
> Passing sadly through the air to the land of shadows.
> But when Aeneas beheld the dying boy's look, his face—

---

[9] From *The Odes of Horace, Newly Translated from the Latin and Rendered into the Original Metres*, by Helen Rowe Henze (Norman: University of Oklahoma Press, 1961), p. 67.

[10] Virgil Georgics, II, 531–534, translated in Gilbert Highet, *Poets in a Landscape* (London: Hamish Hamilton, 1957), p. 69. The Sabines were a hill people conquered by the Romans.

A face that by now was strangely grey—he felt pity for him.
And a deep sigh escaped him.[11]

The career of the poet Ovid (43 B.C.–A.D. 18) was a salutary example of the treatment Augustus reserved for literary figures who failed to extol his moral code. Ovid's early poems in the style of Catullus were very popular with the Roman aristocracy, but he made the mistake of writing a sensual handbook in verse, *The Art of Love*, which decidedly failed to expand on the virtues of family life. As part of a concerted attack on those people he regarded as immoral elements in Roman society, Augustus exiled Ovid in A.D. 8 to a town on the Black Sea; and even Ovid's composition of a superb mythological poem, *Metamorphoses*, was ineffective in ending his banishment.

Livy (59 B.C.–A.D. 17), the great historian of the Augustan age, was more pleasing to Augustus. His long narrative of the *History of Rome*, from its founding to 9 B.C. to where the book breaks off, set out to be didactic, finding in the ancient past of the city the high moral standards that the decadent republic had forgotten (and which, by implication, Augustus was restoring).

The writers of the "silver age" were far more critical and pessimistic. The historian Tacitus (c. A.D. 56–123) too wrote acidic studies, the *Annals* on the Julio-Claudian emperors, and the *Histories* on the Flavian dynasty. While he did not spare even Augustus from condemnation, he was at his sparkling best in his denunciation of the women of the court of Tiberius and Nero. When Augustus's widow Livia died, Tacitus commented: "She was a good match for both her husband and her son [Tiberius]: as cunning as the one, as two-faced as the other." He portrays Agrippina the Elder, the daughter-in-law of Tiberius, as one of the most stubborn, or courageous, women in Rome. When exiled to an offshore island, she starved herself to death. But it is in the malicious portrayal of Agrippina the Younger, the wife of the Emperor Claudius, that he creates his most memorable portrait. After Agrippina married Claudius, Tacitus says, "the country was transformed."

Complete obedience was accorded to a woman—and not a woman like Messalina who toyed with national affairs to satisfy her appetites. This was a rigorous, almost masculine despotism. In public, Agrippina was austere and often arrogant. Her private life was chaste—unless power was to be gained. Her passion to acquire money was unbounded. She wanted it as a stepping-stone to supremacy.[12]

The poet Juvenal (c. A.D. 50–127) was equally free in his criticism. In the sixteen *Satires* he wrote between 100 and 127, he unleashed a storm of invective, couched in elegantly finished verse forms, against the tyranny of emperors and

[11] From *The Aeneid of Virgil*, translated by Cecil Day Lewis. London: Chatto & Windus Ltd. and The Hogarth Press, 1952, pp. 232–233; and New York: Literistic, Ltd. Copyright © 1952 by C. Day Lewis. Reprinted by permission of the publishers.
[12] Tacitus, *The Annals of Imperial Rome*, translated by Michael Grant (Harmondsworth, England: Penguin, 1971), p. 255.

especially of their wives and favorites, the rampant criminality of the Roman population, and especially the squalid overcrowding of a city that had grown excessive in size and ambition.

> This is not all you must fear. Shut up your house or your store,
> Bolts and padlocks and bars will never keep out all the burglars.
> Or a holdup man will do you in with a switch blade.
> If the guards are strong over Pontine marshes and pinewoods
> Near Volturno, the scum of the swamps and the filth of the forest
> Swirl into Rome, the great sewer, their sanctuary, their haven.
> Furnaces blast and anvils groan with the chains we are forging:
> What other uses have we for iron and steel? There is danger
> We will have little left for hoes and mattocks and ploughshares.
> Happy the men of old, those primitive generations
> Under the tribunes and kings, when Rome had only one jailhouse![13]

Roman Architecture and Public Works

During the republic, the Roman architects adopted the basic forms of Greek architecture, at first from the conquered Greek cities of southern Italy and Sicily and later from Greece itself. These forms included the post-and-lintel principle used in the Greek temples and the Doric, Ionic, and Corinthian capitals. From the Etruscans, the Romans took the semicircular arch. Rome's principal innovation in architectural style lay in the combination of the pillar with the semicircular arch.

The arch could be used in rows, sometimes superimposed one upon the other, to form the structure of the great Roman aqueducts, such as those still surviving at the Pont du Gard in France or at Segovia in Spain. Arches could also be used as the outer walls of round or oval buildings, such as the great amphitheaters that were constructed for the gladiatorial games. They thus formed a frame within which the descending rows of stone seats could be constructed, as in the Colosseum. Use of the arch also made possible the vaulting of vast spaces, which could not have been covered either by timber beams or by stone lintels. The so-called barrel vault, which the Romans used to roof over the huge public rooms within their baths and many of their temples, was in reality nothing more than a prolonged arch. Even the dome, which the Romans were the first people to bring into widespread and often spectacular use, could be considered a development of the semicircular arch, since the weight of the dome is transferred directly onto heavy supporting walls. What made possible the construction of such vast domes as that of the Pantheon in Rome, built by Agrippa in 27 B.C. but completely rebuilt by the Emperor Hadrian in A.D. 115–124, was the use of concrete, which became a basic Roman building

[13] Juvenal, *The Satires*, translated by Rolfe Humphries (Bloomington: Indiana University Press, 1958), pp. 44–45.

The Colosseum, Rome *The Colosseum seated 50,000 spectators. Its floor was flooded for staging of mock naval battles but it was mostly used for battles fought by gladiators. (Fototeca Unione, at the American Academy in Rome.)*

material from the second century B.C. The Romans used columns for the interior of their law courts, such as the Basilica Julia, constructed by Augustus in the Roman Forum, and these airy, colonnaded buildings became the usual form for the Roman temple and later a model for the first Christian churches.

In public works as in their architecture, the Romans built to last, especially when they constructed the walls and roads on which they knew their empire to be dependent. Few remains are more suggestive of Roman determination than Hadrian's Wall in the bleak moors of Northumberland in England. About fifty years before Hadrian came to Britain, the Romans had attempted to establish a defense line across the center of Scotland, but the wild Gallic tribes had proved too powerful for the overextended Roman legions. Hadrian ordered the construction of a wall, 30 feet in height and 20 feet thick, that was to run across the narrowest point of northern England, a distance of some 80 miles. Every 2 miles along the wall there was to be a garrison, between every garrison a fortified tower, and every few yards between the towers a soldier. In front of the wall there were to be trenches implanted with sharp stakes. Here was to be the northernmost defense of the Roman empire, at a distance of 1500 miles from the city of Rome.

Great walls like this lay at the end of a highly developed system of roads that were one of the major foundations of Roman military and administrative successes. The roads began at the "umbilical stone" in the Forum of Rome, at the foot of the Capitol Hill, and all mileages were counted from that point. To the south ran the Appian Way, linking Rome with Naples and the former Greek cities of Sicily; to the east, the Emilian Way climbed into the Apennine Mountains and on to the Adriatic coast; to the north ran the Aurelian Way, the great highway to Gaul that skirted the Mediterranean, hanging along the Ligurian cliffs of northern Italy like an implausible ribbon of stone. These roads, totaling 50,000 miles in all, linked Rome with the farthest points of its empire. Along them troops could cover 30 miles a day on foot; and the produce of three continents could be transported to the capital city's swarming population.

Until the eighteenth century, these Roman roads provided the principal highway system in Europe, for they had been built to last. After laying out the line of the road, the Romans dug trenches on each side down to firm ground. Then they excavated the road surface, digging down some 10 feet or more to the subsoil, on which they would construct four layers of foundation—fine earth beaten hard; squared stones joined with mortar; compacted chalk, tiles, and gravel; and finally a handsome outer surface of cut stone, carefully inlaid with smaller carved stones in the gaps between the main paving blocks. Some of these roads are still in use with little repair.

The Cities of the Empire

In the outer provinces of the empire, soldiers and administrators set out to re-create the amenities of the capital city, which meant at the very least a bath, a theater, and an arena. Rome ran a consumer society, and the provinces intended to enjoy themselves too. In Britain the most evocative monument the Romans have left behind are the baths in Bath. The Romans adored hot springs, especially when they found themselves in fog-bound places, and in Bath they had year-round hot springs with a temperature of 105°F. The bath is still kept filled, and the worn stone "diving board" used by several centuries of Roman legionnaries can still be seen. In the congenial climate and countryside of southern Gaul, which is now Provence in southern France, the Romans excelled in building provincial capitals. The great theater of Orange is still in use for drama festivals. The amphitheater of Nîmes is a bullring. And the theater and arena at Arles are still among the best preserved Roman monuments.

It was in the city of Rome itself, however, that the wealth of the empire was most lavishly expended, upon the population of the world's largest city— 1 million in the first century A.D. and perhaps 2 million a century later. Huge aqueducts were constructed to bring fresh water from the outlying hills and, once they possessed unlimited supplies of water, the emperors built magnificent baths, which became great social centers equipped not only with pools but libraries, lecture halls, casinos, and bars. The serious bather took the full treatment. He passed from a room at outside temperature into a lukewarm room and finally into the steam room, where he cleansed his pores through perspiration. Then he took the reverse process, moving from a hot cleansing bath into a warm transition bath and finally into a cold plunge, after which slaves scraped his skin and gave him a massage with oil.

Bread and Circuses

For the entertainment, and perhaps for the pacification, of the 300,000 unemployed, there was a huge chariot arena called the Circus Maximus, below the palaces of the Palatine Hill, from which the emperors watched from a high gallery. Gladiatorial games were presented in the Colosseum. The gladiators specialized in the use of different weapons, such as the sword and shield, the dagger and buckler, and the net and trident. Emperors curried favor by bringing thousands of exotic animals, such as the hippopotamus and the elephant, from distant parts of the empire to be slaughtered, although occasionally the fare was varied by having such self-confessed traitors as Christians massacred by animals or gladiators.

In spite of the magnificence of these public buildings, most of Rome was a squalid, overcrowded mass of tenements. Whereas the wealthy Romans lived in spacious, airy homes, built in colonnades around open courtyards in which flowering bushes grew and fountains played, most Romans lived in vast apartment buildings six to ten floors high. Water had to be carried up from public fountains. Sanitation was almost nonexistent. Garbage was thrown into the street. Typhoid, typhus, and cholera spread in recurrent waves. Malaria was ubiquitous. The dead were piled in noxious pits on the edge of the city. Only the wealthy possessed the means of burial in a formal tomb along one of the roadways leading into the city. It was little wonder that the Roman poor should have found an escape either in the savagery of the games or the consolation of one of the emotional religions, of which Christianity was eventually to prove the most attractive.

THE CHAOS OF THE THIRD CENTURY

The century following the death of Marcus Aurelius in A.D. 180, was a period of renewed conflict and chaos. The most immediate problem was the breakdown of the constitutional system of Augustus, and in particular the constant, violent interference of the army in choice of emperors. The army itself disintegrated into a number of provincial forces, each of which supported the general who would promise them the greatest spoils. Whereas in the first century B.C., leadership of the army could fall to a Pompey or Julius Caesar, in the third century A.D., army leaders were almost without exception feckless, ruthless, and short-lived. Between 235 and 284, only one of the twenty-six emperors installed by the army avoided violent death. Internal order broke down completely. Pirates ravaged the coasts. Brigands roamed the highways. The provincial cities were the first to feel the economic impact of the breakdown of communication and trade. The local aristocracies gave up any pretense of civic patriotism, and sought, mostly unsuccessfully, to protect themselves from economic disaster and physical danger. Manufacturing declined for lack of markets and as a result of the debasement of the currency by the army-appointed emperors.

The countryside declined with the cities. The great estates, which had previously produced a surplus for export, became self-sufficient units. The finest land was retained by the landowners and worked by slaves. The rest of the land was leased out to share-croppers, who thus lacked incentive to improve the land or their methods of farming. The climate may even have worsened, but proof of this is still lacking. Increase in epidemics is certain. In addition to the age-old scourge of malaria, the Germanic tribes, penetrating the empire as welcome army recruits or unwelcome settlers, brought plague. It is possible that the population of the empire had fallen by one-third by the end of the third century.

The decline was briefly halted by two powerful emperors, Diocletian (reigned 284–305) and Constantine (reigned 306–337). Diocletian was another soldier-emperor, who came from Spalato in Yugoslavia. His principal achievement was to break the political power of the army. He modeled his rule on the Persian empire, to the extent of dressing in the ceremonial robes and scarlet boots of a Persian emperor and demanding that even his most powerful subjects prostrate themselves at his feet. He himself, he declared, was the son of Jupiter. To make the imperial administration more efficient, he divided the empire into two parts, retaining the eastern section for himself and appointing his most reliable general as emperor in the west. The two emperors, each of whom took the title of Augustus, were later aided by two junior emperors, known as caesars. The number of provinces was doubled, to make them more manageable in size, but to provide an intermediate level in the administration of the empire they were grouped into twelve dioceses, each of which was placed under a governor. This hierarchical system worked well under Diocletian, and later was incorporated into the administrative structure of the Catholic Church. The army was doubled in size, especially by recruitment of more Germanic soldiers, and its officers were not allowed to move into administrative or political office.

Economically, Diocletian succeeded in stopping the decay, but his solution was to forego all possibility of progress. He tied the peasantry to the land, forbidding them the right to leave the place where they had been born. To stop inflation, he fixed maximum prices and maximum wages. He ordered all groups of the population to follow the profession of their parents. Miners' sons were to be miners, soldiers' sons soldiers, and bakers' sons bakers. He thus gave state sanction to the process that became common in the empire in the fourth century, by which landlords, called *domini*, turned their estates into self-sufficent economic entities. On each great estate, known as a *latifundium*, the land was worked by peasants, known as *coloni*, many of whom were descended from families who had turned over their property to the landlord in return for protection or because they could not grow enough to survive on their own small plots. The peasant houses were often grouped together close to the mansion of the landlord, and the whole complex was called a *villa*. This organization lasted through the Germanic invasions (see Chapter 4), and became one of the elements that fused to form the medieval economic system of village production known as manorialism. After twenty-one years Diocletian was so convinced of the success of his policies that he retired to his 2000-room palace at Spalato overlooking the blue waters of the Adriatic.

Diocletian had not, however, solved the problem of the succession, and upon his death a long struggle for power broke out. The eventual victor was Constantine, the son of one of the two original caesars, who defeated his last rival at the battle of the Milvian Bridge (312) outside Rome. Constantine attributed his victory to the fact that he had ordered his army to draw the cross of Christ on their shields, and immediately after the battle Constantine announced that he had been converted to Christianity, a religion that Diocletian had been attempting to eradicate totally from the empire only twenty years earlier.

Constantine made a number of efforts to make Rome into a Christian city, and although himself baptized only shortly before his death, he attempted to strengthen and unify Christianity throughout his reign. Christianity was recognized as a legal religion within the empire in 313, although the state continued to recognize pagan religions and emperor worship. He began the first church of Saint Peter's on the site of the tomb of Saint Peter on the Vatican Hill, and built another church where Saint Paul was buried. But Constantine soon despaired of turning the pagan city into his ideal of a Christian capital. Moreover, as a native of Yugoslavia, he was well aware of the pervasive decay of those sections of the empire that lay to the west of the Adriatic sea. In 324, he ordered the building of a new capital city of Constantinople, in the heart of the still-prosperous eastern section of the empire. There, with the wealth of the Near East and the eastern Mediterranean, he intended to create a great new, Christian capital. For the next three centuries, the Eastern Roman or Byzantine Empire grew in strength and prosperity, to achieve a golden age under the Emperor Justinian in the sixth century. The Western Roman Empire continued to decay, until it fell prey from the fifth century on to wave after wave of Germanic invaders.

SUGGESTED READINGS

General Introductions

Karl Christ, *The Romans* (1984), provides a good chronological framework, and has illuminating studies on social life, law, religion, and the arts. Michael Grant's *The World of Rome* (1960) and *History of Rome* (1978) are lively overviews, amply spiced with contemporary quotations. R. H. Barrow, *The Romans* (1949), is clear and short, but for greater detail on political developments, see Thomas W. Africa, *The Immense Majesty: A History of Rome and the Roman Empire* (1974).

The Rise of Rome

Rome's debt to the Etruscans can be measured in Massimo Pallottino, *The Etruscans* (1975), Michael Grant, *The Etruscans* (1978), and R. M. Ogilvie, *Early Rome and the Etruscans* (1976), but no writer has brought the Etruscans back to life so successfully as D. H. Lawrence, in *Etruscan Places* (1932). The Greek colonies in Italy are described in A. G. Woodhead, *The Greeks in the West* (1962). Rome under the monarchy and early republic is soundly narrated in H. H. Scullard, *History of the Roman World from 753 B.C. to 146 B.C.* (1980).

The Acquisition of Empire

Rome does not appear to have conquered an empire in self-defense, as Livy implies, in the up-to-date study of R. M. Errington, *The Dawn of Empire: Rome's Rise to World Power* (1972), nor were its goals altruistic, according to the fine analysis of R. Duncan-Jones, *The Economy of the Roman Empire* (1974). William V. Harris shows how Roman society was transformed by the acquisition of empire, in *War and Imperialism in Republican Rome 327–70 B.C.* (1985). The reader can decide whether Carthaginian imperialism was preferable to Roman (it was probably not) in Brian H. Warmington, *Carthage* (1969). Erich S. Gruen shows how Rome influenced, and was influenced by, Hellenistic culture, in *The Hellenistic World and the Coming of Rome* (1984).

The Breakdown of the Republic

The political alliances of the great families are analyzed in Ronald L. Syme, *The Roman Revolution* (1952). Details on the blood-letting and the catastrophic political consequences are provided in H. H. Scullard, *From the Gracchi to Nero*, 5th ed. (1982).

The Empire from Augustus to Marcus Aurelius

Sample the Latin historians themselves—the spice of Suetonius, in *The Twelve Caesars* (1969), translated by Robert Graves, and the scalpel of Tacitus in *The Annals of Imperial Rome* (1959), translated by Michael Grant. Good modern biographies include A. H. M. Jones, *Augustus* (1971); Robin Seager, *Tiberius* (1972); Michael Grant, *Nero* (1970); Stewart Perowne, *Hadrian* (1960); and Anthony Birley, *Marcus Aurelius* (1966). An excellent survey, with fine photographs, is given by J. V. D. Balsdon, *Rome: The Story of an Empire* (1970). Chester G. Starr shows that Rome's institutions made possible its longevity, in *The Roman Empire, 27 B.C.–A.D. 476: A Study in Survival* (1982).

Roman Culture and Society

Try a little of Virgil, *The Aeneid*, especially in the loose translation by the English poet C. Day Lewis (1952). The atmosphere of the Augustan age is felt in Gilbert Highet, *Poets in a Landscape* (1957). R. M. Ogilvie shows how Roman society influenced its literature, in *Roman Literature and Society* (1980). The Roman ability as architects and engineers is proven in Mortimer Wheeler, *Roman Art and Architecture* (1964).

Good introductions to the realities of Roman life include Jerome Carcopino, *Daily Life in Ancient Rome* (1940), and Joan Liversedge, *Everyday Life in the Roman Empire* (1976). The status of women in different classes of society is described in J. V. D. Balsdon's, *Roman Women: Their History and Habits* (1972). Judith P. Hallett demonstrates how upper-class women could exercise power through their families, in *Fathers and Daughters in Roman Society: Women and the Elite Family* (1984).

The Decline of the Empire

For a short, well-documented introduction, see Solomon Katz, *The Decline of Rome and the Rise of Medieval Europe* (1955). The religious crises form the main focus of Peter Brown's beautifully illustrated *The World of Late Antiquity A.D. 150–750* (1971). All the problems are dissected in detail in A. H. M. Jones, *The Decline of the Ancient World* (1966). The most stimulating analysis remains the classic Edward Gibbon, *The Decline and Fall of the Roman Empire*, originally published in 1776–1788 and now available in a one-volume abridgement by Moses Hadas (1962).

part II

The Middle Ages

***Madonna and Child, by Giovanni Cimabue
(1240?–1302?)***   *Mary and the infant Jesus, perhaps the most beloved image in medieval art.*
(Alinari/Art Resource.)

THE MIDDLE AGES

Dates	Political & Military Events	Social, Economic, & Demographic Events	Religion & Philosophy	Art, Architecture, Literature, & Music	Science & Technology
306	Constantine, Emperor (306–337)	Germanic tribes move into Roman Empire			
313			Legal toleration of Christians		
324	Constantinople founded				
325			Council of Nicaea		
378	Battle of Adrianople				
410	Goths sack Rome	Economic decline of Western Roman Empire			
430			d. St. Augustine		
450s	Anglo-Saxons settle in England				
455	Vandals sack Rome				
481	Clovis, King of Franks	Ostrogoths settle in Italy		Ostrogothic churches in Ravenna	
525			d. Boethius		
527	Justinian, Byzantine Emperor (527–65)	Constantinople center of world commerce			
529			St. Benedict founds Monte Cassino		
530s		Law Code of Justinian			
590			Pope Gregory the Great (590–604)	Hagia Sophia	Silk manufacture in Constantinople
622	Muslim conquests in Near East and North Africa		Muhammad begins Islamic religion		Byzantine navy uses "Greek fire"
711	Muslim invasion of Spain		Catholic missionaries in eastern Germany	Mosque, Cordoba	

Date					
732	Charles Martel defeats Muslims at Poitiers, France				
750			Donation of Pepin (basis of Papal States)		
768	Charlemagne, king of Franks (768–814)				
800	Charlemagne crowned emperor of Romans (Holy Roman Emperor)			Carolingian Renaissance Building of Aachen	
843	Division of Carolingian empire				
900s		Feudalism and Manorialism begin	Reform movement in Catholic Church	Norse sagas in Iceland	Medieval agricultural revolution
911		Norsemen settle in Normandy			Viking "long ships"
987	Hugh Capet, King, France (987–96)	Rise of Venice	Russia converted to Orthodox Christianity	*Beowulf*	
1066	William the Conqueror: Norman dynasty in England (1066–1154)	Norman conquest and settlement of England			
1075			Cluniac reform movement Investiture contest begins	Romanesque architecture	
1086		Domesday Book			
1096			First Crusade	*Song of Roland* St. Mark's, Venice	
1100s		Development of English Common Law Rise of a money economy; revival of long-distance trade	Scholasticism begins	Gothic architecture invented	Agricultural development of clay soils; mariners' compass
1122			Abelard, *Sic et Non*		
1152	Frederick I, Barbarossa, Holy Roman Emperor (1152–90)				

(continued)

THE MIDDLE AGES (continued)

Dates	Political & Military Events	Social, Economic, & Demographic Events	Religion & Philosophy	Art, Architecture, Literature, & Music	Science & Technology
1153			d. St. Bernard		
1154	Angevin Dynasty, England (1154–1399) Henry II (1154–89)				
1163				Notre Dame, Paris	
1198			Innocent III (1198–1215)		
1200		Bruges center of North European trade	University of Paris chartered	Arthurian Romances	Textile manufactures in Flanders and North Italy
1204	Crusaders sack Constantinople				
1215	Frederick II, Holy Roman Emperor (1215–50) Magna Carta (England)				
1216			Dominican order founded	Westminster Abbey, London	
1226	Louis IX, France (1226–70)		d. St. Francis		
c. 1272			Aquinas, *Summa Theologica*	Chartres Cathedral Sainte Chapelle	

4

The Foundations of Christian Civilization, 300–600

In the confusion of the third century, the Christian religion, which offered spiritual comfort to the downtrodden, made rapid progress. Persecution gave it martyrs and hastened its spread. Tacitus in the first century could call it "an abominable superstition," although he believed that it would flourish in Rome, "the great reservoir and collecting-ground of every kind of depravity and filth." By the beginning of the third century, the Christian author Tertullian warned that the Christians were already so numerous that they could paralyze the empire. "Imagine the horror you would feel at finding yourselves thus deserted [by the Christians], in the uncanny stillness and torpor of a dying world. You would look in vain for your subjects—the enemy at your gates would be more multitudinous than the population of your empire.[1] At the beginning of the fourth century, Emperor Constantine recognized that his only course of action was to join the Christians and enlist their fanaticism in his service.

The growth of Christianity from the crucifixion of Christ in A.D. 29 to their legal toleration under Constantine in A.D. 313 must first be analyzed, to find the reasons why Christianity should so implausibly have been able to triumph not only over the venerated state religion of the Romans but over the many rival emotional religions that had won millions of converts in the early centuries of the empire. Second, we shall turn to the eastern part of the empire, from the time of the foundation of Constantinople in 324, to examine the transformation

[1] Cited in Joseph Vogt, *The Decline of Rome: The Metamorphosis of Ancient Civilization* (New York: New American Library, 1967), translated by Janet Sondheimer, p. 69.

of that portion of the Roman Empire into the distinctive Byzantine state and of early Christianity into the Greek Orthodox Church. Finally, we shall turn to the decline of the western part of the empire and the concurrent rise of the Catholic Church, of the pope as its head, and of the monasteries as a spiritual refuge in time of invasion.

CHRISTIANITY: THE CENTURIES OF PERSECUTION

Jesus Christ

The earliest account of the life of Christ was written in A.D. 70 by Mark, and his account was used heavily in the expanded accounts written by Mathew and Luke. The spiritual significance of Christ's life was explained by John in about A.D. 100. These four accounts, known as the Gospels, form the first four books in the collection of holy writings that were recognized by the bishops of the Christian Church in the fourth century to be inspired by God in the same way as the Bible of the Jews. They therefore called the Jewish Bible the Old Testament and the new "canon of scriptures" the New Testament. Since the gospels were composed for the avowed purpose of spreading the faith and since they are in many places contradictory of each other, it is difficult to form from them an historically accurate picture of the events of Christ's life.

Nevertheless, the general pattern is clear. Somewhere between 8 and 4 B.C., a young Jewish couple named Joseph and Mary registered the birth of their first child, Jesus, in the city of Bethlehem in the Roman province of Judea, to which they had come for the tax census. Apart from some indications of precocious interest in religious questions, little is reported of the life of Jesus for the next thirty years. About A.D. 26, however, he suddenly embarked on a mission of preaching, in which he attacked the Pharisees and scribes who enforced the Judaic religious laws. By simple sermons couched with the use of appealing parables and by the example of his own life, he preached a message of kindliness, purity, and universal brotherhood. According to the gospel writers, he also performed miracles and thereby enhanced his own reputation as the savior or "Messiah," which the Jewish people had traditionally awaited. It was particularly telling that the prophet Micah (Micah 5:2) had foretold that the Messiah would be from the house of David, like Christ, and be born in the city of Bethlehem.

Christ himself claimed to have come as the savior of the Jewish people, but not, he warned, as a political leader who would bring material prosperity in this world. He was rather, he said, the son of God, who had come to bring them spiritual salvation by sacrificing himself. When he led his followers to Jerusalem in A.D. 29 for the Passover celebrations, the religious leaders tried him before the Sanhedrin, or religious court, for blasphemy, and persuaded the Roman governor, Pontius Pilate, to order his death by crucifixion. After suffering this abominable death on the hillside of Calvary on the edge of Jerusalem, Christ was entombed. Much of the expansive appeal of Christianity ever since has been dependent on the supernatural events that his followers declared occurred during the next few days. On the third day after his crucifixion, women visiting the tomb found that his body had disappeared. Now "resurrected," Jesus was reported to have met and talked with his disciples on several occasions. Forty days later, in his "ascension," he was seen by the disciples to rise to heaven. Fifty days days later, at Pentecost, his disciples received the Holy Ghost or Holy Spirit, and were given the capacity to win converts to the faith in Christ.

Self-appointed prophets had been easily dealt with by the Roman Empire, and Jesus's cause seemed less promising than most, as the religious leaders of his own people had rejected him. Many factors, however, worked in his favor. In the first place, some Jews, feeling oppressed by the Roman authorities and by the Roman puppet ruler Herod, desperately wanted to believe that their Messiah had come to end their nation's subjection. Moreover, Jewish teaching had placed great emphasis on God's intention of using his chosen people to bring redemption or salvation to humankind, which could be identified with that which Christ had promised. The Jews too possessed, in their religious organization of the synagogue, their ritual, and their refusal to compromise their monotheism, instruments that the Christians could use for the propagation of their message. To this Jewish foundation Christ added his own message. His ethical teaching appealed to all the downtrodden. It emphasized their worth as people and their equality, and it promised future rewards. And Christ, by teaching that he was the Son of God, had compelled his followers to make the exclusive commitment to him as the sole mediator with God his father.

The Rise of Christianity

At first Christianity was merely a sect of Judaism, but very few Jews responded to the message of Christ. Non-Jews, or Gentiles, found great difficulty in accepting the demands of the Jewish Law, particularly the regulations concerning kosher food and circumcision. In a crucial decision for the future development of Christianity, the apostle Peter (d. A.D. 67), who as Christ himself had stated was to be the rock on which he would build his church ("Thou art Peter, and on this rock I shall build my church": Matthew 16:18), began to baptize Gentiles without requiring that they should respect the Jewish Law. And shortly afterwards the greatest Christian missionary, Saint Paul (d. A.D. 67), argued not only that circumcision and the culinary laws need not be respected by Gentiles, but that even for Jews the spirit was more important than the law. Paul and the other Christian missionaries then concentrated on carrying the Christian message into the Hellenized provinces of the Roman Empire in Asia Minor and Greece.

Paul, through his speeches and the epistles he wrote to the congregations of the converted, began the long development of Christian theology. Paul emphasized the role of Christ as the redeemer of human beings, who had fallen from grace through the sin of Adam and Eve and thus required Christ's intervention to save them from inborn or "original" sin. He argued that salvation or "justification" was a gift from God in his grace, which the believer must accept in total faith. Performance of good deeds or "works," although praiseworthy, was not alone sufficient to gain salvation (Romans 3:23–28). Although he regarded the celibate life as having higher value than the married life, nevertheless he supported the sanctity of marriage (I Corinthians 7:1–11). Above all, Paul exhorted Christians to "walk in love" for one another in a manner similar to God's love for humankind (Ephesians 5:1–2).

For thirty years, Paul traveled around the Mediterranean world, leaving congregations wherever he preached. Accused of treason, he used his right as a Roman citizen to be tried in Rome itself, where he was probably acquitted after long years of imprisonment. He and Peter, who had moved from Antioch to head the Christian community in Rome, were both arrested during Nero's persecution of the Christians following the fire of A.D. 64. Paul was beheaded outside the city walls. Peter was crucified upside down, and buried in the tiny Christian graveyard on the Vatican Hill.

The Early Church

The next 250 years were a period of organization under persecution. In the early years of this period, the holy scriptures were composed that were to become the New Testament. The Christian Church set out to harmonize its theology not only with the teachings of Judaism, but also with the philosophy of Greece. An increasingly complex ritual was developed, with a religious calendar based on events in the life of Christ, which culminated in the festival of Easter as a replacement for the Jewish Passover. (Christ's Last Supper with his disciples had in fact been the celebration of Passover.) A ritual of worship was also developed, with the Eucharist or the celebration of the last supper as the central ceremony, in which the congregation physically recognized Christ as their savior. ("This is my body. Take and eat in remembrance that Christ died for thee.") Supervision of the congregations and maintenance of the ritual was placed in the hands of a priesthood that, although at first elected by the faithful, eventually became a professional hierarchy.

The most important positions were bishop, priest, and deacon. As the congregations became more numerous, the bishops began to exercise greater authority over all the churches in their city or region in matters of faith and organization; and the doctrine known as apostolic succession was developed, which held that bishops were direct inheritors of the authority that Christ had bestowed on his original apostles. Paul had emphasized the need for the Christian communities to maintain the closest possible contacts; and, as early as the second century, bishops in various areas began to meet in Church Councils to

hammer out common policy with regard to the administration of the Church and on matters of doctrine. Finally, the bishops of Rome, Antioch, and Alexandria were from the early years of the Church regarded as exercising authority over bishops in the West, and were known as patriarchs. The bishops of Constantinople and Jerusalem were by the fifth century recognized as exercising similar authority to the east of the Mediterranean. The bishop of Rome, known as the pope or "papa," claimed by the third century to be superior to the other patriarchs, because he was the successor of Saint Peter, the rock on whom Christ had founded his church (Matthew 16:18); this claim was not recognized by the rival patriarchs. Nevertheless, the formation of a church hierarchy was of great importance in maintaining the unity of the Christian Church and in helping its advance, especially during periods such as between 260 and 302, when the Church enjoyed freedom from persecution and Christianity advanced very rapidly. When Diocletian renewed the persecutions, perhaps one in ten of the population of the Roman empire was already Christian.

At a time when the Roman army was composed increasingly of foreigners from beyond the imperial borders and had thus become almost an alien element within the empire, the Christian bishops had, rather paradoxically, begun to appear as the defenders of the empire. The great Christian writer Origen of

Alexandria (c. 185–254) even argued that God had created the Roman Empire at the exact time in order to provide the universal political framework within which the gospel of Christ could be spread most effectively. They had in short become the supporters of an empire that had persecuted them. Constantine, therefore, found little difficulty in striking an immediately harmonious relationship with the Christian bishops in his empire. In fact, when he moved east to Constantinople, one of his main advisers and his later biographer was Bishop Eusebius of Caesarea.

The supreme role of Christianity was not, however, immediately assured. Constantine tolerated the pagan religions as a matter of statecraft. His son Constantius II (reigned 337–361) welcomed the bishops to his court, but emphasized his own supremacy by exiling them when they disagreed with him. The Emperor Julian even attempted to make the empire pagan again. Only under Theodosius I (reigned 379–395) was Christianity declared to be the sole religion of the empire, and persecution of pagans ordered.

Why had Christianity triumphed, especially over other mystery religions such as the worship of Isis, which also offered a message of universal love, membership in a community open to all regardless of nationality, class, or sex; secret rites; the promise of immortality; and personal closeness to a god in human form? And why, too, had Christianity, a religion of the meek and powerless, triumphed over a religion like Mithraism, which offered a creed of strength?

The second question is easier to answer than the first. Mithraism and a number of other mystery religions excluded certain people from membership, and thus restricted their own numbers. Mithraism not only would not permit women to join, but its rites were so demanding that they kept out those who lacked the capacity for self-denial. When Christianity competed with religions of similar character, it showed that it possessed not only similar qualities but certain crucial advantages in addition. Like the gentler mystery religions, Christianity had in the teachings of Christ a body of moral teachings of great appeal, especially to the poor and the oppressed. It was open to men and women, patricians and slaves, Romans and non-Romans. Perhaps most important of all, it was open to non-Jews as well as Jews. Its early congregations had fostered a sense of belonging, particularly by the care they had extended to their members who were sick or poor.

The Christians, however, also possessed in their Bible not only an accessible description of the life and teachings of their founder and early history, but a link to the centuries-old Judaic tradition. As early as the second century they had formed an organization, extending from the local congregations to the bishops, which permitted them to maintain a unity no matter how widely their converts were spread. Persecution itself helped scare away the less firmly committed, and left those remaining with an increased sense of their own dedication. This unity and heroic commitment gave the early Christians a leverage on the state far greater than their numbers alone warranted.

THE ELABORATION OF CHRISTIAN DOCTRINE

There had been constant disputes about Christian beliefs from the moment Christ died, and as the missionaries carried the message to the widely differing peoples within the empire, it was natural that new interpretations should arise. Moreover, personal rivalries for supremacy among the leading bishops of the Church were often expressed in doctrinal quarrels, so that the victory of one doctrine over another often implied the victory of one bishop over his rivals. It seemed necessary, however, after the recognition of the supremacy of Christianity in the fourth century, for a common doctrine to be worked out. The elaboration of Christian doctrine took two forms—the writings of the Church Fathers and the doctrinal pronouncements of Church Councils.

The Church Fathers

The Church Fathers were theologians whose writings were recognized by the Church as containing the official explanation of the Church's doctrines. Most of the earlier Fathers lived in the eastern section of the empire and wrote in Greek. But in the fourth and fifth centuries the Latin Fathers, who lived in the western section of the empire, were perhaps even more influential. The most important of these were Saint Ambrose, bishop of Milan; Saint Jerome, born in Stridon, Yugoslavia; and Saint Augustine, bishop of Hippo in North Africa. Although they wrote in Latin, all three sought to continue the work of harmonizing Greek philosophy, in which they were thoroughly trained, with Christianity. Jerome translated the New Testament from its original Greek into Latin, and his translation, called the Vulgate, became the official version used by the Catholic Church.

In his brilliant work of theology, *The City of God*, Saint Augustine used the sack of Rome by the Visigoths in 410 as the starting point for a highly influential summation of the Christian view of the relationship of human beings to God. Augustine was convinced, from his experiences as a wild youth given to drunkenness and sexual adventures, that the human being has a natural tendency to sin; and he related, in his *Confessions*, how he himself had been saved from this state of wantonness by the intervention of God. He argued, however, that whether a person is saved or not has been pre-determined by God. This doctrine of "predestination" had already been taught by Paul, and was to be repeated by many Christian writers after Augustine, most notably by the Protestant writer John Calvin in the sixteenth century. Augustine sought to explain all human history in the metaphor of two cities. God, he wrote, had created an earthly city and a heavenly city, a city of God. The earthly city was composed of all beings who devoted themselves to material selfishness, and who thus refused God's desire to save them. The heavenly city was composed of all those who had resigned their selfish impulses and "achieved earthly peace by faith in God, and not for their material betterment." These two cities existed in the past, present, and future; but only in the present, on this earth, did they coexist. In the future, they would be separated. The inhabitants of the earthly city would be punished, and the inhabitants of the city of God would enjoy their permanent reward. "There the virtues shall no longer be struggling against any vice or evil, but shall enjoy the reward of victory, the eternal peace which no adversary shall disturb. This is the final blessedness, this the ultimate consummation."[2]

It has also been argued that Saint Augustine's writings on the position of women reinforced the view of the subordination of the wife to the husband, and of the family structure as woman's support, that was to be predominant throughout the Middle Ages. Whereas Christ had appeared to ignore the subordinate role of woman in the patriarchal family structure enforced by the Judaic religion, Saint Paul had argued that, although women were morally equal to men, their well-being was dependent on their inferior role. Moreover, the Church Fathers, with Saint Augustine the most vociferous among them, had argued that, although marriage was an essential institution within which human passion could be morally expressed, a life of chastity was a higher moral state. For women, this implied the value of a nun's life as a bride of Christ; for men it led to the requirement, finally enforced in the eleventh century, that priests should not marry.

Heresy and Orthodoxy Defined

While the Fathers were developing in the broadest sense a theology for Christianity, the leaders of the Church, faced by the exposition by individual priests or even patriarchs of differing and obviously contradictory theories of what constituted Christian belief, decided in the fifth and sixth centuries that it was necessary to define *heresy*, that which was not true doctrine, and *orthodoxy*, that which was true doctrine. Christ himself had left them with their most persistent problem, by his declaration that, although human, he was the son of God. It was difficult to explain how anyone could be both human and divine (although Roman emperors never seemed to find much problem in doing so), especially in a religion that was avowedly monotheistic. To make matters worse, each of the patriarchs of the principal Christian communities in the east (Antioch, Constantinople, Alexandria) patronized a local school of theology and tended to oppose new ideas suggested by the schools of the rival patriarchs. The tendency toward fragmentation of theological opinion was encouraged. Worse, new ideas were often espoused by provinces that were attempting to break away from the rule of the emperor in Constantinople, especially in Syria and Egypt. The earliest difficulties had been caused by two sects, the Gnostics in the second and third centuries and the Manichaeans in the third and the fourth, which, although not originally Christian, had seen many of their followers join the Christian Church. Both sects abhorred the world of the flesh, and found it difficult to

[2] Saint Augustine, *City of God* (London: Dent, 1945), II, 245.

accept that Christ as a perfect being could have taken human form in anything except outward appearance. The Gnostics were condemned by the Church in the third century and the Manichaeans in the fourth.

Early in the fourth century, new trouble was caused by Arius, a priest in Alexandria, who argued that Christ could not be equal with God, since he had been created by God, nor could he be eternal like God, since there must have been a time when he did not exist. Arius had, moreover, challenged the central Christian concept of the Trinity, which holds that God has three persons, Father, Son, and Holy Spirit, which were equal and eternal. Arius's doctrine, known as Arianism, spread so rapidly that the Emperor Constantine, who had embraced Christianity as a unifying force in the empire, became alarmed. He ordered Christian bishops to meet in the First Ecumenical Council at Nicaea in 325 to establish one position. Led by Athanasius, the patriarch of Alexandria, the council condemned the teachings of Arius, and formulated the Nicene Creed, which remains the basic statement of belief of the Roman Catholic, the Greek Orthodox, and some Protestant churches:

> We believe in one God the Father All-sovereign, maker of heaven and earth, and of all things visible and invisible:
> And in one Lord Jesus Christ, the only-begotten son of God, Begotten of the Father before all the ages, Light of Light, true God of true God, begotten not made, of one substance with the Father. . . .[3]

Arianism remained an expansive force, however, and was carried by missionaries to several of the Germanic tribes that were penetrating the Roman empire.

In the fifth century, Nestorius, the patriarch of Constantinople, taught that Christ had both a divine and a human nature. God was the father of his divine nature and the Virgin Mary the mother of his human nature. The Virgin Mary was thus not the mother of God, but only of Christ's human part. This doctrine infuriated Cyril, the patriarch of Alexandria, whose followers condemned Nestorianism at the Council of Ephesus in 431. Nestorius himself was banned to Egypt, where, unrepentant, he helped found a large number of Nestorian Christian churches.

Shortly after, the priests of Alexandria produced yet another theory, Monophysitism, in which they argued that Christ's divine nature included his human nature. This theory was condemned as a heresy at the Council of Chalcedon in 451. But the doctrine of Monophysitism spread rapidly among the disaffected provinces in Egypt and Syria. Persecution of the followers of Nestorianism and Monophysitism thus helped prepare Egypt and Syria to accept the Muslim Arab invaders in the seventh century as a welcome alternative to the rule of Byzantium.

Seven Church Councils were recognized by the churches of the eastern

---

[3] Henry Bettenson, ed., *Documents of the Christian Church* (New York: Oxford University Press, 1947), p. 37.

section of the empire, that is, by those churches that were to become the Greek Orthodox Church, as having defined the true doctrines of Christianity. Recognition of those doctrines and rejection of the claims of supremacy of the pope in Rome became the essential foundation of the Greek Orthodox Church.

WESTERN CHRISTENDOM: THE ORGANIZATION OF THE CATHOLIC CHURCH

The Rise of the Papacy

The pope in Rome had acted as a mediator, rather than as an instigator, of these doctrinal disputes. In this role, he was welcomed by the other patriarchs, although his claim to supremacy in the Church as the successor of Saint Peter had been rejected contemptuously by them. In the fifth and sixth centuries, the Churches in the West began to follow a different course from those in the East, due essentially to the fact that the power of the Byzantine emperor did not, except for brief periods, extend to Western Europe. After Constantine moved to Constantinople, the capital of the western section of the empire was usually at Ravenna, Milan, or even at Trier in Germany rather than at Rome. As a result, the pope was free to administer Rome as he wished, since the political administration had fallen into his hands by default. The barbarian invasions of Italy, which began with the incursion of the Visigoths in 408 and continued until the end of the Lombard invasions in the eighth century, had the effect of strengthening the pope's importance, since they ended the political power of the Byzantine emperor in Italy. The last Roman emperor in the West, Romulus Augustulus, was deposed in 476 by the Germanic invaders. The Eastern Roman emperor was driven from his last Italian foothold in Ravenna by the Lombards. The wealth, which had previously been spent on the empire, either as a result of taxation or by individual donations to the beautification of their own cities, was now given to the Christian Church, which in the fifth and sixth centuries found itself becoming very rich in land, gold, and other gifts. The popes, moreover, were conducting a highly successful missionary campaign among the peoples entering the empire and even beyond its borders. Between the fifth and eighth centuries, missionaries sponsored by Rome had converted to Christianity the West and East Goths, the Lombards, the Franks, the Angles, the Saxons, and the Celtic Irish.

The freedom of action enjoyed by the pope was most evident during the papacy of Gregory the Great (590–604). Gregory was a Roman aristocrat who had been prefect of Rome and ambassador to the court of Constantinople. He had joined the Church and become a monk. He was chosen pope against his will, but applied himself with enormous energy to the reorganization and disciplining of the Church. He demanded high moral standards of the clergy, enforcing the rule that priests should not marry and strictly punishing anyone guilty of financial misdoing. He was a great teacher, and wrote hundreds of letters of advice to people throughout Europe. He was also a superb administrator who wrote his instructions for the clergy in a simple book called *Pastoral Rule*. His popularity in Italy was great because he was able to buy off the Lombards and to begin their conversion to Catholicism. By seeking to advance the cause of religion, he succeeded in increasing the secular power of the papacy, whether he intended that goal or not.

The popes were to make gestures of subordination to the emperor in Constantinople for several centuries after the death of Gregory, and to maintain relations with the eastern Christian Churches until the final break between the Roman Catholic Church and the Eastern Orthodox Churches in 1054. But in reality, from the sixth century and perhaps even earlier, the Christian Church in the West, under the leadership of the pope, had embarked on its own distinctive road.

Monasticism

Another Christian institution of lasting strength created in these early centuries was the monastery. With its condemnation of the sins of the material world, the Christian Church had always seemed to many to be summoning them to flee from the material world in order to devote their lives wholly to the church. In Syria and Egypt, in the first and second centuries, Christian ascetics had fled into the desert to mortify their flesh. Many found dramatic ways to emphasize their separation from the temptations of the world, such as Saint Simon Stylites, who sat for forty years on top of a 50-foot column. Others went to excess by dressing in skins and living in filth. Saint Pachomius in Egypt, however, in the early fourth century, hit upon the idea of organizing the hermits of Upper Egypt into small groups cooperating in argicultural work, and these communities soon spread across the Mediterranean into Europe. The person responsible for disciplining these groups and for making the institution of monasticism a permament part of Christianity was Saint Benedict of Nursia (died c. 547).

Benedict had himself experienced extreme asceticism by living for three years at the bottom of a pit, but he decided that hard work rather than excessive contemplation was a sign of true humility before God. He led a group of his followers to Monte Cassino in southern Italy, where he founded an abbey that became the model for monasteries throughout Europe. To regulate daily life, Benedict wrote a detailed *Rule*, which had to be followed by all the monks of his order. The monks swore three vows—poverty, chastity, and obedience to the abbot. Work in the fields alternated with reading and prayer. The monks were to sleep in dormitories, where the older ones could help and if necessary discipline the younger. Food and clothing were to be simple but adequate. The monastery was to welcome the poor and Christian pilgrims at all times. Benedict's *Rule* was successful because it was humane, simple, and firm, without being excessively demanding. Benedict, for example, regulated the brethrens' wine drinking:

> *Every one hath his proper gift from God, one thus, another thus.* For this reason the amount of other people's food cannot be determined without some misgiving. Still, having regard to the weak state of the sick, we think that a pint of wine a day is sufficient for any one. But let those to whom God gives the gift of abstinence know that they shall receive their proper reward. If either local circumstances, the amount of labor, or the heat of summer require more, it can be allowed at the will of the prior, care being taken in all things that gluttony and drunkenness creep not in.[4]

Religious orders for women had been created in France, Belgium, and Italy even before Saint Benedict composed his *Rule*. The Irish missionary Saint Columban had encouraged many noble women in northern France to found convents and to encourage their own daughters to become nuns. Although most convents were for women only, Saint Columban's followers formed "double houses," where both men and women were accepted and worked together in both agricultural and intellectual tasks. Saint Benedict's own sister, Scholastica, may also have founded a religious order for women in Italy. The nuns in Anglo-Saxon England and in Germany were, however, at the forefront of the intellectual life of the monastic movement. One of the most famous double houses in England was the Abbey of Whitby, whose abbess, Hild, turned it into a center of learning and teaching. Nuns went from England to help Saint Boniface convert the pagan Germanic tribes. Among them was Lioba, who was not only a busy administrator as abbess of Bischofsheim but also an admired Biblical scholar.

The influence of the monasteries was thus enormous. They opened up new lands by felling forests and draining marshes. Their great libraries were centers of study of the ancient Latin manuscripts and refuges for the intellectuals of the age. They provided schools not only for future Church people but also for lay nobles. In their workshops the arts of the Roman Empire in architecture, sculpture, and metalwork were preserved, while many advances were made in the techniques of weaving, glasswork, brewing, and wine making. The popes themselves became the greatest protectors of the monasteries, especially when the monks' sense of superiority as "regular" clergy (i.e., observers of a rule) over the "secular" clergy (i.e., the priests working in the world) led to rivalry between the two groups within the church.

CHRISTIAN ART AND ARCHITECTURE

From the time of the conversion of Constantine, the Christian Church became increasingly wealthy, both in the stability of the Eastern Roman Empire and in the turmoil of the decline of the Western Roman Empire. This sudden wealth was used in part at least to pay for a vast investment in art and buildings whose

[4] *The Rule of Saint Benedict*, translated by Cardinal Gasquet (London: Chatto & Windus, 1966), p. 74.

glory reinforced the dominance of the Church. The achievements of the Eastern Roman Empire, which culminated in the building of the Cathedral of Hagia Sophia in the sixth century, will be discussed later in the chapter. Christian art and architecture in Western Europe were also vitally important to the strengthening of the church.

Constantine himself began the ambitious program of church building that brought one or more Christian churches into every town. "Who can number the churches?," Bishop Eusebius exclaimed, less than ten years after Constantine had begun the great church of Saint Peter's on the Vatican Hill, on the site of the grave of the first pope. Many churches were converted pagan temples, which had the effect of saving such buildings as the Pantheon from destruction. But many were new.

Although the basilica style of architecture, which the Romans had used for such buildings as the law courts in the Roman Forum, was adopted for the typical Christian church of the fourth century, the form was changed. A Roman basilica had consisted of a rectangular building with an inner hall surrounded by a colonnade. The Christians employed the colonnade only on the two long sides of the building, thus creating a central passageway through which the worshipper would pass. At the western end, they placed the principal doorway, opening onto an anteroom through which one passed into the main nave. At the eastern end of the building, where the altar was placed, they added a semicircular or polygonal apse. This extremely simple building had great advantages. It emphasized the solemnity of the altar, where the sacrament of communion was celebrated. It created a drive toward the east, and thus for

Sant' Apollinare in Classe, Ravenna, Italy   This basilican church was completed in 549, during the Byzantine rule of Ravenna. Its mosaics over the apse, showing Christ as the good shepherd, were added in the sixth and seventh centuries. (Alinari/Art Resource.)

Western Europe, at least, toward Jerusalem. It provided wide wall spaces, which could be decorated with frescoes or mosaics, and an apse that could be dramatically decorated with a representation, often in mosaic, of Christ the Savior. Although some Church leaders questioned the propriety of decorating churches in this way, Pope Gregory the Great settled the question for the Catholic Church: "Painting can do for the illiterate," he said, "what writing does for those who can read." The Christian art of these years can be seen at its finest in the churches of the city of Ravenna on the Adriatic coast of Italy, which was successively capital of the Western Roman Empire, of the Ostrogothic kingdom, and of the Byzantine governors of Italy.

Thus, by the end of the sixth century the Christian Church in the West possessed four features that were to remain as the foundation of its influence throughout the Middle Ages: a developed body of doctrine recognized as divinely inspired; a hierarchy headed by the pope in Rome; disciplined orders of monks and nuns, which offered an attractive alternative to the uncertain life beyond the monastery walls in an age of disorder; and an artistic tradition of great attractive power.

THE GERMANIC INVASIONS OF THE WEST

At the end of the fourth century, both the eastern and western sections of the empire were shaken by new, disruptive forces—the entry into the empire across every section of the northern frontiers of Germanic warrior tribes, of which the most important were the West Goths or Visigoths, the East Goths or Ostrogoths, the Vandals, the Burgundians, the Franks, the Angles, and the Saxons.

Character of the Germanic Tribes

The primary task of the Roman armies in Europe and of the long northern walls had been from the first century A.D. on to prevent the invasion of the empire by the "barbarian" tribes outside. In Scotland and Ireland were the wild, warlike Celts. On the continent of Europe beyond the Rhine-Danube frontier were the many Germanic tribes. Romans were fascinated by the vigor of these warrior bands, which contrasted favorably in their eyes with the pampered luxury of imperial Romans. Although originally nomads, by the first century A.D. the Germanic tribes had begun to settle in villages in the forests, and to develop political and legal institutions that were eventually to be incorporated into the structure of the medieval European states. The principal political bond was loyalty of warrior to king, but in return the king took the advice of his *comitatus* (companions), or council of warriors, by whom he had been originally elected. Disputes were usually settled by a tribal court, in which all the warriors took part. Although decisions usually depended on how trustworthy a plaintiff or defendant was considered to be, certain cases were decided by ordeal. The defendant would be made to walk through fire and, if his wounds healed in a few days, he was considered innocent. Monetary fines were imposed according to a fixed schedule.

Property rights were rudimentary, but careful provision was laid down for protection of women as the property of men, especially during their child-bearing years, when they were considered to be a valuable economic possession. A wife might be captured in battle, or she could be acquired from her relatives. If so, the kin were paid a "bride price," which eventually was transformed into a "bride gift," which was often in land handed over to the woman herself. Tacitus, whose book *Germania* is an important source for our knowledge of the Germanic tribes in the second century, reported that the gifts a bride received were "oxen, horse with reins, shield, spear, and sword. . . . She is coming to share a man's toil and danger." In Germanic society, especially after the tribes had settled inside the Roman Empire, women enjoyed considerable freedom of action. They appeared on the battlefield with the men, although mainly to help the warriors. They were consulted on religious and occasionally on political matters. Their possessions from inheritance or marriage gifts often gave them independent economic power in addition to the administrative power often vested in them by their husbands as estate managers or even as regents of whole kingdoms.

The Huns

The Germanic invasions of the empire were precipitated by the westward movement of a tough, warrior people from Asia known as the Huns. Nomadic tribesmen who fought and, it was said, ate and slept on horseback, they had been a scourge of China since the third century B.C. In their first drive into Europe in A.D. 372, they crossed the Volga in Russia, and brought the East Goths, or Ostrogoths, under their control. The West Goths, or Visigoths, gained permission from the Eastern Roman Emperor to take refuge from the Huns by settling within the empire. Meanwhile the Huns continued their advance into Europe, and under their king Attila (reigned 445–453) they established their base in Hungary. Attila drew tribute from the inhabitants of Russia, Poland, and Germany, as well as from both the Eastern and the Western Roman emperors. When in 450 both emperors refused him tribute, Attila set off with a huge army into Gaul, where he was defeated by an army of Roman troops and Visigoths financed in part by the Eastern Roman emperor. Attila then invaded northern Italy, but spared Rome—partly as a result of the pleas of the pope but primarily because of hunger and disease in his army. He died the following year, and without his leadership the Huns withdrew from Europe. It was thus not the Huns, a people probably of Mongolian ancestry, but the Germanic tribes, who were Indo-European peoples, who were to bring the new ethnic element that was to combine with the Latinized inhabitants of the empire to form the modern nations of Europe.

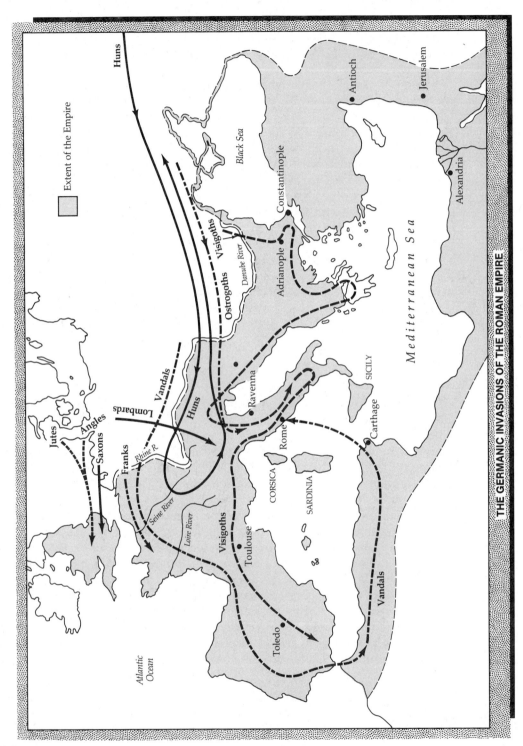

THE GERMANIC INVASIONS OF THE ROMAN EMPIRE

Extent of the Empire

Huns

Black Sea

Antioch

Jerusalem

Alexandria

Constantinople

Adrianople

Mediterranean Sea

Visigoths

Ostrogoths

Danube River

Vandals

Lombards

Huns

Ravenna

SICILY

Rome

CORSICA

Carthage

SARDINIA

Jutes

Angles

Saxons

Franks

Rhine R.

Seine River

Loire River

Visigoths

Toulouse

Vandals

Toledo

Atlantic
Ocean

The Visigoths

The Goths had originally established themselves around the shores of the Baltic Sea, but they had later moved south. One group, the Ostrogoths or East Goths, had settled in southern Russia, where, as we have seen, they were conquered by the Huns. Another, the Visigoths or West Goths, had conquered Rumania, and from there had penetrated the Byzantine Empire itself. Under their king Alaric (reigned 395–410), they had sacked Athens and then moved north to plunder the palace of Diocletian at Spalato on the northern Adriatic. After fifteen years of marauding, they had reached the gates of Rome, whose senatorial aristocracy was too proud, or mean, to buy them off. With little difficulty, Alaric's soldiers breached the walls and sacked the city. Shock waves from their triumph spread throughout the empire. In Constantinople, three days of mourning were declared. "The world sinks into ruin," Saint Jerome wrote. "Yes! . . . The renowned city, the capital of the Roman empire, is swallowed up in one tremendous fire; and there is no part of the earth where Romans are not in exile." The Goths, however, who had been converted to Arian Christianity, spared all the churches, although they set the buildings of the Forum on fire. Alaric showed that he had no intention of attacking the pope, Innocent I, but instead led a procession to Saint Peter's to make gifts of spoils he had saved for the pope. After an excursion to the south, the Visigoths left Italy, crossed southern France, and founded a kingdom in Spain. There they ruled as a hated, alien minority, composing perhaps as little as 2 percent of the population. Only in 589, when they were converted to Catholicism, were they finally able to fuse with the indigenous inhabitants.

The Vandals

The Vandals, after several centuries of wandering throughout central Europe, had crossed the Rhine in 406, fought their way across France, and entered Spain. Opposed by the Visigoths, they made their way into North Africa, where they took the coastal areas of modern Algeria and Tunisia and made Carthage their capital. Building a navy, they were soon able to dominate the western Mediterranean and, in 455, to sack Rome. More thorough in their depredations than the Visigoths had been, they plundered the palaces on the Palatine Hill and even stole tile from the temple roofs. As Arian Christians, they persecuted the Orthodox Christians in North Africa, and were so hated that the expedition sent by the Emperor Justinian in 533 had little difficulty in exterminating them.

The Ostrogoths

The defeat of the Huns had freed the Ostrogoths to move westward. Under their great leader Theodoric (reigned 471–526), they invaded Italy and took as their capital the city of Ravenna of the Adriatic coast. Theodoric was a great admirer of the culture of Constantinople, where he had spent ten years as a hostage. He governed as regent of the Byzantine emperor, although he took the title of King of the Goths as well. More than any other Germanic leader, Theodoric understood the art of coexistence. An Arian himself, he tolerated Catholic Christianity, even though he forbade marriage between Catholics and Arians. He permitted Romans to be governed by Roman law and Goths by Gothic law. One-third of the land and houses were taken by the Goths in return for carrying out all military duties. The Romans were left free to carry on their economic pursuits in peace. Theodoric undertook to reconstruct the monuments in Rome that had suffered from the Visigothic and Vandal attacks, and he set out to make Ravenna into a great new capital. He used the Roman basilica form for the new church of Sant'Apollinare Nuovo, which has a central nave with narrow aisles and a rounded apse at the east end. Its columns are of Greek marble, with beautifully carved capitals; and the wall space is covered with gloriously colored mosaic scenes, mostly from the Bible, which were begun by Theodoric and completed by the Emperor Justinian. For his own mausoleum, he built a circular temple topped by a single stone weighing 300 tons. He employed Latin bureaucrats at his court, and he encouraged the writing of Latin literature, including a *History of the Goths* by his minister Cassiodorus. Another of his ministers was the philosopher Boethius (c. 475–525), who wrote a treatise that became the established authority on the music of the classical world for the next thousand years. Boethius fell from favor and was executed without a trial by Theodoric; but while in prison, he wrote his classic work, *Consolation of Philosophy*, for which he is chiefly remembered.

After Theodoric's death in 526, the Ostrogothic leaders proved ineffective. Nevertheless, they were still able to fight a seventeen-year war against the armies of Justinian in 535–552 before they were finally driven across the Alps to disappear into oblivion. (The property of the Arian churches was then handed over to the Catholic Church, considerably increasing its wealth.)

The Burgundians and Franks

France had been invaded in 430 by a Germanic tribe called the Burgundians, who had settled in the middle Rhône valley. They, however, were conquered by a latecomer among the Germanic tribes, the Franks. The Franks had originally settled between the North Sea and the upper Rhine, and they retained control of this region while engaging in campaigns against the Visigoths and the Burgundians. Under their King Clovis (reigned 471–511), they established control over most of France, where the Romanized inhabitants found it easier to accept them after Clovis, influenced by his wife Clothilde, became Catholic in 496. Left in control of the ecclesiastical framework of France by the new ruler, the Catholic clergy recognized him as a "new Constantine," and blessed the Frankish armies that he led against the Arian kingdoms to the south. The lack of a religious barrier between the Franks and the Romanized inhabitants of France opened the way for an intermingling of peoples more effective than any that had yet occurred. The Germanic language, an Indo-European dialect, was mixed with the rather crude Latin spoken in France to become within several centuries the French language. Constitutional and legal ideas were equally fused. Even methods of farming were combined. Whereas the Franks, like all the Germanic peoples, were masters of felling the forests to open up the heavy clay soils, the romanized Gauls had preferred to farm the chalk soils of the hills. But Clovis's capital, Paris, the old Roman Lutetia, was still a rough, barbarous place.

The Anglo-Saxons

The settlement of Britain was different in character from the penetration of France and Spain. The Germanic tribes of Angles, Saxons, and Jutes that entered England at the beginning of the fifth century had little acquaintance with, and almost no admiration for, the culture of the Roman Empire. Nor did they mingle with the original Celtic inhabitants but drove them further into the mountain fastnesses of Wales and Scotland. They thus did not live as a minority among a highly cultured indigenous population. They opened up the great claylands that had never been farmed. They abandoned the Roman system of government and law, and replaced it with their Germanic system. Only with the missionary expedition of Saint Augustine of Canterbury sent by Gregory the Great in 597 did they accept Christianity. They thus avoided the isolation of Arian peoples like the Visigoths from those they had conquered, and they did not, like the Ostrogoths or the Franks, attempt to absorb the culture of the Roman Empire. When they were Latinized, it was by the Catholic Church. It was only to be expected that life during the early years of Anglo-Saxon settlement in Britain was even more barbarous than that of the France of Clovis.

Three of the barbarian peoples—the Visigoths, the Ostrogoths, and the Vandals—that is to say, the three Arian peoples, had ruled briefly as alien conquerors, and had then disappeared. The Germanic peoples who had accepted Catholicism had, however, come to stay. The Franks and the Anglo-Saxons had crossed the religious barrier that could have prevented their integration into the civilization of Catholic Europe. The Church, which had already asserted its supremacy in the empire, had taken over the barbarian invaders.

EASTERN CHRISTENDOM: THE BYZANTINE EMPIRE

When the Emperor Constantine founded Constantinople in 324, he intended to place his new Christian capital in the most prosperous and culturally advanced section of the empire. Separated by the barbarian invasions from most of the western sections of the empire, the Eastern Roman Empire, which historians call Byzantium after the original Greek settlement at Constantinople, developed a distinctive form of Christian state and society. In the fourth century, the boundaries of this Eastern Christendom embraced all the shores of the Eastern Mediterranean. In the seventh century, however, the advances of the Muslim Arabs into the Near East and North Africa resulted in the survival there of Christianity only among small groups such as the Coptic Christians in Egypt. In compensation, however, Orthodox Christianity was carried by missionaries into the Balkans and into Russia. As a result, when Constantinople itself fell to the Muslim Ottoman Turks in 1453, Orthodox Christianity survived as the religion of the South Slavs of the Balkans, of the Greeks, and of the Russians; and Moscow could claim to be a third Rome, the successor to Constantinople, as Constantinople had been a successor to the first Rome.

The Foundation of Constantinople

Constantine believed that his new city should be planned by, and then governed by, Christ, with him, Constantine, acting as intermediary. He decided to place the city on the shores of the narrow strait of water called the Bosphorus, which links the Black Sea to the Sea of Marmara and thence to the Mediterranean, where Greek settlers in the seventh century B.C. had founded the small colony of Byzantium. Constantine, followed by his city planners, set off himself with a stave, walking westward to indicate where the city boundaries were to be drawn. When asked why he was making the city so large, he replied: "I shall keep on until He who is going before me stops." Christ, not Constantine, was to be the city planner.

During the amazingly short time of six years in which the city was constructed, it became clear that Constantine intended the city to be a combination of Latin Rome, the Hellenistic Mediterranean, and Christianity. Rome itself was reproduced in part in Constantinople. The heart of the new city was the Augustaeum, which corresponded to the Roman Forum. On one side was a huge chariot-racing arena. On the opposite side was the imperial palace. A Senate House was constructed, and all Roman aristocrats were ordered to construct homes identical to those they had in Rome. Constantine followed the Roman habit of placing monumental squares at intervals in the principal streets, in which magnificent columns could commemorate the deeds of the emperors. The constitution was to carry on the traditions of old Rome. The emperor was, in theory at least, to be elected by the Senate, the army, and the people, although Constantine and his successors circumvented the will of the people by associating their chosen successors with them in the exercise of power for years before their death.

To establish Constantinople as a center of Hellenistic culture, Constantine searched the eastern Mediterranean for its treasures. He stripped the temples of Greece for statues to erect in the public square and buildings of Constantinople. He began the establishment of libraries in which the great manuscripts of the Hellenistic world could be preserved and studied; and he required a knowledge of Greek as well as Latin for the bureaucrats of his court.

But above all he intended to found a Christian capital. He brought from the Holy Land all the relics he could obtain, including what were reputed to be the two crosses on which the thieves executed with Christ had died. Eventually, later emperors believed they had brought to Constantinople a phial of Christ's blood, the Lance with which he had been wounded, the Crown of Thorns, and most of the True Cross. Churches were to be the principal monuments of Constantinople, dwarfing even the palace. Constantine's mausoleum was the great church of the Holy Apostles, on which the cathedral of Venice was later modeled. And on one side of the Augustaeum he built the first Hagia Sophia, the Church of the Holy Wisdom, as the cathedral where the patriarch of Constantinople could conduct services and where the emperor was to be crowned.

When the city was dedicated in 330, Constantinople replaced Rome as the capital of the empire; and Constantine unveiled the inscription on the column in the Forum of Constantine: "Oh, Christ, ruler and master of the world. To you now, I dedicate this subject city, and these scepters and the might of Rome. Protect her; save her from all harm."

Justinian (Reigned 527–565)

The second of the great Byzantine emperors—perhaps the greatest of all—was Justinian. In its first 200 years, Constantinople had grown to be a city of 1 million people. Unlike Rome, it was not a parasite, living on the tribute of a captive empire. It had become the center of world trade, profiting from its superb location where the trade routes of Europe, Asia, and Africa met. Two alternative land routes, one crossing southern Russia, another the northern segment of the Persian Empire led Byzantine merchants to Bochara and Samarkand, from where they could follow the silk route to China. Other merchants moved north up the great rivers of Russia in search of furs, iron, and lumber. Central and Western Europe was reached up the Danube valley. But Byzantine merchant ships also traveled down the Red Sea, crossed the Indian Ocean, and bought Indian spices and Chinese luxuries in Ceylon.

Constantinople itself was superbly organized to facilitate world commerce. It provided storehouses, lodgings for foreign merchants, and commercial police. Its gold currency was the principle means of exchange throughout the Mediterranean world, and retained its value unchanged until the eleventh century. Constantinople had also become a great manufacturing center. After monks had smuggled eggs of the silkworm and mulberry seeds from China, which had jealously guarded the secret of silk production for centuries, centers of silk manufacture were founded in the Byzantine Empire, primarily in Syria and at Constantinople itself. The gorgeously designed and colored silk fabrics were manufactured in several workshops in the grounds of the imperial palace. Artisans produced jewelry of gold, silver, pearls, and precious stones, gilded frames for icons (religious images), and carved wooden furnishings. This trade was protected by the Byantine navy, which controlled the waters adjoining the empire.

The one weakness of the Byzantine economy was agriculture. As in Rome, the great aristocrats had bought up estates, forcing the free peasantry from the land. Those who remained had become tied to the soil by state decree. Nevertheless, certain areas remained productive, notably the wheat lands of Asia Minor, the vineyards and olive groves of Greece, and the cotton fields of Syria.

With this wealth Justinian financed an ambitious attempt to reunite the Roman Empire, by reconquering the lands of the West that had fallen to the barbarian tribes. His army was well led and scientifically managed. His cavalry, which consisted of the armored horse and rider called a cataphract, was the most formidable fighting force in Europe. The first expedition led by his able general Belisarius was sent against the Vandal kingdom of North Africa. In 532–534, Belisarius totally defeated the Vandals, captured Carthage, and brought a vast display of captives and spoils back for his triumphal procession in Constantinople. Among the items of gold and jewelry displayed were the treasures from the Jewish Temple in Jerusalem, which had been brought to Rome by Titus in 70. The second campaign expelled the Ostrogoths from Italy and captured their capital, Ravenna. Finally, a third campaign defeated the Visigoths in southernwestern Spain.

These campaigns were brutal and costly in lives and money. According to the *Secret History* which Justinian's official historian Procopius wrote without the emperor's knowledge (and in which he blackened the reputation of the emperor whom he was publicly praising): "[Justinian] so devastated the vast tract of Libya that a traveller, during a long journey, considered it a remarkable thing to meet a single man; and yet there were eighty thousand Vandals who bore arms, besides women, children, and servants without number. . . . The natives of Mauretania [northern Morocco, Algeria] were even still more numerous, and they were all exterminated, together with their wives and children."[5] The control Justinian established in the West was superficial and temporary. In the seventh and eighth centuries, the Lombards took all Italy except the extreme south and Venice. The Visigoths soon retook Spain. The Muslim Arabs conquered North Africa in the seventh century.

While respecting the authority of the pope in the reconquered areas of Italy, in the eastern section of the empire, Justinian intended to maintain Constantine's conception that he was a Christian emperor who, on behalf of Christ, governed both Church and state. (The conception is sometimes called Caesaropapism, since the emperor acted both as caesar and pope.) The patriarch of Constantinople and all other church officials were appointed by the emperor and could be dismissed by him. Matters of doctrine interested him, perhaps too greatly, and he interfered frequently to settle disputes. He punished heretics. Religion also penetrated every aspect of the great cultural revival that Justinian was determined to encourage. The finest writings of the age were the

[5] Procopius, *The Secret History of the Court of Justinian* (Athens: Athenian Society, 1896), pp. 149–51.

books of devotions and the hymnals, although the most elaborate research and argumentation was lavished upon theological polemic. Court ceremonial became more elaborate, in order to emphasize the religious aspects of imperial power. The crown with its cross, the stiff ceremonial robes, the prescribed prostration—which emphasized the awe of the subject at approaching the physical presence of Christ in the person of the emperor—all dramatized the divine position of the emperor. The principal monument of Justinian's reign was to be a great new church of Hagia Sophia, which was not only to symbolize the supremacy of religion in the Byzantine state but also Justinian's triumph over the factions of the city mob in the Nika riots of 532.

The Nika Riots, 532

The one expression of popular will permitted in Constantinople had been the factions called the Blues and Greens, into which the crowd attending the chariot races in the Hippodrome was divided. They acclaimed a new emperor. On race days they petitioned for redress of grievances. Emperors courted their support by giving them ceremonial duties and by having them act as a civilian militia. But the factions easily got out of hand. In 532, when the mob's anger had been roused by taxes for Justinian's wars, they swarmed from the Hippodrome into the streets yelling "Nika" or "Conquer," and set fire to the government buildings around the Augustaeum and even to Hagia Sophia itself. The factions

Empress Theodora and Her Court Ladies, San Vitale, Ravenna   The sumptuous setting probably represents Theodora's rooms in the palace in Constantinople. (Alinari/Art Resource.)

agreed on a new emperor to replace Justinian. Justinian himself was on the point of fleeing when his wife Theodora persuaded him to hold firm: "While it is not proper for a woman to be bold or to behave brashly among men . . . for my part, I consider flight, even though it may bring safety, to be quite useless, at any time and especially now. Once a man has come into the light of day it is impossible for him not to face death; and so also it is unbearable for someone who has been a ruler to be a fugitive."[6] Justinian sent an army to the Hippodrome, where they massacred 30,000 of the crowd. The bodies were later buried in a mass grave at the city gates, as a permanent warning to others. Although the mob was cowed, Justinian was left with a city whose heart was in ruins.

The Rebuilding of Hagia Sophia

Justinian had already been a great builder throughout the empire, and was determined to be remembered for the roads, bridges, walls, aqueducts, hospitals, baths, monasteries, and churches that he had ordered constructed. But for the rebuilding of Hagia Sophia he instructed his engineer-architects, Anthemius and Isidore, to spend without limits. They gave him one of the world's greatest buildings. The new church was planned around a vast central dome, supported

[6] Cited in John W. Barker, *Justinian and the Later Roman Empire* (Madison, Wisc.: University of Wisconsin Press, 1966), pp. 87–88.

Hagia Sophia, Constantinople (537–542)
The building's framework was of brick and stone, but the interior was covered with multicolored sheets of marble. The windows in the 180-foot high dome permitted constant play of sunshine. (Hirmer Fotoarchiv.)

on four enormous columns. But the architects created an undulating, sinuous sense of space in movement, by adding two half-domes to the central dome and by opening out the half-domes with three additional smaller semicircular chapels. As a result, as one enters the building, the worshipper first feels a sense of forward motion typical of basilica architecture; but once one has reached the central dome one feels, as the planners intended, that it is the dome of heaven. Sunlight poured in through forty-two windows at the base of the dome, to illuminate walls covered with brightly colored marble brought from every part of the empire. Rich silken tapestries embroidered with gold and silver hung from an altar of gold inlaid with jewels. Hundreds of silver candelabra hung from beaten brass chains, so that even at night, light from the dome could be seen by sailors. On the day that he dedicated the church, it is said, Justinian declared: "Glory be to God, who has thought me worthy to finish this work. Solomon, I have outdone thee."

Justinian's Law Code

Justinian also felt that he had outdone Solomon in another way, as a lawgiver. One of his first actions as emperor had been the appointment of a commission to make a collection of the existing laws that would end the confusion due to the haphazard growth of Roman law over more than a thousand years. In just over a year the commission issued a succinct summary known as the *Codex Justinianus.* Justinian then demanded that the commission undertake the even more complex task of making sense of the legal opinions of the experts known as jurisconsults. The task was so monumental because of the contradictions and the bulk of these writings that he allowed them ten years. The commission had completed the *Digest,* which summarized more than 2000 books and the opinions of thirty-nine authorities, in less than three! To enable law students to understand the *Codex* and the *Digest,* Justinian then issued a legal textbook called the *Institutes.* Finally, all new laws—now written in Greek rather than Latin—were grouped as the *Novels.* This extraordinary body of civil law exercised enormous effect on the development of Western society. It was in use in the Byzantine empire until 1453. It was the basis of legal study in European universities during the Middle Ages. The Catholic Church embodied its basic concepts in the canon law. Napoleon used it as the basis of his law code in France at the beginning of the nineteenth century, and other European and Latin American countries based their law codes on Napoleon's. It even formed the basis of commercial law in those countries, such as England and its colonies in America, whose common law derived from the Germanic invaders.

Decline After Justinian

The expenses of Justinian's policies greatly weakened the empire, and for the century and a half after his death its territory was prey to attack. In the early seventh century, the Persian Empire succeeded in gaining control of Syria,

Palestine, and Egypt, including the great cities of Antioch, Damascus, Jerusalem, and Alexandria. Although the Byzantine emperors succeeded in recapturing them in a massive counterattack in 622–629, only five years later the Muslim Arab cavalry swept out of Arabia and soon brought the whole of the Near East under their control. By the end of the seventh century, all of North Africa had fallen to them. In 717, they had begun to besiege Constantinople by water and by land.

The Isaurian Dynasty, 717–867

Constantinople was saved by the Syrian general and later emperor, Leo III, founder of the Isaurian dynasty. The new emperors restored the taxation system in the remaining provinces of the empire. Military reorganization was based on the formation of reliable peasant armies recruited primarily in Asia Minor. The navy was armed with Greek fire, a kind of flamethrower first used in the 670s to spray enemy ships with a substance that set them ablaze.

Nevertheless, the empire remained under constant attack. Immediately to the northeast were the Bulgarians, a people formed by the intermingling of the original Slavs of the area with a Hunnic tribe known as Bulgars who had conquered the region. The Bulgarians killed the Byzantine Emperor Nicephorus in battle in 811, the first time an emperor had died in battle since the Visigothic attack in 378. Indigenous Slavs of Russia, under the rule of Vikings, or Norsemen, from Scandinavia, had founded a new state in the Ukraine from which, in 860, they sent a fleet of 200 ships to besiege Constantinople. In Italy, the Lombards again attacked and were defeated by Pepin, the newly crowned king of the Franks and father of Charlemagne. The pope had found a new champion to replace the Byzantine emperor and had received the "Donation of Pepin," an agreement promising the pope direct control over the Byzantine territories in Italy that had just been retaken from the Lombards.

The pope's justification for withdrawing from allegiance to Byzantium was his opposition to the emperor's "iconoclastic" policy. Religious images were widely worshipped throughout the Byzantine empire, as though they had magical qualities, to the annoyance of Emperor Leo III, who decided to order the suspect images broken or destroyed. He thus provoked the "iconoclastic" or "image-breaking" controversy, which wracked the empire for more than a century. Monasteries were the main object of the image breakers, and monks who resisted were even drafted into the army or compelled to marry nuns. Veneration of images was restored in 787, forbidden again in 815, and finally permitted again in 842, thus allowing Byzantine art to continue the Hellenistic tradition in which it had first been schooled.

Michael III, the last Isaurian emperor, was responsible for one significant extension of Byzantine influence—the conversion of the Bulgarians to Orthodox Christianity. But he left an empire once again under siege, when he was murdered by his own chosen successor.

The Macedonian Dynasty, 867–1025

The rule of the Macedonian dynasty was the last period of strength and prosperity of the Byzantine Empire. The emperors renewed the offensive against the Arabs and succeeded in recapturing the island of Crete and large parts of Syria. On their eastern border, they annexed Armenia. After long wars, they finally, in 1018, defeated the Bulgarian armies and annexed the country. In Italy, Byzantine armies also for a brief period in the eleventh century reconquered the South. Perhaps most important of all, however, was the spread of Orthodox Christianity by the work of missionaries.

Two brothers, Saint Cyril and Saint Methodius, had already been sent by the patriarch to Moravia in present-day Czechoslovakia in 864. Although they were unable permanently to prevent German Catholic missionaries from making that region faithful to Rome, they and their followers did develop the Cyrillic alphabet, which was used henceforth for writing down religious works in the Slavic languages of Russian, Serbo-Croat, and Bulgarian. The missionaries from Constantinople were thus given a powerful weapon in the completion of the conversion of the Bulgarians in the ninth century, at a time when the pope was seriously attempting to win them over to Catholicism. The ruler of Serbia (in present-day Yugoslavia) accepted missionaries from Constantinople late in the ninth century, and with most of his subjects accepted baptism.

Most important of all, however, was the conversion in the 980s of Prince Vladimir of the Russian state centered on Kiev in the Ukraine. Vladimir was rewarded with the hand of the sister of the Byzantine emperor. Kievan Russian was thrown open to the religious influence of Byzantium, although Vladimir and his successors were careful not to permit the emperor to exert political influence over them. Nevertheless, in sheer numbers the Christianization of Russia was the greatest addition to Christendom since the conversion of Constantine. During this formative period of their civilization, the Russians were deeply influenced by every aspect of Byzantine culture, and were prepared, at the fall of Constantinople in 1453, to inherit that city's role as the leader of the Orthodox Church.

The Decline and Fall of Constantinople

In the eleventh and twelfth centuries, the empire began again to decline. The Normans drove the Byzantines from southern Italy at the end of the eleventh century. The Seljuk Turks, who had already conquered most of the Arab states from Persia to the Mediterranean, inflicted a major defeat on the Byzantine armies at the battle of Manzikert in 1071, and took Syria and large parts of Asia Minor. The Crusades sent against the Seljuk Turks from Western Europe damaged the Byzantine economy, by opening direct new trade routes from the Near East to Europe, which bypassed Constantinople. In 1204, during the Fourth Crusade, the crusaders even sacked Constantinople itself, and imposed their own line of Latin emperors on Byzantium for the next sixty years. Finally, in the fourteenth and fifteenth centuries, the Ottoman Turks, the strongest of all the series of Turkish tribes who had moved westward from Asia since the tenth century, encircled Constantinople by taking Asia Minor and the Balkans. In April 1453, they mounted their final assault with an army of 150,000 upon a city defended by only 7000 soldiers. Siege guns breached the walls, and the Turkish troops were unleashed within the city to murder and to pillage. The Turkish sultan Muhammad II, then aged only twenty-three, rode slowly through the Forum of Constantine to the Augusteum. He dismounted in front of Hagia Sophia, where he humbled himself before Allah by rubbing a handful of dirt over his forehead. He then attended the first Muslim service in the greatest of all Orthodox churches. And, in the ruins of the Great Palace, he murmured an old Persian poem: "The spider has woven his web in the imperial palace. And the owl has sung a watch-song on the towers of Afrasiab."

SUGGESTED READINGS

General Introduction

The complex interaction of a highly civilized, if declining, empire, with less civilized, but vigorous and innovative, "barbarians," makes the period from the fourth to sixth centuries fascinating in its own right, and not merely as the spectacle of the fall of one of the world's longest-lasting empires. See Peter Brown, *The World of Late Antiquity*, A.D. *150–750* (1971) and Joseph Vogt, *The Decline of Rome: The Metamorphosis of Ancient Civilization*, translated by Janet Sondheimer (1967).

Christianity

Good narratives of the life of Christ and the spread of the early Church include Kenneth S. Latourette, *A History of Christianity* (1953), and J. Daniélou and H. Marrou, *The Christian Centuries*, Vol. 1, *The First Six Hundred Years* (1964). Michael Grant explains the situation in Palestine that led to Christ's crucifixion in *The Jews in the Roman World* (1973). The development of Christian doctrine by the Fathers can be followed in E. K. Rand, *Founders of the Middle Ages* (1928, 1957), and in Peter Brown, *Augustine of Hippo* (1967), the battles over dogma in Henry Chadwick, *The Early Church* (1967).

The Papacy and the Early Catholic Church

Geoffrey Barraclough's beautifully illustrated *The Medieval Papacy* (1968) explains the "emancipation" of the papacy from the authority of the emperors. A lively overview is given in Hugh Trevor-Roper, *The Rise of Christian Europe* (1965). The little-known experience of the city of Rome in the years of confusion after the end of the empire in the West is described in Peter Llewellyn, *Rome in the Dark Ages* (1971). Jeffrey Richards, *Consul of God: The Life and Times of Gregory the Great* (1980), is useful on papal politics but less so on theology. The best study of monasticism is David Knowles, *Christian Monasticism* (1969). For reasons why women entered nunneries, see Eileen Power, *Medieval English Nunneries* (1922).

The Barbarian Invasions

Two excellent surveys, which describe both the invasions and the formation of the Germanic kingdoms, are J. M. Wallace-Hadrill, *The Barbarian West, 400–1000* (1952), and A. R. Lewis, *Emerging Medieval Europe, A.D. 400–1000* (1967). On individual Germanic peoples, see F. M. Stenton, *Anglo-Saxon England* (2nd ed., 1947); Peter Lasko, *The Kingdom of the Franks: North-Western Europe Before Charlemagne* (1971); and E. A. Thompson, *The Goths in Spain* (1969). Justine D. Randers-Pherson, *Barbarians and Romans: The Birth Struggle of Europe, A.D. 400–700* (1983), discusses problems faced by the barbarian kingdoms in coming to terms with the former subjects of the Roman Empire. On the position of women in the Germanic tribes, see Suzanne Fonay Wemple, *Women in Frankish Society: Marriage and the Cloister, 500 to 900* (1981), and Derek Baker, ed., *Medieval Women* (1978).

The Byzantine Empire

Ramsay Macmullen, *Constantine* (1970), is a detailed biography of the founder of Constantinople. Military and economic questions are emphasized in John W. Barker, *Justinian and the Later Roman Empire* (1966). Contemporary quotations bring the period alive in P. H. Ure, *Justinian and His Age* (1951). A fine survey of Byzantine history is given in Speros Vryonis, Jr., *Byzantium and Europe* (1967). More mundane matters are the subject of Tamara Talbot Rice, *Everyday Life in Byzantium* (1967). The beauty of the great capital city of Constantinople can be appreciated in Philip Sherrard, *Constantinople: Iconography of a Sacred City* (1965). André Grabar provides a sumptuous introduction to Byzantine art in *Byzantium from the Death of Theodosius to the Rise of Islam* (1966) and *Byzantine Painting* (1953).

The last days are chronicled in Steven Runciman, *The Fall of Constantinople* (1965).

5

An Age of Invasions, 600–1000

The Romanized inhabitants of continental Western Europe survived the Germanic invasions of the fourth to the sixth centuries with many of their institutions intact. It is misleading to think of those centuries as a period of utter chaos and bloodshed. In fact, the writers of the age produced some of the finest literature written in Latin—the theology of Saint Augustine, the history of Cassiodorus, the philosophy of Boethius. The Visigothic sack of Rome in 410 was exaggerated by Christian writers who wanted to see it as punishment for the city's pagan past. The Germanic invaders were small in number. Where, like the Vandals and the Visigoths, they failed to mingle with the indigenous population, they could be easily overthrown by new invaders. Where they mingled, like the Franks, they accepted Romanization themselves. Thus, by the end of the sixth century, it was possible for many in Western Europe to feel that they had absorbed the worst of the shock of the Germanic invasions. The coins issued by the Roman Senate after the deposition of the last Roman emperor in 476 bore the symbolic slogan, "Rome Unconquered"!

Between the seventh century and the beginning of the eleventh, however, Europe was struck by a series of new invaders. In the eighth century, Muslim Arabs from North Africa penetrated as far as Poitiers in central France before their victorious progress was halted. A nomadic people called the Avars entered Europe from their stronghold in southern Russia at the end of the sixth century, and for the next two centuries dominated the Hungarian plain. Slavic peoples established themselves in the Balkans in the late sixth and seventh centuries, and Bulgarians followed to subjugate the Slavs of the southeastern Balkans in the seventh century.

The eighth century saw a temporary period of stability. The Isaurian dynasty in Constantinople held off the Muslim Arabs in 717, and rebuilt Byzantine power. Under their greatest ruler, Charlemagne (reigned 768–814), the Franks established an empire embracing large parts of Western Europe; and, in 800, Charlemagne was even crowned "Emperor of the Romans" by the pope.

This respite lasted only a century. A third and final wave of invaders struck in the ninth and tenth century. In the Mediterranean, Arabs from North Africa broke the power of the Byzantine navy and established themselves in Sicily. Hungary fell to yet another tribal group from southern Russia, the Magyars, who are the ancestors of the present-day Hungarians. The Vikings, or Norsemen, struck savagely from their Scandinavian homelands. In Russia they drove as far south as Kiev. In the British Isles they settled large areas of the northern coasts. In France they established themselves in Normandy at the mouth of the river Seine. But their most daring expedition took them into the Mediterranean Sea, where they took possession of Sicily from the Arabs.

The third wave of invasions was by far the most disruptive. By the year 1000, European institutions had been totally remodeled to adapt to an age of violent insecurity. Trade, even over short distances, had virtually ceased, and towns had therefore become almost unnecessary. The agricultual village had become the basic nucleus of settled life. Within the village, manorialism, a new form of economic structure based on peasant "serfs" tied to the land, had come into being. Feudalism, a new political system based on the provision of all military, administrative, and legal services by a hierarchy of armed knights bound by ties of personal allegiance, had replaced whatever had survived of Roman provincial government, which, by the second century, had been largely left in the hands of the municipalities. The institutions of manorialism and feudalism, formed during the third wave of invasions, were the fundamental and novel underpinnings of a new age of Christian civilization, which is called medieval.

THE IMPACT OF MUSLIM INVASIONS ON THE WEST

Muhammad and the Foundation of Islam

Muhammad (c. 570–632), the founder of the religion of Islam (meaning "submission" to God) was born in Mecca, an important trading city in Arabia, from which caravans traveled as far north as Palestine and Syria. Muhammad engaged in this trade, and on his journeys became acquainted with the teachings of both Jews and Christians. He married a weathy woman whose business he had been managing. This unexceptional life changed drastically when, at the age of forty, he began to see visions. He believed that the Angel Gabriel had ordered him to reveal the word of God. His visions, which continued for twenty years, were finally collected in the Koran, the holy book of Islam. At first, Muhammad's message was simple: There was only one god, Allah, who was indivisible. (Muhammad was therefore opposed to the Christian doctrine of the Trinity, which he believed implied that there were three gods.) He banned the drinking of alcohol, and, like the Jews, forbade the eating of pork. He permitted men to have up to four wives, and allowed easy divorce for men.

He did however, at least temporarily, raise the status of women in Arabia. He banned female infanticide. He insisted that a man should be able to support all his wives. He urged reconciliation rather than divorce. A woman was permitted to keep a part of her family inheritance as well as the bride-gift made when she married. Perhaps most important of all, women were allowed to worship with men in the mosque during the early years of Islam; many were given a religious education; and some became Islamic scholars. But the seclusion of women was later to be justified by Muhammad's insistence upon female modesty, including covering the body in public; and the subordination of women was considered a command of the Koran, which laid down that "men are in charge of women, because Allah hath made one of them to excel the other."[1]

He proclaimed the giving of alms, the physical resurrection of the body, and the coming of a terrible day of judgment. He expected to make early converts among Jews and Christians, especially since he believed that the Arabs were descended from Ishmael, the elder son of Abraham, and that he himself was the last of a line of prophets including the Hebrew prophets and Christ. The inhabitants of Mecca paid little attention to his early preaching, but in 622 he was invited to act as mediator in disputes in the more northerly city of Yathrib (which he later renamed Medina). There he became chief magistrate and gathered round him a following of militant Bedouin tribesmen, to whom he preached the necessity and rewards of embarking upon a *jihad*, or holy war, against the infidel. Some of the more flagrant infidels were clearly those of Mecca, who had refused his teaching. In 630, he led the Bedouins against Mecca, where he destroyed all the pagan shrines except a sacred black meteorite that had been revered for centuries. Adapted to Muslim worship, the stone was enclosed within a square building called the Kaaba, which became and still remains the center of the Muslim world. The jihad continued, and by Muhammad's death in 632, two-thirds of Arabia had been conquered.

The legacy of Muhammad's teaching was contained in three books: the sayings of Allah as revealed to him, in the Koran; Muhammad's own teachings, in the *hadith*; and a life of Muhammad, called the *sunna*, which was used by the faithful to model their own lives on that of the Prophet. The five principal rules of his new religion were quite simple: belief in one god Allah; prayer five times a day; fasting from dawn to dusk during the month of Ramadan; one pilgrimage at least in a lifetime to Mecca; and charity.

---

[1] Denise Lardner Carmody, *Women and World Religions* (Nashville, Tenn.: Abingdon, 1979), p. 140.

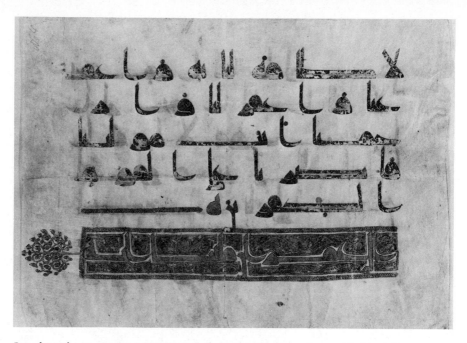

Page from the Koran, Egypt (eighth-ninth centuries) *Muslim artists used highly elaborate forms of abstract decoration in stucco, wood, stone, textiles, and tile. The most favored form of decoration, however, was the transcription of Arabic quotations from the Koran.* (The Metropolitan Museum of Art, Rogers Fund, 1937.)

Although he had created a religion of great expansive power, Muhammad had failed to provide for his succession. The problem was temporarily solved by making his closest companion, Abu Bakr, the *caliph*, or "deputy" or "representative." Abu Bakr successfully won the allegiance of the Bedouins, and was succeeded by other companions of the prophet, Omar (reigned 634–644) and Othman (reigned 644–656). Finally, his son-in-law Ali (reigned 656–661) became caliph. The four caliphs are known as the Orthodox Caliphate. It was a period of tremendous military expansion, especially after Omar had satisfied the army by paying them from the public treasury for their victories. The Arab riders, mounted on their desert ponies and camels, broke out into the Fertile Crescent. One army took Syria and Palestine in 636–637 and Egypt in 640–641. Another swung against Persia, which collapsed in 646. In less than fifteen years, the Arabs had thus taken possession of the Nile Valley and the Fertile Crescent, two of the richest regions in the world; and half a million Arabs left the forbidding deserts of Arabia to settle, and to perpetuate Arab rule, in the conquered regions. In spite of these great victories, the caliphs found difficulty in maintaining their personal power, and Omar, Othman, and Ali were all murdered.

Ali's murderer, Muawiya of the Ummayad family, took the caliphate for himself, and transferred the government to Damascus in Syria. The new center of power was far better located strategically and economically than Mecca and Medina had been. Influenced both by Byzantium and by the cultures of the Fertile Crescent and Persia, the Ummayads were responsible for creating a distinctive culture expressed in architecture, painting, ceramics, textiles, and literature, whose characteristics have remained influential to this day. They also

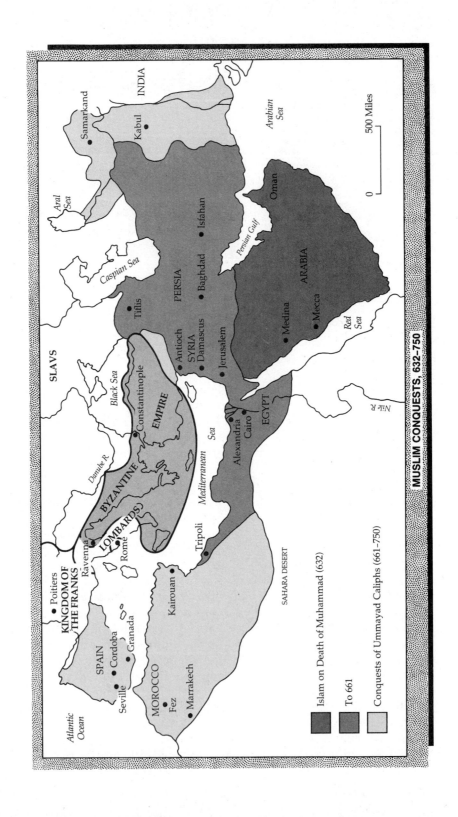

MUSLIM CONQUESTS, 632–750

Islam on Death of Muhammad (632)

To 661

Conquests of Ummayad Caliphs (661–750)

500 Miles

0

encouraged the Arabs to become city builders, not only of Damascus but of new cities founded on the edge of their newly conquered lands.

Dissatisfaction with Ummayad rule grew, especially after the failure to capture Constantinople in 717. They had always been opposed by Shi'ite Muslims mainly in Persia, who believed that only the descendants of Ali could rightfully become caliph, and that therefore the Ummayads were usurpers. But the majority of the Sunni Muslims also were discontented by the eighth century at the failure of the caliph to act as a worthy head of the Muslim religion. Finally, new converts, especially from Christian and Zoroastrian religious communities, were discontented that they had not been fully accepted into Islam by the Arabs. The Ummayads were overthrown in 750, and power was taken by the Abbasid family, who were descended from the uncle of Muhammad.

The Abbasid caliphate, which lasted more than 500 years (750–1258), presided over Islam's greatest intellectual boom. The Abbasids transferred the capital from Damascus to Baghdad on the Tigris River in Iraq. They assuaged discontent with their religious rule by allowing an Islamic clergy, known as the *ulema*, to take over interpretation and enforcement of the religion, which was held to include many of the normal details of daily life. The religious courts thus took over many of the functions that in non-Islamic states were dealt with by the state courts. The caliphs healed the split between Arab Muslims and the converts by abolishing all distinctions between them, opening the bureaucracy and the army to them equally.

The Great Mosque, Kairouan, Tunisia (eighth-ninth centuries) The mosque was completed by the Aghlabid dynasty after they gained independence from the Abbasid rulers of Baghdad in 800. (Art Resource.)

Possession of the Fertile Crescent made the Abbasids economically prosperous. They had taken control of the great cities of Mesopotamia and Iran, which had never undergone the decline of the European or of the Byzantine cities. These provinces produced vast agricultural surpluses of grain, olives, and dates, and new crops such as sugar cane and cotton were introduced. The empire of Islam sprawled across the great trade routes between Europe, Asia, and Africa, and thus could take a large share of the wealth that had previously passed to Constantinople. The Abbasids also borrowed the autocratic ceremonial of the earlier rulers of Persia and Byzantium, especially during the reign of Harun al-Rashid (reigned 786–809). Baghdad became a byword for oriental splendor. In the city center was the caliph's Golden Gate palace, topped by a huge green dome 160 feet high. Nearby was the great palace mosque, where scholars worked on the vast collection of manuscripts the caliphs had brought together. Not only Muslim philosophy was taught. Greek manuscripts from Constantinople were translated into Arabic. Medical research was conducted, and interest in astrology had as a by-product advances in astronomy for which the Observatory at Baghdad was founded. There was even an attempt by the philosopher al-Kindi to make Islamic thought harmonize with the teachings of Aristotle.

In the ninth and tenth centuries the outer provinces of the empire began to break away from the rule of Baghdad. The last descendant of the Ummayads had already been recognized as the rightful ruler of Spain in the eighth century, and the provinces along the North African coast in the area of modern Morocco, Algeria, and Tunisia were independent by 800. By 1000, the only area remaining under control of the Abbasid caliphs was the Tigris and Euphrates valleys. This fragmentation had, however, a stimulating effect on Islamic culture, because many new centers of learning were created in the independent kingdoms into which the caliphate had broken—Cordoba in Spain, Fez in Morocco, Kairouan in Tunisia, Palermo in Sicily, Cairo in Egypt, Samarkand in Transoxiana.

Islam and Western Christendom

The most obvious effect of the military conquests of the Arabs was to reduce vastly the territory under Christian control. The Orthodox Church lost its dominance in the former Byzantine territories of Syria, Palestine, Egypt, and North Africa. The Catholic Church gave up its power in Spain and Portugal. Christian churches did persist in all these areas, in spite of discrimination and at times persecution. Even today, for example, in Egypt there are both Orthodox Christians and Monophysite Christians of the Coptic church. But Christians were a minority that very rapidly grew feebler in numbers. Only in Portugal and Spain were the Christians able to reestablish themselves after centuries of military pressure. The Near East and North Africa had been permanently lost to Christianity.

The hatred of Christian for Muslim became a poison in medieval society. Trade between the North and South of the Mediterranean, which before the seventh century had been a Christian lake, dwindled to almost nothing by 1000. The Catholic Church matched the Muslim concept of the *jihad* with its call for Crusades against Islam, first in Spain in the eighth century and then for the reconquest of Palestine and Syria, the Christian Holy Land, between the eleventh and thirteenth centuries. Christians saw nothing repugnant in selling Muslims into slavery, especially as Muslim pirates were enslaving Christians. The incomprehension between the two civilizations at times seemed to be complete. An Arab geographer wrote that the people of northern Europe were so affected by their distance from the sun that "their temperaments have become chilly and their humors rude. Consequently their bodies are huge, their color pale and their hair long. For the same reason they lack keenness in intelligence and perspicacity, are characterized by ignorance and stupidity. Folly and mental blindness prevail among them. . . ."[2] When Urban II launched the First Crusade, in a fiery sermon at Clermont in France in 1095, he replied in kind:

> An accursed race, a race utterly alienated from God, a generation forsooth which has not directed its heart and has not entrusted its spirit to God, has invaded the lands of those Christians [the Holy Land] and has depopulated them by sword, pillage and fire; it has led away a part of the captives into its own country, and a part it has destroyed by cruel tortures; it has either destroyed the churches of God or appropriated them for the rites of its own religion. They destroy the altars, after having defiled them with their uncleanness. They circumcise the Christians, and the blood of the circumcision they either spread upon the altars or pour into the vases of the baptismal font.[3]

Yet the West, relatively backward in comparison with the civilization of Islam, did receive important benefits from contact with that superior civilization, especially after the first century of Muslim conquest was over. Trade never entirely ceased. At first the principal and almost the sole intermediaries were Jewish merchants, who brought the rough trade goods of Western Europe in exchange for the spices and silks of the East. Soon, however, Venice and the other ports of northern Italy were extending their trade with Constantinople to direct commerce with the Islamic states of the Near East. And the Crusaders' recapture of Palestine and parts of Syria in the First Crusade (1096–1099) gave the apolitical Italians even easier access to the products of the Islamic provinces of the Fertile Crescent. As a result of these contacts, many new products entered Europe. The Mediterranean lands added many new crops to their agriculture, which had previously been based on the olive and the grape, most notably rice, cotton, sugar cane, and citrus fruits. Islamic carpets were highly prized in medieval castles, for their warmth as well as their design, and the techniques used in their production influenced the tapestry makers of Europe. The manufactur-

---

[2] Sa'id al-Andaluse, cited in Philip K. Hitti, *Islam and the West* (Princeton, N.J.: D. Van Nostrand Company, 1962), p. 166.

[3] Robert the Monk's version, in Department of History, University of Pennsylvania, *Translation and Reprints from the Original Sources of European History* (Philadelphia: University of Pennsylvania, 1902), Series I, Vol. I, no. 2., pp. 5–6.

ing of paper was learned from Muslim Spain. The techniques of steelmaking were passed north from Toledo in Spain.

The intellectual debt of Christian Europe was even greater. Few Europeans could reach the faraway libraries of Baghdad, but nearer at hand, in the Ummayad state of Spain, was the great city of Cordoba. Corboba had 3000 mosques, fine hospitals, a splendid university, and libraries of Greek and Arabic manuscripts both in the mosques and in private homes. Christian students and scholars were permitted to reside in the city. Gerbert of Aurillac, the future Pope Sylvester II, studied there, and, according to a rather malicious English chronicler, had even learned "the art of calling up spirits from hell." For West Europeans, Muslim Spain provided access to the books of ancient Greece and the Hellenistic world, even though many were available only in Arabic translation, but many scholars became fascinated with the writings of the Arabs themselves. The troubadours of southern France and Spain were deeply influenced by the romantic poetic tradition in Islamic literature. Prose works, including a description of Muhammad's ascent to Paradise, may have influenced medieval writers such as Dante. Some became so enthralled with the writing of Averroës, a Muslim philosopher who had written a commentary on Aristotle, that the pope had to condemn the heresy of "Averroism" for relying on reason rather than on revelation of God for testing the truth of Christianity.

The Christians were less influenced, however, by Islamic architecture and art, perhaps because of its relationship to Muslim religious practice and regu-

The Patio de los Arrayenes, Alhambra, Granada   *The Alhambra, the fortified palace of the Muslim Nazarite dynasty, was divided into an administrative section, a diplomatic section (where this patio was situated), and a harem. (Spanish National Tourist Office.)*

lation, even though some of its finest achievements were to be seen in the beautiful cities of Cordoba, Seville, and Granada. The main building in Cordoba was the great mosque, which existed primarily for the Muslims to pray the required five times a day. From a tall tower called a minaret, a muezzin called the worshippers to prayer. A wide inner court provided fountains and wash-basins for the purifying ablutions. Within the building, arched colonnades pro-vided a carpeted space on which the barefoot worshippers could prostrate them-selves in the direction of Mecca, as indicated by the highly decorated niche called a *mihrab* in the far wall. (When the Christians reconquered Cordoba, they hacked out a large open area by smashing down the lovely columns of marble and porphyry, and erected—partly out of spite—a cumbersome Christian church in the very heart of the elegant mosque.)

The art of Islam was influential primarily on Western decorative arts, such as calligraphy, since, following Muhammad's proscription of representation of living beings, it was almost entirely abstract, except for the illuminated manu-scripts produced in Persia. The lovely palaces of Seville and especially the Alhambra of Granada, the fortress-palace of the last Islamic rulers of southern Spain, were resplendent with ingenious designs in tile, stucco, glass, wood, and jewelry.

STABILIZATION UNDER THE CAROLINGIANS

The Arab invasion of France had been halted in 732 by Charles Martel, the "mayor of the palace" of the Frankish king. For the past century, the Merov-ingian kings, as the descendants of Clovis were called, had been "do-nothing kings," and power had fallen into the hands of their chief ministers, the mayors of the palace. Of these the two most important were Charles Martel and his son Pepin. Possessing vast estates themselves in eastern Belgium, they were independently powerful and wealthy, and able to profit from the weakness of the kings. Charles Martel had strengthened the Frankish army by adopting from Byzantium the use of the cataphract, the "enclosed" or armored knight on horseback, but he had improved the cavalry's fighting ability by arming them with long lances instead of the arrows used by both the Byzantine and Persian armies. His son Pepin, with the agreement of the pope, overthrew the Merovingian ruler and became king himself in 754. As part of his bargain with the pope, Pepin led the Frankish army to Italy to defeat the Lombards, and handed over central Italy as the Donation of Pepin to the pope.

Pepin's son Charlemagne (reigned 768–814) was the greatest ruler of the dynasty, which is known as Carolingian (from Carolus, meaning Charles). He was the Frankish ideal of a warrior—tall, good-looking, simple in his tastes, lusty in loving, and courageous in battle. Every spring for thirty years he led his armies into battle. He took up his father's campaign against the Lombards, whom he finally defeated, and took for himself the title of King of the Franks and Lombards. He determined to Christianize Germany by force, and fought bloody and successful campaigns against the Saxons in northern and central Germany and the Bavarians in southern Germany. From Austria, he launched a campaign of extermination against the Avars in Hungary, and took from them the spoils of a century of depredation, including the tribute they had compelled Constantinople to pay them. He attacked the Muslims in northern Spain, and was able after tough battles to gain a foothold south of the Pyrenees Mountains from which the long reconquest of the peninsula could be mounted. The result of his campaigns was the establishment of a kingdom that extended from France in the west to Germany in the east and from Holland in the north to Italy in the South.

The Carolingian Renaissance

These conquests led Charlemagne to think of himself as one of the world's great emperors, whose power was excelled only by the Byzantine emperor in Constantinople and the Abbasid caliph in Baghdad. To rival those two capitals, he built a new capital at Aachen in western Germany, where he enjoyed the hot springs. Consciously modeling his actions on those of Constantine at the foundation of Constantinople, he set out to create a new Rome in Germany. He himself designated the sites for his forum, baths, aqueduct, theater, and senate. He brought the statue of the Ostrogoth King Theodoric from Ravenna, to emphasize that he was heir to Theodoric's kingdom. He even considered demolishing the imperial palace in Ravenna, so that he could use its stones for his

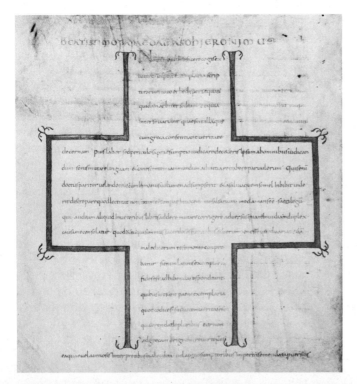

Carolingian Miniscule Script   *Although the Emperor Charlemagne could not read or write, his scholars developed the handwriting known as Carolingian miniscule, which is the basis of modern handwriting in the West.* (The Pierpont Morgan Library.)

palace in Aachen. He had his architects study the descriptions of Constantinople sent by his ambassadors, and he ordered that his own palace chapel be a copy of the great church of San Vitale that Justinian had built in Ravenna. His plans proved futile. His palace was built of wood, like a country farm, and only a few of his lords and merchants built homes around it. City growth stopped when his successors abandoned Aachen as their capital. Only one building has survived, the palace chapel. Although his architects had copied the octagonal ground plan of San Vitale, the new chapel lacked the subtle flow of space created in San Vitale by the semicircular apses and flowing interior passageways. The Palatine Chapel is the monument of a warrior king—clear, uncompromising, and a little barbaric.

Charlemagne's attempt to revive the culture of his empire was more successful. The schools he founded enabled many poor boys to prepare for a career in the church. His minister Alcuin established an educational curriculum that lasted throughout the Middle Ages. It was based on the *trivium* (grammar, rhetoric, dialectic) and the *quadrivium* (arithmetic, geometry, music, and astronomy). Scholars in his monasteries copied classical and early Christian manuscripts and invented Carolingian minuscule, from which the modern form of handwriting is taken. Charlemagne himself made frequent efforts to learn to read and write, but never succeeded.

With the image of Rome so dominant in his thoughts, it was not surprising that Charlemagne should have been crowned Emperor of the Romans on Christmas Day, 800. The events surrounding his coronation have, however, created controversy from that time to the present. While Charlemagne was kneeling at mass in Rome, the pope placed a crown on his head, and the congregation joined in a chorus of acclamation, in the time-honored manner in which emperors of both Rome and Constantinople had received the approval of their people. "To Augustus, crowned by God the great and peaceful emperor of the Romans, life and victory!" Charlemagne may have been displeased that he had been crowned by the pope, since this appeared to acknowledge the superiority of the pope over the emperor. At the very least he believed that the title had made him the equal of the Byzantine emperor, who did recognize him as Basileus, Greek for "king," but refused to call him Roman emperor. (At the time, Charlemagne's followers thought of him as Roman emperor of the West. The title of Holy Roman Emperor was not used for several centuries.) It is uncertain whether Charlemagne had gained anything from the title. It is certain that he had made the same mistake as his father, of misdirecting German efforts toward conquest in Italy, a mistake that his heirs were to perpetuate and that was to waste German resources as well as bring devastation to Italy for the next four centuries.

In 843, the empire was divided by the Treaty of Verdun among Charlemagne's three grandsons, to end the war between them. The western third was the nucleus of the future kingdom of France. The eastern third eventually became the country of Germany. The middle kingdom, however, lacked all unity. The northern half, Lotharingia, comprised the area from Holland to Switzerland and was to be fought over until the twentieth century by the French and German peoples. The southern portion was in Italy, down from the Alps to Rome, excluding the Papal States donated by Pepin. Even within these three kingdoms, authority was taken by local lords, who engaged in perpetual struggles with each other. The brief stabilization under Charlemagne was over, and Europe was once again open to invasion.

THE THIRD INVASION: MUSLIMS, MAGYARS, AND VIKINGS

In the Mediterranean, the Muslim rulers of Tunisia succeeded in the ninth century in defeating the Byzantines, which left them free to take the Mediterranean islands of Corsica, Sardinia, Sicily, and Crete. They were even able to burn the Benedictine monastery at Monte Cassino and to plunder churches on the edge of Rome itself. Their power was brief, however, and the Italian city-states of Genoa and Pisa were able to take Sardinia and Corsica, while the Vikings took Sicily. In that brief period of rule, however, Palermo in Sicily had become a center of Islamic learning.

The Magyars, a nomadic people possibly related to the Turks, crossed the Carpathian Mountains from southern Russia at the end of the ninth century and established themselves on the plains of Hungary, where Charlemagne had exterminated the Avars. For more than fifty years, the Magyars were able to strike with impunity at all parts of Germany, at southern France, and even across northern Italy. They were finally confined to Hungary, after their defeat by the German Emperor Otto I at the battle of Lechfeld in 955, and remained there to become the ancestors of the modern Hungarian people.

The most terrifying of these attacks were by the Vikings, or Norsemen, of Scandinavia. In the eighth century, the Vikings, probably because of overpopulation, food shortages, and internal dissension, began a series of plundering expeditions that increased in frequency and ferocity in the ninth century. They were the finest shipbuilders and navigators in Europe. Their "long ships," designed with carved prows and high sterns, accommodated thirty oarsmen and a total crew of ninety. In these boats, navigating by the sun at day and the stars at night, the Vikings were capable of covering extraordinary distances at great speed and could mount attacks with total surprise. Expeditions from Denmark struck the cities of the North German coast and occupied most of northern England. Other Vikings from Denmark sailed up the rivers of France and Belgium, sacking abbeys and towns as they passed through, until they were finally bought off by the French king with the grant of sovereignty over the province of Normandy, which controlled the mouth of the Seine. In 1060, a group of Norman knights made the dangerous voyage around Spain and Portugal and conquered most of the island of Sicily from the Arabs and southern Italy from the Byzantines; and from Normandy, Duke William mounted his invasion of England in 1066. Groups from Sweden sailed down the Dnieper River in Russia in the ninth century to reach Kiev and even to mount an unsuccessful attack on Constantinople itself. Repelled by the Byzantines, they remained in the Ukraine to found the nucleus of the first Russian state. The most far-ranging expeditions were made by Vikings from Norway, in the eighth century, who sailed to northern Scotland, Ireland, and northern England, and who in the late ninth century settled Iceland. There they composed the Norse sagas, poems about their gods and heroes that for the next two centuries were passed on orally by bards. In the tenth century, expeditions from Iceland explored Greenland and reached America.

Except in Russia, the earliest expeditions of the Vikings were largely destructive. After plundering whatever goods they could find, they set villages and towns aflame. The great literary collections of many of the north European monasteries were destroyed in these raids, as at Lindisfarne in northern England. They were slowly Christianized and by the tenth century were able to intermarry with the Christian populations they had conquered. The Vikings remained, however, among the most vigorous elements in the European population, and, as was proved in Normandy, quickly became astute political organizers. Having mastered the architectural skills of the people they conquered, by the eleventh century the Vikings had created the distinctive forms of Norman architecture in the construction of castles and cathedrals. But for the first 150 years of their incursions into Europe, their effect on Carolingian society was disastrous. For sheer survival, the Europeans were compelled to develop a new framework for their society and their economy.

FEUDALISM AND MANORIALISM

Historians today refer to the new political and military framework as feudalism and the new economic structure as manorialism. Until recently, however, historians used the word feudalism, which is derived from the medieval Latin *feodum*, or fief granted by a lord to his vassal, to describe the whole society from about the ninth to the fourteenth or fifteenth century.

Origins of Feudalism

Feudalism, as a system of government, required that vassals perform services for their lords because of personal obligations agreed to by contract instead of serving an administration paid by the state. It was formed by the combination of several institutions. Personal dependence on a great aristocrat probably derived from the Roman republic and empire. This "client" relation to a "patron" was probably the origin of the feudal notion that a man could become the vassal of a more powerful individual. The owners of the great villas in the late Roman empire, especially after Diocletian, had the same relationship to the inhabitants or *coloni* of their estates, many of whom were bound by law to the land, as did a feudal lord over his manor, most of whose peasants or serfs were also tied to the land. From the Germanic war band was derived the custom of followers who owed their chief personal service and advice. Finally, the concept that military service was due in return for a grant of land may have originated with Charles Martel, who granted estates to warriors in order to give them the economic means to provide themselves with the horse and armor they needed to serve in his new cavalry.

By the ninth century, these different institutions had become fused, primarily as a means of providing local administration and security in the threatening days of the invasions. The system was probably a piecemeal creation beginning at the local level and progressing slowly to become a national system. In one village, peasants might turn over their lands to a lord in return for his protection and its continuing use. The Church, the greatest landholder of all, might grant knights part of their lands in return for their military service and participation in the judicial administration. Local knights, outnumbered by the invaders, might join together under an effective military leader to defend their region or province.

But, when certain lords and especially when kings became powerful enough to demand that lords below them become their vassals, it was possible to impose feudalism from above rather than allow it to grow from below. The most extreme cases—and, indeed, the only case where a fully organized feudal system was imposed on a whole country—occurred as a result of conquest. When Duke William of Normandy conquered England in 1066, he retained legal ownership of all land by right of conquest. He was thus able to share out the land as fiefs, held but not owned by his vassals; and, for any infraction of the contract that the vassal accepted in return for tenure of his land, the king could and did take back the fief.

Feudalism as a System of Government

The feudal system was in the form of a pyramid. At its base were thousands of knights, each of whom had been granted one or more manors, or villages with their inhabitants. In return for the manor, the knight was expected to appear for military service under his lord, normally for forty days a year, equipped with horse, armor, and weapons, and his own personal servants. He was expected to make three gifts to his lord—for the knighting of the lord's son, for the marriage of the lord's daughter, and if necessary for the lord's ransom. He carried out the local administrative duties, such as keeping up the roads, and administered justice in his manor. He was also required to appear at his lord's court when his advice was needed and to participate in the trial of any vassal of his own status.

The lord to whom the knights owed service might himself be the vassal of a greater lord, and might owe that lord services correspondingly greater than those that his own knights owed to him. At the summit of the pyramid was the king, from whom the greatest lords of all held their lands. The system by which the greater lords subdivided their lands among lesser lords, who in turn subdivided their fiefs, was known as sub-infeudation. It led to many complications, since some vassals held lands from more than one lord. It the event of a struggle between his two lords, a vassal was compelled to betray one or the other.

Eventually, the fiefs were regarded as property that could be inherited, provided that the services were rendered and an inheritance fee of one year's revenues was paid. Women could thus inherit a fief, in the absence of male heirs, provided that they sent knights to fulfill the required military service. Many estates were managed by women, some of whom chose to remain single in order to enjoy the wealth and independence their fief gave them. Wives too were often left in charge of the estates when their husbands went on campaign. For the Church as landholder, the obligation to provide knights for war conflicted with the clergy's duty not to take life. This problem was solved by granting lands to lay knights; but the Church resisted vigorously attempts by the king or lay lords to claim the right to name the archbishop or bishop who would be the holder of the fief. Some of the greatest disputes between the Church and the lay lords were caused by the resistance of the Church, not to the need to provide knights but to the interference of laymen in their appointments.

A complicated ceremonial was created over the centuries to create a mystique in the feudal relationship. When receiving his lands from his lord in the ceremony of homage and fealty, the kneeling vassal placed his hands between his lord's and swore that he would be his man ("homage") and would be true to him against all others ("fealty"). The process of becoming a knight was romanticized. After years of serving as a squire to a knight, a young man was permitted at the age of twenty or twenty-one to be dubbed a knight. He spent the night in prayer in the church, took confirmation and communion, and finally before the other knights was presented with his sword by his lord. High moral standards were expected of the knight, as can be seen in many fine medieval poems. The *Song of Roland* of the eleventh century described Charlemagne's campaign against the Arabs in Spain. According to Roland, "For his lord man should suffer great hardships, should endure extremes of heat and cold, should lose his blood and his flesh. Strike with thy lance! And I will strike with Durendal, my good sword which the king gave me. If I die, may he who has it be able to say that it belonged to a noble vassal."[4]

The reality of knighthood was more brutal than Roland's picture. A battlefield in which combatants attacked each other with lance, spear, sword, dagger, and mace was a gory spectacle. On their own estates, many knights engaged in ruthless exploitation of their serfs and, where possible, plunder of their neighbors. Some noble knights were little better than bandits.

The Medieval Manor

The lords and vassals and to a large extent the Church were dependent for their food and many of their other necessities on the peasantry. A fifteenth-century poem explained the function of the three classes of medieval society:

> The work of the priest is to pray to God,
> And of the knight to do justice.
> The farm worker finds bread for them.
> One toils in the fields, one prays, and one defends.
> In the fields, in the town, in the church,
> These three help each other
> Through their skills, in a nicely regulated scheme.[5]

The word *mansus* or manor, meaning a village organized as a unit of production, was first used in the seventh century. The institution may have been derived from the *coloni* system of the late Roman empire, in which unfree tenants worked the lands of a great landowner or *dominus*. Or the manor may stem from the period when free Germanic tribes handed over their lands to a strongman in return for protection. Since in a medieval manor peasants had status varying from slave to free, with many gradations of unfree in between, the institution was probably a very long-term development lasting a number of centuries in which several preexisting systems were combined. Nevertheless, the majority of the peasants on a manor were serfs. They were tied to the land,

[4] C. Stephenson, *Medieval Feudalism* (Ithaca, N.Y.: Cornell University Press, 1942), p. 22.
[5] Cited in Joan Evans, *Life in Medieval France* (London: Oxford University Press, 1925), p. 35. Author's translation.

and could be passed to new owners with the land. But they possessed certain legal rights, including the right not to be dispossessed from their own holding and not to be compelled to render greater services to their lord than called for by contract or custom.

The lord lived in the best house in the village, the manor house, near which was the church and the parsonage. The houses of the villagers, which were often little better than mud-floored huts, clustered nearby, although in some parts of Europe they were scattered among the fields. Woodlands for timber, meadows for grazing, vineyards for grapes were held and worked in common. Most of the land was plowed. At first, this land was divided into two fields, in which one was cultivated and the other left fallow to avoid overcropping. Later, in the north of Europe, the land was divided into three "open fields," with one prepared for spring planting, one for autumn planting, and one left fallow. These open fields were divided into one-acre or half-acre strips. The lord took one-third to one-half of them, and the peasants held several strips in each of the fields. In theory, in this way each peasant obtained a share of both the good and the poor land. The land was plowed in common, using teams of oxen that were communal property. Crops to be planted and the date of harvest were decided by communal discussion. The fields were harvested in common, and the harvest divided according to the amount of land a peasant held. The peasant was required to work three days a week on the lord's land, and at time of harvest was often expected to bring in the lord's harvest first. He was expected to do extra tasks such as maintenance of the roads, and he was required to pay the lord a specified share of his own produce. He even had to pay to grind his grain in the lord's mill, bake his bread in the lord's oven, and squeeze his grapes in the lord's press.

Daily Life on the Manor

The peasant's life was hard. The peasant family lived in a one-room hut, usually with a floor of beaten mud. The only window was a hole in the wall. Beds consisted of a pile of straw, often crawling with vermin, although slightly wealthier peasants might have rough wooden beds. Parents would often live with their married children, and would help in looking after the grandchildren while their parents were away in the fields. Food consisted of vegetables and dark bread, with an occasional piece of meat; and, since water was often polluted, the peasants would drink beer or wine that they made themselves. Few could afford candles, and so they went to bed at dark and rose at dawn.

The wife would share all the tasks in the fields with her husband, except for the heaviest plowing. She was usually responsible for the sheep-shearing. But she also had to do most of the household tasks. She cooked the food and made clothes of rough woollen cloth or of skins. She was frequently pregnant, aged rapidly, and usually died before her husband. At least until the eleventh century, research shows, there were always fewer women alive than men. On one French estate in the ninth century, more female children than male were born, but there were still 104 men to 100 women. On other estates, the imbalance was as high as 132 men to 100 women. If a peasant woman wanted to marry a man outside the manor, either her prospective husband or her own family had to pay a fine to the lord. If she was widowed, she had to get the lord's permission to remarry, usually by proving that her new husband would be able to provide the labor services owing on the land she had inherited from her husband. There are many recorded instances of a lord forcing peasants on his manor to marry, to ensure that able-bodied peasants would be available for the needed labor force. But women, even female serfs, could inherit land in their own right; and, like noblewomen who had inherited a fief, they found that they had a pick of willing suitors or the opportunity to remain single. It was no idyllic condition to be a widow, however, as Geoffrey Chaucer showed in the *Nun's Priest Tale.* The old widow with two young children, he wrote, "ate many a slender meal," and never needed a piquant sauce to stir her appetite. "No dainty morsel passed down her throat. Her diet was as simple as her clothes. Nor had over-eating ever made her sick." And in the deeply compassionate medieval poem, *Pierce the Ploughman's Crede,* there is a portrait of a family plowing in the winter fields behind a team of heifers so thin that every rib was visible:

> His wife went barefoot on the ice so that the blood flowed.
> And at the end of the row lay a little crumb-bowl,
> And therein a little child covered with rags.
> And two two-year olds were on the other side,
> And they all sang one song that was pitiful to hear:
> They all cried the same cry—a miserable note.
> The poor man sighed sorely, and said,
>   "Children, be still."[6]

Yet there were bright spots to the year. The end of harvesting was celebrated with drinking and dancing; and with their share of the harvest the peasants might journey to a nearby town to buy a few goods for their home. On May Day the young men and women spent the night in the fields to welcome in May, and marriages frequently followed. Christmas was twelve days of rejoicing. Families were united in the fields, and times such as fruitpicking were joyful occasions. Troupes of visiting players would sometimes come to the church to present a morality play. Games included a primitive form of football, wrestling, cockfighting, and several kinds of gambling.

Church services on a Sunday were also a form of consolation, although researchers are still uncertain at what point it became normal for villagers to attend church regularly. Those living near the great cathedrals and abbeys, many of which were built in small country towns, had before them a presen-

---

[6] Cited in H. S. Bennett, *Life on the English Manor: A Study of Peasant Conditions, 1150–1400,* 1967, Cambridge University Press, p. 186.

tation of the Biblical message that had been deliberately planned to appeal to, and to be understood by, an illiterate population. Abbot Suger of Saint Denis, near Paris, who built the first Gothic cathedral, relates that enthusiasm for his project was so great that, whenever stone for the columns was cut in a nearby quarry, "both our people and the pious neighbors, nobles and common folk alike, would tie their arms, chests, and shoulders to the ropes, and acting as draft animals, drew the columns up." The Church was undoubtedly a potent intellectual and spiritual force in the peasant's life, even though pagan traditions lingered on in the beliefs in magical rings in the forest and sometimes in witchcraft.

The Medieval Agricultural Revolution

It has been shown recently by historians that conditions of life in Europe were greatly improved by a revolution in agricultural techniques that occurred between the sixth and ninth centuries, and which had been widely spread throughout Europe by the thirteenth century.

The most important change was the substitution of a heavy, wheeled plow for the scratch plow. The scratch plow consisted of a triangular or conical

Plowing. The Month of March This late-medieval prayer book illustrates one of the main technological innovations of the Middle Ages—a wheeled plow, with coulter and mouldboard. The collar, which was developed for horses, is being used on oxen. (Scala/Art Resource.)

plowshare, which scratched a narrow furrow on light soil such as those of the chalky uplands favored by the inhabitants of the Roman Empire and by the Celts. Population pressure after the Germanic invasions made it necessary to open up heavy, clay soil of the plains, and this was done by inventing a new plow, with a knife called a coulter, which cut vertically into the soil, a plowshare that cut horizontally at the roots of the grass, and a moldboard that turned the soil over. Two heavy wheels enabled the peasants to take the plow from field to field and to adjust the height of the cutting blades. To pull this heavy plow required a team of eight oxen, which forced the peasants to work cooperatively. The new plowing technique more than doubled the yield from grain planted. Whereas one measure of grain sown had previously given a yield of 2.5 measures (one of which had to be kept for future seeding), the new technique gave a yield of 4 measures.

The oxen were in many places replaced by the horse after the invention of a new horse collar that enables it to pull loads four or five times heavier than the previous collar, which had restricted the horse's breathing. Iron shoes were nailed to the horse's brittle hoofs. Two to four horses were harnessed in line, thereby enabling them to share the load they were pulling. Since the horse can work longer hours and pull heavier weights than the ox, and moreover can be used for transportation as well, it was soon regarded as worth twice the value of an ox.

The third innovation was the substitution of the three-field for the two-field system in much of northern Europe. By keeping only one of the three fields fallow, the amount of land under cultivation at any one time was increased. The time of plowing was spread by plowing one field in the spring and planting it with oats, barley, or vegetables, and by plowing the other in the fall and planting it with oats or winter wheat. Harvesting at different times of year also reduced the danger of total crop loss.

Finally, new sources of vegetable protein were planted, especially peas and beans, which were added to the more abundant sources of protein in grains, milk, cheese, and eggs. The change of diet as well as the greater abundance of foodstuffs have led some historians to attribute to this agricultural revolution both the increase in population and the exuberance of spirit that became evident in Europe after 1000.

SUGGESTED READINGS

A Rapid Overview

Robert S. Lopez, *The Birth of Europe* (1966), and R. W. Southern, *The Making of the Middle Ages* (1953), are fresh and lively. Christopher Brooke, *Europe in the Central Middle Ages, 962–1154* (1964), is more stolid and has good discussions of economic life and society.

Muhammad and the Impact of Islam

One of the best biographies of Muhammad is W. Montgomery Watt, *Muhammad: Prophet and Statesman* (1974). For an introduction to the history of the Arabs, see the brief study of Bernard Lewis, *The Arabs in History* (1960), or the very detailed, authoritative survey of Philip K. Hitti, *History of the Arabs from the Earliest Times to the Present* (1964). The early expansion is described in Francesco Gabrieli's nicely illustrated *Muhammad and the Conquests of Islam* (1968). W. Montgomery Watt shows Europe's great debt to the Muslims in *The Influence of Islam on Medieval Europe* (1972), and he throws light on the glories of Muslim civilization in Spain in *A History of Islamic Spain* (1965).

Charlemagne and the Carolingian Empire

Peter Munz analyzes the different sectors of Carolingian society, such as the army and the bureaucracy, in *Life in the Age of Charlemagne* (1969). The new capital of Aachen is seen in all its roughness in Richard E. Sullivan, *Aix-la-Chapelle in the Age of Charlemagne* (1963), and Pierre Riché, *Daily Life in the World of Charlemagne* (1978). The struggle to revive learning after the invasions is described in Donald Bullough, *The Age of Charlemagne* (1966). Details of Carolingian political history are elaborated in Rosamond McKitterick, *The Frankish Kingdoms Under the Carolingians, 751–987* (1983). On Carolingian rule in France, see Edward Jones, *The Origins of France: From Clovis to the Capetians, 500–1000* (1982).

The New Invaders

Carlyle A. Macartney, *The Magyars in the Ninth Century* (1930, 1968) is a reliable account of the Magyar campaigns and their settlement in Hungary. More up-to-date accounts of the Viking achievement, both destructive and constructive, are J. Bronsted, *The Vikings* (1963), and Peter G. Foote and David M. Wilson, *The Viking Achievement: A Survey of the Society and Culture of Early Medieval Scandinavia* (1970). On the Norman civilization in Normandy, England, and southern Italy, see David C. Douglas, *The Norman Achievement, 1050–1100* (1969), and for an even broader survey, P. H. Sawyer, *Kings and Vikings: Scandinavia and Europe A.D. 700–1000* (1982).

Feudalism and Manorialism

David Herlihy, ed., *The History of Feudalism* (1971), is a fine collection of sources. Straightforward introductions are given in John Critchley, *Feudalism* (1978), and Carl Stephenson, *Feudalism* (1962). Two superb works on the origins of manorialism as a self-sustaining economic system are M. M. Postan, ed., *The Cambridge Economic History of Europe*, vol. 1, *The Agrarian Life of the Middle Ages* (1966), and Georges Duby, *Rural Economy and Country Life in the Medieval West* (1968). Two older studies of the medieval peasant's life are a fine essay in Eileen Power, *Medieval People* (1951), and H. S. Bennett, *Life on an English Manor: A Study of Peasant Conditions, 1150–1400* (1967). Eileen Power discusses the life of the medieval woman in town and country in her classic essay, *Medieval Women* (1975). Susan Mosher Stuard has edited a collection of scholarly articles, *Women in Medieval Society* (1976).

The technology of the medieval agriculture revolution is explained in Lynn White, Jr., *Medieval Technology and Social Change* (1962), and in Jean Gimpel, *The Medieval Machine: The Industrial Revolution of the Middle Ages* (1976).

Several excellent new studies provide well-documented information on the position of women in the upper levels of early medieval society. Suzanne Fonay Wemple, *Women in Frankish Society: Marriage and the Cloister, 500 to 900* (1981), draws on Germanic law codes. Derek Baker, ed., *Medieval Women* (1978), is particularly useful on Anglo-Saxon England. Pauline Stafford discusses the courts of France, England, and Germany in *Queen, Concubines, and Dowagers: The King's Wife in the Early Middle Ages* (1983).

6

The High Middle Ages, 1000–1300

By the end of the tenth century, the medieval Christian society and civilization of the West had been formed. But it was not yet able to rouse the admiration of longer-established civilizations. The ambassador of the German emperor was told by the Byzantine emperor in Constantinople that even in warfare, German soldiers were of little value. "Your master's soldiers cannot ride, and they do not know how to fight on foot. The size of their shields, the weight of their [breastplates], the length of their swords, and heaviness of their helmets, does not allow them to fight either way. . . . Their gluttony also prevents them. Their God is their belly, their courage but wind, their bravery drunkenness."[1] By the thirteenth century, however, the cities of Europe had displaced Constantinople as the masters of world commerce and manufacturing. In the universities, European scholars were developing a learning as subtle as the classical and Muslim culture that earlier students had traveled to Cordoba to find. Great cathedrals, whose beauty in many cases rivaled that of the Parthenon and Hagia Sophia, reached skyward in a hundred towns. And a Latin emperor installed by crusading European troops—their gluttony barely assuaged by their sack of Constantinople in 1204—was ruling over the Byzantine Empire itself.

The eleventh to the thirteenth centuries mark the apogee of medieval civilization, and it is easy to be awed by its achievements—the abbey of Mont St. Michel rising from the pounding waves of the northern French coast; the intri-

[1] *The Works of Liudprand of Cremona,* translated by F.A. Wright (London: George Routledge, 1930), pp. 241–42.

Mont Saint Michel, France *This Benedictine monastery was founded in 708, on land accessible only at low tide. The monastery was fortified and was never captured in war. (Art Resource.)*

cacy of the stained-glass windows of Chartres cathedral, the secret of which has been lost for half a millenium; the world vision of Dante's poem the *Divine Comedy*; the audacity of the Grand Canal in Venice, the finest of all city streets. But we must remember that this glory had a very mundane foundation. We shall consider first the great economic revival, which made many other achievements possible. Second, we shall see the reestablishment of orderly government and the emergence of new nations under the rule of feudal kings. Third, we shall turn again to the Catholic Church, to examine its profound influence on medieval society and culture and, with less beneficial results, its conflict for supremacy over the feudal monarchies and in particular over the Holy Roman Emperor. With these basic influences established, we can turn to the achievements of a civilization whose creation in the states formed by Europe's invaders could hardly have been foretold in the chaotic days before 1000, when survival rather than civilization was a person's one hope.

THE MEDIEVAL ECONOMIC REVIVAL

The economic revival of Europe was made possible by the agricultural revolution of the seventh to tenth centuries, which, as we saw in the last chapter, had greatly increased the productivity of the land and of its workers. Other factors aided the increase in agricultural production after 1000. There was a marked improvement in the climate for several centuries. Although it has not been explained, the prevalence of plague and other infectious diseases lessened. With the establishment of order in the feudal kingdoms, the peasants were less likely to be killed or to die of starvation than they had been in the pillaging days of the invasions. The growth of population is well documented for England. At the time of the Domesday Book, a survey of the land and its inhabitants drawn up by the Norman conquerors in 1086, the population was 1 million. Three centuries later, it had increased to almost 4 million. Even more spectacular growth occurred in favored areas such as the Rhine Valley, where the population increased ten times in size. More agricultural land was necessary. It was found in a variety of ways. Dikes were constructed in low-lying areas such as the Netherlands to rescue land from the sea or from the flooding of rivers. The lower slopes of mountains were cleared for farming. New villages were created in the middle of the forests, and space for fields hacked out around them, frequently as a planned, well-capitalized move by forward-looking landowners. Vast drainage projects were undertaken, as in the Fens of eastern England. Scrubland was used for the pasturing of cows and sheep. Not only, however, was there a more extensive use of the lands already within the boundaries of the feudal states. New lands were conquered. The crusading Catholics in Spain won back the heart of the Iberian peninsula from the Muslims; and the Germans drove ever further eastward through the sparsely settled lands of the Slavs.

Rural society changed its characteristics during this expansion. The peasants who came to the new villages were attracted there only by the removal of burdens serfs carried elsewhere. Special laws in these villages or towns made it possible for serfs to flee from lords who were too oppressive. One consequence of the increased options available to peasants was that the burdens of serfdom were reduced somewhat even in those areas long settled. Moreover, a form of capitalism entered the countryside. Capital was necessary to open up new villages, to build houses, and to provide seed and animals. The production of a surplus made it possible for the farming population to sell its goods for money, which they could then spend with traveling merchants or in nearby towns for manufactured goods. In short, in the High Middle Ages, a money economy was formed at the village level, a fact that has led historians to assert that the old view that a competitive capitalist economy was created only during the Renaissance in the fifteenth century is untrue. In fact, they assert, the capitalist economy grew slowly throughout the Middle Ages, and extended down to the village level.

The existence of an agricultural surplus first encouraged the revival of short-distance trade, primarily the exchange of the products of the countryside for those of the town. The revival of a merchant class was thus not due to reknotting the ties between Europe and the other continents, which had been interrupted by the Muslim invasions, but rather to the need for middlemen to carry out the bulk trade in foodstuffs, textiles, and timber. Long-distance trade, however, had never entirely ceased, even during the invasions. Wealthy lords and the Church had continued to desire silks, jewels, and spices from the East. And Italian towns such as Venice, Bari, and Amalfi had continued to supply them on a small scale. But in the eleventh century long-distance commerce increased rapidly. The first long-distance merchants consisted of groups such as the Jews, who had never been fully part of feudal society. But others soon came from different sections of society—younger sons of the nobility and especially serfs seeking refuge in those towns where the laws or the civic charter stipulated that a year's residence freed a person from serfdom. "City air makes a person free" was eventually the accepted rule.

Seaports and old towns in strategic locations, such as Florence or Cologne, were among the first to revive. But the traveling merchants soon began to congregate at the points most suitable for trade, such as fords and bridges or at the intersection of major highways, and especially within or just outside the walls of feudal castles or monasteries. Most European cities expanded in this way in a kind of haphazard, unplanned growth. However, kings or great lords with ample resources decided to invest in the foundation of entirely new cities. As the names Newton, Ville Neuve, or Neustadt scattered throughout Europe show, the process transformed the urban map of Europe.

The two most important clusters of cities grew up in north-central Italy and in Belgium. Here the cities, largely free of the controls of feudal kings or lords, combined three economic functions—commerce, manufacturing, and banking. Venice was the driving force in the Italian cities. The city had been created as a refuge in the fifth century from the Gothic invasions, since the small islands on the shallow lagoon at the north end of the Adriatic Sea were easily defensible. The Byzantine authorities in Italy had withdrawn there in 751 after the Lombards had captured their capital city of Ravenna, thereby making Venice the principal intermediary between Constantinople and Europe. At first turning their backs to the land, the Venetians had concentrated on building a superb merchant marine and a fighting navy with which they had taken possession of a line of coastal harbors and islands stretching down the whole length of the Adriatic Sea. Sites for construction had been created by driving thousands of piles into the mud of the islands. Canals had been dug. The great central square of Venice, Saint Mark's, had already been laid out by the tenth century; and the Venetians were rich enough a century later to build a magnificent cathedral modeled upon Justinian's Church of the Holy Apostles in Constantinople. The next two centuries were of extraordinary economic progress. Venice sold salt, which it made in its lagoon. It created large-scale industry for the manufacture of glass, cloth, and armor. It built its own ships in the Venetian Arsenal. And it opened the principal trade route across Europe, linking Venice across the Brenner Pass with Austria and South Germany and thence, down the Rhine, with the Belgian cities. Their empire also expanded. They gained trading privileges in the states established in the Holy Land by the Crusaders at the end of the eleventh century, and a stronghold of their own in Jaffa. In the thirteenth century, they had captured several Greek islands, including Crete, and even administered directly a whole section of Constantinople. This wealth poured into the beautification of Venice, filling it with churches, merchants' homes, libraries, monasteries, and public buildings such as the lovely Doge's Palace overlooking the lagoon.

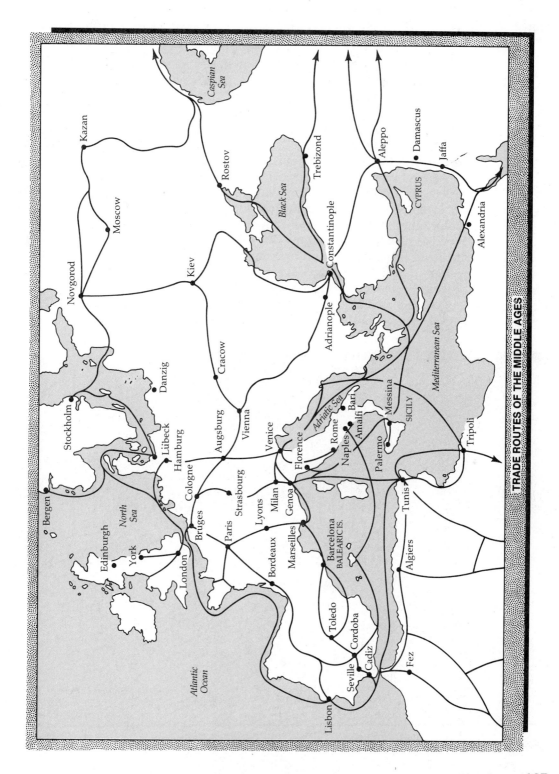

TRADE ROUTES OF THE MIDDLE AGES

167

Other coastal cities fought their way to a share of the Mediterranean trade, especially Genoa and Pisa, which directly challenged the Venetian monopoly; and trade with the coastal cities encouraged the growth of cities inland. Pavia concentrated on the sale of spices and silk. Piacenza supplied Venice with wine and cereals. Milan turned to the large-scale manufacturing of armor and weapons. But of all the inland cities, it was Florence that advanced most rapidly. Florence was the center of a flourishing agricultural region that produced huge surpluses of wheat, olives, and wine. But it advanced most rapidly as a result of its textile industry. The Florentines became superb craftspeople, whose taste and ingenuity produced distinctive cloths that were sought after throughout Europe. They also had a fine talent for business. Buying directly, they concluded favorable purchase agreements with the producers of the premium wool of Spain and England. They set up their own trading offices in foreign countries, in order to sell their products directly, and even ran inns and posthorse stations for their merchants along the major trading routes.

As their prosperity grew, they turned also to banking. Although the medieval Church regarded money as "barren" and banned charging of interest on

Palazzo della Signoria, Florence *The fortified palace was begun in 1299 as residence for the city government. Statues commissioned by the city, including Michelangelo's* David, *were placed in the square below. (Alinari/Art Resource.)*

loans as "usury," its ban was evaded; and, by the late Middle Ages only excessively high interest was regarded as usury. The Florentine merchants made loans at advantageous rates, undertook foreign currency exchange, and soon branched out into tax collection for the papacy and into financial advising and administration for foreign governments. The great buildings of medieval Florence—the Palazzo della Signoria of the city government, the Palazzo del Podestà for the city magistrate, and the Gothic cathedral, were paid for by the city's merchant class, whose guilds controlled the government.

The city of Bruges in Belgium acted as a counterpart, and in fact as the trading partner, of Venice in northern Europe. Well located for access to the many rivers that provided the principal trading routes of northern Europe, Bruges was the main trade center for the exchange of the goods of northern Europe for the eastern goods supplied by the Italian merchants. Even more profitable, however, was the woolen manufacture in Bruges and all the other cities of the surrounding region of Flanders. Each of the cities had its own specialty—Ghent its scarlet cloth, Bruges its finely woven saie, Arras its lightly woven rasch. As in Florence, the wool merchants dominated the social structure of the Flemish towns, and controlled the government through their guilds. They were soon able to win independence from their local lords, and thus, like the Italian cities, they became virtual city-states.

The stimulus of Flanders was felt throughout northern Europe. In England, for example, the main activity of London merchants was the sale of English wool, which went primarily to Flanders and, to a lesser degree, to Italy. In a wider sense, however, the existence of a neatly meshing system of trade routes and markets encouraged the economic development of all areas of Europe. The Scandinavian countries and Russia exported their timber, pitch, and furs. Bordeaux became the port for the shipping of the wines of southwestern France. Toledo shipped its superb steel swordblades throughout the world.

The effect of this economic revival was enormous. Without it, the feudal monarchies could never have established the powerful states within which the modern European nations were formed. The Church could not have drawn a surplus with which it could support increasing numbers of clergy, who ministered as priests, withdrew to the monasteries, or studied and taught in the universities. The great architectural achievements, both religious and secular, could not have been financed. And the great cities, which transformed the self-sufficient, fragmented rural society of the tenth century, could never have developed. Economic prosperity changed the way of life and thought of peasant, town dweller, feudal lord, and cleric.

THE FEUDAL MONARCHIES

In the high Middle Ages, the power of three great feudal monarchies—Germany, England, and France—overshadowed that of all the others.

The Saxon Emperors in Germany

By the end of the ninth century, the German kingdom had broken up into several feudal dukedoms, of which the most powerful was Saxony. The Saxon duke known as Henry the Fowler was named king of Germany by the other dukes in 919. He immediately surprised them by replacing them with his own appointees. With all the German states under his control, he united their armies to begin a great push eastward to colonize new lands beyond the Elbe river and to Christianize the heathen Slavs.

His son Otto I (the Great; reigned 936–973), although an efficient administrator and an ambitious general, was distracted from the problems of northern Europe by the desire to possess the riches of Italy. In 962, he marched on Rome, where the pope proclaimed him Emperor of the Romans, a title that no ruler had thought worth claiming since 924 because of the chaos prevalent in the Middle Kingdom. He married his son, Otto II, to Theophanu, the daughter of the Byzantine emperor, who, as empress and later as regent for her son Otto III, further encouraged the emperors to concentrate on their southern possessions. As a result, by the end of the reign of Otto III, the feudal lords of Germany had been able to regain many of their privileges.

Nevertheless, the Saxon emperors had achieved a great deal. They had stabilized the eastern borders of Germany by creating an effective defense along the Elbe and upper Danube valleys. They had encouraged a great cultural efflorescence in Germany. In the monasteries patronized by them, especially in Saxony and Bugundy, fine works of history had been composed. Beautiful manuscripts had been illuminated in the style of Byzantium. Massive but harmonious churches in the Romanesque style had been built in towns such as Magdeburg and Hildesheim. But there were great weaknesses. The empire was simply too big for one person to rule, as the northern and southern parts were separated by the Alps. It was constantly under attack from the outside by Byzantines, Muslims, Normans, and Slavs. Within, the tendency toward feudal fragmentation was developing rapidly. Perhaps the greatest mistake of all, however, had been the attempt to subordinate the popes to the emperor, usually by picking them and deposing them at will. The papacy was determined to reverse that relationship. In 1075, the Church mounted its counterattack.

Henry IV and the Investiture Contest

Henry IV (reigned 1056–1106), the third emperor of the Salian dynasty, was only six years old when he came to the throne, and during his minority all the forces in Germany opposed to a strong royal power—the cities, the feudal lords, and many of the bishops—increased their strength. Nevertheless, his natural authoritarianism and even truculence led him to behave arbitrarily, not least in his determination to pick bishops who were compliant with his wishes. He had, however, as his opponent Gregory VII (1073–1085), one of the strongest-minded popes of the Middle Ages, who was determined not only to end imperial control over the church but to assert the church's superiority over the empire.

When Henry IV appointed a bishop against the wishes of the pope, Gregory issued in 1075 a decree that forbade future lay investiture, that is, the "investing" or bestowing of authority of his office in the church upon a clergyman by the lay ruler, a practice that in Germany in particular had come to mean the choice of a bishop or abbot by the lay ruler who was granting him his lands. And he followed up this decree a month later with a special papal document, entitled *Dictatus Papae*, in which he made the most explicit and far-reaching statement on papal power hitherto issued. "It is lawful," he declared, "[for the pope] to depose emperors. . . He can absolve from their fealty the subjects of wicked rulers."

Both pope and emperor proved themselves masters of invective. Henry ordered the pope to give up his office, in a letter that began: "Henry, king, not by usurpation, but by pious ordination of god, to Hildebrand now not pope but false monk." Gregory replied by excommunicating Henry, and invited the princes of Germany to appoint another king. Henry crossed the Alps in the dead of winter to the pope's palace at Canossa, where, dressed in the garments of a penitent, he waited barefoot in the snow for three nights for papal absolution. His action, however painful to both his body and his pride, was subtle, because the pope could not refuse him absolution without impairing his own moral prestige. Once absolved, however, Henry returned to Germany to break the princes' revolt, and in 1084 he returned with a large army to capture Rome. In place of Gregory he installed a pope of his own choosing; and, although impelled to retreat to Germany by a Norman army, he left Gregory as a semi-prisoner of his Norman allies. The conflict was finally solved by the Concordat of Worms in 1122, after which bishops were to receive their rings and staffs symbolizing spiritual authority from the pope, but had to do homage for their lands to the emperor. In short, although the pope could appoint the bishops, the emperor could refuse to accept a pope's appointment by refusing to grant the lands.

The Hohenstaufen Dynasty

The temporary accommodation with the pope did not solve the problems of the German rulers. Frederick Barbarossa (Redbeard; reigned 1152–1190), the greatest warrior king of the Hohenstaufen dynasty, saw quite clearly that he had three principal enemies—the princes of Germany, the towns of Italy, and the pope. At first, he tried to work with the pope, and was crowned emperor by him in 1155. He was less successful, however, in his efforts to subjugate the rich cities of northern Italy. He besieged Milan for three years and ordered it destroyed, but merely stimulated an alliance among the Italian cities, which, at the battle of Legnano in 1156, inflicted a crushing defeat on his German cavalry. He eventually reached a compromise settlement with them, allowing them some of the rights they had demanded. He finally solved the problem of the Norman kingdom of the south, which had constantly attacked him, by marrying his son Henry VI to the heiress of the kingdom.

Henry VI's death in 1197 at the age of twenty-three gave the papacy the opportunity to intervene in the disputes among rival German princes over who should be recognized as emperor. The powerful Pope Innocent III (1198–1216) had made the provocative claim that, just as the moon received its light from the sun, so the emperor received his brilliance—that is, his crown—from the pope. He first declared the anti-Hohenstaufen candidate to be emperor. Later, however, he decided that a Hohenstaufen, Henry VI's sixteen-year old son Frederick, would be more pliable; and he was crowned emperor as Frederick II (reigned 1215–1250) in the Palatine Chapel at Aachen. Unknown to Innocent, who died a year later believing that he had finally made the Hohenstaufen dynasty subservient, the accession of Frederick II began the final phase of the confrontation between pope and emperor.

Frederick had little liking for Germany. He wanted only to win the allegiance of the princes and bishops by concessions. His personal interest was in Italy, and especially in his island of Sicily. He himself spoke Italian, Greek, Latin, and French, and he believed in toleration among religions and nationalities. However, his determination to control both Lombardy in the north of Italy and the Italian territories to the south of the Papal States won him the enmity of the papacy, which determined to break the Hohenstaufen dynasty once and for all. The popes supported his rivals in both Germany and Sicily. He was himself excommunicated on four separate occasions. After his death in 1250, the pope handed Sicily to the brother of the French king, who executed Frederick's grandson, the last Hohenstaufen, in the main square of Naples.

During these centuries of disruption, both Germany and Italy broke into many political fragments, and were unable to recover unity until the nineteenth century. The many small states into which the Hohenstaufen empire had broken were to be economically and culturally vigorous. They gave birth to both the Renaissance and the Reformation, and were responsible for much of Baroque art and architecture. Nevertheless, Germany and Italy were not responsible for the greatest intellectual achievements of the Middle Ages. The triumphs of medieval culture were to be the creation of the feudal monarchies that did succeed in imposing a centralized unity—England and France.

Feudal Monarchy in England

Although England had been part of the Roman Empire for 400 years, the results of the occupation were superficial, and the country was easily conquered by the Germanic tribes of Angles, Saxons, and Jutes. These vigorous warriors drove the indigenous Celts into the far western regions of the islands, and undertook with great success the taming of the forests that stretched over central and southern England. After the initial invasions, the Anglo-Saxons governed England well, leaving behind several institutions of lasting importance. Local government through shires was administered jointly by local lords, churchmen, and representatives of the king called shire-reeves or "sheriffs"; the king's law was imposed in local courts; and the Church and great lords were consulted in a central council known as the *witan*. There was even a form of military conscription into a militia called the *fyrd*.

Across the Channel, however, in the Duchy of Normandy, descendants of the Vikings had founded the most efficient feudal state in Europe. In 1066, its duke, William, massed an invasion fleet and an army, and, landing in the south of England, slew the Anglo-Saxon ruler at the battle of Hastings. He immediately imposed efficient, though harsh, Norman rule over the Anglo-Saxons. Huge castles controlled the most strategic cities, such as Dover and London. All land was declared to be the possession of the king, and was redistributed in fiefs among the lords and knights who had invaded with him. Saxon bishops were gradually replaced by Normans, and the new bishops, such as Lanfranc in Canterbury, raised vast, imposing cathedrals in the new romanesque style of architecture, intended to subjugate the spirit of the Saxons as surely as the castles were subjugating their bodies. William also ensured that he would have the most productive system of taxation in Europe by drawing up the superbly detailed land survey known as Domesday Book, which, with its enumeration of the population and their possessions in every part of England, is one of the most precious documents of medieval economic history.

King Henry I (reigned 1100–1135) further improved the efficiency of royal government by recruiting an effective body of civil servants for his treasury, known as the Exchequer, and for his public administration, called the Chancery.

Rochester Castle, England (eleventh-twelfth centuries) The Normans built similar castles throughout England to subjugate the Anglo-Saxons after their defeat in 1066. (Art Resource.)

He also expanded his control over the legal system by sending out "traveling justices," who began the process of hammering out a uniform system of case law that became the foundation of the common law of England and eventually the basis of the law of England's colonies, including the thirteen that became the United States of America.

After a period of chaotic civil war in the middle of the twelfth century, Henry II (reigned 1154–1189), of the Plantagenet or Angevin dynasty, restored order. He further developed the English common law, particularly by using the institution of the jury. (The word "jury" derives from the fact that twelve people from the locality were sworn, or *juré*, to tell the truth on matters with which they had personal acquaintance.) The use of juries was later expanded to include testimony on the state of finances in the locality, and to accuse criminals, and in the thirteenth century the juries were given the task of deciding the guilt or innocence of persons accused of crimes. As his own courts increased their powers, Henry determined to lessen the powers of the courts of the Church, which had been the only legal tribunal within which Churchmen could be tried. His old friend Thomas à Becket, whom he had named Archbishop of Canterbury, opposed him, however. Henry, in a fit of rage, called for someone to rid him of "this pestilent clerick." When four knights did so by murdering Becket at his own altar at Canterbury, Henry claimed his words had been purely rhetorical, but, with the martyrdom and canonization of Becket, Canterbury became the principal place of pilgrimage in England, and Henry was compelled to compromise with the Church by recognizing that clerics would not be tried in the royal courts.

Henry II's successors allowed the powers of the monarchy to weaken. Richard I (reigned 1189–1199) was far more interested in crusading in the Holy Land than in governing England. His brother John (reigned 1199–1216) was opposed by both the pope and the French King Philip Augustus, one of the most subtle feudal monarchs. Philip succeeded in stripping John of most of the possessions in northern France that had been the personal inheritance of either the Norman or the Angevin dynasties. John had, moreover, won the enmity of most of the great lords of England by his financial exactions. In 1215, they compelled him to make public recognition of their feudal rights and privileges in the famous document known as Magna Carta. Most of the clauses of Magna Carta were intended to prevent the king from abusing his powers as feudal ruler. For example, the rights of widows were spelled out. They were to receive their dowries within forty days of their husband's death, and could not be compelled to remarry against their will. But several clauses of Magna Carta were, in the sixteenth and seventeenth centuries, to become the basis for the extension of the freedom of all English citizens. The principle of "no taxation without representation" was developed from the clause: "No scutage or aid, save the customary feudal ones, shall be levied except by the common consent of the realm." The right of a person to be tried by a jury of his or her equals was developed from the clause: "No freeman shall be taken, or imprisoned, or dispossessed, or outlawed, or banished, or in any way destroyed, nor will we go against him, nor send upon him, except by the legal judgment of his peers or by the law of the land."

During the next hundred years, the need of kings for greater revenue from taxes compelled them to call frequently upon not only the great lords but upon representatives of the population at large in what became England's fundamental institution of representative government, the Houses of Parliament. When, in 1265, the nobles revolted against King Henry III (reigned 1216–1272), they called a Parliament of great lords, knights of the shire, and city representatives, which was not recognized as a lawful institution by the king. In 1295, however, King Edward I (reigned 1272–1307), desperate for money to pay for campaigns against the Welsh and the Scots, called a Great Council, in which great lords, knights of the shire, and city representatives were again included. For that reason, the assembly is sometimes called the Mother of Parliaments. Only seven years later, the French followed the English example by calling an Estates General, which was divided into three houses—a First Estate of the clergy, a Second Estate of the nobility, and a Third Estate of commoners. Once the precedent was set of asking a national assembly of some kind for money, kings were compelled to use this device frequently. During the fourteenth and fifteenth centuries in England, the English Parliament was divided into two houses, a House of Lords in which the clergy and the great lords sat, and a House of Commons, in which elected representatives of the knights of the shire and of the burghers, or "city people," sat. Thus, although the powers of the king were restricted institutionally, the country was not fragmented as in Germany or Italy. The rise of an institution like Parliament enabled the English to restrict the power of the monarchy and to take a share in their own government without giving up the national unity that had been created by the feudal monarchy.

The Capetian Dynasty in France

France was the kingdom in which in the twelfth and thirteenth centuries medieval civilization was to reach its height. Yet in the ninth century there seemed little promise of future greatness. The kingdom of the West Franks, created from the western third of Charlemagne's empire at the Treaty of Verdun in 843, had broken up into a number of warring feudal principalities. The most formidable was the Duchy of Normandy, which had been granted to Vikings by the king of France in 911. In the west was the Duchy of Brittany, a land of mists and legends alien to the rest of France in language and culture since its settlement by Celtic refugees from Britain in the fifth century A.D. The Bretons were not to be compelled to become part of the possessions of the king of France until 1532. The rich lands of the valley of the river Loire were broken into a number of small principalities, of which the most important was the County of Anjou. As a result of complex intermarriages among feudal families, when

Henry II became king of England in 1154, he was already Duke of Normandy and Count of Anjou and, moreover, had inherited as a dowry brought by his wife Eleanor the vast province of Aquitaine in the southwest of France.

The counts of Paris who were to unify France were among the weakest of the feudal princes. Perhaps for that very reason, when the feudal lords decided in 987 to elect their king, they picked Hugh Capet, the Count of Paris, to replace the Carolingian dynasty. The Capetian rulers proved, however, almost without exception insidiously clever in the consolidation of their power. They established the principle of hereditary succession for their family by having each ruler ensure that his son was crowned before his father's death. They allied with the Church and the growing towns in their own domain of the Ile de France, the rich lands surrounding Paris, against any recalcitrant feudal lords. And, like the English kings, they created both an efficient system of royal courts and a well-trained bureaucracy in Paris. When Philip II (reigned 1180–1223) became king, the Ile de France was thus in a position to undertake military campaigns against individual feudal rulers in order to increase the territory of the royal "domain," that is, the territory in direct possession of the king of France. Philip was so successful that he became known as Philip the Conqueror, although later generations saw him as the French equivalent of the founder of the Roman Empire and called him Philip Augustus.

Philip continued the work of improving the machinery of government in Paris, which he located in his palace on an island, the Ile de la Cité, in the middle of the Seine River. His principal lords and bishops met occasionally to give him advice in a Curia Regis, or King's Council. A steady monetary income was obtained by fines on such groups as Jews and by forced loans from the towns. Philip's principal effort was, however, to seize the possessions in France of the English King John. Philip succeeded in persuading the pope to condemn John for breaking his feudal allegiance to Philip, which he owed for his fiefs in France. Strong in the moral acclamation of the Church, Philip declared war on John and invaded Normandy. By 1206, he had conquered almost all the English king's possessions in France except Aquitaine.

Philip's grandson, Louis IX (reigned 1226–1270), was to become the most admired monarch of the Middle Ages, both for his saintliness and for his political acumen. He came to the throne at the moment when the French monarchy had reached its greatest prosperity and strength. The revival of commerce throughout Europe had enriched the Parisian middle class. Profiting from the location of Paris on a navigable river that carried goods from eastern France and Germany to the Channel coast, its merchants had engaged in long-distance carrying trade. As the monarchy grew richer, the expenditures of the court on luxury goods had encouraged the growth of many new industries. Parisian craftspeople became experts in the production of robes of linen and silk, jewelry, goldware, crystal, and pottery. Banking expanded, first in the hands of Jews, then of Italians, and finally of the Parisians themselves. Thousands of workers came into the city to work in the docks, the bakeries, the workshops, and the building yards, until the city's population reached almost 150,000. Once again the Capetians profited, by allying with the guilds of the wealthier merchants, to whom they extended protection and from whom they received revenues. They were not, however, able to prevent the exploitation of the poorer workers who, by the fourteenth century, had become rebellious and posed a constant threat to the stability of the kingdom. Perhaps for this reason the Capetians maintained two palaces in Paris, the central palace on the Ile de la Cité, which was at the mercy of the Parisian population, and a highly fortified palace called the Louvre on the edge of the city, from which they could cow the city mob and in whose dungeons opponents could disappear.

Louis loved the old palace on the island, with its sweeping views of the river and its ever-changing traffic. He built there the lovely Gothic Sainte Chapelle to house the supposed Crown of Thorns, which he had bought at exorbitant expense from the Byzantine emperor. Here too he brought together legal experts to whom he entrusted the task of giving legal judgments and of formulating from previous cases a body of law that could be applied uniformly throughout his kingdom. He himself frequently gave judgment, and was so respected that cases were brought to him from all over Europe. This staff of legal experts eventually became the Parlement de Paris, the country's principal law court. At the same time, his financial experts in the palace, whose task was to audit and administer the growing royal revenues, also became institutionalized as the king's treasury. Louis was less successful as a military leader, and the Crusade that he led to Palestine in 1248 was a total failure. The loss of many of his soldiers and the sufferings he witnessed served, however, to increase in him his sense of the obligations of religion. He had learned from his mother a sense of deep piety and personal unworthiness and, as his ill health worsened through his own personal asceticism (he used to beat himself with little chains), his own devotions increased. Throughout Europe he came to be recognized as a saint, and to no one's surprise, shortly after his death the papacy proclaimed him officially a saint. It was hardly surprising, therefore, that France during the reign of Saint Louis, even more than Rome, should have been regarded as the center of Christendom.

THE CATHOLIC CHURCH IN THE HIGH MIDDLE AGES

The Cluniac Reform Movement

The Catholic Church, as we have seen, had been one of the main factors of stability in Europe during the 600 years of invasions that stretch from the Germanic invasions of the fifth century through the Viking invasions of the tenth and eleventh centuries. Grateful lay people had showered it with gifts and money and land. Peasants had commended themselves into serfdom to find safety in its service. The popes had become rulers over large parts of Italy. It was hardly surprising, therefore, that so much wealth had bred corruption. Many monasteries had abandoned the simple life of work and prayer enforced by the Rule of Saint Benedict. Some bishops were engaged in the sale of Church offices, kept concubines, and even provided offices in the Church for their children. Many Church people took more seriously their feudal duties in local administration and military service than their religious obligations. Even some popes were tainted by these habits.

The reaction against this corruption began among the feudal lords. Many nobles founded new monasteries, where the ideals of poverty and devotion could be enforced. Among these monasteries was the Abbey of Cluny in Burgundy, which was founded in 910 by the duke of Aquitaine. Cluny became the center of a great reform movement that spread from France into Belgium and Germany. Its charter forbade all outside interference in the monastery except by the pope. It enforced habits of prayer and ecclesiastical ceremony and the observance of poverty. The rule of the abbot extended not only to his own monks, but to those in the many daughter houses founded to accommodate the growing numbers of people who wished to join the Cluniac order.

Reform reached the papacy itself in the mid-eleventh century, with the appointment of a German reformer as pope. For the second half of the eleventh century, popes attacked clerical abuses such as the sale of Church offices, marriage of the clergy, and keeping of concubines, and excommunicated bishops who refused to reform. In 1059, the power of the Roman nobility and of the emperor over the election of the pope was ended by the decree that henceforth the pope should be elected by the College of Cardinals.

The most far-reaching reforms were carried out by an Italian Benedictine monk named Hildebrand, who became Pope Gregory VII (1073–1085). From 1054, as papal chaplain and later as administrator of the Papal States, Hildebrand had already begun the program of ending corruption and laxity within the church that is known as the Hildebrandine reforms; and as pope he pushed the program with even greater vigor. He severely punished simony, which was interpreted in its broadest sense to mean the sale of any spiritual service such as the performance of a sacrament or of any church office; and he sent legates throughout Europe to force compliance. He regarded clerical marriage as unlawful; from this time the marriage of priests, which had been quite common, became virtually impossible, and celibacy became the rule for all clerics. It was as head of a reformed and reforming church that Gregory VII set out to end what he regarded as the principal cause of abuse within the church, lay investiture; and it was the investiture conflict that, as we saw earlier in the chapter, eventually led to the collapse of his prestige and his expulsion from Rome.

The Crusades

The papacy regained its prestige, however, when, in 1095, Pope Urban II called the feudal nobility of Europe to engage in a Crusade for the liberation of the

Holy Land from the Seljuk Turks, a Central Asian people who had succeeded in conquering most of the Muslim lands stretching from Persia to Palestine by the end of the eleventh century. The harassment of Christian pilgrims to Jerusalem, which the Turks had conquered in 1071, provided the final excuse for the pope to demand their ouster. The response to Urban II's appeal was immediate. He had not only promised military adventure to knights weary of the increasing peace in Europe, but the prospect of great material gain and, in the case of death in battle, immediate absolution for past sins. Three large armies of feudal knights, primarily from France and Germany, met in Constantinople, and in 1096–1099 defeated the Turks in Syria and Palestine and carved out for themselves a number of feudal principalities. To maintain their rule they built vast castles throughout the Holy Land. To exploit their possessions, they offered trading privileges to the Italian trading cities, who thus found a new and easier access to the goods of Asia than that in Constantinople itself.

Muslim power soon revived, however, and later Crusades were far less successful. Although the English King Richard I, the French King Philip Augustus, and the Holy Roman Emperor Frederick Barbarossa participated in the Third Crusade (1189–1192), they captured back only a few minor towns from Saladin, the great Muslim ruler of Egypt who had conquered most of the Holy Land. Frederick Barbarossa drowned on the way to the Holy Land; and Richard was captured and held for ransom in Austria on the way back.

The Fourth Crusade (1202–1204) was diverted by the Venetians, who wanted a reward for transporting the Crusaders to the Near East, into an attack on Constantinople, which was sacked by the Crusaders in 1204. Rather than retake the Holy Land, the Crusaders then seized domains for themselves within the Byzantine Empire, and replaced the emperor in Constantinople with a Latin emperor of their own choice. Venice, with control of a line of Byzantine ports and possession of part of the city itself, gained vast profits from the enterprise. By the end of the thirteenth century, the Crusaders had been ousted from the Byzantine Empire and from the Holy Land.

The Crusades may have increased economic contact between Europe and the Near East, and expanded the desire of the West for Asian luxuries, but they gave the West few other advantages. Little was learned of Muslim culture from the Crusades. Byzantium was dangerously weakened as a bulwark against further Muslim expansion. And, after briefly enhancing the papacy's reputation during the First Crusade, the increasing venality and brutality of the later Crusades soon cast doubt upon the papacy's purity of motive in organizing them.

The Cistercian Reform Movement

In fact, by the twelfth century, the Catholic Church seemed again to be in need of reform. This time, change came from within. The reforming ardor of Cluny had declined, but a new order of monks, called the Cistercians, was founded in 1098 at Cîteaux in Burgundy. The Cistercians turned their backs on the corrupt society surrounding them, seeking out desolate areas in which they could open up new agricultural land. Seven hundred daughter houses were founded, of which the most important was Clairvaux, begun by the most influential of all Cistercian leaders, Saint Bernard (1091–1153). Bernard became the self-appointed guardian of the Church's purity. In letters he castigated even the highest clergy, including the popes, for any lapse in moral or even artistic standards. He called kings to repentance. And by his preaching he created a fervor among the thousands of poorer people who came to hear him.

Innocent III (1198–1216)

Just as the reformed Church of the eleventh century had chosen a powerful pope in Gregory VII, so the reinvigorated Church of the twelfth century found an assertive leader in Pope Innocent III. Innocent, as we saw, had proclaimed the principle of papal superiority over all lay powers. He not only intervened in the choice of Holy Roman Emperor, but also imposed his will on the rising feudal monarchies of England and France. He threw his support to Philip Augustus in the war against King John of England that led to the English loss of most of their possessions in northern France. He forced John to accept an archbishop of Canterbury by placing England under papal interdict, a decree that prevented almost all Church services from being conducted. He ordered Philip to ignore a divorce granted him by the French bishops and to take back his wife.

Innocent sought to crush heresy wherever he saw it. In France he proclaimed a Crusade against the Albigensian heresy, the belief espoused by thousands of Cathars ("pure ones") that the world was a battlefield of good and evil and that the Catholic Church was an agent of the forces of darkness. The Crusade was an excuse for terrible massacres by nobles from the north of France, which were followed by the incorporation of the region of Languedoc into the possessions of the French crown. The court of investigation that was established in 1233 to root out the remnants of the Albigensian heresy eventually became the Catholic Inquisition. Innocent also sponsored the Fourth Crusade against the Muslims in the Holy Land in 1202, which was sidetracked into the capture of Constantinople; but Innocent used the establishment of the Latin Empire there to begin a new missionary effort to persuade the adherents of the Greek Orthodox Church to become Roman Catholics.

To bring the Christian message to the cities, Innocent sanctioned the foundation of two important orders of friars, the Franciscans and the Dominicans. The founders of the two new orders, Saint Francis (1182–1226) and Saint Dominic (1170–1221), both felt that it was necessary to bring the Church back to its ideal of poverty, especially as they felt that even the Cistercians were beginning to succumb to the lure of material wealth. Francis was the son of a rich merchant in Assisi in central Italy, who had spent his early youth, somewhat like Augustine, enjoying the good things of life. After undergoing a traumatic conversion, however, he retreated to the barren, rocky slopes of the mountains behind

Assisi, where he taught to a small group of followers his doctrine of utter simplicity of life in the love of God and recognition of the brotherhood of all living creatures, whether human or animal. His followers were to go out into the world to beg alms, and hence they were known as the mendicant friars (although Francis himself called his orders the Friars Minor). He dismissed the need for learning, and forbade them to have more than the simplest personal possessions. At his death, the order had 5000 members. Fifty years later it had increased to 200,000. It also, however, began to accept gifts of land and to erect substantial houses and churches for the friars. Many Franciscans also became great scholars, thus emulating the ideal that had inspired the teaching of Saint Dominic.

Dominic, a Spanish priest, had become convinced of the need of a new order while attempting to combat the heretical beliefs of the Albigensians of southern France. Dominic found that the Albigensian heretics were highly educated and that the Catholic Church leaders sent against them needed mastery of Church doctrine. While requiring that his followers, like the Franciscans, live in poverty, Dominic also demanded stern mental training in theology.

Both the Franciscans and the Dominicans realized in the thirteenth century that they should not merely preach the doctrine of Christianity, but that they must gain positions of power where that doctrine was being made, namely, in the universities, and especially in the University of Paris.

The Medieval Universities

Education was virtually a monopoly of the Catholic Church from the early Middle Ages on. What little education the feudal nobles received was obtained from their chaplains. Monasteries and cathedrals ran schools, where future clerics could be trained. The university (a word derived from the Latin word *universitas*, and used to refer to a collective body, like a guild, of either teachers or students) was created in Italy. By the twelfth century, there was a well-known university teaching medicine at Salerno and a university teaching primarily law at Bologna. In Paris, the university was originally a guild of teachers who had broken away from the cathedral school with the sanction of the pope. They had established a formal curriculum by the beginning of the thirteenth century. All students began in the Faculty of Arts by studying for five or six years the *trivium* (grammar, logic, and rhetoric) and the *quadrivium* (arithmetic, geometry, astronomy, and music). Successful students were granted the degree of Master of Arts. The more persevering among them could then continue their studies for the doctorate in the Faculty of Medicine, the Faculty of Canon Law, or the Faculty of Theology, depending on whether they intended to become a doctor, a lawyer, or a clergyman. It was study of theology, however, that was regarded as the highest vocation, and it was the theological faculty that stimulated the intellectual debates that most excited the scholars and students of the Middle Ages.

Life for the students was hard. Many of them entered the university at the age of fourteen, and few had many financial resources behind them. They lived in the cheapest attic lodgings they could find near the filthy street called the Street of Straw, where professors rented rooms for their lectures. The first class was at 5 A.M. After a brief snack on a crust of bread for breakfast at 6 A.M., classes continued for the rest of the morning until dinner time at 11 A.M. Afternoon classes were interrupted for a short exercise period. After evening meal at 6 P.M., students were expected to study and pray. Instead, they usually took to the bars and then to the streets, where they let off steam by brawling with each other and by beating up the townspeople. They found companionship in the four "nations" into which all undergraduate students were assigned—France, Picardy, Normandy, and England. The squalor and indiscipline of their life prompted Louis IX's chaplain, Robert de Sorbon, to found a college, with dormitory and study quarters, for the theological students. His original college developed into the principal school of the university, called the Sorbonne, which still houses part of the school of arts and sciences of the University of Paris. And the example of founding colleges was followed by other benefactors in Paris. Whatever the distractions, however, the specter of the final examinations hung over the students constantly. No matter how long they studied, award of the degree that was the passport to future advancement depended on successful performance in an oral examination before a board of faculty members. For most students, preparation for these examinations was largely a matter of learning by heart, from painstakingly copied notes, authoritative texts and commentary. Nevertheless, many of them were aware that in the public debates between the most admired of the professors the doctrines of the Church were taking on new dimensions, especially with the entry of the Franciscans and Dominicans into the intellectual fray in the thirteenth century.

Scholasticism

The leading Christian theologians from the eleventh century on are known as scholastics, or "schoolmen," because they taught in or ran schools; and the theology they taught is known as scholasticism. Although the word scholastic is sometimes used broadly to refer to virtually any Christian theologian or philosopher from the early Middle Ages on, the word refers more specifically to those thinkers, beginning with Saint Anselm in the eleventh century, who attempted to use reason to throw light on questions of faith, who sought to relate the works of the classical scholars, particularly Aristotle, to the established theology of the Catholic church.

In the eleventh and twelfth centuries, two important developments infused new life into the study of theology. First, a new instrument of logic called the *quaestio*, or "question," was developed. It consisted of setting up a proposition and a counterproposition, and pitting the two against each other to establish a conclusion. The method was known as the "dialectic." Second, as a result of translations from Arabic versions of surviving Greek classics, large portions of

Aristotle's writings not previously known in the West had become available. A little later, translations were made directly from the Greek. Aristotle's multitudinous views on ethics, metaphysics, rhetoric, and logic stimulated questioning of the established doctrines, while his massive compilations encouraged some of the finest medieval thinkers to produce their own summations, or *summae*, of a particular field of knowledge.

Professors frequently debated disputed philosophical issues publicly, and students flocked to hear this rather rarefied battle of minds, especially as some of the most charismatic speakers on the university faculties took up the standard for one side or the other. The most popular professor in Paris at the beginning of the twelfth century was Peter Abelard (1079–1142), who won himself many admirers and some irreconcilable enemies by defeating his opponents in argument by brilliant twists of logic. His greatest contribution to the scholastic method was to emphasize that the search for knowledge must begin with doubt and that the tool of logic must be used to advance to faith. He compiled a book called *Sic et non* (*Yes and no*), in which he paired contradictory statements on matters of faith taken from the writings of the Church Fathers and from the Bible. Since Abelard left it to the student to work out how these statements could be reconciled, he won the enmity of Saint Bernard of Clairvaux, who eventually was able to have some of Abelard's writings condemned.

When the Franciscan and Dominican friars gained permission to teach in the University of Paris in the 1220s, they more than anyone else tried to integrate Aristotle's views with Christian doctrine. While conservative thinkers were pressing the pope to ban the study of Aristotle, his cause was taken up by the greatest of the Dominican teachers, Thomas Aquinas (1225–1274), an Italian nobleman who had entered the Benedictine monastery at Monte Cassino and had received further training in Paris under the leading Aristotelian scholar of his day, Albertus Magnus.

Aquinas wrote most of his *Summa Theologica* while teaching at the University of Paris in 1269–1272. Aquinas taught that certain beliefs had to be accepted on faith, but that the reason could be used to elucidate many other areas. The nature of the Trinity could be grasped only by faith, but the existence of God could be proved by reason. The *Summa* consists of a large number of questions, for each of which he states a number of propositions that accord with the Church's teachings. He then suggests many persuasive arguments that counter these propositions. Finally, he propounds his own conclusions, which were so compelling that they eventually came to be accepted by the Catholic Church as the most authoritative statement of its doctrines. The greatness of the book, however, was that all of the propositions form part of an integrated view of the universe in which God and His revelation are related with breath-taking logic to the fate of humanity on this earth. Aquinas's achievement did not silence argument, but stimulated even further debate within the University of Paris and the Church. About fifty years after his death, however, his ideas prevailed, and in 1323 he was canonized, although it was not until the latter part of the nineteenth century that his philosphy was made the official doctrine of the Roman Catholic Church.

Another medieval philosopher whose teachings have been of lasting interest is William of Ockham (?1290–1349). In contrast to Aquinas, however, Ockham was excommunicated for arguing the supremacy of the state over the Church and the superiority of general councils over the pope. In philosophy, he propounded the rule known as "Ockham's razor" that says "neither a thing nor a statement should be more complex than is necessary" or, put another way, "always choose the simplest explanation consistent with the facts." Using his "razor," he argued that all attempts to prove God's existence rationally are too complex to be satisfactory and that belief in God therefore must be grounded in faith, whereas faith is unnecessary for an understanding of nature, which can be explained entirely through the use of reason. This division between faith and reason had the effect of separating natural science from religion and made it theoretically possible for modern science to ignore theological dogma.

Today, Ockham is most highly regarded for his work in logic, in which he carefully distinguished between terms that referred to real things and those that referred to other terms or concepts. The language of science, for example, refers to reality, whereas the terms of logic refer to statements. There are two kinds of statements, he further argued: those that can be proven true by experience, as in science, and those that are proven true by the meaning of the terms themselves, as in logic or mathematics. "The sun rises in the east and sets in the west" is an example of the first kind of statement; "all bachelors are unmarried" is an example of the second. Ockham is considered the last great scholastic.

THE ARCHITECTURE AND ART OF THE HIGH MIDDLE AGES

The Cathedrals

The great cathedrals were in many ways the counterpart in architecture of Aquinas's achievement in philosophy. They embodied a world view that had achieved dominance during the Middle Ages.

From the tenth century on, the buildings of the Church became ever larger. A spate of gifts and land to the Church had given it the financial ability to pay for the great new buildings. The increasing ceremonial of the Church, with its splendid processions of superbly costumed clergy, required a suitable setting. The growing collections of relics of the saints had to be well displayed. And the churches too served many secular functions, whether as a theater for visiting players or as a meeting place of the townspeople for business discussions. And competition among bishops played an important role, especially in the construction of the Gothic cathedrals in the region around Paris.

Romanesque Style

The buildings were mainly variations of the cruciform plan, in which the building literally represented the cross of Christ. A long *nave* running from west to east was crossed by a shorter *transept*. The altar was placed at the east end of the building in a semicircular *apse*. Until the tenth century, the principal buildings were usually somewhat simplified versions of the architecture of the Roman or the Byzantine Empire. In the tenth and eleventh centuries, however, a new style called Romanesque (or, in Normandy and England, Norman) was perfected.

To achieve the size of building desired by the Church, walls were enormously thick, and were supported on the outside by heavy buttresses. Windows were kept small to reduce the strain on the wall. The beauty of the churches lay in the use of round arches in the bays of the nave, which created a sense of flowing movement toward the east, and in the soaring columns that separated the bays and created an upward sense of motion. Round arches were also used to roof over the wide open space of the nave. At first the roof was supported by a series of parallel arches, in what is called barrel vaulting. But in the eleventh century a more complex form of vaulting was invented by the diagonal intersection of two round arches, as in the cathedral of Durham in northern England. Frequently towers were added at the crossing of the nave and transept or on the corners of the west front; and in Germany a very distinctive form of Romanesque architecture was created by adding as many as six towers at the corners of the building.

Sculpture was widely used to decorate the heavy walls. The capitals on the columns were usually carved, either with acanthus leaves as in the Corinthian capitals of the Roman Empire or with a variety of Biblical scenes, flowers, leaves, or allegorical animals. Vast sculptural compositions were placed above the doors of the west front. Over the central door there would frequently be a presentation of Christ in Judgment, with graphic portrayals of the unworthy being dispatched by demons to the torments of hell. So imaginative did many of the sculptures become that they earned the condemnation of Saint Bernard, who held that fascination with "the unclean monkeys . . . the monstrous centaurs . . . the spotted tigers" was distracting monks from meditating on the divine law.

Gothic Style in France

Bernard's wrath was especially roused by the extravagances of Abbot Suger of Saint Denis on the outskirts of Paris. Suger, counselor to the kings of France, loved the arts of the Middle Ages, the paintings, the sculptures, the architecture, and especially the jewels; and, when he decided to rebuild his abbey in 1133–1144, he unashamedly determined to make it the most exciting building in Christendom, a demonstration of the principle that "God is Light." In doing so, he invented Gothic architecture. He did so by combining three basic architectural forms, the pointed arch, the ribbed vault, and the flying buttress. By replacing the round arches of a Romanesque nave with pointed arches, he was able to achieve far greater height without sacrificing strength. By using pointed arches intersecting diagonally in the roof, he was able to build vaults over rectangles instead of the squares that were necessary in Romanesque style, and thus to widen the nave. By using ribs of stone for the vaults of the roof, he greatly reduced the weight of the roof, since only thin masonry was used to fill the spaces between the ribs. Finally, he supported the outside of the wall by thin ribs of stone, known as flying buttresses, in place of the heavy Romanesque buttresses. Since the walls were supporting much less weight, and were themselves supported at points of stress by the flying buttresses, it was possible to make the windows far larger; and Suger filled these spaces with stained glass.

All the bishops who attended the consecration ceremonies at Saint Denis realized the glorious possibilities of this new architectural style, and almost at once a competition began among the bishops of the Ile de France to exceed Suger's achievement. The roof of the cathedral of Noyon, built in the mid-twelfth century, reached 85 feet in height. Maurice de Sully, bishop of Paris, naturally felt compelled to exceed this height. Working closely with the king of France, whose palace faced the site of the new cathedral, he set out to create a

The Ambulatory, Saint Denis Cathedral, France *Gothic architecture was invented in the walkway (ambulatory) around the nave of Saint Denis Cathedral. Here, Abbot Suger combined the pointed arch and the rib vault, supporting them on the outside of the building with rib arches. (Hirmer Fotoarchiv.)*

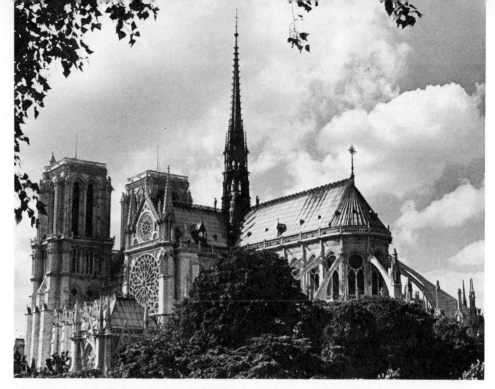

Notre Dame Cathedral, Paris *Flying buttresses support the 115-foot high choir and nave, and make possible the insertion of wide panels of stained glass in all the outer walls.* (Alinari/Art Resource.)

building worthy of Paris's position as capital of the newly powerful Capetian dynasty. Notre Dame de Paris was 130 yards long. Its vaults reached 115 feet, and were 30 feet higher than any previous cathedral. The church could hold 10,000 people. Work began in 1163 and was not completed for almost a hundred years. During that time, however, other bishops had entered the competition. At Chartres, to the south of Paris, the nave was 5 feet higher and 6 feet wider than that of Notre Dame in Paris, and its vast stained glass windows contained the most impressive presentation ever assembled of the Biblical story. In 1211, however, the bishops of Rheims, the cathedral in which French kings were crowned, built a nave 125 feet in height. Nine years later, the nave of Amiens reached 142 feet. And finally, in 1247 the architects of the cathedral of Beauvais attempted to construct a building 157 feet in height. Here at last the Gothic architects had out-reached themselves. The choir fell down the moment it was finished. After being rebuilt, it fell again; and the architects, recognizing that they had sought the unattainable, simply abandoned their effort to complete the building.

Gothic Style in England

The Gothic style spread rapidly from the Ile de France to most of Europe. In England, it was employed as early as 1175 in the rebuilding of Canterbury Cathedral. The English architects did not stay faithful to the French model for long, however. They soon began to decorate the naves with luxuriant stone

187

tracery, which creates in many ways the rather surprising effect of palm trees opening over one's head. In England the use of decorative stone tracery became ever more widespread, and gave the English the leadership in innovation in the Gothic style after the French had brought their desire for height to its furthest possibility. Throughout the fourteenth and fifteenth centuries, the decorative features of England's Gothic architecture became ever more complex. The tracery of the stained glass windows began to resemble the abstract designs of a Muslim wall panel. And in the fan vaults of the fifteenth century the English added a totally new dimension—and the last—to Gothic architecture. The roof of King's College Chapel, Cambridge, is perhaps the most beautiful example of the ongoing vitality of the Gothic style in England at a time when it was already being abandoned in Italy for the new Renaissance style.

Gothic Sculpture, Stained Glass, and Painting

Sculpture and stained glass played an essential role in making the Gothic cathedral carry the Biblical message to the illiterate and literate alike. Within the cathedrals there were many free-standing statues; but it was around the doorways and especially in the composition of the façade of the west front that enormously complex compositions were created. The façade of Notre Dame

Stained Glass, Soissons Cathedral, France *In this scene from the life of Saint Nicholas, three knights are being condemned to death by a consul.* (The Metropolitan Museum of Art, gift of Glencairn Foundation, 1980.)

Cathedral in Paris is one of the finest examples of how sculpture can be integrated with architecture in teaching a specific Christian message. The central doorway represents Christ in judgment. On each side are the apostles; above are angels; and below Christ's feet the wicked are dragged down to hell. Above the doorways is a line of kings of Judah and Israel, and above them Adam on the left and Eve on the right. The two side doorways are devoted to the Virgin Mary, to whom the cathedral is dedicated. The right doorway depicts Mary with her own mother, Saint Anne. The left doorway, the finest in the cathedral, depicts the announcement of the birth of the Virgin, her death and resurrection, and her crowning by Christ himself. The sculptor thus contributed to the cult or worship of her that became a central feature of Catholicism from the twelfth century on. Mary, the image of purity, became the intermediary between impure human beings and her somewhat overwhelming son, the Savior who is portrayed as judge on the central door.

As the cult of Mary developed, sculpture itself lightened and became more human. Figures ceased, as they had been in Romanesque sculpture, to be simply part of the structure of the building, but stood out from the buildings, each with their own individual features, posture, and clothing, as can be seen in the sculptures of Chartres Cathedral.

Gothic architecture made possible the composition of vast pictures in stained glass to fill in the ever larger spaces between the vaults. The artists first made paintings of a series of stories from the Bible or the lives of the saints, often matching stories from the Old Testament on one wall with stories from the New Testament on the other. Using small pieces of glass colored from metal oxides in a melting pot, set within strips of lead, they then reproduced their painting, which was placed in the wall in an iron frame. The result was a new form of art.

Painters in northern Europe especially were employed in the "illumination" or decoration of manuscripts. Here again in the thirteenth century artists developed the ability to portray the individual character and emotions of their figures; but every book page was planned like the façade of a cathedral. The text and the illustrations of the text, usually combined with some sort of abstract or floral decoration, formed a unity. Paris was the center of European book production and of book illumination during the thirteenth century; and it was not surprising that there in the fourteenth century book illuminations became less and less subordinate to the text they were supposed to be illustrating.

MEDIEVAL LITERATURE

Latin was the language of the Church and of university students throughout the Middle Ages, even when the students were composing their irreverent "goliardic" or satiric verses, which praised drunkenness, gambling, and wenching. but as the modern European languages took form, many new works of literature were written in the vernacular, or local dialects of the different European peoples. The vernacular tongues came into existence as a result of the mixing of the languages of conquerors and conquered in some regions. For example, English is the result of grafting onto an Anglo-Saxon base a good many French words carried by England's early rulers. The word "language" itself is French in origin. English also contains Latin, Danish, and Old Norse words. The word "gift," for example, is from Old Norse.

Among the earliest literary works were *chansons de geste*, French epic songs of heroic deeds, which described the triumphs and defeats of the feudal warriors. The earliest epic we have knowledge of is the Anglo-Saxon *Beowulf*, written in England in the tenth century, but probably composed in the early eighth century. The poem describes Beowulf's battles with such beasts as the water monster Grendel and later with a dragon. In French literature, the emperor Charlemagne inspired the greatest number of epic poems. The *Song of Roland*, written in France before 1100, is the tale of Charlemagne's war against the Muslims in Spain. It celebrates the feudal loyalty of the emperor's vassal Roland, who dies bravely in defense of the rear guard of Charlemagne's army as it is treacherously attacked by an overwhelming Muslim force at the pass of Roncesvalles in the Spanish Pyrenees.

The most elegant medieval narratives are the verse romances of King Arthur and the knights of the Round Table, written by the French poet Chrétien de Troyes for Marie de Champagne, daughter of Eleanor of Aquitaine. Both Eleanor and Marie were great patrons of the wandering poets known as troubadours, who composed lyric poems of courtly love celebrating the usually unconsummated and frequently unrequited love of a knight for someone else's wife. Marie herself was a fine poet who is credited with composing at least twelve romances.

The courtly style spread rapidly to Germany, where a poet who celebrated love, or *Minne*, came to be called a *Minnesinger*. In Germany also the Arthurian legend was a source of inspiration for courtly romances. The great poem *Parzival*, by Wolfram von Eschenbach, describes how Arthur's pure knight, Sir Percival, finds the Holy Grail, which medieval Christians believed to have miraculous healing powers and later assumed to be a chalice containing Christ's blood. The Germans also turned to their own legends, and in the *Nibelungenlied* of about 1200, recounted the stories of the Rhinemaidens and of the panoply of gods in Valhalla headed by Wotan.

One of the most important medieval poems was the *Divine Comedy* of Dante Alighieri (1265–1321). Dante was both a scholar and a statesman. He had studied theology, classical philosphy, and the poetry of the troubadours of Provence. Using Latin, he had written a defense of the use in literature of the vernacular Italian language. In Florence, he had allied himself with the faction supporting the emperor against the faction supporting the pope, and, while his faction held the upper hand, had served in the city government as councillor, elector, and prior. In 1302, however, his own group was exiled, and he spent the rest of his life in the service of different princely states in Italy. He remained faithful to the emperor in the continuing quarrels with the papacy, and justified secular authority over papal claims in a treatise entitled *On Monarchy*. His greatest work, written while he was moving about in exile, is a long, three-part poem he called *Comedy* but which since the sixteenth century has been called the *Divine Comedy*.

The poem, which is an allegorical journey in the realms through which a soul passes after death—Inferno (Hell), Purgatory, and Paradise (Heaven)—was as much a summation of medieval thought as Aquinas's *Summa Theologica*. As the poet Virgil guides him through these realms, Dante describes hundreds of people whom he meets—the great writers of antiquity, the heroes, the leaders of the Church (many of whom he consigns to Inferno), the traitors such as Brutus and Judas, and many of the Florentines he knew personally and on whom he took a vindictive revenge. He lays out the whole scholastic scheme of virtues and vices and of punishment and salvation. And in Paradise, to which he is guided by Beatrice, whom he had loved platonically since glimpsing her as a youth, he leads up to a vision of God himself. By his command of the Tuscan dialect of Italian, which he used with marvellous subtlety and variety, Dante had succeeded in proving that the vernacular language could equal and even exceed Latin as a vehicle of human thought and artistic pleasure.

THE ACHIEVEMENT OF THE HIGH MIDDLE AGES

The High Middle Ages, from the eleventh through the thirteenth centuries, saw the creation in Europe of one of the most distinct and most integrated forms of culture in world history. Its characteristics were the predominance in almost all intellectual activity of the enormously powerful Catholic Church; the stabilization of politics and social power in the hands of a warrior class of feudal knights; an economic upsurge made possible by a revolution in agricultural techniques but brought to new heights by the development of commercial and industrial activity in rapidly growing cities; and the consolidation of new national groups, formed by the intermingling of different ethnic groups within newly stabilized political boundaries.

This synthesis was achieved at great cost, however. The conflict between church and state left Germany and Italy politically fragmented until the nineteenth century. Divergent opinion was ruthlessly suppressed as heresy, even when, as in the case of the Albigensians, it was supported passionately by large numbers of people in whole regions of the continent. Feudal monarchies consolidated their kingdoms as a consequence of many wars, both small and great. Finally, we must recognize that as with all agricultural societies, the glittering achievement of the Middle Ages was based on the hardship of the peasant's life, for whom, as a medieval plowman says, "the labor is indeed great." Yet, despite the high cost, the cultural and intellectual achievements of the High

Middle Ages were very real and very much to the benefit of contemporary and future European generations.

During these three centuries, Europe enjoyed a great economic boom. Not only was production greatly increased on existing farmland, but vast new areas of forestland were brought under the plow. Cities grew as trading centers, at first for local trade and then increasingly for long-distance trade within Europe and with other continents. Financial activities rapidly followed commercial, and small-scale artisan crafts were expanded to become, in many instances, large-scale industrial production involving thousands of workers. The city had become the driving force of European economic life.

The warrior class, which had become dominant during the age of invasions, was reorganized into a hierarchical aristocratic structure, in which a direct link was established between the right to hold land and the duty to carry out state service, in military or administrative tasks. But with the enforcement of internal peace within the new national states, the monarchs, as heads of the feudal structure, were increasingly able to exercise powers independent of the aristocratic class because they received an independent monetary income, conducted affairs of state through a bureaucracy, and, through a royally appointed judiciary, enforced a uniform legal system. As state boundaries became more certain, groups within regions began to coalesce. The appearance of national languages, although frequently with very significant regional variations or dialects, became the most outstanding expression of the national divergences that were henceforth to play an enormous role in European political and cultural history.

The preeminence of the Catholic Church gave to the period its most distinctive characteristics. After a thousand years of intellectual debate, the Catholic church, established firmly as the arbiter of belief in the West, made determined efforts to have its truth prevail, and, although debate over contrary truths continued within the universities, the approved arguments did not represent an effort to discover new truths but rather were intended to insure further acceptance of the validity of what was already believed. Nevertheless, where the advance of knowledge was not seen as a danger to religious orthodoxy, cultural advances were revolutionary. Nowhere was this more true than with architecture. At no period of history has building in stone advanced more rapidly than in the extraordinary progression from the heavy churches of early Romanesque to the lightly soaring cathedrals of High Gothic. The great cathedrals more fully than anything else symbolize the complex harmony of medieval Catholic culture.

SUGGESTED READINGS

General Introductions

Comprehensive coverage based on the most recent scholarship is provided by Christopher Brooke, *Europe in the Central Middle Ages, 962–1154* (1964), and John H. Mundy,

Europe in the High Middle Ages, 1150–1309 (1973). Robert W. Southern, *The Making of the Middle Ages* (1967), is more analytical, and is especially insightful on social change.

The Economic Revival

Helpful introductions by prominent European scholars include R. H. Bautier, *The Economic Development of Medieval Europe* (1971), which emphasizes the importance of trade with Asia and Africa; and Carlo M. Cipolla, *Before the Industrial Revolution: European Society and Economy, 1000–1700* (1976), which sees a gradual transition from the medieval to the early modern economy. On commerce, see R. S. Lopez, *The Commercial Revolution of the Central Middle Ages, 950–1350* (1976); on agriculture and the society of the villages, see Georges Duby, *The Early Growth of the European Economy: Warriors and Peasants from the Seventh to the Twelfth Century* (1974); and on technology, see Jean Gimpel, *The Medieval Machine: The Industrial Revolution of the Middle Ages* (1977). Documents on the history of cities are collected in John H. Mundy and Peter Riesenberg, eds., *The Medieval Town* (1958). But it is more revealing to study individual cities, in such fine works as Frederick C. Lane, *Venice: A Maritime Republic* (1973); Christopher N. L. Brooke, assisted by Gillian Keir, *London, 800–1216: The Shaping of a City* (1975); or William H. Bowsky, *A Medieval Commune: Siena Under the Nine, 1285–1355* (1981).

The Medieval Monarchies

Sidney Painter, *Rise of the Feudal Monarchies* (1951), is still helpful. The fragmentation of political power in Germany is analyzed in Geoffrey Barraclough, *The Origins of Modern Germany* (1963), which is the best study of the Holy Roman Empire in the Middle Ages.

The great Hohenstaufen emperors have inspired good biographies, notably Peter Munz, *Frederick Barbarossa: A Study in Medieval Politics* (1969); and Thomas Curtis Van Cleve, *The Emperor Frederick II of Hohenstaufen: Immutator Mundi* (1972). The investiture contest is explained in Brian Tierney, *The Crisis of Church and State, 1050–1300, with Selected Documents* (1964).

The constitutional development of England is the main focus of G. O. Sayles, *The Medieval Foundations of England* (1948). The consolidation of monarchical power is described in the well-documented biography by David C. Douglas, *William the Conqueror and the Norman Impact upon England* (1964), and its squandering away in Sidney Painter, *The Reign of King John* (1949).

The standard work on the French monarchy is Robert Fawtier, *The Capetian Kings of France* (1960). Amy R. Kelly, *Eleanor of Aquitaine and the Four Kings* (1950), not only throws light on Eleanor and her daughter Marie, but on the French and English dynasties into which she married. Marion Facinger shows the reduction in the queen's power in *A Study of Medieval Queenship: Capetian France, 987–1237* (1968).

The Medieval Church

Geoffrey Barraclough, *The Medieval Papacy* (1968), is a fine, short introduction, and can be supplemented by Robert W. Southern, *Western Society and the Church in the Middle Ages* (1970). David Knowles, *The Monastic Order in England* (1951), is relevant to the monastic reform movements throughout Europe. Knowles, with D. Obolensky, provides an equally authoritative and broader survey in *The Middle Ages* (*The Christian Centuries*, Vol. II) (1968). David Knowles sets scholasticism in relation to classical thought in *The Evolution of Medieval Thought* (1962).

For the great cathedrals, see K. J. Conant, *Carolingian and Romanesque Architecture, 800–1200* (1959), and George Henderson, *Gothic* (1967), both of which are well illustrated. The building of the great cathedral of Paris is described in Allan Temko, *Notre Dame of Paris* (1955).

The cult of the Virgin is described in Marina Warner, *Alone of All Her Sex: The Myth and the Cult of the Virgin Mary* (1976), and Geoffrey Ashe, *The Virgin* (1976).

part III
The Birth of the Modern Age

The Gattamelata, Padua, Italy, by Donatello   The first free-standing equestrian statue since Antiquity. (Alinari/Art Resource.)

THE BIRTH OF THE MODERN AGE

Dates	Political & Military Events	Social, Economic, & Demographic Events	Religion & Philosophy	Art, Architecture, Literature, & Music	Science & Technology
1294			Pope Boniface VIII (1294–1303)		d. Roger Bacon
1295	Model Parliament in England	Marco Polo returns from China			
1302			Bull *Unam Sanctam*		
1309		Periodic famines in Europe, population decline	Babylonian captivity of Papacy (1309–1378)		Gun powder used in warfare
1321				Dante, *Divine Comedy*	
1337	Hundred Years War begins				
1347		Black Death; economic depression			
1351				Boccaccio, *The Decameron*	
1358		Peasant revolt in France Rise of cities in central and southern Germany		Petrarch, *Sonnets*	
1366				d. Giotto	
1378			Great Schism (1378–1417)		
1381		Peasants' Revolt in England			
1387		Prosperity of German and Swiss cities		Chaucer, *Canterbury Tales*	
1400s	Military expansion of Ottoman Turks		Conciliar movement in Catholic Church	Renaissance begins in Italy	
1414			Council of Constance (1414–1418)		
1415	Battle of Agincourt				
1434	Cosimo de' Medici in power, Florence	Portuguese round Cape Bojador			Portuguese develop caravel ship

Date					
1440				d. Jan van Eyck	Gutenberg: invention of printing
1453	Turks take Constantinople				
1455	Wars of Roses in England (1455–1485)				
1469	Lorenzo de' Medici in power, Florence				
1485	Henry VII, King, England: Tudor Dynasty (1485–1603)				
1492	Spanish take Granada	Columbus discovers New World	Pope Alexander VI (1492–1503)		
1497		Vasco de Gama's voyage to India (1497–1499)		Manueline culture in Portugal	
1500s			Christian Humanism	Renaissance in France begins	Copernicus, *Comentaries*
1504	d. Queen Isabella, Spain				
1509	Henry VIII, King, England (1509–1547)		Erasmus, *Praise of Folly*		
1510	Portugal takes Goa	Spain legalizes slave trade		d. Botticelli	
1512					
1513			Machiavelli, *The Prince*		
1517			Luther posts Theses in Wittenberg		
1519	Charles V, Holy Roman Emperor (1519–1556)	Magellan sails around world (1519–1522)		d. Leonardo da Vinci	
1521			Diet of Worms		
1530	Pizarro conquers Peru		Confession of Augsburg		
1534			Henry VIII, Supreme Head of Church in England		
1536			Calvin's *Institutes*	Michelangelo's *Last Judgment*	

(continued)

THE BIRTH OF THE MODERN AGE (continued)

Dates	Political & Military Events	Social, Economic, & Demographic Events	Religion & Philosophy	Art, Architecture, Literature, & Music	Science & Technology
1540		French and British exploration in North America	Jesuits founded		
1545			Council of Trent (1545–1563), reform in Catholic Church		
1546					Tycho Brahe (1546–1601)
1556	Philip II, Spain (1556–1598)				
1558	Elizabeth I, England (1558–1603)			Dome and nave of St. Peter's, Rome, begun	
1562			French Wars of Religion begin		
1564					Galileo (1564–1642)
1568	Revolt of Netherlands against Spain begins	Dutch acquire overseas empire			
1571					Kepler (1571–1630)
1576				d. Titian	
1588	Defeat of Spanish Armada				
1589	Henry IV, France (1589–1610)		Lutheranism spreads in Scandinavia		
1598			Edict of Nantes		
1600		English East India Company French expansion in Canada		Shakespeare's principal tragedies	
1603	James I, England (1603–1625)				
1604				Cervantes, *Don Quixote*	

7

Decline and Rebirth, 1300–1500

The great economic boom that began about 1000 and had provided the material foundation for the cultural achievements of the High Middle Ages ended at the beginning of the fourteenth century. For the next 200 years, the European economy was struck by three devastating scourges—famine, plague, and war. Population had fallen more than a third by the end of the fourteenth century, and did not return to the level of the year 1300 until the beginning of the sixteenth century.

During this long economic recession, several of the most basic institutions of medieval Europe were transformed. The papacy's growing materialism damaged its spiritual prestige, and during the so-called Babylonian Captivity of 1309 to 1378, when the pope resided in Avignon under the influence of the French king, its power to influence lay rulers virtually disappeared. The feudal monarchs cast off their reliance on an increasingly anachronistic feudal nobility, whose military value had been undermined by the new technology of longbow, pike, and gunpowder, and instead based their strength on efficient taxation and well-trained civil servants. England, France, and Spain were all governed by these "New Monarchs" at the end of the fifteenth century, although Italy and Germany remained politically fragmented. Finally, faced with economic recession, the cities renewed their business techniques and embarked on new forms of commercial and industrial activity, and were able to create new sources of wealth in spite of the recession. In the late Middle Ages, the middle class of the cities became the chief patrons of a vigorous cultural life.

Thus, although we often speak of the fourteenth and fifteenth centuries as the decline or waning of the Middle Ages, in fact, especially in the cities of

Northern Europe, medieval culture entered a new phase of creativity. Gothic architecture of the late Middle Ages, known as perpendicular in England and flamboyant in France, created new forms by decorative rather than structural innovation. Catholic piety expressed itself in mysticism in the writings of Margery Kempe and Thomas à Kempis and also in a more sinister way in the persecution of women as witches. Sculptors such as the German Tilman Riemenschneider (c. 1450–1531) brought a new realism to the depiction of the sufferings of Christ and the saints. And Flanders, and particularly the city of Bruges, took the lead in a new form of painting combining meticulous realism with Christian symbolism. In the works of Jan van Eyck, Hans Memling, and Roger van der Weyden, the Flemish artists brought the medieval synthesis to a glorious finale.

In Italy, however, the wealthy governing class of the vast commercial and industrial cities was patronizing in the fifteenth century a new cultural movement that we now call the Renaissance, or "rebirth." The term "Renaissance" implies that the classical culture of ancient Greece and Rome had been "reborn" in Italy, which is precisely the way the citizens of Florence conceived the new age in which they were living. In their cities, and especially in Florence, the Italians believed that they had left more than a thousand years of Church-dominated civilization to bring to life again the culture of the ancient world. Although we no longer believe that the Renaissance was a clear break with the Middle Ages, and in fact see the persistence in the Italian cities of such medieval traits as religious piety and intolerance and the respect for hierarchical organization of society, we recognize that the predominant characteristics of Italian society and culture in the fifteenth century were new. The more significant of the new traits were the revival of Greek and Roman cultural forms and their transformation into new forms of art and literature; predominance of lay rather than ecclesiastical influence and an emphasis on the material rather than the religious aspects of life; and a passionate belief in the dignity of the human being. While the northern Europeans were lamenting the catastrophies of their age, and like the French poet François Villon were sighing for "the snows of yesteryear," the Italians were rejoicing in the fresh, heady spirit of their new vigor. "Now, indeed," wrote the Florentine business leader Matteo Palmieri, "may every thoughtful spirit thank God that it has been permitted to him to be born in this new age, so full of hope and promise, which already rejoices in a greater array of nobly gifted souls than the world has seen in the thousand years that have preceded it."

THE ECONOMIC RECESSION OF THE LATE MIDDLE AGES

The Three Scourges

The underlying causes of Europe's population decline and consequent economic recession were famine, plague, and war. By the early 1300s, Europe's population growth was outstripping its agricultural productivity. Population had doubled between 1000 and 1300, and as a result, marginal land on hillsides or on sandy wastes had been brought into cultivation. Much of this land was beginning to lose its fertility. Moreover, previously fertile soil had been overcropped, often because the practice of allowing the soil to lie fallow for a year had been neglected. Also, the exhausted soil had been insufficiently fertilized and was in many areas turning to dust. The climate too, after three fairly benign centuries, was again turning harsh. Harvests over large regions were destroyed by huge rainfalls, floods, or drought. Crop failures produced famines throughout the fourteenth and fifteenth centuries. The worst in the medieval period occurred in 1315–1317, when the harvests throughout the continent failed for three years in succession. Cities suffered the worst effects. In the textile-producing town of Ypres in Belgium, one-tenth of the population starved to death. Localized famines occurred almost every year, but could be mitigated by importing food from unaffected regions. But famines affecting all Europe occurred every few years, and left a weakened population vulnerable to disease and especially to the pestilence, the Black Death, that struck in 1347.

The Black Death was a combination of bubonic plague, characterized by high fever and suppurating sores, and pneumonic plague, affecting the lungs and causing death within three or four days. The Black Death had originated in Constantinople in 1334, and had reached southern Europe by December 1347, carried by fleas on infected rats. Many of them may have traveled on the ships of returning Crusaders. From Italy and southern France, it spread northward and westward, reaching Paris by June 1348. By June 1349 it was in London and Cologne. Six months later it was in Scotland and Denmark. By the end of 1350 it had reached Russia. Its effects were far from uniform. Some villages suffered relatively few deaths. In others, almost the whole population was wiped out. But it was almost always more devastating in the cities than in the countryside. Florence lost 50,000 out of a population of 80,000. It also seems certain that women, weakened by child-bearing and poor food, were more likely to die than men. Recent research has demonstrated that whereas there were more women than men in Florence in 1300, by 1450 there were 25 percent more men than women.

The horror of the disease was described by the Florentine author Giovanni Boccaccio (1313–1375) in the *Decameron*, a collection of 100 sometimes funny, sometimes sad stories told by a group of Florentines who had fled to the supposedly pure air of the country to escape contamination:

> In its early stages both men, and women too, acquired certain swellings, either in the groin or under the armpits. Some of these swellings reached the size of a common apple, and others were as big as an egg, some more and some less. . . . Then the appearance of the disease began to change into black or livid blotches, which showed up in many on the arm or thighs and every part of the body. And just as the swellings had been at first and still were an infallible indication of approaching death, so also were these blotches to whomever they touched.[1]

[1] Cited in David Herlihy, ed., *Medieval Culture and Society*, translated by David and Patricia Herlihy, (New York: Walker, 1968), p. 217.

The plague recurred in one area or another almost every year, with major outbreaks at least every generation throughout the fourteenth and fifteenth centuries. The large, unsanitary cities were always the worst hit. There were twenty outbreaks in London in the fifteenth century; and in 1665, when the plague seemed to have receded throughout most of Europe, London suffered a new outbreak that killed 90,000 people.

Finally, warfare affected every part of the continent. The Ottoman Turks were penetrating into Eastern Europe. They captured Constantinople in 1453 and Athens in 1456, and by the 1480s were in Hungary. Their fleet meanwhile was attacking the south of Italy. The Grand Dukes of Moscow were fighting a long battle to throw off the control of the Mongols of the Golden Horde, which was not successful until 1480. In Eastern Europe, the Teutonic Knights were engaged in a bloody battle with the Slavic peoples to gain estates for themselves and to spread Christianity. The English and the French were locked in the Hundred Years War (1337–1453). The Catholics of Spain completed in 1492 the 800-year struggle to oust the Muslim Arabs. There was war not only against foreign enemies but civil war also. In England, noble families competed for control of the throne, the worst conflict being the War of the Roses (1455–1485), in which the Tudor family finally triumphed.

Some of the bloodiest clashes occurred during the many uprisings of peasants and artisans in the century following the Black Death. Social unrest was due in part to the sense of fear and insecurity caused by the plague and famines. But there were more immediate economic and social causes of discontent. In the economic recession following the plague, landlords had attempted to recoup their revenues by raising rents, reviving feudal dues and labor services, and using force to prevent the flight of their serfs. Employers in the cities had laid off workers and tried to freeze the wages of those remaining, refused workers the right to their own guilds, and manipulated taxes to their own benefit. Governments had attempted to pay for their wars by increasing tolls and taxes.

There was a similarity in the pattern of revolt throughout Western Europe. Revolts often began in the countryside in the more prosperous areas, where peasants objected to losing gains they had already made. It spread quickly to the artisans and laborers in the cities, who believed that the reduction of population ought to have led to improvement in the position of those surviving; and urban leaders usually came forward to take over the direction of the peasant movement and to link it to the urban uprising.

Although there were uprisings in Flanders, Languedoc, Italy, Catalonia, and Sweden as well, the two greatest revolts were the Jacquerie in the area around Paris in 1358 and the Peasants' Revolt in England in 1381. The Jacquerie was named after the French slang word for a peasant, Jacques Bonhomme. Under the leadership of Guillaume Karle, peasants went on a rampage in the countryside, murdering nobles and burning castles, while in Paris and other cities artisans rose against their employers. Within a few weeks, however, the nobles had temporarily patched up their differences and counterattacked with great brutality. In the ensuing slaughter more than 20,000 peasants and city workers were killed. In England, Parliament had ordered the freezing of wages, both for peasants and for urban workers, at pre-plague levels by the Statute of Laborers (1351), and the regent of the kingdom, John of Gaunt, had strictly enforced the law. Led by Wat Tyler, Jack Straw, and John Ball, as many as 100,000 peasants and workers revolted and marched on London. They sacked John of Gaunt's palace, freed the prisoners in the jails, took the Tower of London, burned the homes of the rich, and killed the Archbishop of Canterbury. The young King Richard II met them personally, and granted their demands for the end of serfdom, labor services, and head taxes. Believing themselves satisfied, the peasants dispersed. The king, however, first had Wat Tyler murdered and then withdrew his concessions; the nobles then set about punishing the rebels with great severity.

The Decline of the Papacy

Far from being a moral bulwark in a time of widespread suffering, the papacy slumped to one of its lowest levels. The great wealth accumulated by the Church had undoubtedly encouraged many without a spiritual vocation to enter the Church, especially the younger sons of kings or nobles, and they had continued to practice nepotism, that is, the offering of appointment in the Church to their relatives. Monastic orders frequently enjoyed their material comforts, and forgot their vows of poverty, chastity, and obedience.

Widespread disillusionment with the behavior of the clergy finds expression in one of the great books of late medieval literature, *The Canterbury Tales* of Geoffrey Chaucer (1340–1400). Writing in England in the fourteenth century, Chaucer based some of his tales on the popular French verse stories called *fabliaux*, which usually satirized merchants, priests, lawyers, and so on. Other tales were borrowed or suggested by the great Italian and French writers of his day. Chaucer, however, went far beyond the frequently bawdy *fabliaux* and used considerable imagination with his other sources. Placed within a frame of a pilgrimage to the shrine of Saint Thomas in Canterbury Cathedral, the tales are told by the travelers as they journey together. As each pilgrim tells his or her tale, Chaucer builds a vivid panorama of medieval society; but it is the clerics who above all feel the bite of his wit. The pretty little Prioress is demure and sentimental, but she lavishes more attention on her lap dogs than on the poor and seems more concerned with her appearance than was thought proper for a nun. The monk is praised not for his saintliness but for his stable of horses and for his bridle, "jingling in a whistling wind as clear, and also as loud, as does the chapel bell." And as for the Friar, "He knew the taverns well in every town. / And every innkeeper and barmaid / Better than a leper or a beggar."

The greatest outrage roused by the Church's actions was directed at the pope himself. Popes had been distracted from their religious duties by their interference in disputes among lay rulers and by their vast judicial and administrative tasks. But when Pope Boniface VIII (1294–1303) attempted to assert his supremacy over the tough French King Philip IV (the Fair; reigned 1285–1314), he disastrously overreached himself. In 1302, in the papal bull *Unam Sanctam*, the pope asserted that papal power, the spiritual sword, was superior to royal power, the material sword. "Both the material and spiritual swords are in the power of the Church. . . . It is fitting moreover that one sword should be under the other, and the temporal authority subject to the spiritual power. . . . We, moreover, proclaim, declare, and pronounce that it is altogether necessary to salvation for every human being to be subject to the Roman pontiff." Instead of seeking forgiveness, Philip sent an army to Italy, which captured Boniface. The pope died shortly afterwards, and his successor forgave Philip. Far from satisfied, Philip enforced the election of a Frenchman as Pope Clement V (1305–1314).

Finding Rome in disorder, Clement moved the papal court from Rome to Avignon in southern France, which was eventually purchased as a papal fief. Clement and the following six popes were all French, and all resided in Avignon, where they blatantly favored French clerics over those of other countries. English and German Catholics were particularly outraged at the vast sums of money required to build a huge new papal palace in Avignon. In 1378, the Italian Pope Urban VI ended the so-called Babylonian Captivity in Avignon by bringing the papal court back to Rome. This move only made matters worse, since a conclave of French cardinals then elected another Frenchman as pope in Avignon, thus beginning what is called the Great Schism.

The Conciliar Movement

When neither pope proved willing either to resign in favor of the other or to permit the election of a new pope, the cardinals of the Church took matters into their own hands. Accepting a theory propounded at the University of Paris by the chancellor, Jean Gerson, a follower of William of Ockham, and other theologians, the cardinals decided that a General Council of the Church, at which all bishops were represented, could act with greater authority than the pope alone. The original doctrines of the Church, they argued, had been developed in church councils, like that at Nicaea, and God would continue to prevent any new church council from falling into doctrinal error. The basic thrust of this "conciliar movement" was thus to make Church government more representative and to restrict the powers of the newly developed papal monarchy. In 1409, cardinals supporting both the pope in Rome and the pope in Avignon met at Pisa, and attempted to end the schism by naming a new pope, Alexander V, and deposing the other two. The popes refused to be deposed, however, and the result of the Council of Pisa was that three popes disputed their right to the title.

A new church council met at Constance in 1414–1417 to end this proliferation of popes, which had become a scandal to all Catholics. The council first declared its own supremacy over the pope: "The Council of Constance, an ecumenical council, derives its power direct from God, and all men, including the pope, are bound to obey it in matters of faith, of ending the schism, and of reforming the Church in head and in members." They displayed their own reforming zeal by inviting John Huss (1369–1415), a Czech reformer who was asserting the supremacy of Biblical authority over the teaching of the clergy, to Constance on a safe conduct pass and then burning him for heresy. Finally, in 1417, the council chose a new pope, Martin V, persuaded two of the other popes to resign, and deposed the third.

The reformers among the bishops and cardinals attempted to use the next council, held in Basel (1431–1449), to win even greater power within the church. They ordered restrictions on the pope's power to tax the church. When Pope Eugenius IV ordered them to attend a new church council at Ferrara, many refused to go. He then declared the Council of Basel to be schismatic, and the council in turn declared him deposed. In 1449, however, the remaining members of the Council of Basel agreed to recognize Eugenius's successor, Nicholas V, as the legitimate pope, and the conciliar movement collapsed.

The movement had failed primarily because of its own internal divisions arising from the political ambitions of its members. The popes were able to wait until the reforming zeal directed at their own power and income had subsided in order to reestablish their preeminent position. But they had in fact won a hollow victory, because they had lost the chance to reform the church from within.

Catholic Mysticism

The pope also failed to harness the passionate search for a new spirituality that inspired vast numbers of clerical and lay people in the fourteenth and fifteenth centuries. The Franciscan and Dominican friars took the lead in bringing an experience of mystical religion, the experience of direct communion with God, to lay people. They authorized the foundation of communities of lay men or women called Beghards or Beguines, but some of their teachings later won them criticism from the papacy. One group of followers of Saint Francis, known as the Fraticelli, became so extreme in their proclamation of a coming age in which the Church hierarchy would be unnecessary that they were condemned by the second of the Avignon popes, John XXII. One of the most influential of the new groups was the Brothers of the Common Life of Modern Devotion. In houses for men or women, both clergy and lay people lived together, emphasizing the interior life of the spirit without recourse to public expressions of religion such as pilgrimages or fasting. A book of devotional practice, *The Imitation of Christ*, written for the Brethren by Thomas à Kempis in 1425, became the most popular religious book in Europe after the Bible.

Women were very active in the mystical movement. Saint Catherine of Siena (1347–1380) led the movement for restoration of mystical devotion within the church, castigated leading Churchmen for materialism, and was instrumental in 1377 in persuading the pope to return from Avignon to Rome. Saint

Bridget (c. 1300–1373), a Swedish noblewoman, founded her own order of Bridgettines, and wrote a widely popular book describing her spiritual visions. In England, Margery Kempe (d. 1438), a mother of twelve children, dressed in white robes, went on a pilgrimage to the Holy Land, wrote meditations, received visions, and, when censured by the clergy, responded by criticizing them.

The Church was most concerned, however, by two direct attacks—by the followers of John Wycliffe (d. 1384) in England, known as Lollards, and the supporters of John Huss in Bohemia, called Hussites. Wycliffe was a theologian at Oxford University who criticized not only the papal revenues paid by England and the vices of the pope and cardinals but also the very institutions and dogma of the Church. He held that the clergy needed no more property than their clothes and food; that the state of grace of a clergyman affected his ability to serve the sacraments; and that the Bible alone expressed the will of God. More than a century before Luther, he was thus stating several of the crucial Protestant challenges to the Catholic Church. The English monarchy found Wycliffe's teaching useful as long as the pope was in Avignon; but when the Lollards began to proclaim the egalitarian ideas that were expressed in the Peasants' Revolt, the king joined with the pope in 1401 in condemning them as heretics. The Church attempted to deal with the Hussite movement by burning Huss at the stake in 1415, primarily because he refused to renounce his support of several of Wycliffe's theses, which had been condemned. The well-armed Hussite forces in Bohemia were, however, able to force the Council of Basel in 1431 to make a number of concessions to their demands for religious change.

The New Monarchy

The "New Monarchs" of the Late Middle Ages created the modern form of state. The feudal state had been based on the assumption that the power of the monarch was enforced by a hierarchy of vassals, each of whom owed personal allegiance to his lord in return for the grant of a fief. By the fifteenth century, in England, France, Spain, and a number of smaller states, the rulers had claimed *sovereignty*, the right of the government to control the governed by such instruments of state power as taxation, law courts, police, and bureaucracy. Changes in military technology ended the usefulness of the feudal knight in the fourteenth and fifteenth centuries. Important new weapons were the longbow, the pike, and gunpowder. The armored knights attacking on horseback were helpless against arrows shot by archers from the powerful longbows, and found it suicidal to charge against a pike, a long stave to which a sharp metal head with a point and carving blade had been affixed. Gunpowder had been used in China as early as the ninth century, but it was only introduced in Europe in the early fourteenth century. Small guns were used in the first battles of the Hundred Years War between France and England, and were immediately able to blast away the great horse that had made the feudal knight so fearsome. As guns increased in size, artillery was also used for the siege of fortified cities. As their military usefulness decreased, the knights were given a largely ceremonial role, and the pageantry of chivalry developed into a romantic, nostalgic art. The New Monarchs found that the tournaments, the courts of love, and the ceremonial of such newly founded orders of knights as the Order of the Golden Fleece of the Duke of Burgundy served to provide a function and justification for a nobility whose wealth was no longer justified by their military service.

Increasingly unwilling to use their nobility for military purposes and unable to take back the fiefs they had been given, the kings turned more and more to raising monetary revenues. They increased feudal dues, imposed fines in their law courts, forced cities to make them loans, and increased customs duties. With this income they were able to build professional armies, often composed of mercenaries from foreign countries, and to employ in civil administration career bureaucrats from the middle class and the Church, who were dependent on the kings for their advancement.

The creation of a strong monarchy in France was hampered by its long war with England. The Hundred Years War (1337–1453) had begun when King Edward III of England claimed the throne of France in the hope of getting back much of the territory that had been seized from King John by Philip Augustus. In savage fighting on both land and sea, the English were at first successful in reestablishing their control over large areas of France. After temporary setbacks, English hopes again revived under King Henry V (reigned 1413–1422) when he invaded France and won the great victory of Agincourt (1415). England's ally, the duke of Burgundy, was then able to take possession of Paris and to capture the French king. Although a peasant girl, called Joan of Arc, was able to inflict some defeats on the British armies before she was captured and condemned to death for heresy, the real foundations for a lasting French victory were laid by King Charles VII (reigned 1422–1461). Charles created the New Monarchy in France, with its revenues, its bureaucracy, and its professional army; and by 1453 he had driven the English out of every part of France except the port city of Calais. The structure of the New Monarchy was completed by King Louis XI (reigned 1461–1483), whose guile, amorality, and administrative genius made him an ideal monarch in the eyes of such political theorists as Niccolò Machiavelli.

After its early victories against France in the Hundred Years War, the English monarchy had been weakened by quarrels among the nobility, which culminated in civil wars, known as the Wars of the Roses (1455–1485). These wars were fought between the nobles supporting the House of Lancaster, whose symbol was a red rose, and those supporting the House of York, whose symbol was a white rose. The nobles profited from the weakness of the kings to build themselves huge castles, and to take personal power in their own regions. But the victory of Henry Tudor in 1485 at the Battle of Bosworth Field ended these pretensions. Proclaiming himself King Henry VII (reigned 1485–1509), the new king immediately set about creating the New Monarchy in England. He enlisted his administrators from the Church and the middle classes, and consulted Parliament as little as possible. He squeezed out the greatest possible monetary revenues, by exploiting every possible source of income, and by avoiding foreign wars. At the time of his death, he had brought stability to England after years of chaos, and had left to his successors of the Tudor dynasty one of the most strongly entrenched monarchies of Europe.

Spain was united as a result of the marriage in 1474 of Ferdinand of Aragon and Isabella of Castille, who together as the Catholic monarchs created the New Monarchy in Spain. The bellicose nobility was in 1492 used to defeat Granada, the last remaining Arab kingdom in Spain, and was pacified with the grant of former Arab lands. Ferdinand and Isabella then sought to enforce Catholic uniformity. Jews and Arabs who refused to convert were expelled. The Spanish Inquisition was used to discover heresy among Catholics. The army was reorganized to include pikemen and gun soldiers who could be used against disobedient members of the feudal nobility.

By 1500, the New Monarchs of England, France, and Spain had become the most important political and military powers in Europe.

The Cities in Recession

Whereas the royal response to the challenge of political survival during the military and economic transformation of the late Middle Ages was to create the bureaucratic structure of the New Monarchy, the cities responded to the problems of economic recession by a profound renovation of their methods of doing business. It is undeniable that the cities suffered greatly, perhaps even more than the countryside, from the three scourges of the period. During times of famine they had to search farther and farther afield for sources of food. The plague struck the unsanitary, densely crowded populations cramped within the city walls with even greater force than in the villages. Barcelona's population dropped by two-thirds, for example, and some cities were reduced to one-tenth of their previous population. Gunpowder made sieges of cities more damaging. Moreover, the fall in population throughout Europe reduced the market for urban manufactured goods, especially for the cloth that was the staple product of the majority of cities. Attempts to keep down wages in order to compete for the remaining markets provoked widespread rioting in many of Europe's major cities in the late fourteenth and fifteenth centuries. International trade probably dropped even more than local trade, and may even have fallen to less than two-fifths of the level before the Black Death.

Nevertheless, the cities survived, and even prospered, in spite of the economic recession. For this prosperity, which was responsible for some of the most beautiful buildings ever erected in Europe—the city hall of Bruges, the palace of the Doge by the lagoon in Venice, the cathedral-like churches of East Anglia in England, the palaces of the patriciate in Florence—there are many explanations. Food was probably cheaper for the city dwellers, since there was a shift in the terms of trade in favor of the cities. Agricultural prices were falling slightly at a time when the price of manufactured goods was rising rapidly. More important, however, was the renovation of business techniques undertaken throughout Europe by the urban class.

The Italians pioneered new methods of forming business partnerships. They abandoned the temporary partnerships common previously, which were disbanded after each business venture, and formed instead companies lasting several years that could employ resident agents in the cities with which they were trading. Family-run companies like those of the Bardi and Medici families in Florence were more efficient in pooling savings and sharing in profits by issuing shares.

Written records improved. Newsletters circulating among vast companies such as the Fuggers in Augsburg were more informative sources of political information available than the reports of ambassadors, especially as the profitability of company enterprises was dependent on knowledge of political change. Bookkeeping improved. Arabic numerals replaced the clumsy Roman numerals, making bookkeeping simpler. Double-entry bookkeeping, in which profit and loss could immediately be compared, made accounting more efficient.

New instruments of banking offered new sources of profit. For example, a company would accept money on deposit at its home office, and issue a "bill of exchange" that could be turned in for cash, often in a foreign currency, at one of the company's other branches. Some companies, which had begun as commercial businesses, found that their banking activities were a source of even greater profit, especially if they were named by the papacy or a monarchy to collect their taxes. In one of the most notable business transactions, Charles V bribed his way to election as Holy Roman Emperor with a loan of 543,000 florins from the Fuggers.

Some cities found it necessary to diversify or completely change their economic basis. Milan, for example, gave up textile manufacturing, and instead became an armaments manufacturer capable of outfitting a small army at a moment's notice. Some previously backward regions became highly developed, most notably south Germany and Switzerland, which were able to open up markets in the expanding areas of Eastern Europe. A union of seventy mostly northern German cities called the Hanseatic League broke Denmark's control of the mouth of the Baltic Sea, and grew wealthy by supplying western Europe with the timber, herring, and furs of Scandinavia and western Russia.

Nevertheless, the two areas that had been predominant in the trade of the High Middle Ages—the Low Countries and north-central Italy—remained the pivots of European commerce and manufacturing. In the Low Countries, especially in Flanders, medieval culture enjoyed a last flowering. In Italy, medieval culture was largely abandoned, and replaced by the new culture of the Renaissance.

Late Medieval Culture in Flanders

Flanders fostered every art of the late Middle Ages. The principal manufacturing cities such as Bruges and Ypres built Cloth Halls in flamboyant Gothic, usually with tall belfries from which the citizens could be summoned to the central city square in times of danger. The wealthy merchants built comfortable homes in buff-colored brick. Church music was advanced in the masses of writers such as Guillaume Dufay. Altars were decorated with realistic sculptures in wood or alabaster by artists such as Claus Sluter. But the art form that was most prized was painting. The most important patron was the duke of Burgundy, who held court in Bruges as well as in his other capital in Dijon. The local cloth merchants purchased religious paintings, while the Italian colony in Bruges, headed by the representatives of the Medici company, had the artists paint portraits of themselves. Artists from all over the Low Countries joined together in the artists' guild in Bruges, and created there the Flemish style, which lasted with little change for almost a century. The Flemish school included such painters

Giovanni Arnolfini and His Wife, by Jan van Eyck (c. 1380–1441) Van Eyck's portrait of the Italian merchant and his wife is a piece of medieval symbolism, with the dog meaning faithfulness, the candle Christ, and the crystal beads purity and innocence. (Reproduced by courtesy of the Trustees, The National Gallery, London/ Art Resource.)

as Roger van der Weyden, who was the favorite painter of Charles V, the portrait painter Hans Memling, and the painter who did most to create the style of the school, Jan van Eyck (c. 1380–1441).

With van Eyck, the artist became a prominent social figure who could move at the highest levels of the ducal court. He dressed his servants in livery and took pride in the good living his fees made possible. He gave up the medieval artist's habit of anonymity, and signed his protraits. (He often added, *Als ich Kann*—the best I could.) In one painting, he even showed himself in the mirror. At first glance, van Eyck's intimate, realistic paintings of the interiors of Flemish houses, with the owners posed among their possessions, appear similar to the Dutch interior paintings of the seventeenth century. But van Eyck is still a medieval painter, because he insists subtly on the Christian symbolism of all the objects in his paintings. In the portrait of the Italian merchant Giovanni Arnolfini and his wife, every material object has a meaning. The little dog is the sign of faithfulness. The fruit on the side dresser reminds one of the Garden of Eden. The mirror is a symbol of purity. And the lighted candle in the chandelier represents Christ as the light of the world.

The fifteenth century was the swansong of Flanders. The port of Bruges was silting up. The demand for Flemish cloth was declining. The center of North European banking was shifting northward, first to Antwerp and then to Amsterdam. And the center of North European artistic inspiration was shifting too. After 1500 no great artist was born in or moved to Bruges, which became an intellectual and economic backwater.

THE RENAISSANCE IN ITALY

Just as we can pinpoint the beginning of Gothic style in architecture with the reconstruction of the Abbey of Saint Denis by Abbot Suger in 1129, so we can state with some assurance that the cultural movement we call the Renaissance (simultaneously in architecture, sculpture, painting, literature, and philosophy) was born in Florence in the first thirty years of the fifteenth century. The Renaissance was created for, and financed by, the patriciate of Florence. In 1419–1426, Brunelleschi built the first building in Renaissance style, the Foundlings' Hospital, for the silkweavers' guild. When Masaccio died in 1428, at the age of twenty-seven, he had already transformed the medieval style of painting into a new art form, with its mastery of perspective and the intimate portrayal of individuals wracked by the trials of life on this earth. His friend, Donatello, had restored the realism of Greek and Roman sculpture, combining it with a psychological insight that was to be the Renaissance's essential contribution to the harmony of classical sculpture. And the chancellors of Florence, who were unique in Italy in that they were scholars called to active political roles, had proclaimed a new philosophy that we have come to call "civic humanism," in which the Athenian polis and the Roman Republic were seen as ideals of independence and freedom that it was the task of Florence to uphold in Italy.

The Patriciate of Florence

The culture of the Florentine Renaissance was essentially different from that of the Middle Ages because its patron, the Florentine patriciate, was different in character from the Church leaders who were the principal patrons, or at least the principal influence on, medieval art. The foundation of the wealth of this patriciate in the thirteenth and fourteenth centuries was in woolen textiles. At first great wealth was made by the members of the wool finishing guild, who bought cloth from all over Europe and then reworked it in a distinctively Florentine style for resale. By the fourteenth century, however, Florence had taken over the manufacturing of cloth itself. Members of the wool manufacturing guild were buying wool directly from the sheepowners in Spain and in England and buying dyestuffs from the East. Workers flooded in from all over Italy to find employment in the vast workshops in the many tasks of cloth production, from carding, combing, beating, spinning, and weaving to the final finishing of the beautiful patterned fabrics for which Florence became famous.

Sensitive as always to changes in the market, the Florentines had embarked upon silk manufacture through the silk manufacturers' guild in the fifteenth century, and were thus able, at a time when competition from England and Flanders was cutting into their woolen markets, to rebound with increased vigor. Wealth from textiles enabled many of the companies to diversify into banking, which was organized through the bankers' guild. The papacy was the main patron of the bank owned by the Medici family, but many other companies also engaged in the profitable transfer of money, the granting of loans, and frequently in manufacturing or even mining themselves. The ruling class of bankers and textile manufacturers was closely allied to the professional and intellectual classes, such as the doctors and lawyers, and together as members of what were called the great guilds they formed an oligarchy that was able to manipulate political power without holding a total monopoly of it.

By the end of the thirteenth century, the patriciate had written for Florence a constitution by which they were able to control the governing body of twelve priors, for whom a massive palace had been constructed on the central square of the city. Like the senatorial aristocracy of the late Roman republic, the Florentine patriciate divided up into closely knit family alliances, which frequently engaged in open warfare with each other in the city streets. Family palaces were in fact built like fortresses, with towers within which the family could withstand a siege. Marriage was a highly important political and economic ceremony, since it was the main method for gaining access, or offering access, to a position within the city's power structure. Women were thus required to fit their notions of a husband to a family's political ambitions, but within the family the woman

Lorenzo de' Medici, by Andrea del Verrochio (c. 1435–1488) Verrochio trained many young artists in his workshop in Florence, including Leonardo da Vinci. He was frequently employed by the Medici family. (National Gallery of Art, Washington, D.C.; Samuel H. Kress Collection, 1939.)

gained a position of considerable power and trust. Some indeed took over the administration of the family fortunes.

By the early fifteenth century, the most important family grouping was that of the Medici, which had strength in the principal textile guilds and in banking. After defeating a rival faction in 1434, Cosimo de' Medici (1389–1464) became the unofficial ruler of Florence. His wealth from textiles and banking enabled him to maintain a vast network of supporters in the city. The democratic process was maintained in form but manipulated in practice. Ballot boxes were stuffed with the names of his supporters. Opponents were exiled, ruined by taxation, or on rare occasions executed. The working class was entertained with lavish processions and tournaments, and appeased with jobs and charity.

Upon Cosimo's death, his son Piero ran the Medici political system for five years; and, upon his death, Lorenzo de' Medici (1449–1492), then twenty-one years old, became head of the family. Lorenzo restricted the exercise of power even more narrowly, but he continued the family's great public entertainments, encouraged new commercial ventures, and worked for the maintenance of peace among the Italian states. Mainly under his patronage, Florentine culture reached new creative heights.

The Florentine patriciate were generous patrons of artists and scholars, many of whom were from their own families. As members of the guilds, they helped pay for the building of the cathedral and many new churches; and as part of the city government they showered commissions on artists and scholars. Individual patrician families also gave commissions themselves, believing, like the ancient Romans, that their reputation with posterity would depend on the works of art and learning that they left behind. Family mausoleums were particularly favored as an investment in the future. Michelangelo himself, the greatest genius of the Renaissance, was called upon to build the mausoleum for the Medici family. Altar pieces were commissioned that depicted not only Christ and the saints but the members of the Florentine families that had paid for the commission. Writers were paid to compose frequently fulsome biographies. Machiavelli's great book, *The Prince*, whose amoral advice on the art of government became the bible of the New Monarchs, was written in the hope that it would restore him to favor with the Medici rulers of Florence in the early sixteenth century.

The values evident in the new art were the values of the patriciate. The patricians, as self-made business people, admired human individuality, and demanded that it should be represented in art and literature. They were down-to-earth manufacturers and bankers, and had none of the medieval Church's disregard for the material world. They wished to see material quality in what they purchased, and they desired that the material world should be displayed in all its glory and complexity in the works they commissioned. They admired the play of the intellect, which was essential in their own work; and they supported, and often took part in, gatherings of intellectuals to debate challenging themes of philosophy. Finally, the patriciate, deeply aware of the problems of governing a city-state, called upon their scholars to furnish them with the lessons of the Athens of Pericles and the Rome of Cicero. Thus, the patriciate did not need to be courted by its artists and scholars. It was already attuned to the message they were to teach.

Precursors of the Florentine Renaissance

Of all the Italian cities, Florence was probably the best prepared intellectually for the reception of a new cultural movement. Gothic architecture had never taken full hold in Italy, and especially not in Florence. The vast churches built in the thirteenth and fourteenth centuries, although they displayed Gothic pointed arches, were in fact more like ancient Roman basilicas with calm wide naves, bare simple walls, and completely rational appearance. The architects did not seek to drive toward heaven in vaulting rooflines, nor did they elucidate the mysterious complexities of religion in their decoration.

The contribution of the medieval writers of Florence was also to prepare the way for the Florentine search for individualism. Although Dante's *Divine Comedy* is a summation of the Catholic cosmology, his study of the foibles of the individuals he meets on his journey from the Inferno to Paradise are psychologically insightful portraits. The fine poet Francesco Petrarch (1304–1374) was patronized by the papal court in Avignon and considered himself an expert on the early Christian writers, yet he had already advanced partway to the ideals of Renaissance humanism. He immersed himself in the writings of Virgil and Cicero, and developed an interest in the ruins of ancient Rome. He himself was proud of his ability to write in Latin, in which he addressed a series of

Letters to the Ancient Dead to such classical authors as Homer and Livy. He was one of the first to realize that the monastic libraries contained vast numbers of ancient manuscripts of the classical writers that had not been known for centuries. He was even able to find manuscripts of some of the lost speeches and letters of Cicero. He thus took an important part in reviving the interest in classical Greece and Rome that was a fundamental feature of the Renaissance. His own writings in Latin were disappointing, but when he turned to the composition of poems in Italian to Laura, a married woman to whom he paid suit for twenty-one years, he proved the lyrical elegance of which the Italian language was capable. His own individualism gave him so great a desire for international fame that he happily accepted the crown of laurel leaves bestowed on him as poet laureate in 1341, in a revival in Rome of the ceremony the ancient Greeks had celebrated at the games in Delphi.

Petrarch's student and friend, Giovanni Boccaccio, copied him in studying Greek and seeking to popularize Greek writings in Italy. But, also like Petrarch, he is remembered primarily for his contribution to the development of literature in the Italian language. His early poetry was written to celebrate his love for a woman he called Fiammetta. Its frank delight in physical joys was in sharp contrast with Petrarch's etherealized love for Laura. In the *Decameron*, a work that was influential in establishing Italian prose style, the realism of his portrayal of human foibles became even more marked. With the *Decameron*, the world of the medieval courtly romance had been decisively rejected.

Florence's favorite medieval artist was Giotto (1266–1337), a painter of enormous personal charm and infectious ethusiasm. Giotto is generally recognized

The Epiphany, by Giotto di Bondone (1266–1337) *The Epiphany festival commemorates the visit to the stable where Christ was born, of the three Wise Men, who are seen recognizing him as the savior of the Gentiles. (The Metropolitan Museum of Art, John Stewart Kennedy Fund, 1911.)*

as having brought the technique of painting from the flat, two-dimensional, immobile appearance that typified Byzantine art to dramatic realism of the style sometimes called naturalism. Giotto painted in fresco, that is to say, wall paintings done on freshly laid plaster so that the colors set as the plaster becomes firm. He planned his scenes carefully to achieve the greatest possible drama. He made his figures appear three-dimensional, by using perspective and by foreshortening the limbs of his figures. Above all, he sought to present the individual emotions of each of the characters portrayed. He was enormously successful. The wealthy of most of the cities of Italy begged him to paint for them. But the Florentines, recognizing, as the Renaissance patrons were to do later, that an artist of his genius could excel in every form of art, appointed him master mason of the city. His lasting memorial in Florence is the beautiful Gothic belltower in brightly colored marble that stands beside the cathedral.

The Early Florentine Renaissance, 1400–1430

It was Brunelleschi's Foundlings' Hospital that announced most forcibly that a new age had arrived. Brunelleschi (1377–1446) had begun his career as a goldsmith and sculptor. Disappointed, however, that he had not won the competition to sculpt the doors of the Baptistery next to the cathedral in Florence, he went off to Rome with his friend Donatello. [The competition was won by Lorenzo Ghiberti (1378–1455), who produced two doors so beautiful that Michelangelo declared that they were worthy to be the Gates of Paradise!] In Rome, Brunelleschi studied the ruins, measuring columns, capitals, and arches, in order to discover the mathematics of ancient Roman architecture. When he returned to Florence, he won the competition for a design for a vast dome that would complete the unfinished cathedral. He constructed a Gothic dome, with an inner and outer shell held firm by hidden chains, but he did not wish to be always a Gothic architect. He believed his opportunity to become a classical Roman architect had come when in 1419 he was commissioned by the silkweavers' guild to erect a Foundlings' Hospital as a home for abandoned children.

Florence already had several charity homes for abandoned children but needed more. To house the few who could be accepted into the new hospital, Brunelleschi created a design composed of traditional Roman architectural motifs. For the facade he used nine elegant arches with Corinthian capitals, above which Andrea della Robbia placed a series of terra cotta sculptures of abandoned babies in swaddling clothes. A strong architrave created a horizontal line above the arches, and the stability of the pattern was completed with nine pedimented windows and a strong roofline of brightly colored tile. The building, however, does not resemble a Roman building, even though the arches and pediments and even the sculptured busts are motifs common in Roman architecture. The careful, spatial pattern that Brunelleschi worked out by painstaking mathematics was different from the Roman conception of harmony; and the lightness of this portico differs totally from the heavy, weight-bearing function of Roman arches.

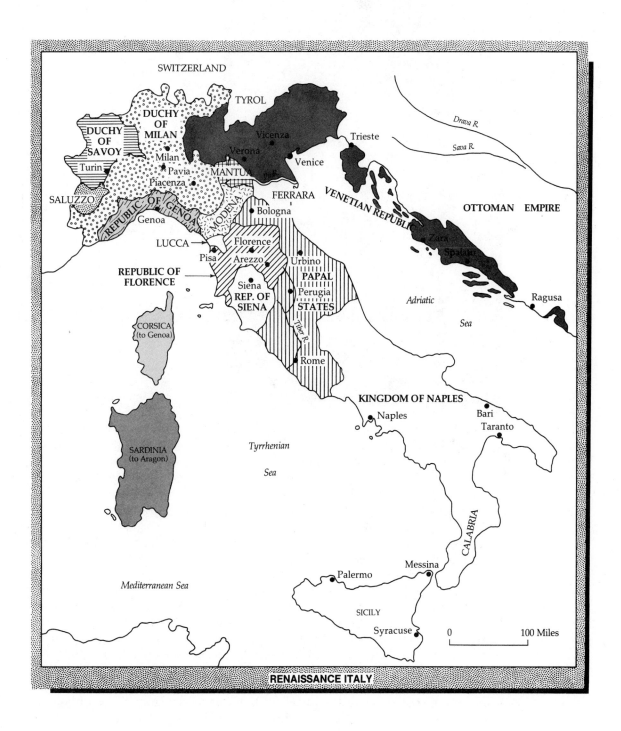

SWITZERLAND

TYROL

DUCHY OF MILAN

DUCHY OF SAVOY

Turin

Milan

Pavia

Piacenza

SALUZZO

MANTUA

Vicenza

Verona

Venice

Trieste

Drava R.

Sava R.

VENETIAN REPUBLIC

OTTOMAN EMPIRE

REPUBLIC OF GENOA

Genoa

MODENA

FERRARA

Bologna

LUCCA

Pisa

Florence

Arezzo

Urbino

REPUBLIC OF FLORENCE

Zara

Spalato

Ragusa

CORSICA (to Genoa)

Siena

REP. OF SIENA

PAPAL STATES

Perugia

Tiber R.

Rome

Adriatic

Sea

SARDINIA (to Aragon)

KINGDOM OF NAPLES

Naples

Bari

Taranto

Tyrrhenian

Sea

CALABRIA

Mediterranean Sea

Palermo

Messina

SICILY

Syracuse

0   100 Miles

RENAISSANCE ITALY

The Expulsion of Adam and Eve from the Garden of Eden, by Masaccio (1401–1428) By changing the shading between the despairing figures and the hovering angel, Masaccio created a sense of dimension known as "atmospheric perspective." (Alinari/Art Resource.)

Brunelleschi had in fact created a Roman-inspired form of architecture that was unique, and it was to set the pattern for the distinctive style of the early Renaissance. Moreover, the Foundlings' Hospital was set on a newly cleared square, not like so many medieval buildings on an irregular space formed by haphazardly knocking down buildings. The harmoniously designed, perfect square, with complementary buildings on each side, became one of the principal notions of Renaissance town planning.

Masaccio (1401–1428) was the first of the great Renaissance painters, and, even though he was killed in 1428 at the age of twenty-seven, other painters came to Florence to study his work for the next century. He was regarded as a natural successor to Giotto, whose technique of monumental figures set in dramatically conceived backgrounds he had mastered. But Masaccio had made several crucial advances in the technique of painting. He used what was called atmospheric perspective in addition to the more mathematical linear perspective that had been worked out by Brunelleschi. He used changes of atmosphere to suggest movement through distance. For example, in his painting, *The Expulsion of Adam and Eve from the Garden of Eden,* vague swirling clouds change in their consistency, and separate the angel floating in the sky from the earthbound figures of Adam and Eve. Second, Masaccio brought to fulfillment the portrayal of the emotions of human individuals that had been begun by Giotto. The heartbroken suffering of Adam and Eve as they are expelled from Eden into a sinful world, their innocence lost, is movingly portrayed, while the modeling of the figures has given them almost a sculptural quality.

Masaccio had undoubtedly learned a great deal of human anatomy from his close friend, the sculptor Donatello (1386–1466), who dominated the sculpture of the early Renaissance with the authority that Michelangelo was to wield later. Donatello had little time for medieval sculpture, but he had studied ancient Roman sculpture. Yet, like Brunelleschi in architecture, he created a new style of art that transcended his Roman models. He had observed with a sharp artist's eye the variations of individual expression and almost the very language of the body, as he showed in the statue of Saint George, which he completed as a commission for the armorer's guild. His portrait busts of Florentine merchants showed a psychological insight that has no trace of flattery. And when he was commissioned to sculpt an equestrian bronze statue of a mercenary leader for the main square of Padua, he took the newly discovered Roman statue of Marcus Aurelius for his model but created an apotheosis of brutal strength and restrained authority that outshines his model. Thus, these three friends—Brunelleschi, Masaccio, and Donatello—could be said to have been the principal forces in creating the Renaissance style.

It is possible, however, that they were so immediately accepted because Florence had already become the center of humanism. Humanism was originally a term applied to a person who taught grammar and rhetoric in the medieval university, but when taken up by the scholars of the Renaissance it applied in general to a person whose principal study was the humanities. And it came to imply that the study of the human being rather than of religion was central to their interests. The first Renaissance humanists had sought to further their study of the humanities by reviving the purity of the classical Latin and Greek languages and of the classical texts and by rediscovering classical texts that had been lost. Study of Latin had gone on throughout the Middle Ages, but now an effort was made to prune the language of the many medieval usages that had crept in. The study of Greek was aided by the emigration to Florence in the half-century preceding the Turkish capture of Constantinople in 1453 of many of the leading Byzantine scholars, who taught Greek and who brought with them many Greek manuscripts unknown in the West. Linguistic study developed such prestige that many scholars became antiquarians, interested more in the authenticity of texts than in the creation of new literature. The Florentine humanists were, however, determined to apply the lessons of classical scholarship to their own city's government. These so-called civic humanists drew from their study of the Roman republic the essentially Renaissance idea that the purpose of the state, and in particular of Florence, was to ensure individual freedom and political participation. In reality, however, as we saw, the rule of the Medici family was a barely disguised oligarchy.

Florentine Culture Under the Medici

The power of the Medici was seen almost at once in the erection of many splendid family palaces on the city's narrow streets. The Medici, as always, set the standard for others when they commissioned Michelozzo (1396–1472) to build a palace in keeping with their new grandeur. Michelozzo's palace respected the realities of life in Florence. From the outside it looked like a massive fortress, with huge rusticated blocks of stone broken only by cell-like windows on the ground floor, but with light and airy upper floors beyond the reach of marauding crowds. Within, however, was a lovely open courtyard, surrounded by a cloister, and beyond a secluded garden where Lorenzo supported a school of art for the talented youth of Florence. Here, it was said, Michelangelo was brought to learn his trade; and it was for Lorenzo that he carried out his first important commission.

The palaces were the residence of a single family, indicating a greater emphasis within Florentine society on the nuclear rather than the extended family; but the emphasis on the privacy of parents and children did not destroy the family clans in which distant relationships were recognized and upheld both as a matter of morality and self-interest. Within the home a woman was undoubtedly highly respected, and often given administration of the family finances relating to the household. But, as recent research has shown, the inward-turning palace in a real sense cut women off from contact with the public life beyond the palace walls and thus restricted both their physical and mental horizons.

The city palaces of the Medici and the other Florentine patrician families became centers of artistic and literary patronage. Walls were covered with frescoes. Oil paintings hung in the chapels and reception rooms. Intellectuals were invited to conduct discussions on philosophic topics, in which the family and their guests participated vigorously.

Cosimo de Medici invited a young scholar, named Marsilio Ficino (1433–1499), to take charge of a program of classical translation he was sponsoring, and in 1462 gave a villa on the outskirts of the city as a center for the study and discussion of the "new philosophy." At this villa, known as the Academy, Florence's artists, humanists, and political leaders met under Ficino's guidance to discuss the philosophy of neo-Platonism, which was Ficino's main interest. As a result, Ficino's views came to influence the circle around the Medici. Ficino had studied first Plato and then the Egyptian philosopher Plotinus, an exponent of Plato in the third century A.D. whose writings were known as neo-Platonism. Ficino argued that Plato's theory of ideas was crucial, but that the ideas existed in the mind of God. Human beings felt an urge to reach God, and displayed this urge in their search for two of the central ideas in the mind of God—beauty and love. Hence Ficino arrived at the splendidly Florentine conclusion that a person pursuing beauty and love was in fact seeking communion with God. He also implied, however, that the beauty and the love must have some ethereal quality to them and must not be too tied to this material world.

One of the finest expositions of this philosophy was *The Oration on the Dignity of Man* by Pico Della Mirandola (1463–1494), who also was a member of the Florentine Academy. Pico was a precocious scholar who knew Latin, Greek, Hebrew, and Arabic. Not bound by either linguistic or religious restraints, he sought the qualities that are possessed by all individuals as human beings. All people, he argued, have within themselves a share of the divine idea. Everyone has been given by God the ability to become whatever one wishes. But the highest goal should be the achievement of the contemplative life, in which the drive for material success has been set aside.

It was Sandro Botticelli (1444–1510) who brought neo-Platonism into painting, with his allegorical representations of Simonetta Vespucci in *Primavera* and *The Birth of Venus*. Simonetta was a young, married woman in the Medici circle who was idolized by the men of the court, and in particular by Lorenzo's brother Giuliano. Simonetta died of tuberculosis. Giuliano was murdered by conspirators. Hence when Botticelli placed Simonetta in *The Birth of Venus* as Venus rising on a seashell from the waves, he depicted a woman only partially of this earth, ideally beautiful and yet totally unreachable.

Ficino's views were formulated as a code of behavior for the aristocrats of the noble courts of Italy in *The Book of the Courtier*, written in the small ducal court of Urbino by Baldassare Castiglione (1478–1529). The book ostensibly describes a week of conversation in 1507 at the court of the great art patron Giudobaldo da Montefeltro, on the nature of the ideal courtier. Some of the participants bring up the most obvious requirements of a Renaissance courtier, such as military prowess, and even athletic ability in swimming and wrestling. In short, the courtier must first be a fine physical specimen. He must also, however, have a fine mind, trained in the classics and able to handle the complexities of philosophical discussion. Finally, however, the humanist Cardinal Bembo demands that the courtier should be a neo-Platonist, in whom the pursuit of love becomes an immaterial linking, not so much of man and woman, but rather of human beings with God. Little less was demanded of the women in the court than of the men, for Baldassare's courtiers dismiss through mockery the medieval notion of the natural inferiority of women. The potential greatness of women, they argue, is only too obvious when one studies the achievements of rulers like Isabella of Castile. Nevertheless, her counterpart at court to the "robust and sturdy manliness" of the male must be "a certain soft and delicate tenderness, with an air of feminine sweetness in her every movement."

Lorenzo de' Medici was only forty-four when he died in 1492; and, in a lovely poem, he had already given a premonition of his early death.

How sweet is youth,
Yet it flies from us.
Be happy now, if you wish to be happy.
One cannot be sure of tomorrow.[2]

[2] Cited in Nikolaus Pevsner, *An Outline of European Architecture* (Harmondsworth, England: Penguin Books, 1963), p. 184. Author's translation.

But the Florentine Renaissance seemed already to have run its course. In 1494, led by the visionary monk Girolamo Savonarola (1452–1498), the Florentine masses revolted and expelled the Medici. Books and paintings were burned, as the Florentines followed Savonarola's call to repentance after their century of materialism. Although Savonarola himself was burned at the stake in Florence after being condemned by the pope, Florence itself never regained its position as leader of the Renaissance. However, two of Italy's greatest artists, Leonardo da Vinci and Michelangelo Buonarroti, who had received their early training and commissions in Florence, and many lesser figures, were about to carry the Florentine message more widely afield.

The Spread of the Renaissance in Italy

Throughout the fifteenth century, and especially after 1494 when the French king invaded Italy to enforce his dynastic claim to Naples, the Italian states were engaged in political rivalries that often culminated in brutal wars. Many of the states fell into the power of mercenary captains, who fought with each other and often with the armies of the papacy. These rulers, however, who engaged in every political trick within their states and used force without compunction to win their ends outside, were lavish patrons of art and intellectuals who attempted to vie with the Florentine patriciate in the beautification of their own cities.

One great dynasty was the Malatesta of Rimini on the eastern coast of Italy, for whom the Florentine Leon Baptista Alberti redesigned a great church with

Ginevra de' Benci, By Leonardo da Vinci (1452–1519) The psychological penetration of Leonardo's portraits is exemplified in this insightful painting of a young Italian noblewoman. (National Gallery of Art, Washington, D.C.; Ailsa Mellon Bruce Fund.)

a facade in the form of a Roman triumphal arch. In niches constructed along the walls, Sigismondo Malatesta, who had been excommunicated several times for his crimes, buried the famous humanists of his court, and above the main door he instructed Alberti to omit all reference to God and instead to write simply, "Sigismondo Malatesta." Such a patron felt no need of the deity in his church. The ruthless Sforza family in Milan were especially fortunate in attracting to their service the multifaceted genius of Leonardo da Vinci (1452–1519).

Leonardo's brilliance took him into every artistic and intellectual activity of the Renaissance, and his visionary imagination took him into realms that were not to become reality until the twentieth century. He was trained as a painter in Florence, but by the time he reached Milan he was already an expert engineer, sculptor, musician, and scientist. In Milan he designed churches and drew plans for ideal cities. He painted *The Last Supper* in fresco on the wall of a Milan church, creating a dramatic scene in which he penetrated the differing emotions of the disciples at the moment when Christ announces that one of them will betray him. His interest in botany led him to place Ginevra de' Benci against a background of carefully observed trees and plants in his portrait of her. He studied anatomy in the Milanese hospitals, designed festivals for the court, reclaimed swamps, and designed fortifications. His *Notebooks* from his Milan days and his later residence in France were crammed with the observations and inventions with which his brain teemed—among thousands a design for an airplane and for a submarine, detailed botanical drawings of plants and flowers, and a dissection of the human eye. The extraordinary variety and quality of everything Leonardo did marked him as one of the greatest minds of that, or any, age.

Michelangelo and the Roman Renaissance

The popes and cardinals of Rome replaced the Florentines as the principal patrons of the Renaissance at the end of the fifteenth century, and, under their patronage, the Renaissance changed character. The leaders of an immensely wealthy institution, they wanted vast and lavishly decorated churches that would impress the thousands of pilgrims thronging to the holy city; and for themselves many of the popes and cardinals, as offspring of some of the richest families of Italy, wanted new palaces that would emphasize the grandeur of their role. In contrast to the artistic innovations of Florence, the patrons in Rome sought monumental expressions of power. The greatest monument was to be the city itself. Rome was embellished with wide avenues smashed through medieval streets, with hundreds of new churches, with statues, and with fountains. In paintings of the artists patronized by the popes, such as Raphael Sanzio (1483–1520), the emphasis is on the grandiose and majestic. Raphael's carefully planned frescoes in the Vatican palace illustrate in rich and balanced colors such uplifting themes as transubstantiation, and the springlike freshness of feeling and color evident in the paintings of the Florentine Botticelli are replaced by the heavy colors of a Roman summer.

Michelangelo's genius, however, transcended his age. In his early youth Michelangelo Buonarroti (1415–1564) had been influenced by the discussions in the Academy with his friends Ficino and Pico della Mirandola, and the sense that the artist, in seeking beauty, is also seeking God remained deeply embedded in his thought. "Had my soul not been created godlike," Michelangelo wrote, "it would seek no more than outward beauty, the delight of the eyes. But since that fades so fast, my soul soars beyond, to the eternal forms." When he sculpted a statue, he always considered that, far from shaping a statue from stone, he was liberating a preexisting statue from the stone that encased it. He was in fact profoundly religious, as can be seen in the heartbreaking statue called the *Pietà* in which, at the age of twenty-five, he depicted Christ lying lifeless in the arms of the Virgin Mary.

The pope who stimulated him to some of his greatest effort and caused him his greatest frustrations was Julius II (pope, 1503–1513). Julius' overweening pride led him to commission Michelangelo to create for himself one of the largest tombs in Europe. Merely to choose the marble, Michelangelo labored for eight months in stone quarries. Yet when he had barely begun the work, Julius sent him instead to paint the vast ceiling of the Sistine Chapel in the Vatican Palace. For four years, Michelangelo lay on his back on scaffolding, covering the ceiling with frescoes containing a neo-Platonic manifesto of the soul's journey from the material to the divine. Taking scenes from the Book of Genesis, Michelangelo depicted first the Drunkenness of Noah, in which the human soul is imprisoned in the flesh. In the center was the Creation of Adam, the moment when God's finger brings spiritual life into the body of man. And at the far end, in a picture of total spirituality, was God the Creator. Upon Julius's death, Michelangelo returned to his former patrons, the Medici of Florence, for whom he created a superb funeral chapel and library. In 1543, he was finally back in Rome, acting as superintendent of the Vatican buildings. He then had freedom to remodel the very skyline of Rome. For the summit of the Capitol Hill, he designed three harmonious palaces and a courtyard, in which he placed the ancient classical statue of the emperor Marcus Aurelius. His greatest project, however, was to redesign the dome of Saint Peter's, whose soaring dome dominates Rome today.

In a sense, by the mid-sixteenth century, Rome had followed Michelangelo in a return to spirituality. Popes of the High Renaissance such as Julius II had spent extravagantly the income they had gained from such traditional revenues as fees from newly appointed bishops, income from Church lands, and judicial charges; but, faced with the huge cost of rebuilding Saint Peter's Cathedral, they had been forced to intensify the sale of pardons, or "indulgences," for sins of the living and the dead. This extravagance had provoked a revolt in Germany and other countries of northern Europe which, by the 1520s, had challenged the very existence of the Catholic Church in large parts of the continent (see Chapter 8). This tension within the Catholic Church found expression in Michelangelo's paintings and in the deliberate disharmony of much of his architecture. Above all it is evident in the *Last Judgment*, a huge fresco that

Studies for the Libyan Sibyl, by Michelangelo (1475–1564) On the sides of the Sistine Chapel ceiling, Michelangelo painted Old Testament prophets and sibyls, or prophetesses, of the ancient world, to show the link between antiquity and Christianity. (The Metropolitan Museum of Art; purchase, 1924, Joseph Pulitzer Bequest.)

he painted in the 1530s for the rear wall of the Sistine Chapel in which the tormented damned are consigned by hideous demons to unspeakable horrors. Out of the tension came the successful reform movement within the Church we call the Catholic Reformation. But for Michelangelo himself the sense of doom, of unrelieved sadness, had become predominant. He expressed his utter melancholy in three statues of the Entombment of Christ, the most despairing of which he intended for his own tomb.

The Venetian Renaissance

While Rome returned to its spiritual goals, one city of Italy remained loyal to the bright, materialistic pursuits that had originally stimulated the Florentine Renaissance. Venice was still a world apart, secure in its lagoons, especially after the defeat of the Ottoman Turks at the sea battle of Lepanto in 1571. It had found new sources of trade after the fall of Constantinople to the Turks; but, more important for the city's artistic development, many of the rich merchant families had begun to spend their wealth on buildings and art rather than risk investing it in new trading ventures. Although Venetian artists painted many religious scenes, they reveled in the myths of the classical world, which they depicted sensuously and dramatically.

The greatest masters of the Venetian school were Titian Vecelli (1487?–

1576), Paolo Veronese (1528–1588), and Tintoretto (1518–1594), whose real name was Jacopo Robusti. Titian excelled in both allegorical and religious painting, but among European royalty he was especially in demand for his insightful, though flattering, portraits. He painted both Charles V and his son Philip II, who made him the official court painter of Spain. Titian became rich enough to return to Venice to live like a prince in his own right. Veronese too painted large numbers of religious paintings, but by specializing in scenes of festivals he was able to portray the contemporary Venetian patriciate that employed him. In his paintings, courtiers in the latest fashions sit in magnificently decorated palaces, partaking of banquets of exotic delicacies, while in the background musicians play and dogs caper. On one occasion the Inquisition even required him to change some details of a banquet, which they considered unsuitable for a religious theme.

Tintoretto was said to have attempted to combine Michelangelo's skill in drawing with Titian's use of color, but his own genius is evident in the drama that infuses all his religious paintings. He became immensely popular in Venice, and was often employed to decorate the Doge's palace and the neighborhood churches. His greatest achievement was a series of fifty-six large paintings that he executed for the Scuola di San Rocco, one of the charitable institutions founded by the Venetian patriciate to educate the poor and look after orphans. Faced with the task of making fifty-six paintings in one place look different, Tintoretto constantly changed his color schemes, shifted the point from which

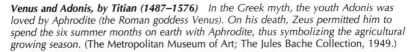

Venus and Adonis, by Titian (1487–1576) *In the Greek myth, the youth Adonis was loved by Aphrodite (the Roman goddess Venus). On his death, Zeus permitted him to spend the six summer months on earth with Aphrodite, thus symbolizing the agricultural growing season. (The Metropolitan Museum of Art; The Jules Bache Collection, 1949.)*

the painting is viewed, and even changed the philosphical character of each painting. In short, he was an innovator at a time when it seemed that such artistic perfection had been achieved by Titian and Michelangelo that all one could hope to do was adopt their way of painting.

THE RENAISSANCE MOVES NORTH

The Renaissance passed only slowly from Italy to the countries north of the Alps, which were still experimenting with the possibilities of late Gothic culture. Communication was difficult, and travel, especially in the unsettled conditions of the late fifteenth century, was dangerous. Nevertheless, some northern patrons were already avid to display their modernity by patronizing artists and architects from Italy who were masters of the new styles.

The Art of the Northern Renaissance

Curiously enough, the very first signs that these patrons were aware of the Italian Renaissance came when they built their own tombs. The French king and many aristocrats had tombs in Italian style built as early as the mid-fifteenth century. King Henry VII of England, the founder of the New Monarchy there, was buried in Westminster Abbey in a marble tomb sculptured by a fellow student of Michelangelo from Florence. It stands today in stark incongruity with the intricate Gothic vaulting overhead.

Slowly a kind of hybrid architecture developed throughout northern Europe, in which Renaissance versions of ancient Roman motifs were incorporated into the newest buildings. The most favored motif of all was the Roman triumphal arch, which was affixed to the front of building after building, in a way that would have shocked the stricter Italian architects. Italian artists found it easier and easier to obtain employment in the North, and indeed some of the greatest Italian artists were lured to the courts of the North.

Northern artists were soon acquainted with the artistic changes of the early and High Renaissance, and were especially impressed by the mastery of perspective and of the presentation of the human anatomy. Some of the more adventurous went to learn for themselves in the schools of Italian painters. Possibly the most important of these journeys was that made to Venice in 1505 by the German painter Albrecht Dürer (1471–1528) from Nuremberg.

Dürer was already then one of the finest artists of northern Europe. He had mastered all the late medieval crafts. He was a superb painter in oil and water color, and had already become one of the greatest copper engravers and masters of woodcuts of all times. His style, although still predominantly medieval in character, had developed a terrifying intensity, which he used in such engravings as *Saint Michael's Fight Against the Dragon*. In Venice, he became acquainted with early Renaissance concepts, especially of perspective and anatomy. He also encountered there the neo-Platonic notion that the painter must seek to present in material form the idea of beauty. Dürer never lost the north European intensity of religious feeling, which he, and many other north European artists, sought to give expression to through their new skills. This can be seen in such engravings as Dürer's *The Knight, Death, and the Devil.* In this picture, in spite of the boldness of the knight riding through the demon-filled forests, one is left with a sense of mystical discomfort.

The northern artists were profoundly uneasy at the state of the Catholic Church, and many, most notably Dürer and the portrait painter Lucas Cranach, immediately flung themselves into the service of Martin Luther when he led the revolt against the Catholic Church (see Chapter 8).

Christian Humanism

In an even more direct sense, the humanists of northern Europe prepared the way and helped advance the religious reformation. Scholars in the north were fascinated by the rediscovery of classical literature, both Latin and Greek, and sought themselves to develop the clarity of Latin style that typified the work of the Italian scholars. Many north European scholars went to Italy to study, and others learned from Italian business people in the north of the philosophical discussions in the patrician courts and households of the Italian cities. Most important, however, in the diffusion of the new knowledge was the invention of the printing press and the widespread use of paper.

Until this time, all books in Europe were written by hand on parchment (sheepskin), or on papyrus, and thus books were rare and costly. The Chinese had invented paper in the second century A.D., and its use had been adopted from them by the Arabs in the eighth century. Only in the fourteenth century, however, was paper of fiber, silk, or cotton manufactured in Western Europe. The Chinese too had invented printing, by use of carved wooden blocks, in the eighth century A.D., and in the tenth century knew how to use movable type. However, the large number of characters in the Chinese language made it simpler for them to use only a full block for each page of text. Thus, when Johann Gutenberg of Mainz, about 1450, invented a method of printing using movable type cast in molds for the letters of the alphabet, it was a European innovation, and its use spread rapidly through Germany and from there to Italy. Although the first books were printed in expensive editions that resembled medieval illustrated manuscripts, the pent-up demand for books almost immediately made printing for a mass market highly profitable, and by the end of the century cheap editions were pouring from almost a thousand presses. By 1500 between 6 and 10 million books had been printed. The most important single weapon for challenging any authoritarian regime, ecclesiastical or secular, was thus ready at hand. By far the most popular book to be printed was the Bible, which had already appeared in translation in Germany long before Luther used his own translation as his support in justifying his attack on the pretensions of the pope to dominance in the Christian Church.

Sir Thomas More, by Hans Holbein the Younger (c. 1497–1543) When painted in 1527, More was still highly regarded by King Henry VIII. After he refused to accept Henry's leadership of the Church of England, he was beheaded. (The Frick Collection.)

Most northern humanists were Christians who sought by studying the classics and the Bible to find a deeper understanding of the meaning of religion. Their very piety made them reformers. Sir Thomas More (1475–1535) in England, for example, although a confirmed Catholic who was executed for refusing to convert to Protestantism, nevertheless wrote a sharp indictment of his own age in his book *Utopia*. *Utopia* was a description of an ideal state in which property would be owned in common and religion could be followed freely.

The most influential of the humanists was the Dutch scholar Erasmus (1466–1536). Born in Rotterdam the illegitimate son of a priest, he was raised by a lay order called the Brethren of the Common Life, who instilled in him the lasting belief in the "philosophy of Christ," a gentle Christianity that condemned all war and criticized the inequities of wealth and class. Eventually he entered the Church himself as a priest. He mastered Greek and Latin, and read widely in classical literature, the Bible, and the writings of the Church Fathers. He decided that the New Testament in use contained numerous errors, and published a revised version based on the earliest texts he could find together with a Latin translation and commentary. These books made him the foremost religious scholar of his day, and most of the Protestant reformers were to use his texts as the basis for their translations of the Bible into the vernacular.

Erasmus even seemed prepared to become a reformer himself, when he published in 1511 a scathing attack on the abuses of his age, known as *The Praise of Folly*. In it he lashed out especially at the sale of pardons by the papacy, which he felt was demeaning the Church and excusing the worst forms of sin. But like More, he refused to leave the Catholic Church. The two great scholars had immense influence on the movement of religious reform that was to dominate most of the sixteenth century, yet they themselves, when confronted with a choice, were unable to join that movement they had done so much to unleash.

SUGGESTED READINGS

The Transformation of the Middle Ages

The economic recession provoked by the scourges of the fourteenth and fifteenth centuries is analyzed in Harry A. Miskimin, *The Economy of the Early Renaissance, 1300–1460* (1969), and somewhat more technically by Raymond de Roover, *Business, Banking, and Economic Thought in Late Medieval and Early Modern Europe* (1974). The plague's economic and environmental impact is analyzed in Robert S. Gottfried, *The Black Death: Natural and Human Disaster in Medieval Europe* (1983). On the plague in England, see Philip Ziegler, *The Black Death* (1969). The psychological reaction to the fluctuating threat of disease is explained in the path-breaking work of Philippe Ariès, *Western Attitudes Toward Death: From the Middle Ages to the Present* (1974).

Guillaume Mollat, *The Popes at Avignon, 1305–1378* (1963), is a good introduction to the Babylonian Captivity. Popular religious fervor could become mysticism, as shown in Rufus M. Jones, *The Flowering of Mysticism* (1939), or seek sacrificial victims, as illustrated by Norman Cohn's *Europe's Inner Demons: An Inquiry Inspired by the Great Witchhunt* (1975).

The origin of the New Monarchies in France and England is discussed in Joseph R. Strayer, *The Medieval Origins of the Modern State* (1970), whose brilliant but brief analysis may be filled out by a biographical study such as S. B. Chrimes, *Henry VII* (1973), or P. M. Kendall, *Louis XI* (1971). Desmond Seward studies the transformation of the French and English monarchies, as well as the military campaigns, in *The Hundred Years' War: The English in France, 1337–1453* (1978).

Two excellent surveys that prefer social and intellectual analysis to chronological narrative are Denys Hay, *Europe in the Fourteenth and Fifteenth Centuries* (1966), and Steven Ozment, *The Age of Reform, 1250–1550* (1980).

The Renaissance in Italy

One should begin with the expansion of the cities in the High Middle Ages in Daniel Waley's *The Italian City-Republics* (1969), and J. K. Hyde, *Society and Politics in Medieval Italy: The Evolution of the Civil Life, 1000–1350* (1973). Then, plunge into the maelstrom of Florentine life. Gene Brucker, *Renaissance Florence* (1969), is a fine synthesis. Good political analyses include J. R. Hale, *Florence and the Medici: The Pattern of Control* (1978); Nicolai Rubinstein, *The Government of Florence Under the Medici (1434–1494)* (1966); and Alison Brown, *Bartolomeo Scala, 1430–1497, Chancellor of Florence: The Humanist as Bureaucrat* (1979). Cecilia M. Ady, *Lorenzo dei Medici and Renaissance Italy* (1962), provides a brief acquaintance with Il Magnifico. For the "little people," see Samuel Kline Cohn, Jr., *The Laboring Classes of Renaissance Florence* (1980). The role of ritual ceremonies in keeping the working class loyal is discussed in Richard C. Trexler, *Public Life in Renaissance Florence* (1981). Ian Maclean, *The Renaissance Notion of Woman* (1980), is a complex analysis of how people viewed woman, from the legal, philosophical, and even medical points of view. Hannelore Sachs's well-illustrated *The Renaissance Woman* (1971) treats education, family life, and work.

The artistic achievement is described, with many examples, in Jacques Lassaigne and Giulio C. Argan, *The Fifteenth Century: From Van Eyck to Botticelli* (1955). Kenneth Clark does justice to the most varied genius of the age in *Leonardo da Vinci* (1976).

Peter Partner, *Renaissance Rome 1500–1559* (1976) is more interested in political and economic background than in the artists.

Finally, although his theses have been under constant attack for two decades or more, Jacob Burckhardt's *The Civilization of the Renaissance in Italy* (1867) is still worth reading for the freshness of his defense of the individualism and materialism that he perceived as the core of the Renaissance achievement.

Northern Humanism

The religious preoccupations of the northern scholars are emphasized in Johan Huizinga, *Erasmus and the Age of the Reformation* (1957, 1984), and Myron P. Gilmore, *The World of Humanism, 1453–1517* (1952). Erwin Panofsky, *The Life and Art of Albrecht Dürer* (1955), is a masterly analysis of the greatest of the northern artists, and his *Early Netherlands Painting* (1953) is the classic study of Roger Van der Weyden and Jan van Eyck.

8

The Two Reformations

The Florentine Renaissance had been sharply and almost fatally interrupted by the outburst of religious fanaticism provoked by Savonarola in 1494–1498 (see p. 222). Although Savonarola's death at the stake was soon followed by a resurgence of the humanistic culture of Florence under the late Medici rulers, the years of religious turmoil had been a significant reminder that the mass of Europeans were far from abandoning the call of religion. On the contrary, the deep piety of the fifteenth century, seen from one end of the continent to the other in such varied forms as the tormented wood carvings of Veit Stoss in Germany, the devotional meditations of the English mystic Margery Kempe, or the austere discipline of the Franciscan nuns known as Poor Clares, was evidence of a deep thirst for a return to the spirituality of the early Church.

To those demands the Renaissance papacy appeared oblivious. Its prestige and its moral fervor had slumped disastrously during the Babylonian Captivity in Avignon and the Great Schism that followed; and the marvelous artistic achievements of giants like Raphael and Michelangelo, which it had purchased, had merely increased among the pious a disgust with its worldliness and among the worldly a fury at the financial expedients necessary to pay for this Roman magnificence. The final blow was the decision by Pope Leo X (1513–1521) to permit the renewed sale of indulgences, which were considered pardons of temporal punishments due for sin and the remission of time in purgatory. They are not the same as absolution of guilt but were sold by clerics as if they were. In 1517, Martin Luther, a German friar and professor of theology at the University of Wittenberg, launched the Protestant Reformation by nailing to the

Martin Luther, by Lucas Cranach the Elder (1472–1553) Cranach, the court painter of Wittenberg, painted portraits of Luther at all stages of his career and designed woodcuts to carry more widely the Protestant message. (IN/Germanisches Nationalmuseum, Nürnberg from German Information Center.)

door of the Wittenberg church ninety-five theses, which not only condemned the sale of indulgences but explicitly questioned some of the most fundamental claims of the pope to exercise divine authority on behalf of Christ.[1]

Although the consequences of Luther's act were not immediately recognized—the pope had merely remarked on hearing of the theses, "Friars bickering as usual"—the revolt against Rome advanced rapidly. Soon changing its character from an attempt to reform the Church to a revolution against it, the Protestant Reformation passed through three main stages. In the first place, new religious doctrines were developed that could be substituted for long-established doctrines of the Catholic Church. It was therefore important for the Protestant Reformation that its first leaders should not be political insurgents but learned theologians. Martin Luther (1483–1546), who led the Protestants in Germany, taught theology at the University of Wittenberg and later produced a superbly written and highly influential translation of the Bible into German. Huldreich Zwingli (1484–1531), who began the Reformation in Switzerland, was a priest in the principal church in Zürich, argued with Luther as an intellectual equal, and opened the first rift in the Protestant ranks by refusing to accept all of Luther's version of Christianity. Perhaps the most refined thinker of the Protestant Reformation was John Calvin (1509–1564), a Frenchman who made

---

[1] The word Protestant originates in the *Protestatio* or protest of a minority of the delegates at the imperial Diet of Speyer in 1529, who objected to the recess of the diet after it had forbidden any further religious innovation in Germany.

the Swiss city of Geneva his center, and whose great work, *The Institutes of the Christian Religion,* was one of the most learned and most influential books of the sixteenth century.

Second, Protestantism required the political and, more important, the military support of secular rulers against counterattacks by the Catholic Church. For Luther, the situation was ripe for revolt in many of the states into which Germany was divided. Many princes supported Luther, most notably the Elector of Saxony, in which Wittenberg was located. The reasons for accepting Protestantism by many princely rulers were not primarily religious. Acceptance of Lutheranism provided a good excuse for throwing off the controls of the Holy Roman Emperor and for refusing the financial demands of the pope. The governing bourgeoisie of many German cities were also ready to support the new religion. To them, Luther cried, "Poor Germans that we are—we have been deceived! We were born to be masters, and we have been compelled to bow the head beneath the yoke of tyrants." The federal constitution of Switzerland made it possible for specific cantons, especially the wealthier and urbanized ones, to support Zwingli and even to fight a civil war against the Catholic cantons in which Zwingli himself was killed. With the arrival of Calvin in Geneva, however, the center of Swiss Protestantism passed to the city-state of Geneva. In a very short time, Protestantism gained strongholds from which Catholics could not dislodge it.

The third stage was the expansion of Protestantism from its original centers to neighboring countries and even across the oceans. The process of expansion was twofold. In certain cases foreign rulers felt the same desire as the German princes to establish in their kingdoms both financial independence and their own moral authority. Henry VIII founded the Anglican church in England as his own version of Protestantism, while the Scandinavian kings were prepared to accept Lutheranism when Luther organized his church so as to readily support the secular power. But Protestants were also proselytizers. From the start they sent out missionaries burning with the desire to make converts. The German Lutherans were even able to find many new supporters in Austria, whose ruler, the Emperor Charles V, had undertaken to extirpate Protestantism on behalf of the pope. The most effective missionaries were the Calvinists, who found in Geneva a superb training ground in which they studied with as much fervor as twentieth-century revolutionaries how their doctrines could be spread in a sort of underground conspiracy. These missionaries succeeded in spreading Calvinism to the Netherlands, Scotland, parts of France, and England; and, as Puritanism, it was carried by English Calvinists to England's colonies in North America.

Perhaps because the early efforts of the Catholic rulers and of the Renaissance popes to crush Protestantism were so unsuccessful, the Catholic Church undertook its own Reformation, which used to be called the Counter-Reformation but is now more generally known as the Catholic Reformation. (The word Counter-Reformation is still used occasionally, but only to denote the efforts of the Catholic Church to *counter* the advance of Protestantism.) A far-reaching program was undertaken to end the Church's preoccupation with material goals, and especially the nepotism and financial abuse that had caused so much sympathy for Protestantism. The Church's doctrines were reaffirmed, and the doctrinal changes demanded by the Protestants finally rejected. New weapons were refined for the struggle against Protestantism, notably the drawing up of an Index of Forbidden Books; widespread use of the Roman and Spanish Inquisitions against heresy; and the foundation of new and learned orders of monks, like the Jesuits, to lead the struggle. Catholic and Protestant engaged in a competition that soon passed from a doctrinal confrontation to a military struggle that lasted until the end of the Thirty Years War in 1648.

THE ESTABLISHMENT OF A PROTESTANT THEOLOGY

Martin Luther

Luther first believed that he was no different from many reformers who had appeared to call the Church to reform in periods of decline. He said that when he visited Rome in 1511 he was appalled: "Godlessness and evil are great and shameless there. Neither God nor man, neither sin nor modesty, are respected. So testify all the pious who were there and all godless who returned worse from Italy."[2] Luther was, however, suited in character to be a revolutionary rather than a reformer. Like his own father, he was stubborn and, in both appearance and opinions, bullnecked, a man of towering rages and fierce independence.

Luther's father had sent him to the University of Erfurt to study law, but Luther, knocked to the ground one night by a bolt of lightning, promised Saint Anne, the local patron saint, that he would become a monk. He went about finding his own salvation in his own fashion. He tried mortification of the flesh, but found it unsuccessful: "I was a good monk," he said later, "and I kept the rule of my order so strictly that I may say that if ever a monk got to heaven by his monkery it was I. If I had kept on any longer, I should have killed myself with vigils, prayers, reading, and other work." He then tried to study his way to salvation, seeking the answer in the Holy Scriptures, on which he lectured from 1512 on at the University of Wittenberg.

Luther slowly came to realize from his study of the Bible that he disagreed with one of the basic doctrines of the Church, the need to do good works in order to achieve salvation. His own efforts to do good had proved worthless in removing the deep sense of sin that afflicted him. Suddenly one day, he said later, he realized that the answer lay in Saint Paul's Epistle to the Romans, in the sentence, "The just shall live by his faith." The concept of justification by

---

[2] Hans J. Hillerbrand, ed., *The Reformation: A Narrative Related by Contemporary Observers and Participants* (New York: Harper & Row, 1964), p. 25.

faith was the entire answer to the problem of sin. His concept of justification by faith, that is, achieving salvation by the personal grace of God granted through personal trust in God, led him to reject some of the basic teachings of the Catholic Church. These teachings can be summarized as good works are necessary for salvation, the Catholic priesthood must act as an intermediary between God and human beings, and the teachings of the Church over the centuries must be regarded as a source of divine truth in addition to the Bible.

When John Tetzel, a rapacious seller of indulgences, appeared on the borders of Saxony in 1517, Luther was thus already prepared not only to attack the abuses but also some of the basic claims to power of the Catholic Church. When Luther found that some of his own parishioners in Wittenberg had purchased indulgences, he composed ninety-five propositions, or theses, for debate, and posted them publicly on the door of the castle church. Some of the theses were direct criticisms of Tetzel: "They preach only human doctrines who say that, as soon as the money clinks into the money chest, the soul flies out of purgatory." Other theses criticized the doctrine of "superfluous merit" that was the basic justification for the sale of indulgences. This doctrine held that Christ's life had been so perfect that he had left behind an excess of merit that could be used by the pope to lessen the sufferings in purgatory of those whose lives had been less than perfect. A believer could gain an indulgence by good works or a money payment. Others criticized the pope for using German money to build Saint Peter's. Leo X, the urbane son of Lorenzo de' Medici, preferred to let the matter drop, but members of the German clergy demanded further action. For the next three years Luther debated his theories openly with leading theologians sent against him by the Catholic Church, and succeeded in two areas: (1) in winning the support of some German clerics and nobles; (2) in making clear that his opinions were heretical.

In June 1520, the pope ordered Luther to recant or face excommunication. By then, however, Luther was beyond compromise. In several short, incisive pamphlets, he had already called for revolt against the Catholic Church. In *An Address to the German Nobility* he demanded that the German princes carry out a thorough reform of the Catholic Church in their states. In *The Babylonian Captivity of the Church*, he challenged the position of the Catholic hierarchy as an intermediary between human beings and God, seeing it rather as an obstacle to the individual's achievement of salvation by faith. He even demanded the abandonment of five of the Church's seven sacraments, and produced his own interpretation of the doctrine of transubstantiation, the doctrine that in the communion service the bread and wine were changed into the body and blood of Christ. Upon receiving the papal bull of excommunication, he led a group of students and professors out to burn it publicly, and wrote a scathing rejection of the pope's criticism entitled *Against the Accursed Bull of the AntiChrist*.

The pope appealed to the new Holy Roman Emperor Charles V (reigned 1519–1556) to take action against Luther. Luther was protected, in spite of his excommunication, by the Elector of Saxony. Charles met with all the German

The Emperor Charles V on Horseback, by Titian *Charles is shown attacking the Protestants at the battle of Mühlberg in 1547. (The Prado, Madrid.)*

princes and representatives of the cities at Worms in 1521, where he personally argued with Luther. Once again Luther refused to recant: "Unless I am convinced by the testimony of Scripture or by evident reason (for I trust neither in popes nor in councils alone; since it is obvious that they have often erred and contradicted themselves) I . . . cannot and will not recant." The young emperor replied in a classic justification of reliance on tradition and authority:

> You know that my ancestors were the most Christian Emperors of the illustrious German nation, the Catholic kings of Spain, archdukes of Austria, and the dukes of Burgundy, who all were, until death, faithful sons of the Roman Church. Always they defended the Catholic faith, the sacred ceremonies, decretals, ordinances, and holy rites to the honor of God, the propagation of the faith and the salvation of souls. It is certain that a single monk errs in his opinion which is against what all Christendom has held for over a thousand years to the present. . . . I am resolved to act and proceed against him as a notorious heretic, asking you to state your opinions as good Christians and to keep the vow given me.[3]

Zwingli in Zürich

Meanwhile, in Switzerland, Huldreich Zwingli's views had gone through a somewhat similar evolution to Luther's. Zwingli, during his studies in the Universities of Vienna and Basel, had come to admire the writings of Christian

---

[3] Cited by Hans J. Hillerbrand, ed., *The Reformation: A Narrative Related by Contemporary Observers and Participants* (New York: Harper & Row, 1964), p. 94.

humanists such as Erasmus, and had demanded that the Church end its abuses. During his service as priest in Zürich he had undertaken a long study of the Bible and, like Luther, had decided that all religious truth lay in the Holy Scriptures. All the Catholic hierarchy and its ceremonial were, in his opinion, unnecessary for salvation, for which only justification by faith was needed. Between 1522 and 1525 he persuaded the Zürich city council to carry through their own reformation, to renounce the authority of the Catholic Church, to remove the relics and even the stained glass windows from the churches, and to adopt a new, simplified form of worship. The council, however, with Zwingli's support, made Zürich into a kind of theocracy, a state governed by a church, in which the government excommunicated heretics, punished immorality, employed spies for its marital court, and ran a form of state welfare system.

Luther and Zwingli slowly drew apart on matters of doctrine and strategy, in spite of the obvious value of coordinating their forces against the Catholic counterattack. Luther and Zwingli could not agree on the central doctrines of transubstantiation. Zwingli saw the communion service as a memorial of Christ's last supper. Luther, although he disagreed with the Catholic belief that the bread and wine were transformed into the body and blood of Christ, nevertheless held that Christ was present in the bread and wine. An attempt in 1529 to persuade the two to find a compromise broke down in failure, and Luther abandoned Zwingli when the Catholic cantons attacked. Zwingli, aided by only 2500 men, died in battle; and the remaining Zwinglians united with the Calvinist church in 1549.

The Anabaptists

The Anabaptists were a radical sect, many of whose members were former Zwinglians who wished to found what they regarded as a more purified church than that of Zwingli himself. They held that all lay people, male or female, were equally members of the priesthood, and women were very numerous in the early congregations, supporting the movement with funds and on occasion preaching publicly. The Anabaptists demanded that baptism should be delayed until adulthood, when one had learned "repentance and amendment of life." Since almost everyone had been baptized as a child, the sect became known as "rebaptists" or Anabaptists. They also believed that all property should be owned communally and that society as well as religion needed to be reformed. Both Catholics and Lutherans engaged almost immediately in savage persecution of the Anabaptists, who were tortured, hanged, burned, and drowned. (The Anabaptists should not be confused with the Protestant denomination called Baptists, which was founded by John Smyth in Amsterdam in 1608.) The primary reason for their persecution in Germany was that they were among the leaders of the Peasants' Revolt of 1524–1525 and incurred Luther's wrath for not accepting his authority. The Anabaptists might have disappeared had they not been brought back to their original simplicity of life by a Dutch leader named

Menno Simons (1496–1561). His followers, called Mennonites, founded new communities in America, Eastern Europe, and Russia.

Calvin in Geneva

John Calvin became acquainted with Luther's teachings while studying philosophy, law, and linguistics in France. Like Luther, he experienced a "sudden conversion," and was compelled, during the persecution of suspected Lutherans in Paris, to flee to Basel in Switzerland. He began work on *The Institutes of the Christian Religion,* and published the first edition in 1536 when he was only twenty-seven. The book was at once recognized as one of the most important statements of Protestant belief.

On many points, Calvin agreed with Luther. He held that the only way to know God was by studying the Bible. He rejected salvation by good works, and held that human beings must accept the grace of God displayed by the death of Christ on the cross. Far more than Luther, however, he held that the powers of God were absolute, and that his ways were unintelligible. Most of all, he emphasized the doctrine of predestination, that God has decided in advance who will be damned and who will be saved: "Eternal life is foreordained for some, and eternal damnation for others." Since only a few people would be saved, Calvin suggested that, in addition to the certainty of one's own faith, a person might apply three tests to see if one were among the elect destined for salvation, "a confession of faith, an exemplary life, and participation in the sacraments of baptism and the Lord's Supper."

It was essential for the elect to establish their church on this earth as a visible expression of the eternal organization that linked believers in the present with those in both the past and the future. This church was to undertake tasks normally considered part of the state's duties, including education, supervision of business conduct, and even eligibility for state office. It was only to be expected, therefore, that the Calvinist church would eventually take over the state, as it did in Geneva under Calvin's guidance.

Calvin also created a hierarchical structure of ministers, deacons, and so on, which could exist where the state was either indifferent or intolerant. The personal life of every Calvinist was the responsibility of the community. Hard work was the duty of everyone. Ostentatious spending was to be discouraged, if not actually forbidden or even punished. Accumulation of wealth was not condemned, especially since wealth was to be used in the service of others, such as the old or the sick (though not of the shiftless poor, who were clearly not among the elect).

Luther, Zwingli, and Calvin had thus created new theologies that, though based on the long tradition of Catholic theology, were incompatible with the teachings of the Church. The theologies could not be practiced in new churches. But in the sixteenth century, an age when religious diversity was not tolerated, creation of a new church implied enormous changes in the lives of all members

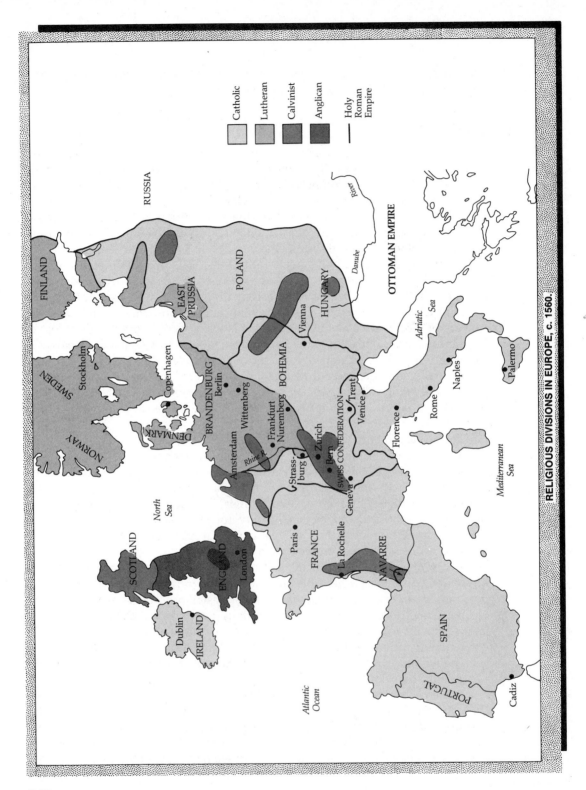

RELIGIOUS DIVISIONS IN EUROPE, c. 1560.

Catholic   Lutheran   Calvinist   Anglican   —— Holy Roman Empire

RUSSIA

FINLAND

EAST PRUSSIA

POLAND

HUNGARY

Vienna

BOHEMIA

Danube River

OTTOMAN EMPIRE

Adriatic Sea

SWEDEN

NORWAY

Stockholm

Copenhagen

DENMARK

BRANDENBURG

Berlin

Wittenberg

Amsterdam

Frankfurt

Nuremberg

Rhine R.

Strass-burg

Zurich

Bern

SWISS CONFEDERATION

Geneva

Trent

Venice

Florence

Rome

Naples

Palermo

Mediterranean Sea

North Sea

SCOTLAND

ENGLAND

London

Dublin IRELAND

Atlantic Ocean

Paris

FRANCE

La Rochelle

NAVARRE

SPAIN

PORTUGAL

Cadiz

of a state in which there was to be a new church: in politics, in finance, in class relationships, in education, and in culture. The Protestant Reformation could therefore be successful only if its adherents wanted changes in many other spheres as well as in religion. This situation existed in large parts of Germany and Switzerland; and there Protestantism established its original base.

PROTESTANTISM ESTABLISHES A TERRITORIAL BASE

The first territorial base of Protestantism lay in Germany and Switzerland, in a territory shaped like a diamond, with the cities of Wittenberg, Frankfurt, Augsburg, and Geneva as its four points. Although it had previously taken little part in the major events of European history, this area was now ready to step forward into a central role. The region possessed four characteristics that made it the ideal first home of Protestantism: It was rich. It was politically fragmented, so that hundreds of individual rulers felt free to make their own individual choice of religion. It was highly educated, especially in the writings of Christian humanism. And finally, it possessed a deep Christian piety, which made the abuses of the Renaissance Church intolerable to it.

The wealth of Germany and Switzerland had increased greatly in the fifteenth and sixteenth centuries. Many of Europe's important trade routes crossed this territory, most notably the great route linking northern Italy to the cities of Flanders. The development of the resources of the Baltic countries and Eastern Europe opened vast opportunities to the manufacturing and trading cities of Central Germany. Further profits were made in mining and banking; Luther's own father had made a fortune from copper and iron mines. Germans were partly responsible for the exploitation of the silver, iron, and copper mines of Austria and Hungary.

Even more important was the shift of the center of European banking from Florence and central Italy to south Germany. The group most responsible for this shift was the Fugger family of Augsburg, the principal bankers for the Holy Roman Emperor. The fortune of the Fuggers was probably ten times as large as that of the Medici a hundred years earlier; and the German bankers had established a strong foothold in Antwerp, the new banking center of the Low Countries. German bankers controlled the export of Spanish colonial goods to Germany. The German countryside, too, was prosperous. It had recovered from the Black Death and was growing wealthy from supplying the expanding cities. This wealth was to be of great importance in giving the area the ability to withstand the Catholic powers.

Political disunity made possible the rapid acceptance of Protestantism. Germany was divided into more than 300 states, many of which resented their subordination to the Holy Roman Emperor in Vienna. A few could not be weaned away from Catholicism. States such as Bavaria, dependent on and vulnerable to attack from the Holy Roman Emperor, were unlikely to turn Protestant. But a large number of German cities were very willing to throw off the control of local bishops, and were supported in this by the artisan class, who frequently resented the exactions of the Church and its moral laxity. Several great cities became both intellectual and military centers of Protestantism. Strassburg on the Rhine was won over to Lutheranism by several humane ex-monks who brought their wives to the city. Cities with great universities, like Heidelberg, were soon persuaded by the professors to follow the Protestant wave. The city of Nuremberg became Lutheran under the influence of the great painter Albrecht Dürer and the poet Hans Sachs. Two-thirds of the German cities were Protestant by 1531.

The princely states moved even more rapidly to accept the doctrines of Luther. Luther's patron Frederick the Wise, Elector of Saxony, probably prevented Lutheranism from being wiped out in its infancy by refusing to hand Luther over to the papal authorities. Princes who turned Protestant often had material rather than spiritual goals. They invariably confiscated the property of the Church and, with Luther's agreement, established state churches that recognized the prince's supreme authority. By 1531 the princely states of most of north and central Germany had become Lutheran.

In Switzerland, as we saw, it was the cities that took the lead in accepting Zwinglianism, and Protestantism had great difficulty in penetrating the rural cantons. In fact, the rural cantons almost succeeded in wiping out Protestantism when they defeated Zwingli's small army in 1531. But Protestantism persisted in the cities of Basel and Bern and spread from there to the city of Geneva.

The intellectual classes within this region had been prepared for the acceptance of Protestantism by the writings of the Christian humanists, most notably those of Erasmus, who made possible new translations of the Bible by issuing his authoritative Greek text of the New Testament and had turned many against Church abuses with his satirical *Praise of Folly* (1511).

The printing press spread widely throughout Germany the writings of the Protestant theologians; by 1530, one-third of a million copies of Luther's works had been published. The region's artists joined in the propagation of the new religion. Lucas Cranach (1472–1553), who was the court painter of the Elector of Saxony, became an immediate admirer of Luther and painted portraits of him at all stages of his career; and he produced many works of Protestant propaganda in woodcuts, a technique by which hundreds of copies of pictures could be printed from wood blocks. Even more influential was Dürer, who was not only one of Germany's finest painters but undoubtedly Germany's greatest printmaker. Dürer became one of Luther's greatest supporters. In 1521, fearing that the pope had put Luther to death, Dürer wrote in his diary: "I know not whether he lives or is murdered, but in any case he has suffered from the Christian truth. If we lose this man, who has written more clearly than any other in centuries, may God grant his spirit to another. . . . O God, if Luther is dead, who will henceforth explain to us the gospels? What might he not have written for us in the next ten or twenty years?"[4]

Here then was a region that was prepared, mentally and emotionally, to accept the doctrines of Protestantism, and had the capacity, economic and military, to fight for those doctrines.

NEW CONVERSIONS TO PROTESTANTISM

Spread of Lutheranism

The three decades after Luther's posting of the ninety-five theses were a period of great opportunity for the Protestants. Until the Catholic Church had carried through a far-reaching reform program from within, it could not wage a spiritual competition with the Protestants. As a result, during these three decades it had to rely on the strength of the rulers who remained faithful to it, most notably the Holy Roman Emperor Charles V. Charles, however, was faced by a vast number of other problems even more threatening to his power than the Lutherans. The Turkish Sultan Suleiman the Magnificent (reigned 1520–1566) was in control of Hungary, and his armies reached the gates of Vienna itself in 1520. The French king, although committed to maintenance of Catholicism in France, was quite prepared to aid the German Protestants as a means of weakening the Holy Roman Empire. The princes in south Germany had little desire to strengthen the Holy Roman Emperor by throwing all their strength under his leadership to defeat their fellow princes who had turned Protestant. Finally, Charles's empire was simply too big for him to control (see Chapter 9). Thus, as Charles attempted to pull together military forces that could compel the Protestant states of Germany to abandon Luther and Lutheranism, he was constantly frustrated by the revival of one threat or another in different parts of his wide empire.

Luther took advantage of this situation to create an organized church that, while satisfying the demands of the German princes, would at the same time make his version of Christianity available and appealing to the average person for whom Catholicism had often seemed a distant and alien creed. While taking refuge in the Wartburg castle in Saxony, he had composed a beautiful translation of the Bible into German, and had planned a new form of worship in which the congregation could participate in the singing of melodious hymns, many of which were composed by Luther himself. He also simplified the system of sacraments, recognizing only baptism and communion. Books and sermons, made available to Lutheran ministers by printings in the thousands, provided a homespun but powerful basis for their sermons, which became the central feature of the Lutheran church service.

In spite of his own revolt against the Catholic Church, Luther did not accept

[4] Roland Bainton, *Here I Stand* (New York: Abingdon Press, 1950), p. 92.

the right of individuals to choose whatever form of religious belief they wished. Religious tolerance was far from his concept of religious freedom. He recognized that the survival of Lutheranism was dependent on the goodwill of the rulers, and hence it became far more important for the ruler to be converted than for the majority of his subjects to decide.

In fact, Luther gained the goodwill of the majority of the princes in Germany, and lost the support of many of the poor, by harshly condemning the desperate revolt of the peasantry in 1524–1525. Seeing south Germany ravaged by nothing less than a class war, in which the peasants, supported by many of the workers of the cities, fought desperately to regain lands that had been confiscated from them and to throw off harsh obligations owed to landlords, Luther publicly called for the savage reprisals taken by the upper classes, in which as many as 100,000 peasants may have been killed.

Lutheranism was thus especially appealing to rulers intent on creating in their own states the type of New Monarchy adopted in England and France in the late fifteenth century. In 1527 the kings of Sweden and Denmark broke with the Catholic Church, and in both cases used the break as an excuse for confiscating the Church's property. Denmark adopted Lutheranism as the national church a decade later, and, since Norway and Iceland were ruled by Denmark at that time, both countries also became officially Lutheran. Lutheranism became the official church of Sweden in 1593; and Finland, a possession of Sweden, also became Lutheran. There was a good deal of popular support for Lutheranism in Scandinavia, which made the actions of the rulers more easily acceptable. Many Scandinavian students had become sympathetic to Lutheranism while studying in German universities, especially in Wittenberg, which trained the new church leaders of all the Scandinavian countries. Moreover, Lutheran doctrines were also spread into Scandinavia by merchants from the towns of Hanseatic League, making the middle class of the Baltic seaport towns among the earliest converts to Lutheranism.

The English Reformation

The English adoption of Protestantism was almost totally different, even though there had been frequent criticism of papal abuses in the fifteenth century and some of the principal Christian humanists had been English or, like Erasmus, had worked in England. England was probably receptive to the introduction of Lutheranism, which had been a subject of debate at Cambridge University. The second Tudor king, Henry VIII (reigned 1509–1547), was not prepared, however, to follow the example of the Scandinavian kings. He wanted both to remain a Catholic and to be head of his own church. Apparently he was deeply worried that he was being punished by God for marrying his brother's widow, Catherine of Aragon, by being given a daughter, the future Queen Mary, but no son. Ending his marriage to Catherine was, however, a very difficult process, even though kings had often been able to persuade the pope to annul their marriages. Catherine was politically important in her own right. She was the daughter of Ferdinand and Isabella of Spain and, more important, the aunt of Emperor Charles V. Moreover she was blameless in character and deeply religious, and was determined to fight against any annulment procedures that Henry might institute.

Henry found that he could not persuade the pope to annul his marriage, and eventually decided to accept the suggestion of his advisers, Thomas Cromwell (1485–1540) and Thomas Cranmer (1489–1556), that he make himself the head of the Church in England. The scheming politician Cromwell was given the task of breaking opposition within the Church and among Catholic lay people. Cromwell forced legislation through Parliament making Henry supreme head of the Church of England, and dissolving the monasteries. Their lands and possessions were shared among the king and his leading supporters in Parliament, who were thus given a material incentive to continue their support of the new religion.

Cranmer married Henry to Anne Boleyn, a lady in waiting of Catherine, in January 1533, and two months later, as Archbishop of Canterbury, declared that Catherine's marriage was invalid. Anne disappointed Henry by giving him a daughter, the future Queen Elizabeth, instead of a son. Henry then established a baleful precedent for his future treatment of his wives by executing Anne for treason. (His third wife died in childbirth. His fourth, whom he married for political reasons, was divorced. His fifth was executed soon after. His sixth outlived him.) Cromwell, who had persuaded Henry to execute Anne, was

Henry VIII, by Hans Holbein the Younger Painted in 1540, Henry VIII displays the determination, and perhaps the inner wilfulness, of a man who has successfully broken with the pope and has already divorced two wives and executed one. (Galleria Nazionale d'Arte Antica/Art Resource.)

himself beheaded for treason later. Henry had established a church entirely in keeping with his own absolutist tendencies; and he did not permit Cranmer, who was an admirer of Zwingli, to make any doctrinal changes.

Only after Henry's death, during the regency of his son Edward VI (reigned 1547–1553), was Cranmer able to introduce significant features of Protestantism into the Anglican church. During that time he wrote a Declaration of Faith of Forty-Two Articles, which recognized the Bible as the source of religious truth and accepted justification by faith, and a beautiful *Book of Common Prayer*. Although Catherine of Aragon's daughter, Queen Mary (reigned 1553–1558), attempted to bring England back to obedience to the pope, Elizabeth (reigned 1558–1603) again restored the Anglican church, but in so humane a way that the majority of her subjects had no difficulty in accepting it. After King James VI of Scotland became ruler of England as James I (reigned 1603–1625), an attempt was made to compel the Calvinist Scots to accept the Anglican religion, but this was unsuccessful. The Anglican church was carried to the English colonies in North America where, after the American Revolution, it became the Episcopalian church. But no other efforts were made to spread the Anglican church. It was created as a national church and as such it was not a religion that sought converts beyond Britain and its empire.

Calvinist Geneva

Calvinism, on the other hand, was conceived from the start as a proselytizing religion. Calvin's writings presented a doctrine that was far more international in character than Luther's. In Geneva, which was controlled by Calvin from 1536 to 1538 and from 1541 to 1564, Calvinism had a city that was both a model for the Calvinist life on this earth and an organizing center for the missionary activity that was to spread Calvinism to other parts of Europe. It took Calvin several years before he was able to persuade the city council of Geneva to become the instrument of his purposes. He did not believe that the church should govern the city, but that the city government should do what the church wished. He interfered in elections by preaching special sermons just before elections, and he supported those factions in the city government that were sympathetic to his views. Eventually the other factions were driven out, and the city government became totally supportive of the Calvinist ideal, not only of religion but of the state.

It is important to remember, however, that the Calvinist church itself was an essentially democratic organization, whose hierarchical structure provided a flexible means by which lay people influenced the policies of the church. At the base of the hierarchy was the congregation, which elected both its minister and a number of lay elders, who worked with the minister in the administration of the local church. In each region, the ministers and one elder from each congregation formed the presbytery, which controlled the church's property and confirmed in his position a minister elected by the congregation. A synod, composed of representatives of the presbyteries, supervised both the presbyteries and the congregations. Finally, there was a national assembly, in which both lay people and ministers were represented, whose regular meetings were a final court of appeal for the whole national church and the highest supervisory body in the church. Thus the lay members of the congregation felt themselves represented at each level of the church hierarchy. In Geneva itself, the highest administrative body within the church was the Consistory, which was made up of twelve lay persons, picked from the elders of the congregations, and the ministers.

The Calvinists set out to convert Geneva into a model city, a "city of saints," which could be held up to the rest of the world as an example of the value of the Calvinist way of life. In many ways Geneva became an ideal of social justice. Relief was provided for the poor. The sick were cared for in the City Hospital. Provision was made to support widows and orphans. Calvinist refugees from all over Europe were welcomed, and many settled permanently, enabling the town to broaden its economic base with new industries such as silkweaving. Each group of refugees was permitted to maintain its national Calvinist church. Education was especially supported. The clergy were expected to be highly trained in religious studies and in the writings of Calvin himself. Calvin became one of the two professors of theology in the newly founded Genevan Academy, a college that was soon regarded by Catholics as a school specializing in the training of religious revolutionaries.

The moral strictures of the Genevan government were harsh. The use of spies and informers was universal; and the Consistory was instructed to "admonish amiably those whom they see leading a disorderly life, and where necessary to report to the assembly who will be deputized to make further correction." Every small crime against Calvinist morality was harshly punished, from dancing and playing cards to kissing in public or laughing in church. Those found guilty of blasphemy had their tongues pierced; and heretics were burned at the stake. The subordination of women to men was sharply enforced. Two or three women regarded as witches were burned at the stake every year. And Calvin, in spite of his loving marriage based on his recognition of his wife as an intellectual equal, laid down as a principle that women were inferior to men: "Let the woman be satisfied with her status of subjection, and not take it amiss that she is made inferior to the more distinguished sex." Geneva in fact was in many ways a hard, unbending place. The physical beauty of the churches was defaced, their stained glass broken and the statues smashed. As refugees poured in, the city became crowded within its ramparts; but it remained a fortress, the principal stronghold of the elect. As such it was revered by its admirers and hated by its detractors.

Spread of Calvinism

Geneva's influence was very soon felt by its neighbors, especially in the nearby regions of Germany, where the University of Heidelberg became a center for

Calvinist studies. Calvin's home country of France was especially receptive to his doctrines, which spread rapidly among the trading classes of the Atlantic seacoast. One of Calvin's most important converts was Jeanne d'Albret, Queen of Béarn and Navarre in the Pyrenees. Her son, Henry of Navarre (1553–1610), was educated as a Calvinist, and he became for several years the leader of the Huguenots, as French Calvinists were called. When, by one of the quirks of dynastic inheritance, Henry, who was a member of one of the minor branches of the French royal family, became heir to the throne of France, he renounced Calvinism and became a Catholic; but he remained sympathetic to Calvinism throughout his reign. The French-speaking area of Belgium was also receptive to Calvinism, which advanced rapidly through the large cities and expanded northward into the Dutch cities.

Scotland was converted to Calvinism by John Knox, who had been trained in Geneva. The Scottish parliament was strongly anti-Catholic, and in 1560 Knox had little difficulty in persuading it to renounce Catholicism and to accept a Calvinist declaration of faith that Knox had written.

Calvinism also soon spread into the relatively tolerant Anglican church in England. At first the Calvinists believed that it was not necessary to break with the Anglican church, but simply as "Puritans" to insist on the purification by the Anglican church of the remaining relics of popery. They were, however, persecuted by the Stuart kings, James I and Charles I. As a result, a number of them fled to the Netherlands, and in 1620 a small group of them, who later became known as the Pilgrim Fathers, set out on the *Mayflower* to found a new Calvinist commonwealth in North America.

THE CATHOLIC REFORMATION: THE PROTESTANT ADVANCE HALTED

Reform Within the Catholic Church

By the middle of the sixteenth century many Catholics were concerned that so little had been achieved by their efforts to stop the expansion of the Protestant churches. Many concluded that their strategy up to that point had been wrong. Luther's excommunication, for example, had made him a hero in Germany. The attempts to debate with him had given him a forum in which to expound his doctrines of a Scripture-based religion. Even the representatives chosen to debate with him had been conservatives, who seemed merely to be reasserting the need for unquestioning obedience to the authority of the Catholic Church and uncritical acceptance of the way of life of the members of the clergy. The call to arms of the south German princes had indeed produced a civil war in Germany, but one in which the Protestant forces had fought the Catholics to a standstill; and the only result of the fighting had been, in the Peace of Augsburg (1555), an agreement that the rulers of German states had the right to choose either Catholicism or Lutheranism as the religion of their subjects. In some ways the agreement, from the Catholic point of view, was worse even than total toleration, since Catholics whose ruler turned Protestant would have to forsake Catholicism or emigrate. The armies of Charles V, moreover, while supposedly fighting on behalf of the pope, had taken the opportunity in 1527 to sack Rome, and had forced the pope to flee from his capital in fear of his life. The refusal to compromise with Henry VIII had led to his ouster of the Catholic Church from England. Virtually all the attempts to fight back against Protestantism had inflamed either local or national patriotism against the Catholic Church.

After the middle of the century a new strategy for dealing with Protestantism had been developed, which was to prove far more effective. Real reform within the Catholic Church was the key. A few popes in the first half of the century had made some half-hearted attempts at reform. Legal proceedings in the Church courts had been made more efficient and less costly. Abuses such as sale of Church offices had been punished. The more venal of the Church's administrators had been removed. But after 1550 a new type of pope was chosen. These were men who were not members of the powerful Italian patriciate but from poor families, who had risen by their own efforts and had sympathy for the austere morals of the clergy of Spain. These popes proved to be genuine reformers. By 1600 almost all of the corruption that had provided the original impetus to Protestantism had been removed from the Church. With this change of atmosphere in Rome, the influence of the spiritual reformers became strong. Whereas the mystics of the fifteenth century had been compelled to withdraw within themselves because the Church was unreceptive and even threatened persecution, now the spiritual leaders found an audience throughout the Catholic Church. The most important of these leaders came from Spain. Saint Teresa of Avila and Saint John of the Cross wrote books of spiritual meditation that became classics in their own time. But it was Ignatius Loyola (1491–1556) who was to envisage how the new fervor could be turned into a powerful weapon that could not only drive back Protestantism but also spread the Catholic religion to parts of the world where neither Catholicism nor Protestantism had ever been heard of.

Loyola and the Jesuits

Loyola was the son of a weathy family in the north of Spain, who after years of riotous living had almost lost his life as the result of a dangerous wound received in battle. His long convalescence and his struggle with death gave him a sudden interest in religious matters. He studied deeply all the devotional literature he could find, not only the Bible but the lives of the saints and the writings of the Spanish mystics. He most admired Saint Francis and Saint Dominic, who had stepped forward to save the Church in an earlier age: "Suppose I should do as Saint Francis did, what Saint Dominic did," he said. Like Saint Francis, he withdrew into the isolation of a cave in the mountains of Spain, where for a year he sought to reach God through meditation. Eventually he felt that he had achieved communion with God and that he knew how to help others to do the same.

In his famous book, *Spiritual Exercises*, Loyola laid down a disciplined course of meditation lasting four weeks during which the serious searcher after spiritual enlightenment would be brought exercise by exercise closer to the understanding of the presence of God. Each of the senses would be involved in the exercises, as in the meditation on death, where the meditator is invited to think of the sounds of his own funeral, the smell of his own corpse, and the pallor of his body. The purpose of the discipline was to compel the believer, in small steps, to subordinate his or her will to that of God; to force the physical flesh into subordination, to accept the reality of one's own sin, and finally to achieve release through the understanding of the greatness of Christ's passion on the cross. In the course of the exercises, there was to be meditation at five specific times of day—at midnight; in the early morning; before or after mass; at the evening service; and before the evening meal.

But Loyola was far more than a mystic, and his powers of organization extended far beyond the ability to organize spiritual meditation. He was still a soldier, though now a soldier enlisted in the cause of Christ, and he saw that the Church no less than the state needed an army, a spiritual one. Loyola knew that Spain did not offer him the opportunity to organize the new force on the lines he desired. He had himself been investigated and imprisoned by the Spanish Inquisition; and he did not wish his new organization to be placed under the authority of the Spanish hierarchy. He went directly to the pope and proposed the creation of a new order of monks. It was to have the pope himself as the supreme head of the order, which was to be known as the Society of Jesus, or Jesuits. The head of the order, known significantly as the General, was to be responsible to the pope alone.

The Society of Jesus was given two principal tasks, to combat Protestantism and to spread Catholicism among the heathen. Education, as Saint Dominic had required for his order three centuries earlier, was to be the main weapon of the order. Loyola required many years of testing before he would permit a person to be accepted fully into the Jesuits. As the order expanded, many Jesuit colleges, universities, and seminaries were founded. The most important was at Douai in Belgium, which was the principal training ground for Jesuits being sent into the Protestant countries of the north. Loyola had decided to fight Geneva by its own methods, and Douai soon became as much feared by Protestants as Geneva had been by Catholics. Jesuits too were soon being appointed as royal confessors, and became influential as royal advisers, especially in matters of foreign policy. But the Jesuits were far from neglecting Loyola's command to spread the word to the heathen. Jesuits moved fearlessly to all parts of the world, following the far-ranging trading vessels of the Portuguese and Spanish fleets. They established a stronghold in the Portuguese enclave in Hiroshima in Japan, for example, and were partly responsible for the fact that 300,000 Japanese had become Christian by 1600. The travels of their most famous missionary, Saint Francis Xavier, took him to Goa, Malaya, the pearlfishers of the Comoro Islands, and to Japan. Many of these missionaries died on their journeys or were executed during their missionary efforts.

The Roman and Spanish Inquisitions

More than any other force, the Jesuits were responsible for halting the spread of Protestant doctrine, but the Church possessed other weapons as well. The pope had authorized the foundation of a papal inquisition in 1233, to destroy the Albigensian heresy in France. In 1542, with the specific purpose of combating Protestantism, Pope Paul III passed the powers of the papal inquisition over to a body called the Congregation of the Inquisition, or Roman Inquisition, which became better known as the Holy Office. This body was given authority to investigate, to use torture, and to punish.

Even greater powers were possessed by the Spanish Inquisition, which had been established by Ferdinand and Isabella in 1478 and grudgingly recognized by the papacy. Its purpose was originally to ensure that Jews and converted Moors were sincere in their conversion to Christianity; but under two famous Inquisitor Generals, Tomás de Torquemada and Ximénex de Cisneros, the Spanish Inquisition extended its activity greatly. It believed that those influenced by the teachings of the northern European humanists, especially by Erasmus, might easily be led into heresy. It attacked a group of Catholic mystics known as the Illuminists, and it had little difficulty in detecting the few people in Spain who had been converted to Protestantism.

The violence of the Spanish Inquisition increased until its methods of inquiry, and especially its public burnings at the stake, became the symbol to Protestants throughout Europe of what they felt to be the true face of the Catholic Church. Although the Roman and Spanish Inquisitions were able virtually to eliminate Protestantism in Italy and Spain, it is very possible that reaction against their methods had the effect of increasing the determination of Protestants not to permit the reestablishment of Catholicism in their own countries.

In a similar way, the establishment in 1559 of an Index of Forbidden Books, a list of books containing heretical doctrines that Catholics were not permitted to read, was effective as the first form of censorship after the invention of printing, and did succeed in preventing most Catholics in Spain and Italy from reading such books as the works of Erasmus. Yet the Index may have encouraged more adventurous Catholics to read heretical works they might not otherwise have read, and it provided Protestants with yet another example of what they regarded as danger to freedom of thought posed by the reforming papacy.

Art and the Reformations

Many Protestants from Luther on had regarded the art of the High Renaissance in Rome as proof of the Catholic Church's absorption with materialism, and had denounced the extravagant decoration of the churches, the innumerable paintings of saints and the Virgin that seemed to them to border on idolatry, and the almost pagan style of depicting God and Christ. In deliberate contrast to the Catholic Churches, all Protestant churches of whatever denomination were designed to be simple, austere, and functional. They were almost totally lacking in paintings or sculpture; and, where Catholic churches were converted to Protestant use, iconoclastic crowds smashed the heads off statues and white-washed frescoes. Art was placed at the service of Protestant expansion, in such forms as the woodcuts of Lucas Cranach or the engravings of Albrecht Dürer. But there were very few commissions given for religious paintings. Painters therefore turned to acceptable subjects. Portraiture remained at a very high level. In England, the royal family and many noble and intellectual leaders were painted by a series of perceptive artists, who extended from Hans Holbein the Younger (c. 1497–1543) at the court of Henry VIII to Nicholas Hilliard (1537–1619). In the Netherlands, paintings of everyday life known as *genre* paintings remained popular. But in the hands of a great artist like Pieter Brueghel the Elder (c. 1525–1569), genre painting achieved unparalleled drama. Using for his own purposes the styles that the Flemish had mastered in the fifteenth century, Brueghel presented scenes of peasant life of extraordinary complexity, as in his *Children's Games.* He deliberately overemphasized, almost in a satirical way, the roughness and even the grotesqueness of peasant ways, as in *A Country Wedding,* where huge platters of food are carried in on rough, improvised serving trays. But he could also strike the chill of horror into the observer when he

The Massacre of the Innocents, by Pieter Brueghel the Elder (c. 1525–1569) *Brueghel set in a Flemish village in the Biblical scene of the murder of the babies of Bethlehem ordered by Herod to ensure the death of Christ.* (Kunsthistorisches Museum, Vienna.)

turned to scenes of inhumanity, as when the soldiers in a wintry Flemish village prepare to murder babies in his *Massacre of the Innocents.*

In Italy, the Catholic Church decided to meet Protestant criticism by turning art even more directly to the dramatization of the church's message. Michelangelo took the lead when he painted the *Last Judgment* for the back wall of the Sistine Chapel. Completed in the 1530s at the request of Pope Paul III, its writhing figures, tormented in their passage to hell, were a direct image of the fate of unbelievers. But few Roman artists of the sixteenth century, working in a deliberately discordant, unbalanced style called Mannerism, were able to achieve the artistic quality reached in the High Renaissance. Only Tintoretto in Venice, working on vast religious paintings, was able to turn the drama of the new style to the full service of the Catholic Reformation. The great north Italian painter Caravaggio (c. 1565–1609) broke with Mannerism by turning to a bold, aggressive naturalism in which he dramatically presented the Church's teaching in such paintings as the *Death of the Virgin.* Despite the differences between them, both Caravaggio and the Mannerists prepared the way for the most powerful artistic expression of the Catholic Reformation, the Baroque style of the seventeenth century (see Chapter 11).

The Final Confrontations

The conclusion of the Council of Trent (1545–1547, 1551–1552, 1562–1563) reconfirmed the Protestants in their conviction that compromise with the Catholic Church was impossible. The pope had called the Council to consider Church doctrine that had been challenged by the Protestants, and some Catholic leaders had even suggested that some small changes might be made. After long consideration, the Council rejected every Protestant position, and reaffirmed the traditional stand of the Church on all matters of doctrine. The Council stated that not only the Bible but the findings of popes, Church Councils, and the Church fathers were also sources of religious truth. It denied that faith was sufficient in itself, but that good works were also necessary and efficacious in bringing salvation. Priests were forbidden to marry. Divorce was rejected. And, the final blow of all, the Council held that indulgences were effective in reducing time in purgatory.

Almost all the wars of the century following the Council of Trent were influenced, if not actually caused by, the confrontation between Catholic and Protestant, as we shall see in the next chapters. The political struggles among three aristocratic factions for control of the French monarchy, which convulsed France between 1562 and 1598, were infinitely more bloody than they might have been because one faction was Calvinist. Philip II of Spain began the long, unsuccessful war of 1566–1648 to crush the revolt of his Dutch subjects not primarily to retain the riches of the Netherlands within his empire, but to crush Dutch Calvinism. When he sent his Armada against England in 1588, it was in part to restore Catholicism there. The final and most destructive phase of this religious confrontation—and the one in which nonreligious motives most clearly influenced those participating in what was ostensibly the final showdown between Catholic and Protestant—was the Thirty Years War.

The war began in 1618 with the attempt of the Habsburg ruler Ferdinand II (King of Bohemia, 1617–1637; Holy Roman Emperor, 1619–1637) to wipe out Calvinism in Bohemia. When the Czech Protestants were joined by several German states, Ferdinand destroyed their armies in 1620. Fighting broke out again in 1625 when the Danish king came to the aid of the German Protestants, but Ferdinand decisively defeated him and drove his forces back into Denmark. By 1629, it looked as though Ferdinand intended to wipe out Protestantism in Germany. His very successes roused the other European powers against him, including Catholic France, whose virtual head of state, Cardinal Richelieu, helped support an invasion of Germany by the Lutheran king of Sweden, Gustavus Adolphus. Destruction became universal in Germany, as Swedish and German Protestant armies clashed with the Catholic forces of Ferdinand and the south German princes. When the death of Gustavus Adolphus in battle seemed likely to bring a breathing space for the combatants, Richelieu intervened openly on behalf of the Protestants. When peace was made at Westphalia in 1648, it was to recognize a permanent stalemate in the religious confrontation. In Germany, rulers were permitted to choose whether they (and their subjects) would be Catholic, Lutheran, or Calvinist. In short, a whole century of fighting had done almost nothing to change the relative strength and geographic hold of the Protestant and Catholic forces in Europe. The Thirty Years War had shown, however, that for seventeenth-century statesmen like Cardinal Richelieu, the cause of religion had yielded precedence to the cause of national power.

SUGGESTED READINGS

General Introduction

De Lamar Jensen, *Reformation Europe: Age of Reform and Revolution* (1981), is an excellent survey. The religious aspects of the Reformation are emphasized in Owen Chadwick, *The Reformation* (1964), the political background in G. R. Elton, *Reformation Europe, 1517–1559* (1963). A. G. Dickens, *Reformation and Society in Sixteenth Century Europe* (1966), is lucid and well illustrated.

The Protestant Reformation

The standard biography of Luther is Roland H. Bainton's well-written *Here I Stand: A Life of Martin Luther* (1960). One of the earliest and most stimulating attempts at "psychohistory" is Erik H. Eriksen, *Young Man Luther: A Study in Psychoanalysis and History* (1962). For reappraisals by, respectively, a great French and a great German historian, see Lucien Febvre, *Martin Luther: A Destiny* (1955), and Gerhard Ritter, *Luther* (1963).

Two thorough studies of Zwingli are Jacques Courvoisier, *Zwingli: A Reformed The-*
ologian (1964), and G. R. Potter, *Zwingli* (1976), which explains how the Swiss Confederation divided on religious lines.

Calvin's ideas are traced in François Wendel, *Calvin: The Origins and Development of*
His Religious Thought (1963); the city of saints that he dominated, in E. William Monter,
Calvin's Geneva (1967). Calvin's economic ideas are sympathetically described in W. Fred
Graham, *The Constructive Revolutionary: John Calvin and His Socio-Economic Impact* (1971).
Philip Benedict, *Rouen During the Wars of Religion* (1981), shows why urban groups turned
to Calvin.

The Catholic Reformation

For a well-documented account by a Catholic scholar, see H. Daniel-Rops, *The*
Catholic Reformation (1961). A. G. Dickens, *The Counter Reformation* (1969), is short and
reliable, but may be supplemented by M. O'Connell, *The Counter-Reformation, 1560–1610*
(1974). Jean Delumeau, *Catholicism Between Luther and Voltaire: A New View of the Counter-*
Reformation (1977), sees similarities between the two Reformations. For the founder of
the Jesuits, see P. Dudon, *St. Ignatius of Loyola* (1949). On the leading woman mystic,
see Stephen Clissold, *St. Teresa of Avila* (1979).

The Religious Wars

Richard S. Dunn, *The Age of Religious Wars, 1559–1689* (1979), is a good textbook.
The religious wars in France are covered briefly in John E. Neale, *The Age of Catherine de*
Medicis (1962). Full-length treatments of the Thirty Years War are Cicely V. Wedgewood,
The Thirty Years War (1961), and Georges Pages, *The Thirty Years' War* (1970).

Women in the Reformation Era

Roland Bainton, the doyen of Reformation scholars, discusses the part played by
individual women in different parts of Europe in three studies, *Women of the Reformation*
in Germany and Italy (1971), *Women in the Reformation in France and England* (1973), and
Women of the Reformation: From Spain to Scandinavia (1977). On the Protestant witch hunts,
see H. C. Eric Midelfort, *Witchhunting in Southwest Germany, 1562–1684* (1972), and Alan
D. MacFarlane, *Witchcraft in Tudor and Stuart England* (1970).

Joyce L. Irwin, *Womanhood in Radical Protestantism, 1525–1675* (1979), argues that
Anabaptists believed in the subordination of women. Natalie Zemon Davis shows that
Calvinism appealed to women in the cities, in *Society and Culture in Early Modern France*
(1975).

Steven Ozment, *When Fathers Ruled: Family Life in Reformation Europe* (1983), contrasts
the loving relationships within the Lutheran family with what he perceives as a repressive
role of the father in the late Middle Ages.

Good biographies of individual women involved in one way or another in the
religious turmoil include Garrett Mattingley, *Catherine of Aragon* (1941); Walter Cecil Rich-
ardson, *Mary Tudor: The White Queen* (1970); and Nancy L. Roelker, *Queen of Navarre:*
Jeanne d'Albret (1968).

9

The Overseas Discoveries
and the New Empires

Throughout the Middle Ages the major part of European trade had been in bulk goods necessary for feeding and clothing the inhabitants of the continent—cereals, dried fish, wool, finished cloth, and timber. But the greatest profits had been made on luxury goods, small in bulk but incredibly difficult to obtain from the farthest corners of the globe. From China along the aptly named Silk Route had come the most prized fabric of all, as well as many other Chinese luxury goods such as ceramics and lacquerware. From India and the Spice Islands (Moluccas) of southeast Asia had come the cloves, cinnamon, and other spices that were used to add flavor to salted fish and dried meat, the staple foods of the European upper and middle classes for most of the year. These spices were transported by one or another of two major routes. Some were carried by ship across the Indian Ocean and up the Red Sea or the Persian Gulf for shipment from the Near East. The other route was overland to the Fertile Crescent and thence to the Mediterranean coast. From West Africa came pepper and, far more important, the gold of Guinea, which was carried across the Sahara Desert by the camel caravans of Arab merchants to the North African coast.

By the beginning of the fifteenth century, however, Europeans were becoming dissatisfied at the rising prices of these goods. The increased costs were due in part to charges that were exacted by those who controlled the routes, and in part to the enormous difficulty of getting the goods across oceans, through deserts, and over mountains. Trade with Ming China in the fourteenth and fifteenth centuries passed across the Mongol-controlled territories of Russia and Iran. The Ottoman Turks controlled most of the Fertile Crescent and large parts of Eastern Europe even before they took Constantinople in 1453, and they imposed exceptionally heavy tolls on goods bound for Europe from China or India. The Muslim Arabs controlled the whole coast of North Africa and dominated the cities of sub-Saharan Africa, at the southern end of the caravan routes, such as Timbuktu. The Italian cities, located as they were in the central Mediterranean, felt they had no choice but to strike the best bargains they could with the Turks of Asia Minor and the Arabs of North Africa and then pass the costs along to their customers in northern and western Europe. But in the fifteenth century the rulers of Portugal and Spain realized that their coasts on the Atlantic ocean, which had seemed little more than the end of the known world, presented them with a marvelous opportunity. They were in a position to be the first European powers to trade directly with the gold suppliers of Africa, the spice producers of south and southeast Asia, and the silk merchants of East Asia as well as to gain access to new sources of such economically significant goods as fish, whale and seal oil, timber, grain, and sugar.

Europeans had been trying to break out of their small continent throughout the Middle Ages. The Vikings had opened the North Atlantic. The Crusaders had established an overseas empire in the Holy Land. Venice and Genoa had conquered island empires in the Mediterranean. The great discoveries of the fifteenth century have to be seen as a continuation of this effort, just as the technological advances in navigation have to be seen as a refinement of such earlier instruments as the compass and astrolabe produced by medieval scientists. It is also important, however, to see the explorations and discoveries as reflecting the mental attitude that became dominant during the Renaissance— most notably the determination to know more about every aspect of the physical world and confidence in the capacity of human beings to achieve whatever goals they embarked upon.

However, the difficulties as well as the rewards were greater than the early explorers realized. Despite the compass and astrolabe, navigation and shipbuilding had to be further developed so that wooden, sail driven ships could cross thousands of miles of uncharted oceans. Violent opposition to the voyages by empires threatened with the loss of long-established trade monopolies had to be overcome. The sporadic violence of more primitive peoples, who were rightfully suspicious of the early explorers, had to be met and dealt with. Goods suitable for exchange with the traders in Africa or Asia had to be obtained. Finally, once the original expedition had been made and trading contracts established, a more settled form of economic and political presence had to be established thousands of miles from the home country. All of these difficulties were overcome by the Portuguese and the Spanish in the fifteenth and sixteenth centuries, at least a century before any other Atlantic power possessed the ability or the will to seek a share for themselves of the profits and risks of overseas exploration and empire.

The new era opened in 1415 when the Portuguese launched a sudden sea

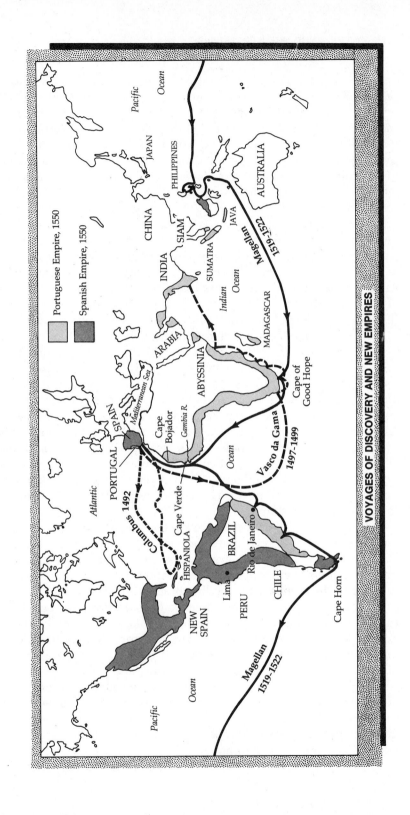

VOYAGES OF DISCOVERY AND NEW EMPIRES

Portuguese Empire, 1550

Spanish Empire, 1550

Pacific Ocean

JAPAN

PHILIPPINES

CHINA

SIAM

INDIA

SUMATRA

JAVA

AUSTRALIA

Indian Ocean

MADAGASCAR

Magellan 1519-1522

ARABIA

ABYSSINIA

Cape of Good Hope

SPAIN

PORTUGAL

Mediterranean Sea

Cape Bojador

Gambia R.

Atlantic Ocean

Columbus 1492

Cape Verde

HISPANIOLA

Vasco da Gama 1497-1499

NEW SPAIN

BRAZIL

Rio de Janeiro

Lima

PERU

CHILE

Cape Horn

Magellan 1519-1522

Pacific Ocean

Christopher Columbus, by Sebastiano del Piombo (1485–1547)
Columbus's four voyages to America left him wealthy but embittered at his failure to sail far enough west to reach Asia or Japan. (The Metropolitan Museum of Art, gift of J. Pierpont Morgan, 1900.)

and land attack on the Arab city of Ceuta on the Mediterranean coast of Morocco. Quickly developing magnificent maritime technology, the Portuguese concentrated for the next century on the exploration of the islands of the Atlantic and the coast of West Africa, where they established trade and slave stations. In 1497–1499, the Portuguese expedition of Vasco da Gama sailed around Africa and across the Indian Ocean to the spice port of Calicut in southern India. From then on the whole world opened to the Portuguese. In 1500 an expedition on the way to India lost course and discovered Brazil. In 1510, the Portuguese took Goa on the coast of India; in 1511, Malacca on the coast of Malaya; and in 1515, Hormuz at the mouth of the Persian Gulf. In 1547, they opened trade with Japan; and in 1557, they were allowed to establish a trading post at Macao in China. The Portuguese, with a population of only 1 million, made no effort to create a large territorial empire, but concentrated on establishing fortified trading stations at points crucial for the maintenance of trade. By the end of the sixteenth century, Portugal was enjoying a prosperity greater than at any other time in its history.

Spain entered the competition for overseas trade and empire after its unification under Ferdinand and Isabella. The first expedition sent out by Spain was led by the Genoese sea captain Christopher Columbus (1451–1506) in 1492. Columbus, although convinced he had discovered the Indies, had in fact found the Bahamas and other Caribbean islands; but later expeditions showed the Spaniards that they had found a vast continent whose existence had been hitherto unsuspected and which presented an almost impassable barrier to establishment of a westward sea route to Asia. But the Spanish also realized that this new continent and its neighboring islands offered enormous potential for economic gain, especially as its highly civilized Aztec and Inca empires could be easily overthrown by a handful of brutal soldiers. The Spanish decided to profit from what they had found rather than regret what they had not. The Aztec empire was defeated in 1517–1519 and the Inca in 1530–1532; and by the 1550s the Spanish were in control of a vast empire stretching from Florida and what is now the southwestern United States almost to the tip of South America, with only Brazil remaining in Portuguese hands.

THE PORTUGUESE TRADING EMPIRE

Early Portuguese Discoveries

When the Arabs were finally ousted from Portugal in 1250, it was one of the poorest countries in Europe. Its agriculture was backward. There was almost no manufacturing. Only fishing presented any significant source of income. Isolated at the southwestern tip of Europe on the edge of the Atlantic Ocean, it had little trade, and as late as the fourteenth century the country's capital of Lisbon had a population of only 40,000. In 1385, however, the throne was seized by John of Aviz (reigned 1385–1433), a bastard son of the previous king. He and his successors of the house of Aviz were determined to transform their poverty-stricken kingdom into a prosperous, efficient state. John's third son, Henry, who is known to everyone except the Portuguese as Prince Henry the

Prince Henry the Navigator, by Nuno Gonçalves About 1460, Gonçalves painted the Veneration of Saint Vincent, *portraying not only Henry and the royal family but a wide range of Lisbon citizens, from knights to beggars.* (Museo Nacional de Arte Antiga/ Scala-Art Resource.)

Navigator (1394–1460), was the person most responsible for making Portugal into a great maritime power. He had taken part in the attack on Ceuta, and while in this Moorish city had become fascinated with the tales of the great cities of sub-Saharan Africa. Henry was also much taken with the possibility of circumventing the Arab-dominated caravan routes across the Sahara desert and reaching West Africa by sea. From the reports he received in Ceuta he realized, perhaps before any other European leader, that in sub-Saharan Africa there existed great trading empires with rich cities whose wealth had been barely tapped by Europeans. But he also saw that, given the necessary maritime technology, the Portuguese were the people who could most easily establish those contacts by sea.

Henry moved to the southwestern coast of Portugal, at the point where Portugal is closest to Africa, and gathered round him a group of experts to whom he assigned specific tasks in the development of maritime technology: chart making, instrument design, and perfection of ocean-going vessels. To assist his maritime ventures, he secretly obtained copies of sea charts drawn up by Italian and Catalan sailors, as well as their most advanced instruments such as the compass and astrolabe. His ship builders developed the caravel, a ship capable of riding through the Atlantic storms and of reaching speeds hitherto impossible for oar-driven galleons.

Year after year he sent out expeditions to explore the coast of Africa and the nearer islands of the Atlantic. Prevailing winds swept an early expedition in 1419 to the island of Madeira, and soon after the more distant Azores were reached. Madeira and the Azores were annexed to Portugal, their timber felled and shipped to Lisbon, and sugar, grain, and grapes planted. Other expeditions crept slowly down the African coast. In 1434 a Portuguese expedition rounded Cape Bojador in southern Morocco, beyond which it was thought lay a boiling sea from which flames leapt and a sun so hot that white men turned black in its rays. When a Portuguese expedition reached Cape Blanco in 1441, it brought back gold dust and black Africans who were baptized and sold into slavery. This act symbolized the mixed motivation of both Portuguese and Spanish exploration—a humane desire to convert the heathen and an urge to make profit at whatever human cost!

By Henry the Navigator's death in 1460 the Portuguese had opened a lucrative trade in gold, slaves, and ivory with the states of West Africa, and had founded flourishing colonies in Madeira and the Azores. But the later rulers of the house of Aviz, especially King John (reigned 1481–1495) and King Manuel (the Fortunate; reigned 1495–1521) were unsatisfied with the profits of Africa alone. They wanted to reach the Indies by sailing around Africa. Africa proved to be thousands of miles longer than they had dreamed, and the realization after they had crossed the Gulf of Guinea that the African coast turned southward for thousands of miles was a bitter disappointment. In 1487 King John therefore gave Bartholomew Dias the task of discovering the southern tip of Africa and, if possible, sailing on to India itself. Dias found the Cape of Good Hope but was compelled by the threat of mutiny by his crew to return to Portugal.

King Manuel the Fortunate

Manuel, however, was even more ambitious than John, and he saw that the voyage of Dias had put the Portuguese within reach of their goal of gaining a monopoly of oceanic trade with the Indies. He commissioned a fleet of four ships and 170 men under the command of Vasco da Gama (1469?–1524) for a voyage to India, and gave them the best equipment and charts available. All Lisbon knew the significance of da Gama's voyage, and the whole city turned out to see him embark. Da Gama sailed first to the Canary and the Cape Verde Islands, and then, daringly forsaking the coast, he set off across the Atlantic in a gigantic semicircle that, after four months at sea, brought him to land at the Cape of Good Hope. He then followed the East African coast until he reached the Arab-dominated city-states on what is now the coast of Kenya. There he picked up an Indian pilot, who took him across the Indian Ocean to the spice port of Calicut. His arrival caused little stir in a city accustomed to the arrival of great fleets from the Near East, even though he was the first European to have reached India by sailing around Africa; but he managed to get a load of spices with which he returned to Lisbon in September 1499. The cargo of spices paid for the voyage several times over, and proved to Manuel the vast potential for Portugal in exploiting the new trade route. Manuel took for himself a monopoly of the spice trade, and assigned the ground floor of his royal palace on the Lisbon seafront to the handling of the spice cargoes.

Manuel immediately sent out a second expedition under Pedro Alvares Cabral (1460–1526), a friend of Vasco da Gama. Cabral struck west of da Gama's course across the Atlantic and landed in Brazil, which he claimed for Portugal. He then recrossed the Atlantic and continued around South Africa to Madagascar and Mozambique, and crossed the Indian Ocean to Calicut. There, however, the Indians objected to his attempts to convert them to Catholicism and to his efforts to found a trading post, and he reacted by bombarding the city. He finally withdrew with a profitable cargo of spices, but on his return was reprimanded for his use of force.

Cabral's discovery of Brazil is still a subject of controversy. The Portuguese said that he had been blown off course by storms; but it is now suspected that Portuguese sailors had sighted Brazil earlier, and that Cabral was secretly assigned to claim it.

Manuel immediately set out to profit from the new annexation. Not only would Brazil be a useful point for ships taking the wide circle across the Atlantic to the Indies, but its "brazil" wood (senna) was especially suitable for dyestuffs. (The country was named after the wood.) The Portuguese soon established themselves among the Indian tribes of the coast of Brazil and sent back to Portugal, under royal monopoly, the precious wood. Plantations of sugar cane and manioc were started as well.

The later expeditions sent by Manuel to the Indies were heavily armed, so that they could break the Muslim control of the trade of the Indian Ocean; and fortified trading posts were created at crucial points such as Hormuz at the mouth of the Persian Gulf and at Mozambique on the East African coast. But the key to Portuguese control of the Indian Ocean was the capture of Goa on the coast of India in 1510, which became so wealthy as the main transshipment point for Asian spices, silks, ceramics, and pearls that it was known as the Golden Babylon of the East or simply as "Golden Goa."

Even access to Indian trade was insufficient for Manuel. New expeditions pressed on toward Southeast Asia. Malacca on the coast of Malaya was seized, giving the Portuguese access to the spice trade of Indonesia and the Moluccas, where they established forts. In 1547, they reached Japan, where they were permitted to trade through the southern port of Nagasaki. In 1557, the Portuguese were granted by the Chinese emperor the right to establish their own fortified city at Macao, a small peninsula at the mouth of the Pearl River.

Character of Portuguese Overseas Settlements

In their overseas settlements, the Portuguese wanted where possible to create a replica of Portuguese society at home. For this reason, the government encouraged the emigration of women from Portugal to join the administrators, soldiers, and merchants in all the Portuguese-held territories except in Asia, where the cost and health hazards were considered prohibitive. In Madeira and the Azores, settlement was entirely Portuguese, and the seclusion of women, traditional in Portugal, was imposed. Even working women had to wear black veils to prevent exposing themselves in public; and the well-to-do were expected to keep busy within the home. In Africa, conditions were so unsettled that women achieved great freedom, often sharing even in the skirmishes with the local peoples resentful of Portuguese incursion. The numbers of Portuguese women in Africa were so small, however, that traders and soldiers intermarried both with Muslim Moroccan women and with black women of the West African coastal states. In Brazil, on the other hand, large numbers of Portuguese women settled, partly because the Portuguese administration required "purity of blood" in the wives of its high officials. Within the cities segregation of women was practiced, but in the countryside a more egalitarian society developed. Women on the sugar plantations wielded considerable influence as household managers, and often upon the death of their husbands took over management of the plantation itself. In Asia, with an almost total lack of suitable Portuguese brides, the Portuguese men either had harems or married local girls of mixed or entirely Asian blood. The children of these marriages, as Eurasians, were however subject to discrimination by both the Asians and the Portuguese. Thus within the Portuguese empire a kind of racial hierarchy developed, the infinite gradations of which were scrupulously noted as a method of assigning individuals their places within colonial society.

Manueline Culture

Manuel felt that the great trading expeditions had made him one of the greatest monarchs of Europe. He took for himself the grandiose title of "Lord of Guinea and of the conquest of navigation and commerce of Ethiopia, Arabia, Persia, and India." His capital city of Lisbon had grown to a population of 100,000; and he set about beautifying the city to make it worthy of his new wealth and prestige. He built churches, convents, and palaces, in an exotic architectural style that came to be called Manueline. Sculptures, inspired by the shells, the foliage, and the animals of the new empire and even the ropes and sails of the ships, swarm over all the doorways and windows of the buildings in a startling fretwork of stone.

Fifty years after Manuel's death, the expedition of da Gama which he had sponsored inspired the writings of Portugal's greatest poet, the *Lusiads* of Luiz Vaz de Camões (1524–1580). Camões modelled his poem on Virgil's *Aeneid*, and he made clear in the opening lines that Portugal's achievement was no less brilliant than that of Rome:

This is the story of heroes, who leaving their native Portugal behind them opened a way to Ceylon, and further, across seas no man had ever sailed before. They were men of no ordinary stature, equally at home in war and in dangers of every kind; they founded a new kingdom among distant peoples and made it great. . . . Let us hear no more then of Ulysses and Aeneas and their long journeyings, no more of Alexander and Trajan and their famous victories. My theme is the daring and renown of the Portuguese, to whom Neptune and Mars alike give homage. The heroes and the poets of old have had their day; another and loftier conception of valor has arisen.[1]

The Results of Portuguese Imperialism

The possession of empire was a mixed blessing for the Portuguese. After the first relatively easy assumption of control of the Indian Ocean and the sealanes to East Asia, the Portuguese found it increasingly difficult and costly to maintain a monopoly. The power of Venice revived rapidly after 1520, and it regained part of its former share of the spice trade. It thus was able to offer serious competition to Portugal on the European markets, with the result that the price of such spices as pepper fell during the sixteenth century and reduced the profits of both competitors.

Moreover, for many Portuguese citizens, the possession of a trading empire was directly harmful. More than 150,000 black slaves had been sold in Lisbon by 1500, and slaves had replaced Portuguese servants in many of the wealthier houses in Lisbon. The wealth pouring in made it seem unnecessary to develop manufactures in Portugal, since the empire provided the means to buy them elsewhere. Agriculture declined because part of the rural population was drained off to provide labor for the empire. The influx of gold from Guinea and from the Spanish possessions in America caused sharp inflation, the causes of which were not diagnosed by the economists of the day. Inflation was especially damaging to the large segments of the population that lived on fixed incomes.

Perhaps the worst blow to the Portuguese empire came when the country was ruled by Spain, between 1580 and 1644. Spain, absorbed with innumerable struggles in Europe and the Mediterranean and more interested in its own empire in America than in the Portuguese empire in Asia, left the way open for other European countries to establish a foothold in the East as well as for the Muslims to reassert their power against the Portuguese. Thus a century of seeming glory had left behind problems that would dog the country for centuries to come, and contribute to Portugal's economic backwardness at a time when Western Europe was making enormous commercial and industrial advances.

SPAIN'S EMPIRE IN THE AMERICAS

Spanish Voyages of Discovery

Spain entered the colonial struggle almost a century after Portugal. Until the marriage in 1469 of Ferdinand of Aragon (king, 1479–1516) and Isabella of Castile (queen, 1474–1505), the country had been divided into several states whose

---

[1] From Luis Vaz de Camões; *Lusiads,* translated by William C. Atkinson (Harmondsworth, England: Penguin Classics, 1952), p. 39.

main effort for seven centuries had been to oust the Arabs. Ferdinand and Isabella completed this reconquest in January 1492, with the capture of Granada, the last Muslim state in Spain. They were well aware that Portugal would probably soon reach India by sailing round Africa, and so, only seven months after the capture of Granada, they took the gamble of sending Columbus westward across the Atlantic "to discover and acquire islands and mainland in the Ocean Sea," by which they meant China and Japan. They hoped that Columbus would discover a westward route that would enable the Spanish to forestall the Portuguese, and would at the same time open up new regions far from Europe where their rambunctious, crusading army could be employed usefully, now that the fighting was over in Spain. Neither they nor Columbus knew that the vast continent of America blocked their way to Asia. In fact, although Renaissance geographers in Italy had published maps showing that the world was round, they had been considerably misleading not only by omitting America but by showing the total sea distance from Europe to Asia by a westward route as far shorter than it was in reality.

It was not surprising, therefore, that when Columbus, after thirty-three days of sailing from the Canary Islands, saw land in the Bahamas, he assumed that he had reached the outer islands of Asia. He collected evidence of the products of the islands, which included some gold trinkets, unusual plants, and fruits, as proof that he had reached the Indies. He then continued on in search of Japan, but found instead Cuba and Hispaniola. His flagship was wrecked, however, and he returned to Spain in March 1493, still unaware that he had discovered America. Ferdinand and Isabella sent him back immediately with a larger fleet and colonists, whom he settled on Hispaniola. Returning in 1498, he explored the mainland of South America along the coast of Venezuela.

Finally, in 1502, he followed the coasts of Costa Rica and Honduras in Central America.

Although Columbus himself stubbornly refused to believe he was not exploring the Indies, the Spanish rulers decided that they had better profit from the fact that they were the firstcomers from Europe to a land of considerable economic potential. In 1494, Spain signed with Portugal the Treaty of Tordesillas, splitting the non-Christian world between them on a line 270 leagues to the west of the Cape Verde Islands. Although the agreement gave Portugal Africa and India, it left to Spain all the Americas except Brazil; and the Spanish proceeded at once to begin the exploitation of the Caribbean Islands, which offered the possibility of raising tropical goods such as sugar for Europe. Large numbers of settlers were at once sent out to the islands where, by disease and hard labor, they virtually wiped out the native Indian population. For that reason, they were authorized to introduce black slaves from Africa. The first Spanish settlement on the continent itself was made on the Isthmus of Panama, where Balboa founded the city of Darien; and in 1513, Balboa led the first European expedition to see the Pacific Ocean.

The Spanish were still determined to reach Asia by sailing westward, and they sponsored the voyage of Ferdinand Magellan in 1519 that was to find a route around the tip of South America. Magellan, with enormous difficulty, did succeed in rounding Cape Horn through the stormy straits that were named after him; and, crossing the Pacific Ocean, he reached the Philippine Islands, which he claimed for Spain. Magellan was killed by hostile natives. Although his expedition completed the circumnavigation of the globe, they had to report to the Emperor Charles V that it was impossible to establish a regular sea route around Cape Horn. The Spanish then waited almost half a century before trying once again for a westward route. They took control of the Philippines in 1542. In 1568–1569 they found an easy route from Acapulco on the Pacific coast of Mexico to the Philippines, and immediately established the practice of sending one galleon a year to pick up spices and other goods for transshipment to Europe across Mexico. Even then, however, Spain's impact on the spice trade was very small, and the Spanish made little effort to extend their presence in Asia beyond the Philippine Islands.

Pre-Columbian Civilization

At the time that Magellan's expedition was circumnavigating the globe, a Spanish *conquistador* named Hernán Cortés (1485–1547) had found, and conquered, the great Aztec empire in Mexico. The Indians whom the Spanish had defeated were descendants of peoples who had crossed a great land bridge linking Asia to America across what is now the Bering Strait, and had spread throughout North and South America as early as 25,000 B.C.

Perhaps the most creative of the Indian peoples had been the Mayans who, between the fourth and ninth centuries A.D., had erected vast temple complexes in the Yucatán peninsula of Mexico and in Guatemala. The Mayans cleared the jungle around their cities, and raised vast fields of maize (corn), beans, squash, potatos, cocoa, and tobacco. Within their temples, they created superb sculptures in stone, mural paintings, ceramics, and precious metals, and to serve a religion based on astrology they developed highly skilled astronomical methods. Their calendar was more accurate than the Julian calendar of the Romans. Their civilization revived in the eleventh and twelfth centuries, and their traditional arts flourished again in a new ceremonial center at Chichén Itzá. But when the Spanish reached the Yucatán in the sixteenth century, the Mayan temple-cities had already been abandoned for several centuries, and were disappearing into the jungle.

Of the many civilizations that had flourished in America, unknown to Europe and Asia and knowing nothing of Europe and Asia, only two remained important at the time of the Spanish incursion—the Aztec empire in Mexico and the Inca in Peru. Cortés and his troops were at first overwhelmed at the splendor of the capital city of the Aztec Emperor Montezuma (1480?–1520). It had between 100,000 and 200,000 inhabitants; and some historians have even asserted that it was larger than any contemporary city in Europe. It was linked to the land by three vast causeways, and divided into rectangles by wide streets lined with canals. Its palaces and temples shone white in the sunshine across the blue waters of the lake, while its colorful markets astonished even those who had seen Constantinople.

The Conquest of Mexico and Peru

Cortés, who had at first been welcomed by Montezuma, took him prisoner, ordered the destruction of the Aztec temples, and seized vast quantities of gold and silver. Many of the lovely Aztec brooches, statues, and other artifacts were melted down for easier shipment to Spain, thus inflicting an irreparable loss to our knowledge of Aztec and earlier Mexican civilizations. Montezuma was killed by his own people for accepting Cortés's demands, and Cortés was driven from the city in great danger. He returned three months later, however, with the help of one of the neighboring peoples who had suffered at the hands of the armies of the Aztecs in their search for sacrificial victims. Using cannon as well as other European weapons, Cortés fought his way back into the city, destroying it block by block, and filling the canals with the rubble of its buildings. He immediately began the reconstruction of the city in European style on the same site. (The foundations of the Aztecs' great temple were rediscovered only in 1978, just yards from where Cortés built a huge new cathedral as an affirmation of the replacement of the Aztec religion by Catholicism.)

Similar treatment was given to the Inca emperor Atahualpa (1500?–1533) by Francisco Pizzaro (1470?–1541), who led a Spanish expedition to the Andes in 1530. Welcomed by Atahualpa, Pizzaro made him prisoner, and after seizing all his treasure had him executed. Pizzaro took the fortified Inca capital city of

Cuzco by siege, and within two years had taken over the whole of the Inca empire. Other conquistadores seized additional areas of North and South America during the first half of the sixteenth century, inflicting great suffering on the Indian population.

Society in the Spanish Empire

In the New Laws of 1542–1543, an attempt was made by the Spanish government to mitigate the exploitation of the Indians by the system of *encomienda*, in which Indians were compelled to work for a lord, usually a Spaniard but occasionally an Indian leader, in return for being made Christian and given protection. It was extremely difficult to restrain the holders of the great estates, however, and Spanish America remained at least until the nineteenth century an area in which the Indians were exploited for the benefit of a small landed class. The political organization was somewhat better than the economic. Spanish possessions were divided into two viceroyalties, New Spain, which covered all possessions north of Panama and was governed from Mexico City; and Peru, which included all South America and was governed from Lima. Large numbers of new cities were founded, almost always in superbly chosen locations. Some were administrative capitals, others missionary bases, others mining or manufacturing cities. Surprisingly, only about 100,000 people emigrated from Spain throughout the sixteenth century to conquer, administer, Christianize, and exploit this empire.

The percentage of women among these emigrants is uncertain, but from the third voyage of Columbus, when thirty women were carried to the Caribbean, the Spanish government determined to encourage their settlement. Spanish viceroys, unlike the Portuguese, were expected to bring their wives, to help set a social tone that would be akin to that of Spain itself in their capitals of Mexico City and Lima. Here, and in the richer regional centers such as the mining city of Potosí in Bolivia, both the administrative elite and the commercial and banking classes attempted to uphold high standards in learning and art. On the plantations, too, as in the Portuguese empire, Spanish women were welcomed as helpmates and often became estate administrators. Women even accompanied their husbands on military expeditions, and found themselves engaging in physical labor to help the expeditions survive. The Church also welcomed women in its missionary work. Convents were founded in the early years of the conquest, both for women emigrating from Spain and for the daughters of the conquistadores themselves. These nuns acted as teachers not only for the Spanish but for the Indian women also, and some became respected scholars and creative writers. The finest poet of the colonial period may have been the nun Juana Inés de la Cruz, who worked in a convent in Mexico City in the seventeenth century.

Many Spanish men married Indian women or kept them as concubines because of the shortage of Spanish brides. Cortés himself had lived with an

Indian woman called La Malinche during the struggle with the Aztecs, and had used her as his interpreter. Some of his leading soldiers married into the Aztec nobility, including even the daughters of the Emperor Montezuma. But for the majority of Indian women, who went through the sufferings of life on the plantations and the decimation of the Indian population, and for the black slave women brought in to repopulate the landed estates, there is little or no documentation of the undoubted hardships of life during the first three centuries of Spanish rule.

Economic Effects of Spanish Imperialism

The economic system of the Spanish empire was very shaky. At first Indian and then black African labor was used on the great estates to grow sugar and tobacco in the tropical areas and to grow cereals and raise animals in the inland areas. The Spanish, however, were far more interested in exploitation of the mines. In the 1540s rich veins of silver were discovered in Mexico and Bolivia, thereby greatly bolstering the revenues of the Spanish crown, which took 20 percent of all bullion sent back to Europe. But very few in America profited from the export of this bullion except a few wealthy Spaniards or native Creoles (Spanish born in the Americas); and the price paid in human lives was enormous. The population of Mexico may have fallen from 11 million to 2.5 million by 1600 as a result of overwork and disease.

The conquest and exploitation of its American empire helped make Spain the predominant power of the second half of the sixteenth century in Europe.

Casa de Pilatos, Seville, Spain (c. 1500) After the defeat of the Muslims in 1492, Spanish architects incorporated Muslim decoration, such as tiles and stucco, into buildings in Renaissance style. (Spanish National Tourist Office.)

To pay for the sugar, tobacco, hides, and bullion, Spain sent to the Americas wine, oil, flour, and manufactured goods such as cloth and metal tools. The prosperity within Spain was most evident in the port of Seville, which had been given a monopoly on trade with the Spanish empire. The merchant class of Seville built lovely palaces in Moorish style, erected a vast new cathedral, and constructed huge port facilities along the river for the hundred or more ships sailing to and from America each year. But this rosy picture did not last. The Spanish began to buy more and more manufactured goods abroad rather than produce them at home for use in the American trade. The vast influx of bullion into Spain caused rapid inflation. Prices in Spain quadrupled during the sixteenth century, causing terrible suffering for the peasantry, and making it necessary for the monarchy to receive an unending supply of bullion to cover its debts. Philip II in particular lived beyond his means, and was forced on several occasions to declare bankruptcy. Moreover, the arrival of the annual treasure fleets on which the royal income depended was coming under increasing danger each year from English, French, and Dutch pirates, who were often supported by their home governments.

SPAIN DURING THE PERIOD OF THE COLONIAL CONQUESTS

Two rulers of Spain experienced the power and the problems brought by possession of the new colonial empire—Charles (king of Spain as Charles I, 1516–1556; Holy Roman Emperor as Charles V, 1519–1556) and his son Philip II (reigned 1556–1598). When Ferdinand and Isabella had married their daughter Joanna to Philip the Handsome, son of the Holy Roman Emperor Maximilian I, neither Joanna nor Philip was in direct line to inherit a throne. But all the more senior claimants died, and as a result Charles, the son of Joanna and Philip, inherited the Netherlands in 1506; Spain, Naples, Sicily, and the Spanish empire in 1516; and Austria and parts of south Germany in 1519, as a result of which (and through bribery) he was also elected Holy Roman Emperor. Thus, although Charles's deepest interest was in Spain, he was inevitably involved in the affairs of almost every part of Europe.

Charles V

Charles's problems proved insuperable. In 1520, the Spanish cities rose against him, in protest against his financial exactions and restriction of their powers of self-government. After putting down the revolt, Charles attempted to show his intention to give predominance in his own policies to Spain by transferring the rule of Austria and his German possessions permanently to his younger brother Ferdinand and his successors. As Holy Roman Emperor and a faithful Catholic

Philip II, by Titian The portrait, painted when Philip was 24, was sent to his future wife, Mary Tudor of England. (Giraudon/Alinari-Art Resource.)

he was, however, compelled to spend most of the 1520s in fighting Protestantism in Germany. He could not concentrate his efforts there because, as ruler of a large part of Italy, he had to fight against another Catholic king, Francis I of France, who was attempting to take Naples. It was little surprise that the German Protestants made great progress militarily, and were able in 1555 to force recognition of the right of individual rulers to become Lutheran. It was also not surprising that Charles could not cover his expenses without taking vast loans from German bankers. In 1556, disgusted with the endless frustration, he abdicated the Spanish throne in favor of his son Philip, and retired to a life of religious meditation in a monastery in a remote part of Spain.

Philip II

Philip inherited Spain and its American colonies, the Spanish Netherlands, and parts of Italy. He also inherited the leadership of the Catholic Reformation. Philip embodied in many ways the best virtues of a Spanish noble. He was dignified, pious, frugal, and hard-working. In fact many of his officials found him too hard-working, since he insisted on reading all the state papers himself. (The delay in receiving orders from Spain gave support to a favorite saying in Spanish America: "If death came from Spain, I should be immortal.") But he was firmly committed to the ideals of the Catholic Reformation and was determined to make Spain purer even than Rome. The Spanish Inquisition did not spare the nobility nor even the Church leaders in Spain. The primate of Spain himself was imprisoned for seventeen years and his books found to contain heresy. The Index banned even the books of Sir Thomas More, who had died for Catholicism. Converted Jews and Muslims were placed under strict supervision of the Inquisition. Protestants were burned in public ceremonies.

The symbol of Philip's reign was the vast, mournful Escorial palace, which he built on the outskirts of Madrid, the city he had chosen as the new capital of Spain in 1561. The main part of the palace was a monastery and mausoleum for Philip's family, with only a small portion of the building devoted to living and working quarters for Philip and his government. The style was severely classical. Almost all exterior ornamentation was omitted. Philip's bedroom opened into the chapel through a small opening, so that even when ill he could participate in the church services. Here, isolated from the life of his people and saddened by innumerable personal tragedies, which included the death of four wives and of his son and heir, he planned the moves against the North European powers and the Turks that brought his country to bankruptcy.

During the 1560s and 1570s, Philip's first goal was to break the Turkish control of the sea lanes of the Mediterranean, especially those linking Spain with his possessions in Italy. Philip joined with Venice and Genoa to put together a fleet of 208 galleys, which in 1571 met the Turkish fleet at Lepanto off the coast of Greece. In a bloody battle the Christian fleet succeeded in destroying almost all of the Turkish vessels, and freed 150,000 galley slaves. Nevertheless, the long-term results of Lepanto were disappointing. The Turks easily rebuilt their navy. The eastern Mediterranean remained under firm Turkish control, and North African corsairs, or pirates, preyed constantly in the western Mediterranean.

Philip's second aim was to intervene in France to halt the advance of Calvinism and to support the conservative Catholic forces led by the Guise family, who were conspiring to take the French throne. France suffered for more than thirty years from a threefold confrontation among the Guise faction, the moderate Catholic supporters of the monarchy, and the Calvinists, which was made worse by Spanish intervention.

These civil wars are known as the French Wars of Religion (1562–1598), but they were just as much a struggle among factions for political power as a battle between opposing faiths. During the vastly complicated infighting, victory seemed to go capriciously from side to side. The more fanatical Catholics, supported by Catherine de Médicis, wife of Henry II and mother of the following three kings, seemed to have put an end to the Calvinist cause by murdering, on the eve of Saint Bartholomew's Day, 1572, 20,000 Calvinists in Paris and other French cities. The Protestants, however, regrouped in even greater strength, and found a new leader in Henry Bourbon, the king of Navarre. Philip then vastly increased his financial support of the Guise faction, but found his money wasted when the French king succeeded in having the duke of Guise murdered. But a Guise supporter then murdered the king himself, and, in an ironic turn of events, the throne passed to Henry of Navarre, the leader of the Calvinists. Henry IV converted to Catholicism in order to become king, supposedly justifying his apostasy with the remark, "Paris is worth a mass." During his reign, however, the Protestants of France were able to exercise freedom of worship in a number of fortified towns as guaranteed in Henry's Edict of Nantes (1598). Thus, after an enormously expensive intervention, which had included the use of Spanish troops, Philip had seen the French throne pass to one of his avowed enemies.

Philip's third task, and his greatest debacle, however, was his attempt to put down the revolt of the Netherlands. Charles V had inherited the seventeen provinces of the Netherlands (consisting approximately of present-day Holland, Belgium, and Luxembourg) as part of the Burgundian possessions of his grandmother Mary. The reign of Charles V had brought great prosperity to the Netherlands, since it opened the Spanish market for their cloth, metalwork, arms, cereals, and naval goods, and gave them easy access to Spanish raw wool and the tropical goods of the Spanish empire in America. Protestantism had not been harshly repressed. The principal complaint of the Netherlands against Charles had been his demand for taxes. The reign of Philip proved much more repressive. Philip intended to crush Protestantism, to break the political power of the Netherlands' aristocracy, and to tax the merchant class heavily. Although he appointed his wise and conciliatory half-sister, Margaret of Parma, as regent in 1559, Philip also sent other advisers and the Inquisition to carry through the repression he had ordered. As a result, in 1566 a Calvinist revolt broke out in the Flemish-speaking part of the Netherlands, during which mobs sacked Catholic churches and smashed their statues and windows.

Margaret called in German mercenary troops, who carried out mass executions. But Philip, still unsatisfied, sent in a Spanish army under the cruel and stupid Duke of Alva to engage in even harsher repression. Counts Egmont and Horne, two of the leaders of the revolt, were captured by trickery and executed. Alva also attempted to use extreme taxation to break the opposition of the merchants, and he moved the Council of Troubles, the body handling the unrest, to Amsterdam to bring the Dutch into obedience. The Dutch, however, took to the sea to harass the Spanish fleets bringing reinforcements, and, calling themselves the Sea Beggars, maintained bases in the Rhine delta from which they could attack virtually any part of the coast. Behind the dikes and great rivers, the Sea Beggars formed a political movement that found a great leader in the nobleman William the Silent, of the house of Orange.

Alva was forced to flee from Amsterdam, and for a time it looked as though the whole of the Netherlands would be united in independence. Philip, however, found at last a first-class general in Alessandro Farnese, duke of Parma. Using experienced Spanish troops, Parma broke the resistance of the Flemish cities. William the Silent was assassinated in 1584, after Philip had offered a large bribe for his murder. By then, however, the war in the Netherlands was becoming impossibly expensive for Philip. Queen Elizabeth of England had sent a small army to help the Dutch, and had unleashed her ships to pillage the Spanish fleets and colonial settlements. Her favorite privateer, Sir Francis Drake (1540?–1596) had been knighted when he returned from a three-year circumnavigation of the globe, loaded with booty from Spanish ships and colonies.

Philip decided that the way to solve all his problems at once was by one massive campaign—the destruction of the English fleet by a Spanish Armada, the invasion of England, and the restoration of Catholicism there, which he expected would be followed by the collapse of Dutch resistance. The Armada sailed up the English Channel in July 1588, constantly under attack by the smaller but faster English ships commanded by Drake. When the Spanish took refuge in Calais, Drake forced them out by sending in fireships. The Spanish commander finally broke off the engagement, and, caught by a tempest, was forced to sail around the north of Scotland back to Spain. Only one-half of the Spanish fleet returned home. Although Philip rebuilt his fleet and continued sea battles with Britain and land battles in both France and the Netherlands, the defeat of 1588 ended any hope that he could extricate himself from his interlocking problems. After the death of Philip, peace was made with the English in 1604. In 1609, a truce recognized the independence of the seven northern Dutch provinces of the Netherlands, which was reaffirmed in 1648 after a renewal of the fighting.

Spain's Golden Age

As his political problems accumulated, Philip turned to art as well as to religion for consolation. He purchased many religious paintings from Venice executed in the late Renaissance style, and he recalled Titian to Spain. As his official painter, Titian created the style of the court portrait, flattering presentations of members of the royal family and nobility that were often sent to other royal courts as gifts. During Philip's reign, Spain was home to the greatest religious painter of the late sixteenth century, El Greco (1541–1614), an artist from Crete who had been trained in Venice. There he had learned the style of Tintoretto, which he later combined with elements of the Byzantine style that he learned in Crete. As a result, he created paintings that were totally individual in appearance. His *Baptism of Christ*, for example, is carried out in swirling, ethereal color, with the main scene up front, close to the viewer, and the skies resplendent in their joy at the event.

Philip was not fond of the literature that was delighting the crowds in Madrid, even though this was the greatest age of Spanish drama. In 1598, the year of Philip's death, the first play of Lope de Vega (1562–1635), who was to become Spain's most popular playwright, was produced. Like his contemporary William Shakespeare, de Vega filled the stage with real human beings in the throes of passion, of hate or of love, and his audiences worshipped him. He responded by writing 1500 plays, of which the most famous is *Fuenteovejuna*, the story of a town called Fuenteovejuna, whose hated chief official is murdered.

When questioned about who did the murder, every villager gives the same answer, "Fuenteovejuna." Another dramatist, Miguel de Cervantes (1547–1616) had turned to writing after losing the use of his sword hand at the battle of Lepanto. But he had not had much popular success until he wrote one of the world's most charming and penetrating novels, *Don Quixote*, which was published in 1604. The bumbling, lovable knight, whose brain has become addled with reading tales of chivalry and who goes out with his steward Sancho Panza to rescue damsels in a world menaced by dragons, was immediately recognized as one of the greatest creations in the world of literature.

It is perhaps telling that Spain's finest novel should be about a man who has chosen to live in the past. Philip's reign had been in one sense an attempt to set the clock back, and it had failed. He had had the opportunity to lay the foundations in Spain itself for future economic growth; and he had done nothing. The peasantry was poor and oppressed, the nobility isolated and repressive, the Church purified but persecuting. An exploitative colonial system had been institutionalized, and would result in continuing suffering for centuries to the native Indian population. And even the wealth of the Americas, by destroying the Spanish price structure and by postponing the creation of economic development at home, had prepared the precipitous decline of Spain in the next two centuries.

LATER ENTRANTS INTO THE COMPETITION FOR COLONIES

Voyages from Northern Europe

The maritime powers of northern Europe had no intention, even in the late fifteenth century, of allowing Portugal and Spain a monopoly of the profits from overseas trade and empire. The new contenders were the English, the French, and the Dutch. Beginning far behind the Iberian powers in maritime research and technology, the northern European countries had to go through something of the same painful process of development, except where secrets could be bought or stolen. In 1497, only five years after Columbus had shown the existence of the American continent, the English King Henry VII sent the Italian sailor John Cabot (1450–1498) to the north of the American continent, beginning the long and fruitless efforts to find a northern passage to Asia. Cabot discovered Newfoundland and Nova Scotia, and the following year he reached Delaware Bay. An English expedition even visited the Caribbean Islands in 1527, but brought back the news that the Spanish were so firmly entrenched that it was impossible for the English as yet to hope to gain a foothold. The British therefore concentrated in the sixteenth century on exploring the African coast, where the Portuguese seemed less strong. In the 1550s, four expeditions sailed to the coasts of Ghana and Benin. They quickly realized that it was not only possible to obtain gold but that the African chiefs were willing to sell them slaves who were captives from neighboring peoples or even their own subjects, whom the English could then resell to the Spanish colonies in the Caribbean and on the American mainland—either legally with a permit or illegally, at greater profit.

The French concentrated their early expeditions on North America. King Francis I sent the Florentine Giovanni da Verrazzano to find a northern passage to Asia in 1523. He reached America at the coast of the Carolinas, and sailed north as far as Maine. Systematic knowledge of what was to become French Canada was collected by the Breton mariner Jacques Cartier, who made several voyages to the Saint Lawrence valley between 1534 and 1541, where he explored the sites of the future cities of Quebec and Montreal. He did not, however, find gold but only iron pyrites, which greatly disappointed his sponsors. The French therefore largely abandoned their efforts to open up North America for almost half a century.

The English under Queen Elizabeth continued to search for a northern passage to China, even attempting to find a northeast passage around the northern coast of Russia. The result of that voyage was the founding of the London Muscovy Company, which opened trade with Russia. Sir Humphrey Gilbert claimed Newfoundland for England in 1583. And in the early 1600s, Henry Hudson, a Dutch sailor in the service of England, reached the Arctic icepack at Spitsbergen and later explored the great bay that was named after him. The English, however, were becoming more impressed with the possibility of establishing settlements in the vast area in America that lay to the north of Spanish control. In 1584 and 1587, Sir Walter Raleigh, the half-brother of the explorer Humphrey Gilbert, was given charters by the queen to establish settlements at Roanoke Island in Virginia. Both failed almost at once, and the only lasting effect of Raleigh's venture was perhaps the introduction of tobacco into England. The colonizing movement in England did receive new stimulus from the exciting travel book of Sir Richard Hakluyt, *The Principal Navigations, Voiages, Traffics, and Discoveries of the English Nation* (1589), which urged the English to abandon the search for the northern passage and to seek immediately to settle the inviting lands of coastal North America.

Even before 1600, the Dutch too were beginning to force their way into a share of overseas trade. They already possessed the best ship for coastal trading, the flyship, which enabled them to undercut all other European shippers. In the late sixteenth century, however, they also developed large ocean-going vessels with which they intended to challenge Portugal's monopoly of Asian trade during its union with Spain. Many of Portugal's navigation secrets were published by Jan Huyghen van Lindschoten, who had worked in Goa in the service of the archbishop. His book *Itinerario* gave detailed instructions not only on how to sail to India but also the Americas; and it was used by the English as well as the Dutch. In 1594 the Dutch founded the Company of Far Lands, which sent out a small fleet of four ships the next year, under the leadership of a tough sailor named Cornelius Houtman, who had lived for many years in Lisbon. The fleet reached Java and the Moluccas without much difficulty, and brought back a cargo of pepper and mace and the knowledge that the Portuguese hold on their overseas trade was very shaky.

So many Dutch groups organized expeditions to Asia that the Dutch government compelled them all in 1602 to join together in one company named the United Netherlands Chartered East India Company, which became one of the most successful and longest-lived commercial companies in history. The company was given the sole right to trade between the Cape of Good Hope and the Straits of Magellan. Moreover, it was authorized to make war, build forts, capture foreign ships, and coin money. Very quickly the Dutch broke the Portuguese control. They made treaties with the local princes and were permitted to build forts, of which the most important was Batavia (now Djakarta) on the island of Java.

The Dutch then made war on the Portuguese and forced them out of Malaya and Ceylon. To scare away the English, they massacred their merchants at Amboina in the Moluccas. When Dutch ships reached Japan, they were permitted to replace the Spanish and Portuguese as the sole agent for Japanese trade with Europe, since the Japanese had become weary of the successful propagation of Christianity by the Jesuits and friars. For 200 years after 1646, the Dutch settlement at Nagasaki was to be Japan's only contact with Europeans and with the knowledge Europe was accumulating from the scientific revolution of the sixteenth century to the industrial revolution of the eighteenth. Finally, in 1652, the Dutch took possession of the Cape of Good Hope and established their own settlement at Capetown. The British and French made almost no attempt to settle in Asia during the seventeenth century, and contented themselves with a few small trading posts on the coast of India. For almost a century, therefore, the Dutch were the principal trading power in Asia, and the profits they reaped were the foundation of their golden age of culture in the mid-seventeenth century (see Chapter 10).

Dutch Colonization in North America

The seventeenth century was a period of intensive settlement of North America by the northern European powers. Here again the Dutch were determined to take a share. In 1621, Calvinists in Amsterdam, wishing to strike directly at the Spanish in America, formed the West India Company for the explicit purpose of attacking Spanish ships and colonies and seizing a share of Spain's trade. The company even succeeded in capturing the whole Spanish treasure fleet in 1628. As in Asia, they sought small, strategically located ports. In the Caribbean they took the tiny island of Curaçao. At the mouth of the Hudson River, they bought the tip of Manhattan Island from the Indians and named it New Amsterdam. (New Amsterdam was seized by the English in 1664, and renamed

New York after the Duke of York, who had led the capture.) The West India Company never had the success of the East India Company, and it remained only a minor source of income for the Dutch merchants. The French and British were determined, by contrast, to make their principal effort in the North American mainland and in the Caribbean.

The French in North America

The French returned to the regions they had explored earlier in the century, sending missionaries, administrators, and fur traders. The most important of their leaders was Samuel de Champlain, who founded Quebec in 1608. Other French missionaries, such as Fathers Marquette and Joliet, and explorers, such as La Salle and Frontenac, established a superficial French control over the Saint Lawrence Valley and over the Great Lakes as far as Lake Superior. A French colony was founded in 1669 in Louisiana at the mouth of the Mississippi.

The British in North America

British settlement progressed in the vast area left vacant between the French settlement in Canada and the Mississippi Valley and the Spanish settlement in Florida. King James I divided the right to colonize this area between two companies, the London Company and the Plymouth Company. Jamestown in Virginia was begun by the London Company in 1607, and after great hardships became the first English settlement to survive. The Plymouth Company failed to found a colony in the more northerly areas assigned to it; but in 1620 the Pilgrim Fathers landed at Cape Cod and founded the first settlement in New England. Nine years later English Puritans were authorized to form a Company of Massachusetts Bay, which, during the persecution of Puritans by Charles I and Archbishop Laud, moved all its stockholders to Massachusetts, where they were joined during the next decade by thousands of religious refugees.

By the end of the seventeenth century the pattern of settlement in the British colonies was clear. In the colonies of New England there were religious settlements, mostly Puritan, which had been founded as refuges for the elect. Land was held individually after assignment by the township. There was considerable self-government through the colonial assemblies and the local township meetings. In the southern colonies, from Maryland to the Carolinas, settlement had been by large trading companies whose main purpose had been profit. Material incentives had been offered to those who would settle. After Virginia became a royal colony, it offered large estates to anyone bringing settlers from Europe—50 acres for every person brought in. Very soon the pattern of landholding in large plantations worked by African slaves became predominant. In the "middle" states, from Delaware to New York, there was a mixture of large estates and family farms; many different religions; and considerable industry and commerce. Perhaps the most unusual colony was Pennsylvania, founded by the Quaker William Penn (1644–1718) as a refuge for fellow Quakers, an offshoot of Puritanism whose pacifism invited constant persecution. But he also opened the colony to any who would come, promising rental of a 200-acre farm for one penny an acre or sale of a large estate for £100.

Thus the English colonies on the mainland of North America invited large-scale settlement, and it was hardly surprising that in the eighteenth century they should have refused to be bounded by the sparsely settled possessions of the French and the Spanish.

The opening up of overseas trade and the establishment of colonial empires between the fifteenth and seventeenth centuries were a revolutionary new departure in Western history:

1. It shifted the center of European economic and political strength away from the Mediterranean lands to those on the Atlantic Ocean or the Baltic Sea. Although some Italian cities were still able to stage a brief revival in the sixteenth century, the relative decline of Mediterranean Europe in comparison with western and northern Europe had begun.
2. Portugal and Spain, as the firstcomers into the new colonial venture, reaped the profits before any other European power. Both enjoyed a century of prosperity greater than any they had previously known. Spain, far larger in population and territory than tiny Portugal, was able to use its new wealth to gain the predominant political and military position in Europe for much of the sixteenth century. Both countries were able to finance—and encourage—the production of the finest art, architecture, and literature in their history.
3. Both Portugal and Spain, however, suffered from the mistakes they made in the use of their new wealth and power. Neither reinvested at home to create further economic development and employment, either in agriculture or industry, in preparation for a time when the profits from spices and precious metals would dry up. Spain in particular exploited its colonies mercilessly, and by wiping out a good part of its Indian population in America it not only committed a colossal act of inhumanity but failed even in a selfish way to profit from the existence of a highly civilized, hard-working population that in many ways was superior to the soldiers who subjugated them.
4. The opening of Asia to European trade and, increasingly, to conquest changed the character of world history. Japan and to a slightly lesser degree China were strong and distant enough to be able to maintain isolation from the Europeans when they wished. But the rest of Asia was to fall increasingly under European influence. In Africa, the arrival of the Europeans not only expanded the scourge of slavery, but severely weakened and in certain instances completely destroyed indigenous states with highly developed cultures.
5. The penetration of the Dutch into Asian trade did not appreciably alter the system of trade and influence established by the Portuguese. But the settlement of the English and, to a less important degree, of the French in

North America led to the opening up of an area whose economic potential was to prove infinitely greater than that of the Spanish in Central and South America.

SUGGESTED READINGS

General Surveys

J. H. Parry, one of the most informative historians of the overseas discoveries, provides a brief introduction in *The Establishment of the European Hegemony, 1714–1715* (1961) and more specialized treatment of maritime technology in *The Age of Reconnaissance* (1963). If you would like to marvel at the progress in ship design, see also Parry's beautifully illustrated *The Discovery of the Sea* (1974).

The Portuguese Trading Empire

C. R. Boxer shows how Portuguese society was affected by the overseas riches in *The Portuguese Seaborne Empire, 1414–1825* (1969), whereas its impact in Asia is discussed in Bailie W. Diffie and George D. Winius, *Foundations of the Portuguese Empire, 1415–1580* (1977). The life of Lisbon and the court is developed in down-to-earth detail in A. H. de Oliveira Marques, *Daily Life in Portugal in the Late Middle Ages* (1971). The best account of the spread of Portuguese and Spanish art into their new possessions is George Kubler and Martin Soria, *Art and Architecture in Spain and Portugal and Their American Dominions, 1500 to 1800* (1959).

Spain's Empire in the Americas

Let Columbus tell his own story, in *The Journal of Christopher Columbus*, translated by Cecil Jane (1960), but Samuel E. Morrison tells it for him very entertainingly in *Admiral of the Ocean Sea* (1942).

J. H. Parry, *The Spanish Seaborne Empire* (1966), explains the importance of Seville for trans-Atlantic trade.

The position of women in the Spanish colonial empire is studied in James Lockhart, *Spanish Peru, 1532–1560: A Colonial History* (1968), and Asunción Lavrin, ed., *Latin American Women: Historical Perspectives* (1978). C. R. Boxer, *Women in Iberian Expansion Overseas, 1415–1815: Some Facts, Fancies and Personalities* (1975), is anecdotal rather than synthetic.

On Aztec civilization before the destructive arrival of Cortés, see Jacques Soustelle, *The Daily Life of the Aztecs on the Eve of the Spanish Conquest* (1955). John Hemming describes the destruction of Inca civilization in *Conquest of the Incas* (1970). Pierre Vilar shows how importation of bullion weakened the Spanish economy in *A History of Gold and Money, 1450–1920* (1976).

Spain Under Charles V and Philip II

Stanley G. Payne relates social and intellectual developments to political change in *A History of Spain and Portugal* (1973). Equally reliable is John H. Elliott, *Imperial Spain, 1496–1716* (1963). Elliott shows that one can learn a lot about a colonial power by studying its colonies in *The Old World and the New, 1492–1650* (1970). Karl Brandi, *Charles V* (1939), is still sound. Philip II can be followed through the broader study of his reign, in John Lynch, *Spain Under the Habsburgs*, Vol. I, *Empire and Absolutism, 1516–1598* (1963), or in the biography by P. Pierson, *Philip II of Spain* (1975). Garrett Mattingley, *The Armada* (1959), and David Howarth, *Voyage of the Armada* (1982), place the sea battles in their political context. Philip II's palace tells much about the king who built it, in George Kubler, *Building the Escorial* (1982). An understanding of sixteenth-century Spain can be enhanced through Bartolomé Bennassar's studies of the development of Spanish mental attitudes, *The Spanish Character: Attitudes and Mentalities from the Sixteenth to the Nineteenth Century* (1979). Better yet, read Miguel de Cervantes, *Don Quixote* (many editions). Melveena McKendrick shows that Lope de Vega's plays are a rich mine of information about Spanish attitudes to women, in *Woman and Society in the Spanish Drama of the Golden Age* (1974).

Later Colonial Empires

C. R. Boxer analyzes Dutch society as well as the overseas explorations and trade in *The Dutch Seaborne Empire, 1600–1800* (1965) and *The Dutch in Brazil* (1973). The weakness of New France, France's American empire, is explained in George W. Wrong, *Rise and Fall of New France* (1970). For an introduction to the vast literature on the early British colonies in North America and the West Indies, see John Bowle, *The Imperial Achievement* (1974), and Cyril Hamshere, *The British in the Caribbean* (1972). For a recreation of the slave experience on one of the French West Indian islands, see the contemporary classic by André Schwarz-Bart, *A Woman Named Solitude*, translated by Ralph Manheim (1973).

Finally, for fresh insights into the place of European imperialism in the structure of the world economy, there are three ambitious and challenging works: Immanuel Wallerstein, *The Modern World-System: Capitalist Agriculture and the Origins of the European World-Economy in the Sixteenth Century* (1974); E. L. Jones, *The European Miracle: Environments, Economics, and Geopolitics in the History of Europe and Asia* (1981), which is less prolix than its title; and Eric R. Wolf, *Europe and the People Without History* (1982). Fernand Braudel, *The Mediterranean and the Mediterranean World in the Age of Philip II* (1972), is encyclopedic, but everyone should at least taste a little of its vast learning.

part IV

The Age of Absolutism

***Louis XIV, by Hyacinthe Rigaud
(1659–1743)*** *The Sun King at age
63, after four decades of absolute
rule.* (Musée National du Louvre/
Alinari-Art Resource.)

THE AGE OF ABSOLUTISM

Dates	Political & Military Events	Social, Economic, & Demographic Events	Religion & Philosophy	Art, Architecture, Literature, & Music	Science & Technology
1600s				Baroque architecture	
1602		Dutch East India Company founded			
1610	Murder of Henry IV, France Louis XIII, France (1610–43)			d. Caravaggio	
1618	Thirty Years War (1618–48)				
1625	Charles I, England (1625–49)				
1628					Harvey proves circulation of the blood
1636				Corneille, *Le Cid*	
1637					Descartes, *Discourse on Method*
1640				d. Rubens	
1642	English Civil Wars (1642–48)				d. Galileo
1643	Louis XIV, France (1643–1715)				
1651			Hobbes, *Leviathan*		
1660	Charles II, England (1660–85)				
1665				d. Poussin	
1667				Milton, *Paradise Lost*	
1669				d. Rembrandt	
1673				d. Molière	

Date				
1675			d. Vermeer Wren, St. Paul's Cathedral, London	
1680			d. Bernini	
1685	James II, England (1685–88)	Louis XIV revokes Edict of Nantes, France		
1687				Newton's *Principles*
1688	Glorious Revolution, England	Dominance of oligarchy in Britain		
1689	Peter the Great, Russia (1689–1725)			
1690		Locke's *Essay Concerning Human Understanding*		
1699			d. Racine	
1714	George I, Britain (1714–27)			
1715	Louis XV, France (1715–74)			
1717			Watteau *Embarkation for Cythera*	
1733		Voltaire, *Philosophical Letters*		Mechanization of textile production in Northern England
1738		John Wesley begins Methodist movement		
1740	Frederick II, Prussia (1740–86); Maria Theresa, Austria (1740–80)		Rococo churches in Germany, Austria; Balthasar Neumann (1687–1753)	
1748		Montesquieu's *Spirit of the Laws*		
1750			d. Bach	
1751			Diderot's *Encyclopedia*	

(continued)

THE AGE OF ABSOLUTISM (*continued*)

Dates	Political & Military Events	Social, Economic, & Demographic Events	Religion & Philosophy	Art, Architecture, Literature, & Music	Science & Technology
1756	Seven Years War (1756–63)	British annex French possessions in India and North America		Mozart (1756–91)	
1759				Voltaire, *Candide* d. Handel	
1762	Catherine the Great, Russia (1762–96)		Rousseau, *Social Contract*	Winter Palace, Saint Petersburg Gluck, *Orfeo*	
1774	Louis XVI, France (1774–92)			Goethe, *Sorrows of Young Werther*	
1776		Fiscal breakdown in France	Adam Smith, *Wealth of Nations*		
1780	Joseph II, Austria personal rule (1780–90)				
1789	Beginning of French Revolution				

10

Power and Glory in the Seventeenth Century

In the late Middle Ages the most successful rulers, the New Monarchs, had ceased to derive their power primarily from the personal allegiance of a hierarchy of landed nobles and had instead based their power on a highly trained bureaucracy, a professional army, and independent powers of revenue raising. In the sixteenth century the successors of the first New Monarchs had continued the process of increasing their personal powers, and several had reached the point where they could exercise despotic rule. The most outstanding examples were Charles V and Philip II, the successors of Ferdinand and Isabella in Spain; Henry VIII, the successor of Henry VII in England; and Francis I of France, who expanded the powers taken by Louis XI. At the end of the sixteenth century and throughout the seventeenth century, however, no uniform type of despotic rule developed throughout Europe. On the contrary, the forms of government in Europe become far more varied than those that had existed in the High Middle Ages or even in the early sixteenth century.

Four basic types of government can be distinguished during this period. In Russia, which was only freed from Mongol rule in 1480 by the ruler of the principality of Moscow, despotic rule was consolidated into a form of government we call autocracy, in which virtually no constraints from within the state were placed on the power of the ruler by the constitution, by the Church, or by the legal system. A second form of government, absolutism, reached its highest development in France during the reign of King Louis XIV. An absolute monarch threw off the institutions such as representative parliaments or legal

287

codes that in the Middle Ages had fettered royal powers, but did not exercise unlimited powers because he still recognized the authority over him of duty to God, traditional restrictions on the area within which government should operate, and the necessity to compromise with the most powerful of his subjects, especially with the nobility. The English created a third form of monarchical government, limited monarchy, in reaction against the attempts of the first two kings of the Stuart dynasty, James I and Charles I to take for themselves powers of absolutism similar in some ways to those of the French monarchy. In this type of monarchy, which was complete in England after the Revolution of 1688, the king continued to exercise certain executive powers, but the principal decision making in government was done by the nobility and the wealthiest of the middle class through parliament in a form of oligarchy. Finally, the Dutch, after declaring the independence of the United Provinces or Dutch Republic from Spain in 1581, created a form of democracy in which all citizens theoretically shared power, but which in fact was dominated by the wealthiest of the middle class of its cities. Hence we shall call this form of government middle-class republicanism. In this chapter we shall examine in turn the creation and influence on state development of autocracy in Russia, absolutism in France, limited monarchy in England, and middle-class republicanism in the Netherlands.

THE CREATION OF RUSSIAN AUTOCRACY

Early Russia

Both geography and history have set the Russian people apart from the mainstream of European civilization. The East Slavs, who are the most numerous nationality of the Russian people, spread into the vast steppes of Russia from Novgorod in the north to the Ukraine in the south by the ninth century A.D., and were separated from intense Westernizing influence by the Western and South Slavs of Eastern Europe with whom they were frequently at war. The East Slavs were incorporated in the first Russian state around Kiev on the Volga River by Viking settlers known as Varangians in the ninth century. (The word for Russia is probably derived from the Viking word Russ, or Rhos, which was the name of one group of Varangians.)

The Varangians rapidly intermingled with the Slavic population and left virtually no imprint of Viking ways. They were responsible for bringing the East Slavs into close contact with the Byzantine Empire, by opening up the route from Kiev to Constantinople. The Kievan state accepted Greek Orthodox Christianity in 986, and thereby definitively separated Russia from the evolution of Catholic Europe. Kievan Russia naturally looked to Byzantium for its culture, and hence developed a deep interest in the ritual, the theology, and the monasticism of the Byzantine church. The monarchs also inherited a state church willingly subordinated to the secular power at the very time the pope was challenging the authority of the emperor in Western Europe.

Tatar Yoke

Kievan Russia was easily defeated by the Mongols, or Tatars, of the so-called Golden Horde, under Batu Khan in 1237–1240, and most of its cities were destroyed. Mongol rule, which lasted until the late fifteenth century, further estranged the Russians from the evolution of Western Europe. Although the Mongols permitted Russian princes to continue to rule, provided they paid the required tribute, Mongol ways of life became deeply rooted among the Russian people. Monarchical power was unrestricted by any respect for individual rights. Violence by governmental officials was normal. Women were secluded from all social life. And even in appearance, the Russians modeled themselves on Mongols, in their baggy clothing, long hair, and beards.

The prince of Moscow, the ruler on whom the Mongols most relied for collection of tribute, was able eventually to oust his masters. The city of Moscow had been founded as frontier settlement in the twelfth century, but had developed rapidly because of its fine central location within the river networks of European Russia. Its importance had been enhanced in the early thirteenth century when the metropolitan of the Russian Orthodox Church settled there. The Muscovy rulers were able to annex large numbers of the surrounding principalities and thereby increase their own military strength. They inflicted a first military defeat on the Tatars at Kulikovo in 1380. But only in 1480 was Ivan III (the Great; reigned 1462–1505) able to force them back as far as the northern shores of the Black Sea.

Ivan III

Ivan III founded the absolutism of the Russian monarchy. After the fall of Constantinople in 1453 and the subsequent end of the Byzantine Empire, he took the Byzantine emperor's title of *autocrator*, the Byzantine symbol of the double-headed eagle, and Constantinople's forms of court ceremonial. He accepted the declaration of a Russian monk that, with the fall of Constantinople, Moscow had become a third Rome: "Two Romes have fallen; the third stands; and a fourth one there shall not be." He married Sophia, the niece of the last Byzantine emperor, who claimed to be heiress to the Byzantine throne, and brought her to Moscow to help instill in the Muscovite nobility a modicum of the social graces of the Byzantine court. He thus felt that both religiously and politically he had a claim not only to succeed to the power of the Byzantine emperor but actually to annex the Byzantine Empire itself. With such imperial pretensions, he was determined to spread his power in every direction. He took over the vast territories of Novgorod, which extended as far as the Ural Mountains, and seized border territories of the neighboring state of Poland-Lithuania. He also inaugurated Russia's drive to the east, when Russian pioneers crossed the Ural Mountains and began the colonization of Siberia. This overland Russian drive toward the North Pacific must be seen as the equivalent of the seaward journeys of the Western European powers. When the Russian explorers and settlers reached the Sea of Okhotsk in 1638, they had already traveled one-third as far again as the sailors who crossed the Atlantic Ocean. Rather than acquire colonies, one Russian historian remarked, Russia colonized itself.[1]

To maintain his power at home, Ivan III created a new service nobility, by the grant of large estates to a class called *pomietchiks*, who retained their lands only during their lifetime in return for specific services to the ruler. Eventually these lands became hereditary. In addition, the hereditary nobility were compelled to render service, and thus both the hereditary and service nobility became similar in character in that their position in society and their wealth was dependent on service to the ruler. Ivan began the process of tying the peasants to the land as serfs, to ensure that they would pay their taxes to the state and give their labor to the nobility.

In keeping with his imperial ambitions, Ivan called to Moscow a group of Italian architects to transform his old fortress-palace of the Kremlin in the center of Moscow. They built a magnificent crenellated wall of red brick, 4.5 miles long and 60 feet in height, broken at intervals with imaginatively decorated watch towers. Within the wall they raised a breath-taking group of cathedrals whose bell-shaped domes were gilded with gold leaf, and fine palaces for Ivan and for the head of the Orthodox Church. In a short time, the Kremlin had become one of the most dramatic imperial residences in the world.

Ivan the Terrible

Control was difficult to maintain, however, as the empire expanded rapidly. Tsar Ivan IV (the Terrible; reigned 1534–1584), who was the first ruler officially to use the title of tsar (or caesar), responded to the challenges facing him by resorting to savage violence to break resistance. He created Russia's first sinister secret police, the *oprichnina* or "separate kingdom," a private army of black-uniformed sadists who roamed uncontrolled through Russia on black horses decorated with dogs' heads. Ivan's own temper was so uncontrolled that on one occasion he killed his own son and heir, while several of his seven wives were either sent to monasteries or murdered. Ivan regarded the nobles as his irreconcilable enemies, and constantly sought to break their power by annexation of their lands, by exile, or even by execution. Many of the hereditary nobility were forced to settle on the frontiers, and the service nobility were given many of their lands.

Ivan seized many of the remaining territories of the Tatars in southeastern Russia, and he began the military conquest of Siberia. Although unable to break Swedish and Polish control of the Baltic, he opened trade relations with England by granting trading rights through the northern port of Archangel.

Ivan's vicious rule was followed by three decades of chaos known as the

---

[1] Cited in E. L. Jones, *The European Miracle: Environments, Economies, and Geopolitics in the History of Europe and Asia* (Cambridge: Cambridge University Press, 1981), p. 74.

Time of Troubles, in which the nobles attempted to reassert their power and neighboring countries tried to annex the border provinces. To end this state of confusion, Michael Romanov, grand-nephew of Ivan the Terrible, was chosen tsar in 1613 in an assembly dominated by the nobles. Although Michael was able to drive out the foreign armies, for most of the seventeenth century the power of the nobility increased at the expense of the tsar. In 1649, the assembly approved the legal enserfdom of the peasants, and divided all Russian society into strictly defined levels of class. Foreigners were penned up in ghettos in the large cities to prevent the spread of their modernizing influences. Even the patriarch, as the metropolitan of Moscow was known after 1589, challenged the power of the tsar over the Russian Orthodox Church. Some progress against these tendencies was made by Tsar Alexis (reigned 1645–1676); but it was his son Peter (the Great; reigned 1682–1725) who was to see in the reinforcement of autocracy the key to the modernization of the Russian state.

Peter the Great

Peter grew up in the foreign section of Moscow, where he became fascinated with Western technology as well as with military and naval science. He also became disgusted with the power and the backwardness of the Russian nobles, the intrigues of the Church, and the excessive political power of the palace guard called the *streltsi*. At the age of seventeen, he carried out a coup against

Peter the Great, by Jean-Marc Nattier (1685–1766) As his armor emphasizes, Peter was deeply concerned with strengthening Russia's army, which he personally led to victory in the Great Northern War with Sweden. (Novasti Press Agency.)

the regent, his half-sister Sophia Alekseyevna, whose brutal government had alienated important groups within the powerful palace guard. Sophia was despatched to a convent; and Peter set out to enforce his will against all opposition. A brilliant, headstrong, cruel giant of a man, 6 feet 8 inches tall and possessed of massive strength and self-confidence, he personally executed the rebels among the palace guard when they attempted to overthrow his government during his first journey to Western Europe in 1697–1698. The trip had, however, already provided him with the knowledge and the manpower he needed for the modernization of his country. Often in disguise he had visited factories, barracks, and naval bases, and had even for a time worked himself in the shipyards of Amsterdam. Everywhere he had recruited foreign technicians, architects, and military experts for work in Russia. The trip had also taught him that the European powers were unwilling to help him attack Turkey, but would watch with favor if he were to humiliate the rising power of Sweden.

He declared war on Sweden in 1700, with the specific goal of winning for Russia Swedish territories on the Baltic that could provide Russia with an ice-free port as a "window on the West." In this Great Northern War (1700–1721), although he was aided by Poland and Denmark, he was at first unsuccessful in his battles with the brilliant young King Charles XII of Sweden; but in 1703 he was able to seize the mouth of the Neva River, which flows into the Gulf of Finland and thence into the Baltic. Here he decided to create a new capital city for Russia.

Saint Petersburg

The site of Saint Petersburg was decidedly unpromising, a marshy wasteland where thousands of his workers died of dysentery. After the city plan had been laid down, the police informed the nobles the size of the houses they were to build in Saint Petersburg; and all nobles were compelled to serve in the bureaucracy, the army, or the navy. Noble cadets were required to enroll in his military and technical schools or in the Naval Academy. By excellence of performance, nobles could rise through the new Table of Ranks, a division of the nobility into fourteen grades. The Table at the same time provided an entry into the nobility for talented members of the middle class. A commercial section of the city was carefully laid out, and the trading community of Archangel compelled to settle there. Artisans were assigned specific streets, such as the Street of the Cannonmakers.

In this city Peter intended to establish selectively everything he regarded as best in Western Europe. The city plan of the original island on which the city was founded was copied from Amsterdam and London. The government ministries that lined the river bank was modeled on the Swedish civil service, which he had come to admire while fighting against Sweden. The new army was modeled on those of Sweden and Prussia, the navy on those of England and the Netherlands. France provided the model of social life. Even the style of dress had to be similar to that of France. The old Muscovite robes were banned; and Peter himself shaved or cut the hair of those who refused to look like the French nobility.

Peter saw that the status of noble women and their role in society must be completely transformed if Russia was to be Westernized, and that in particular the seclusion of women practised in old Muscovite society had to be ended. The women in his palace could no longer be kept in a separate section of the building. As early as 1699 he had scandalized the nobles in Moscow by ordering them to bring their wives to a palace dinner with dancing. In Saint Petersburg after 1718, he put the end of women's segregation in the hands of the head of police. All the nobility had to attend "assemblies" three times a week in which for at least five hours men and women took part in conversation and played games. He ordered that men and women should be allowed to choose their own spouses. He was particularly determined that noble women should be well educated, and began the experiment of sending Russian noble women to the small German courts to learn Western ways of behaving. Paradoxically, the newly elegant nobility despised Peter's own wife Catherine for what they felt were her peasant ways; but their daughter, the Empress Elizabeth (reigned 1741–1762), was one of the most accomplished women in Saint Petersburg.

Slowly a pastel-colored, harmonious city grew up in the northern rains. Saint Petersburg was different from any city in Russia, and as the creation of one despot drawing on a nation's resources for the creation of a totally new Baroque city, it was different even from the cities of Western Europe. No previous city, not even Constantinople, had been so totally planned; and its character as the ideal Baroque city was maintained by the rulers of the next two centuries as the city expanded southward.

Saint Petersburg had, however, divided Russia into two societies—a Westernized group, composed primarily of the nobility and a section of the middle class, had adopted continental European ways of thought and values and often spoke French in preference to Russian. To them the society seemed to offer unlimited privilege. Against them, however, was ranged the vast majority of the Russian people and especially the peasantry, whose tax burdens were increased to provide for Peter's new creation and for the privileges of its inhabitants. While Peter had succeeded in modernizing one segment of Russian society at an incredible pace and had thereby made Russia one of the leading powers of Europe, he had at the same time, by creating an inseparable gap between the two segments of Russian society, left a weakness from which Russian society would never recover before the Revolution of 1917.

THE ABSOLUTISM OF FRANCE'S SUN KING

No European monarch possessed, or even sought, the autocratic powers of the Russian tsar. The ideal form of royal government that most tried to achieve was the absolute monarchy of Louis XIV (reigned 1643–1715) in France. Absolutism was not the sole creation of Louis XIV, however, but rather a slow accumulation of power, with frequent setbacks, from the reign of Louis XI at the end of the fifteenth century on. Louis XI had given France the basic characteristics of the New Monarchy, that is, a professional army, a reliable income from taxation and other sources, the power to legislate, and control over the Catholic Church. Although he was distracted by his unprofitable wars in Italy, Francis I (reigned 1515–1547) consolidated the powers taken by Louis XI. The Wars of Religion were, as we saw, a bitter civil war in which not only Catholics and Protestants warred but factions within the nobility competed for control of the crown. Nevertheless, they can be interpreted as a serious if misguided attempt by the French monarchy to end the threat to monarchical power presented by the existence of the fortified cities of the Calvinists and by the lack of national uniformity in religion.

Henry IV and Louis XIII

It was, however, the cynical charmer Henry IV (reigned 1589–1610) who was able to restore both order and royal predominance. Henry recognized that it was wiser for the king to ally with the 15 million Catholics of the kingdom than with the 1 million Calvinists, whose leader he had been; and he had converted to Catholicism (for the third time) in 1593 in order to be accepted in Paris as king. At the time, however, he recognized that religious toleration was a far better method of creating unity under the monarchy than the mutual intolerance of the religious wars. The Edict of Nantes of 1598, which granted religious toleration to the Huguenots and the right to maintain their fortified cities, won the loyalty of the most intelligent and hard-working section of the population. The middle class, moreover, of whom the Huguenots were a vitally important segment, were also delighted at the economic policies instigated by Henry's chief minister, the duke of Sully. Sully believed that France should as far as possible be self-sufficient in both industry and agriculture. By frugal expenditure and careful accounting, he maintained the value of government bonds, and he gave the government a fiscal surplus. The foundation of new industries was encouraged, especially in such luxury goods as silk, lace, and glassware.

Henry and Sully were particularly careful to encourage the reconstruction of the center of Paris. They created two lovely residential areas, one at the tip of the Ile de la Cité, where an equestian statue of Henry looked out over the ships coming up the river Seine, and a superb square now called the Place des Vosges, where Henry himself sold houses to carefully selected members of the new bureaucracy. They thus began the tradition of urban planning that was to make Paris the most harmonious of all European capital cities. Although Henry later had the reputation of being the most popular of all French kings, he was not admired by all his subjects. In 1610, he was assassinated by a fanatical Catholic, leaving his nine-year-old son Louis XIII (reigned 1610–1643) as king and his wife Marie de Médicis as regent.

The Triumphal Entry of Henry IV into Paris, by Peter Paul Rubens (1577–1640) *This preliminary sketch for an oil painting shows the Paris crowd greeting Henry IV in 1594, after his conversion to Catholicism.* (The Metropolitan Museum of Art, Rogers Fund, 1942.)

Marie proved an incompetent administrator, and France was only rescued from incipient anarchy when power was taken by the brilliant, tough-minded Cardinal Richelieu, in 1624. Louis XIII, who had little taste for government, allowed Richelieu (1585–1642) to run the administration until his death. Richelieu gave the French monarchy an efficient bureaucratic foundation for absolutism. He gave almost unlimited power in local administration to thirty middle-class officials called *intendants*, each of whom governed one of the thirty *généralités* into which Richelieu divided France. In Paris, Richelieu ran the government from his own palace, which he constructed next to the Louvre, working through a royal council composed of his own nominees from the middle class. The nobility were thus bypassed both in central and local government. Richelieu also increased the military strength of France by building a new navy, with separate fleets operating on the Mediterranean and Atlantic coasts of France, and by modernizing the French artillery. He also took away the right of the Huguenots to fortify their cities, although he did permit them to maintain their worship.

The Frondes

Reaction against Richelieu's innovations came during the rule of his hand-picked successor, Cardinal Mazarin (1602–1661), an Italian who controlled the government from 1642 to 1661. Mazarin was the lover, and may have been the husband, of Louis XIII's widow, Anne of Austria, who theoretically ran the government on behalf of her son, the five-year-old Louis XIV. Mazarin lacked the prestige and force of character of Richelieu, and infuriated the nobility by his devious ways of government. In 1648–1652, in the Frondes, a nationwide series of uprisings named after the slingshots of Paris children, it seemed that the monarchy might well be stripped of many of the powers it had gained during the past 150 years. On one occasion, the Paris mob flooded into the Louvre palace, and forced the young king to run for his life from his own bedroom. Louis XIV's distrust and hatred of the Paris crowd and of the nobles who had unleashed it against the monarchy was perhaps the dominant theme of French government for the rest of his reign. After the royal armies had restored order in 1652, he waited impatiently for the opportunity to remodel monarchical power free of the control of a chief minister like Richelieu or Mazarin.

The Nature of French Absolutism

This opportunity came in 1661, upon the death of Mazarin. Louis at once took personal power, and acted for the rest of his reign as his own chief minister. The situation within both Europe and France could not have been more ideal for the reassertion of the power of the French king. Within France all classes were weary of the insecurity and economic chaos resulting from the lack of strong government under Mazarin, and were glad to accept the assertion of royal power.

In Europe too the situation was ripe for a demonstration of French strength. The Austrian empire was harassed by renewed attacks of the Ottoman Turks, who besieged Vienna itself in 1683. Germany had not recovered from the Thirty Years War. The Dutch were weakened by naval rivalry with England. The English were convalescing from their own civil wars. Only France, with a population of 18 million and a rich agriculture, a strong indutrial base, and a modernized army and navy, was in a position to dominate Europe.

The assertion of absolute royal power was justified by the theory of the divine right of kings, which had been propounded at the end of the sixteenth century by a group of political philosophers known as the *Politiques* and was elaborated with great eloquence in the sermons and writings of Bishop Jacques-Bénigne Bossuet, the most influential preacher and political philosopher of Louis's reign. The *Politiques* had argued that the king was governed by the will of God and was responsible only to God, and therefore should exercise "supreme power over citizens and subjects, unrestrained by law." Bossuet justified the king's absolute power by the teachings of the Bible, but also because it was the guarantee of order in human affairs. This was expressed by Bossuet in the slogan, "One king, one faith, one law." He went on to explain: "It is necessary to obey princes as justice itself, without which there is neither order nor an end to affairs. They are gods and participate in some manner in the divine independence."[2]

Louis believed that he had been chosen by God to rule France, and that he was accountable to God for the conscientious fulfillment of the duties of mon-

---

[2] Bishop Jacques-Bénigne Bossuet, *Political Economy Drawn from Holy Scripture*, cited in *History of Western Civilization, A Syllabus* (Stanford: Stanford University Press, 1940), p. 35.

archy. He saw in himself the embodiment of France, and in his own actions the primary source of French well-being. From his birth, he was known as the "Sun of France," an image frequently used earlier for the pharaohs of Egypt, and throughout his reign the image of Louis as the rising sun dominated the official representations of the monarch, who was now known as the "Sun King." Only from him, acting like the sun as the source of life, could France prosper, he believed. Hence, he concluded that only through his exercise of absolute power could efficient government be achieved. He warned his son of the sufferings of France's neighbors, which were governed by popular assemblies:

> The more you grant [the popular assembly], the more it demands; the more you caress it, the more it scorns you; and what it once has in its possession is retained by so many hands that it cannot be torn away without extreme violence. Out of so many persons who compose these great bodies, it is always the least sensible who assume the greatest license . . . so that a prince who wants to bequeath lasting tranquility to his people and his dignity completely intact to his successors cannot be too careful to suppress this tumultuous temerity.[3]

Louis was like Philip II of Spain in that he worked harder himself than any of his own civil servants; but, also like Philip, he was a poor administrator in that he was unable to delegate authority. He never called a representative assembly, and he rarely consulted his nobility. He believed correctly that they wished to replace the centralized power of the king with a decentralized administration controlled by the nobility in their own regions of the country. Louis governed through a small group of bureaucrats, drawn mostly from the middle classes, whose orders were executed in the provinces by the *intendants*. In other words, Louis based his power on Richelieu's creation.

Louis's "absolute" power was, however, far from unrestrained. Louis had to respect long-established customs and rights. City charters could not be revoked. The elected assemblies in the provinces could not be entirely bypassed. The courts of magistrates, known as *parlements*, in Paris and in the provinces, retained not only their judicial functions but also significant political powers, including the right to register, and thus bring into force, royal edicts. The guilds retained considerable powers in the regulation of economic life. Moreover, and perhaps most important in the long run, the nobility and Church leaders were able to frustrate the king's efforts to make them pay direct taxes and thereby prevented him from solving the financial crisis in the later part of his reign.

The Palace of Versailles

The key to understanding Louis XIV's conception of government was his construction of a new palace at Versailles, which, from 1681, was to act as the capital of France in place of Paris. Versailles served a number of purposes. It

---

[3] Louis XIV, *Mémoires for the Instruction of the Dauphin*, translated by Paul Sonnino (New York: Free Press, 1970), pp. 130–131.

protected the king from a resurgence of mob violence in Paris, such as he had experienced during the Frondes; and at the same time, by emphasizing the remoteness of the monarch, it enhanced his prestige. Versailles, too, the largest and most splendid palace in Europe, served to impress upon visiting foreigners the greatness of the French king and the power of his kingdom. Moreover, the palace, filled with the luxury products of French art and industry—tapestries, glass, furniture, paintings, sculptures—served as the most persuasive advertisement possible for French products. The establishment of all government ministries in Versailles gave the king immediate access and easy control over all the work of administration.

But Versailles was most immediately useful as the final measure by which the French monarchy humbled and controlled its own nobility. Since the nobility had been deprived of political power and local administrative duties under Richelieu, they were given instead by Louis XIV expensive ceremonial functions to perform at Versailles, a whole ritual of time-consuming and frequently demeaning attendance around the king's person. Selected groups of nobles were expected, and indeed fought for the privilege of being able, to attend the king's *lever*, the ceremony when he got out of bed, washed his face on an oiled cloth, and drank a glass of wine and water. A similar number were given the dubious privilege of seeing him go to bed at his *coucher*. The king checked from his balcony in the royal chapel whether all his nobles were attending mass in the morning, and many a noble found that his retention of a royal pension or grant of a new estate was dependent on his ability to exchange a few whispered words with the king at some meaningless ceremony.

Colbert and Mercantilism

Louis was fortunate in having the services of one of France's finest economics ministers, Jean Baptiste Colbert (1619–1683). Colbert was the foremost exponent in Europe of the economic theory called mercantilism, to which all European powers subscribed to some degree. Mercantilism was an economic theory that grew up piecemeal between the sixteenth and eighteenth centuries, and no one person ever became its authoritative exponent. Nevertheless, acceptance of its basic principles by almost all European governments had great influence not only on economic policy but also on foreign policy and war.

Mercantilists were impressed by the fact that Portugal and Spain, because of their supply of gold and silver bullion, were able to buy whatever they wished, and they identified bullion with national wealth. It followed that the goal of a state should be to amass bullion. This could be done only by either possessing mines or exporting more goods than are imported, with the difference being paid in gold or silver. Emphasis was therefore put on industry that could produce goods for export, and regulations were enforced to maintain the quality and low cost of goods produced for export. State interference in the economy was regarded as essential to maintain an easy flow of goods within the country, to foster new industry, and to ensure a supply of the raw material essential for manufacturing. Colonies were acquired as a source of raw materials that the home country could not produce and also to act as a captive market for the goods produced by the home country.

The most negative aspect of mercantilism was the belief that the amount of trade possible in the world was limited and that therefore a country could increase the extent of its trade only at the expense of its neighbors. In the last resort, war was to be used to seize part of a neighbor's trade or to destroy part of its capacity to export. It was felt, as a result, that a nation should be constantly ready to go to war. Certain features of mercantilism, such as the encouragement of new industry, acted to stimulate economic growth, whereas others, such as the accumulation of bullion, which added to internal inflation, were detrimental to economic growth.

While Colbert ran the French economy, the beneficial effects counterbalanced the detrimental ones, especially because Colbert was unconvinced of the value of war in increasing national well-being. The tax system was made more efficient and more just, although the clergy and nobility still largely escaped the payment of taxes. Trade was encouraged by the construction of new roads and canals, including a canal linking the Atlantic and Mediterranean coasts of France. New industry was encouraged, and strict royal regulations enforced by an army of inspectors ensured that the quality of French goods was the highest in Europe. French overseas trading companies were helped with government financial and military aid to expand their control in Canada and the Mississippi Valley and increase their trade in India and West Africa. Colbert could not, however, prevent the king from taking a number of actions that were deeply damaging to the French economy.

Louis could not tolerate the persistence of Calvinism in his kingdom, even though the Huguenots were making a great economic contribution as well as holding vitally important offices in the army and navy. He attempted to convert them first by billetting troops upon them, and, when this failed, in 1685 he revoked Henry IV's Edict of Nantes. Rather than become Catholic, 100,000 Huguenots left France, in conditions of appalling hardship, to find new homes among France's enemies. Many of France's most experienced soldiers and sailors, its most skillful artisans, and its most forward-looking business people took up residence in England and its American colonies, the Netherlands, and Prussia, bringing with them skills, capital, and often industrial secrets that could later be used against France.

The Wars of Louis XIV

It was Louis' four wars, however, that were to be the greatest strain on the French economy. Louis regarded the achievement of *la gloire*, military glory, as essential for his own reputation, especially where military victory would enhance the security and expand the boundaries of France. His first war, the War of Devolution (1667–1668) against Spain, was short and successful, and enabled him to straighten the dangerous bulge in the northeastern border of France by annexing part of the Spanish Netherlands. The second war, the Dutch War (1672–1678), had several purposes. He wished to wipe out Calvinism in the Netherlands, to destroy the Dutch as economic rivals to France, and to gain from Spain, the somewhat unlikely ally of the Netherlands, the important frontier province of Franche Comté. The Dutch held off the French invasion by breaking the dikes to flood the central part of their country, and thus won time to put together a coalition with Spain, England, Austria, and several German states that fought the French to a standstill. The French, however, were still able to hold Franche Comté at the treaty in 1678. During the peace that followed, Louis trumped up legal pretexts for seizing most of the German province of Alsace, and even sent his army to intervene on the right bank of the Rhine. These actions provoked his third war, the War of the League of Augsburg (1689–1697). The Dutch again put together a coalition that blocked any further French annexations.

Louis' last war, the War of the Spanish Succession (1702–1713), was due to his attempt to ensure that his second grandson inherit the throne of Spain, which had been bequeathed to him by the Spanish king, in preference to the other claimant, the second grandson of the Austrian Emperor. Lous fought for eleven years against a massive coalition of almost every major power in Europe, and lost important battles to the Austrians in Italy and to England in Germany and the Spanish Netherlands. In 1713, with a swollen national debt and Paris on the verge of rebellion once more, Louis was forced to accept the compromise Peace of Utrecht. Although Spain and its American colonies were to pass to Louis' grandson, the thrones of France and Spain were never to be united. Austria was compensated by the grant of the Spanish Netherlands and of Spanish possessions in Italy. Britain was given Gibraltar and the island of Minorca, as well as the sole right to the supply of slaves to the Spanish empire. France ceded Nova Scotia, Newfoundland, and Hudson Bay to Britain. Twenty-eight years of war had thus given France a defensible frontier in the east and northeast, but the cost had been enormous.

Literature and the Arts

Louis intended that France should also dominate the culture of Europe; his cultural imperialism was in many ways far more successful than his military adventures. French art and literature were to dominate Western culture for the coming two centuries. During the first half of the seventeenth century, French writers had begun to set new standards of literary excellence. Paris' favorite playwright at this time was Pierre Corneille (1606–1684), who specialized in historical dramas. His most exciting play, *Le Cid*, was a romantic drama about an eleventh-century Spanish military commander at war with the Arabs. But his influence was even greater in his later plays, when he turned to dramatization of historical events in ancient Rome.

Ancient Rome was to be the dominant influence on French culture in the later seventeenth century. Both Colbert and Louis XIV intended in their rebuilding to make Paris a new Rome. When the city wall of Paris was pulled down in demonstration that France was militarily impregnable, great new triumphal arches like those of the Roman Forum were erected where the city gates had been. A new façade to the Louvre palace was designed with vast wings, interspersed with Corinthian columns, on either side of an overwhelming triumphal arch. A French version of Roman architecture thus became a perfect demonstration of the power of French absolutism and a reminder that its predecessor was the grandeur of the Roman Empire.

The painters most favored by Colbert were gathered together in the Academy of Painting at the Louvre palace, and were expected to choose topics from classical antiquity as the subject of many of their paintings. The pattern of this new school of French painting was set by two Frenchmen who settled in Rome, Nicolas Poussin (1594–1665) and Claude Lorrain (1600–1682).

Although Poussin was at first influenced by the melodramatic style of the Mannerists and the color of the Venetians, by the late 1630s he was developing the rational, highly formal style that was to be the model for much French painting in the seventeenth century. Like others of his time, Poussin used tales from classical antiquity as subjects for his paintings, as in *The Rape of the Sabine*

The Rape of the Sabine Women, by Nicolas Poussin (1594–1665) *According to legend, the women of the nearby Sabine tribe were abducted to provide wives for the warriors of Rome's founder, Romulus.* (The Metropolitan Museum of Art, Harris Brisbane Dick Fund, 1946.)

Louis XIV, by Antoine Coysevox (1640–1720) Coysevox contrasted the swirling clothes and billowing hair with the firm composure of the monarch's face. (Lauros-Giraudon/Art Resource.)

Women. Even his landscapes refer to classical events. As with all his works, his landscape paintings created a sense of mathematical planning, order, and coherent form.

It was Claude Lorrain, however, who became the predominant influence on French landscape painting. He too made classical allusions in his sunlit landscapes of the rolling hill country near Rome, usually showing dignified people in meadows overlooked by classical temples, or harbors where mist and sunlight are used to dissolve the barriers between land and sea. Lorrain created a style that had a long-lasting influence on landscape painters even into the nineteenth century, as in the paintings of Turner. In the later seventeenth century, painting and sculpture became unimaginatively conventional and served largely to glorify the court of Louis XIV. Charles Le Brun, who had the title "First Painter to the King," covered the ceilings of Versailles with grandiose classical depictions of Louis' military triumphs, while the sculptor Antoine Coysevox provided numerous Baroque portraits of the king as well as compositions of winged horses or mythical heros for the palace gardens.

Jean Baptiste Racine (1639–1699), the greatest tragic dramatist of the reign of Louis XIV, frequently wrote on the Roman themes favored by the king and Colbert, but he broadened the scope of his plays by turning to classical Greece, and finally, at the urging of the king's last wife, Madame de Maintenon, wrote on biblical themes for her newly founded girls' school. Like all other aspects of life at Versailles, the poetry in the plays of the classical playwrights followed strict rules of composition, which, though elegant, could become artificial in the hands of lesser writers. In Racine's hands, however, they were a marvellously supple instrument for the expression of human emotions. For example, in his play of the same name, Phèdre laments how she has fallen tragically in love with her own stepson immediately after her marriage to his father:

> I saw him. I blushed. I went pale before him.
> A deep agitation rose in the depths of my soul.
> I could no longer see. I could not speak.
> I felt my whole body go cold and turn to fire.
> I recognized the fearsome flames of Venus,
> The unavoidable tortures in the blood
> When she pursues one . . .
> I fled everywhere to avoid seeing my love. Oh, height of misery,
> My eyes found him again—in the features of his father.[4]

Yet Versailles was far from being totally humorless. The favorite comic playwright of the court, Molière (1622–1673), was a scathing satirist of contemporary foibles. In *Tartuffe* he criticized those who took religion to excess; in *Les Femmes Savantes*, the pretensions of women whose learning has gone to their heads; in *L'Avare (The Miser)*, the middle-class obsession with the amassing of money; in *Le Bourgeois Gentilhomme*, the foibles of a middle-class social climber. Molière was a great writer because he never lost sight of the human feelings of the people whose failings he is holding up to ridicule, as when the miser in *L'Avare* laments the loss of his money:

> Thief! Thief! Murderer! Killer! Justice, just heaven! I am lost, I am killed! Someone has cut my throat, someone has stolen my money! Who can it be? What has happened to him? Where is he hiding? What can I do to find him? Where shall I run? Where shall I not run? . . . Alas! my poor money, my poor money, my dear friend, they have taken you away from me! And, since you have been taken away, I have lost my support, my consolation, my employment; everything is finished for me, and I have nothing more to do in the world! Without you it is impossible to live. It is over. I am finished, I am dying, I am dead, I am buried. Is there no one who wants to bring me back to life by giving me back my money?[5]

Thus Versailles, while it centralized French culture, also put its particular stamp of classicism in the grand manner on French art. A whole generation of artists was trained at the palace—in painting under Charles Le Brun, in landscape gardening under André Le Nôtre, and in architecture under the principal architect of the palace itself, Louis Le Vau. With the death of Louis XIV, Versailles, although it remained the administrative center of the country, ceased to be the dominant influence on its intellectual or cultural life. Paris, reclaiming control of French culture, was able to perpetuate the French leadership of Western literature and art into the nineteenth century.

---

[4] Jean Racine, *Phèdre*, act I, scene 3. Author's translation.
[5] Molière, *L'Avare*, act IV, scene 7. Author's translation.

THE ESTABLISHMENT OF LIMITED
MONARCHY IN ENGLAND

Limited Absolutism of the Tudors

When Henry VII (reigned 1485–1509) seized power in England with his victory at the Battle of Bosworth Field, he at once set out to ensure that his dynasty, the Tudor family, would possess the means to govern England without interference from the nobility and so far as possible without recourse to Parliament for grant of taxes. He was aided by the fact that in the Wars of the Roses many of the leading nobles had been killed and in the absence of heirs their lands had passed to the crown. He made use of high fines imposed on nobles suspected of lack of loyalty either to bring them into submission or, in some cases, to ruin them financially. Using the royal household for collection of the king's traditional revenues, such as customs duties and income from the royal estates, he was able to build up a large surplus, which he was careful not to squander on military adventures on the continent.

His son, Henry VIII (reigned 1509–1547) was far less restrained in the use of the powers Henry VII had left him. In the early years of his reign he fought successful wars with the Scots and the French, but after 1514 he devoted himself to the increase of his powers inside England. As we saw, his desire for a divorce from Catherine of Aragon drove him to break with the papacy, and led him, at the suggestion of his adviser Thomas Cromwell, to have Parliament declare him Supreme Head of the Church of England. He expanded the powers of the royal judicial court created by his father and known as the Star Chamber after the stars painted on the ceiling of the courtroom. Henry used the Star Chamber to take swift action outside the rules of common law.

In 1536–1539, Henry dissolved the wealthy monasteries of England, and confiscated their lands and possessions. These properties were then sold piecemeal over the following years, primarily to those in Parliament who had loyally supported the king's attack on the Catholic Church. By this means he not only vastly increased the wealth of the crown, but he also created a large group of supporters whose fortunes were tied to the maintenance of the Reformation in England. By the 1530s, Henry VIII appeared to possess tyrannical powers. He could behead two of his own wives on specious charges of treason; and leading subjects, whether widely admired like Sir Thomas More or widely feared like Thomas Cromwell, could be executed when they fell from his favor or opposed his will.

Henry VIII's position could, however, be called despotism by consent. He was aware that his power depended on the collaboration of two vitally important groups: the justices of the peace who administered local government and the members of Parliament who had been enriched and strengthened by carrying through Henry's Reformation. Unlike the continental states, local government in England was carried out by unpaid local squires, usually the wealthiest landowner in each parish, who had been given greater powers by Henry VII as a method of reducing the powers of the old nobility. This class elected from among its own group the knights of the shire, who represented the country districts in the House of Commons in Parliament, including among these representatives younger sons of the nobility. (The eldest son of a noble family inherited the title and sat in the House of Lords.) The cities, which had retained many of the rights of self-administration, also sent representatives to the House of Commons. Thus, a class of landowners and city merchants, who came to be called the "gentry," possessed the political ability to take action against the king if sufficiently opposed to his policies.

Most important of all, the sixteenth century saw a continual increase in the wealth of the gentry. Merchants in London and the provincial cities continued to profit from export of England's great staple, woolen cloth, as well as the cod that was being fished in great quantities off Newfoundland. Stockholders in such companies as the Muscovy company, which had been welcomed to Russia by Ivan the Terrible, as well as others who financed the plundering expeditions of sailors such as Drake in the late sixteenth century, were growing wealthy. High food prices and rents increased the incomes of the landowners. Moreover an administrative class comprising the wealthier lawyers and government officials had joined with the landed gentry and the mercantile class in pouring money into what has been called England's first industrial revolution. Great technological advances were being made in the coal mining industry, and as the forests were cut down, coal was used increasingly as an industrial fuel. Advances were also made in working such metals as brass, iron, and lead, and new techniques made the manufacture of unfinished cloth more profitable. By 1588, when the threat of the Spanish Armada was ended, there was a substantial class of wealthy landowners, merchants, financiers, and industrialists who felt themselves to be economically and even socially independent of the monarchy, and believed themselves capable of running the government themselves.

Queen Elizabeth (reigned 1558–1603) attempted to work with the nobility and gentry, and until the danger from Spain subsided she succeeded. She negotiated with Parliament a religious settlement that adopted a mild form of Protestant theology, recognized the queen as "supreme governor" of the church, and used fines to punish noncompliance. She picked excellent ministers, most notably Sir William Cecil, Lord Burghley, and toward the end of her reign his son Sir Robert Cecil. She attempted to avoid making enemies on the continent by choosing any one of several foreign suitors, but kept all dangling as long as she could. In the end, she married no one. Her aid to the Dutch in 1585 and the defeat of the Spanish Armada in 1588 undoubtedly raised Elizabeth's popularity to its highest point with the English people, and helped stimulate a great outpouring of national patriotism, but the cost brought Elizabeth into conflict with Parliament. No longer seeing the necessity for emergency taxes, Parliament became more recalcitrant when asked for revenues, and only the aging queen's popularity and prestige enabled her to gain her way. Nevertheless, on one occasion she was compelled to appear in Parliament personally to ask for funds. "I know that I have the body of a weak and feeble woman," she told the kneeling politicians, "but I have the heart of a king, and of a king of England, too."

The Elizabethan Age

The self-confidence of the English in the late sixteenth century, which Elizabeth herself had done so much to promote, was expressed in a cultural exuberance different from anything England had experienced before. In architecture a totally unselfconscious style evolved, especially in building country manor houses for the gentry. No attempt was made to form a unified conception such as that of the great palaces of the French nobility in the Loire Valley. The English architects borrowed whatever pleased them from countries they had visited or pattern books—classical columns and triumphal arches, traditional English timber and plaster, Flemish strapwork. The result suited the taste of the new gentry: comfortable, unaffected, charming, as can be seen in such a building as Longleat House in southern England. In music it was the age of the English madrigal, a form adopted from Italy but further developed for the choirs of the English churches and colleges by composers such as William Byrd and Thomas Tallis. The freshness of the age, its delight in the discovery of the natural world, echoes in the poems of Edmund Spenser (1552?–1599), as in this evocation of England's wild flowers:

> Bring hither the Pink and purple Columbine,
>   With Gillyflowers:
> Bring Coronation and Sops in wine,
>   Worn of paramours.
> Strew me the ground with Daffadowndillies,
> And Cowslips, and Kingcups, and loved Lilies:
>   The pretty Pawnce,
>   And the Chevisaunce,
> Shall match with the fair flower Delice.[6]

But it was in the theater that Elizabethan England excelled. Two theaters were opened in London in 1576, and immediately attracted not only large and often boisterous audiences but brilliant writers. One of the earliest favorites among the 300 or more playwrights of the late sixteenth and early seventeenth centuries was Christopher Marlowe (1564–1593). Writing frequently in blank verse, Marlowe filled his plays with passion and violence, developing gory tales of people of strong personality destroyed by their own actions, as in his most famous play, *Tamburlaine the Great*, which recounts the life of the Mongol ruler Tamerlane.

William Shakespeare (1564–1616), the supreme genius of English literature,

[6] Edmund Spenser, *The Shepherd's Calendar. July*, 1. 99.

became known in London by 1592 as an actor and playwright. He joined the Lord Chamberlain's company in 1594, and wrote plays designed for the actors of that company for the next twenty years. He did well from his writing, bought a country house and part-ownership of two principal London theaters, and retired to Stratford in 1613. During his involvement with the theater, he wrote 37 plays, 154 sonnets, and 3 nondramatic poems.

Shakespeare, said Ben Jonson, a rival playwright, "was not of this age, but of all time." In his work, he had covered every aspect of the human experience. He could make the buffoonery of Sir John Falstaff endearing, as when the fat knight decides that honor is not for him:

> What is honour? A word. What is that word, honour? Air. . . . Who hath it? He that died o' Wednesday. Doth he feel it? No. Doth he hear it? No. It is insensible then? Yea, to the dead. But will it not live with the living? No. Why? Detraction will not suffer it. Therefore I'll none of it: honour is a mere scutcheon [heraldic shield]: and so ends my catechism.[7]

With sympathy, he portrays the overly ambitious Lady Macbeth, who goads her husband into killing the king and usurping his throne. In madness, she sees her hands spattered with the blood of her victim and realizes that "all the perfumes of Arabia will not sweeten this little hand" (*Macbeth*, v.i.56). In perhaps his darkest tragedy, he shows the descent of King Lear from the despot that can bear no contradiction to an impotent dependent, "a poor, infirm, weak, and despis'd old man" abandoned by the daughters to whom he had given his kingdom. And it was Shakespeare who best summed up Elizabethan pride in their country, in the lines of John of Gaunt in the play *Richard II*:

> This royal throne of kings, this sceptered isle,
> This earth of majesty, this seat of Mars,
> This other Eden, demi-paradise. . . .
> This blessed plot, this earth, this realm, this England.[8]

The Early Stuarts

Elizabeth's successor, her cousin James VI of Scotland, who became King James I of England (reigned 1603–1625), was totally unable to understand the delicate balance that had enabled the Tudors to give the appearance of enjoying absolute powers. In reaction against the strict controls imposed on him by the Puritan clerics during his reign in Scotland, James had come to believe in the divine right of kings, which, he thought, would be respected in England. He wrote a book on the theory, and on every possible occasion lectured Parliament about it. "That which concerns the mystery of the King's power," he explained, "is not lawful to be disputed; for that is to wade into the weakness of princes, and

[7] *Henry IV, Part I*, v.i.131
[8] *Richard II*, II.i.40.

The Puritan, by Augustus Saint-Gaudens (1848–1907) The determined strength of the seventeenth-century Puritans of England and its colonies is caught dramatically in this bronze statue by the leading American sculptor of the nineteenth century. (The Metropolitan Museum of Art, Bequest of Jacob Ruppert, 1939.)

to take away the mystical reverence that belongs unto them that sit in the throne of God." Such sentiments were not well received in a legislature that had no respect for his ability as an administrator or for the officials he appointed. Worse in James's eyes, the English Calvinists, or Puritans, were gaining increasing numbers of seats in Parliament, even though he had warned them as early as 1604 that, if they did not conform, he would harry them from the land.

The trial of strength between king and Parliament began over the raising of revenue. James, increasingly unable to subsist on the monarchy's traditional revenues because of the continent-wide inflation, tried to raise money without consent of the legislature by "benevolences," or gifts, which it was impossible for individuals to refuse, and by imposition of new customs duties. When Parliament objected to his revenue raising or criticized his foreign policy, James would dismiss it. His son, Charles I (reigned 1625–1649), granted inadequate funds by Parliament for the conduct of wars against Spain and France, felt compelled to resort even more to imposition of forced loans and other revenue-raising devices that Parliament felt were illegal.

In 1628, the legislative body presented the king with the Petition of Right, which listed a number of the king's actions, such as imprisonment of citizens without trial, that they wanted him to stop. Furious, Charles attempted for eleven years (1629–1640) to govern without Parliament. He was fairly successful in increasing his income by such measures as taxing the inland towns for construction of a navy, but his desire for religious conformity, encouraged by William Laud, the reactionary archbishop of Canterbury, increased the anger of the Puritans in England and of the Presbyterians in Scotland. When the Scots went to war with England in 1638 rather than accept a new Anglican Book of Prayer, they destroyed the precarious balance of Charles' finances. He called Parliament in 1640 to ask for funds to fight the Scots, but dismissed it after three weeks when it refused him money until he accepted a long list of reforms.

Charles summoned a new Parliament in 1640, known as the Long Parliament because it sat on and off until 1660. For two years, virtually every group in Parliament united in dismantling the instruments of royal absolutism. The king's chief minister was tried for treason and executed. Laud was also arrested, and later beheaded. Laws were passed requiring the summoning of the legislature at least every three years, giving it control over extraordinary expenditures, and abolishing several special courts used by Charles to raise revenue. By the end of 1641, Parliament had already made England into a limited monarchy.

The Civil Wars

The religious question broke the unity of Parliament. The Puritans demanded that Parliament abolish bishops, and remodel the Anglican church on Calvinist lines. These demands split England into two sides, which saw the only solution to their disagreement as civil war. Although the opposition to the king was known as the Parliamentarians, about one-third of the members of the House of Commons and a majority of the House of Lords sided with the king, who had set up his banner at the loyal city of Oxford. His supporters, known as Cavaliers or royalists, consisted primarily of the large landowners of the north and west and their tenants, all sincere Anglicans, and many who believed in monarchy for religious or more practical reasons. The Parliamentarians were supported to a large extent by the merchant and working classes of the cities, the many smaller landowners of the east and south and almost all Puritans.

The Puritans were themselves divided, however, between the Presbyterian majority, who wished to form a church similar to that in Scotland, and more radical groups, including the Independents, the Diggers, and the Levelers. The Independents, of whom the most important was Oliver Cromwell (1599–1658), wished to allow each congregation complete autonomy, and thus they were also known as Congregationalists. The Diggers wanted communal ownership of property, the Levelers universal manhood suffrage.

Cromwell, a country squire from eastern England who had served in the House of Commons since 1628, persuaded the Parliamentarian leaders to completely reorganize their forces in 1645 into a New Model Army under his leadership. That June he defeated the king's forces at the Battle of Naseby, and in 1646 Charles surrendered.

Puritan Rule

The victors then split between the Independents, who wanted further religious change, and the Presbyterians who joined with the royalists and the Scots in fighting a second civil war on behalf of the king. Cromwell had no difficulty in defeating them, however, and he decided that peace could be restored only with the execution of the king. Charles was tried for treason by Parliament, after all except sixty Independents had been excluded. He was found guilty and beheaded outside his own palace in London in 1649. The king's death did not bring political stability. From 1649 to 1653, England was governed as a Commonwealth by the legislative body known as the Rump Parliament, and by a council of state dominated by Cromwell. The monarchy and the House of Lords were abolished; and Cromwell led the army to Ireland and Scotland, where he put down revolts with great savagery. When the Dutch objected to English attempts to exclude them from the carrying trade to England, Parliament declared war on the Netherlands. Cromwell tired of the Rump Parliament's inability to establish any coherent policy, replaced it by an even more ineffective body known as the Barebones Parliament, and finally took power himself as the Lord Protector of England.

Cromwell, as a devout Puritan, found himself in a quandary, since he wanted both to restore parliamentary government representative of the people as a whole and at the same time to institute the rule of the godly. He ended by governing through the only instrument he trusted, the Puritan army. The English soon wearied of this military dictatorship. Taxation was high, to pay for the expensive war against the Dutch; and life, patterned on that of Calvin's Geneva, was joyless. Theaters and alehouses were closed, the Sabbath was mournful, and the slightest moral transgression such as dancing was severely punished. When his weak son Richard became Protector upon Cromwell's death in 1658, a group within the army itself joined with a number of leading aristocrats in calling for the return of Charles I's son, Charles II, as king.

Charles II (reigned 1660–1685) showed his political subtlety by declaring himself willing to accept all the restrictions on royal power imposed in 1640–1641, and by guaranteeing a general pardon except for a few regicides responsible for his father's death. In 1660, Charles was welcomed back with public rejoicing. Puritan rule had thus succeeded in restoring the popularity of the monarchy.

The Restoration

Charles II was well aware that the pretensions to absolute rule of James I and Charles I had ended with the execution of his father. He accepted a financial subsidy from Louis XIV, but he was wise enough never to challenge Parliament openly. Instead he built up a party of his own supporters within Parliament, known by their detractors as the Tories. Although himself secretly a Catholic, he cultivated the support of the Anglicans, and endorsed the harsh measures taken against the Puritans, who were finally ousted from the Church of England

and declared to be Nonconformists, or Dissenters, and liable to exclusion from many public offices and from teaching.

In taste, Charles admired the France of Louis XIV, and led his aristocracy in the adoption of the styles in music, painting, architecture, and dress of Versailles. English opera came into its own with the works of Henry Purcell. Once again, the English theater flourished, although the majority of the plays tended to appeal to an aristocratic audience rather than to the wide variety of spectators of Shakespeare's day. The most popular plays by such playwrights as William Wycherley were comedies of manners, in which the foibles of the aristocrats themselves were presented in a satirical and frequently bawdy manner. The aristocrats were also satirized by the playwright and poet John Dryden (1631–1700), in epic poems in which many contemporary political figures could easily be recognized. Dryden sought to bring into English verse the clarity and order of the French writers of the seventeenth century, but the result was frequently somewhat artificial, especially when in the following century the style was picked up by lesser writers.

It was, however, a Puritan who was the greatest literary figure of an age whose standards he despised. John Milton (1608–1674) had been a powerful pamphleteer for the Puritan cause, as well as for some causes less acceptable to the Puritans, such as the right of divorce for incompatibility and the freedom of the press from censorship. Cromwell had used him as a secretary for foreign affairs. The pressure of work left him totally blind, but using secretaries he turned in the years of the Restoration to the composition of a great epic poem, *Paradise Lost*, which was completed in 1665. The opening of the poem is a painting in words describing the fall of Satan:

. . . Him the Almighty Power
Hurled headlong flaming from th'ethereal sky
With hideous ruin and combustion down
To bottomless perdition, there to dwell
In adamantine chains and penal fire
Who durs't defy th'Omnipotent to arms.[9]

The Glorious Revolution

Charles' pig-headed brother James II (reigned 1685–1688) failed to understand how the civil wars had changed the relationship of king to legislature in England. He openly admitted that he was a Roman Catholic, and tried to appoint Catholics to leading positions in the army and administration. He attempted to avoid parliamentary control over taxation by accepting further subsidies from France. When his new son, born in 1688, was baptized a Catholic, Anglicans and Puritans in England united against him, and invited William of Orange, the *stadholder* of the Netherlands and husband of James' Protestant daughter

[9] John Milton, *Paradise Lost*, bk. i, lines 44–49.

Mary, to invade England in order to rule England jointly with his wife. James fled to France, and his few supporters were quickly subdued.

With the "Glorious Revolution" thus successfully completed, Parliament passed a series of acts laying the constitutional basis for limited monarchy. In the Bill of Rights of 1689, Parliament declared William and Mary legal sovereigns, thus implicitly establishing the legislature's right to choose the king, and laid down such basic rights of English citizens as the right to trial by jury and free elections. The king was forbidden to tax without consent of Parliament, to maintain a standing army during peace time, or to suspend laws. The right of the legislature to choose the king was further demonstrated in 1701 when Parliament passed the Act of Settlement, requiring that the throne should pass to Sophie of Hanover, the granddaughter of James I, and her successors, if James II's daughter Anne, the next in line, should die childless.

Although the king theoretically retained control of the executive after 1688, in fact a system of cabinet government developed during the next fifty years. The king found it essential to work through ministers who could persuade Parliament to accept legislation he desired, and it was thus a very short step to appointing leaders of one party as royal ministers. The most important of these ministers came to be called the prime minister, or first minister.

What England had achieved during the seventeenth century was still far from being a complete democracy, in which all citizens would participate in the choice of government. It was a system whereby the well-to-do of England had gained predominance; but because they had also fought for certain rights for all citizens, such as the right to hold property, the way was open for the eventual participation of all citizens in the government process.

MIDDLE-CLASS REPUBLICANISM IN THE NETHERLANDS

After Spain had recognized the independence of the seven northern provinces of the Netherlands at the truce of 1609, the Dutch proceeded to create a new state that was a model for Europe in economic prosperity, religious toleration, and intellectual creativity.

Although Dutch society was the freest in Europe, the structure of government was far from being a true democracy. Power lay undisguisedly in the hands of the wealthiest merchants and financiers of the great cities. Constitutionally, the country was a federal union of the seven constituent provinces, each of which sent members to a federal assembly called the States General. The States General elected the head of a federal executive who was known as the *stadholder*. In 1579, William of Orange (the Silent; 1533–1584) had been chosen the first stadholder of the United Provinces, as the country was called, and after his assassination five years later his son Maurice of Nassau (stadholder 1584–1625) had been chosen. He was succeeded by his brother Frederick Henry (stadholder 1625–1647), whose son Prince William II was stadholder from 1647 to 1650. The States General were determined, however, that the house of Orange should not establish a hereditary dynasty, and in particular that they should not be able to convert the position of stadholder into that of king. As stadholders, the house of Orange did command the army, but they did not establish foreign policy, and they had little influence on internal policy, which was largely within control of the local assemblies in each of the provinces and of the city governments. After William II's death, the opponents of the house of Orange from the province of Holland, which itself was dominated by the city of Amsterdam, were able to prevent the appointment of his son as stadholder and for a time to abolish the office itself. Only during the extreme danger in the French invasion of 1672 was the office reinstated and William III (who became king of England in 1689) appointed stadholder. In 1702, the position was again abolished, only to be restored in the middle of the eighteenth century when the house of Orange was recognized as hereditary stadholders. In 1815 they were appointed kings.

The Calvinist Oligarchy

Thus real power in the Netherlands was held by the States General, but the States General was dominated by one province, Holland, which paid more into the federal budget than the other six provinces combined. Holland was, in turn, controlled by Amsterdam, and Amsterdam was run as a merchant oligarchy. The city government of Amsterdam consisted of a sheriff, four burgomasters, nine aldermen, and thirty-six city councilors, known as the regents. They were chosen, like the representatives to the local and national assemblies, by franchise open only to the wealthy middle classes.

In reality, as in Renaissance Florence, a very small number of powerful families controlled all aspects of government. The most important aspect of this oligarchy was its religious tolerance. Although they were Calvinist and emphasized their devotion to Calvin's ideals of self-restraint and social service in their dress, manner of life, and their service to charity, they refused the demands of the more extreme Calvinist ministers. They insisted on toleration for other Protestants and Jews, and made no attempt to prevent private worship by Catholics within their own homes. They refused to go along with the preachers' demands that they ban drinking, dancing, and the theater, and after the 1650s even abandoned sober clothes and adopted instead the latest fashions in silk and lace imported from their arch-enemy France.

Dutch Economic Development

The second characteristic of the oligarchy was that it placed the development of the economy above all other interests. In their view, toleration was not only morally correct but also financially profitable. Jews and other refugees had brought capital and industrial skills that opened new forms of manufacturing and trade. Control of foreign policy was also an instrument of economic policy. The merchants of Amsterdam, for example, refused to support the Stadholder Frederick Henry when he wanted to reconquer Antwerp from the Spanish, because they had no desire to see Antwerp revive as a rival to Amsterdam itself. They interfered in the wars between their neighbors, such as that between Sweden and Denmark, solely to protect their investments, and supplied weapons to both sides, even during their own war of independence.

Control of the government by the merchants enabled them to take those actions that allowed government and private finance jointly to create instruments essential to the growth of Dutch commerce. The States General, as we saw, had forced the different companies competing for a share of the East Indian trade to join together in 1602 in the Dutch East India Company and similarly had formed the Dutch West India Company nineteen years later. In Amsterdam the government closely supervised the operation of three financial institutions that became the basis for Dutch domination of Europe's financial life for the next two centuries. The Amsterdam Exchange Bank became the main depository of capital from all over Europe. The Amsterdam Lending Bank displaced the Italians as the principal source of business loans. Finally, the Amsterdam Stock Exchange set Europe's commodity prices.

Class Harmony

There was very little protest within the Netherlands against this oligarchic form of government. The poorest sections of the population in the cities were helped

The Concert, by Jan Vermeer (1632–1675) Vermeer emphasized the play of light from an unseen window on the folds of silken dresses and on the books and musical instruments. (Isabella Stewart Gardener Museum/Art Resource.)

in innumerable private charitable institutions, such as orphanages, alms houses, and hospitals, although there was always a large number of very poor people, including beggars, unemployed, and refugees, whose sufferings could make them riot. The working class were quite well housed in such picturesque quarters as the new Jordaan district of Amsterdam, which was a favorite place for painters like Rembrandt to live. The expanding economy in the seventeenth century enabled them to find work at reasonable wages. The middle classes were equally secure. Preachers, lawyers, shopowners, and teachers all found a good living in the country's growing cities. Intellectuals found that the Netherlands was the country in Europe most open to freedom of inquiry. Universities such as that of Leiden became great centers of medical and scientific research, and freedom from state interference enabled the Dutch printing industry to become the largest in Europe. Although the nobility were unable to influence the government, they were able to maintain their large estates in the countryside, and grew wealthier from feeding the cities. The Dutch experienced a great surge of national pride in what they had achieved under their oligarchy. They were so proud of their home life—the restrained harmony of their marble-tiled rooms, the sturdy dignity of their wooden furniture, their sober gowns embellished only with lace or ruffles—that they paid their finest painters to depict this way of life. The charm of Dutch daily life was immortalized in the paintings of such artists as Jan Vermeer, Pieter de Hooch, and Meindert Hobbema (see Chapter 11).

Dutch Decline

The end of Dutch economic expansion was signaled about 1660 with the end of growth of population, which became stable for the next century and a half. The Dutch had taken part in too many wars in the seventeenth century—the war for independence, the struggles with Portugal and Spain for colonial empire, three wars with England, and the long wars with Louis XIV. Moreover, the economic rivals of the Netherlands, driven by the mercantilist view of the limited nature of international trade, were determined to seize a greater share of Dutch commerce. The British gained their Atlantic fisheries and drove the Dutch from New Amsterdam. French and British merchant navies undercut the Dutch in the coastal carrying trade. The Portuguese fought to regain a share of their lost trade in the East Indies. Worst of all, the Dutch had invested primarily in overseas trade, land, and interest-bearing bonds, and had made no preparation to share in the new industrial revolution, based on coal and iron, that began in England in the early eighteenth century. By the late seventeenth century, Dutch creativity had spent itself; but their golden age had left a message to Western civilization: that greatness does not depend on military power or centralized rule or even abundance of resources but rather on freedom of thought and activity—a message that Peter the Great failed to learn in the shipyards of Holland.

SUGGESTED READINGS

General Surveys

Henry Kamen makes good use of economic quantification in explaining the influence of recession, in *The Iron Century: Social Change in Europe, 1550–1660* (1971), while the complications of political infightings are elucidated in Carl J. Friedrich, *The Age of the Baroque, 1610–1660* (1952), and J. B. Wolf, *The Emergence of the Great Powers, 1685–1715* (1951).

Russia Through Peter the Great

Good biographies of the tsars who created the Russian autocracy include J. L. I. Fennell, *Ivan the Great of Moscow* (1962); Harold Lamb, *The March of Muscovy* (1948); B. H. Sumner, *Peter the Great and the Emergence of Russia* (1951); and M. S. Anderson, *Peter the Great* (1978). On Saint Petersburg, see Harold Lamb, *The City and the Tsar: Peter the Great and the Move to the West, 1648–1762* (1948). The peasant role in Russian society is sympathetically analyzed in Jerome Blum, *Lord and Peasant in Russia* (1961). On the nobles before Peter, see Robert O. Crummey, *Aristocrats and Servitors: The Boyar Elite, 1613–1689* (1983).

France from Henry IV to Louis XIV

Roland Mousnier discusses Henry IV's role in the creation of French absolutism in *The Assassination of Henry IV* (1972), and Richelieu's taming of the nobility is detailed in A. D. Lubinskaya, *French Absolutism: The Crucial Phase, 1620–1629* (1968). The best biography of the Sun King is J. B. Wolf, *Louis XIV* (1968). For economic and social background, see Pierre Goubert, *Louis XIV and Twenty Million Frenchmen* (1970). Life at Versailles is scintillatingly re-created in W. H. Lewis, *The Splendid Century* (1953). The role of literature in aristocratic society is explained in David Maland, *Culture and Society in Seventeenth Century France* (1970). The criticism of learned women is explained by Carolyn Lougee, *Le Paradis des Femmes: Women, Salons, and Social Stratification in Seventeenth Century France* (1976).

England in the Sixteenth and Seventeenth Centuries

The ability of the Tudors to maintain despotism with the support of Parliament is explained in G. R. Elton, *England Under the Tudors* (1960), but biographies such as J. J. Scarisbrick, *Henry VIII* (1968), and J. E. Neale, *Queen Elizabeth I* (1952), bring out more clearly how important was the intangible force of personality. The breakdown of the Tudor constitutional system under the early Stuarts is traced to its social roots in Lawrence Stone, *Causes of the English Revolution, 1529–1642* (1972), and in his *The Crisis of the Aristocracy, 1558–1641* (1965). The radical elements in the Puritan forces receive full treatment in Christopher Hill, *The Century of Revolution, 1603–1714* (1961). The attitude of women to the civil war is analyzed in K. V. Thomas, "Women and the Civil War Sects," *Past and Present* (April 1958), pp. 40–62. On Cromwell, see C. V. Wedgwood, *Oliver Cromwell* (1956), and Christopher Hill, *God's Englishman* (1970).

The debate over the nature of the English family in the seventeenth century, stimulated in part by attempts to describe the close relationship of Charles I to his queen, Henrietta Maria, can be followed in Lawrence Stone, *The Family, Sex, and Marriage in England, 1500–1800* (1977), and Antonia Fraser, *The Weaker Vessel* (1984). Stone's views are rejected by Ralph A. Loubrooke, *The English Family, 1450–1700* (1984), who sees no basic change in family relationships in the seventeenth century.

Seventeenth-Century Netherlands

Politics and culture are superbly intertwined in Charles Wilson, *The Dutch Republic and the Civilization of the Seventeenth Century* (1968). C. R. Boxer shows the importance of Amsterdam in the creation of a Dutch trading empire, in *The Dutch Seaborne Empire, 1600–1800* (1965). The social structure of two great trading cities is compared by Peter Burke, *Venice and Amsterdam: A Study of Seventeenth Century Elites* (1974). Bertha Mook uses paintings to document Dutch family life, in *The Dutch Family in the 17th and 18th Centuries: An Exploratory-Descriptive Study* (1977).

The investment in painting by Dutch burghers is described in Deric Regin, *Traders, Artists, Burghers: A Cultural History of Amsterdam in the 17th Century* (1976), and John Michael Montias, *Artists and Artisans in Delft: A Socio-Economic Study of the Seventeenth Century* (1982).

II

From the Scientific Revolution to the Enlightenment

By the late seventeenth century, a new world view had gained acceptance. Many (but by no means all) Europeans had come to believe that the world is governed by natural laws, and that those laws can be discovered by the application of reason to observed data. This belief was due above all to the fact that verifiable laws had been discovered that seemed to govern the working of the physical universe and the human mind. Two centuries of experimentation and observation by astronomers and physicists, during a period of vast intellectual change that we call the scientific revolution, had begun with the publication in 1543 of Nikolaus Copernicus's astronomical treatise *On the Revolutions of the Heavenly Bodies* and had culminated in 1687 in Isaac Newton's subtly simple explanation of the relationship of all physical matter and motion in his book, *The Principles of Mathematical Philosophy*. At almost exactly the same time, John Locke appeared to have explained in an equally mechanistic way the psychology of the human mind.

For the next 100 years, from the late seventeenth to the late eighteenth century, intellectuals known in France as *philosophes* and like-minded thinkers in many other countries undertook to find the natural laws that the scientific revolution appeared to suggest existed throughout the physical universe, including even the operation of human society. Their work embraced religion, law, psychology, sexual inequality, education, economics, and political philosophy. It was widely spread not only through their own books and travels but also by the publication of the 28 volumes of the French *Encyclopedia*, in which

Denis Diderot, by Carl van Loo (1705–1765) In spite of the immense work of editing the 28-volume Encyclopedia, *Diderot also wrote plays, novels, and philosophical works.* (Musée National du Louvre/Scala-Art Resource.)

the leading *philosophes* collaborated. The more practical of their ideas—but not their call for greater political equality—were applied with moderate success by several monarchs who are known as the Enlightened Despots.

The culture of the seventeenth and most of the eighteenth century displays the same self-confidence that characterized the work of the pioneering scientists and philosophers. The Baroque style was formulated in Italy at the end of the sixteenth and the beginning of the seventeenth centuries, and spread to the northern countries, accommodating itself there to the more classical styles derived from the Renaissance. In place of the tension and sense of insecurity that the Mannerist artists and architects had sought to create during the last three-quarters of the sixteenth century, the Baroque artists and architects were magnificently confident in the grandeur of their approach. The massive scale, the unrestrained color, the direct appeal to the senses were manifestations of a new certainty of purpose, whether it lay in the glorification of a monarch or of a religion. For all its exuberance and its emotional display, the Baroque style was, however, rational. It was deeply influenced by mathematics and especially by geometry. In the palaces, the churches, the frescoes, and especially in the great city plans, one sees an endless fascination with mathematical relationships and geometric forms—squares, ovals, circles, convex and concave curves, and especially the search for the infinite, whether in a hallway of matched mirrors or a ceiling fresco that opens a palace ballroom to a heaven inhabited by gods and angels.

Paris took the lead in the eighteenth century in the modification of the Baroque style into a softer, more delicate, and less emotionally overpowering

319

variation, called Rococo, which, however, reached its greatest heights in the courts and churches of south Germany and Austria.

By the late 1770s, most of the *philosophes* were dead, and there were already signs that this age of certainty was coming to an end. Writers such as Rousseau in France and Goethe in Germany were giving emotion primacy over reason, and preparing the way for the replacement of the Enlightenment by a new cultural movement called Romanticism. Even though the American and French revolutions are often considered to be the final outcome of a century of belief in the perfectibility of politics, the resort to violence to achieve that progress was in itself a confession that progress was far from inevitable; and the decline of the French Revolution in the 1790s from its early idealism into imperial expansion and military dictatorship cast doubt for many upon the belief in reason and progress that had made the early part of the eighteenth century such a stimulating period in which to live.

THE SCIENTIFIC REVOLUTION

Origins of the Scientific Revolution

It is not true that there was no interest in science during the Middle Ages. Works of both Greek and Arab science had been obtained from the Muslims, especially in Spain, and there had been a deep interest in Arab medicine. The advances in logic that had been made by the scholastic philosophers had led to rigor of argument in handling not only philosophical ideas but facts about the nature of the physical universe.

Although the Church had proclaimed the dogma that the universe was governed by laws that God had created, and that He could set aside, it had also accepted the writings of a number of classical thinkers as orthodox truth about the nature of the universe. For example, the Church accepted Ptolemy's view that the sun, stars, and planets moved around the earth in crystalline spheres, of which the outermost one, called the *primum mobile*, kept everything in motion. It accepted the teachings of the Greek physician Galen on the workings of the human body. Above all the Church accepted the teachings of Aristotle on a very large number of matters, including his views on physics and in particular his view that in their natural state objects will remain at rest.

Yet it was obvious to many medieval thinkers that there were inconsistencies or even mistakes in some of the classical views. Dissection, which had been permitted on a limited number of corpses in the fourteenth and fifteenth centuries, had, for example, shown that Galen was wrong in many details.

During the Renaissance, the orthodox theories came under renewed scrutiny for several reasons. The publication of hitherto-unknown works by classical scientists, especially Archimedes, proved that the ancient thinkers had been debating conflicting theories themselves, and had not been in agreement on one body of scientific theory. Alchemists, obsessed since ancient time with the belief that they could transmute base metals into silver and gold, had made considerable progress in chemical experimentation, and in fact are regarded as the forerunners of modern chemistry. The most important alchemist of the sixteenth century, Paracelsus, argued that each disease was different, contrary to Galen's view that all diseases were caused by humors in the body, and had proposed the use of metals such as mercury or iron in their treatment. Astrology, the attempt to divine the supposed influence of the planets on human events, became extremely popular in the Renaissance, and helped further knowledge of the stars and planets. Perhaps most important of all, the work of careful observation and measurement, which was at the basis of the achievements of the engineers, architects, military planners, and scientists, had brought experimenters to the point where they were ready to formulate a new procedure of finding and testing knowledge, which we call the scientific method.

Scientists had been aware since ancient times that instead of beginning with the acceptance of an established truth such as might be required by religion, they must begin with skepticism, a questioning of truths. Scientific inquiry follows the procedure of first observing the phenomenon to be studied; next establishing a hypothesis; then experimenting to test the predictions derived from the hypothesis; and finally accepting the hypothesis as probably true, modifying it to correct for errors revealed by the experiments, or discarding the hypothesis as false and developing a new one.

The Church had paid little attention to how scientists worked until the Council of Trent (1545–1563) had reasserted the truth of all traditional Catholic doctrine in preparation for the battle against Protestantism. Now in competition with a rival theology, the Church felt compelled to oppose a method of establishing knowledge that questioned accepted Church authorities. When Galileo Galilei not only published a book showing that the Ptolemaic view of the universe accepted by the Church was wrong but also stated flatly that scientific knowledge could not be based on the authority of the Bible, he was forced by the Church to recant (see pp. 323–24).

The Church could, however, not stop the scientific revolution because in the seventeenth century several factors combined to speed its advance. First, several inventions made possible more accurate observation and experiment. The Dutch had developed great skill in the making of lenses. To aid navigation, they had invented the telescope, which was immediately used by astronomers such as Galileo in Italy. The realization that two lenses together could magnify far more effectively than one led not only to the telescope but also the microscope, which was also invented in Holland. Among the many scientific tools invented at about the same time were the barometer, the pressure gauge for measuring pressure of air or gas, the thermometer, and the air pump.

Second, scientists realized that in order to describe and explain the working of the physical universe, they would need new forms of mathematics. Galileo wrote that the language of the universe "is written in the mathematical language, its characters are triangles, circles, and other geometrical figures, without the aid of which it is impossible to understand a word of it, without which one wanders vainly through a dark labyrinth."[1] Arabic numerals had replaced Roman numerals in the late Middle Ages. But in the seventeenth century a number of mathematical advances of great importance were made. The Scottish mathematician John Napier invented logarithmic tables, which cut in half the time spent on mathematical calculations; and he invented the use of decimals for dealing with fractions. In 1637 the French philosopher and mathematician René Descartes developed analytical geometry, a method by which geometric relationships could be expressed in algebraic formulae. At the end of the seventeenth century, Isaac Newton and the German philosopher Gottfried Wilhelm Leibniz apparently invented differential or infinitesimal calculus at about the same time.

Change was most rapidly achieved in medicine, where the benefits were immediately demonstrable. As we saw, Renaissance painters had already made considerable progress in understanding human anatomy, and Andreas Vesalius had published a medically important textbook of anatomical drawings in 1543 that brought into question Galen's doctrines. When the experimental method was applied in the seventeenth century, the views of Galen were rapidly disproved. One of the most important advances was made by the English physician William Harvey, who was able to show that the heart operates as a pump, forcing the blood through the veins, and that the blood circulates through the body. The Dutch scientist Antony van Leeuwenhoek used the microscope not only to examine drops of water and to show the existence of protozoa, but also to examine blood corpuscles.

Advances in Astronomy

A far greater battle had to be fought with the Catholic Church in order to force changes in astronomy. For the Church, astronomy was not merely an understanding of the movements of the planets and stars, but it was also an interpretation of the position of the earth in Christian cosmology and of the relationship of all matter. It was on the issues raised by astronomy that the Church stood most firmly behind the teachings of Aristotle and Ptolemy, especially in holding that the sun revolved around the earth and not the earth around the sun. Both technology and mathematics were needed to establish a more accurate astronomy. Nikolaus Copernicus (1473–1543), a Polish clergyman, although lacking advanced scientific instruments, was able to show mathematically that the explanation of the universe was much simpler if one accepted that the earth moved around the sun rather than the other way around. This simpler explanation was in keeping with the requirements of Ockham's razor, which was one of the dominant criteria of rational thought by Copernicus' day.

[1] Cited in F. Sherwood Taylor, *A Short History of Science and Scientific Thought* (New York: Norton, 1963), p. 138.

Since he had no hard data, however, Copernicus' theory made very little impression at the time. Tycho Brahe (1546–1601), working in Denmark with more accurate instruments, was able to observe the movements of the planets, although he did not come to believe in a heliocentric view. His observations, however, were studied by Johannes Kepler (1571–1630), who was something of an eccentric but also a brilliant mathematician. Although he was trying to describe what he believed to be the music of the spheres, Kepler arrived at three important laws of planetary motion that are still largely accepted. His first showed that the planets travel in ellipses, and that the sun is the center of one focus of the ellipse. His second law described mathematically the motion of the planets, namely, that a line drawn from the planet to the sun sweeps over equal areas in equal times. Finally, in his greatest achievement, he showed that one simple mathematical formula can give the time taken by a planet to complete its orbit: the squares of the period of the orbit are proportional to the cubes of their mean distance from the sun.

The Italian astronomer Galileo Galilei (1564–1642) attacked Aristotle frontally, and thereby earned himself the suspicion of the Church. He had obtained one of the new Dutch telescopes and made painstaking observations; and he became convinced that almost every aspect of the Aristotelian system was wrong. He challenged first Aristotle's concept of motion, namely, that a body would be at rest unless moved by an external force. Galileo held instead to the principle of inertia, that a body would continue moving unless stopped by an external force. He argued in his scintillating and easily comprehensible book, *Dialogue Concerning the Two World Systems—Ptolemaic and Copernican*, that there are no

Galileo Galilei (1564–1642), by an Unidentified Artist Galileo's astronomical research was fundamental in proving that the earth and planets move around the sun, a view he was forced by the Inquisition to recant. (Library of Congress.)

crystalline spheres, and that the earth revolves around the sun. He was called before the Roman Inquisition at the age of seventy and agreed, under threat of torture, to withdraw his views.

Galileo's work was carried on by Sir Isaac Newton (1642–1727), who was born in the year Galileo died. In fact, many people said later that the soul of Galileo had passed into the body of Newton. By the time he was twenty-three, Newton had already made highly important contributions to science. In his own modest description:

> In the beginning of the year 1665 I found the method for approximating series and the rule for reducing any dignity [power] of any binomial to such a series [i.e., the binomial theorem]. The same year in May I found the method of tangents of Gregory and Slusius and in November had discovered the direct method of Fluxions [the elements of differential calculus], the next year in January had the Theory of Colors, and in May following I had entrance into the inverse method of Fluxions [integral calculus], and in the same year I began to think of gravity extending to the orb of the moon. . . . and having thereby compared the force requisite to keep the Moon in her orb with the force of gravity at the surface of the earth, and found them to answer pretty nearly. All this was in the two years of 1665 and 1666, for in those years I was in the prime of my age for invention, and minded mathematics and Philosophy more than at any time since.[2]

With his mathematical tools established, Newton drew up a vast synthesis that brought together in a harmonious mathematical system not only an explanation of planetary motion but of the nature of matter and of its gravitational attraction. In his book, *The Mathematical Principles of Natural Philosophy*, published in Latin in 1687, he showed that all bodies attracted each other by a law of gravitation, and showed mathematically the nature of this attraction in three laws of motion. His most important formulation was that the force of attraction of all bodies is directly proportional to the product of their two masses and inversely proportional to the square of their distance apart. Newton's explanation of the universe was more elegant and more comprehensive than any previous description, and it struck the age as a revolutionary discovery. The poet Alexander Pope wrote:

> Nature and Nature's Laws lay hid in night,
> God said, Let Newton be! and all was light.[3]

Newton's impact was so great because physics was the first field of human knowledge in whcih an apparently irrefutable demonstration was made that natural laws govern the universe and that they can be discovered by human reason. Newton's laws of motion had virtually no practical purpose at the time, but the effect of his demonstration was incalculable. It led directly to the many-sided inquiries that constituted the Enlightenment of the eighteenth century.

[2] Cited in Ibid., p. 125.
[3] Alexander Pope, "Intended for Sir Isaac Newton," *Epigrams*.

Eighteenth-Century Science

The principal scientific advances in the eighteenth century were made not in astronomy or physics but in chemistry, where once again the experimental method proved its value. Joseph Black, a Scottish professor, was able to demonstrate that air was not a simple substance but was made up of several gases. Joseph Lavoisier in France became the founder of modern chemistry with his theory that all substances are made up of a very few basic elements, of which he himself described oxygen, hydrogen, and twenty-one others. Advances were also made in biology, as a result of careful work of classification and synthesis. In Sweden, Carl Linnaeus created the system of classification of animals and plants that is still in use today. In Paris, Georges de Buffon, the director of the state-run botanical garden, wrote a vast synthesis of all biological knowledge.

The eighteenth century became the age of the popularization of scientific knowledge. Two academies spearheaded this movement, the Royal Society for Improving Natural Knowledge, founded in England in 1662, and the Academy of Sciences, founded in Paris in 1666. Bernard de Fontenelle, who was secretary of the Academy of Sciences for forty-two years, was instrumental in France in spreading the gospel of science, through his talks at Parisian salons and especially by his book, *Plurality of Worlds*. Voltaire, after spending two years in England at the order of the French government, also helped spread acceptance of science by making the work of John Locke and Isaac Newton well known through his *Philosophical Letters*.

Science in the eighteenth century still seemed comprehensible to the average educated person, and it became a form of mass entertainment. The upper and middle classes of London, Paris, and many other cities poured into salons and lecture halls to hear talks on medicine, astronomy, or physics. As a result, the belief in the inevitability of scientific progress and the supremacy of human reason became deeply rooted. The Age of Reason therefore also became the Age of Optimism. Nowhere was that optimism more evident than in eighteenth-century Paris during what became known as the Age of Enlightenment.

THE EIGHTEENTH-CENTURY ENLIGHTENMENT

Preeminence of Paris

Paris was the center of the eighteenth-century Enlightenment. Its foremost place in the intellectual life of Europe was recognized in virtually every country. (The English recognized the importance of French thought but remained distrustful of it.) Several factors came together to give Paris this position.

First, France was still, as it had been under Louis XIV, the richest and the most populous country in Europe. The nation therefore had the economic base and the broad population necessary to support the scientists and philosophers, to buy the books and paintings, and to finance the academies, laboratories, and botanical gardens that were necessary for the intellectual advances that constituted the Enlightenment.

Second, in the evolution of France since the twelfth century, Paris had increasingly absorbed the greater part of French talent in almost every sphere, not only intellectual and artistic but economic, administrative, military, legal, and social. The greatness of Paris was paid for by the relative impoverishment of the French provinces; Paris, however, had been made into a magnet not only for France but for the rest of Europe as well. Moreover, the court of Versailles, which during the reign of Louis XIV had drawn off much of the intellectual life of Paris, had ceased to compete after the death of the Sun King. Neither Louis XV nor Louis XVI had the desire to dominate the intellectual life of France as had Louis XIV. As a result, Versailles lumbered on as the administrative center of the country, but intellectual life returned to its traditional home in Paris.

Third, Paris acted as a kind of hothouse for the European intellect. The French educational system had created a large educated class that delighted in the discussion of philosophical ideas. Moreover, in Paris there was an interplay between intellectuals of whatever class and the nobility and the upper middle class of the city. The institution of the *salon*, a gathering in a private home at the invitation of a hostess, provided an organized setting for the interchange of ideas. Whereas in London much of the intellectual interplay took place in taverns among men, in Paris the company was chosen and the conversation directed by women who had as their goal the interaction of the finest minds in France. These hostesses included the Marquise Anne-Thérèse de Lambert, who entertained philosophers such as Charles Louis de Montesquieu and comic writers such as Pierre Marivaux; Alexandrine de Tencin, mother of the *philosophe* and mathematician Jean d'Alembert, an unfrocked nun who also worked as a government spy, and wrote several novels; and Madame Marie-Thérèse Geoffrin, whose highly coveted invitations were given to painters like Antoine Watteau on Mondays and leading *philosophes* like Denis Diderot on Wednesdays. It was in salons like these that the young Wolfgang Amadeus Mozart astounded Europe with his wizardry on the piano, Montesquieu introduced the influential political treatise, *The Spirit of the Laws*, and the Abbé Antoine-François Prévost read aloud his novel, *Manon Lescaut*.

Finally, the intellectual leaders of Paris not only exercised their influence outside France by their books, but were in constant demand to go personally to bring the thinking of Paris abroad. Diderot stayed for five months with the dictatorial Catherine the Great of Russia, without greatly changing her thinking. She did, however, offer to publish in Russia the great *Encyclopedia* that he and d'Alembert had edited when it came under criticism of the French censor. Voltaire lived in the palace of Frederick the Great of Prussia for three years. Thus the ideas of the French Enlightenment spread throughout Europe, and became the common intellectual currency of the continent. There were exceptions however. The English remained suspicious. German philosophy was simultaneously attracted and repelled by the blandishments of Cartesian thought. And in art and architecture the south Germans and Austrians went far beyond the original model of Parisian Rococo. But in general the eighteenth-century Enlightenment was the work of France and of France's admirers.

The Church Under Attack

The first task of the Enlightenment was to clear away the obstacles to future progress, the most obvious being Christian dogma. The very claim that reason was supreme represented a rejection of the Christian assertion of faith. In a sense René Descartes' (1596–1650) *Discourse on Method*, which had taught that doubt was the origin of certainty in knowledge, justified the questioning approach of the Enlightenment. Descartes began the *Discourse* with the assertion, "I think, therefore I am." Using reason alone and refusing to accept any assumptions on faith, he proceeded to test what was real in the universe. He ended with a belief in God, but he reached it by reason and not by faith.

Later writers were far more destructive. In his *Historical and Critical Dictionary*, Pierre Bayle, a rationalist philosopher, sharply criticized the Church for its persecutions, and argued in favor of the toleration of all religions. The most outright attack on the Church was led by Voltaire (1694–1778) with his cry, "Crush the infamous thing." To Voltaire, a glaring example of the persistence of bigotry into the Age of Reason was the torture and public execution of a Huguenot merchant named Jean Calas on the implausible grounds that he had strangled his elder son in order to prevent him from becoming a Catholic. Voltaire made the Calas case known all over Europe, not only to force the righting of the wrong to the Calas family but to publicize the danger of a persecuting Church. Even when the Enlightenment thinkers supported religion, most argued in favor of deism, a theory that God had created a perfect world governed by natural laws and had then stepped aside to leave human beings to use their reason to find the correct way of life. The deists rejected any idea that morality should be laid down by the Church, but argued that the moral law was just like any other natural law and could be discovered by reason. Since God had stepped out of the universe, the deists naturally rejected miracles. Only a few Enlightenment thinkers were atheists. Most were content to be deists or to remain within the ranks of a tolerant church such as the Anglican.

Legal Reform

The second sphere in which it was obvious that natural law was not followed was in the legal sphere, and especially in punishment. The article on torture in the *Encyclopedia* argued that torture was not only cruel but ineffective in establishing truth: "An ancient writer has also said quite sententiously that those who can stand the question [torture] and those who do not have enough strength to stand it lie in an equal way."[4] Punishment, the *philosophes* argued, should be made to fit the crime, an original idea in an age which believed that the more severe the punishment, the less likely people would be to commit even minor crimes. The Italian philosopher Cesare Beccaria even argued in *On Crimes and Punishments* that punishment should reform the criminal as well as protect society.

Psychology

At the basis of this approach was an entirely new concept of human psychology, which owed its origin to the English thinker John Locke (1632–1704). Locke's *Essay Concerning Human Understanding* was widely admired in France. In this work he argued that at birth the mind of a child is a *tabula rasa*, a blank surface, and that it acquires all knowledge by receiving impressions through the senses. No knowledge is innate. The sense impressions are organized by reason until the human being possesses a coherent view of the outside world. It followed from this argument, as French psychologists such as Etienne de Condillac argued, that, since all knowledge is derived from the environment, the character of a human being could be changed by controlling his or her environment. The Swiss thinker Claude Helvétius went further, and argued that an environment in which pain would be minimized and pleasure would be maximized would be a natural environment, that is, one in accord with the laws of nature. These views became known as utilitarianism after they had been expressed in their most extreme form by Jeremy Bentham in England. In his *Principles of Morals and Legislation* (1789), Bentham even argued that it was possible to make specific calculations so that the amount of pain and pleasure given by any legislative act, or indeed by any act, could be assessed.

Equality of Women

Some, though not all, of the *philosophes*, thought that one specific example where human law had not followed natural law was in the relation between the sexes. The hostess Marquise de Lambert published a book on the status of women in which she argued that lack of education spoiled "all those dispositions that nature has given women. . . . We destine them to please and they only please us by their graces or their vices."[5] The *Encyclopedia* argued that the sexes were naturally equal and that marriage was a civil contract that should recognize this

---

[4] Denis Diderot, *The Encyclopedia: Selections*, edited and translated by Stephen J. Gendzier (New York: Harper Torchbooks, 1967), p. 246.

[5] Cited in Shirley Jones, "Madame de Tencin: An Eighteenth Century Woman Novelist," in Eva Jacobs et al., eds., *Woman and Society in Eighteenth Century France* (London: The Athlone Press, 1979), p. 214.

equality rather than institutionalize inequality. Other writers argued that, since the environment controlled the nature of the human being, ancient Athens, with its seclusion of women in the home, had in fact stultified their development. By contrast, in Renaissance Italy, where women had been given equal access to society, they had become philosophers. The most extreme argument in favor of this equality, free of the restricting influence of society, was the novel of Bernardin de Saint Pierre, *Paul et Virginie*, in which he described the life of two youngsters growing up on an island in the Indian Ocean, free of the artificial restrictions of European society.

Education

Education, in the hands of the Church, appeared to the *philosophes* to be a manipulation of the environment in an adverse way to produce stunted human beings. The Enlightenment pressed for the expulsion of the Jesuits from France in part to get them out of French education. The *philosophes* began with the view that the child was naturally good and that the less done to interfere with this goodness the better. Moreover, since nature, in the sense of the unspoiled countryside, was the best environment, the ideal education consisted of permitting a child to grow up away from society, and especially away from the corruption of cities—in the countryside where the most natural instincts would flourish. The most influential book on education was the novel *Emile* by Jean-Jacques Rousseau (1712–1778), which became a virtual handbook for child rearing in the eighteenth century. Rousseau argued that for twenty years a boy should be sent into the countryside with a tutor to grow up in kindness and simplicity. A girl should be raised at home by her mother, who should employ sympathy rather than discipline and should concentrate on the development of her emotions. Rousseau did not, however, argue in favor of full equality of the sexes and concluded with the recommendation that married women should be secluded in something like the Athenian practice.

The Physiocrats

The most far-reaching plans for change in accordance with the natural laws were in economics and politics. The French economists were known as physiocrats, which meant believers in "government by nature." They felt that the economic system had laws as valid as those of the Newtonian physical universe, but that those laws had been vitiated by state interference. It was therefore essential that the state step out of economic life, except for a necessary minimum of regulation needed to permit the natural laws to work. It should "let be, let happen" *(laissez-faire, laissez-passer)*. It should avoid duties, tolls, export bans, or harmful taxation, so that an economic system would come into being in which all individuals were free to produce and trade for the maximum profit to themselves. The physiocrats were, however, not great admirers of industry or even of commerce, and held that the only real production of wealth was by agriculture. This led them to point out that the French economic system was being ruined by the exploitation of the peasantry, who, by unfair taxation and other burdens, were prevented from following their natural inclination to produce more. French thinkers never fully accepted the capitalist system. It was Adam Smith, a Scottish economist, who published in 1776 the most influential justification of capitalism, *The Wealth of Nations*.

Political Philosophy

In politics, French political writers decided that the English had created a sound political system, and thus much of the French political writing of the early eighteenth century attempted to explain what was good in the English system. John Locke had provided them with a persuasive set of fundamental principles in his *Two Essays of Civil Government*, which he had written in justification of the overthrow of King James II in the Glorious Revolution of 1688. Locke had argued that all human beings were born with "unalienable rights" to life, liberty, and property. They created a government to perpetuate enjoyment of these rights in organized society, and entered into a "social compact" with that government. Should the government break the compact, then the citizens had the right to replace that government with another. These views were embodied in Thomas Jefferson's Declaration of Independence in 1776, although Jefferson substituted for Locke's inclusion of property as a right the view that human beings had also an inalienable right to the "pursuit of happiness."

French visitors returned from England in the early eighteenth century to report that the social compact was working. Voltaire wrote in his *Philosophical Letters* that England was a country where natural rights were respected and social harmony had been achieved. Montesquieu (1689–1755), in his *Spirit of the Laws*, set out to show why. Although his book was a vast study of all the presumed influences that affect political systems (e.g., hot countries favor despotism, cold countries democracy), the most influential part of his book was his argument that the English system worked because of the separation of powers. In England, he said, there was a balance among the legislature, the executive, and the judiciary, and this separation should be the basis of all democratic constitutions. He was, however, wrong about the English constitution, since the relations between the legislature and the executive were lubricated by bribery, and the English were in fact working toward a more unified system in which an executive cabinet would be part of the legislative parliament. Nevertheless, the value of separation of powers was accepted by the founding fathers of the United States and was made the central idea of the Constitution that they produced in 1787.

Perhaps the most far reaching of the political philosophies presented by the Enlightenment thinkers was Rousseau's *Social Contract*. Rousseau seemed to begin the work with a call for revolution: "Man is born free, and everywhere he is in chains." The chains, Rousseau argued, were the bonds of society and government—private property, the judicial system, the bureaucracy, the privileges of the upper class. These repressive forces had taken away the human being's natural rights. Rousseau, however, went on to argue that, even in a democratic society, a majority can tyrannize over a minority. He then asked how one can form a society in which every individual is free. His ingenious answer led directly to the justification of dictatorship. Every individual, he said, has two wills—an individual will, which is the desire for self-gratification, and a general will, which is the desire for the well-being of the whole community. An individual feels the full well-being of which he or she is capable only when fulfilling both the individual and the general will at the same time. If one fails to achieve either, one has a sense of unfulfillment and therefore, concluded Rousseau, one is not free. Government is instituted to interpret and enforce the general will. Where a person's individual will is in conflict with the general will as interpreted by the government, then the government has the duty, for that person's sake as well as for the sake of the community, to make that person follow the general will. In Rousseau's great paradox, this means nothing less than that the individual will "be forced to be free." Rousseau thus achieved the most subtle justification of absolute power, that a despotic government does good by forcing people to do what is best for themselves.

Enlightened Despotism

Although the French monarchy showed little enthusiasm for applying the political program of the Enlightenment, there were many rulers in Europe who were determined to do so, most notably Frederick II of Prussia, Catherine II of Russia, and Joseph II of Austria. These rulers, however, ignored the fact that the political ideal of the Enlightenment was the spread of liberty and equality. Instead, they took from the Enlightenment only those lessons that taught efficiency, and they treated the *philosophes* as apostles of scientific administration. To found an absolutism that was more secure because it was more effective, these Enlightened Despots were quite prepared to apply reason to learn what the *philosophes* considered to be the natural functioning of those areas of society that would enhance the powers of despotism, namely, law, economics, education, and even religion.

To begin their program of increased efficiency, these rulers first consolidated their power and centralized their governments. Power was grounded on a professional military loyal to the monarch, although usually drawn from the aristocracy, and a secularized administration that derived its authority solely from the crown. One of the first practices followed by almost all enlightened despots was to introduce religious tolerance, which had the effect of allowing members of minority denominations to hold office in the government. This action tied bureaucrats more closely to the monarch and reduced ecclesiastical influence on administration.

As a means of increasing their economic base, and hence their power, many absolute rulers tried to expand their territories by conquest. Frederick II of Prussia, for example, seized the rich province of Silesia from the neighboring state of Austria, and fought two long wars in order to hold on to it. To encourage trade within their states and therefore further enhance their economic strength, most monarchs removed tariffs between provinces and regions within their domains, built and repaired roads and canals, instituted uniform taxes collected by royal officers, and subsidized new industries. To encourage their citizens to transfer their allegiance from local lords to the central government, the monarchs revised their legal codes to make them uniform across the country and, where possible, removed corrupt judges. To further attach the populace to the crown and to lessen the hold of the churches, the autocrats often set up secular schools and opened them to larger numbers of individuals than had previously had access to education.

Although the motives and achievements of these despots are open to much justifiable criticism, it is undeniable that they made lasting changes in the administration of their states. But very little progress was made in sharing power with the growing middle class who profited from the reforms, and thus the despots failed to achieve a basis of middle-class support that might have made their reforms self-perpetuating.

Literature and the Enlightenment

Many of the leading writers of the eighteenth century used their abilities as novelists or poets to popularize the teachings and the demands of the Enlightenment. The satirical novel was a particularly effective tool. In *Gulliver's Travels*, the Anglo-Irish clergyman Jonathan Swift used the imaginary journeys of his hero to Lilliput, a land of tiny people, and to Brobdingnag, a land of giants, to describe in ludicrous form the foibles both of the English political parties and of various intellectuals with whom he was warring. His most savage attack, however, was on mankind itself, who are described as vicious Yahoos in a land he visits on the last of his journeys, where only the horses have decency. When Voltaire turned to the satirical novel in his *Candide*, he was equally scathing on the foibles of human society. He has his young hero Candide suffer virtually every tribulation that afflicted the society of his day, from torture by the Inquisition to capture by brutal German foot soldiers, and concludes with the moral that, rather than be involved in the crimes and follies of the world, one should withdraw to "cultivate one's garden."

The rhyming couplets favored by most poets of the early eighteenth century were a particularly effective instrument of satire, especially in the work of Alexander Pope. Perhaps Pope's most ambitious work was a long poem entitled *An*

Essay on Man, in which he argued the Enlightenment view of the need to find and follow the laws of nature, especially in human conduct.

> All nature is but art unknown to thee,
> All chance, direction which thou canst not see;
> All discord, harmony not understood;
> All partial evil, universal good;
> And, spite of pride, in erring reason's spite,
> One truth is clear, Whatever is, is right. . . .
> Know then thyself, presume not God to scan,
> The proper study of mankind is man.[6]

The Pre-Romantics

It was, however, perhaps first in literature that the Enlightenment's pursuit of reason was abandoned, and the foundations laid for the cultural movement called Romanticism. The basis of the Romantic attitude had been laid by Rousseau, with his emphasis on the value of human emotions, the glory of unspoiled nature, and the corrupting influence of society. His novel *Emile* had become a virtual guidebook for the would-be Romantics in France in matters of education, while his *Confessions*, with their unashamed revelation of the author's deepest emotional experiences, set a pattern of personal introspection that exercised great influence on the younger writers of his day. In Germany, for example, Rousseau was much admired by the group of writers known collectively as the *Sturm und Drang* ("storm and stress") movement, which, between 1766 and 1780, preached the value of genius, of creative freedom, and the importance of feeling.

One of the most influential German works of this period was a novel, *The Sorrows of Young Werther*, by Johann Wolfgang von Goethe (1749–1832). The novel describes a young man who eventually commits suicide, just as Goethe himself may have been contemplating doing at this time, out of rejected love. It created the prototype of the self-pitying and self-destructive hero who was to become the central character of innumerable plays and novels in the first half of the nineteenth century, although Goethe himself was to turn in *Faust* with far greater subtlety to the self-examination of an individual who passes from indulgence to salvation.

Rousseau's love of nature found a counterpart in England, where William Wordsworth (1770–1850), living among the rugged beauty of the northern lake district, saw in the deep contemplation of nature a way to the understanding of God. In *Lyrical Ballads*, published jointly in 1798 with his friend Samuel Taylor Coleridge (1772–1834), Wordsworth attempted to show that simplicity of language could be highly effective in expressing the emotions evoked by waving fields of flowers or the views of distant mountains. Coleridge, however, had

[6] Alexander Pope, *An Essay on Man*, Ep. i, lines 284–89; Ep. ii, lines 1–2.

moved even further from the rational society of the eighteenth century in the supernaturalism of *The Rime of the Ancient Mariner* and the exoticism of *Kubla Khan*, a poem probably written under the influence of opium.

> In Xanadu did Kubla Khan
> A stately pleasure-dome decree:
> Where Alph, the sacred river, ran
> Through caverns measureless to man
>   Down to a sunless sea.[7]

Perhaps the most revolutionary of the pre-Romantic English writers, in his rejection of both the form and content of the classical writers of the eighteenth century, was the visionary poet William Blake (1757–1827). Like Rousseau and Wordsworth, Blake despised the industrial city and admired the charm of the unspoiled countryside. He rejected established religion and turned to the occult. He relied on his own intuition rather than preset rules, both to shape the engravings with which he illustrated his poems and in setting the form of the verse itself. As a result, his work, which was little known in his own time, has an extraordinary evocative power, as in his description of the sunflower, unable ever to join the sun it follows daily, as a symbol of human frustration:

> Ah, Sun-flower! weary of time
> Who countest the steps of the sun;
> Seeking after that sweet golden clime,
> Where the traveller's journey is done;
>
> Where the Youth pined away with desire,
> And the pale Virgin shrouded in snow,
> Arise from their graves and aspire
> Where my Sun-flower wishes to go.[8]

THE BAROQUE AND ROCOCO STYLES IN ARCHITECTURE AND ART

During the centuries of the scientific revolution and the Enlightenment, European architecture and art were dominated by two styles that appealed to the emotions rather than to reason—Baroque and its charming offspring, Rococo.

The word "Baroque," which in Italian means odd-shaped, was originally used at the end of the eighteenth century to disparage the style of art and architecture developed in Italy in the seventeenth century, but is now used without negative connotations as a description of the style and sometimes in an even broader sense of the whole society of the seventeenth century. The

---

[7] Samuel Taylor Coleridge, *Kubla Khan*, lines 1–5.
[8] William Blake, *Ah, Sun-Flower! Songs of Experience.*

Baroque style gradually replaced Mannerism at the end of the sixteenth and the beginning of the seventeenth century. After first appearing in Italy, it passed to Spain and Portugal and then to Germany and Austria. In France, England, and the other northern countries, which had remained true to the classicism derived from the Renaissance, its influence was also strongly felt, and it became possible to see in even the largely classical buildings features that are typical of the Baroque style of southern Europe.

In a similar way, Baroque style in painting spread northward from Italy to the other Catholic countries. Although many artists, even in Italy, retained such individuality of style that it would be incorrect to label them as painters of the Baroque school, it is also true that the Baroque style influenced even such countries as the Netherlands, which had continued in the tradition of the naturalist style of fifteenth-century Flanders.

In the early eighteenth century, the Baroque style in architecture and art was transformed into the Rococo style, which remained in vogue until the 1770s. Rococo also appealed to the emotions, but it was more delicate, subdued, and perhaps more lacking in intellectual content than the Baroque.

Character of Baroque Style

Baroque style in both architecture and art had three main characteristics—intense movement, theatricality, and direct emotional impact. To achieve these, the Baroque artists employed a number of different devices. First, they were determined to exploit to the full the possibilities of mathematics, and especially of geometry. They utilized the straight line, opening up enormously long vistas down roadways or canals. The square and the rectangle were widely used forms for real estate development, especially in London and Paris. The circle was adopted not only for domes but also for the intersection of a number of streets, which could thus be made to form a star. But the most favored shape was the oval. The oval brought into architecture and even into city planning a sense of luxurious elegance. A half-oval could be used to present a row of city houses as a gracious crescent. Employed in the ground plan of a Baroque church, it created a sense of undulating motion, a source of delight to the eyes and of disorder to the mind. Finally, Baroque artists were fascinated by the concept of infinity. Streets became enormously long, especially as they were designed more for the pleasure of travelers in horse-drawn carriages than for pedestrians. Alleyways through formal gardens were prolonged by canals until they disappeared over the distant horizon.

The second method of achieving the Baroque artist's goal was trickery. Baroque artists were masters of illusion. Facing mirrors were used to create a sense of space within a building. Ceilings were painted to represent the sky, with humans at the base looking wonderingly through floating columns toward a heaven filled with saints and cherubs. Statues were not placed in carefully planned niches, but, painted in vibrant colors, swarmed along the walls as

The Ecstasy of Saint Theresa, by Giovanni Lorenzo Bernini (1598–1680) The angel is about to plunge into the heart of the mystic St. Theresa the arrow that will unite her to Christ. (Alinari/Art Resource.)

though they were alive. Optical illusions were frequently used. Passageways become narrower to create an illusion of great length. Holes were pierced in walls to permit the sun to enter like a floodlight. Altars were disguised as theater stages, with a sculpted audience on either side viewing the drama within.

The most basic strategy, however, was to appeal to the emotions through the senses. Since the purpose of many buildings and paintings was to emphasize the greatness of the Catholic Church or of kings and nobles, vast size was often used to overwhelm the observer. The Italian architect Giovanni Lorenzo Bernini (1598–1680) had set the standard with his vast colonnade at the entrance to Saint Peter's Cathedral in Rome, a masterpiece that magnified the size of an already enormous building. The appeal to the emotions could be more direct. The materials of buildings and the colors of paintings were picked for their immediate impact. In Bernini's marble statue, *The Ecstasy of Saint Theresa*, rays of sunlight are picked up by shafts of gilded metal as the saint swoons before an angel announcing her union with Christ. Other favorite materials were marble of many colors, alabaster, painted stucco, gold, and even tin. When Bernini designed the vast canopy over the high altar of Saint Peter's, he employed so much bronze in its twisting columns that he had to use metal stripped from the imperial Roman Pantheon. Decoration became an essential part of Baroque art, and not simply an addition to architecture as it had been during the Middle Ages and even in the Renaissance.

Baroque Architecture

It was in Rome that the new style was first accepted, perhaps because it had been foreshadowed in the later work of Michelangelo. It was Bernini, the greatest Baroque architect and sculptor, who used it to transform the appearance of Rome even more thoroughly than Michelangelo had been able to do. The popes, who were busy creating beautiful vistas by cutting new streets through the medieval quarters of Rome, employed Bernini and many other artists to build new churches decorated with sculptures at the intersections of the new roads. Bernini too gave Rome one of its most charming features, the large number of fountains, such as the Fountain of Rivers in the Piazza Navona, many enlivened with his statues of pagan gods.

Bernini was brought to Paris by Louis XIV to design a new façade for the Louvre palace, but the French were not yet prepared for the outright exuberance and expense of Bernini's Baroque style. Baroque therefore entered France as an influence on the prevailing classical style rather than as a totally new style. Both the façade of the Louvre, eventually designed by Claude Perrault, and Versailles itself, were built with restrained color, balanced façades, and attention to the correct use of classical motifs. Yet Versailles was still essentially Baroque in feeling, in its size, its interior color, its sculptures, its mirrors and fountains, and its landscape design.

Saint Paul's Cathedral, London, by Christopher Wren (1632–1723) *Wren's nave is severely classical, incorporating a triumphal arch, but combines harmoniously with the baroque curves and niches of the towers on the west front. (Michael Holford.)*

The same must be said of many buildings in England in the seventeenth century, even though many architects took pains to avoid the tricks of Baroque style. Inigo Jones, one of the best architects of the early seventeenth century, even blamed Michelangelo for the excesses of Italian architecture, and in the new palace that he began on the Thames riverfront for Charles I, he was very restrained. England's greatest architect of the late seventeenth century, Sir Christopher Wren (1632–1723), was far less so. He enlivened even the most staid buildings, such as the Royal Naval College in Greenwich, with features that broke the strict classical façade, such as towers with bulbous domes. Even his supreme achievement, Saint Paul's Cathedral, whose west front is constructed around an enormous triumphal arch, incorporates undulating Baroque curves into the side towers. By breaking the four-square appearance of his buildings, Wren was thus able to create the tension that is essential to Baroque. Wren's most ingenious achievement was the fifty-one city churches that he designed after the great fire of London of 1666, because by playing with geometric forms in the spires that dominated all the churches, he created a totally different appearance for each at a minimum cost.

Baroque Painting

The Mannerist painters of the sixteenth century, especially Tintoretto and El Greco, had already pointed to the direction in which Baroque artists would move. Both had used color and design to create tension and excitement rather than balance and harmony, and both, having created the emotional appeal they were seeking, had left their canvases with a strangely unfinished appearance that was deliberately intended to be disturbing. From about 1600, however, Rome once again became the center of European painting for a generation, and it was there that the Baroque style, in painting as in architecture, was fully worked out as a consciously formulated style.

A school of painters gathered around Annibale Carracci (1560–1609) who, in his use of light in almost a theatrical sense and in his direct appeal to the emotions, was one of the first Baroque artists. Both Italian and foreign artists came in large numbers to Rome between 1600 and 1630, because it was regarded as the center of the art world. Of the artists who studied the new art in Rome at this time, by far the most important was Peter Paul Rubens (1577–1640).

Rubens worked in Mantua and Rome between 1600 and 1608, and returned to Antwerp a master of all the methods (and tricks) of Italian Baroque—the use of color; the setting of figures in vast complicated patterns; the depiction of light shining on rich fabrics or precious metals; and above all the illusion of infinite space filled with bodies in violent, twisting motion. But he had also developed his own, distinctive method of depicting the human face and form and of using a dramatic story to paint a deeper philosophical meaning. Rubens became the favorite painter of Catholic rulers and indeed of some Protestant ones as well, since his style was so perfectly in keeping with the grandiose

The Purification of the Temple, by El Greco (1541–1614) *El Greco's portrayal of Christ driving the moneylenders from the Temple is one of the finest examples of Mannerist art, with its distorted figures, its whirling motion, and its discordant colors.* (The Frick Collection.)

vitality of the age. He maintained a workshop in which large numbers of students would transfer onto vast canvases the small sketches with which he met his commissions. Then, when they had finished, he would add some final touches that invariably turned the picture into an irrefutable Rubens masterpiece. He was so admired that he was sent from court to court to perform diplomatic tasks as well as to paint the portraits and the allegories for which he was admired. Perhaps the most ambitious of all his projects was twenty-three enormous paintings depicting the life of Marie de Médicis, the vainglorious mother of Louis XIII. His most touching portraits were, however, of his second wife Helen Fourment, who was sixteen when she married the fifty-three-year-old painter.

Rubens' pupil, Anthony Van Dyck (1599–1641), became the court painter of the English King Charles I, and he painted many of his best portraits of the king and other nobles of his court. Van Dyck had learned from Rubens a mastery of color, especially in depicting rich materials and the appearance of the human face. Rubens also had met the finest Spanish painter of the Baroque period, Diego Velázquez (1599–1660), and had even persuaded him to go to Rome to study. As court painter in Madrid, Velázquez, like Van Dyck, specialized in portraits of the royal family and the court. But Velázquez was a person who loved all humanity, as he showed in his paintings of the poor water sellers in the streets of Seville and the dwarfs and jesters of the court. His ingenuity in composition is displayed in perhaps his best-known painting, *Las Meninas* (*The Ladies in Waiting*). This charming painting shows the artist at work in his studio painting the king and queen, who are visible only in a mirror on the back wall, while the little Princess Margarita and her ladies break in unexpectedly to see what is happening.

Dutch Art

In the Netherlands in the seventeenth century, the influence of Baroque could be seen in the artists' use of color, in the ability to create a sense of motion, and at times in a subdued theatricality. But the Dutch artists remained true to the tradition of naturalism, which they had inherited from Flemish artists of the late fifteenth century, such as van Eyck.

The scope of Dutch painters was severely restricted by the patrons to whom they catered. The Calvinist church did not buy large religious tableaux of the kind commissioned by the Catholic Church. Nor were individual Calvinist patrons permitted to glorify themselves in portraits like those of the Catholic court painters. The great merchants ordered pictures of themselves as members of the city government or of the administrative body of some charity institution. The middle classes purchased subdued and dignified portraits of themselves and their families. Occasionally, patrons like the house of Orange ordered religious paintings for their own homes. But by far the most widely purchased paintings were of scenes of daily life in the countryside, the city streets, or private homes. These *genre* paintings, as they were called, were usually small enough to hang on the restricted wall space of a Dutch house, and were regarded by the average Dutch person as an investment that could be readily turned back into cash.

Artists specialized in one type of painting, for which they could become known and thus command a higher price. Some painted landscapes, others ships at sea, still others farm scenes. Still lifes of bowls of fruit or flowers were very popular, as were harmonious scenes of family life in the home, especially with women painters who could work on them in their own homes. Rachel Ruysch, for example, who was the daughter of a botany professor, was one of the most admired painters of meticulously observed compositions of flowers, which were often enlivened with lizards and snakes.

The master of the Dutch interior was Jan Vermeer (1632–1675). Vermeer's paintings were all deceptively simple. Light from a window at one side of the painting falls on an unassuming scene—a servant pouring milk, a young girl having a music lesson, a lady reading a letter. There is no drama and no tension. Yet every detail is rendered to perfection: the tiles, the music instruments, the crinkled maps on the wall, even the studs in the chair; and washing over this comfortable scene is the muted light that makes the humblest detail a source of delight.

The Supremacy of Rembrandt

Rembrandt van Rijn (1606–1669) began his career by painting a series of portraits of well-to-do Dutch burghers, either individually or in groups, and immediately earned a reputation for his psychological insights, his mastery of the depiction of light, and, like Rubens, his ability to organize figures in large group scenes. Rembrandt loved his early years of prosperity in the 1630s and 1640s, when he was inundated with commissions. He bought a fine house and a large art collection, and married the wealthy daughter of a prominent burgomaster.

Rembrandt's style perfectly suited the taste of Amsterdam, where he lived, and even his large religious allegories usually found purchasers. His style was rich and full, and clearly influenced by the "dark and light" painting methods of Italy and Spain. But he was always totally personal in style, even in the group portraits commissioned by the corporate bodies of Amsterdam, such as the famous *Night Watch*. (When the picture was cleaned, however, it was discovered that it was a scene set during the day and not at night!) The painting depicts one of the militia guards patrolling the streets of Amsterdam. The figures are so skillfully arranged that the captain and his lieutenant seem to move forward toward the onlooker, while the lances and pikes of the guards in the rear jostle together as they follow the drummer. But Rembrandt has achieved his own unique impression by his sparing use of color, which illuminates only the captain's red sash, the lieutenant's yellow uniform, and a girl's dress.

After the death of his wife Saskia in 1642, Rembrandt's joyful way of life broke apart. He fell into debt, and, declared bankrupt, was forced to sell his house and art collection. Commissions dropped off, as the mercantile oligarchy

Self-Portrait, by Rembrandt van Rijn (1606–1669) Rembrandt painted himself at all stages of his career, from his carefree youth to the dark days, as here in 1659, when personal tragedies overburdened him. (National Gallery of Art, Washington, D.C.; Andrew W. Mellon Collection.)

The Embarkation for Cythera, by Antoine Watteau (1684–1721) *Watteau's most famous painting shows a party of courtiers setting off for the island of love, where Venus was born in the foam of the sea.* (Art Resource.)

became more ostentatious in its tastes while Rembrandt probed the nature of the human soul. His mistress, Henrijke Stoffels, with whom he had lived for twenty years following Saskia's death, died in 1663, his only son Titus in 1668, and Rembrandt himself a year later. Yet Rembrandt triumphed over all his sorrows, as can be seen in his extraordinary series of self-portraits, the depiction of a man bowed with suffering and yet capable of learning from sorrow a deeper understanding of the nature of life. It is perhaps for this reason above all that Rembrandt is regarded as one of the greatest painters who ever lived.

Rococo Style

In the early eighteenth century, both architecture and art changed in character. Paris had replaced Rome as the arbiter of style, and it was in Paris that the Baroque style was transformed into the Rococo. Rococo broke with the Baroque style by giving up the absorption with grandeur and seeking instead an elegant intimacy achieved through smallness of scale. The fascination with geometric patterns and sheer size was replaced by a love of intricate decoration, especially in the use of *rocaille* (rock patterns) and *coquille* (shell shapes), whose encrusted irregularities were usually painted in muted pastel colors.

   The pioneer of the new style was Antoine Watteau (1684–1721), a Flemish painter who lived in Paris. Watteau, who died of tuberculosis at the age of thirty-seven, painted scenes of undisturbed happiness in paintings such as *The Embarkation for Cythera*. Aristocratic men and women in shimmering silks and

342

taffeta while away sunny afternoons in leafy glades in total contentment. It is an idealization of the way of life of the nobility that seduces rather than overwhelms.

Two of the favorite painters of eighteenth-century France, Jean-Honoré Fragonard and François Boucher, followed Watteau's style, as did many others of the period. Women painters were extremely popular in eighteenth-century Paris. Fragonard's sister-in-law, Marguérite Gérard, painted scenes of aristocratic life in the style of the Dutch interior painters. Queen Marie Antoinette, by her patronage, spurred the careers of Anne Vallayer-Coster, who specialized in still-life paintings of flowers and fruit, and of the prolific portrait painter, Elisabeth Vigée-Lebrun, who has left more than 600 paintings, including several of Marie Antoinette herself.

Painters were frequently called upon to paint frescoes or wall panels, because in a Rococo room every feature had to harmonize. Paris in fact became the center of the minor arts. Artists were called upon to design doorknobs, mantelpieces, clocks, curtains, saltcellars, and chandeliers. As a result there was a kind of unity within a Rococo palace or church despite the extravagant decoration characteristic of the style.

The French, however, made little effort to adjust their architectural style, the predominant classicism of Versailles, to accommodate these new decorative arts. The greatest architectural achievements of the Rococo style were in Austria and south Germany, where the spatial design of palaces and churches was entirely reworked. The patrons were the rulers of the many independent states and the abbots of the wealthy monasteries. Rather than bring in Italian or French architects, they employed Germans and Austrians, such as Balthasar Neumann (1687–1753). Entering one of their buildings, one is in an entirely new world, as can be seen in Neumann's great pilgrimage church of Vierzehnheiligen near Bamberg. Here Neumann has linked together a series of ovals and circles, thereby doing away completely with the rectangular floor plan; and he has created something more akin to a ballroom than a church, a fantasy of creams, pinks, and blues in which a multitude of painted and sculpted figures surge riotously toward the skies. In Germany and Austria, and perhaps nowhere else, Rococo became a great architectural style, as can be seen in such achievements as the Zwinger palace in Dresden, the Schönbrunn palace in Vienna, or the great monasteries like Melk, which dominate the valley of the Danube.

MUSIC FROM THE BAROQUE TO THE CLASSICAL

Just as painting became an integral part of the architecture of the vast new palaces, churches, and theaters, music developed into a form that was integrated perfectly with the other art forms within a Baroque architectural setting.

With the development during the Renaissance of new instruments and the advance in techniques of composition, European music had changed parallel to the style changes of architecture and art. Polyphony, the blending of several lines of melody, was developed during the late Middle Ages and reached its highest form in the choral writings of Giovanni Palestrina in the sixteenth century. The most typical creation of the Baroque age of the seventeenth and eighteenth centuries was opera, which combined drama, orchestral music, and song so as to satisfy the typical Baroque passion for grandeur and illusion. Frequently retelling the myths of the classical world or the events of Greek and Roman history, the Baroque opera composers, such as George Frederick Handel in his *Julius Caesar* of 1724 or Cristoph Gluck in his *Orfeo* of 1762, gave their singers the opportunity to display the virtuosity of the human voice in long melodious lines decorated with innumerable trills. The late Baroque instrumental style, which combined polyphony with development of homophony, the progression of chords in different keys, reached its height in the orchestral, choral, and organ works of Johann Sebastian Bach (1685–1750).

The Baroque style was replaced about the middle of the eighteenth century by the classical. By then the orchestra had assumed its modern form, especially as the result of the improvement of stringed instruments and the use of such wind instruments as the oboe, bassoon, and flute. By the time of Franz Josef Haydn (1732–1809), Vienna had become the center of European orchestral music; and the symphony, as perfected by Haydn, had become the most admired musical form. The style was known as classical because it followed strict rules of composition, in the relation of keys, presentation of themes, and structure of movements, and because it eschewed any blatant emotionalism. As was evident in the works of Wolfgang Amadeus Mozart (1756–1791), these rules far from stifled expression, but rather could be used to express joy, sadness, tension, and humor. In such works as his *Jupiter* symphony or his finest opera, *Don Giovanni*, Mozart brought the classical style to its highest perfection.

THE SCIENTIFIC AND ARTISTIC ACHIEVEMENT

The seventeenth and eighteenth centuries, at least in intellectual and cultural terms, had been an age of increasing certainty and optimism. The authority of the thinkers of antiquity, as modified and upheld by the Catholic Church, had been successfully challenged. The scientific method had gained wide acceptance as the most reliable means of establishing truth about the nature of the physical world. Tools had been developed by which new knowledge could be discovered, both through such technological creations as the microscope and such intellectual tools as analytical geometry and calculus. Great advances had been made in individual fields of science such as astronomy, medicine, and physics. The attempt to discover laws applicable to human society comparable to those being discovered in the physical world had made the thinkers of the eighteenth-century Enlightenment conceive over-arching theories for law, penology, economics, psychology, education, and politics, and propose far-reaching programs of reform of those abuses their polemics had identified.

In culture a similar sense of confidence had produced an art and architecture lacking the distortions of Mannerism. Although there were great stylistic variations between north and south, Catholic and Protestant, and individual artists and architects, almost everyone displayed a confidence in the purpose of their undertakings. This assurance was most evident in the great churches built as monuments to a resurgent Catholicism or in the vast monasteries secure in their seemingly unlimited wealth; in the enormous palaces like Louis XIV's Versailles and the many attempts by other rulers to emulate the Sun King's achievement; or in the huge canvases painted by Rubens for the glorification of Marie de Médicis. Looking back after the French Revolution had shattered the self-confidence of aristocratic society, many observers asked themselves regretfully whether they would ever again live in an age of such self-assurance.

SUGGESTED READINGS

The Scientific Revolution

Alfred R. Hall surveys the principal stages in the emergence of the new scientific outlook in *The Scientific Revolution; 1500–1800: The Formation of the Modern Scientific Attitude*

(1966), and *From Galileo to Newton, 1630–1720* (1963). Herbert Butterfield is especially helpful in explaining the astronomical advances, in *The Origins of Modern Science, 1300–1800* (1965). Biographies of the leading scientists include Thomas S. Kuhn, *The Copernican Revolution* (1966); James Stephens, *Francis Bacon and the Style of Science* (1975); Stillman Drake, *Galileo at Work: His Scientific Biography* (1978); and Edward N. Andrade, *Sir Isaac Newton* (1958). Thomas S. Kuhn, in *The Structure of Scientific Revolutions* (1965), emphasizes the changing mental attitudes that made possible scientific advance.

The Enlightenment

Straightforward introductions to the leading thinkers of the eighteenth century are provided by George R. Havens, *The Age of Ideas* (1955), and Kingsley Martin, *French Liberal Thought in the Eighteenth Century* (1954). Carl Becker, *The Heavenly City of the Eighteenth Century Philosophers* (1969), challenges the reputation of the *philosophes* for rationality, while Peter Gay, *The Enlightenment: An Interpretation* (1966–1969), sees them as revolutionary innovators. Elizabeth Fox-Genovese analyzes the economic thought of the physiocrats in *The Origins of Physiocracy: Economic Revolution and Social Order in Eighteenth Century France* (1963). The best biography of the publisher of the *Encyclopedia* is Arthur Wilson's *Diderot: The Testing Years, 1713–1759* (1957), while a good selection from the multitudinous articles in the *Encyclopedia* is given in Denis Diderot, *The Encyclopedia: Selections* (1967). Voltaire's correspondence is widely quoted in Owen Aldridge, *Voltaire and the Century of Light* (1975), but one should sample Voltaire's writings more extensively in B. R. Redman, ed., *The Portable Voltaire* (1977). Everyone will enjoy the satire of Voltaire, *Candide* (1966), in Joan Spencer's modern translation. Jean-Jacques Rousseau made his principal contribution to political theory in *The Social Contract* and to education in *Emile*. For a balanced biography, see George R. Havens, *J.-J. Rousseau* (1978).

Baroque and Rococo Architecture and Art

The relationship of Baroque to Renaissance art is analyzed in the fine introduction by Frederick B. Artz, *From the Renaissance to Romanticism: Trends in Style in Art, Literature, and Music* (1975). The general features of Baroque style are surveyed in Victor L. Tapie, *The Age of Grandeur: Baroque Art and Architecture* (1960). To see the national differences within the style, turn to Rudolf Wittkower, *Art and Architecture in Italy, 1600–1750* (1958); Anthony Blunt, *Art and Architecture in France, 1500–1700* (1953); and Judith Hook, *The Baroque Age in England* (1976).

Afred Cobban, ed., *The Eighteenth Century: Europe in the Age of Enlightenment* (1969), is gorgeously illustrated, but should be supplemented by Stephanie Faniel, *French Art of the Eighteenth Century* (1957). Donald J. Grout, *A History of Western Music*, 3d ed. (1980), has a reliable summary of musical development in the seventeenth and eighteenth centuries.

12

The Old Regime

The phrase "old regime" is used to describe the social and governmental structure of Europe as it was before the French Revolution of 1789. The prevailing features of this regime were the dominance of privileged upper classes, composed of aristocrats, high church leaders, and the wealthy middle class; the exploitation of the vast peasant majority and the much smaller urban working class for the benefit of this privileged elite; and economic and military competition among the states dominated by these privileged classes for an even greater share of the wealth of the world, as a result of increased trade and territorial annexations.

Rococo art summarized the ideals of this elite—rich, elegant, good mannered, untroubled, the art of a society in which unchallenged wealth had brought peace of mind and the capacity for happiness. Thinking of the halcyon days before the bloodshed of the French Revolution, the French diplomat Talleyrand remarked, "He who has not lived before 1789 has not known how sweet life can be."

The old regime was at its height in the years between the Peace of Utrecht of 1713, which ended the War of the Spanish Succession, and the beginning of the French Revolution in 1789. During this period, a major shift took place in the balance of power among the European states. In Eastern Europe, Prussia and Russia became the dominant powers, while Poland and Turkey went into sharp decline. Austria, which seemed during the first half of the century to be threatened with a similar decline, recovered, and by the late eighteenth century was once again a significant force in international affairs. In Western Europe,

Britain became the leading imperialist power overseas, while at the same time embarking upon the argricultural and industrial advances that would make it the foremost economic power in the world by the beginning of the nineteenth century. France, suffering economically from the cost of the four wars fought by Louis XIV, overextended itself by seeking to expand its power simultaneously on the continent and overseas.

This evolution in the power balance inside Europe was hastened by a series of wars that left many, if not all, the participants in great financial difficulties.

Although several powers were able to stave off the worst of their internal problems by employing strategies recommended by the thinkers of the Enlightenment, none undertook a far-reaching reform program calculated to remedy the deep social problems of the old regime.

In this chapter, we shall consider first the changes in the international balance of power; second, the wars that helped bring about that change; and third, the failure of the societies of the old regime, and especially that of France, to make the internal reforms necessary to solve the financial problems their wars had caused or at least exacerbated.

A CHANGING BALANCE OF POWER

The Decline of Poland and Turkey

In the sixteenth and seventeenth centuries, Poland had been a powerful state. Successful wars had made it the fourth largest state in Europe, with a population of 11 million. But its military successes had been a source of its undoing. The eastern third of the country was predominantly Russian-speaking, and was regarded by the Russian government as rightfully part of Russia. The western sections of Poland included a large German-speaking population. Hence, the Polish state suffered from constant strife between the national groups that composed it, while both Prussia and Russia could claim to intervene on behalf of the German-speaking or Russian-speaking minorities, respectively.

The Polish nobility was perhaps the most backward in Europe. It kept the majority of the peasant population in serfdom. It elected its own king, usually from among competing foreign candidates. The royal government was, however, paralyzed by the constitution, which gave every single nobleman who was a member of the national assembly the right to veto any piece of legislation. The Polish government proved completely unable to resist when, in 1772, the rulers of Russia, Prussia, and Austria each annexed a large slice of Polish territory on their own borders. In new partitions in 1793 and 1795, the three predators shared out what was left of Poland, which disappeared from the map as an independent state.

The siege of Vienna in 1683 was the last great expansionist campaign of the Ottoman Turks. The sultans of the eighteenth century were corrupt and lethargic, and unable to exercise control over the Muslim clergy or over the grand viziers who ran the administration. The janissaries, a standing army whose principal purpose was to defend the sultan's household, interfered constantly in politics. The governors of the provinces, barely supervised by the sultan, grew rich through extortion. Perhaps most important of all, the military effectiveness of the Turkish army and navy was dropping in relation to that of its European enemies, Russia and Austria. From the late seventeenth century on, the Turks were forced to cede one European province after another to Austria or Russia. In the late eighteenth century, Russia even conceived a plan of abolishing the Ottoman Empire entirely, and of taking Constantinople for Russia. Such an action would have infringed all concepts of a balance of power among the European states, and hence it was opposed not only by Austria but also by France, which was increasingly becoming the guarantor of the Turkish Empire against Russian ambitions.

The Rise of Prussia

The nucleus of the state of Prussia was the Mark of Brandenburg, which sprawled across north Germany from the Elbe River to the Oder, with its capital in the small town of Berlin. Its land was low-lying, sandy, hard to farm, and lacking in defensible borders. By reason of the very difficulty of creating a viable society under these conditions, the peasantry had become hard-working and self-denying, and its nobility stern, disciplined, and devoted to the well-being of the state. The ruling family, the Hohenzollern, ran a harsh but efficient government.

The foundations of Prussian economic development and military power were laid by the Elector Frederick William I (the Great; ruled 1640–1688). He put an end to the provincial assemblies, and took the power of taxation for himself. He strictly enforced the serfdom of the peasants, and gave the aristocrats a monopoly of officers' positions in his reorganized army. He set an example of religious toleration by welcoming Polish Jews and the French Huguenots expelled by Louis XIV. He encouraged local industry, improved agriculture, and built better roads.

His son, King Frederick I (reigned 1688–1713) was permitted to become king as reward for joining the coalition against Louis XIV; and he called his new kingdom Prussia. In his desire, like the other monarchs of Europe, to emulate the French, he began the monumental rebuilding of Berlin, and invited artists and scientists to move there.

King Frederick William I (reigned 1713–1740) reaffirmed the brutal military traditions of the Great Elector. He spent his resources on doubling the size of the army and building a war treasury rather than on culture. It seemed, however, that when his son Frederick II (ruled 1740–1786) became king, he would reverse all his father's policies.

Frederick appeared to be the very opposite of his father. He loved music,

Frederick II of Prussia *In spite of his powdered wig and elegant clothes, Frederick's sharp features and wrinkled skin earned him the nickname of "Old Fritz."* (German Information Center.)

literature, and the French language. He had run away as a youth to avoid the rigid military discipline his father was imposing upon him. As king he built a lovely new palace in Rococo style at Potsdam, to which he invited Voltaire; and he corresponded with the *philosophes* in Paris. But Frederick was to show that he believed he could combine the militarism of his father Frederick William I with the cultural goals of his grandfather Frederick I.

Shortly after becoming king, he seized the province of Silesia from Austria. Later in his reign he joined with Austria and Russia to begin the partitions of Poland. These actions, however, he regarded as essential for the well-being of his state, since the territorial annexations gave Prussia a broader economic base, a doubled population, and more defensible frontiers.

To encourage non-Lutherans to participate in Prussian economic development, he permitted toleration of Catholics and Jews; while other enlightened despots were expelling Jesuits, he welcomed them. He was especially interested in the improvement of agriculture. New crops, such as turnips, were introduced and so were new tools such as iron plows. He drained marshland, and brought in immigrants to turn heathland into arable farms. Primary schools were founded in the villages to provide a minimum literacy—and no more. His most notable successes were his legal reforms. Frederick tried to stamp out corruption among the judges, restricted the use of torture, and reworked the legal codes.

The limits of both his desire and his ability to change the character of Prussian society were also evident. He refused to abandon mercantilism and imposed high tariffs to reduce imports. He made no effort to limit the burdens of serfdom on the peasantry, and supported the landlords in tying the peasantry ever more firmly to the land. Given the services of a cooperative aristocracy, he saw no reason to challenge the basis of their power. Nevertheless, his economic and social reforms, following the military build-up of his father, enabled Prussia to survive fifteen years of war against the leading armies of Europe.

The Russia of Catherine the Great

Peter the Great, as we saw in Chapter 10, had begun the modernization of the Russian administration, economy, and military forces, and the westernization of Russian culture. After his death in 1725, no Russian ruler until the accession of Catherine II (the Great; 1762–1796) attained even a shadow of the power Peter had wielded. Reigns were frequently short, cut off by disease or assassination. The death of a ruler was followed by a struggle of factions within the imperial palace to name the new ruler. For a time, the old Russian nobles appeared on the point of undoing Peter's reforms, but they were ousted by the service nobility. In spite of this political infighting around the ruler, however, the modernization of Russia, although slowed, was not stopped. Foreign culture—first German, then French—remained influential at the court. The nobility continued to do service to the state, even though the obligation to do so was abolished in 1762. The army remained one of the most powerful in Europe.

In 1762, the nobility deposed and later murdered Tsar Peter III, and made

Catherine the Great, by S. Torelli
Although Catherine took pride in consulting the philosophes, she enjoyed not only the trappings but the reality of autocratic power. (Novasti Press Agency.)

his wife Catherine (who probably connived in the plot) empress. She remained bound to the nobility for the rest of her reign, with the result that, in spite of her claim to be a reformer, she achieved nothing that was against the interests of the aristocracy.

As empress, Catherine seemed at first determined to win the reputation throughout Europe of being, in Voltaire's phrase, "the North star." She exchanged letters with the leading *philosophes*, wrote satirical plays in French, and used Montesquieu's ideas as the basis for a manifesto she issued at the beginning of her reign calling for basic reforms of Russian law and administration. An assembly representing nobles, middle classes, and free peasants met to consider documents of grievances sent in from all parts of Russia; but, after a year and a half of debate, Catherine packed them off home with nothing achieved.

She then attempted reform by despotic decree, enlisting the help of Diderot, whom she brought to Saint Petersburg. To improve administration, she divided Russia into fifty provinces of a more manageable size than the old units, and put them under the administration of aristocrats. Towns were given some rights of self-government. Newspapers were founded, but were not permitted to express criticism of the government. She was especially interested in the education of girls. In Saint Petersburg she founded separate schools for girls of the aristocracy and the middle class; and in the provinces she started several hundred elementary schools for both boys and girls. To show that women were at least the equal of men in intellectual capacity, she appointed a brilliant noblewoman, Princess Dashkova, director of the Academy of Sciences. Finally, she took over the property of the Russian Orthodox Church, and turned over much of its land and serfs to aristocrats.

Most of the reforms were, however, window dressing, skillful propaganda that enhanced her reputation in the West. The reality of her reign was to be seen in her treatment of the serfs. She made grants of state lands, with their serfs, to leading nobles. She permitted serf families to be broken up. Landlords were allowed powers of physical punishment of their serfs, and could even exile them to Siberia. Discontent boiled over in 1773–1775 in the greatest peasant uprising in Russian history, the rebellion led by the Cossack Pugachev. Hundreds of thousands of peasants joined Pugachev, who seized large parts of the Volga Valley and even for a time threatened Moscow. The revolt was finally defeated by the Russian army, and Pugachev was executed.

In spite of the shortcomings in Catherine's reform program, Russia was far stronger at her death than it had been thirty years earlier at her accession. She had restored the central position of the absolute monarchy, even if it was more than ever tied to the nobility. She had encouraged economic growth with remarkable success. The number of factories in Russia had tripled during her reign, and Russia was Europe's principal iron producer at the end of the eighteenth century. She had encouraged foreign immigration to uninhabited regions of Russia, settling thousands of German colonists in the Volga River Valley. Above all, she had maintained the strength of the Russian army and navy.

Catherine added more than 200,000 square miles of territory to the Russian empire, increasing its population by 12 million.

The Restoration of Austrian Power

The Thirty Years War, which ended in 1648, destroyed any possibility of the Habsburg rulers of Austria using their position as Holy Roman Emperor to create a unified German state. Instead the Habsburg monarchs decided to concentrate their ambitions on turning their own hereditary family possessions in southeastern Europe into a powerful, multinational state. The Habsburgs controlled the original family holdings in Austria; the Czech-speaking kingdom of Bohemia; and the kingdom of Hungary, from which it finally expelled the Turks in 1699. At the end of the War of the Spanish Succession, the Habsburgs were given Belgium and Lombardy.

To ensure unity among these national groups, the Habsburgs insisted on the primacy of the Catholic religion and acceptance of the hereditary right of the Habsburg family to rule. Although each of the separate Habsburg possessions retained its own assemblies representing primarily the nobility, the Emperor Leopold I (1658–1705) was able to supervise them through imperial councils responsible to him. He also built up a standing army with troops recruited in the German-speaking provinces. The army was further increased by Charles VI (reigned 1711–1740), who was, however, distracted from governmental affairs throughout his reign by his ultimately successful efforts to get the local assemblies inside his empire and the other European governments to recognize his only child, his daughter Maria Theresa, as his heir.

Upon her accession, however, Frederick II of Prussia claimed, and seized, the rich Austrian province of Silesia. Her inability to recover Silesia persuaded Maria Theresa (reigned 1740–1780) that Austria should adopt at least some of the reforms that were making Prussia so formidable a rival. The Austrian administrative system was rebuilt on the Prussian model, with a Directorium to supervise administration, a Council of State as a central advisory body, and a High Court of Justice as a final court for the whole empire. To bring uniformity into administration, she used German-speaking Austrians as much as possible. Army reforms were also copied from Prussia. Conscription was introduced, training schools founded for officers, and Prussian military tactics learned. Deeply concerned with the well being of the peasantry, she freed the serfs on the crown lands, and was disappointed that almost no aristocrats followed her example. Finally, she supported establishment of elementary schools, the improvement of high schools, and modernization of the University of Vienna.

The pace of reform picked up slightly after 1765, when, upon the death of Maria Theresa's husband Francis I, her son Joseph II became Holy Roman Emperor and co-ruler of Austria. Joseph II believed that the power of the monarchy should be used to force his subjects to accept in a short space of time the reforms proposed by the Enlightenment thinkers. Maria Theresa, however, dampened his impatience until her death in 1780. But in the last ten years of his life, from 1780 to 1790, Joseph proceeded at a breakneck pace to transform his empire.

Joseph was zealous in attacking the power and wealth of the Catholic Church. By making education secular, he ended the Church's control over the schools. He granted religious toleration to Protestants, Jews, and members of the Greek Orthodox Church, and opened to them entry into the educational system and to public office. He shut down almost a third of the empire's enormously wealthy monasteries, and used their resources to finance schools, hospitals, and aid to the poor. He also roused the bitter opposition of the non-German sections of his empire, by a program of Germanization of the administration. In attempting to end serfdom, he won the enmity of the aristocrats throughout the empire. He granted the serfs personal freedom, including the right to marry without the lord's permission and to move freely off the land. Just before his death, he attempted to change the labor services due to a landlord into a fixed monetary payment. Finally, he continued his mother's educational reforms, setting up teachers' training schools, improving secondary education, and using the University of Vienna to train his civil servants. By his death, one-quarter of all Austrian children attended school, which was perhaps the highest percentage in all Europe. Joseph died at the age of forty-nine, worn out by the frustration of seeing many of his reforms blocked by the aristocracy.

Maria Theresa and Joseph II had, however, achieved a great deal. The Austrian empire had avoided disintegration; and annexations in Poland had compensated in part for the loss of Silesia. Centralized administration had been made more efficient, and the non-German nobility strengthened in its personal loyalty to the throne. State revenues had been restored, and the conditions of life for the peasantry improved. Without these reforms, it is doubtful if so heterogeneous a state could have survived, as it did, until 1918.

Older Nation-States in Western Europe

The eighteenth century was the golden age for the British oligarchy that had consolidated its political power at the Glorious Revolution of 1688. The oligarchy, which comprised no more than 5 or 6 percent of the population, was composed of the great landowners, the gentry or squires, the well-to-do business classes, and the professional classes. Local government was in the hands of justices of the peace drawn from the local gentry. City government was in the hands of the merchant class. The House of Lords had a membership mainly of 200 great nobles. In the House of Commons, the wealthiest landowners and business people predominated, since a majority of the elections were decided by a few powerful families. The loose interest groups within Parliament, known as Whigs and Tories, were less and less divided by principle, but were becoming coalitions of politicians competing for power and the control of government patronage that power brought. Stable government was achieved, however, under a number of outstanding political leaders who, with the king's backing,

Chairing the Member, by William Hogarth (1697–1764) *Hogarth's series of etchings satirizing a parliamentary election begins with the bribed and drunk voters at the polls and ends in a brawl around the victorious candidate.* (The Metropolitan Museum of Art.)

maintained strong discipline over their faction in Parliament, not least by judicious dispensing of government contracts, jobs, and pensions. The master of this art of political manipulation was Sir Robert Walpole, who ran the British government from 1721 to 1742 and possessed the powers of a modern prime minister.

Within this oligarchy, there was considerable mobility, especially between the mercantile and the landed classes; and, perhaps as a consequence, the oligarchy as a whole was far more committed to money making than were the French upper classes. Agricultural improvements provided one important source of increased revenues. The opportunity for investment in Britain's industrialization (see Chapter 14) was also seized by many of the great landowners. But in the early eighteenth century the greatest opportunity for rapid profits lay in overseas ventures, particularly in the West Indian and East Indian territories that were already or would soon be in British possession. As a result, Parliament neglected the British army, which was recruited mainly from among continental mercenaries, but maintained the largest and most experienced navy and merchant marine in Europe. The British, in short, had made a conscious decision that the nation's effort should be concentrated on overseas expansion rather than diverted to overambitious efforts to interfere militarily in continental affairs. The wisdom of this decision was shown in the wars at mid-century, which left Britain the supreme colonial power.

France had been left exhausted by the wars of Louis XIV, and showed few signs of recovery until administration was entrusted by King Louis XV (reigned

1715–1774) to Cardinal Fleury in 1726. As chief minister until his death in 1743, Fleury restored efficiency to the central government, blocked the interference of the nobility, and encouraged economic development by improving the roads, sponsoring new industry, and opening up trade with the Muslim Near East. Commerce was also expanded with France's overseas colonies, especially the sugar islands in the Caribbean, and the merchant marine increased in size to handle the growing trade. Cities along the Atlantic seaboard, such as Bordeaux, boomed from their function as traders and processors of the tropical goods pouring into France and as increasingly important participants in the African slave trade. At the same time, however, the French army was maintained as the largest on the continent, and in fact was oversupplied with officers drawn from among the nobility.

By mid-century, France was faced with a fundamental choice. Since it had been unable to carry through social and fiscal reforms at the expense of the entrenched nobility and clergy, it needed to choose whether to devote its efforts to maintaining and perhaps increasing its influence on the continent of Europe or to shift its resources to buttress a greater effort, in competition with Britain, for hegemony overseas. Rather than make this choice, the French government attempted to carry out both policies at the same time. As a result, it succeeded in neither.

WAR AT MID-CENTURY

The territorial rivalries of the Eastern European powers and the Franco-British struggle for supremacy overseas merged at mid-century in two great wars: the War of the Austrian Succession, 1740–1748; and the Seven Years War, 1756–1763.

New Imperial Rivalries

In the eighteenth century, Spain and Portugal, the two powers that had first acquired overseas colonies, were desperately attempting to hold onto the possessions they had left. Spain, with the gold and silver mines of the Americas nearly worked out, favored establishment of large plantations worked by the Indian population and African slaves. Portugal concentrated on development of Brazil and on maintenance of trade in the Far East and Africa through its remaining settlements of Goa in India and on the coastal areas of Angola and Mozambique in southern Africa. The Dutch, who had been forced out of North America by the British in the seventeenth century, kept only small trading settlements in the Caribbean and Guiana, and concentrated their efforts on the development of the spice trade of the East Indies. The French and British, however, were determined to expand their colonial empires.

The French were preparing for eventual conflict with Britain in North America by creating a strong naval base at the mouth of the Saint Lawrence River and a series of forts along the Saint Lawrence and Great Lakes and in the Mississippi Valley. Although the French population of this vast area was very small, it was obvious that the purpose of the forts was to prevent the British from expanding westward beyond the Appalachian Mountains. At the same time, the French were striking alliances with local princes in India in order to restrict the activity of British trading stations, and perhaps ultimately to oust the British East India Company entirely.

The War of the Austrian Succession

War began in 1739 when Britain attacked Spain on the grounds that it was maltreating British sailors while searching their ships for contraband. France at once joined the war on the side of Spain. This colonial war, however, merged in 1740 with the continental struggle known as the War of the Austrian Succession.

Immediately after Frederick II of Prussia had seized the Austrian province of Silesia from the new Empress Maria Theresa, the Austrian throne was claimed by the rulers of Saxony, Bavaria, and Spain, on the ground that a female did not have the legal right to inherit the Austrian empire. Once again, France came to the aid of Spain and declared war on Austria. Only Britain and the Netherlands supported Maria Theresa. The Austrians, however, succeeded in holding back all their opponents. In 1748, both the continental and colonial wars ended in compromise. The British and French retained the fortified centers they had captured from each other. Frederick kept Silesia.

The Seven Years War

For the next seven years, the European states jockeyed for diplomatic advantage and prepared for a new war. The Seven Years War (1756–1763) was, however, very different from the previous war because a so-called diplomatic revolution preceded it. Britain abandoned Austria, and allied instead with its arch-rival Prussia. The Austrians, whose principal goal was the return of Silesia from Prussia, persuaded Russia, France, and Spain to join them in an alliance against Britain and Prussia. Frederick survived by shifting his armies desperately from frontier to frontier, supported with British money but not with British troops. He may, however, have been on the point of final collapse when in 1762, the new Russian tsar, Peter III, an emotionally unstable person who was an admirer of Frederick, shifted sides and offered Russian aid to Prussia. Once again, in spite of vast expenditure of money and lives, Austria failed to regain Silesia.

Meanwhile, the British, led by the fine wartime leader William Pitt from 1757 to 1761, won control of both the Atlantic and the Mediterranean, and were quickly able to conquer most of the French islands in the Caribbean. In India, the British took control of the rich province of Bengal, whose ruler had allied with the French. All the French trading posts were occupied without difficulty.

The Death of General Wolfe, by Benjamin West (1738–1820) *The British commander Wolfe was killed in his successful capture of the city of Quebec from the French in 1759.* (National Gallery of Canada, Ottawa; gift of the Duke of Westminster, 1918.)

In North America, the British first took the French forts in the Mississippi Valley. The Saint Lawrence Valley was taken as a result of the capture of Quebec in 1759 and Montreal in 1760. In the peace treaties that ended both the continental and colonial fighting, the French were allowed to keep two sugar-producing islands in the Caribbean, their West African slave centers, and their trading posts in India. But the British annexed all French possessions in North America to the east of the Mississippi River, except for the province of Louisiana, which was given to Spain.

The two great wars of mid-century had profound effects on the participants. Frederick the Great had added a rich province to his kingdom, but he had paid a very heavy price, widespread destruction where the invading armies had fought and the loss of half a million Prussian lives. But Prussia had established itself as a major rival to Austria for hegemony in Germany, and had begun the process by which, within 100 years, it would drive Austria from Germany entirely. Russia had nothing to show for its participation, except an increase in the state debt. Austria was also deeply indebted and had suffered heavy human losses, but it had survived; and, partly as a result of the reforms undertaken by Maria Theresa and Joseph II after the war, was soon able to recoup its strength. Britain was apparently the major gainer from the wars. It had driven the French from Canada and from all territory east of the Mississippi, and had won a free hand to expand its power in India. It had gained a number of Caribbean islands. But it too had spent heavily on the wars, partly for the campaigns in North America and India and partly in large subsidies to Frederick the Great. Government expenditures more than tripled in 1756–1761 alone. The government began during the Seven Years War and continued afterwards measures to compel the British colonies in North America to pay for their own defense; and these unwise moves (see Chapter 13) were to be the direct cause of the revolt of the American colonies in 1776. France was, by all measures, the greatest loser from the wars. It not only lost its territories in North America. It also lost the possibility of expanding in India. Even during the War of the Austrian Succession, it had trouble paying the costs of the fighting. Partway through the Seven Years War, the French government told the Austrians that it was bankrupt. The French foreign minister informed the king, after France had accepted Britain's terms for peace: "The humiliating peace of 1763 has given rise to the opinion in every nation that France has no longer any strength or resources. . . . It is enough to read the Treaty of Paris, and particularly the negotiations which precede it, to realize the ascendance which England has acquired over France and to judge how much that arrogant nation savors the pleasure of having humiliated us."[1] France was to obtain its revenge by aiding the British colonies in America gain their independence; but that effort was to push France into a fiscal crisis that made possible the revolution of 1789.

THE SOCIETY OF THE OLD REGIME

National Differences

When we turn to the societies that fought these wars and struggled with the problem of paying for them, we are first struck by the enormous differences among them.

The most obvious contrast was between Western and Eastern Europe. In Western Europe, the manorial system had broken down as early as the fourteenth and fifteenth centuries, leaving the peasantry free to acquire or rent land or to become paid employees. In Eastern Europe, the landlords had tied the peasantry more firmly than ever to the land as serfs, and greatly increased their dues in labor and goods. The power exercised by Eastern European landlords, as well as the duties they rendered to the state, were different from those of their counterparts in the West. Systems of government also varied enormously, from Russian autocracy to Dutch republicanism; and the differences became wider throughout the eighteenth century as, on the one hand, the British possessing classes increased their political power while, on the other, despotisms like the Prussian state increased their controls over even the wealthiest of their subjects.

Economically, too, the European states were following divergent courses.

[1] Cited in C. B. A. Behrens, *The Ancien Régime* (New York: Harcourt, Brace and World, 1967), p. 158.

The British again were at one extreme, as they began to revolutionize their agricultural and industrial techniques, while at the same time achieving dominance in colonial trade. At the opposite extreme lay the Poles, whose aristocracy seemed determined to prevent the development of commerce and to overburden their own agricultural producers with excessive demands for labor services and feudal dues.

These differences, and indeed many more—because regional and local diversity was a principle respected throughout eighteenth-century society and enforced by long-standing custom—are important because they explain why the various parts of Europe reacted in different ways to the call to revolution that was to sweep the continent in the last three decades of the century.

Continent-Wide Similarities

It can, however, be argued with some plausibility that the similarities among these societies were as important as, or even more important than, the differences. Or, to put it another way, the political and social characteristics to which we refer as the old regime were common to virtually all the states of Europe (with the exception of Britain and the Netherlands).

The term "old regime" was first used in France in the early 1790s to denote the society that was being transformed by the revolution that had begun in 1789, and hence it came to refer to French society as it was throughout the eighteenth century. But historians have broadened the usage of the term to apply to the society of Europe as a whole, because they see important similarities between the society of France and that of the other continental European states.

With the exception of a few small states, every country was governed by hereditary rulers, usually kings or emperors.

Organized religion played an important part throughout society. An established church was usually supported by the state, which excluded nonmembers from public office and often from higher education. Attempts to enforce uniformity varied greatly, however. The penalties on dissenters from the Church of England, whether Catholic or nonconforming Protestants, were largely political and social. In France, however, Protestant preachers could be punished by death. Men attending Protestant assemblies could be sent to the galleys and women to life imprisonment. The privileged position of the clergy, both Catholic and Protestant, encouraged the entry into the ministry of many with little vocation; and many churches were like the French, which in its upper levels at least had become, as Alfred Cobban remarked, "a system of out-door relief for the aristocracy." Literature in both Catholic and Protestant countries abounds with satirical descriptions of cynical, self-serving priests and parsons, with whom the everyday lives of most people were intimately involved, through the required rituals of baptism, marriage, and burial, and through education. By the last third of the century, there were many signs of widespread revolt against the despiritualized churches. Organizations within the churches held responsible for the corruption were attacked; in 1773 the pope even disbanded the Jesuits. New churches, such as the Methodist church in Britain, were formed to restore spiritual fervor. In the villages, however, there was a resurgence of old practices, such as the midsummer's night festival, that verged on the pagan.

A hereditary nobility, often divided between those deriving their status from military service in medieval times and those later appointed for state service, enjoyed a privileged position in this hierarchical society. In the whole of Europe, the nobility may have numbered about 4 million, while its upper ranks, the great magnates, included no more than 5000 families. The primary income of the nobility was from land, in the form of rents or income from sale of produce. A second source was pensions or grants from the ruler, which were usually obtainable only by those with regular access to the ruler at court. A third was salaries, usually drawn by younger sons from the professional positions that the nobility increasingly kept for members of its own ranks—the officer corps of the armies, the higher ranks of the bureaucracy, and the upper levels of the Church hierarchy. In all countries the nobility were set apart in fiscal, judicial, and other rights by their rank. In most countries, they paid few or no taxes. As a result, throughout Europe, it was the peasantry who carried the financial burden the other classes had used their privileges to avoid.

Other social groups also possessed privileges as a long-standing right. Guilds and corporations within the cities controlled manufacturing and trade. In the cities each trade or specialized craft had its own guild, such as the silversmiths,

The Forge, by Francisco Goya (1746–1828) *After years of success as Spain's court painter, Goya turned to the sufferings of ordinary people, whether in their working lives or in the disasters of war. (The Frick Collection.)*

the drapers, or the printers. Each was organized as a hierarchy, rising from apprentices to journeymen to masters, and imposed strict controls on recruitment into the guild. It also exercised minute control over quality of product and prices, and could use these powers to maintain monopoly and exclude competition. Although the purpose was a guaranteed income and stable production, the effect was to drive competitors into the countryside where guild regulations could be avoided. Small-scale entrepreneurs breaking into the textile trades, for example, would "put out" raw materials to be spun and woven in the homes of villagers.

Provincial assemblies or estates and such judicial bodies as the French parlements possessed rights that monarchs found hard to deny. The nobility of Austria and Hungary, for example, could use their control of the manorial courts to block the monarchy's attempts to reform serfdom.

Finally, throughout Europe, it was in the cities that the forces of change were gathering that would eventually challenge the privileged classes. Here were gathered a middle class that, growing wealthy from commerce or manufacturing, felt its way to social or political advancement blocked. Here also was a growing working class prone to violence when its food supply or its employment was threatened.

It was in France that the forces of revolution made the most far-reaching effort to transform the old regime, and for that reason it is useful to examine in more detail the characteristics of French society during the reigns of King Louis XV and King Louis XVI.

Condition of the French Peasantry

Of France's population of 26 million in 1789, 22 million were peasants. The hereditary nobility owned 20 percent of the land, the clergy 15 percent, and the middle classes 30 percent—that is, 8 percent of the population owned 65 percent of the land. The remaining 35 percent of the land was owned by the peasantry. But only one-half of the peasants were landowners, and they usually had plots so small and infertile that it was impossible to support a family from their produce. As a result, both the landless peasants and many peasant landowners worked most of the time on land owned by others, as day laborers, sharecroppers, or renters, and developed a passion to take legal possession of the land they worked.

The peasantry was bitterly annoyed at the burdens that seemed to be placed upon it alone, both for the support of the state through taxation and the support of the idle rich through their labor and payment of customary dues. The state imposed upon the peasantry the major part of the land tax, which had to be paid by each village in a lump sum. It was collected by fellow villagers, who spent the year spying on the others, and could be foiled only by extreme ingenuity in hiding one's produce. The state also imposed an array of indirect taxes that were even harder to avoid. They included a salt tax, evasion of which could be punished by imprisonment or service in the galleys, and excise taxes on wine, tobacco, and leather. Finally, the state required the peasants to work on the roads and, if selected by lot, to do military service. The Church also was paid between one-twelfth and one-twentieth of the peasant's produce, and more than half of this payment was used to support absentee bishops. The local landlords, whether they were hereditary aristocrats or middle class people who had recently purchased the land, also collected customary dues, such as payments for use of the mill or winepress. In addition, the lord enjoyed the right to hunt over the peasant's land and to graze animals on part of it.

For all these payments, the peasants saw no direct benefit to themselves. The state's income was spent almost entirely on the military, on interest on the state debt, and on pensions for the aristocracy. Attempts to alleviate rural suffering, as in times of famine, were small and ill-financed. The Church was increasingly derelict in its social duties during the eighteenth century. The landlords, who were the class most hated by the peasantry, did little for their localities, unlike the English gentry, who as justices of the peace were responsible for administration and justice in their own districts.

The growth in the peasant population by some 2 million in the twenty years before the revolution increased the danger of famine. Social historians, working on the charitable attempts to relieve the consequences of the poverty and on the crime born of desperation, have documented the results of this widespread destitution. Children were the worst sufferers. Unwanted children were exposed to die, or were handed over to orphanages. Professional porters walked hundreds of miles to Paris to deposit babies in the city's foundlings' hospitals. Peasant women facing starvation trained their children to be beggars or became full-time beggars themselves. Many became prostitutes. Others joined the hundreds of gangs of thieves and smugglers who roamed the countryside. The existence of deep poverty in every part of the country was one of the most dangerous challenges to the stability of the old regime.

Working-Class Grievances

The urban working class of France, which may have numbered a little over 2 million by the middle of the century, had its own grievances against the social system. The first and overriding consideration was a fear of lack of food, and especially of bread. Before the eighteenth century, grain sales had been localized, and strictly supervised by the authorities. Before sales to outsiders, the local poor had been permitted to buy their necessities at fixed, fair prices. In the eighteenth century, however, the growth of national marketing through large-scale jobbers, while theoretically permitting greater economic efficiency, worked to the disadvantage of the poor. Crops were bought up even before being harvested. Prices fluctuated wildly in relation to supply, and short-term rises of 300 percent were common. Urban riots in France throughout the eighteenth century coincided with rises in the price of bread or with outright famine,

especially for the one-third of the urban population eking out a marginal existence at a level of bare subsistence. Usually, the mob would seize the food
supplies, put them on sale at what it regarded as a fair price, and sometimes
pay the merchant the proceeds. But as the century progressed the riots became
increasingly violent, especially in Paris, which, as by far the largest city, was
the most difficult to keep supplied. In the Flour War in 1777, the mob seized
the markets and granaries of central Paris, until the government turned the
military against them to restore order.

Second, the workers were discontented at the low wages paid, especially
to day laborers, and at the difficulty of advancing in those crafts controlled by
the surviving guilds. The most excitable of the urban poor were workers employed at or below subsistence wages. Riots were frequent among such groups
as the women in the fishmarkets, artisans in trades such as furniture making,
and dockworkers. Fear of unemployment frequently united these groups against
their employers. When famine and unemployment threatened, as in Paris in
1787–1789, radical leaders could easily find a readily manipulable crowd that
could be launched against the established authorities.

The Bourgeoisie

The French bourgeoisie grew steadily richer during the eighteenth century,
especially between 1730 and 1770. The middle class was sharply divided between those engaged in the professions, especially in law, and those engaged
in business, commerce, and finance.

The prestige of the professional groups remained higher than that of the
business classes, since the French middle class knew that for upward mobility
in society, and especially entry into the nobility, it was essential to move out
from what was regarded as sordid money making. Most successful business
people sought to send their children into the professions and to buy landed
estates for themselves.

Despite the damaging effect of this attitude upon French economic growth,
the French business classes were taking advantage of every opportunity to
increase their wealth. They profited from government inefficiency, since private
individuals were paid by the state to carry out many of the functions that it
was incapable of fulfilling. Even taxes were collected privately, by the "farmers-
general" and an army of collectors. Private financiers supplied the ships for
overseas colonization, uniforms and weapons of the army, and even bullion for
the currency.

The middle class also profited from the economic measures taken by Colbert
and carried on by his successors to a lesser degree in the eighteenth century.
Better roads and canals had improved internal trade. Private companies varying
from luxury manufacturers to owners of coal mines and iron foundries were
subsidized by the government. Acquisition of an overseas empire especially
enriched the merchant class of the cities of the Atlantic and Channel coasts.
Profits came from the Canadian fur trade and the fisheries off Newfoundland.

But the greatest wealth derived from the sale of West African slaves in the Caribbean and from the sale in France of sugar from the islands of Martinique and Guadeloupe and of the tropical products of India. The British, moreover, had not annexed the most profitable of the French possessions in the Caribbean, West Africa, or India, and these profits continued after the Seven Years War. Thus the French middle class was relatively content with its economic position.

However, in the middle of the century they found that their social advancement was being blocked by the upper nobility, which had previously been open to new recruits from the more successful of the middle classes. This increased restrictiveness was part of a Europe-wide movement by the nobility to safeguard their privileges and to regain part of the power they had lost to the monarchy in the previous two centuries. Advancement into the higher levels of the army, the Church, the legal profession, and especially into the royal court was deliberately restricted to members of the upper nobility. A barrier was erected against the social ambitions of the middle classes and even of the lesser nobility, who as a result ceased to be socially conservative. These groups accepted the political reforms advocated by the Enlightenment thinkers, and were prepared to support profound constitutional changes that would open again to them the way of social advancement. This resentment against the privileged class coincided with the breakdown of the financial administration of the state, as a result of the accumulated expenses of the European and overseas wars. Since the middle classes held most of the government bonds that had been sold to finance the wars, they were personally threatened by the possible bankruptcy of the state, and they therefore felt it was essential that the country be given an efficient administration controlled by them as a way of safeguarding their own financial security.

Church Privileges

The privileged classes remained impervious to this growing disaffection. The Church was deeply divided between the small number of archbishops, bishops, and abbots drawn mainly from the nobility, who lived in Paris and Versailles rather than in their dioceses, and the lower clergy, who carried out all the pastoral duties. The lower clergy were deeply embittered at the need to collect tithes for their absentee superiors, whose income has been estimated to exceed that of the lower clergy by 140 to 1. At the same time, the bright young clerics in the seminaries and cathedral chapters were outraged that newly enforced restriction of higher ecclesiastical rank to those of noble rank had for the first time cut off the possibility of advancement to those of poor or middle-class backgrounds.

Divisions Within the French Nobility

The French nobility probably numbered about 400,000, but a few hundred, known as *Les Grands* (The Great), possessed the major share of the class's wealth. They lived in Versailles and Paris, maintained hundreds of servants, and took part in the expensive social life of the court. As a result of their presence near the king, they were able to take a large share of the perquisites of the court, such as the high appointments in the Church or of provincial governorships. The nobility was, however, increasingly determined to profit from the weakness of King Louis XV and try to regain the political powers it had lost under Richelieu and Louis XIV. In their battle to retain their fiscal privileges against the reforming efforts of the leading finance ministers of both Louis XV and Louis XVI, the nobles reasserted their political independence from the monarchy. By doing so, they prevented the financial reform of the state, which meant above all equitable taxation, and thereby made revolution inevitable.

Reform Plans Foiled

The administrative structure of the French monarchy in the eighteenth century has been described as resembling "a palace that had been built piecemeal by adding rooms and wings without any renovation of the original structure or any attempt to harmonize the whole."[2] A centralized absolutism, working in the provinces through governors called intendants, backed by a largely middle-class bureaucracy, had tamed the nobility and ended most of its political powers. The Estates General, the representative body that had met regularly from the fifteenth to the early seventeenth century, had held its last meetings in 1614, and was no longer considered a potential source of opposition to royal power. Appointments in the Church had been confided to the king by the pope since 1516, enabling him to circumvent another potential source of opposition. But the apparently firm structure of French absolutism, in the final mold given to it in the seventeenth century by Cardinal Richelieu and Louis XIV, contained many mechanisms by which the will of the king could be frustrated, not least when he might seek to increase royal revenues by reforming the country's social and financial structure.

Ecomomic changes could be hampered by local laws respecting commerce and by the powers of the guilds. A number of provinces, mostly on the French borders, administered many of their own affairs through provincial parliaments, called estates, dominated by the local aristocracy and clergy. More important, however, were the assembly of the Catholic bishops and archbishops, which retained the right to grant (or deny) the king a gift for the support of the state, and the judicial bodies known as parlements in Paris and the provinces.

The parlements had been created, in the thirteenth century in Paris and in later centuries in the provinces, for the purpose of supervising lower courts and registering royal decrees, as well as carrying out such police matters as control

---

[2] Gordon Wright, *France in Modern Times: From the Enlightenment to the Present*, 3d ed. (New York: W. W. Norton, 1981), p. 8.

of censorship or religious observances. But they had developed a political role by refusing at times to register royal edicts on grounds that they contravened previous royal rulings or the traditional constitution and by issuing a "remonstrance" stating their reasons for their refusal. The king, in turn, could force them to register his edict by appearing in person, or by intimidating them by exiling individual members or the whole parlement to another part of the country. The Church hierarchy and the parlements were throughout most of the eighteenth century able to foil the monarchy's plans for tax reform.

In 1749, to cover the costs of the War of the Austrian Succession, the government imposed a 5 percent tax on all sources of income. This was the first time that the nobility and clergy had been required to pay a direct tax, and the crown intended to impose it regularly in peacetime. Faced by the united opposition of the nobility, the clergy, and the professional classes, the government was forced to drop the tax. Even more opposition was roused by the new series of taxes imposed to pay for the Seven Years' War, since they included not only the 5 percent tax but also a tax on the income from government office, and were followed by far-reaching administrative reforms. In 1774, however, the new King Louis XVI bowed to the opponents of the fiscal changes, and dismissed the reforming ministers.

He was still, however, faced with the urgent need for income. Minister after minister tried new methods of increasing state revenues, each finding his reform plans opposed by the nobility in the court or by the lawyers in the parlements, as the state moved closer to default. Finally, in 1786, faced with

"Equality Before Taxation." The cartoon shows how the burden of the national debt would be carried equally by nobles, clergy, and the "third estate" of all other citizens if all paid a national tax. (French Embassy Press and Information Division.)

the vast expenses of participation in the American War of Independence, which tripled the interest owing on the national debt, the finance minister proposed to the king that, instead of forcing through reforms against the will of the privileged classes, he should persuade them to tax themselves. The king called an Assembly of Notables, composed of the nobility, the upper clergy, and high administrators, which met in 1787. This assembly demanded that power should be dispersed among the provincial assemblies, which they themselves could dominate, and refused the tax reforms.

Disappointed in the Assembly of Notables, the king tried to force the parlement of Paris to register a new land tax that applied equally to all classes. The parlement won wide popular support by refusing the edict on the grounds that there should be no taxation without representation. The king thereupon capitulated, and accepted the demand of both the Assembly of Notables and the parlement that he should call the Estates General, through which the upper classes believed they could constitutionally take the power of governing France. The First Estate, or assembly, representing the clergy, and the Second Estate, representing the nobility, were to be chosen directly by the clergy and nobles in the provincial assemblies. For the Third Estate, theoretically representing everyone else, all male taxpayers over the age of twenty-five were to choose local electors who would then meet to pick the actual representatives to be sent to Versailles. The electors picked almost entirely middle-class professional people, such as lawyers or local officials, as well as a few clergy and even lesser nobles. This Third Estate, dominated by the discontented middle classes, was quickly to take over the Estates General and change a movement for reform into a revolution.

SUGGESTED READINGS

General Introductions

The similarities between the monarchies of the eighteenth century are clear in Mathew S. Anderson, *Eighteenth Century Europe, 1718–1789* (1976), and Reginald J. White, *Europe in the Eighteenth Century* (1965). The hierarchical division of society is analyzed by William Doyle, *The Old European Order, 1660–1800* (1978).

Eighteenth-Century Wars

Two older surveys are still useful: Penfield Roberts, *The Quest for Security, 1715–1740* (1947), and Walter L. Dorn, *Competition for Empire, 1740–1763* (1940). A more recent synthesis is Geoffrey Symcox, *War, Diplomacy, and Imperialism, 1618–1763* (1974).

The Old Regime

C. B. A. Behrens, *The Ancien Régime* (1967), is a subtle introduction to French society. On the different classes, see Franklin L. Ford, *Robe and Sword: The Regrouping of the French Aristocracy After Louis XIV* (1953); Elinor G. Barber, *The Bourgeoisie in Eighteenth Century*

France (1967); Olwen Hufton, *The Poor of Eighteenth Century France 1750–1789* (1972); and Jeffrey Kaplow, *The Names of Kings, The Parisian Laboring Poor in the Eighteenth Century* (1972). There are good essays on the status of women in the old regime, and in particular on Diderot's less-than-enlightened views on this one issue, in Eve Jacobs et al., eds., *Women and Society in Eighteenth-Century France* (1979), and Paul Fritz and Richard Morton, eds., *Women in the 18th Century and Other Essays* (1976).

For the old regime as it existed in the other states of Europe, a detailed introduction is given in E. N. Williams, *The Ancien Régime in Europe: Government and Society in the Major States 1648–1789* (1970). Essays on individual countries are grouped in Albert Goodwin, ed., *The European Nobility in the Eighteenth Century* (1967). The varying conditions of the peasantry can be compared in Jerome Blum, *European Peasantry from the Fifteenth to the Nineteenth Century* (1978).

The Enlightened Despots

John G. Gagliardo, *Enlightened Despotism* (1967), is a brief, sound introduction. On the predecessors of Frederick the Great in Prussia, begin with the scholarly survey of Francis L. Carsten, *The Origins of Prussia* (1954); make the acquaintance of the true founder of Prussian absolutism, in Ferdinand Schevill, *The Great Elector* (1947); and enjoy some of the idiosyncracies of King Frederick William I, in Robert R. Ergang, *The Potsdam Führer*, (1941; 1972). Gerhard Ritter gives a penetrating analysis of Frederick's motives in *Frederick the Great* (1968). The most comprehensive biography is George P. Good, *Frederick the Great: The Ruler, the Writer, the Man* (1947). On Prussia's principal institution, see Gordon Craig, *The Politics of the Prussian Army, 1640–1945* (1964).

Catherine II's foreign policy is emphasized in G. S. Thomson, *Catherine the Great and the Expansion of Russia* (1962), her policies at home in Isabel de Madariaga, *Russia in the Age of Catherine the Great* (1981). The early reforms in Austria are described in C. A. Macartney, *Maria Theresa and the House of Austria* (1969). The ambitious failures of her son are praised by Saul K. Padover, *The Revolutionary Emperor, Joseph the Second, 1741–1790* (1934; 1967), and briefly summarized in T. Blanning, *Joseph the Second and Enlightened Despotism* (1970).

part V

Revolution and Reaction

Liberty Leading the People, July 28, 1830, by Eugène Delacroix (1799–1863) *The union of the classes of Paris in the overthrow of the reactionary King Charles X.* (Musée National du Louvre/ Giraudon-Art Resource.)

REVOLUTION AND REACTION

Dates	Political & Military Events	Social, Economic, & Demographic Events	Religion & Philosophy	Art, Architecture, Literature, & Music	Science & Technology
1760	George III, Britain (1760–1820)	French and British exploration of South Pacific			Factory system spreads in Britain
1764					Hargreaves' spinning jenny
1769					Watts' steam engine
1770				d. Boucher	
1776	American Revolution (1776–1783)				
1783	William Pitt the Younger, Prime Minister, Britain				
1785				David, *Oath of the Horatii*; Mozart, *Marriage of Figaro*	
1787	U.S. Constitution adopted				
1789	Meeting of French Estates General; Taking of the Bastille	Serfdom and feudal dues abolished in France			
1790			Civil constitution of the Clergy, France; Burke, *Reflections on the Revolution*		
1791				d. Mozart	Metric system adopted, France
1792	Louis XVI deposed (France)				
1793	Reign of Terror in France (1793–94)				Eli Whitney's cotton gin
1798			Malthus, *Principles of Population*	Wordsworth, Coleridge, *Lyrical Ballads*	

Date	Politics	Society/Economy	Religion	Arts & Letters/Music	Science & Technology
1799	Napoleon seizes power, France				
1801		Napoleon reorganizes French legal and administrative system			Jacquard loom (France)
1802	Temporary peace (1802–1803)		Napoleon's concordat with Pope	Chateaubriand, *Genius of Christianity*	Krupp company develops crucible steel
1804	Napoleon crowned emperor, France				
1805	Battle of Austerlitz; Battle of Trafalgar			Beethoven, *Third Symphony (Eroica)*	
1806	Abolition of Holy Roman Empire				
1807	Treaty of Tilsit of France and Russia	Napoleon imposes Continental System			Fulton's steamship, New York
1808	French invade Spain	Nationalist revolt against Napoleon begins			
1809	Metternich, Chancellor, Austria (1809–48)			d. Haydn	
1811		Luddites attack machines (England)			
1812	French invade Russia; U.S. declares war on Britain				
1814	Louis XVIII, France (1814–24)				
1815	Battle of Waterloo; Congress of Vienna	Corn Laws, Britain; industrialization begins in Europe			
1819	Carlsbad Decrees	Factory Act, Britain			
1829			Catholic Emancipation Act, Britain		
1830	Revolution in France; Louis Philippe, (1830–48)		Conservative Catholic reaction in France	Hugo, *Hernani*; Delacroix, *Liberty Leading the People*	Rocket railroad locomotive

(continued)

REVOLUTION AND REACTION (continued)

Dates	Political & Military Events	Social, Economic, & Demographic Events	Religion & Philosophy	Art, Architecture, Literature, & Music	Science & Technology
1832	Reform Bill, Britain			d. Goethe	
1833		Abolition of slavery in British Empire			
1835	Ferdinand I, Austria (1835–48)			Rebuilding Houses of Parliament, London	
1837	Victoria, Britain (1837–1901)		d. Fourier		
1840	Frederick-William IV, Prussia (1840–61)	Chartist agitation, Britain	Proudhon, *What is Property?*; Blanc, *Organization of Work*		French railroad system begun (1840s)
1844			Engels, *Condition of the Working Class*		Morse's telegraph
1845					
1846		Repeal of Corn Laws, Britain			
1848	Revolutions throughout Europe Francis Joseph, Austria (1848–1916)		*Communist Manifesto*		

13

The Atlantic Revolution, 1776–1815

The Enlightenment thinkers had been misleadingly reformist in appearance. Their revolutionary views on virtually every aspect of human society had been discussed calmly in the urbane atmosphere of Rococo living rooms with the very nobility whose privileges would be swept away if the Enlightenment's ideas were put into practice. Their views had even been espoused in principle by despotic rulers to whom such notions as the equality of all human beings or the derivation of power from the consent of the governed were anathema. But polite discussions in salons and the selective application of the Enlightenment's ideas by despots were insufficient. In many parts of Europe and North America, large numbers of people were determined to carry out what one recent historian has called a "democratic revolution" whose purpose was to assert "the principle that public power must arise from those over whom it is exercised."[1]

Revolutions inspired by this principle broke out in a chain reaction— in Corsica in 1755; in the thirteen British colonies of North America in 1776; in France and Belgium in 1789; in Poland in 1791; in Holland in 1795; in Italy in 1796; in Switzerland in 1798; in Latin America between 1810 and 1825; and in Spain in 1812. Since these revolutions on both sides of the Atlantic were all based on the demand that government should be responsible to the governed, historians have spoken of these revolutions as one "Atlantic revolution," and, borrowing a term first used in Spain in the 1820s, have labeled those demanding

[1] Robert R. Palmer, *The Age of the Democratic Revolution; A Political History of Europe and America, 1760–1800, Vol. 1. The Challenge* (Princeton, N.J.: Princeton University Press, 1969), p. 185.

parliamentary self-government "liberals." Of these revolutions the most important and the most closely connected were the American and the French revolutions.

In 1792, the revolutionary government of France declared a crusade for the extension of the democratic revolution into the despotic countries of Europe. At first welcomed by liberals in the countries they invaded, their rule soon provoked resentment, especially after the revolutionary government had been converted into a barely disguised dictatorship by Napoleon in 1799. Opposition to Napoleonic rule stimulated the forces of nationalism in almost every country of Europe. In countries already united, such as England or Spain, nationalism merely roused the determination to fight more strongly against the French. But in areas where peoples did not possess their own nation-state, the sentiment of nationalism become revolutionary in a political sense. These areas were of two kinds. In the one, a nation was divided into a number of smaller states, and desired to be united. In the other, one state was formed of a number of different nationalities who desired the break-up of that state into its component nationalities. Germany and Italy were the principal examples of the former. Germany was divided in 1789 into more than 350 states; Italy was fragmented into ten. The Austrian empire was the foremost example of the latter. In the Austrian empire, ruled by a German-speaking minority, were Poles, Rumanians, Czechs, South Slavs, Italians, and Hungarians, all of whom desired their own nation-state. Most nationalists were strongly liberal at least until the middle of the nineteenth century, and when they opposed French rule under Napoleon I, it was on the grounds that the French had ceased to be liberal.

The conservative monarchs of Europe enlisted the forces of nationalism to defeat the French, but from 1815 on, under the leadership of the Austrian chancellor, Prince Clemens von Metternich, engaged in a reactionary policy of conservatism whose purpose was to combat at the same time both liberalism and nationalism. In this chapter we shall consider the advances of liberalism through the American and French revolutions, and the nationalism roused in opposition to French rule. In Chapter 15 we shall turn to the attempts of conservatism to combat liberalism and nationalism.

THE LIBERAL REVOLUTION IN THE THIRTEEN COLONIES

Americans in the thirteen British colonies were fascinated by a minor revolt that broke out in 1755 on the small island of Corsica in the Mediterranean and by its charismatic leader Pasquale Paoli, who was attempting to oust the Genoese who had misgoverned the island for the past four centuries. Paoli created a democratic government at the inland town of Corte, founded a new university, and called a representative assembly. Paoli's cause was publicized with great effect in England and America by James Boswell, who wrote a paean to Paoli after visiting him at his new capital. Boswell saw Paoli as the Enlightenment personified, and his cause was taken up in France by such *philosophes* as Voltaire and Rousseau. The Genoese responded by selling Corsica to France in 1768. The French, who had acquired Corsica in part to counterbalance their losses in North America, sent a large army, which easily defeated Paoli's tiny force in 1769. Paoli himself escaped to England, and in his noble character remained for many the reminder that the liberal revolution had begun.

Causes of the Revolution

Meanwhile, the thirteen American colonies were moving toward revolution for their own reasons. Until 1763, most white colonists in America had been largely satisfied with their status. Land was plentiful since settlers could move westward. Even in the cities there were few poor, and as a result virtually every American colonist had the feeling that economic betterment was available in reward for effort. There is even some evidence that women enjoyed greater property rights and freedom to engage in business as well as greater equality within the family than in Europe; but there is, however, no evidence that they supported the revolution against British rule to safeguard their status as women. Moreover, the colonists enjoyed widespread political power. They had been able to cut back the strength of the royal governors and of the nominated upper houses, and in most colonies an elected lower house exercised considerable power. These assemblies, as well as such local government institutions as town meetings, were places where new people could rise to political importance.

Of all the societies of the eighteenth century, the American colonies represented a place where the citizens felt they already possessed the right of self-government and social and economic freedom. Moreover, although the British government had embraced the theory of mercantilism, it had wisely, or perhaps unthinkingly, permitted the colonies to go their own way, without enforcing very strictly the various curbs on colonial production and trade that should have been an essential part of mercantilist policy. Even where the colonies had grievances, they varied enormously from colony to colony. The planters of the South were deeply in debt to London merchants, and would gladly have repudiated those debts. Philadelphia and Boston merchants had turned to smuggling to avoid restrictions on the area where they could trade. Frontiers people objected to measures to protect the Indians. But despite common complaints, it seemed unlikely that the colonists, spread thin in a new land more than 1200 miles long, would ever collaborate sufficiently to throw off British rule.

After the annexation of the French possessions in North America in 1763, however, the British government decided to tighten up its administration in America, and thereby persuaded the colonists that it was undertaking a sinister program to deprive them of the economic and political liberties they already enjoyed. In this sense the American revolution was a conservative (but liberal) revolution against an innovating British government. To protect the Indians, the British government prohibited settlement by the colonists beyond the Appalachian Mountains. They thereby annoyed not only the frontiers people, but all who had intended to open up western land or merely to invest in it. To pay for the British army that was defending the colonists in America, the British government passed the Stamp Act, which was to raise revenue by the sale of stamps to be fastened to legal documents and newspapers. To the colonists the Stamp Act was "taxation without representation," the imposition through the enforced purchase of the stamps of a tax for which they had not voted. A similar criticism was made of the imposition of import duties that were collected on goods such as tea coming into the colonies. The most unwise act was, however, the British attempt to coerce the colonies into obedience, after mobs had attacked the stamp sellers and thrown a load of tea into Boston Harbor. When the government closed the port of Boston, it seemed the final proof that the British intended to destroy all the colonists' cherished freedoms, and it led directly to the revolution against British rule.

By that point, the colonists were ready not merely to demand a change in British policy but to break their ties with the British people. Benjamin Franklin wrote:

> When I consider the extreme corruption prevalent among all orders of men in this old, rotten state, and the glorious public virtue so predominant in our rising country; I cannot but apprehend more mischief than benefit from a closer union. I fear that they will drag us after them in all the plundering wars which their desperate circumstances, injustice, and rapacity may prompt them to undertake; and their wide-wasting prodigality and profusion is a gulf that will swallow up every aid we may distress ourselves to afford them.[2]

The coastal cities were the force that organized the united effort of the colonists. The cities were in close contact with each other through correspondence societies and through coastal trade. Through their clubs, they had absorbed the teachings of the Enlightenment thinkers, especially the view of John Locke that government enters a "contract" with the governed for the main purpose of safeguarding their "unalienable rights" to life, liberty, and property; and they had decided that Britain had broken that contract.

Many men from the cities' middle classes were prepared to lead mob violence through societies such as the Sons of Liberty, in order to get the insurrection started, while women planned the boycott of British goods through the Daughters of Liberty. Philadelphia was recognized as the city that must organize the revolution, even though it was in Boston and the nearby towns of Lexington and Concord that the first shots of the war were fired. Hence, it was in Philadelphia that the Continental Congress met in 1774 to demand that the British recognize their right to legislate for themselves. In 1776, after two years of

[2] Cited in Bernard Bailyn, *The Ideological Origins of the American Revolution* (Cambridge, Mass.: Harvard University Press, 1967), p. 136.

The Second Continental Congress, by Edward Savage (1761–1817) *Meeting in the State House in Philadelphia, the Congress representing the thirteen colonies approved the Declaration of Independence on July 4, 1776.* (National Portrait Gallery, Smithsonian Institution, Washington, D.C.)

fruitless negotiation with the British, a second Continental Congress decided that a complete break with Britain was the only course of action possible. On July 4, 1776, it adopted the Declaration of Independence written by Thomas Jefferson, which not only proclaimed that "all men are created equal" but broadened Locke's definition of "unalienable rights" to "Life, Liberty, and the Pursuit of Happiness." They thereby gave notice to the world that the ideas of the Enlightenment had ceased to be debating topics for drawing rooms, and had become revolutionary doctrines that could bring about change, by war, if necessary.

The Revolutionary War and the Constitution

The British appeared to have far superior forces, 50,000 British troops and 30,000 German mercenaries against a colonial army of 5000, backed by local militia and headed by such inexperienced generals as the Virginia squire, George Washington. The British generals proved incompetent, however; European strategies and tactics were ineffective in the American terrain; and supplies had to be obtained over 3000 miles of ocean. And, after the first major British defeat at

379

Saratoga in 1777, the French and later the Spanish joined the war on the colonists' side. The French fleet was partly responsible for enabling the Americans to pin down the main British army at Yorktown in 1781, where it was forced to surrender. Although Britain held on to its other possessions against French and Spanish attack, in 1783 it conceded independence to its thirteen American colonies. The American colonists had thus established, to the satisfaction of all supporters of the Enlightenment, that it was possible for a small people to win the right of self-government against a major imperial power.

By adopting a new federal Constitution in 1787, the members of the Constitutional Convention showed how the political theories of the Enlightenment could be used as the framework for a practical, republican form of government when a new nation determines to make a fresh start. They took from Montesquieu the view that there should be a separation of powers among the legislature, the executive, and the judiciary, and that there should be "checks and balances" by which one power within the constitutional framework would prevent abuses by another. But, for efficiency of government, they gave both the president and the senate stronger powers than most Enlightenment political philosophers would have favored. Yet by encouraging the electoral principle in the widest sense and by adding ten Amendments to the Constitution in 1791 that constituted a "bill of rights" guaranteeing individual liberties, the Constitution makers believed that they had made impossible an abuse of their powers by either the executive or the legislature and created an instrument of government that was not only idealistic but workable.

The successful conclusion of the war of the American revolution and the reassertion at the Constitutional Convention of 1787 that constitutional power derives from the people caused a shock wave to pass through Europe. Europeans accepted what the Americans themselves believed, that they had fought for liberties they already possessed against a government that was trying to take them away. But the fact that the Americans were a people of immigrants from several European countries living in a new environment gave their revolution a more universal appeal than if they had been solely English. It was, in the European view, humanity in the highest sense of the Enlightenment that was carrying through the revolution, and not simply a group of English colonists.

THE FRENCH REVOLUTION

Nowhere was the impact of the American revolution felt more deeply than in Paris. French *philosophes* had believed, especially since the publication by the French author, Hector Saint-Jean de Crèvecoeur, of *Letters of an American Farmer*, that the American environment also had the qualities of unspoiled nature that the explorer Louis Antoine Bougainville had found in Tahiti in 1768. The American colonists had skillfully played upon this notion. The most effective pro-

The Oath of the Horatii, by (Jacques Louis David (1748–1825) *In the seventh century* B.C., *the three Horatius brothers swore to defend Rome in single combat with three rival warriors. David's picture (1785) was interpreted as an allegory of American self-sacrifice.* (Musée National du Louvre/ Giraudon-Art Resource.)

pagandist had been Benjamin Franklin, who had been sent by the Continental Congress as its representative to the French government. Franklin's simple kindliness and homespun wisdom were precisely the kind of natural gentility the French expected of a product of the American environment. Franklin slipped from salon to salon, spreading the message of the American revolution. French soldiers, such as the Marquis de Lafayette, returning from the war in America, confirmed that American society was just as the French wanted to believe it. A great wave of pro-American feeling spread through France in the 1780s. France's finest sculptor, Jean-Antoine Houdon, carved busts of Franklin and Washington, and in 1785 the painter Jacques-Louis David (1748–1825), who was leading a classical revolt against Rococo painting, summarized the feeling of admiration for America's sacrifices in the painting *The Oath of the Horatii.* What was important in the immediate sense was the fact that helping the Americans had brought the French government to the edge of bankruptcy, which the king hoped to avert by asking for the grant of taxes by the Estates General, the traditional parliament of the country, which had not met since 1614. In August 1788, the king ordered elections to be held for an Estate General that was to meet in

Versailles in May 1789. In that way, he unwittingly called into being the body that was to begin the revolution.

Causes of the Revolution

In the ten years between the meeting of the Estates General and the seizure of power by Napoleon in 1799, the revolution went through four principal phases, each of which brought new leaders, with new programs, into power. The first phase, constitutional monarchy from 1789 to 1792, was dominated by the middle class, the group most imbued with the ideals of the Enlightenment. In the second phase, from 1792 to 1793, France was ruled by the Girondins, a provincial group dedicated to the increase of personal freedom in France by a reduction of the power of Paris and the spread of the democratic revolution throughout Europe by the force of arms. During the third phase in 1793–1794, France was goverened by a dictatorship of the lower middle class and working class of Paris, in a Reign of Terror dominated by the Jacobin party. Finally, between 1794 and 1799, middle-class rule was restored, but proved both corrupt and inefficient.

The goals of each group in French society remained quite constant throughout this ten-year period. The nobility wanted a return to the economic privileges and political power they had enjoyed before the reign of Louis XIV. The middle classes desired an efficient financial administration, the end of barriers to their own advancement in society, and political power. The working class in the cities demanded a secure food supply and regular work. The peasants sought the abolition of feudalism, lower taxes, and more land. Women demanded legal and political equality, educational opportunity, greater rights within the marriage, and the possibility of divorce.

But it is important not to oversimplify a very complex situation. Revolution developed a force of its own. Once revolution had started, it seemed impossible to stop the movement to greater and greater political extemism, which had the effect of producing an equally violent conservative reaction. The fluctuating fortunes of the war in Europe produced constant political agitation. Personal ambition underlay seemingly incongruous political alliances. Lust for power or blood may have provoked some of the more extreme violence. And once again the central role of Paris underlay every situation.

To control Paris was to control the course of the revolution; and hence it was in the streets of Paris that the greatest confrontations took place. Each new phase of revolution began with a takeover of Paris by force. The constitutional monarchy came to an end when a Paris mob stormed the Tuileries palace in August and massacred all prisoners in the jails in September 1792. Girondin rule ended when the Paris mob drove the Girondins out of the Convention assembly. The Reign of Terror was stopped when its leader Robespierre was overthrown by a Paris uprising. And the middle-class rule of the Directory ended in 1799 when Napoleon seized control of Paris.

The Tennis Court Oath, by David *On June 20, 1789, the Third Estate, finding its meeting hall closed, adjourned to the royal tennis court where they swore never to disband before a constitution was written.* (Giraudon/Art Resource.)

Constitutional Monarchy, 1789–1792

When the Estates General met in May 1789, an effort was made to copy the procedures of 1614, with the members of the estates even dressing in the same costumes. The First Estate represented the clergy, and included many parish priests as well as the upper hierarchy of the Church. The Second Estate represented the aristocracy, but included many poorer nobles from the provinces and did not represent merely the higher nobility from Versailles. The Third Estate, which was twice the size of each of the others, was supposed to represent the rest of the French population, but consisted mainly of lawyers, administrators, and intellectuals. The Third Estate was deeply imbued with the reforming ideals of the Enlightenment, and intended to put them into force. They found, however, that the king had very little enthusiasm for them or for reform. He refused to let the three estates meet together and vote as one assembly, as the Third Estate demanded. The Third Estate replied in June by declaring that it was the National Assembly, and invited the other estates to join it. The First Estate agreed to do so, and the king, fearing growing violence in the provinces and the threat of intervention from Paris, ordered the nobles to join as well. The new assembly, which had taken the title of National Constituent Assembly, immediately declared that it proposed to write a constitution for the kingdom.

383

Violence in Paris and the provinces, however, was sweeping the revolution into more radical courses than the reformers in Versailles had expected. The crowd in Paris, dangerously short of food, was roaming the streets, arming itself with weapons from gunsmiths and armories. Increasingly extreme leaders were speaking out in the municipal government. When the king gathered mercenary Swiss and German troops near Paris, the crowd, told by its leaders that the king was about to massacre them, stormed the state prison of the Bastille, where they murdered most of the guards. The Bastille, which had symbolized to most French people the worst aspect of royal despotism, was torn down stone by stone, even though only seven prisoners had been found in it.

The situation was even more serious in the provinces, where the peasantry had begun burning chateaux, destroying feudal records, and seizing stocks of wheat. The National Assembly decided to appease the peasants; in a dramatic session on the night of August 4, 1789, they attempted to pass a large part of the reform program of the Enlightenment. They abolished serfdom and put an end to feudal dues. Tithe payments to the Church were forbidden. All classes were to pay taxes. Advancement in the army and navy was to be open to all, irrespective of class. On August 27, with a gesture toward the American Revolution, the Assembly passed the Declaration of the Rights of Man and of the Citizen. These rights included freedom of speech, press, and assembly; freedom from arbitrary arrest; and the "sacred and inviolable right" to enjoy one's own property. (When in 1791 Olympe de Gouges issued a Declaration of the Rights of Woman and the Citizen, she was not at first taken seriously. In 1793, she was guillotined.)

These gestures meant little to the working class of Paris. In October, led by the women who worked in the central markets of Paris, a large crowd, which swelled in size as it moved, set off for Versailles to rescue the king from his evil counselors, and to heal the breach that Louis XIV had opened when he moved the government to Versailles. After spending the night on the cobbles of the palace, they smashed in, killed several guards, and forced the king and queen into their coach. In a long, slow procession, the crowd pulled the royal family back to Paris and installed them in the Tuileries palace.

The National Assembly joined them a few days later, and pressed on with its reform program. In November 1789, the lands of the Church were confiscated, and used to back a new paper currency. In July 1790, the Civil Constitution of the Clergy laid down that the clergy should be elected by all citizens, Catholic or not, and that the clergy should receive state salaries. When the pope threatened to excommunicate all clergy who took an oath to the Civil Constitution, an important barrier was erected between faithful Catholics and the revolution, which was not removed until Napoleon struck a concordat with the pope in 1802. A new constitution was written based on the separation of powers among the executive, the legislature, and the judiciary, but granted the vote only to so-called active citizens who owned a specific amount in property. All women and the rest of the male population were known as "passive citizens."

The old provinces of France were abolished, and replaced by eighty-three departments of almost equal size whose officials were to be elected. Religious toleration was granted to Protestants and Jews. Torture was banned. Women were to reach majority at twenty-one like men, were to have an equal share in inheritance with their brothers, and when married were to have a right to share in the administration of their property and in the way in which their children were brought up. Disputes within families were to be mediated by "family tribunals," on which, however, women could not sit. The years when reforms were flooding from the National Assembly were the high point of the revolution, especially as the economy was improving and the food supply had stabilized. In England, the poet William Wordsworth expressed the feeling of hope that many in Europe felt at the extraordinary progress made in transforming the despotism of France:

> From that time forth, Authority in France
> Put on a milder face . . .
> . . . in the People was my trust,
> And in the virtues which mine eyes had seen.
> I knew that wound external could not take
> Life from the Young Republic . . .
> . . . and her triumphs be in the end,
> Great, universal, irresistible.[3]

The impression that France's underlying problems had been solved was misleading. Radicals in the Jacobin Club, the largest political club in France, with 2000 branches in Paris and the provinces, were preparing the organization that was to carry through an egalitarian revolution by implementing a puritanical dictatorship of lower-middle-class leaders backed by the Parisian mob. At the same time, aristocrats were leaving the country in increasing numbers to find refuge and military support in the courts of Germany and Austria. Thus the constitutional monarchy was already threatened from within and without when the king destroyed all hope of making the constitution work by attempting to flee the country. He was captured near the German border, and brought back to Paris as a semiprisoner. Thus, when the Legislative Assembly, elected under the provisions of the new constitution, met in September 1791, the prospects of maintaining the constitutional monarchy were already poor.

Girondin Rule

Only a third of the members of the Assembly supported the continuance of the monarchy, and a battle for power ensued between the Girondin group and the Jacobins. The Girondins were mostly provincial leaders, and the group was named after the southwestern department of the Gironde, from which many came. The Girondins wanted to take strong measures against the nobles who

[3] William Wordsworth, "Preludes," 11.1–2, 11–14, 16–17.

had fled, by confiscating their property, and to crack down on the clergy who were not cooperating with the revolution. They also wanted to bring Paris under the control of the provinces, and to reduce the powers of the central government over the economy. The government's principal effort, they felt, should be to extend the revolution to other countries. Against them stood the uncompromising Jacobin revolutionaries, led by Georges Jacques Danton and Maximilien Robespierre, who were determined to take over the government.

The Girondins prevailed on the king to declare war on Austria and Prussia, believing that popular revolution would break out in those countries and end the danger they represented to the revolution in France. The French armies, however, sustained immediate defeats on the frontiers. Paris boiled over in fear and anger. In August 1792, the crowd besieged the Tuileries palace. The assembly suspended the king, and he was transferred to the Temple prison under control of the Paris city government. In September the crowds roamed through Paris, massacring all prisoners regardless of whether they were aristocrats or not.

In this atmosphere of intimidation, elections were held for a new assembly called the Convention. The Girondins won a majority of the seats from the provinces, the Jacobins most of the seats for Paris. For the next year, the Girondins dominated the revolution. They abolished the monarchy on September 21, 1792. They attempted to increase civil rights. When they introduced divorce, there was one divorce for every three marriages in Paris. The powers of local government were strengthened in the departments. They extended the war by promising to help any people attempting "to recover their liberty." Crushing defeats were inflicted on the Prussians and Austrians; and French troops occupied Belgium, the Rhineland, and Savoy. Euphoric with victory, the Convention found the king guilty of treason, for engaging in counterrevolutionary plots with foreign governments, and he was beheaded by the guillotine in January 1793 in the main square of Paris. Well aware of the adverse international reaction to the execution, the Convention declared war on Britain and Holland in February 1793 and on Spain in March. This time they had overreached themselves. The war on the northern frontiers turned unfavorable, and a large royalist uprising broke out in western France. The Jacobins seized their opportunity, and unleashed the Paris crowds against the Girondins in the assembly. Most of them fled or were arrested, and the Jacobins took over the government.

The Reign of Terror

The government of the Reign of Terror (1793–1794) was a tightly knit dictatorship of radical leaders who had assumed the role of forcing France to reform. They worked through a system of committees, of which the most important was the Committee of Public Safety, and they were backed by Jacobin clubs throughout the country. Their methods at first seemed necessary to save France from invasion. Universal military conscription, a *levée en masse,* was adopted.

"Representatives on Mission" were sent out into the provinces to punish disloyalty. One of the more bloodthirsty of these representatives organized mass drownings in the Loire River of those he considered guilty of treason. Large numbers of troops were sent to put down the royalist uprising. All the country's resources were placed under central control, and a system of food rationing and maximum price laws was introduced. These measures helped bring victory at the frontiers, and in a short time French troops had again occupied Belgium, the Rhineland, and Savoy.

The Jacobins then proceeded with the remodeling of France. Christianity was replaced by the worship of reason and then later by worship of a supreme being. The Christian Sunday was abolished, and a new ten-day week instituted with provision for civic rather than religious holidays. One holiday was called Maternal Tenderness Day. Women were in fact expected to resume their traditional social roles, and to abandon the wild activism they had shown in the earlier days of the revolution. The Jacobins viewed the murder of one of their most uncompromising leaders, Marat, by a woman named Charlotte Corday as proof of the need to end women's political participation, and all women's political clubs were banned. The months were renamed. The three winter months, for example, became Nivôse, Pluviôse, and Ventôse (Snowy, Rainy, and Windy).

Like so many dictators, the Jacobins ended by quarreling among themselves for preeminence. In the struggle for power, Danton and his followers, and later Hébert and his supporters, were guillotined by Robespierre. Robespierre had,

Marie Antoinette Being Led to Execution, by David   David sketched the former queen as she passed below his window on the way to the guillotine in October 1793. (Documentation Photographique de la Réunion des Musées Nationaux.)

however, inspired such fear for their own lives among the members of the assembly that they turned the hungry Paris mob against him. The more moderate members of the Convention then ordered his arrest, and he was guillotined two days later on 8 Thermidor of the new calendar or July 26 of the old. Throughout France there was a shudder of relief that the Terror was over; and in a violent campaign known as the Thermidorean reaction, all those suspected of collaboration with the Jacobins were hunted down and jailed or executed.

The Directory

The final phase of the revolution was government by a corrupt middle-class body called the Directory, which was nevertheless greeted by the French people as a welcome change from the dictatorial puritanism of Robespierre. A few attempts by the Paris crowd to reassert its power were easily defeated, either by the middle-class militia called the National Guard or by the army. In October 1795, an ambitious young general from Corsica named Napoleon Bonaparte was called in to mow down a Paris uprising with a "whiff of grapeshot," an action that won him promotion to command of the French army in Italy and thus brought him rapidly within reach of supreme power.

NAPOLEON AS CONSUL AND EMPEROR

It seemed unlikely that the young general would be able to take over the government only four years later. Corsica had been French only one year when Napoleon was born there in 1769, and he always spoke Italian better than French. He had attended military school in France on a scholarship, but his progress had been held back by his lack of noble background. He had, however, won a reputation as an artillery officer, and had made good political connections in Paris by marrying Joséphine de Beauharnais, the mistress of one of the leading members of the Directory. In Italy in 1796–1797, he proved to be a brilliant general, and he displayed his precocious self-confidence by writing the peace treaty with Austria himself. His popularity in France became enormous when it was learned that he had made northern Italy into a republic and earned Austrian recognition of French annexation of Belgium and the left bank of the Rhine. Sent to Egypt in 1798, he was less successful. Although he won the Battle of the Pyramids against the Egyptians, his fleet was destroyed by the British Admiral Horatio Nelson, and his army was defeated in Palestine. The French armies in Europe were doing even worse, however, and Napoleon was asked by some members of the Directory to come back secretly to France to seize power. He abandoned his army in Egypt, and took power in a brilliantly executed and bloodless coup in December 1799. The French gave an overwhelming vote in favor of the conversion of the government from the Directory into a Consulate, in which Napoleon, as First Consul, would exercise virtually supreme power.

Napoleon's Internal Reforms

Napoleon was made consul for life in 1802 and emperor in 1804, in each case by overwhelming votes of support in plebiscites. The support was due not only to the fact that he had won new military victories in Italy, but to the fact that during the five years of the consulate he had carried through a far-reaching program of reforms in France itself. During this period, he claimed that he had consolidated and made permanent the reforms that the French had originally carried out the revolution to obtain.

His most immediate aim was to restore orderly government in France after the repression of the Terror and the corruption of the Directory. He accepted the framework of local government created during the constitutional monarchy, with the division of France into departments, cantons, and communes, but ended the election of local officials. All officials were to be appointed from Paris, and were to be responsible directly to the central government. He governed with the advice of a Council of State, a body of professional administrators. The bureaucracy was reorganized into a coherent series of ministries, of which the most important was the Ministry of the Interior, whose purpose was to maintain internal order. Stability of government finance was restored by imposition of a large number of indirect taxes and by a partially successful attempt

The Emperor Napoleon, by Jean A. D. Ingres (1780–1867) After his coronation as emperor in 1804, Napoleon attempted to combine the pomp of the ancient Roman emperors with the ceremonial grandeur of France's absolute monarchs. (Musée de l'Armée/Art Resource.)

to make everyone pay direct taxes. Control of the French currency and of internal credit was placed in the hands of a newly created Bank of France, whose 200 shareholders came to constitute the élite of the French financial class. A new law code called the Napoleonic Code completely reorganized the French legal system, but on conservative lines. The preservation of the family as the basic social institution was a paramount goal. Causes for divorce were sharply limited. Although a woman retained an equal right of inheritance, she required her husband's permission before she could make a will or gifts. "The wife owes obedience to her husband" was the code's prescription for family harmony. Finally, Napoleon brought internal religious peace. Ever since the passage of the Civil Constitution of the Clergy, not only large numbers of the clergy but many faithful Catholics had become disaffected from the state. Napoleon persuaded the pope to sign a concordat in which he recognized the nationalization of Church property and permitted Napoleon to nominate the clergy. In return, freedom of Catholic worship was fully restored, and religious orders, including Jesuits, again allowed to operate. (The pope accepted Napoleon's invitation to officiate at his coronation as emperor, but Napoleon crowned himself.)

France thus became the most centralized country in Europe, and Paris's position of preeminence was made even greater than during the old regime. Napoleon regarded centralization as essential to maintenance of the personal controls that he saw as necessary to orderly government. He was proud, for example, that at any moment of the day he knew exactly what was being studied by every school child in France. By this centralization, he considered that he had given every social class what it had really wanted in 1789. The middle classes had financial stability, efficient administration, and the opportunity to rise. The peasants were secure in the possession of their new lands, and the permanent abolition of feudal dues was written into the Napoleonic Code. The working classes of the cities had work, even if the principal employment in France lay in supplying and serving in Napoleon's armies. Even the old nobility had been welcomed back to serve with the newly created Napoleonic aristocracy in the imperial court and armies. Napoleon believed that of the vaunted revolutionary triad—liberty, equality, fraternity—he had at least given equality and fraternity, and thus he had appeased, if not satisfied, even the liberals.

THE NATIONALIST REVOLT AGAINST NAPOLEON

As long as the armies of France could pose as the crusaders for liberalism, they received considerable support from within the countries against whom they were fighting; and even Napoleon was not at first regarded as an old-style French imperialist. As late as 1805, a great lover of freedom like Ludwig van Beethoven was able to consider dedicating his third symphony to Napoleon although at the last minute he decided not to do so. As Napoleon restricted local powers of self-government, and in particular as he replaced native rulers with members of his own family, it became possible for the forces of nationalism to be turned against him by the very conservatives he claimed originally to have come to oust.

French Support of Liberal Reform

During the 1790s, the French undoubtedly did a great deal to encourage reform in the countries they invaded. In all the areas that came under their control they abolished feudalism, modernized the central and local governments, provided equality of opportunity in education and government, guaranteed human rights, and redistributed part of the wealth of the Church. Revolutionary armies set up republics in Holland, Switzerland, and northern Italy; and in them the native middle class was given power.

Italy was particularly receptive to French influence, since virtually every one of its states, with the exception of the modernizing government of Piedmont-Sardinia in the north, was governed by some form of out-of-date despotism. The old maritime republics of Genoa and Venice were governed by self-seeking oligarchies that had lost touch with their own citizens. Milan was governed directly by the Austrian emperor. The pope was regarded as an enemy of all modernity. The kingdom of Naples and Sicily was a byword for inefficiency and privilege. Hence, in all the cities of Italy, the middle class was ready for any aid the French could give them in overthrowing their own governments. The Cisalpine republic created by the French in northern Italy was especially important. There, in the capital city of Milan, for three years republicans from all over the peninsula gathered to coordinate their plans for the liberalization of all Italy. Soon after setting up the Cisalpine republic, the French armies drove out the pope and set up a Roman republic. When the king of Naples and Sicily came to the aid of the pope, the French easily defeated him, and turned southern Italy into a republic. The middle-class reformers in Naples then wrote a modern constitution, adopted French administrative practices, and tried to abolish feudalism.

Napoleon As Reformer

As first consul, Napoleon seemed intent on continuing the program of reform in Europe. He simplified the political geography of Germany by abolishing all the states of the imperial knights and most of the free cities and the states of the Church. He was particularly careful to increase the size of Prussia in order to have a counterweight to the power of Austria in Germany. His plans were interrupted in 1803, however, when Britain and Austria, his implacable enemies, went to war against him once more, with the aid of Sweden, Russia, and a number of smaller German states. For two years Napoleon concentrated on putting together a fleet and army for the invasion of England; but, deciding in 1805 that the danger from the Austrian and German forces had become pressing, he moved his army rapidly into Germany. He won a minor victory over the Austrians at Ulm in October, and then occupied Vienna. In December, he won his most brilliant victory at Austerlitz, where he totally destroyed the Austrian army. Any possibility of invading England had, however, been ended when Nelson destroyed both the Spanish and French fleets at Cape Trafalgar off the coast of Spain in October 1805. From that point, Napoleon dominated the continent and Britain the seas, in a classic stand-off in which each power could only search for a weak spot of the enemy to exploit.

Even now Napoleon had not completely lost his reputation as a reformer. In 1806 he created a new German state, a Confederation of the Rhine that linked fifteen western and southern German states in a federal union. The confederation included such important states as Bavaria, Baden, and Württemberg, the area of Germany that was most sympathetic to French culture and that considered itself heir to the cultural legacy of the Roman empire. In 1806 Napoleon swept aside the armies of Prussia, which had belatedly and unwisely entered the struggle against him, in the battles of Jena and Auerstedt, and occupied Berlin. When he defeated the Russian forces at Friedland in 1807, the capricious Tsar Alexander I turned into an uncritical admirer of Napoleon. Meeting with Napoleon at Tilsit, he agreed to permit Napoleon to continue his remolding of Europe's geography even further eastward. Prussia lost half its territory. Its Polish lands were joined to a section of the tsar's to create the Duchy of Warsaw, and a completely new Kingdom of Westphalia was formed in Germany, from territory of Prussia and smaller German states, and given to Napoleon's brother Jerome.

In Italy, too, Napoleon continued to rework the political structure. In 1804 he united almost all of northern and central Italy into a Kingdom of Italy, and appointed Eugène de Beauharnais, brother of his wife Joséphine, as viceroy. Eugène governed with exemplary efficiency for the next ten years. Administration was improved, education modernized, public works expanded, and the Napoleonic law codes introduced. Perhaps most important, the administrators from the different states incorporated into the Kingdom of Italy gained experience in working together in a common administration. Napoleon annexed most of the papal states, and brought the pope to France. Finally, the French armies took over southern Italy in 1806, and made Napoleon's brother Joseph king. Joseph introduced the usual Napoleonic benefits such as better roads and the French law code. When Joseph was sent two years later to be king of Spain, Napoleon chose as the new king his brother-in-law Marshal Joachim Murat. Murat, who was rather stupid and vainglorious, tried to make himself the champion of Italian nationalism. He deserted Napoleon after his defeat in Russia in 1812–1813, and tried to persuade the Italians that he could unite Italy. He even declared war on Austria in 1815, but was captured and executed. Neither Joseph nor Murat made much headway in persuading the Italians that they were liberators, however, and the king of Naples was accepted back by the mass of the population with as much indifference as they had shown at his ouster.

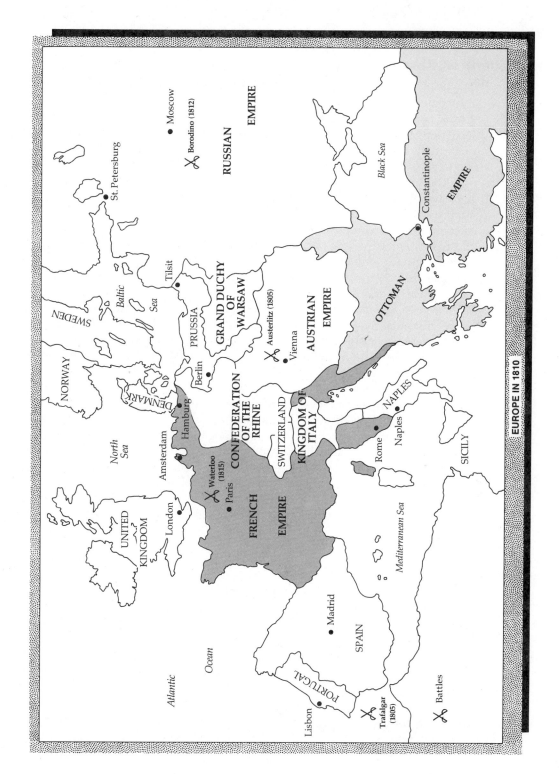

RUSSIAN EMPIRE

Moscow

Borodino (1812)

St. Petersburg

Black Sea

Constantinople

OTTOMAN EMPIRE

Tilsit

Baltic Sea

SWEDEN

PRUSSIA

GRAND DUCHY OF WARSAW

Austerlitz (1805)

Vienna

AUSTRIAN EMPIRE

NORWAY

Berlin

DENMARK

CONFEDERATION OF THE RHINE

SWITZERLAND

KINGDOM OF ITALY

NAPLES

Hamburg

North Sea

Amsterdam

Waterloo (1815)

Paris

FRENCH EMPIRE

Rome

Naples

SICILY

Mediterranean Sea

UNITED KINGDOM

London

Atlantic Ocean

Madrid

SPAIN

PORTUGAL

Lisbon

Trafalgar (1805)

Battles

393

The Nationalist Revolt

The year 1807 was the last when Napoleon was able to win support from within the countries he had defeated. Between 1807 and 1814, there was a constant rise of national feeling against him, caused by his restriction of the powers of local self-government, by his establishment of new kingdoms ruled by members of his own family, and above all by the ban on all trade with Britain known as the Continental System.

The nationalist revolt began in Portugal and Spain. Following the defeat of his navy at Trafalgar, Napoleon had decided that he must try a new strategy against the British—to cut off all their trade with continental Europe and thereby to bring Britain to bankruptcy and perhaps to revolution. In 1806, he instituted the Continental System, by which he forbade all ports on the continent of Europe to trade with Britain. European countries were, however, heavily dependent on Britain for manufactured and for tropical goods, especially as the British navy in the Atlantic and Mediterranean controlled all merchant vessels trading in those waters. All European countries, including France, at first evaded the Continental System by smuggling. In 1807, however, the Portuguese government, which traditionally had maintained close ties with Britain, officially refused to cooperate in the system. Napoleon decided to make an example of that small country, and he himself led a large army across Spain to attack Lisbon. The Portuguese royal family fled to Brazil, and the British immediately sent an expeditionary force under Arthur Wellesley, the future duke of Wellington, which established itself near Lisbon. The Spanish, objecting to the passage of a marauding French army across Spain, began to attack the French troops in guerrilla bands. Napoleon then captured the Spanish royal family by trickery, forced their abdication, and made his brother Joseph king of Spain.

Napoleon's high-handed tactics were completely unsuccessful. Both the Portuguese and Spanish rose against him, led by clergy and nobles, in nationwide revolt that for six years held down 300,000 French troops in the Iberian peninsula.

Napoleon Defeated

Seeing Napoleon pinned down in Spain, in April 1809 the Austrians again declared war. For Napoleon it was becoming increasingly difficult to put fresh armies in the field after so many years of fighting. He scraped together a new army of whom half were unwilling conscripts, and defeated the Austrians at the battle of Wagram. The Russians, who had not aided the Austrians, took panic, massed an army on the borders of the Grand Duchy of Warsaw, and refused to collaborate in the Continental System. Napoleon thereupon made his greatest error. He decided to invade Russia. With an army of 450,000 men, he set off for Moscow in June 1812. Except on one occasion, at Borodino, the Russians refused to give battle, but withdrew slowly, leaving only scorched earth in the territories Napoleon must cross. Napoleon reached Moscow with

Napoleon's Retreat from Moscow, by Jean L. E. Meissonier (1815–1891) *The many paintings of dramatic scenes from Napoleon's career made after his death helped to create an overly romantic popular image of him that is known as the "Napoleonic Legend."* (Giraudon/Art Resource.)

a half-starving army, and found the city in flames. In October, fearing the coming of the Russian winter in a city stripped of supplies, he began the disastrous retreat from Moscow. Caught by an early Russian winter and constantly harrassed by Russian troops, the French army was decimated. Only 30,000 soldiers had returned to Poland by December. Napoleon deserted them, and rushed back to France to raise more troops for what was to prove a final campaign in Germany. This time he faced an entirely new Prussia.

Deeply chagrined by the territorial losses in 1807, the Prussian monarchy had decided to carry through a "revolution from above." The leaders of this modernization program were the chief ministers Henrich von und zum Stein (from 1807 to 1808) and Karl August Hardenberg (from 1810 to 1822), who set out to carry through important reforms they considered had been omitted by Frederick II. The serfs were emancipated and given a share of the land. The medieval guilds were abolished to provide greater freedom of industrial activity. Careers in commerce and industry were opened to the nobility. Advancement in the army, which had previously been a preserve of the nobility, was made dependent on merit only. The model for the army reform, which included military conscription, was the French revolutionary army. To whip up public enthusiasm for this program, the government encouraged all the intellectual groups to stir up both Prussian and German nationalism. The historian Johann Gottlieb Fichte, in his *Addresses to the German People,* appealed to the university students and others to prepare to sacrifice themselves "to the devouring flame of higher patriotism." The ideal was taught of a national community to which the individual must be subordinated; and France was presented as inimical to everything Germany stood for. The university of Berlin in particular was expected to inculcate these doctrines in the new generation of Prussian leaders.

In encouraging nationalism, the Prussian government thus took a calculated gamble, which could easily have led to the sweeping away of Prussia itself and of the other conservative monarchies in a united democratic state of Germany. But in the crisis of 1813, when the last campaigns were being fought against Napoleon, military results were what counted. At first the Prussian armies suffered a number of minor defeats at the hands of the new French army. Then, in October 1813, the combined armies of Austria, Prussia, and a number of German states decisively defeated Napoleon at the Battle of Leipzig, a battle that came to be called the Battle of the Nations. Meanwhile the forces of Wellington had fought their way through Spain and had entered France itself. Although Napoleon wanted to fight a last desperate campaign in France, his own marshals forced him to abdicate. He was permitted by the victorious allies to become the sovereign of the tiny Italian island of Elba, from which, ironically enough, he could see his native island of Corsica, where the Atlantic revolution had begun.

The Hundred Days

The allied armies occupying Paris restored Louis XVIII, the younger brother of the executed King Louis XVI, as king. (Louis XVII, the son of Louis XVI, had died in prison in Paris in 1795.) While the allies were deliberating in Vienna on how to set the clock back in Europe after the disastrous changes brought about by the French, Napoleon suddenly escaped from Elba in March 1815, and was welcomed back to France by his armies. Louis XVIII fled to Belgium, to take refuge behind the army of Wellington, which was near Brussels. Napoleon issued an entirely new constitution in the vain hope of appearing more liberal than before. To deal with the British threat, he set off for Belgium with an army of only 100,000 men. In the final battle of his career, he was soundly defeated at Waterloo by a combined British and Prussian army. Napoleon returned to France and abdicated once again. To his surprise and fury, the British took him as a prisoner to the remote island of Saint Helena in the South Atlantic, where he died in 1821.

The allies, when they returned to Vienna, were well aware that they had defeated France but not yet the forces demanding self-government and national independence. The example of the successful revolt of the thirteen British colonies and the foundation of the United States was soon to be followed by all the Spanish and Portuguese colonies on the mainland of Central and South

America. The experience of running their own governments, even if under French control, in the various satellite republics set up by the revolutionary armies in Europe had given the citizens of backward monarchies a heady taste of the meaning of democracy, while even in the kingdoms established by Napoleon the benefits of efficient and fair government were not likely to be quickly forgotten. Louis XVIII, brought back in the "baggage trains of the allies," could not ignore the political changes of the past quarter-century; he at once accepted the role of constitutional monarch, and left untouched most of the legal and administrative reforms of Napoleon. Perhaps most important of all, nationalism had become a passionate force in large parts of Central and Eastern Europe, encouraged by military victory, and threatening the existing political status quo in Italy and Germany. Thus the defeat of Napoleon was, in the eyes of the conservative monarchies, only a first step to the necessary suppression of liberalism and at the very least to the restraining and redirecting of the force of nationalism. Between 1815 and 1848, therefore, the conservative powers attempted to enforce a program that, if it could not wipe out these revolutionary forces, could at least keep them under strict control.

SUGGESTED READINGS

The Atlantic Revolution

The thesis that all the revolutionary outbreaks of the period 1760 to the 1820s were part of an "Atlantic revolution," whose purpose was to make governments responsible to the governed, is convincingly argued in Robert R. Palmer, *The Age of the Democratic Revolution; A Political History of Europe and America, 1760–1800. Vol. 1. The Challenge* (1959), and Jacques Godechot, *France and the Atlantic Revolution of the Eighteenth Century, 1770–1799* (1965).

Revolution in the Thirteen Colonies

The causes and course of the revolution are described in detail in John R. Alden, *The American Revolution, 1775–1783* (1962). Bernard Bailyn, *The Ideological Origins of the American Revolution* (1967), shows that the colonists believed they were fighting to retain liberties they had possessed before 1763, and not to win self-government for the first time. Samuel Bass Warner, Jr., *The Private City: Philadelphia in Three Periods of Its Growth* (1968), is a model study in the new urban history, and is especially useful for showing the legacy of the revolutionary events in the future development of Philadelphia. For a new analysis of the role of cities in the revolution see Gary Nash, *The Urban Crucible: Social Change, Political Consciousness, and the Origins of the American Revolution* (1979).

The thesis that women in colonial America were better off than women in Europe and would thus support the revolution as a defense of their status is argued by Roger Thompson, *Women in Stuart England and America: A Comparative Study* (1974), and opposed by Mary Beth Norton, *Liberty's Daughters: The Revolutionary Experience of American Women, 1750–1800* (1980). For a brilliant overview of the role of women in American life from the revolution on, see Carl Degler, *At Odds: Women and the Family from the Revolution to the Present* (1980).

The French Revolution

The injustices within the old regime that brought France to revolution are analyzed in Pierre Goubert, *The Ancien Régime: French Society, 1600–1750* (1973). A more detailed portrayal of the urban and rural poor is given by Olwen Hufton, *The Poor of Eighteenth Century France, 1750–1789* (1972). For a Marxist interpretation of their role in the revolution, see Albert Soboul, *The Parisian Sans-Culottes and the French Revolution, 1793–94* (1964). Georges Lefebvre, in his concise *The French Revolution from Its Origins to 1793* (1962), argues that in fact the revolution was a series of separate class revolutions for entirely different goals. George Rudé, *Paris and Its Provinces, 1792–1802* (1975), is particularly useful for an understandng of the Girondins. The failure of the Directory to solve the problems left behind by the Terror is documented in Martyn Lyons, *France Under the Directory* (1975). For a survey of women's role in the revolution, see Olwen Hufton, "Women in Revolution 1789–1796," *Past and Present*, no. 53 (November 1971), pp. 90–108; and Jane Abray, "Feminism in the French Revolution," *American Historical Review*, 80 (April 1975), pp. 43–62. There are good introductions to the documents illustrating the role of women in the French revolution in Darline Gay Levy, Harriet Branson Applewhite, and Mary Durham Johnson, *Women in Revolutionary Paris, 1789–1795* (1979).

Napoleon

The extraordinarily varied interpretations by historians of the career of Napoleon are weighted in Pieter Geyl, *Napoleon: For and Against* (1949). His reforms in France are described in Louis Bergeron, *France Under Napoleon* (1981). Two standard biographies are Georges Lefebvre, *Napoleon* (1969), and Felix Markham, *Napoleon* (1963). The rise of nationalism in opposition to the French invasions can be followed in Markham's *Napoleon and the Awakening of Europe* (1954). On Prussia, see Walter M. Simon, *The Failure of the Prussian Reform Movement, 1807–1819* (1955). On Italy, see Emiliana P. Noether, *Seeds of Italian Nationalism, 1700–1815* (1951).

14

The Industrial Revolution

The industrial revolution that began in Britain in the eighteenth century and spread to large parts of Europe by the middle of the nineteenth century proved in the long run to be even more profound in its effects than the liberal and nationalist revolutions. New sources of power were exploited, first by the harnessing of rivers and then by the use of steam. Machinery of increasing size and technical sophistication, manipulated by relatively unskilled workers, replaced the male and female craft workers who had carried out production in their own homes or workshops. The factory became the basic productive unit. New forms of transportation were developed to supply the vastly expanding demand for raw materials, and the even greater need for an inexpensive means of speeding the new products to their markets at home and overseas—first canals, then roads, and finally steamships and railroads. Improvements in agriculture were linked to changes in industrial production. Changes in animal breeding, in crop choice, and in farm machinery made agriculture more productive, while the presence of a growing urban market for farm products induced the wealthy to sink capital into improvements in farming and to buy out, or drive out, many of the less productive independent farmers. In the industrial areas a new type of society came into being, composed of two antagonistic classes, a working class that felt itself to be exploited and a class of owners and managers that drew off an increasing share of the national income. From the antagonism between these two classes was to come, by the end of the nineteenth century, a confrontation that was far more shattering in its results than even the Atlantic revolution had been.

A Manchester Cotton Mill in 1842   With the development in the eighteenth century of power-driven machines, textile workers no longer did spinning and weaving in their village cottages but were employed in huge, bare factory buildings in industrial cities. (Mary Evans Picture Library.)

THE EARLY INDUSTRIAL REVOLUTION IN BRITAIN

Reasons for Britain's Lead

Britain was the first country in Europe to industrialize, because it alone possessed in combination all the prerequisites for this massive economic and social change. First, it was ideally suited geographically to becoming the world's first industrial power. In an age when the transportation of mass goods could be carried out only by water, it possessed fine harbors on all its coasts. Every inland town had easy access to the ports, either by navigable rivers or by easily constructed canals. Rich deposits of coal and iron were well located in southern Wales, northern and central England, and central Scotland. Fine clay deposits made possible the development of a pottery industry. The Pennine Mountain range, which ran down northern England, offered a double advantage. Its fast-flowing streams could easily be harnessed for water power. Atlantic storms striking the western slopes ensured a continually damp climate for Manchester and other textile towns in which cotton threads could be easily worked, while the eastern slopes enjoyed a drier climate that was more suitable for woolen manufacture.

Second, by the beginning of the eighteenth century, Britain possessed the world's largest merchant marine, which it had developed not only for trade with its colonial empire but to participate in Baltic trade, in African slave trade, and in the Asian spice trade. With 6000 merchant ships, Britain already had the means to sell its manufactured products in all parts of the world.

Third, Britain possessed a mercantile class with great commercial expertise and accumulated capital. The wealthy middle class in England, like that earlier in Amsterdam, had become experts in banking, insurance, commodity markets, and joint stock ventures, and they were well aware of the great profits to be made by investing risk capital. The nobility, too, unlike the aristocracy of France, had, at least since the sixteenth century when many had acquired their estates under the Tudors, worked their own estates for profit. They had thus amassed capital that they were accustomed to invest, through Britain's well-developed banking system, in commercial ventures. Thus both the mercantile class and the aristocracy possessed capital and financial acumen, which prepared them to use the banks to transfer the wealth made in the South of England in agriculture and commerce to the North for foundation of industry.

Fourth, British agriculture had been undergoing profound change at least since the seventeenth century, which would greatly increase food output in Britain. The lead had been taken by aristocratic landowners who copied Dutch agricultural techniques and crop rotation, which were widely popularized in the eighteenth century by such aristocrats as Charles Townsend and Jethro Tull. The most important of the changes had been the adoption of the turnip and clover, which restored the nitrogen to the soil that had been taken out by cereals, and thus made it possible to end the habit of leaving a third of the land fallow and at the same time provided winter feed for animals. Scientific stock breeding also made it possible to increase the size of sheep and cattle, and thus the amount of meat available for consumption. Agricultural machinery was also improved, notably by Tull, who introduced a drill that could plant seeds individually and a hoe drawn by a horse. The medieval system in which each worker owned a number of individual strips of land in different fields was ended by the "enclosure," as a result of hundreds of acts of parliament, of the strips and of common land as consolidated farms. As many as 50,000 small farmers may have lost their land to the new capitalist owners, although many stayed on in the countryside either as tenant farmers or as hired laborers. Some drifted into the cities, but their numbers may not have been as great as historians supposed until recently. As a result of the agricultural changes, Britain remained able to feed its growing population until the 1780s.

Fifth, the British constitutional system, as a result of the changes in the seventeenth and eighteenth centuries, was highly supportive of industrialization and agricultural modernization. The classes with capital to invest were also in control of the government. After the revolution of 1688, the monarchy was never able to challenge the dominance of Parliament, the mouthpiece of an oligarchy that comprised not more than 6 percent and perhaps only 3 percent of Britain's population. Although the House of Commons was elected, most of its seats were in the control of a small number of wealthy aristocrats, and in the few constituencies with relatively free elections, bribery usually established the outcome. Moreover, since there was no redistribution of seats as population shifted, large areas of the North were virtually unrepresented, and rapid industrial growth could proceed there with virtually no regard for its consequences to the environment or to the well-being of the workers. Members of the gentry ran local government as justices of the peace, and the leading merchants ran the cities. Moreover, membership in the professions, such as law and medicine, was also restricted to this small governing class. After Parliament summoned the Elector of Hanover to become King George I (reigned 1714–1727), upon the death of Queen Anne, the oligarchy's predominance was assured. Throughout the reigns of George I and George II (reigned 1727–1760), that is, the period when industrialization began on a large scale, power was held by the Whigs, who were a coalition of the urban financial and commercial classes with some of the wealthiest landowners. While Robert Walpole was chief minister (1721–1742), he worked out the basis of what became the English cabinet system of government, in which a group of ministers, headed by a prime minister, ran the executive and dominated the legislative branch through its own political party. But the ministers of the Tory party, which was supported primarily by the landowning classes and was favored by George III (reigned 1760–1820), made no essential change in the oligarchic structure of government or in the laws concerning banking, company formation, and trade that encouraged industrialization. The restriction of power to a small oligarchy was not to be changed until the reform of the parliamentary system itself was begun in 1832; and, from the economic point of view, the essential importance of the predominance of the oligarchy was that it favored development, and intended to profit personally from it. This privileged class failed to realize that industrialization would bring into being the two classes that would challenge its predominance, the northern capitalist and the industrial proletariat.

Development of Industrial Technology

The cotton industry of Lancashire was the first segment of British production to be run on industrial lines, and its driving force was the city of Manchester. At the beginning of the eighteenth century, Manchester was already an important textile town, producing goods of wool, linen, silk, and cotton. Its production was, however, held back by the fact that the women who spun the cotton thread in their own cottages in the countryside could not keep up with the weavers, who used a mechanized loom imported from Holland in the late seventeenth century. The imbalance became even worse when John Kay invented an even more efficient weaving machine called the flying shuttle, which used two hammers to drive a shuttle from side to side across lines of thread. As his entry in a nationwide competition for invention of a spinning machine that would similarly increase the rate of production of the spinners, James Hargreaves patented a "spinning jenny," which made it possible for a spinner to spin eight threads at once. Shortly afterwards, Richard Arkwright, with his "water frame," harnessed water power to the new spinning machines, and made it possible for spinners to produce more thread than the weavers could handle. Finally, Edmund Cartwright invented the power loom, which brought the productivity of the weavers into balance with the spinners. None of these inventions required great scientific knowledge, but were the product of ingenious craftsmen usually working with simple carpenters' tools. But the inventions revolutionized the textile industry, and the creation of the factories in Manchester and other northern cities almost immediately stimulated other industrial change.

In 1769 James Watt invented a steam engine that could be used in place of water to power the textile machinery. Previously, steam engines had employed atmospheric pressure to drive the piston down into the cylinder. Watt used steam to drive the piston in both directions, thereby saving greatly on fuel, and he later converted the up-and-down motion of the piston into a rotary motion suitable for driving machines. The steam engine soon replaced water power in the mills, and was widely used for pumping in the mines. Increased coal production was needed to power the steam engines, and canals were soon constructed to carry the coal to the factory towns and the finished products to their markets. In a canal-building mania in the late eighteenth century, the British

Rotative Steam Engine of James Watt and Mathew Bolton, 1784 Watt's development of the mechanism to convert the vertical thrust of his steam engine's piston into rotary motion made his invention invaluable for pumping in the mines and for driving textile machinery. (The Science Museum, London.)

constructed vast numbers of canals, the most important being the Grand Trunk
Canal, which linked the northern industrial towns to London and the other
southern cities. Road transport was also improved with the invention of a new
method of surfacing using broken stones and by the grant to individuals of the
right to collect tolls on sections of road they had improved.

The use of the steam engine to drive ships was pioneered in the United
States, where in 1807 Robert Fulton proved the feasibility of the steamship as
a means of passenger and goods transportation by sailing up the Hudson River
from New York to Albany in thirty-two hours. Soon, steamships were in wide
use on rivers and lakes in North America and in Europe and for short sea
voyages, but the steamship was not efficient enough for ocean travel until the
engines and propellors were improved in the 1850s and 1860s. In 1829 an even
more important application of the steam engine was made, when George Stephenson demonstrated a railroad locomotive called the Rocket on a trial track
near Manchester. Railroad mania then succeeded canal mania. Between 1829
and 1843, 1900 miles of railroad were built in Britain, and all its major cities
were connected by rail. The need for iron for railroad tracks and steam engines
revolutionized the metallurgical industry. The smelting of iron ore was greatly
improved with the development of the blast furnace in the 1820s. In 1856, Henry
Bessemer invented his converter, which made it possible to manufacture steel
inexpensively by blowing air through molten pig iron. Steel then began to
displace cast iron as the principal industrial metal. Shortly after, high-grade
steel was made by the Siemens-Martin, or open hearth process, which used
scrap iron as well as pig iron and thus permitted the industry to cannibalize its
worn-out products.

Social Problems of Industrialization

In the industrial towns of Britain, a new form of society came into being,
composed of two classes only, owners and workers; and Manchester was universally recognized as the epitome of this society. The Manchester millowners
were usually people who had worked their way up within the factory system,
often beginning as spinners or weavers. The knew every detail of the industry
themselves, worked extremely hard, took risks with their capital, and expected
a high return. Not all of them were the blatant exploiters whom Friedrich Engels
was to denounce in 1845 in *The Condition of the Working Class in England*. Robert
Owen, who became a convinced socialist and founded model factory communities in Scotland and the United States, began his career in Manchester. Many
of the business leaders were Nonconformist Protestants (i.e., members of a
Protestant church other than the Church of England), who believed in thrift,
in hard work, and to a lesser degree in charity. Almost all, however, accepted
the doctrines of laissez-faire as they had been persuasively argued in 1776 by
Adam Smith in *The Wealth of Nations* and refined by later economists such as
David Ricardo (see pp. 410–11).

Throughout the nineteenth century, England's novelists bitterly denounced the self-righteousness of these businessmen. No one was more effective in holding them up to scorn than Charles Dickens, and Josiah Bounderby of Coketown, in Dickens's novel *Hard Times*, became for his readers the image of those hard-faced men:

> He was a rich man: banker, merchant, manufacturer, and what not. A big, loud man, with a stare, and a metallic laugh. A man made out of coarse material, which seemed to have been stretched to make so much of him. A man with a great puffed head and forehead, swelled veins in his temples, and such a strained skin to his face that it seemed to hold his eyes open, and lift his eyebrows up. A man with a pervading appearance on him of being inflated like a balloon, and ready to start. A man who could never sufficiently vaunt himself a self-made man. A man who was always proclaiming, through that brassy speaking-trumpet of a voice of his, his old ignorance and his old poverty. A man who was the Bully of humility.[1]

The essential truth that underlay Dickens's picture was demonstrated by the many commissions that studied conditions in the industrial towns from the 1800s on. One report in 1842 found that the average age of death of the workers in Manchester was seventeen! Working conditions for children and women were particularly bad. Child labor was at first considered necessary for a profitable operation. Small children from the age of six were employed for up to fourteen hours a day to repair threads or sweep up cotton waste in the factories, or to drag tubs of coal on all fours through the narrowest shafts of the mines. They had to be beaten with belts to keep them awake. All suffered lung problems from the fluff or dust, and were stunted from malnutrition. After the employment of children under the age of nine was forbidden in the Factory Act of 1819, women were employed in increasingly large numbers. They worked in temperatures of up to 120 degrees in linen factories, because the heat was good for the fabric, and breathed metal filings in metal-polishing workshops. Their tuberculosis rate in the mills was three times the national average. Yet some women even protested against the Factory Acts that were passed to protect them, because by keeping them out of dangerous work it restricted their possibility of higher wages. Work for men was heavy, repetitive, long, and ill-paid. They had little chance of advancement, and no time, energy, or opportunity for further education. It has been argued that real wages did in fact rise during the first half of the nineteenth century, by 25 percent between 1800 and 1825 and 40 percent between 1825 and 1850. But the workers remained bitterly discontented throughout England, and protested continually in ways that ran the gamut from smashing their machines to seizing their own city by riot.

The cities were a blot on the landscape. Workers' houses were thrown up in vast terraces, with little effort to provide sanitation, water, or fresh air. Whole families lived in cellars, or in windowless backrooms. As a result, the towns were swept periodically by epidemics of cholera, typhus, and typhoid, from

---

[1] Charles Dickens, *Hard Times* (Boston: Houghton Mifflin, 1894), p. 14.

Child Labor in the Coal Mines *Young children were employed to haul tubs of coal through shafts too narrow for adults. The average age of death in Britain's industrial cities in the 1840s was seventeen.* (Mary Evans Picture Library.)

which even the owners did not escape. Until the 1830s, the industrial towns of Britain had virtually no self-government, and hence no controls were placed on the industrialists or the profiteering builders. The air was filled with dust and smoke. Mountains of slag grew up around the mining villages. The factories poured their waste products into the rivers, which were thereby totally poisoned, even though they were used for drinking water. The factories, railroads, and docks were built along the river banks. Hillsides were sliced open for railroad cuttings. The workers' housing constantly shook to the movement of the trains and echoed to the noise of the factories. The owners avoided the necessity to make improvements by building capacious homes miles away in the countryside.

Amenities were slow to come. At first the Nonconformist sects built a few churches; and the Methodists, founded by John Wesley in 1738, were reputed to have done much to prevent revolution in Britain by turning people's thoughts to the rewards their sufferings would win in the life after death. A few parks were created in the middle of the nineteenth century; and Manchester even opened a university in 1851. But it was enormously difficult to improve cities that had been developed with total disregard for the human beings who lived and worked in them.

THE FIRST PHASE OF INDUSTRIALIZATION ON THE CONTINENT

Reasons for Delayed Industrialization

There were many reasons why the countries on the continent of Europe lagged behind Britain in the eighteenth century in adopting industrialization. The predominant attitude among the aristocracy, and even among many of the successful middle classes, was unfriendly to business; and, as we saw, even those who made money in business hastened to invest it in land, and to move their children into some other, more socially prestigious profession. The guilds in the cities also erected barriers against new methods of production that would put their members out of work, while the peasantry preferred to scrape a living from their farms rather than move into the towns. The expansion of trade was hampered by innumerable tolls and customs barriers, both within and between countries. There was a reluctance to build canals across national borders, or to make rivers that crossed into foreign countries navigable. Unlike Britain, the deposits of raw materials were poorly located. The richest coal seams, which stretched in one geologic formation from the north of France to the Ruhr in Germany, were divided among France, Belgium, Luxembourg, and several German states. Governments discouraged the growth of cities, because they were regarded as centers of political unrest. The frequent wars hampered commerce and investment in manufacturing. Perhaps the most important factor, however, was that the British already possessed a strong lead in industrial production, and could easily undercut any infant industry on the continent. The hunger for British goods had been demonstrated by the widespread participation in smuggling during Napoleon's Continental System, which did not prove an important stimulus to continental manufacturing—not least because the British navy controlled the supply of non-European and even of much European raw materials in Napoleon's empire.

Beginning of Industrialization on the Continent

After 1815, the situation in several parts of Europe became more favorable to industrialization. The European population was growing, from 192 million in 1800 to 274 million in 1850. This rapid increase was due partly to better medical care, especially of young children and older people, and partly to the more settled conditions after the end of the Napoleonic wars. But there had also been a marked improvement in the food supply. Many of the improvements that the British had adopted in the seventeenth and eighteenth centuries were taken up in Europe. Land was enclosed to form more efficient farms. Scientific breeding of animals carried on the research begun in Britain. Better types of cereal grain were developed. Many peasants were forced to sell their land, and moved into the cities where they formed a laboring proletariat available for industrial employment. There were no continent-wide wars, and under the guidance of the Austrian Chancellor Clemens von Metternich, the principal countries of the continent collaborated in the maintenance of order and the suppression of discontent.

Several governments decided, after studying the example of Britain, that it was essential for them to encourage industrialization. The first task, they felt, was to learn from Britain. Commissions were sent to study British industrialization, and large numbers of industrial spies were employed to steal secrets that the British would not sell. Governments organized competitions for industrial inventions, held industrial exhibitions, and founded schools of science and technology. The French government led the way in improving transportation. Napoleon I had built hundreds of miles of canals and roads. Another 1800 miles of canals were built between 1815 and 1848. The steamboat was widely used on France's rivers. The Belgian government was the first to see the potential of the railroad, and built two intersecting lines across the country. In the 1840s, the French embarked on an even more ambitious scheme of railroad construction. They planned a country-wide system of railroads, constructed like a bicycle wheel with Paris as its hub. The government provided the tunnels, bridges, and railbed, while private companies provided the track and equipment. The system was complete by the 1860s. Germany, in spite of the changes brought about by Napoleon, was still divided into more than thirty states; but many of them had begun to recognize the disadvantages for economic development of this political fragmentation. A number of separate customs unions were formed, gradually coalescing by the 1850s into a unified German *Zollverein* or customs union under Prussian leadership and comprising almost all the German states except Austria. With freedom of goods thus guaranteed, the Germans created a national railroad system, which began a profound transformation of the economy by linking the aristocratic, semifeudal estates of the east with Berlin and the industrializing areas of the Rhineland.

British capitalists, seeking even higher returns than were available at home, began to invest in the new industrial areas of France, Belgium, and Germany after 1815, and many British workers were lured by higher wages to bring their trade secrets and skills to the continent. Among many large-scale projects, the British built the important railroad down the Seine Valley from Paris to Rouen, opened one of the largest coal mines in the Ruhr in Germany, and built Europe's largest engineering factory in Belgium. Europe's entrepreneurs immediately proved themselves the equal of those in Britain, and some of the most important of Europe's industrial companies had been founded by the early 1820s. The Krupps of Essen in Germany was already making steel in crucibles. The de Wendels in Lorraine had begun to open up France's principal source of iron ore. The Borsig company in Berlin was making locomotives. Europe's banks expanded to meet the needs of the industrial companies. The Rothschild family, which had established family-owned banks in Frankfurt, Paris, Vienna, London, and Naples, proved adept at shifting capital across national boundaries, and did much to bring into being a genuine system of international banking in Europe. Other bankers, such as the Pereire brothers in France, concentrated on such opportunities as railroad building within the national economy. German banks were particularly successful in gathering the savings of the middle classes for investment in industry, and the bankers frequently took a direct role in the management of the new companies.

By 1850 Britain was still by far the world's greatest industrial power, producing two-thirds of its coal and one-half of its iron and cotton cloth. But several regions of Europe had developed an industrial base, which enabled them to compete with the British at least within their own national markets. Belgium was probably the most advanced of the continental countries. It possessed a small but unified market, rich resources in coal and iron ore, and a skilled working and managerial population. In France, industrialization was well advanced in the coal field areas of the north, in Lorraine and some isolated areas of the central mountains, and especially in Paris. Within the Austrian empire, there were new factory districts in the suburbs of Vienna, in Budapest and western Hungary, in the Po Valley of northern Italy, and in Bohemia. The principal German industrial districts were located near or on the coal and iron ore deposits of the Ruhr Valley, the Saar, and Saxony, but Berlin was also becoming a manufacturing center.

The Europeans learned nothing from the British example of the dangers of unplanned industrialization. Newly industrialized cities such as Liège in Belgium, Lille in France, and Essen in Germany were as ugly and polluted as the worst English cities. The health of the factory workers was as bad as in Manchester. The king of Prussia woke to the disastrous effects of life in factory towns when his provinces in the industrial Rhineland failed to find enough healthy recruits to fill their quota for the army. The workers were especially vulnerable to harvest failures, such as that of the potato and wheat harvests in the Austrian empire in 1846–1847, which precipitated the uprisings that overthrew the Metternich government in 1848. And Europe was also becoming accustomed to the same dismal portrayal of workers' suffering, in government reports or more lurid denunciations in fiction or political propaganda, as in Britain. A member of the French Academy of Medicine described the scene at a factory gate in 1840:

> One should see them coming into the town every morning and leaving it every evening. Among them are large numbers of women, pale, starving, wading barefoot through the mud . . . and young children, in greater numbers than the women, just as dirty, just as haggard, covered in rags, which are thick with the oil splashed over them as they toiled by the looms.[2]

And it was two Germans who, in 1848, wrote the most influential indictment of industrial capitalism, *The Communist Manifesto:*

> Our epoch, the epoch of the bourgeoisie, possesses, however, this distinctive feature: it has simplifed class antagonisms. Society as a whole is more and more splitting up into two great hostile camps, into two great classes directly facing each other: Bourgeoisie and Proletariat.[3]

---

[2] Cited in Jürgen Kuczynski, *The Rise of the Working Class* (New York: McGraw-Hill, 1967), p. 59.

[3] Cited in Contemporary Civilization Staff of Columbia College, Columbia University, *Introduction to Contemporary Civilization in the West: A Source Book* (New York: Columbia University Press, 1957), pp. 390–91.

REFORMING THE INDUSTRIAL SYSTEM

Economic Liberalism

An important body of theory called economic liberalism was enthusiastically adopted by the new industrial middle class, and used as justification not of government interference in the industrial system but of a decrease of governmental control. Political liberalism, as we saw, was the doctrine that human beings had the right to govern themselves through representative institutions. When adopted by the industrial middle class, it was restricted to mean the right of the propertied class to rule. The original attack on mercantilism, as a doctrine that justified many forms of state interference in the economic system, had been led by Adam Smith (1723–1790) with his famous book, *The Wealth of Nations.* Smith had argued that there was a natural harmony in the working of the economic laws, provided that there was no state interference. Individuals, he said, possessed the ability to trade, that is, to exchange goods with each other for their mutual benefit. In a system where the state did not falsify prices by interference, entrepreneurs realized which goods were in demand by the consumer, and concentrated on producing them. When demand changed, entrepreneurs shifted their production to supply the new needs. But the entrepreneurs, in competing with each other, were stimulated to raise quality and lower prices. Moreover, employers would be forced to compete for workers who were free to withhold their labor until wages were satisfactory. Thus, if the government restricted itself to maintaining national defense, internal order, and adequate public works, the employer, the worker, and the consumer would all profit.

Later political economists, aware of the growing class antagonism in the factory towns, were less optimistic about the harmony of interest among the classes, but continued to argue for the benefits of a totally free working of the economic system. They were deeply influenced by the views of Thomas Malthus (1766–1834) in his *Essay on the Principles of Population.* Malthus had tried to show that any increase in the worker's standard of living leads the worker to have more children, who then consume the surplus and bring the family back to subsistence level again. Worse, the additional workers resulting from the increase in population would enter the labor market, and thereby bring down wages again. The inevitable result would be the constant threat of starvation, unless the numbers of the working class were kept down by war, misery, or self-restraint. No incentive should be given to an increase in population, he implied, either by raising wages or by supporting the poor in comfortable idleness through charity, especially as population tends to increase geometrically, while the food supply increases only arithmetically.

The *Principles of Political Economy,* by David Ricardo (1772–1823), was deeply imbued with these pessimistic theories. Ricardo believed in the "iron law of wages," which was particularly appealing to the northern factory owners in England. "The natural price of labor," Ricardo wrote, "is that price which is necessary to enable the laborers, one with another, to subsist and perpetuate their race, without either increase or diminution." In short, the worker should be paid just sufficient to stay alive and have children, and no more. As a result, Ricardo recognized, there would be a built-in antagonism between the employer and the worker within the industrial system. Ricardo also argued a law of rent. He thought that rent was established according to the cost of producing on the poorest land farmed, and that therefore the majority of landowners who held the better land were receiving a far higher share of society's wealth than they deserved. There was thus an antagonism between the landlord and the industrialist, who would receive a greater and more equitable share of society's wealth if cheaper food were available for his workers as a result of the reduction of the rent paid to the landlords.

The British middle classes believed quite seriously, therefore, that the industrial system would be improved if they could reduce state interference in industry and state protection of the landowning class. They objected to the Navigation Laws, which required all British goods to be transported on British ships, and to the vast array of import duties. In particular, they wanted the end of the high duties on imported cereals (or corn, as the British called them), which had been imposed to protect the British landlords. During the first half of the nineteenth century, import duties were reduced on a very large number of goods on a piecemeal basis, but the northern English manufacturers had to put together a powerful Anti-Corn Law League to pressure parliament to repeal the Corn Law. Faced by the great Irish famine of 1845–1846, caused by failure of the potato crop, a Tory government finally repealed the law in 1846. By the early 1850s, Britain had abandoned the last vestiges of mercantilism, and had adopted free trade. Its example was followed, however, by only a small number of European countries, including Belgium, the Netherlands, and Switzerland.

Pragmatic and Humanitarian Reform

The business classes, however, were not able to obtain total end of state interference in the internal workings of the economy, especially as the evidence of working-class suffering accumulated. Some of the earliest reforms were called for in Britain by groups compelled by deep religious feeling, who demanded an end to the more palpable abuses of the system. Frequently, they were supported by the landowning class, who demanded reform in the industrial sphere to counterbalance the concessions the industrialists were compelling them to make. An attempt was made as early as 1802 to protect the morals and health of children in factories. But the use of child labor was effectively restricted only by the Factory Acts of 1819 and 1833. The work of women and children was cut down to ten hours a day six days a week, by the Ten Hours Act of 1847; and this act had the practical effect of restricting men's work to ten hours as well. Since in many cases the local justices of the peace, who were retired factory owners, were left to administer the laws, it is doubtful whether they were universally applied.

The accusation that the industrial city was inefficient, not least because of its health conditions, led to more pragmatic reforms, especially when the industrial cities were given representation in Parliament after 1832. Municipal governments were established in the 1850s, and they set out to improve the water supply and sanitary conditions, to open parks and hospitals, and to build schools. But it must be emphasized that these reformers were merely attempting to modify the working of an industrial system that, in its basic form, they approved.

Radicalism

When the industrial classes had argued for political liberalism, it had been for the extension of the suffrage to their own class; and once they themselves had the suffrage, they were not willing to share it. When the liberal premier Guizot of France was asked what his message was for those who were excluded from voting by high property qualifications, he replied, *"Enrichissez-vous"* ("Get rich"). Even after the Reform Bill of 1832, only one in five of England's male population had the vote. To the "radicals," or "democrats" as they were sometimes called, real reform was only possible by an extension of the suffrage to all males; and a few middle-class women radicals argued that it should be extended to all females also. Many of the radicals in England had been sympathetic to the ideals of the French revolution, and when they organized demonstrations and occasionally riots to demand wider representation, the government replied with force. Eleven people were killed by the troops in the so-called Peterloo Massacre in Manchester in 1819; and this demonstration was followed by the passage through Parliament of the Six Acts, which restricted freedom of the press and assembly. The government justified these laws the following year when it uncovered the Cato Street Conspiracy, a radical plot to murder the cabinet and establish a provisional government. Disappointed with the Reform Bill of 1832, the radicals drew up a People's Charter in 1838, demanding universal male suffrage, annual elections, equal electoral districts, and payment for members of the House of Commons. Their followers, known as Chartists, collected millions of signatures on a petition presented to Parliament in 1839, which was ignored. Some of the more violent of their leaders were arrested after confrontations between workers and soldiers in the Welsh mining districts. The movement revived in the distress of the 1840s, and a last attempt was made to pressure Parliament by calling half a million workers to demonstrate in London in 1848. The leaders finally called off the procession, which already looked as though it would be poorly supported, when the government refused them a permit. The Chartist movement petered out, but in the series of reform bills passed between 1867 and 1918, universal male suffrage was achieved. Partial female suffrage was passed in 1918, and universal female suffrage in 1928.

Radicalism on the continent was centered in Paris, not least because the constitution of 1830 had granted the suffrage to only 170,000 people, even

The Peterloo Massacre, 1819 *Cavalry atacked a peaceful crowd attending a political reform meeting at St. Peter's Fields, Manchester, killing eleven people and injuring 400.* (Mary Evans Picture Library.)

though the radicals had rallied the working class in the overthrow of the Bourbon monarchy (see Chapter 15). Moreover, Paris offered refuge to exiled radicals from all over Europe. The liberal government became increasingly uneasy at the activity of these political groups, and, after an attempted assassination on the life of King Louis Philippe, banned radical organizations and imposed censorship of the press. Rather than draw up a petition, like the English Chartists, the French radicals began to organize "reform banquets" in 1847–1848, in which their leaders, such as the poet Alphonse de Lamartine, demanded universal suffrage and payment of the members of the French Assembly. After the government banned a reform banquet in February 1848, the Parisian crowds rose in revolt, overthrew the king, and made France a republic. Lamartine became president of a provisional government, and universal suffrage was adopted. The radical experiment lasted only until June, because almost at once a division appeared between the radicals, such as Lamartine, who wanted only political reform, and the socialists, such as Louis Blanc, who wanted social reform to accompany the political changes. The radicals lost most of their support when they permitted the army to shoot down workers on the streets of Paris in the bloody "June Days"; and the French turned, in the presidential elections of December 1848, to Louis-Napoleon Bonaparte, the nephew of Emperor Napoleon I, to save them from the extreme leaders of both political radicalism and social reform.

Utopian Socialism

Socialism, as a theory of the collective ownership of society's wealth, had existed at least as early as classical Greece. In *The Republic*, for example, Plato had argued for the collective ownership of all property. In the sixteenth century, Sir Thomas More, in describing the perfect state in his book, *Utopia*, forbade the private ownership of property. Rousseau had taken the theory even further in arguing that private property was the single cause of all the evils within a society:

> The first man who, having enclosed a piece of land, took it into his head to say, "This belongs to me," and found people simple enough to believe him, was the true founder of civil society. What crimes, wars, murders, what miseries and horrors would have been spared the human race by him who, snatching out the stakes or filling in the ditch, should have cried to his fellows: "Beware of listening to this imposter; you are lost if you forget that the fruits belong to all and that the earth belongs to none."[4]

In the late eighteenth and early nineteenth centuries, however, socialism was presented as an alternative to capitalism in the running of the new industrial society. Socialism never rejected the industrial system, even though many of the first inchoate protests by workers against their exploitation began with the smashing of their machines. The socialists believed that the industrial system could be made more humane if it were run on totally different principles. Some of the earliest socialists believed that the new system could begin piecemeal. Robert Owen, who had made a fortune in Manchester, bought the largest spinning factory in Scotland, at New Lanark, and there he attempted to create a model socialist community to prove that the antagonism between the classes could be ended without impairing the profits of the enterprise. He built attractive factory buildings, housing for the employees, and free schools. He argued that under these conditions his employees would work harder, and he paid them higher wages than his competitors. People came from all over Europe to see this extraordinary experiment, but he himself eventually became disillusioned, especially after the failure of his attempt to found a similar community in the United States.

The idea of a harmonious industrial community was pioneered in France by Charles Fourier (1772–1837), a somewhat eccentric traveling salesman and amateur philosopher. Fourier believed, like all the early socialists, that the basic problem of industrial society was inefficiency. As an amateur mathematician, he suggested that society should be divided into communities, called *phalanstères*, each composed of 1620 people. Within these communities, all persons would be assigned to do the work for which they were fitted and which they would enjoy. (Children, who enjoy playing in dirt, were to clean the streets!) Fourier also believed strongly in the equality of the sexes. His communities would have provided day care to enable women to have equal opportunity with men, and he would have allowed the easy grant of divorce. Although Fourier

[4] Cited in Alexander Gray, *The Socialist Tradition: From Moses to Lenin* (London: Longmans, Green, 1947), p. 81.

appealed publicly for funds to start such a community (and supposedly came home daily at noon for ten years to meet any prospective investor), no one ever supported him. Several communities in the United States, however, were inspired by his ideas.

Other theorists believed that socialism could be started only on a national basis. Of these perhaps the most influential was Claude de Saint-Simon. Saint-Simon believed in collective planning in order to make industrial society more just and more efficient. He argued that it was possible to make a fresh start because the French Revolution had wiped out obsolete institutions. Once the remaining idle groups, namely, the nobles and soldiers, had been abolished, the industrial middle class was to take over control of the administration, but work in favor of the laboring class. An elite of intellectuals and artists was to ensure the moral advance of society. In endeavoring to show how society should be run on scientific lines, Saint-Simon came up with many ideas that were to be applied by the governments of the Second Empire between 1852 and 1870. Among them were the foundation of credit institutions, the use of technocrats in government, and even a proposal for constructing a Suez Canal. Saint-Simon exercised a wide influence in France, and one of his pupils, Auguste Comte (1798–1857), was the founder of the scientific study of society, which he named sociology. Other followers unfortunately brought discredit on the movement by turning it into a wild religious sect, engaging in various eccentric orgies.

By the 1840s, many socialists had rejected the view that the capitalist and the worker could be reconciled. Pierre-Joseph Proudhon (1809–1865) believed, like Rousseau, that private property should be abolished. In the opening paragraph of his book, *What Is Property?*, published in 1840, he argued that property was "theft." Individuals who owned property had stolen it from the collectivity, and as a result had established a tyranny over others that was similar in kind to that of the slave owner over the slave. In place of this tyranny, Proudhon believed that those who worked should be given possession, but not ownership, of the land or factory, both of which would remain the property of the whole community. Associations of workers would join voluntarily with other associations to form worldwide federations. Once society had become a federation of producers, the state would no longer be necessary, and would therefore disappear. In this way, Proudhon became the forerunner of the Anarchist movement. Only in a society such as that proposed by Proudhon, added the French labor organizer and theorist Flora Tristan, would the emancipation of women become possible. The exploitation of women and the exploitation of the worker were part of the same process, and could be ended only by the same means.

Louis Blanc (1811–1882), in *The Organization of Work*, a scathing attack on the workings of the liberal economic system, argued that no improvement was possible as long as capitalists ran the system on competitive rather than cooperative principles. In order to transform the present system gradually, he proposed the formation of "social workshops," supported with capital from the state. These workshops would provide good working conditions and high wages, and would therefore attract the best workers away from private capitalists. They would be so efficient that they would force the private owners to turn their factories over to the state. In the course of time, society would become composed of harmonious units of production. During the revolution of 1848 in France, national workshops were established, but the result was to discredit Blanc's theories. Thousands of unemployed workers flooded into Paris, where they were given meaningless work, often simply digging holes and filling them in again. The middle classes became disturbed at the danger of having so many dispossessed workers in Paris, and forced the government to close many of the workshops. Refusing to disband, the workers, aided by many Parisians, set up barricades, and fought a bloody but hopeless battle during the so-called June Days against the regular troops sent by the provisional government to suppress them. The failure of the national workshops and the battles of the June Days were of great importance in the history of socialism, because they seemed to many to demonstrate decisively that the early socialist notion that the reconciliation of classes could be achieved by the gradual remodeling of the industrial system was fallacious. Karl Marx later labeled these early socialists "utopian," implying that they were unrealistic dreamers. The way was open for the theory of "scientific socialism" as propounded by Karl Marx himself, which held as one of its basic premises that "the history of all hitherto existing societies has been the history of class conflict."

MARX AND THE FOUNDATION OF COMMUNISM

Karl Marx (1818–1883) was born in Trier in western Germany, the grandson of rabbis and the son of a lawyer who had converted to Christianity when Karl was six. He at first intended becoming a lawyer himself, but after studying law at the universities of Bonn and Berlin, he was won over to the attractions of German philosophy. He was particularly impressed with the philosophic ideas of Georg Wilhelm Friedrich Hegel (1770–1831), who had argued that history was the working out of the purposes of God through a process called the dialectic. Every state of society, which he called the thesis, brings into being its opposite, which he called the antithesis. As a result of the confrontation of the two, the thesis and antithesis fuse to form the synthesis. Marx liked the notion of the dialectic, but believed that it was not the will of God that set the process in motion. He urged that economic rather than nonmaterial forces caused the thesis and antithesis to form. In short, he adopted what became known as the theory of dialectical materialism. Failing to obtain a university post after completing his doctorate at the University of Berlin, he took up journalism in the Rhineland; but the authorities were so appalled by his atheism and his revolutionary fervor that he was compelled to seek refuge, first in Paris and then in Brussels, where he met Friedrich Engels (1820–1895). Engels supplied Marx with first-hand knowledge of industrial conditions in England, which enabled him to bring his philosophic theories into touch with practical realities, and together they worked out the ideas they were to formulate in 1848 in *The Communist Manifesto*, which they wrote for the Communist League, a small international group of revolutionary-minded workers.

In the *Communist Manifesto*, the struggle between classes has become the basis of the dialectic; and the classes at different periods of history are seen to have formed as a result of the changing character of the means of production. In every society, except the original primitive tribe where all property was owned in common, Marx and Engels held, there have been two classes—the exploiter and the exploited. As the means of production change as a result of technological advances, growth of population, or new forms of investment, new classes are created that challenge the dominance of the previous ruling class. Marx and Engels pointed in particular to the Middle Ages, when the commercial middle class of the towns challenged the predominance of a landed aristocracy over unfree serfs. But the eventual triumph of the middle class by the time of the French Revolution led to a new class conflict, that of the industrial owner and the proletariat.

Marx explained the exploitation of the working class by industrial owners through his labor theory of value. The value of all goods was due entirely to the amount of labor time expended on their production. The worker, however, was paid only a small portion of the market value of the goods he or she produced. The difference between the wages paid the worker and the price at

Karl Marx (1818–1883) As a youth, Marx was slight and poetic in appearance. In later life, he developed the physique and beard suitable to the patriarchal role he had assigned himself in the workers' revolution. (German Information Center.)

which the goods were sold, which Marx called "surplus value" and we would call "profit," was appropriated by the owner as legalized exploitation. The process of history, however, was working in favor of the proletariat and would lead inevitably to the final victory of the workers. Industrial ownership was falling into fewer hands as a result of competition among the capitalists, and the proletariat was becoming increasingly numerous and more pauperized. More goods were being produced than could find buyers among the exploited workers, and as a result there were frequent crises of overproduction. The system was thus disintegrating, but the process could be hastened by the activity of an elite of workers, the communists, whose study of the evolution of the historic process would enable them to know the point at which pressure could be applied, by revolutionary activity, to bring about the overthrow of the exploiting class.

Once revolution was successful, the working class would set up a "dictatorship of the proletariat," during which a classless society was to be created. All property was to be brought under public ownership and managed for the common good. But during this transition stage, when workers' attitudes would still be influenced by their indoctrination during the capitalist regime, wages would still be paid in relation to the work performed. During the dictatorship of the proletariat, a complete mental transformation of the workers was to take place. Slowly, a new form of person would arise, for whom cooperation and not competition was the normal way of life. In this society, the motto would be "from each according to his ability, to each according to his need." The subjection of women would be ended, since their exploitation within the family had been due to the existence of private property. Crime would disappear, and the police force would be abolished. When communist regimes existed throughout the world, the army would no longer be necessary. Eventually the very institution of the state would "wither away." And, since society would have become classless, the very process of the dialectic, which had set everything in motion, would halt, since there would no longer be one class to war with another.

After the failure of the 1848 revolutions throughout Europe, Marx settled in London, where he worked out in enormous detail his economic theories. The first volume of *Capital* appeared in 1867, the remaining volumes after his death. At the same time he helped found the First International Workingmens' Association, as a federation of revolutionary workers' groups from all countries that was to work for the overthrow of bourgeois society. Bickering among the members and government persecution led to its disbandment in 1876. A second International, founded in 1889 after Marx's death, although better organized, still could not overcome the quarrels among the different groups of revolutionaries, and in particular failed to heal the breach between the Social Democrats, who believed that the new society could be achieved peacefully through participation in the democratic process, and those, like Marx himself, who saw revolution as the only possibility.

The Marxist analysis of the historical process has been frequently criticized.

The explanation of all human motivation by reference to materialist forces has been challenged as an oversimplification of reality, by omitting such motives as patriotism, religion, or even simple generosity. Changes in the means of production are held to be caused by human ingenuity as much as by the working of economic forces. Even the predicted failure of the capitalist system as a result of its own internal contradictions has been shown not to have occurred. Moreover, many critics have argued that it is impossible to bring about a perfect society by such imperfect means as revolution and proletarian dictatorship, or to compel human beings to become perfect by state controls. To some the very notion of a classless society is as "utopian" as the early socialist dreams that Marx ridiculed. Yet no criticism can deny the power of Marxist thought. Social and historical analysis, for example, has been indelibly affected by such concepts as the permanence of class conflict and the significance of economic motivation. Moreover, as a call for political action, Marxism proved to have an attractive force that no other form of socialist theory possessed, because it was at the same time a denunciation of exploitation, an explanation of the historical process, a plan for revolution, and a blueprint for a new and more noble society.

SUGGESTED READINGS

Origins of the Industrial Revolution

The fullest treatment of the impact of the early inventions is given in Paul Mantoux, *The Industrial Revolution in the Eighteenth Century* (1961). A concise but authoritative survey is given by T. S. Ashton, *The Industrial Revolution, 1760–1830* (1964), and by Phyllis Deane, *The First Industrial Revolution* (2d ed., 1980). Deane joins with W. A. Cole to apply modern economic theory to the quantification of the progress of industrialization, in their *British Economic Growth, 1688–1959: Trends in Structure* (1962).

Manchester as the Prototype of the Industrial City

Asa Briggs, *Victorian Cities* (1968), pp. 88–138, explains why contemporaries regarded Manchester as a symbol of Britain's industrialism. Friedrich Engels uses his experience in managing his father's factory in Manchester as the basis for his classic indictment, *The Condition of the Working Class in England*, first published in 1845. Steven Marcus, in *Engels, Manchester, and the Working Class* (1975), analyzes the influence of Manchester on the growth of Engels' theories that he expounded to Karl Marx. Salford, a suburb of Manchester, is the subject of Robert Roberts, *The Classic Slum* (1971). Dickens's slashing attack on all northern capitalists provides lurid entertainment and still rouses indignation in *Hard Times* (1854).

Changes in slum housing over time are discussed in Enid Gauldie, *Cruel Habitations: A History of Working-Class Housing, 1780–1918* (1974).

The Spread of Industrialism to the Continent

W. O. Henderson, *Britain and Industrial Europe 1750–1870* (1965), emphasizes the British role in stimulating European industrialization, which is analyzed in his *The Industrial Revolution on the Continent* (1967), and in Sidney Pollard, *Peaceful Conquest: The*

Industrialization of Europe, 1760–1970 (1981). For a left-wing description of the condition of the workers in Europe, see Jürgen Kuczynski, *The Rise of the Working Class* (1967). It should be compared with the superb study of E. P. Thompson, *The Making of the English Working Class* (1963), which describes the rise of a proletarian class consciousness.

Utopian Socialism

Alexander Gray, *The Socialist Tradition: From Moses to Lenin* (1947), includes a good overview, but for a more detailed treatment, turn to G. D. H. Cole, *Socialist Thought*, vol. 1, *The Forerunners, 1789–1850* (1955).

Economic Liberalism

Adam Smith himself is persuasive in *Inquiry into the Nature and Causes of the Wealth of Nations* (1776). For a good selection from the writings of the liberals, see John Plamenatz, ed., *Readings from Liberal Writers, English and American* (1965).

Radicalism

John Plamenatz examines the reasons for radical failure in France in *The Revolutionary Movement in France, 1815–1871* (1952). The reasons why Britain's radicals failed to become revolutionary are given in Mark Hovell, *The Chartist Movement* (1925), and Norman Gash, *Aristocracy and People: Britain, 1815–1865* (1980).

Marx and Marxism

Good lives of Marx include Isaiah Berlin, *Karl Marx* (1948), and Franz Mehring, *Karl Marx* (1962). For a manageable selection from Marx's voluminous writings, see Robert C. Tucker, ed., *Marx-Engels Reader* (1972). *The Communist Manifesto* is indispensable reading.

Women and Industrialization

Louise A. Tilly and Joan W. Scott argue, in *Working Women in Nineteenth Century Europe* (1979), that women became more dependent on men as home life was separated further from the workplace. Patricia Branca, *Women in Europe Since 1750* (1978), is a thorough and reliable survey of women's changing roles during the industrial age and of the rise of the women's movement. On the non-industrial employment of women, see Lee Holcombe, *Victorian Ladies at Work: Middle-Class Working Women in England and Wales, 1850–1914* (1973) and Theresa M. McBride, *The Domestic Revolution: The Modernization of Household Service in England and France, 1820–1920* (1976).

15

The Conservative Reaction, 1815–1848

When the powers that had defeated Napoleon met in Vienna in 1814–1815 to write a peace treaty that would restore the tranquility of monarchical Europe, they believed that the two forces they must repress were liberalism and nationalism. The armies of the French Revolution and of Napoleon had taught the subjects of the conservative monarchs that they had the right to use force to remodel their societies and to reconstruct their states. Such disruptive ideas, the peace makers believed, could be robbed of their power of subversion only by the imposition of a system of controls based on an equally powerful ideology—which they called "legitimacy." The principal exponent of this doctrine was Prince Clemens von Metternich, Austrian Chancellor from 1809 to 1848; and he was, to a very large extent, able to unite the conservative powers of Europe in a concerted effort to put down liberalism and nationalism both within their own states and in other countries until finally, in 1848, those forces erupted in a continent-wide revolution.

THE CONGRESS OF VIENNA, 1814–1815

When Napoleon abdicated for the first time in 1814, the rulers or leading ministers of the countries who had defeated him and the representatives of the restored king of France, Louis XVIII, met in Vienna to hammer out a peace settlement. Although they had expected to complete their work within a month,

The Congress of Vienna, by Jean Baptiste Isabey (1767–1855) *Metternich, who chaired the Congress, is standing, in elegant white breeches. The French representative Talleyrand is seated with his arm on the table at the right.* (Reproduced by gracious permission of Her Majesty Queen Elizabeth II.)

they met almost continuously until June 9, 1815, when they signed the final protocol, nine days before Napoleon's final defeat at Waterloo. The peace conference became a gigantic festival in which the Austrian Emperor Francis I (Holy Roman Emperor as Francis II, 1792–1806, Austrian Emperor 1804–1835) acted as host to the aristocracy of all Europe. The city provided a sumptuous setting. Francis gave receptions in the Hofburg palace in the city or in Schönbrunn palace on the edge of Vienna. Austria's nobility entertained in such Baroque city palaces as that of Count Rasumovsky, the patron of the composer Ludwig van Beethoven who conducted several performances of his own works for guests of the conference, and even produced a new performance of his opera *Fidelio.* For those with less cultivated tastes, the emperor's entertainment committee put on military parades, firework displays, ice skating parties, and great balls. Every night at dinner in the Hofburg, forty tables were set for the guests, and 1400 horses were available in the imperial stables for their use.

This entertainment was necessary to amuse the majority of the delegates because the principal decisions of the conference were being made by a very small group of statesmen meeting in Metternich's private offices in the Chancery. Tsar Alexander I personally represented Russia. The British were first represented by the foreign minister, Robert Stewart Castlereagh, and later by the duke of Wellington; Prussia by its chief minister, Prince von Hardenberg; and France by the brilliant, cynical diplomat Talleyrand. Metternich's political philosophy was largely accepted by the congress, although the British at times demurred from its more extreme formulations. Metternich was already one of the most experienced diplomats in Europe. From 1806 to 1809 he had been the Austrian representative in Paris at the request of Napoleon himself, who enjoyed the intellectual duel with the young man whose opinions ran directly counter to his own; and it was during those years in France that Metternich became convinced that Napoleon's claim to be the heir to the Revolution was totally justified. "The Austrian power," he wrote, which he himself represented, was the true guarantor of "the general peace and political equilibrium" against everything Napoleon stood for. Metternich had won the total confidence of the Emperor Francis I, who preferred his hobbies of making chain mail and cooking toffee to the work of administration. Metternich was therefore in a strong position to direct the congress in the direction he wished it to follow.

The first principle of the peace settlement was "legitimacy," which meant the restoration to power of rulers with both a hereditary claim and a conservative attitude toward government. Metternich believed that Louis XVIII in France possessed those qualities, and he opposed the exaction of revenge on France for the conflict into which the French Revolution and Napoleon had plunged Europe. A lenient peace treaty had been concluded with the French king in May 1814, which had permitted France to retain some of its territorial annexations in Europe and had imposed no indemnity; but, because of the enthusiastic welcome given by the French people to Napoleon upon his return from Elba, it was decided, after the Vienna congress was over, to impose a second, harsher treaty in November 1815. This time the French were compelled to pay a large indemnity, to support an army of occupation for five years, and to return the territories they had annexed. Nevertheless, the preservations of France as a viable, conservative monarchy remained one of the basic principles of the peace settlement. The even more conservative kings of Spain and of the Two Sicilies were also restored to power.

The British, Russians, Prussians, and Austrians had already agreed in March 1814 to form a Quadruple Alliance, whose representatives were to meet regularly for the following twenty years to ensure that France would keep the peace terms they imposed on it. In November 1815, they renewed this alliance. The purpose of the alliance was to safeguard legitimacy in Europe, since the four powers promised not only to meet in the case of renewed aggression by France but also to consider measures "for the repose and prosperity of the peoples and for the maintenance of the peace in Europe." This Quadruple Alliance later became confused in the minds of many people in Europe with the Holy Alliance which Tsar Alexander I persuaded the Austrian emperor, the Prussian king, and eventually most of the powers of Europe except Britain, to sign. In addition to a declaration that they would follow Christian concepts of "Justice, Charity, and Peace," they agreed that, "regarding themselves as compatriots . . . [they

would] lend aid and assistance to each other on all occasions and in all places,"
for the maintenance of the social order. It was, however, as members of the
Quadruple Alliance and not because of the reactionary social philosophy of the
Holy Alliance that the conservative monarchies agreed to use their armies to
suppress movements for representative government.

The second principle of the settlement was what Metternich called "equilibrium," and in some ways this principle countervened that of legitimacy. To
establish political stability and a balance of power, the great states believed that
it was wiser to have only strong, conservative monarchies rather than restore
every small state as it had existed in 1789. The two ancient maritime republics
of Genoa and Venice, which had been abolished by Napoleon, were not revived.
The tiny German states, such as the free cities and the principalities of the
imperial knights, which Napoleon had handed to their stronger neighbors, were
not restored. Prussia was strengthened by annexation of parts of Saxony and
of the Rhineland. Although a kingdom of Poland was re-created, it was not
made independent but placed directly under the rule of the tsar, who was also
made ruler of Finland. Austria was given Venice and regained Lombardy, and
was made president of a German Confederation that was to replace the Holy
Roman Empire abolished by Napoleon in 1806.

The third principle of the Congress was to surround France with a number
of strong buffer states, which would prevent its armies from committing future
aggression. On France's northeastern border, Belgium, the former Austrian

*Count Clemens von Metternich, by Sir
Thomas Lawrence (1769–1830)*   In his elegance and good looks, Metternich seemed to
his conservative supporters to symbolize the
continuance of the aristocratic ideals of the old
regime. (Reproduced by gracious permission of
Her Majesty Queen Elizabeth II.)

Netherlands, was united to Holland, whose stadholder became king of the Netherlands. Prussia was to control the Rhine frontier bordering on France. To block the southeastern frontier, Piedmont-Sardinia was given Genoa, Savoy, and Nice.

The peace settlement of 1815 has been criticized for ignoring the national feelings of the peoples who were placed under foreign rule regardless of their wishes, and of retaining in power or restoring to power the most reactionary governments in Europe. But this was precisely what the conference set out to do, believing that only in this way could the peace of Europe be assured. "Unmoved by the errors of our time—errors which always lead society to the abyss," Metternich wrote later, "we have had the happiness in a time full of danger to serve the cause of peace and the welfare of nations, which will never be advanced by political revolutions."[1] Except for the union of Belgium and Holland, which broke apart in 1831, the peace settlement was to last without major change until 1848.

METTERNICH AND THE CONCERT OF EUROPE, 1815–1848

The loose alliance that had been formed at the Congress of Vienna came to be known as the Concert of Europe, and the system of political repression came to be called, to the annoyance of Metternich himself, the Metternich System. Although the victorious powers at the congress had taken as their overriding goal the supervision of France, within three years the restored monarchy of France had been welcomed into the alliance, which was expanded into a Quintuple Alliance. Although the alliance authorized military intervention by the Austrians for the suppression of liberal revolution in Naples in 1821 and by France in Spain in 1823, it soon became clear that the most imminent threats to legitimacy from liberal and national revolutionaries were in the Austrian empire, in Germany, and in the Russian empire.

The Fragility of the Austrian Empire

The country that was most vulnerable to the attacks of liberalism and nationalism was Metternich's own, the Austrian empire. In 1815, this empire had two basic weaknesses, the unrest of subject nationalities under the rule of German-speaking Austrians and the resentment of the peasant majority at the small but extremely wealthy aristocratic landowning class. From about 1830 on, with the onset of industrialization, a third source of discontent appeared, the anger of exploited urban workers against the industrial owners.

The Austrian empire was a ramshackle creation. In this empire of 30 million people, only one-quarter spoke German, but the administration of the empire

[1] Prince Clemens von Metternich, *Memoirs* (London: Bentley, 1888), I, 175.

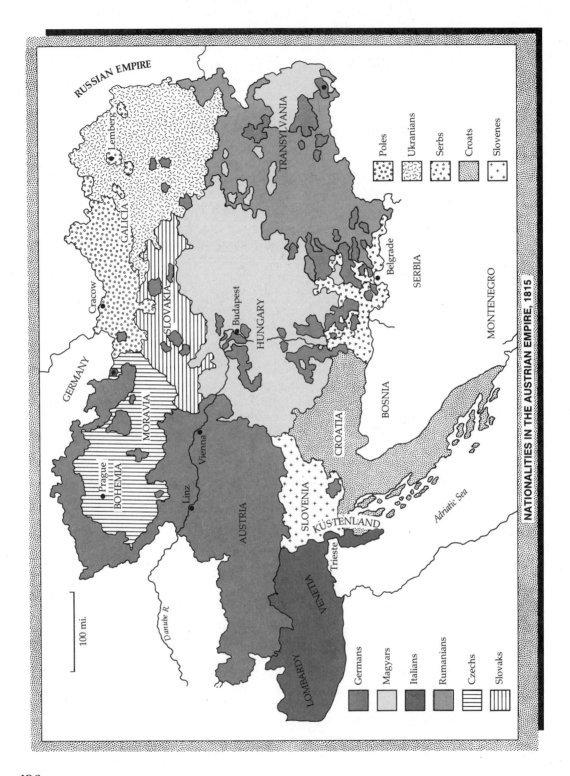

RUSSIAN EMPIRE

GALICIA

Lemberg

Cracow

GERMANY

SLOVAKIA

MORAVIA

Prague

BOHEMIA

Linz

Vienna

AUSTRIA

Budapest

HUNGARY

TRANSYLVANIA

Belgrade

SERBIA

MONTENEGRO

BOSNIA

CROATIA

SLOVENIA

KÜSTENLAND

Trieste

VENETIA

LOMBARDY

Adriatic Sea

Danube R.

100 mi.

Poles

Ukranians

Serbs

Croats

Slovenes

Germans

Magyars

Italians

Rumanians

Czechs

Slovaks

NATIONALITIES IN THE AUSTRIAN EMPIRE, 1815

was dominated by a largely German-speaking class of bureaucrats centered in Vienna but working also from regional capitals such as Prague and Budapest. National feeling was very strong among all the subject nationalities, and increased in fervor during the early nineteenth century, especially as the Romantic movement influenced students and professors in the universities, artists and writers, and members of the professional classes. As long as it remained a largely cultural phenomenon, nationalism could be kept under control by various expedients of censorship and occasional arrests. Metternich was, however, aware of the danger of the grievances spreading to the aristocrats, and he made efforts to encourage the non-German nobles to enter the upper level of nobility, which dominated the court life of Vienna. In the Hungarian noble Count Stephen Széchenyi, for example, Metternich found a collaborator who sought the economic development of Hungary within the unity of the Austrian empire. Within the Hungarian assembly, Széchenyi worked for the modernization of Hungarian transport, especially roads and bridges, reclamation of wastes, and the founding of industry; and he strongly opposed the nationalist Louis Kossuth, who was Metternich's greatest critic in Hungary. Metternich also had plans to appeal to the non-German aristocrats by the constitutional renovation of the empire. He wished to set up a new council of state broadly representative of the national groups within the empire, and on one occasion proposed that the chancery in Vienna be divided into six separate national groups. He was unable to persuade either Francis I or his successor, Ferdinand I (reigned 1835–1848), to accept any of these plans.

Metternich saw peasant revolts as less dangerous than nationalist revolts. Metternich even felt that discontent in the countryside would ensure the loyalty to the empire of the non-German aristocrats, who needed the empire's support to maintain their privileged positions. A nationalist uprising in Poland in 1846, for example, failed when the Polish peasantry used the opportunity presented by the involvement of their landlords in the uprising to attempt to gain control of their lands.

The rise of an urban working class between 1830 and 1848 proved more destabilizing than peasant discontent. The construction of railroads had encouraged the founding of manufacturing plants in cities such as Budapest and Prague, as well as the development of mining in Bohemia. But the most rapid industrial growth had been in the outer suburbs of Vienna, whose population increased by 100,000 in the 1830s and 1840s as migrants from the countryside moved in to take jobs in the construction industry and textile plants. When large numbers of these workers joined the demonstrations of students and intellectuals against Metternich in March 1848, the chancellor was compelled to resign.

Before 1848, however, Metternich's secret police and prisons were sufficient to keep order within the Austrian empire. Only when liberal, nationalist, and social revolt occurred almost simultaneously throughout the empire was there an opportunity for revolution to be successful.

Russia Under Alexander I and Nicholas II

During the first half of the nineteenth century, Russia alternated between half-hearted efforts at reform and whole-hearted and largely successful repression. The nationalist threat to the empire came primarily from within the enlarged Polish state. Inside Russia itself, demands for some kind of constitutional, more broadly based government were expressed largely by the Westernized aristocracy of the Saint Petersburg court. To Tsar Paul I (reigned 1796–1801), repression and isolation from Western influences was the solution. He was murdered by his own guards, who hoped that the new tsar, Alexander I (reigned 1801–1825) would agree to share power with the aristocracy. At first working through a committee of personal friends who all admired the West, he attempted to reorganize the government on Western lines, founded several new universities, and encouraged aristocrats to free their serfs. As the war with Napoleon progressed, the tsar became more fanatical in religion and more repressive in politics. The universities and schools were strictly controlled, and almost half a million peasants were forced into "military colonies," in which they both acted as soldiers and worked the land. Alexander's repressive attitude roused opposition among the young aristocrats who had come to know Europe during the campaigns against Napoleon, and they formed secret societies: the Northern Society in Saint Petersburg, which wanted a liberal monarchy along British lines, and the more radical Southern Society in Kiev, which wanted the murder of the tsar, a centralized republic, and the grant of the land to the serfs. When Alexander I died unexpectedly in December 1825, there was confusion as to whether the throne should pass to his younger brother, Constantine, or to the even younger brother Nicholas in whose favor Constantine had secretly renounced the throne. Profiting from the confusion, the Northern Society called upon the garrison of Saint Petersburg to revolt, but, when they did, Nicholas had them shot down by loyal troops. A revolt by the Southern Society was foiled by the arrest of its leader. This so-called Decembrist revolt reconfirmed Nicholas I (reigned 1825–1855) in his conservatism, and throughout his reign he intensified the repression of all liberal forces.

Discontent in Poland was the next to erupt. Although the Poles had been allowed to have their own army and administration, they had become increasingly resentful in the last years of the reign of Alexander I at the officials he appointed and at strict police controls. Secret societies were founded in the universities and army academies. In November 1830, army cadets in Warsaw seized control of the city and, joined by aristocrats and gentry, formed a provisional government. They received almost no support from the peasantry, however, nor from Britain and France, from whom they had expected immediate aid. Nicholas sent a strong Russian army into Poland, which captured Warsaw and engaged in vicious reprisals against the leaders of the revolt. Thousands fled the country as Nicholas ended Polish autonomous administration, closed several universities, and placed the army in control.

Within Russia itself he was even more repressive. The "Third Section" of the chancery was set up as a kind of political police, with power over all aspects of Russian life. Censorship and controls over the universities were increased. Thus repression made it possible to avoid the desperately needed reforms, especially improvement of the conditions of the serfs, and to postpone plans to modernize the economy.

The Repression of German Liberalism

Metternich saw in Germany three separate dangers—nationalist revolution for the union of the country and the ouster of Austria from Germany, a liberal revolution led by university professors and students for the abolition of conservative monarchy, and a social revolution by the peasantry for the annexation of the land of the aristocrats. He used the assembly of the German Confederation as a means of maintaining Austrian representation inside Germany and as a way of palliating German discontent by establishing certain common policies such as defense. But the king of Prussia and several conservative German rulers were deeply worried at the activity of German student organizations, which had demonstrated by burning books of conservative writers. In 1819, Metternich seized the excuse of the murder by a demented student of a reactionary playwright to push through the German Confederation passage of the Carlsbad Decrees, which banned the student groups, instituted press censorship, and ordered the police to root out subversives in the universities. New demonstrations in 1832 for establishment of a republic in Germany once again gave Metternich the excuse to push through the diet of the German Confederation measures restoring the power of the few German princes who had been compelled to grant constitutions. In Germany by 1833, discontent had been forced underground. There were, however, signs that the "Metternich system" was beginning to break down.

Fissures in the Metternich System

In 1821, the Greeks revolted against the Turks, who had occupied Greece since the fifteenth century. Their uprising was greeted throughout Western Europe not only as a Christian battle against Muslims but as a liberal and nationalist crusade. For Metternich, the revolt posed a difficult quandary. While sympathizing with them as Christians, he could hardly condone their determination to overthrow an established government. He reconciled himself not to intervene on behalf of the Turks by the consideration that the Turkish empire was not part of the Concert of Europe as it had been formed in 1815. Greek independence was recognized in 1829 after the destruction of the Turkish fleet by the British and French and the invasion of the Turkish provinces of Moldavia and Wallachia (now part of Rumania) by Russia. The principles of legitimacy were, however, upheld by the offer of the new Greek throne to the son of the king

Massacre at Chios, by Eugène Delacroix *Delacroix's depiction of the Turkish attack on the Greek population of the island of Chios in 1822 was intended to stir sympathy in France for the cause of Greek independence.* (Musée National du Louvre/Alinari-Art Resource.)

of Bavaria, whose family had the hereditary right to rule in southern Germany if not in Greece and who could be relied upon to govern in a suitably conservative manner.

In 1830–1831, the successful revolt of the Belgians against the Dutch, under whom they had been unwillingly placed by decision of the Congress of Vienna, split the Quintuple Alliance wide open. When the Dutch King William I appealed to the great powers for military aid in bringing the Belgians back under his control, the Russians, Prussians, and Austrians appeared willing to comply with his request. The French government, however, warned that it would not tolerate the appearance of their troops in an area on the French border. A compromise was reached with the offer of the Belgian throne to the German prince Leopold of Saxe-Coburg-Gotha, the uncle of the future Queen Victoria of England, which was accepted by all the great powers. In an ironic reversal of their positions, the Russians, Prussians, and Austrians authorized the British and French to send military forces to eject a Dutch army that William had sent for the reconquest of Belgium.

After 1831, there were no further successful attempts to overthrow the established governments of Europe before the continent-wide revolts of 1848. But for all the appearance of placid somnolence, the suppressed resentment continued to build toward continent-wide revolution.

LIBERALISM IN BRITAIN AND FRANCE, 1815–1848

Liberalism, in the sense of the greater participation of the industrial middle classes in the control of the government and the introduction by government of the laissez-faire principles of economics, advanced rapidly in Britain and France at the very time that Metternich was striving to oppose its progress in Eastern and Central Europe and in Spain. Britain and France differed from the other continental powers in several important ways. First, they were not seriously threatened by the demands of nationalism. Both countries had been nation-states since the Middle Ages. The demands of regional minorities such as the Welsh or the Bretons would not become significant until the mid-twentieth century. The Scots and Welsh were quiescent under British rule, and the Irish could be held down by force, although they did present a constant problem to British governments throughout the nineteenth century. Second, the aristocrats of both countries were prepared, or could be forced, to share power with the rising middle class. Third, the pressure of the lower middle and working classes for increased political participation for themselves could be harnessed by the upper middle classes in their own favor, without the grant of the broadened suffrage that the radicals were demanding.

Britain Under Tory Rule, 1815–1830

To suppress working-class unrest during the economic depression that followed the end of the Napoleonic wars, the government of the Tory party in Britain embarked upon a policy of reaction that paralleled the policies of Metternich on the continent. As we saw in Chapter 14, the government had used force against such demonstrations as that in Peterloo Fields at Manchester in 1819, and had severely curtailed public liberties. In 1822, however, the government was broadened by the admission of several reformers, who changed the direction of British policy. The remodeled government refused to support the attempts of the Quintuple Alliance to put down liberal revolutions. Tariffs that restricted British trade were abolished. The formation of trade unions was permitted. In 1829, the Tory government forced through Parliament the Catholic Emancipation Act, by which Catholics were permitted to hold public office and to sit in Parliament for the first time since those rights were withdrawn in the anti-Catholic reaction during the reign of Charles II. The Tories, in spite of their proclaimed opposition to social change, had thus succeeded in allaying part of Britain's discontent.

Parliamentary Reform

The successful revolution of July 1830, which brought the liberals to power in France, influenced the elections in Britain that year. The victory of the Whigs brought to an end almost fifty years of Tory rule. The Whigs determined that it was time for the monopoly of power by what they regarded as conservative-minded landlords to be ended. In the Reform Bill of 1832, they gave the vote to all who owned or leased property whose annual rental value was at least ten pounds. This measure increased the number eligible to vote by only 200,000, thus extending the suffrage only to include the upper middle class. Second, the constituencies were redistributed, 168 seats being taken from the rural areas of the south and given to the new industrial areas of the north, for the specific purpose of enabling the new industrial owners (but not the workers employed by them) to be represented in Parliament. The Reform Bill thus gave the industrial middle class an important share in power. Other reforms followed. The Factory Act of 1833 forbade child labor below the age of nine. Slavery was abolished in the British Empire (and the owners compensated). The Municipal Corporations Act permitted cities to carry out local administration through elected councils. It did, however, require seven years of agitation by the Anti-Corn Law League and the impact of the Irish famine of 1845–1846 to force the abolition of the Corn Laws through Parliament; and it was the Tory government of Robert Peel, which came to power in 1846, rather than a Whig government, that passed this reform.

In 1848, in spite of the Chartist agitation, Britain was able to pass virtually unscathed through the year of revolutionary agitation that was shattering governments all over the continent. By admitting the upper middle class to a share in political power, Britain's aristocracy had prevented them from uniting with the lower middle and working classes in agitation to overthrow the domination of the aristocracy itself.

The Restoration in France, 1814–1830

When Louis XVIII was restored to the French throne in 1814, he realized that it was impossible to restore the absolute powers the monarchy had wielded before 1789. He granted a constitutional charter, setting up a two-house legislature. The Chamber of Peers was nominated by the king, the Chamber of Deputies chosen by an electorate of about 100,000 who met high property-owning qualifications. The so-called Ultra-Royalists, composed largely of nobles returning from exile and of conservative clergy, won the election of 1815, however, and sought to set back the clock to 1789 by punishing revolutionary and Bonapartist leaders for treason and for attempting to regain their own property. They were forced out in 1816, after their supporters had engaged in an orgy of revenge known as the White Terror. A more moderate government ran France for the next four years, but after 1820 policy was dominated by Louis XVIII's younger brother, who became king as Charles X (reigned 1824–1830).

Charles was determined to exclude the upper middle classes from power, even though the industrial revolution was gaining a foothold in France, and he relied almost entirely on the Church and the more extreme members of the aristocracy. He compensated the aristocrats financially for their losses during the Revolution, with funds obtained by lowering the interest on government bonds, and welcomed the Jesuits into France again. Extreme Catholics were placed in leading positions in the university and secondary schools. As a result, the middle classes became outright opponents of the restored monarchy, and sought supporters among the urban working classes for the eventual overthrow of the monarchy and its conservative supporters.

The Bourgeois Monarchy of Louis Philippe

When, in 1830, Charles X attempted to change the constitution by restricting the suffrage even further, Parisian rioters forced the flight of the king, with the goal of establishing a republic, but the wealthy middle classes forestalled them by forming a provisional government that offered the throne to the cousin of Charles X, the duke of Orleans, who became king as Louis Philippe (reigned 1830–1848). Under this so-called July or Bourgeois Monarchy, France was governed by the upper middle classes. The new government issued a charter, which expanded the suffrage from 100,000 to 170,000, thus bringing into the ruling class a slightly less wealthy segment of the upper middle classes. The well-to-do middle classes of France, however, were not prepared for significant reform in the industrial system. A Factory Act was passed but not enforced. Uprisings by the workers in Lyons and Paris were put down with great brutality by government troops. Censorship was reinforced on the newspapers, on the grounds that it was necessary to protect the king, on whose life several attempts had been made. The Bourgeois Monarchy was in fact facing considerable opposition from outside the assembly. Legitimists wished to restore the reign of Charles X. Bonapartists, influenced by the "Napoleonic legend," a rosy portrayal in books, poems, and the press of Napoleon as a persevering reformer, wanted to restore the Bonaparte dynasty. Students and some of the more radical-minded of the working classes wanted to establish a republic, and a few admirers of the utopian socialists hoped to transform France's whole economic and social system as a result of revolution. Even within the Chamber of Deputies, there were demands for widening of the suffrage and further social reforms. With no solid base of support beyond their own restricted class, it would take only three days of rioting in February 1848 before the monarchy of the upper bourgeoisie was overthrown.

THE REVOLUTIONS OF 1848

Causes of the Revolutions

Only Britain and Russia remained immune to the revolutions that spread throughout Europe in the spring of 1848, Britain because it had implemented just sufficient reform, Russia because its repression was efficient and the reformers disorganized. Beginning with an uprising in Sicily in January, the European states were shaken during the next four months by almost fifty separate revolutions. Although each of these revolutions was influenced by local causes of discontent, the revolutions also had in common opposition to the conservative alliance orchestrated by Metternich through which the demands for political and social reform had been frustrated since 1815. The demands of the revolutionary leaders were primarily for representative democracy and national rights, sometimes together, sometimes separately. The former wanted above all an extension of the suffrage, as well as the grant of such political rights as freedom of assembly, freedom of the press, reduction of police powers, and reduction of the privileges of the aristocracy. They were divided between the liberal middle class, which would be satisfied to extend the suffrage only to property owners, and the radicals, who demanded universal suffrage, usually within a republican government. The nationalists, who up to this point were usually liberal or radical in their political views, were active mainly in Italy and Germany, where they demanded the formation of a unified nation-state, and in the Austrian empire, where they wished autonomy or even independence of the individual national groups within the empire. A third pressure for reform came as a result of the widely felt suffering among the poor in all parts of Europe. Europe's rapidly growing population had made it increasingly difficult to provide an adequate food supply. When harvests of potatoes and cereals failed, as they did in 1845 and 1846, famine threatened in many parts of Europe, and not merely in those regions where the crop was grown. The consolidation of farms on the continent for more efficient production had forced part of the rural population to move into the cities, where they faced social discrimination and the constant danger of unemployment. As industrialization advanced in such cities as Vienna and Milan, an urban working class expressed the same grievances against the industrial owners that had been voiced earlier in the textile and mining towns of Britain. Thus, to the demands for self-government and national self-determination, the working class added their demand for a more secure and cheaper food supply, steady and fairly paid work, and better living conditions. By failing to undertake the piecemeal reforms that saved the British government, the conservative adherents of the Metternich system on the continent had made revolution inevitable.

Early Revolutionary Victories

Revolution began in Palermo in Sicily on January 12, and the king was almost immediately forced to grant a liberal constitution. From there the uprisings spread to many of the other states of Italy.

On February 22, after the French government banned a public banquet, which had been called to demand universal suffrage, crowds began to demonstrate in the streets of Paris. The next day, when royal troops fired on the

Meeting of the Frankfurt Parliament, September 1848 *The Parliament, elected by male suffrage in Germany and Austria, wrote a federal constitution that was never adopted by the separate German states.* (Bildarchiv Preussischer Kulterbesitz.)

crowds, killing a number of demonstrators, the demonstrations became more violent. On February 24, King Louis Philippe fled into exile, and the radicals, led by the poet Alphonse de Lamartine, set up a provisional government. During the following weeks, the government passed a number of far-reaching reforms. France was made into a republic, and a new constitution was written creating a 900-member assembly elected by universal male suffrage. The socialists were appeased by establishment of national workshops that would provide work for the unemployed.

When news of the ouster of the French king reached the Austrian empire, it sparked revolution in every part of the empire. In Budapest on March 3, the popular Hungarian nationalist leader Louis Kossuth made a speech in the assembly demanding autonomy and a change in the constitution of the Austrian empire. On March 11, an assembly of Czechs meeting in Prague made similar demands. On March 13, students in Vienna joined with local deputies in demanding reforms, but later, when they were joined by discontented workers from the city's slums, the troops opened fire on the crowd, converting a peaceful demonstration into a violent uprising. That evening the emperor, fearing for his own life, promised to grant all the demands of the crowds. Metternich resigned, and left Vienna in disguise. Once he was gone, the emperor agreed to the constitutional changes demanded by the Hungarians and Czechs; and, when revolution broke out in Milan in the Austrian province of Lombardy, he withdrew the Austrian troops from the city, leaving it in the hands of the revolutionaries. Determined to add Lombardy to his own kingdom, Charles Albert, king of Piedmont-Sardinia, then declared war on Austria and invaded Lombardy.

On March 18, crowds demonstrating in Berlin for constitutional change in Prussia were also fired on by the troops. Rioting broke out, and the king withdrew the troops from Berlin and granted a liberal constitution. Rulers in several other German states were compelled to follow his example. The nationalists seized the opportunity to organize the calling of an all-German parliament, elected by universal male suffrage, which met in Frankfurt on May 18. This assembly of intellectuals, which had set itself the task of writing a constitution for a unified Germany, lacked all practical political experience, however, and was hampered from the start by the animosity of the conservative rulers. Although the Frankfurt Parliament attempted to act as a German government, and even declared war on Denmark, it had no independent power. Nevertheless, in May 1848, it looked as though the revolutions throughout Europe had been largely successful. Constitutions had been granted in almost every conservative state. Concessions had been made to the nationalists in both Germany and Austria. Even the workers had won the institution of national workshops in France, and had been given employment on public works projects in Austria.

The Revolutions Repressed

From June 1848, however, the counterattack of the conservatives was even more successful. In France, fearing the danger of violence from the laborers in the national workshops, the government had agreed to the suppression of the workshops. In protest the Parisians began to erect barricades in the working-class districts. The government called in the tough General Louis Eugène Cavaignac to use the regular army to force the workers into submission. In the bloody June Days, Cavaignac bombarded the city and then unleashed his soldiers, supported by thousands of peasants from the countryside, to massacre the Parisian insurgents. Martial law was declared, and up to 12,000 Parisians were exiled to the French colonies. Neither Cavaignac nor Lamartine profited from this action. When they ran as candidates in the presidential elections of December 1848, they were defeated by Louis-Napoleon Bonaparte, the nephew of the Emperor Napoleon I, who seemed to many to offer an ideal compromise. As the heir of Napoleon, he offered order and military glory. But he had earlier written a book called *The Extinction of Pauperism*, which correctly showed that he intended to apply the teachings of Saint-Simon if he ever came to power. And he had cultivated the peasants by promising better relations with the Catholic Church. With his overwhelming election victory—he received the votes

The Emperor Francis Joseph of Austria (reigned 1848–1916) *During his 68-year reign, Francis Joseph struggled unsuccessfully to hold together the quarrelling nationalities that made up the Habsburg inheritance. (Bildarchiv Preussischer Kulterbesitz.)*

of 5.5 million of the electorate to only 2.4 million votes for all other candidates together—France was able to avoid the extremes of the conservative reaction that were to afflict the rest of Europe.

In Austria, the government determined that only extreme force could repress the revolutionaries. It ordered its generals to bombard rebellious cities, including Vienna itself, into submission. After the cities were taken, army troops massacred thousands of citizens and engaged in widespread plunder. Once the rebellions were crushed, the government tried to win upper-middle-class support by passing some legal and economic reforms and by having the Emperor Ferdinand I abdicate in favor of his nephew Francis Joseph (reigned 1848–1916).

In November 1848, the king of Prussia felt strong enough to send his troops back into Berlin, and he dismissed the constituent assembly and withdrew the Prussian delegates from the Frankfurt Parliament. His army was then sent to aid other rulers in Germany put down the revolutionaries in their states. The Frankfurt Parliament collapsed in June 1849, when the last members dispersed to their home states.

The revolutions of 1848 had failed for several reasons. In the first place, the conservative governments had control of the armies, whose generals had remained loyal. Against this force, no impromptu revolutionary militia could in the long run be successful. Second, the liberals and radicals had quarreled among themselves, most notably over the extent to which the suffrage should be extended, and with the social reformers, whose demands for far-reaching economic change had been refused. Third, the nationalists, particularly in Germany, had proved to be ineffective revolutionaries. They had quarreled with each other, and often shown themselves unwilling to grant to others rights of self-government they were demanding for themselves. Finally, the industrial revolution was not advanced enough to have created a sufficiently large class of deprived workers who could carry through a revolution by themselves, without the aid of the middle classes or of the peasantry. Hence, almost nothing had been achieved that survived the repression that began in June 1848 and was virtually complete by the end of 1849. Perhaps the most dangerous result of the failure was that the nationalists in Germany and Italy decided to abandon the democratic reformers, and seek their goals by alliance with the established monarchies.

SUGGESTED READINGS

General Surveys, 1815–1848

Eric Hobsbawm suggests many penetrating insights, from a left-wing viewpoint, in *The Age of Revolutions, 1789–1848* (1964). J. R. Talmon's *Romanticism and Revolt: Europe 1815–1848* (1979), is judiciously balanced, a nice achievement when dealing with such an age of confrontation.

Metternich and the Conservative Reaction

Whether one agrees with Metternich or not, it is hard not to be fascinated by his urbane elegance as seen in G. de Bertier de Sauvigny, *Metternich and His Times* (1970). His diplomacy is tellingly analyzed in Henry A. Kissinger, *A World Restored* (1964). The problems facing the Habsburg monarchy in the early nineteenth century appear insoluble, as perhaps they were, in Robert Kann, *The Multinational Empire* (1950), and C. A. Macartney, *The Habsburg Empire, 1790–1918* (1969). On Metternich's capital, see Ilsa Barea, *Vienna: Legend and Reality* (1966).

The repression of discontent in Russia is described in Hugh Seton-Watson, *Imperial Russia, 1801–1917* (1967), while for detailed studies of the Decembrists, see Anatole G. Mazour, *The First Russian Revolution* (1957), and Marc Raeff, *The Decembrist Movement* (1966).

Liberal Advances in Britain and France

Good introductions to British history in the nineteenth century include Asa Briggs, *The Making of Modern England, 1783–1867: The Age of Improvement* (1959), and David Thomson, *England in the Nineteenth Century* (1950). Cecil Woodham Smith's *Queen Victoria* (1972) is an entertaining biography. Her study of the Irish potato famine, *The Great Hunger* (1963), is considerably less amusing.

Frederick B. Artz, *France Under the Bourbon Restoration, 1814–1830* (1931, 1963) is still useful. For a fine modern appraisal of the 1830 revolution, see David Pinckney, *The French Revolution of 1830* (1972). For the quintessential liberal statesman, see Douglas W. Johnson, *Guizot* (1963).

The Revolutions of 1848

The events in the different countries of Europe can be compared in Priscilla Robertson, *The Revolutions of 1848* (1952), and Francois Fejtö, ed., *The Reopening of an Era, 1848: A Historical Symposium* (1948). Detailed studies of the individual revolutions that not only analyze national grievances but bring alive the drama and suffering of the uprisings include: on France, Georges Duveau, *1848: The Making of a Revolution* (1966); on Austria, R. John Rath, *The Viennese Revolution of 1848* (1957); on Germany, Lewis B. Namier, *1848: The Revolution of the Intellectuals* (1946). Perhaps the best description of all is to be found in Gustave Flaubert's novel, *A Sentimental Education,* first published in 1869, which correctly indicates how chaotic events were after the first Parisian demonstration on February 22, and how little the average person knew about what was going on.

part VI

The Age of Nationalism and Imperialism

Prince Otto von Bismarck (1815–1898) *Bismarck's ruthless determination to dominate European politics in the late nineteenth century won him the nickname "Iron Chancellor."* (IN-Press/Bundesbildstelle from German Information Center.)

THE AGE OF NATIONALISM AND IMPERIALISM

Dates	Political & Military Events	Social, Economic, & Demographic Events	Religion & Philosophy	Art, Architecture, Literature, & Music	Science & Technology
1850s		Fall in death rate			Steel replaces iron in construction
1851		Great Exhibition, London		d. Turner	
1852	Second Empire, France (1852–70)			Rebuilding of central Paris	
1853	Crimean War (1853–56)			Wagner, *Ring of the Nibelung* (1853–74)	
1856	Congress of Paris			Flaubert, *Madame Bovary*	Bessemer process for steel
1859	Italian War (1859–60)	Suez Canal begun	Churches oppose theory of evolution	Millet, *Angelus*	Darwin, *Origin of Species*
1861	French intervention in Mexico	Emancipation of Russian serfs			
1862	Bismarck, Chancellor, Prussia				Pasteur's germ theory of infection
1866	Austro-Prussian War Italy annexes Venice	Burton and Speke to East Africa Growing terrorism in Russia		Dostoevsky, *Crime and Punishment*	Nobel invents dynamite
1867	Disraeli, Prime Minister, Britain Formation of Dual Monarchy, Austria-Hungary	U.S. purchases Alaska		Marx, *Capital* (1867–94)	
1870	Franco-Prussian War French Third Republic founded	Scramble for Africa begins		d. Dickens	
1871	Second German Empire founded		Anti-Catholic laws in Germany (1871–73)		
1874		Britain founds Gold Coast colony		First Impressionist exhibition	

Year					
1876					Alexander Graham Bell's telephone
1878	Congress of Berlin				
1879	Dual Alliance (Germany, Austria)				Edison's electric light bulb
1880s		Cartels in U.S.		Post-Impressionism in art. Symbolism in literature.	
1886					First Daimler-Benz automobile
1888	William II, Germany (1888–1918)				
1890	Dismissal of Bismarck	Russian industrialization begins		d. van Gogh	
1894	Nicholas II, Russia (1894–1917)	Dreyfus affair, France (1894–1906)			
1898	Spanish-American War	U.S. annexes Philippines			
1899	Boer War (1899–1902)				
1900s				First motion pictures	
1901	Edward VII, Britain (1901–1910)				
1903					Orville and Wilbur Wright's airplane
1905	Revolution in Russia		Separation church and state, France		
1914	First World War (1914–18)				
1917	March Revolution, Russia; November Revolution, Russia				
1919	Paris Peace Conference				

16

The Zenith of the European Nation-State, 1848–1914

Repression of the 1848 revolutions, while successful in the short run, could not postpone for long the resurgent demands for greater political participation by both the middle and working classes and the determination of national or ethnic groups to form nation-states of their own. In Germany and even to some extent in Italy, middle-class liberals were compelled to accept the leadership of conservative and often militaristic nationalists to gain the national unification that both countries achieved in 1870–1871. In Britain, the wealthy middle class that had profited from the parliamentary reform of 1832 was forced to allow broad political participation and far-reaching social reforms. In France, Louis Napoleon Bonaparte, reigning as Emperor Napoleon III from 1852 to 1870, attempted first to win support by economic reform and military adventure but finally resorted toward the end of his reign to increasing democracy. Austria, unable to restore the efficacy of the Metternich system without its founder, attempted to save its empire from disintegration by sharing rule of the smaller nationalities between the German-speaking Austrians and the Hungarian Magyars. Even in Russia, Tsar Alexander II had neither the ability nor the wish to continue the repressive policies of Nicholas I, and attempted to solve the dual problem of inefficient agriculture and discontented peasants by abolishing serfdom in 1861, a step followed in 1864 by granting some local self-government to elected assemblies.

THE UNIFICATION OF ITALY AND GERMANY

The Kingdom of Piedmont-Savoy

The failure of the revolutions of 1848–1849 in Italy discredited the revolutionary leaders, not only for their inability to resist the Austrian and French armies but by the way in which they had run the republics they had founded. Although a number of conservative Catholics held that the only way left to unify Italy was as a federation under the pope, a majority of Italian nationalists decided after 1848 that constitutional monarchy under the rule of the king of Piedmont-Savoy was preferable. Many factors were in favor of the leadership of Piedmont. The state, which consisted of Piedmont itself, the territory of the old republic of Genoa, the island of Sardinia, and the two French-speaking provinces of Savoy and Nice, had a solid economic base in the agriculture and industry of the upper Po Valley. Its king, Charles Albert, had won support of the nationalists by his attack on the Austrians in Lombardy in 1848 and of the liberals by granting the most democratic constitution in Italy. The new King Victor Emmanuel II (king of Piedmont, 1849–1861; king of Italy, 1861–1878) had found in Count Camillo Cavour, a Piedmontese noble and industrial entrepreneur, the statesman of genius who could unify Italy under Piedmont.

Because of his admiration for the British constitution and of his willingness to work with the Piedmontese parliament, Cavour has often been presented as a well meaning liberal, and contrasted favorably with the conservative Prince Otto von Bismarck, who united Germany under Prussia. Cavour, however, had a great deal in common with Bismarck in his approach to national unification, which both knew would be achieved only by diplomatic guile and military force. Cavour's first actions as premier of Piedmont were to modernize the economy of Piedmont. He built railroads and purchased steamboats, founded new industries and banks, abolished most of the monasteries and confiscated their lands. The size of the army was increased and its equipment improved.

Italy Unified

Cavour found an ally willing to help his new army oust the Austrians from Italy in the new French emperor, Napoleon III, who, as the descendant of the Corsican Bonaparte family, felt personal sympathy for the Italian cause. By dangling in front of Napoleon III the offer of ceding Savoy and Nice to France, Cavour gained Napoleon III's promise to intervene against the Austrians if they could be made to appear the aggressors in a war with Piedmont. Cavour provoked the Austrians into invading Piedmont in April 1859, by massing his army at the border with Lombardy. The French armies rushed to Piedmont's support, and defeated the Austrians at the battles of Magenta and Solferino. To Cavour's fury, Napoleon III, however, aghast at the cost in French lives and under

Guiseppe Garibaldi (1807–1882) *Garibaldi was idolized for his many efforts to unify Italy. In 1860, with a thousand "red shirts," he conquered Sicily and Naples, which he handed over to King Victor Emmanuel II.* (Bildarchiv Preussischer Kulturbesitz.)

Catholic pressure at home not to permit an attack on the Papal States, made a separate peace with the Austrians, giving to Piedmont Lombardy but not Venetia. However, insurrections orchestrated by Cavour broke out in several central Italian states, which at their request were then united to Piedmont. To assuage Napoleon, who had not expected this sudden increase in the size of Piedmont, Cavour then ceded Savoy and Nice to France.

When an insurrection broke out in Sicily, Cavour secretly permitted the colorful nationalist Giuseppe Garibaldi to sail from Piedmont with a thousand volunteers, known as his "red shirts," to aid the uprising. Within weeks, Garibaldi was in control of southern Italy and seemed prepared to march on Rome to drive out the pope. To forestall him, Cavour sent the Piedmontese army, under the personal command of the king, through the Papal States to meet Garibaldi north of Naples. There, in a dramatic meeting, Garibaldi, who had been a staunch supporter of republicanism, handed over to the king the territories he had conquered. They were united to the enlarged state of Piedmont as the kingdom of Italy, with Victor Emmanuel as king and Florence as its capital. Venetia and the area around Rome still remained to be annexed, however. Cavour himself died three months later, and did not live to see the final completion of his work. Venetia was annexed with Prussian help in 1866, and Rome was finally incorporated into Italy in 1870.

Italy After 1871

The unification of Italy did not prove the panacea the nationalists had hoped for. Although the suffrage was gradually extended until in 1912 all males over the age of thirty could vote, parliamentary democracy did not work well. Catholics had been forbidden by the pope to participate in the politics of the new state, and the pope himself had retired into self-imposed imprisonment within the Vatican, from which no pope was to emerge until a new agreement was reached with the Italian state in 1929. Parties lacked a coherent ideology, and power fell into the hands of a series of strong political manipulators, who were able to put together parliamentary majorities based largely on the self-interest of the deputies. Regional patriotism remained strong, adding a further obstacle to the creation of genuine national political parties.

The deepest weakness of the state was the economic and social division between north and south. The united kingdom, created as it had been under Piedmont, favored the industrializing north at the expense of the rural, semi-feudal south. Tariffs, for example, favored the import of cheap food for the industrial workers of the north, but kept industrial goods expensive so that imports could not compete with northern products. State investment in such public works as harbors, roads, and the telegraph was spent largely in the north. With a higher birth rate than the north, the south found itself wracked by chronic problems of overpopulation and underdevelopment, and after 1890 the poor southern peasants saw emigration as the only salvation. Between 1890 and 1914, 5 million Italians emigrated, primarily to other parts of Europe and to North America.

Italy nevertheless attempted to play a role in world affairs that was beyond its means. In 1882, it joined the German and Austrian empires in the formation of the Triple Alliance, a supposedly defensive military pact. The Italians too had attempted to take part in the European scramble for Africa. They had established colonies along the Red Sea coast at Eritrea and Somaliland by 1895, but had been ignominiously defeated when they attempted to conquer the kingdom of Ethiopia in 1895–1896. After the French forestalled them by taking Tunisia in 1881, they turned their ambitions to the neighboring area of Tripoli (present-day Libya), which they succeeded in annexing after fighting a brief war with Turkey in 1911–1912.

Germany After the 1848 Revolutions

German nationalists were appalled that, while a state like Piedmont-Savoy could unite Italy, their own country remained split into more than thirty independent states. The failure of the Frankfurt Parliament in 1848–1849 had shown the impossibility of uniting Germany through liberal means, but, if Germany was to be united, like Italy, under one of its member states, the problem was whether that state should be Prussia or Austria. To unite under Prussia implied choosing the *kleindeutsch* (small German) solution, which required the ouster of Austria. If unification was under Austria, the choice was for the *grossdeutsch* (greater Germany) solution, which posed the problem of what would be done with Austria's non-German possessions. Princes restored to their autocratic powers in 1848 showed little interest in either solution. Even Prussia's King Frederick-William IV (reigned 1840–1861) seemed more interested in whittling down the already small powers granted to a lower legislative chamber by the Prussian constitution of 1850 than in undertaking expansionist policies within Germany. King William I (king of Prussia, 1861–1888; German emperor, 1871–1888) found, however, that the middle-class liberals in the lower house of the legislature were deeply suspicious of any attempt to increase the power within the state of the landowning gentry of the eastern regions of Prussia and were willing to use their right to vote the budget to block any such attempt. In 1862 the Prussian government proposed to double the size of the regular army, whose officer corps was a virtual monopoly of the landowning gentry, while at the same time abolishing the militia officered by the middle classes. Seeing its own position challenged while that of the aristocrats was being bolstered, the lower house refused to vote the budget providing tax revenues for the army changes. William I, determined to break this liberal opposition, called in Otto von Bismarck (1815–1898) as chief minister to handle the crisis.

Bismarck and German Unification

Bismarck was the archetype of the East German aristocrat, a wealthy landowner who admitted quite frankly: "I am no democrat and cannot be one. I was born and raised as an aristocrat." He was far more, however, than a diligent administrator of his estates. He had represented Prussia at the assembly of the German Confederation, and had been Prussian representative to Russia and France. Called back from Paris in 1862 for the purpose of cowing the lower house, he told them, just two weeks before he dissolved the parliament: "It is not by speeches and majority resolutions that the great questions of our time are decided. That was the great mistake of 1848 and 1849. It is by blood and iron." He collected taxes without the consent of the Prussian parliament, and carried through a complete modernization of the expanded army's weapons and tactics. Working with the army's principal reorganizers, the marshals Albrecht von Roon and Helmut von Moltke, he had within two years made the Prussian army the strongest in Europe. Bismarck then felt free to work toward the unification of Germany under Prussia by methods even more Machiavellian than Cavour's.

He won the friendship of Russia by encouraging it to crush a revolt in Poland in 1863, and by permitting it to pursue Polish fugitives onto Prussian territory. To try out the new Prussian army and to embroil Austria in northern Germany, Bismarck persuaded Austria to join Prussia in a war on Denmark. The excuse was the Danish king's attempt to annex the province of Schleswig, which, with the neighboring province of Holstein, had been under Danish

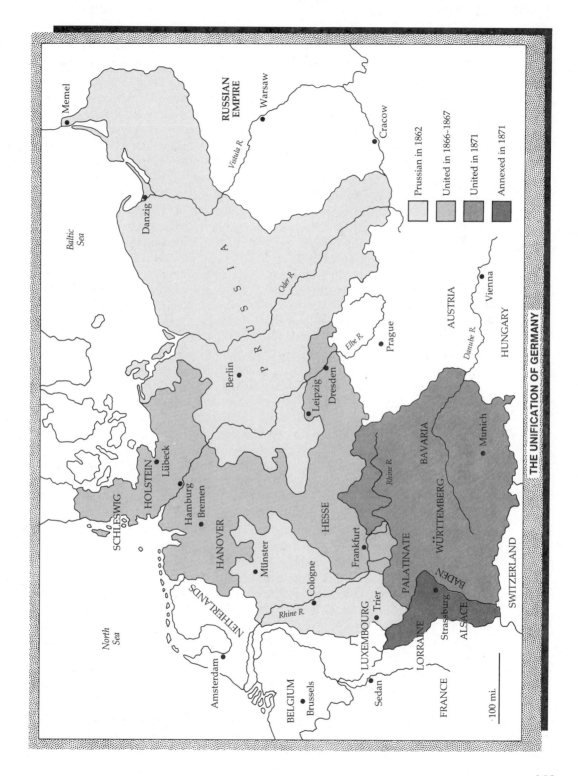

THE UNIFICATION OF GERMANY

Prussian in 1862
United in 1866–1867
United in 1871
Annexed in 1871

RUSSIAN EMPIRE

Memel

Warsaw

Cracow

Danzig

Baltic Sea

Vistula R.

Odar R.

P R U S S I A

Berlin

Prague

Elbe R.

Leipzig
Dresden

AUSTRIA

Vienna

Danube R.

HUNGARY

BAVARIA

Munich

Rhine R.

WÜRTTEMBERG

BADEN

SWITZERLAND

HESSE

Frankfurt

PALATINATE

Strasburg

ALSACE

LORRAINE

FRANCE

Sedan

Trier

LUXEMBOURG

Cologne

Rhine R.

Münster

HANOVER

Bremen
Hamburg

Lübeck

HOLSTEIN

SCHLESWIG

North Sea

NETHERLANDS

Amsterdam

BELGIUM

Brussels

100 mi.

overlordship since 1815. (The majority of the population of Schleswig was Danish, whereas the majority in Holstein was German.) Denmark was easily defeated by the Prussian army, and at the peace Bismarck insisted that the two provinces should be placed under joint Prussian and Austrian rule, with the Prussian army occupying Schleswig and the Austrian, Holstein.

The poor performance of the Austrian army was clear proof to Bismarck that Prussia could easily defeat it, if no major power came to its aid. He was already sure of Russian benevolence. He entered into an agreement with the new kingdom of Italy, promising it Venetia if it would attack Austria upon an outbreak of hostilities between Austria and Prussia. Finally, he hinted to the Emperor Napoleon III that, for remaining neutral, France would be rewarded with the gift of an unspecified territory in the Rhineland. He then provoked Austria into a declaration of war on Prussia, by denouncing its administration of Holstein. To Napoleon III's horror and amazement, the Prussian army defeated the Austrians overwhelmingly at the Battle of Königgrätz in 1866, bringing the war to an end in less than seven weeks. Resisting the army's demand for imposition of a humiliating peace on Austria, Bismarck demanded only the cession of Venetia to Italy and the end of the German Confederation and thus of Austrian representation within Germany. In place of the German Confederation he united all the north and central German states in a North German Confederation, under the presidency of the king of Prussia, cleverly winning support for this move by permitting universal male suffrage for election of members of the lower house of the Confederation. Prussia annexed outright the states of Hanover, Hesse-Kassel, Nassau, and Frankfurt, in order to link its Rhenish provinces with the main body of Prussia.

Bismarck then ended the constitutional crisis in Prussia, which he had precipitated himself by collecting taxes illegally, by presenting to the parliament an indemnity bill that gave him retroactive authorization to have collected the taxes in 1862–1864. Most of the liberals joined with the conservatives in enthusiastically endorsing the bill, and even voted Bismarck himself a huge sum of money in gratitude for the successful war. The vote destroyed any hope that the German liberals could become an independent force in the new state, and indeed any possibility that they could be the backbone of true democracy in Germany. Opposition to Bismarck's policies was to come in the future primarily from the expanding Social Democratic party and only rarely from the middle-class liberals, who found that the new state offered them vast economic opportunities.

Four South German states—Württemberg, Baden, Bavaria, and part of Hessen-Darmstadt, all Catholic states that had fought on the side of Austria against Prussia in 1866—were, partly at the insistence of France, not included in the North German Confederation. Nevertheless, Bismarck's principal purpose for the next four years was to persuade them to join voluntarily in a unified Germany. He also believed that France would go to war to prevent such a Germany from being created. He therefore worked to ensure that this war would be

A Dog and Cat Butcher During the Siege of Paris, 1870–1871 *During the four-month siege of Paris in the Franco-Prussian war, Parisians were reduced to eating zoo animals and even household pets. (Mary Evans Picture Library.)*

fought when Prussia rather than France was fully prepared, and in such circumstances that the south German states would regard the war as a German crusade in which they would rally to the cause of Prussia. Napoleon III played into Bismarck's hands by demanding for France a piece of German territory on the left bank of the Rhine, Luxembourg, or Belgium in compensation for Prussia's vast annexations. Bismarck refused privately, humiliating Napoleon, but kept the secret documents for publication when their exposure would do the most harm to France with German public opinion.

Hence Napoleon III was already deeply incensed when Bismarck agreed to allow the cousin of King William I to accept a Spanish offer to become their king. King William I, to Bismarck's annoyance, felt that the French objection, that France would be surrounded by territories under the control of members of the Prussian royal family, was quite reasonable, and agreed that his cousin should withdraw his candidature. The French unwisely refused to leave the matter there, and sent their ambassador to William I while he was vacationing at the spa town of Bad Ems to demand categorically that he never permit a Hohenzollern to take the Spanish throne. The king politely refused this request, and sent a detailed description of his conversation by telegram to Bismarck in Prussia. Bismarck and his dejected military advisers were at dinner, despairing of ever provoking France into a war, when the Ems telegram arrived. Bismarck saw that the telegram could be doctored to make it appear that the Prussian king had rudely snubbed the French emissary. When the telegram was released to the newspapers that evening, it produced the desired effect. With crowds demonstrating in the streets of Paris in favor of a war with Prussia, Napoleon III declared war.

The south German states, seeing this as an act of French aggression against Germans and impressed at the documents Bismarck now published of France's earlier demands for German territory, placed their armies under the command of Prussia. The German forces moved rapidly into eastern France. Almost three times the size of the disorganized French armies and far better equipped with modern weapons, they surrounded one large French force at Metz, and defeated another large army at Sedan, where they took Napoleon III prisoner. Napoleon abdicated when the parliamentary leaders in Paris declared France a republic. Republican efforts to raise new armies merely prolonged the fighting for several weeks, and Paris, which had undergone a four-month siege and bombardment by the German army, surrendered in January 1871.

Creation of the Second Reich

While Paris was still under bombardment, Bismarck succeeded in persuading the south German states to join with the North German Confederation in a new *Reich* (empire). The king of Prussia was declared German emperor or Kaiser in a ceremony staged, for the further humiliation of France, in the Hall of Mirrors of the Palace of Versailles on January 18, 1871. The constitution of the North German Confederation was adopted with little change for the new empire. The executive was to be headed by a chancellor, who was to be responsible directly to the emperor. An upper house, or *Bundesrat*, was to represent the member states. A lower house, or *Reichstag*, was to be chosen by universal male suffrage, but Prussia was assigned two-thirds of the seats. No civil rights such as freedom of speech or assembly were guaranteed in the constitution. The *Reichstag* had very little power over the army and navy, but it did have the power to review the budget. As a result, although the chancellor theoretically worked only with the emperor, in reality he found it necessary to establish a working relationship with the *Reichstag*.

The new empire at once asserted its strength by imposing on France a punitive peace treaty. The province of Alsace and most of Lorraine, German-speaking regions that contained France's principal iron ore deposits and some of its richest agriculture, were annexed by Germany. The French were required to pay an indemnity of five billion francs in gold. German troops, after a triumphal march through Paris, were to remain in occupation of France until the indemnity was paid. Moderate treatment of Austria after its defeat in 1866 had made it possible for it to become an ally in the future. The deliberate demeaning of France after a war in which the French had lost 140,000 lives, and especially the annexation of Alsace-Lorraine, ensured that the French would be the Germans' irreconcilable enemy. For the next four decades, all European diplomacy was based on the assumption that a new war between France and Germany would eventually take place. Bismarck was to wrestle for the next nineteen years, as chancellor of the German Empire, with the unstable international situation that he himself had been most instrumental in creating.

Effects of German Unification

Unification acted as an immediate stimulus to the German economy. Whereas the removal of customs barriers between the German states had merely freed internal trade within Germany, the new empire created an economic union by making possible free movement of population and capital as well. Berlin became the economic center of the new Germany, acting to transmit capital accumulated in the agricultural East to the booming industrial areas of the Ruhr and the Rhineland in the West and to the iron and steel industries of Alsace-Lorraine. The banks favored the growth of trusts in industry, especially so that they themselves could exercise a controlling interest in such large-scale operations as those necessary in heavy engineering and mining. German scientific progress was harnessed to technological inventions for industry, in such industries as steel and chemicals. Germany moved rapidly to the forefront in the electrical industry. Railroads were extended to link every part of the country, and a large merchant marine was constructed. The efficiency of the German school system ensured that the German working class was the best educated in Europe. As a result of advances in medicine and the growing availability of medical care, the population rose rapidly, from 40 million in 1871 to 68 million in 1914, in spite of the emigration of large numbers during the 1880s and 1890s.

This prosperity supported an ever-growing army, which became the predominant influence on the society of the new empire. Acceptance into the officer corps was regarded as essential to entry into high society, and the emperors emphasized that discipline and the military virtues were essential to the well being of the state. "The only nations which have progressed and become great," proclaimed William II (reigned 1888–1918), "have been warring nations. Those which have not been ambitious and gone to war have been nothing."

Since most young men were drafted into the army for two or three years of service, and forced to remain in the reserves for more than twenty years, the army was able to put its imprint on every class of society. Since, moreover, the constitution made the army leaders responsible only to the emperor, they enjoyed a freedom of interference in policy making that was unique among the European states. This power was exercised above all by the German general staff, a select corps of officers responsible for planning German strategy. Under Count Alfred von Schlieffen, between 1895 and 1905, the general staff began preparations for a preemptive war against France. The Schlieffen plan, which was complete by 1905, called for a two-pronged attack against France across neutral Belgium, which was to wipe out French military forces within a few weeks.

After the *Reichstag* agreed in 1899 to endorse the creation of a large German war fleet, the German navy also became a source of pressure on the government and a source of danger to German policy making. Whereas the army saw France as the primary danger, the navy saw that it was necessary to challenge Britain on the seas and as a result pushed a reluctant Britain in 1904 into the alliance with France, which helped bring Britain into the First World War on France's side in 1914.

Bismarck as German Chancellor, 1871–1890

Bismarck, whose policy had been to unify Germany by upsetting the established balance of power in Europe between 1862 and 1871, had now become Europe's supreme conservative—in a sense, the new Metternich. Regarding Germany as a "satiated power," he used every diplomatic means at his disposal to ensure that the new balance of power would not be disturbed. He believed that only five European powers mattered—Germany, Austria-Hungary, Russia, France, and Britain; and his goal was to ensure that Germany would always be firmly allied with two of them, while preventing the remaining two from allying together.

At first Bismarck considered that the natural allies of the new German Empire were the equally conservative emperors of Russia and Austria. After both had been fêted in a joint state visit to Berlin, it was agreed in 1873 to form the Three Emperors League, in which the three nations promised to repress radicalism within their states and to work together to establish a common policy on European problems. The alliance was almost immediately threatened by the distrust between Austria and Russia. In 1877, Russia, fighting on behalf of the independent south Slav states of Serbia and Montenegro and of the Greek Orthodox Christians in Turkish-controlled Bulgaria, had imposed a crushing defeat on the Turkish armies. Both Austria and Britain were fearful that this defeat would leave Russia supreme in the Balkans. Bismarck therefore offered himself as an "honest broker" to mediate between his two allies, Austria and Russia.

At the Congress of Berlin (1878), Russia was compelled to reduce its demands, and a small Bulgarian state was created rather than the large one desired by Russia. Austria was compensated by being given administration of the two Turkish provinces of Bosnia and Herzegovina, which Serbia had wanted to annex. Britain, which had taken no part in the war, was allowed to annex the Turkish island of Cyprus.

Although the Congress of Berlin, which was dominated by Bismarck, appeared to be a great triumph for his diplomacy, in reality it marked the end of his ability to manipulate the European state system. Russia's anger at Bismarck's apparently pro-Austrian intervention was so obvious that in 1879 Bismarck concluded a secret Dual Alliance with Austria, which was broadened into the Triple Alliance in 1882 by inclusion of Italy. Having recognized that there was a possibility of the eventual conclusion of a Franco-Russian alliance, Bismarck made one of his greatest errors by agreeing under pressure of German business groups that Germany should take for itself territories in Africa and the South Pacific, thus challenging Great Britain overseas. As his alliance system crumbled, he accepted increases in the size of the German army as the ultimate safeguard, a policy even more calculated to drive the French, Russians, and British into each other's arms.

Within Germany, Bismarck believed he could also play off one political group against another. His allies within the *Reichstag* were the National Liberal party, which represented the big business groups that were profiting from the economic boom, and the Conservatives, who represented the great landowners of eastern Germany. In the early 1870s, he considered that his greatest enemy was the Catholic Center party, against which he decided to wage a campaign called the *Kulturkampf* ("culture struggle"). To Bismarck the Catholic Church was a danger, not only because it could interfere with the centralizing goals of the new German government, but because it encouraged the south German states to maintain their ties with Austria. In a series of anti-Catholic laws, he expelled the Jesuits, put strict controls on education, including even the education of Catholic priests, and dissolved many Catholic organizations. His measures, which were denounced by the papacy, united the Catholics of Germany against him.

Always realistic, Bismarck abruptly changed course at the end of the 1870s. He relaxed most of the anti-Catholic laws, and turned his attention to the defeat of an even more imposing threat, that of the newly founded German Social Democratic party, which, in the election of 1877, had received half a million votes. After two assassination attempts on the emperor (which were not, however, carried out by socialists), Bismarck pushed through the *Reichstag* the anti-Socialist laws, which banned the party from holding meetings or publishing newspapers, but did not prevent it from running candidates for the *Reichstag*. Although the socialist leaders went into exile, the socialist vote continued to increase throughout the 1880s.

Bismarck then tried a new tactic, state socialism. To show that the state could safeguard workers' well-being better than the socialist party, he brought in a state program of accident, old-age, and illness insurance. He did not succeed, however, in destroying the appeal of the socialist party to the working classes. After the anti-Socialist law was allowed to lapse in 1890, the Social Democratic party received 1.4 million votes. In 1903, it received 3 million. In 1912, with a vote of 4.2 million, it became the largest party in the *Reichstag*. Bismarck's internal policy was thus as lacking in coherence as his foreign policy, and the brash young Emperor William II believed that he personally could govern far better than the seventy-five-year-old chancellor. In March 1890, he provoked Bismarck into resigning.

The Germany of William II

Under William II, the power of the German army in politics increased greatly. At times, the military seemed capable of overthrowing chancellors by use of backstairs influence with the emperor himself. Its funds were increasing, so that it could afford ever-growing purchases of guns and equipment from the steel and chemical companies of the Ruhr and Rhineland. After 1898, when the *Reichstag* passed the first naval bill, the navy became a new source of pressure on the government, especially as it received enthusiastic public support as a result of clever propaganda campaigns directed by Navy Secretary Alfred von Tirpitz. The emperor himself exulted in Germany's military prowess, and undoubtedly helped heighten international tension by his bellicose pronouncements. Nothing pleased him more than to denounce the "Yellow Peril." "Thousands of Chinese will shiver if they feel the iron fist of the German Empire lying firmly on their back," he boasted.

Yet the Germany of William II was far more than a militaristic autocracy. Within the legislature, the rise of the Social Democratic party indicated that the German working class had at last found a means of making its strength felt. German intellectual life was among the most fruitful in Europe. In both the sciences and the humanities, German universities were at the forefront of Eu-

German Emperor William II (reigned 1888–1918) William II's penchant for self-dramatization was reflected in his choice of uniforms. His bellicose oratory helped maintain tension between Europe's competing military alliances. (Ullstein Bilderdienst.)

ropean research; and German artists and dramatists were engaging in path-breaking work that was strongly disapproved of by the emperor and his court. Germany was a deeply divided society that was to find unity once again, as it had previously, by European war.

CHANGE IN THE CONSERVATIVE EMPIRES: AUSTRIA AND RUSSIA

After 1849, the stability of the Austrian empire continued to be upset by the demands for greater political democracy and for autonomy or independence of the non-German nationalities within the empire. After the revolutionary movements were crushed throughout the Austrian empire in 1849, Emperor Francis Joseph turned immediately to a policy of repression, which was entrusted to the minister of the interior, Alexander Bach. Hungary and Bohemia were placed under the direct rule of bureaucrats sent by the ministry of the interior and known as "Bach's Hussars." These bureaucrats attempted to push the policy of Germanization. One military defeat after another, however, forced the emperor into a policy of concessions. After the Austrian armies were defeated by the forces of France and Piedmont in Italy in 1859, Austria was forced to cede Lombardy to Piedmont; and, to win back popularity after the ignominy of the defeat, Francis Joseph decided in 1861 to grant an Imperial Diploma, which set up an imperial parliament called the *Reichsrat* chosen by regional parliaments or diets. The diets themselves were chosen by a complicated electoral system that gave predominance to large property owners and to German-speaking citizens. The imperial parliament was given the power to initiate and vote on laws, but was not given control over the imperial cabinet, which remained responsible directly to the emperor. The Hungarians and Poles refused to cooperate with this new system, and as a result the German-speaking groups exercised even greater power than before.

The Austro-Hungarian Compromise

After Austria had been defeated by Prussia in 1866, and had been compelled to recognize Prussian leadership in Germany, the Austrian government reluctantly decided to try to disarm the nationalists within the empire by granting the demands of one national group, the Magyars of Hungary. In 1867, by the so-called Compromise, the empire was broken into two parts, an Austrian and a Hungarian section. Francis Joseph was to be emperor of Austria and king of Hungary. The foreign affairs, army, and treasury of both sections were to be administered by three joint ministries. Each section of the empire was to have its own parliament and cabinet government. But the suffrage was so restricted as to give predominance within the Austrian section to the German-speaking inhabitants and within the Hungarian section to the Magyars.

The Compromise was not a success. In the Hungarian section, nationalists such as Louis Kossuth still demanded complete independence for the Magyars. Peasants still felt exploited by the landlords and working people by the industrialists, regardless of their nationality. Rule by Magyars was no more satisfactory to the other nationalities than rule by German-Austrians. The South Slavs (Croats, Serbs, and Slovenes) began to look to their fellow nationalists in Serbia for the creation of a unified South Slav state. There was also great annoyance among the Czechs and Poles, although some of Francis Joseph's ministers proved adept at disarming opposition by granting some cultural autonomy to these groups.

After 1893, with the resignation of the skillful premier Count Edward Taaffe, the attack of both nationalists and liberals was renewed. A new movement, the Young Czechs, was founded to work for the autonomy of Bohemia. Poles agitated for the creation of a Polish national state. Even the German-speaking Austrians demanded greater powers of self-government. Perhaps most important, the cause of greater political participation was taken up by the Austrian Social Democratic party, founded in 1888 and increasingly strong in the imperial legislature.

Reform in the Russian Empire

In Russia as in Austria, military defeat forced the government to appease discontent by introducing a far-reaching program of social and economic reforms. Russia had declared war on the Turkish empire in 1853 in support of Orthodox Christians in the Turkish Balkan provinces, and had invaded Moldavia and Wallachia. To Russia's surprise, Britain and France came to the support of Turkey to prevent the establishment of Russian hegemony in the Balkans, and attempted to seize the Crimean peninsula of Russia, with its important port of Sebastopol. In what then became known as the Crimean War (1853–1856), the British and French eventually defeated the Russian armies and took Sebastopol, in campaigns in which 500,000 men were lost. At the Congress of Paris in 1856, Russia was compelled to withdraw its forces from the Balkans, and was forbidden to maintain a war fleet in the Black Sea.

Tsar Alexander II (reigned 1855–1881) recognized the need of Russia to modernize after this military defeat, although he was personally in favor of continued autocracy. The centerpiece of his reform program was the emancipation of Russia's serfs, who constituted one-third of the peasant population. The serfs were not only freed and became full citizens, they were granted the land they had tilled for themselves, although not the land they had worked for their lord. The government compensated the landlords, and required the peasants to pay back the government in forty-nine annual redemption payments. Worse, however, the government did not give the land directly to the peasants but to the commune, or village, to which the peasant was bound to ensure his payment of taxes and redemption payments.

Three years later Alexander permitted the cities to have municipal councils and the provinces to have local governments, which were to carry out such local functions as education, public works, and sanitation. Although the peasants were represented in the local governments, the election process was planned in such a way as to give predominance to the upper and middle classes. The court system was reformed in the same year, and trial by jury was introduced. Finally, in 1874, compulsory military service for all citizens replaced the draft of army recruits by quotas upon the peasantry.

The Rise of Violent Opposition

The reforms did not win the tsar the support of the peasants, who felt aggrieved that they had been given only what they considered the worst land and that they could not leave the communes. Although the middle classes were pleased with the formation of the local councils, they were disappointed when, after the first assassination attempt on Alexander in 1866, he dropped plans for the calling of a central parliament, or *Duma*. Disillusionment with the nature of the reforms led to increasingly violent opposition within Russia. In the 1850s and 1860s, many young intellectuals called "nihilists," believers in "nothingness," demanded the total renovation of Russian government, church, and society. The nihilists attempted to win supporters among both the aristocracy and the peasants, and many of the idealists among them, who were known as "populists," engaged in a "go to the people" campaign in which they worked in the villages and tried to build a base of peasant support. The peasants, however, were unimpressed, and often denounced the populists to the police.

A violent wing of the nihilists turned to terrorism, and in March 1881 succeeded in killing the tsar with a bomb. As a result, the new Tsar Alexander III (reigned 1881–1894) restored the traditional Russian policy of repression. The secret police arrested thousands, and either executed them or sent them to exile in Siberia. Harsh censorship was imposed on the press, and strict supervision was exercised over the schools and universities. Non-Russian nationalities (Poles, Finns, Ukrainians, and Jews) suffered virulent persecution. In turn, repression provoked new demands for reform, which, during the reign of Nicholas II (reigned 1894–1917) were expressed by a growing number of political parties that succeeded in organizing in spite of the ban on their activity.

Reform Demands Under Nicholas II

The Constitutional Democrats, founded in 1902, wanted a constitutional monarchy similar to Britain's, with universal suffrage and redistribution of the land to the peasants. The Social Revolutionaries continued the populist work among the peasants, and used terrorism to further their goal of giving the land to the people who worked it. The Social Democrats, founded in 1898, were followers of Marx who, however, split in 1903 into two wings. The Bolsheviks, or "majority," led by Vladimir Ulyanov, who used the pseudonym Lenin, wanted a centralized, disciplined party. The Mensheviks, or "minority," wanted to give local groups greater independence.

When Russia suffered defeat and great losses in its 1904–1905 war with Japan, the authority of the government broke down and the outlawed political parties began to operate openly. Workers went on strike, and peasants burned the houses of landlords. After the shooting of peaceful demonstrators in the square in front of the Saint Petersburg imperial palace in January 1905, the whole country joined in revolution. The tsar capitulated and issued the October Manifesto in which he promised the election of a *Duma* by universal male suffrage. Under the provisions of a constitution granted in 1906, the first *Duma* was elected. Although the Constitutional Democrats, the most moderate of Russia's political parties, won the largest representation, the tsar did not work seriously with the *Duma*, and dismissed it after only ten weeks. A second *Duma* met only a little longer, and after its dismissal the tsar reduced the representation of the peasants and workers in future elections. Although the change made the future *Dumas* more docile, the tsar had in reality destroyed the one genuine hope of retaining his throne, by sharing power with parties committed to parliamentary democracy rather than to revolution.

VICTORIAN BRITAIN

Queen Victoria

The prestige but not the power of the monarchy in Britain was restored by Queen Victoria (reigned 1837–1901). During her reign, Britain exercised greater world influence than at any other period. George III had been mentally incapable of ruling toward the end of his life. His son, George IV (reigned 1820–1830), while cutting something of a splash in society with his extravagant living and ambitious building projects, exercised little political influence. William IV (reigned 1830–1837) was a mediocrity. But Queen Victoria, with her sense of religious propriety and her sober self-discipline, was to be the patron of a new age, especially after her marriage in 1840 to the dedicated young German prince, Albert of Saxe-Coburg-Gotha.

Victoria embodied and thereby magnified all the virtues that the British middle class claimed to admire in the mid-nineteenth century—self-denial and hard work, veneration for the family, subordination of the wife to the husband, pride in one's nation, and a sense of responsibility for the well-being of those less privileged by class or color. Many of these values were to be rejected in the great release from Victorian morality that seized England after her death; but for a large part of the nineteenth century, these ideas were the cement that fused together at least the British middle classes in the self-confidence and self-congratulation that typified the Victorian age.

Queen Victoria and Prince Albert in 1854 Victoria and Albert, with their nine children, exemplified in their own lives the central tenet of Victorian morality, the sanctity of the family as the mainstay of social values. (The Bettmann Archive.)

Mid-Victorian Prosperity

From 1815 to 1848, British society seethed with discontent, whether of farm laborers losing their land, workers exploited in the mills and mines, or middle classes yearning for a greater share of political power. But a variety of reforms, such as the Reform Bill of 1832, abolition of the Corn Laws, and the early Factory Acts, had alleviated much of this discontent. After 1848, Britain embarked upon twenty-five years of real prosperity. The basis of this prosperity was continuous investment in heavy industry intended to supply both the home and the world markets. Capital, accumulated as a result of the industrialization and agricultural reforms of the eighteenth century, could now be invested in new industries at home or could be shifted overseas to the British Empire or to such developing areas as Latin America. The farmers continued to mechanize and to improve seed and livestock, and found they were in no way harmed by abolition of the Corn Laws. Even the workers discovered that their real wages were rising sufficiently so that they could perceive a genuine improvement in their standard of living, while the newly founded local governments were making a moderately successful attempt to improve the facilities of the cities in which the workers lived.

The Great Exhibition of 1851, held in London in a superb building of cast iron and glass called the Crystal Palace, symbolized the confidence of the mid-Victorian age. All the industrial countries of the world were invited to send their products for exhibition side by side with Britain's. Millions came from Britain and Europe to gaze with astonishment upon the wondrous products of an industrial revolution that could produce not only gas cooking ranges and electric clocks but steam engines designed to look like Doric temples.

Rivalry of Liberals and Conservatives

The political system also adapted to the new age. The Whigs were replaced by the Liberal party, a coalition of well-to-do landlords and urban industrialists, backed by the newly enfranchised middle classes, while the Tories changed their name to Conservatives. In the 1860s, both the Liberals under the leadership of William Gladstone and the Conservatives under Benjamin Disraeli realized that they would have to support wider political suffrage and a renewed program of reforms. In 1866, the Liberals brought in to Parliament a Reform Bill that would have extended the vote to the better-paid workers in the cities, but the bill was defeated. The Conservatives won the elections that followed, but Disraeli, sensing that there was widespread public support for extension of the suffrage, decided to take for the Conservatives the credit for passing a new Reform Bill. In 1867, he pushed through Parliament the Second Reform Bill, which gave the vote to most city workers and to large numbers of farm workers. The new voters, however, threw out the Conservatives in the elections of 1868, and returned Gladstone to office as prime minister.

In his "Glorious Ministry" of 1868–1874, Gladstone rewarded his new supporters with a long series of reforms. In 1870, the Education Act made schooling compulsory for children up to the age of thirteen. Entry to the civil service, which had previously been a preserve of the well-to-do classes, was opened to all through competitive examination. And the officer corps of the army was no longer restricted to the upper classes. Finally, the secret ballot was introduced for parliamentary elections. Gladstone's great reforming ministry was followed by an almost equally effective one under Disraeli, between 1874 and 1880. Disraeli increased the powers of the trade unions, gave municipal governments the right to build municipal housing after slum clearance, and improved public health facilities. His principal activity, however (see pp. 496–502), was encouragement of British imperialism. Gladstone's second ministry, from 1880 to 1885, was responsible for the Third Reform Bill in 1884, which extended the vote to all male adults, including the farm workers previously excluded. The dramatic political dialogue between Gladstone and Disraeli personalized the confrontation between the two political parties. Nationwide political campaigns, fought for the first time by party leaders outside their own constituencies, roused widespread public interest in the use of their new voting power.

A final series of reforms was passed by the Liberals between 1906 and 1914. Workers were to receive accident compensation and sickness and unemployment insurance. Peaceful picketing was made legal, and a procedure was set up for establishing minimum wages. To cover the increased social expenditures, the Liberals introduced new taxes, including a tax on inheritances and on profits from increased real estate values. When the hereditary House of Lords, which was largely Conservative, rejected the budget, the Liberals decided that its powers would have to be reduced by Act of Parliament. In 1911, the House of Lords lost the right to veto a money bill, and its power of veto of other bills was reduced to two years only. (The House of Lords voted to accept the reduction of their powers proposed by the House of Commons only when the government threatened to have the king create enough new lords willing to vote the bill through the upper chamber.) The Liberals finally passed the Irish Home Rule Bill giving Ireland its autonomy in 1914, only to shelve it when World War I broke out.

British parliamentary democracy had achieved far broader participation in the nineteenth century than that of any other European country, but the economic and social difficulties of the British working class produced by two centuries of industrialization were far from being solved. Those problems might well have been attacked successfully, had not the program of reforms begun by the Liberals in 1906 been interrupted by the First World War.

FRANCE: FROM THE SECOND EMPIRE TO THE THIRD REPUBLIC

The election of Louis Napoleon Bonaparte (1808–1873) as president of the Second French Republic in December 1848 had been a repudiation by the majority of the French people of the leaders who had carried through the revolution of February 1848 and the repression of the June Days. But it was not a return to reaction. The French people saw in Louis Napoleon a successor to the Emperor Napoleon I, whom they had, under the influence of the propaganda of the Napoleonic legend, come to see as a guarantor of the gains made during the French Revolution and as a promise of a restoration of order and military glory. As president, Louis Napoleon attempted immediately to fulfill these wishes. He renewed relations with the Catholic Church by sending a French army to restore the pope to power in Rome. He appealed to conservatives by strengthening the army, and welcomed royalists into his service. With promises of government support for economic development, he won over the middle classes. Finally, even when, on December 2, 1851, he carried out a coup d'état, he did it as the champion of democracy against the parliament, which had attempted to reduce the suffrage by 3 million voters.

His new constitution of 1851 made him president for ten years, with controlling power over a two-chamber legislature. Within a year, his police was in such firm control of the country, and his popularity was running so high, that he felt secure in asking the country to approve, in a national plebiscite, his becoming Emperor Napoleon III. (Napoleon I had abdicated in 1815 in favor of his son, Napoleon II, who died in 1832 without having reigned.)

Napoleon III's Economic Policies

As emperor, Napoleon III showed that he was a sincere follower of the ideas of Saint-Simon. He believed that the secret to economic development was the provision of cheap credit through government-sponsored banks. He founded a bank to aid real estate development and another to assist in financing large-scale industrial undertakings. A nationwide system of savings banks made it possible for the savings of many small investors to become available for such projects at home as the expansion of the railroad network and for loans to foreign governments. Napoleon III had also, however, accepted the liberal belief in the value of free trade. He negotiated the reduction of tariffs with many European countries, and in 1860 signed a free trade treaty with Britain. He also supported implementation of one of Saint-Simon's favorite schemes, the construction of the Suez Canal, which was carried out by Ferdinand de Lesseps, a French engineer, between 1859 and 1869, with more than half the capital supplied by small French investors. He even began to explore the possibility of constructing a Panama canal.

The Rebuilding of Paris

Both the desire for national prestige and the Utopian Socialist belief in the use of public works for reduction of unemployment provided motives for Napoleon

Boulevard des Capucines, Paris, by Claude Monet (1840–1926) In his reconstruction of Paris, Haussmann began a vast new Opera House at the intersection of the Boulevard des Capucines and a wide new Boulevard Impérial. (The Nelson-Atkins Museum of Art, Kansas City, Missouri. Acquired through the Kenneth A. and Helen F. Spencer Foundation Acquisitions Fund.)

III's massive reconstruction of Paris, which he entrusted to Baron Georges Haussmann. Haussmann was given powers to open up the crowded, unsanitary slum areas of Paris by constructing 85 miles of new boulevards, frequently cut through the working-class areas that had been centers of insurrection in June 1848. His new facades imposed a uniformity on Parisian architecture that many thought the height of elegance, but others found monotonous. In building a vast new Opera House, Haussmann even attempted to create, in a revival of Baroque architecture, a distinctive style for the Second Empire. Beneath the city he constructed a network of storm drains, and, in emulation of ancient Rome, provided Paris with a new supply of pure drinking water that helped reduce Paris's epidemics of cholera. The most successful new projects were the huge new parks created at each edge of the city, which were planned to act as the lungs of Paris. Private capital poured into the city's rebuilding. Vast new department stores were constructed, with huge domes of colored glass. Theaters were built for light operas, music hall dancers, and serious dramas. Just as the construction of Versailles in the seventeenth century had attracted to France the aristocratic tourists of that century, so Haussmann's renovation made Paris the center of a huge tourist industry, which was made possible for the first time by the railroads.

Foreign Policy of Napoleon III

Napoleon's first ventures into foreign affairs seemed to be equally successful. After France had intervened with Britain against Russia in the Crimean War, he was able to host in Paris the most glittering peace congress since Metternich's in Vienna, and to pose briefly as the new arbiter of European diplomacy. Napoleon III's armies defeated Austria in 1859. Not only had he permitted Piedmont to take Lombardy, but, with the cession to France of Savoy and Nice, he made the greatest permanent expansion of France's continental possessions since the reign of Louis XIV. Moreover, Napoleon III began again the extension of the French Empire in Asia. In 1858–1859, using the excuse of protecting Vietnamese Christians, he seized the whole coast of southern Indochina, including the port of Saigon. In 1860, the French even joined with the British in attacking Peking, to force the Manchu dynasty to increase their diplomatic and commercial privileges in China.

The success of these policies up to 1860 had made the French people acquiesce willingly in the absolutist constitution which left all power in the hands of the imperial court and a strictly controlled civil service. After 1860, however, Napoleon's policies, both internal and foreign, began to break down. The free trade policy caused great difficulty for French industry, which could not compete with British manufacturers. When Napoleon attempted to turn Mexico into a French satellite by imposing upon it the Habsburg prince Maximilian as emperor, his plans were thwarted both by the military resistance of the Mexicans and by the pressure of the United States. After French armies were withdrawn,

Maximilian was captured and shot. In Europe, meanwhile, Bismarck was easily able to manipulate Napoleon into remaining neutral during the Austro-Prussian war of 1866, with the vague promises of helping Napoleon restore his own prestige by annexation of some German territory.

As his plans crumbled, rather than increase his absolutism within France, Napoleon democratized his empire. In 1860–1861, he gave the legislature greater control over finance, and in 1867 he had his ministers report directly to it on their policies. In 1869–1870, the legislature was permitted to initiate legislation and to vote on the budget; and these changes were approved by the French people in a plebiscite by a vote of 7.3 million to 1.5 million. France might well have become a constitutional empire similar to Britain if these changes had been given time to work.

Napoleon, however, in seeking to turn the withdrawal of the Hohenzollern candidate to the Spanish throne into a French diplomatic triumph, had fallen into the trap set for him by Bismarck. When he declared war on Prussia in 1870, France was totally unprepared for a war against the revitalized Prussian armies, and thus he was personally blamed for the French defeat in the early weeks of the war. After his capture by the Prussians at Sedan in September 1870, Napoleon III was deposed by a group of parliamentary leaders in Paris, who set up a Provisional Government of National Defense. They made France a republic, called new elections in February 1871, and led a majority in parliament who sought peace as well as the restoration of a non-Bonapartist monarchy. The new government under Adolphe Thiers signed the peace treaty with the Germans in May, which gave up Alsace-Lorraine to Germany.

The Paris Commune

In Paris, however, the elections had given a majority to those favoring continuation of the war and the maintenance of a republican form of government. Before the peace was signed, the Parisian working classes and many from the middle classes rose in revolt, to prevent implementation of peace and to force the ouster of Thiers' government. The leadership of the revolt was taken by a coalition of anarchists, Utopian and Marxist socialists, and moderate republicans, who declared Paris' municipal government, the Commune, to be the city's only legitimate administration. The Communards, as the supporters of the Commune were called, became progressively more revolutionary in their actions, beginning a program for taking over the property of the very wealthy and attacking the Catholic Church. Thiers, preoccupied with ending the war with Germany and unprepared for the Parisian uprising, at first withdrew the troops loyal to his government from Paris, but, after two months of skirmishing around the city's boundaries, he sent the army back into Paris in May. In a week of vicious street-to-street fighting, as many as 20,000 Parisians were killed. Forty thousand more were later sent into penal servitude overseas.

Both the actions of the Communards and the manner in which Thiers suppressed the revolt exacerbated France's internal divisions. The property-owning classes tended to view all reformers as opponents of the system of private property itself, who would be willing to use violence to achieve social change. The reformers saw the established authorities as ruthless utilizers of state power, and especially of the army, to prevent change in the status quo. The conflict between Paris and the rest of France, deeply rooted in French history since the Paris-based Capetian monarchy had started unifying the country, was inflamed by the street battles and by the executions and deportations that followed. The new republic faced a very difficult task in finding a constitutional mechanism by which these conflicts could be resolved.

Foundation of the Third Republic

The National Assembly undoubtedly favored the restoration of monarchy, but was unable to choose between rival claimants to the throne. The Assembly therefore completed the writing of a republican constitution, in which power lay chiefly with a lower house or Chamber of Deputies, elected by universal male suffrage, and that controlled the cabinet. The new system proved very unstable. There was a deep-seated division between conservatives, who favored some form of monarchy, increased power to the Catholic Church, and a stable economic system based on the small provincial towns and the peasantry, and the republicans, who wanted reduction of Catholic power, social reform, and urban economic development. Rather than form two parties, as in England, these groups split into a large number of political parties, which fought constantly over government policy and ministerial appointments. Many politicians used their position to engage in shady financial dealings, and the frequent revelation of these scandals tarnished the reputation of the republican form of government. The extreme conservatives became so disenchanted in the 1880s that they threw their support behind a glamorous but shallow general, Georges Boulanger, in the hope that he would rally enough military support to overthrow the republic. The Boulanger supporters were, however, outsmarted by the government, which summoned Boulanger to trial for treason. The general's nerve broke, and he fled to Belgium, where he committed suicide.

The threat from the right did little to force the supporters of the republic into stable political coalitions. Although attempts were made to link the moderate republican parties into a coalition in the 1880s and 1890s, neither of these efforts was successful, and the constant change of governments continued. The only clear line of policy uniting the republican groups was anticlericalism. The public schools had been secularized in the 1880s, and no members of the clergy were permitted to teach in them. In 1901, no religious order was permitted to operate without state authorization, thousands of Catholic clergy were forced to leave the country, and hundreds of Catholic schools were closed. In 1905, the concordat that Napoleon I had signed with the papacy was repudiated, and the Catholic Church was separated completely from the state. Under the pressure of the growing socialist party, the republicans finally turned to social reform. In 1903, health standards for factories were established and enforced. In 1904, workers were given a ten-hour workday. And in 1911, old-age pensions were introduced.

The Dreyfus Affair

The anti-Catholic clerical campaign was in part a republican reaction against the greatest scandal of the Third Republic, and Dreyfus Affair. In 1894, Captain Alfred Dreyfus, the only Jew on the French general staff, was arrested for selling secrets to the Germans, convicted on the basis of forged documents, and sent to Devil's Island prison in French Guiana. His conviction was exploited by the conservatives as a means of attacking the republic, but also was the occasion for an anti-Semitic campaign that was encouraged by extreme Catholics. When the army refused to re-try Dreyfus after the documents had been shown to be forgeries, France became sharply divided between the Dreyfusards and the anti-Dreyfusards, who disagreed not only on the innocence or guilt of Dreyfus himself, but on their attitudes toward the army, the Catholic Church, and the very existence of the republic itself.

The campaign to clear Dreyfus was spearheaded by the brilliant political strategist and future prime minister, Georges Clemenceau, (1841–1929) and supported by many leading French intellectuals, including Emile Zola, who published in the newspaper edited by Clemenceau an influential polemical attack on the military court, entitled *J'accuse* ("I Accuse").

The Dreyfusards eventually triumphed. Dreyfus was released in 1899, and finally exonerated in 1906. But the damage done in fomenting deep divisions in French society was far from repaired when France faced the problem in the 1900s of establishing a nationally supported policy for handling the increasingly threatening confrontation with Germany and its allies.

SUGGESTED READINGS

General Surveys, 1848–1914

Stimulating introductions are given by A. J. P. Taylor, *The Struggle for Mastery in Europe, 1848–1918* (1954), and L. C. B. Seaman, *From Vienna to Versailles* (1963). For clear, detailed exposition, see Norman Rich, *The Age of Nationalism and Reform, 1850–1890* (1977), and Felix Gilbert, *The End of the European Era, 1890 to the Present* (1984).

Unification of Italy and Germany

The best study of Bismarck's diplomacy is Otto Pflanze, *Bismarck and the Development of Germany: The Period of Unification, 1815–1871* (1963). For a German account, in an abridged form, see Erich Eyck, *Bismarck and the German Empire* (1958). Denis Mack Smith sees Cavour as not unlike Bismarck, in *Italy: A Modern History* (1969), and *Cavour and Garibaldi* (1954).

The tormented politics of postunification Italy are analyzed in Christopher Seton-Watson, *Italy from Liberalism to Fascism, 1870–1925* (1967), Germany's political difficulties in A. Rosenberg, *Imperial Germany: The Birth of the German Republic, 1871–1918* (1964). On the Kaiser, the best biography is Michael Balfour, *The Kaiser and His Times* (1964). His schizophrenic capital city is evoked in Gerhard Masur, *Imperial Berlin* (1971). Gordon Craig dissects German political behavior in *Germany, 1866–1945* (1980). W. L. Guttsman, *The German Social Democratic Party, 1875–1933* (1981), shows that the socialists created a subculture even more than a political party.

Victorian Britain

The idiosyncracies of Britain's reigning monarch are described in Elizabeth Longford, *Queen Victoria: Born to Succeed* (1965). The Victorian Age is sparklingly analyzed in G. M. Young, *Victorian England: Portrait of an Age* (1936), and Asa Briggs, *Victorian People* (1954). British political developments are explained in Robert K. Webb, *Modern England: From the Eighteenth Century to the Present* (1968). The duel that enlivened British politics in the late nineteenth century is entertainingly captured in Philip Magnus, *Gladstone* (1954), and Robert Blake, *Disraeli* (1969). Geoffrey Best, *Mid-Victorian Britain, 1851–1875* (1971), explains the economic structure that put so many women and children to work. New insights into the motivation of Victorian women are presented in Patricia Branca, *Silent Sisterhood: Middle Class Women in the Victorian Home* (1975).

France: From Second Empire to Third Republic

The enigmatic emperor is favorably appraised in F. Simpson, *Louis Napoleon and the Recovery of France* (1975), and in a more balanced way in J. M. Thompson, *Louis Napoleon and the Second Empire* (1954). David Thomson, *Democracy in France Since 1870* (1969), unravels some of the tangle of French politics under the Third Republic. For the anticlerical campaign and its deeper significance, see John McManners, *Church and State in France, 1870–1914* (1972). Modern scholarship on the Dreyfus affair is presented in Douglas Johnson, *France and the Dreyfus Affair* (1967).

17

Society and Culture in the Nineteenth Century

The eighteenth century had seen the birth of the industrial revolution in Britain. The nineteenth century saw the expansion of industrialization throughout the continent of Europe and to parts of other continents, most notably to North America. As the century progressed, the process of industrialization changed in character. Although the original industrial revolution, based on coal, iron, and textiles, remained central to manufacturing production, a second revolution, based on steel, electricity, and chemicals, enormously diversified industrial output. The volume and variety of goods increased, stimulating the disorderly growth of cities as centers of both production and consumption.

The advance of scientific knowledge and technology not only spurred on industrial progress but also made possible a revolution in health care, which had the effect of continually reducing the death rate. The European and North American populations grew at an unprecedented rate, and indeed faster than that of any other part of the world.

Scientific progress was closely linked to industrial change, especially in those fields such as chemistry where new instruments improved experimental ability or where scientific discovery could most easily be applied industrially. But the field of science in which advances of knowledge caused the most startled public reaction was biology. Darwin's demonstration of the theory of evolution in 1859, with its challenge to the Biblical explanation of creation, roused an aggrieved reaction among some Christian churches that is still resounding.

Literature was deeply concerned with the social changes brought about by industrialization. At first, during the Romantic movement in the first half of the century, most literary works attempted to escape the change by turning to a preindustrial past for its themes or by seeking in the exploration of human emotions a flight from the rationalist world of scientific reality. But from the middle of the century, the Realist and Naturalist schools of writers found in the new society a rich subject for study. In the 1880s, they were attacked by the Symbolist writers, who held that art should exist for art's sake and not as a commentary on social reality.

Painting went through a similar course of development as literature. Until about 1850, the Romantics appealed directly to the emotions in their dramatic use of color and exploration of exotic themes, or turned art into a lyrical exploration of the beauties of nature. Again, from mid-century, pictorial Realism stimulated artists to explore such themes as the suffering of the poor or the hypocrisy of the ruling classes. In the 1870s, however, the Impressionists pioneered a new style of painting, delighting in the capacity to render through color the immediate impression of objects and happenings. The Post-Impressionist painters of the 1880s and 1890s in turn attempted to bring painting back to presentation of the permanent rather than the transitory and to endow their paintings with an emotional insight they felt lacking in the Impressionists.

Architecture and music remained faithful to Romanticism far longer than literature or painting. By the 1830s, architects seemed convinced that only by reviving the styles of the past could they save architecture from corruption by the progress of industrialism, with the result that the styles favored were neo-Gothic, neo-Renaissance, neo-Hellenic, and even neo-Muslim. Only when architects recognized the potential of the new industrial materials, and especially of steel, glass, and concrete from the 1870s on, did the century create its own distinctive style of building. Composers, liberated by Beethoven from the constraints of the classical style, found Romanticism a source of infinite variety for most of the century.

THE GROWTH OF TECHNOLOGY, BUSINESS, AND CITIES

Impact of Advancing Technology

Coal, iron, and textiles remained the basis of industrialization in the nineteenth century as they had in the eighteenth. But throughout the century there was enormous growth in the numbers of mines being worked and textile mills being established. The most significant advances, however, were in iron and, later, steel production. In this area, technological developments occurred throughout the nineteenth century. In the second half of the century, steel replaced iron as the primary construction material and was used in the manufacture of rails and cars for trains, machines and machine parts, steam engines, and girders for bridges, buildings, and, at the end of the century, skyscrapers.

Technological advances not only affected daily life through the production of steel, but it also had a marked impact on ordinary living and working conditions through advances in electricity and chemistry. Factories made extensive use of electricity, and both workplaces and homes had electric light. Trains, and street cars, and modern household appliances, such as refrigerators and washing machines, were powered electrically. Communications also advanced rapidly, as electricity made possible the invention of the telephone, telegraph, and radio.

The communications industries were also affected by rapid advances in chemistry. Wood pulp was treated chemically to produce cheap papers for books, newspapers, and magazines, enabling publishers to cut costs and print large editions at reasonable prices for a growing literate public. Chemistry was also important in the advance of photography, especially in developing plates and printing pictures taken by a camera. Other industries affected were textiles because of the manufacture of artificial or synthetic dyes and fabrics; soap because an alkali was developed to mix with fatty acids and produce more lather than in the past; and finally armaments because of the invention of dynamite and poison gas.

Development of Business Organizations

As technology produced an increasing amount of goods for consumption, the organization of businesses began to change radically. Because nineteenth-century manufacturing processes brought together so many different components—for example, steel is made from iron, which is first mined, then melted in furnaces fueled by coal, then, as steel ingots, shaped for the marketplace in rolling mills, and finally shipped to customers—formerly small, individually owned businesses expanded into giant corporations. A prime instance is the transformation of the holdings of the small entrepreneur Andrew Carnegie into the U.S. Steel Corporation. Starting as a modest investor in iron production, Carnegie turned his iron enterprises toward steel manufacturing and formed the Carnegie Steel Company, which then bought up steel plants, rolling mills, iron ore mines, coke ovens, ships, and railroads, eventually supplying almost 50 percent of the steel needs of America. When J. P. Morgan wanted to take over Carnegie Steel, he joined with H. C. Frick, Carnegie Steel's former chief, to create the U.S. Steel Corporation and thus control what had become a vast industrial empire.

To assure a ready supply of money—capital—for these expanding companies, governments relaxed earlier restrictions on joint stock companies and accepted the principle of "incorporation," which involved the concept of "limited liability." In the view of the law, a corporation is the same as a person and can therefore buy goods and services and owe debts. If the corporation cannot pay its debts and goes into bankruptcy, its owners, because of their limited liability, lose only the amount of their investment, unlike a sole proprietor, who can lose everything he owns if his business goes bankrupt. Because of the comparative safety of corporations, they were able to attract large amounts of investment capital and, during prosperous times, grew at phenomenal rates.

This growth was aided and abetted when a corporation, like the Krupp armaments firm, gained such complete control of a market that it could eliminate competition and fix prices for its goods. When monopolistic control of this sort was exercised jointly by an international group of corporations, the combination was called a "cartel" and brought enormous profits to its members.

The booming industries and international combinations of the nineteenth century generated a new elite of enormously wealthy investors—called "capitalists" by Marxists and other critics—who moved easily across national boundaries and around the world in pursuit of profit or pleasure. The actual running of their corporations was left to "managers," who formed a new and powerful class and whose interests were not always identical with those of the "owner-investors." For example, investors often wanted a quick return on their money, whereas managers may have wanted to plow profits back into their companies for future growth. As a result, there often were raging battles for control that sometimes proved beneficial and other times disastrous, but in either case created an environment of instability and uncertainty. By exploiting the inherent unsteadiness of the investment-stock market, shrewd speculators like James Fisk, Jay Gould, and J. P. Morgan gained control of giant enterprises and made huge fortunes.

Increasing Population and Developing Cities

The radical changes in technology and business organization affected ordinary working people in many ways. Even though working-class discontent remained high throughout the nineteenth century, all statistics show that real wages (that is, purchasing power) and living conditions were improving markedly. One indication of this improvement is the sharp upturn in the population—there were about twice as many people living in Europe at the end of the nineteenth century as at the beginning—and another, related, indication is the sharp decline in the death rate for the same period, especially among children.

Some of the growth in population and decline in death was due to major advances in the medical sciences, hygiene, and nutrition. But it was also due to the success of labor groups and early unions in efforts to gain for workers a "living wage," to limit the working age of children, and to reduce the number of hours they and adults had to work. Higher wages brought more food and better housing than in the early days of the industrial revolution, when workers were barely able to earn a subsistence income. Limiting the working age of children reduced health hazards for the young and increased their chances for survival. The health of workers, and hence their life span, was increased by regulating the safety and health conditions under which they worked, and by reduction of working hours which, in the United States for example, fell from 16 hours at the beginning of the century to 10 at the end.

The political strength of the lower classes increased as the rural populations left the farms and villages to flood into the cities in response to the magnetic pull of industrialism. In 1800, London had a population of 860,000 and Paris 550,000; by 1900, London's population had grown to 4.1 million and Paris's to 2.7 million. As early as 1850, there were more people living in cities than in the rural areas of England. The nineteenth century saw a major population shift in most industrialized countries.

To meet the surge in population, cities expanded in every direction at a rapid rate. This expansion was aided by the construction of railroad lines radiating from the cities and bringing commuters into vast stations strategically located at the periphery of urban centers. Able to afford the cost of commuting daily, the middle classes abandoned the cities to the less affluent and moved to the suburbs. The less affluent working poor, meanwhile, were able to move to the edge of their cities after construction of subways and streetcar lines. Real estate developers bought up large tracts of undeveloped, marshy, and unsanitary lands on which they built vast complexes of six- or seven-story tenements into which working-class families were packed.

Nevertheless, conditions, even for the workers, were improving, especially in the second half of the nineteenth century. The cities, which since the seventeenth century had been restricted within huge defensive bastions erected to withstand the blast of artillery, were opened up, once it was clear that the new military technology of war had made the walls useless. Almost every city of Europe, large and small, pulled down its walls, and used the space made available around the central core of the city to form a circle of tree-lined boulevards that became a favorite place for the upper classes to ride on horseback or in carriages and for the other groups to stroll. The most ambitious rebuilding scheme was undertaken in Vienna, where in place of the walls the city government constructed the magnificent Ringstrasse, a wide roadway around the inner city lined with parks, coffee shops, theaters, museums, and government buildings.

Urban Amenities

Municipalities were also catering to the desires of their citizens for education and leisure. Increasingly during the century, the European countries recognized the need to provide a free public education, at least at the elementary level. France set the example in 1833, by requiring construction of primary schools throughout the country, and by 1870 almost every country had such a system. Secondary schools followed more slowly, and were usually fee-paying. Universities were founded in many of the new industrial cities.

Theaters too ceased to be a preserve of the wealthy. As early as the 1800s

Carriage at the Races, by Edgar Degas (1834–1917) *The Impressionists often painted scenes of contemporary Paris. Degas' subjects included ballet dancers, cafe scenes, and the horserace tracks. (Museum of Fine Arts, Boston; 1931 Purchase Fund.)*

in Vienna, the middle classes had become the major patrons of the classical composers, through the purchase of tickets for concerts, thus displacing the aristocratic patron. The Italian opera house, perhaps the major institution in every small Italian city, was filled with an audience drawn from every group in society. The lower middle classes of Berlin patronized the serious drama of protest that appalled the imperial court. Lighter entertainment was provided by the English music halls and the French vaudeville; and, as early as 1895, the first movie in Paris was attended by large, enthusiastic audiences.

Sports too appealed to all groups within the city's population. Every city built a horse-racing track, with comfortable boxes and restaurants for the well-to-do, moderately priced seats for the middle classes, and cheap standing room for the poor. Polo fields were available for the rich. Soccer became a mass sport in Europe, attracting crowds of up to 100,000 by 1900, while in the United States football and baseball won enthusiastic followings. In Germany, gymnastics was popular from its first encouragement by the Prussian state as a means of preparing youth for the war of liberation against Napoleon I.

Finally, the age of the mass consumer market began. In the early days of the industrial revolution, workers had frequently been forced to buy their few needs in food and clothing from the company-owned store. By the end of the nineteenth century, they were being wooed as a consumer by dazzling displays of goods presented, in radiantly lit department stores, along great shopping streets like the Nevsky Prospekt of Saint Petersburg, Regent Street in London, and Fifth Avenue in New York.

THE TRIUMPH OF SCIENCE

It was hardly surprising that the age of industrialization should have seen major advances in science, since the progress of industry had at once furnished advanced technological tools for experiment and led to the immediate utilization of scientific discoveries with practical applicability. Many scientists, however, resisted the lure of seeking only discoveries that would bring immediate reward, and pressed on with the work of formulating the fundamental principles that would explain the disparate phenomena of the material world.

Applied and Theoretical Chemistry

Chemistry had lagged behind the other sciences in the seventeenth and eighteenth centuries, largely because of the primitive nature of scientific equipment available. At the end of the eighteenth century and in the first half of the nineteenth, several important breakthroughs were achieved.

The last of Aristotle's theories to undergo scientific scrutiny, his view that matter is composed of the four elements of earth, fire, air, and water, was finally abandoned in the 1770s. The French chemist Antoine Lavoisier, working with oxygen, which had just been isolated, showed that, in such phenomena as burning and rusting, an element combines with oxygen without any loss of matter. He thus not only demonstrated the nature of combustion (which he also showed to take place in a similar way in breathing) but postulated the principle that matter is indestructible. He went on to argue that Aristotle's elements were compounds of simpler elements, and he listed thirty-two of these basic substances.

The English chemist Joseph Priestley backed up this work by demonstrating experimentally many of the basic combinations of elements, such as carbon monoxide and sulfur dioxide. Once the basic elements were considered to be composed of atoms, as suggested by John Dalton, an amateur scientist in England, progress was rapid. Dalton himself showed that it was possible to determine the weight of the atoms composing an element; and, in 1869, the Russian scientist Dmitri Mendeleev drew up a periodic table, in which he grouped elements according to weight and properties, and even predicted the existence of several not then known but soon discovered. The periodic table was further extended at the end of the century with the discovery of an inert gas called argon, which was followed almost immediately by the discovery of helium, krypton, neon, and xenon.

The study of organic chemistry, that is, the study of the substances that constitute the bodies of animals and plants, made rapid progress in the nineteenth century, and was separated from the study of inorganic chemistry or research in the substances forming nonliving things. It had been thought that only living organisms could produce the substances in animal or vegetable tissues; but in 1828, the German chemist Friedrich Wöhler proved that he could make urea in his laboratory. Understanding of the complex molecules formed by the atoms of carbon was central to advances in organic chemistry. The theory of valence, developed at mid-century, made it possible to describe the bonds formed by atoms in the creation of compounds such as benzene. Large numbers of organic substances were isolated in the later nineteenth century, and the basic subdivision of organic compounds into proteins, fats, and carbohydrates was established.

Much of the research in chemistry proved to have practical application. By 1850, textiles were being bleached with chloride of lime, coal gas had been brought into use as a means of lighting, and the invention of the process of vulcanization, combining rubber with sulfur under heat, made possible the use of rubber for many industrial purposes. Nitrocellulose had been discovered in 1846, and, after many dangerous experiments, was used to make dynamite by Alfred Nobel in 1866. Nobel thus became the founder of the modern high-explosives industry. Other inventions helped improve the quality of life. Wood pulp was used to make inexpensive paper. Black-and-white photography was invented. Synthetic dyestuffs made colorful ready-to-wear clothes available at low prices.

The work in organic chemistry of the French scientist Louis Pasteur (1822–1895) had great value for both industry and medicine. In working on fermentation in wine, beer, and milk, he invented the process known as pasteurization, a method by which disease-carrying organisms can be destroyed by rapid heating and cooling of those liquids. While working on bacteria, he proved conclusively that germs are the cause and not the product of disease. Upon hearing of Pasteur's experiments, the English surgeon Joseph Lister used carbolic acid to kill germs, and thus made surgery far safer. Finally, Pasteur began work on vaccination, and was able to develop an effective vaccine against rabies.

Study of Energy

The study of the nature of energy led both to formulation of general laws and to industrial application. In the eighteenth century, heat, light, electricity, and so on were regarded as "imponderables" or "fluids," weightless substances that flowed in and out of other bodies. If a body was hot, for example, it was thought to contain "calorific fluid." No relationship was perceived between heat and light or between electricity and magnetism. Benjamin Thompson, Count Rumford, an American who had moved to Europe at the time of the American Revolution, was able to show that heat was not a substance but rather a form of motion or of energy. In the 1840s, the English physicist James Joule and the German Hermann von Helmholtz showed that all forms of energy, such as heat and light, were interchangeable, and that, with the correct apparatus, they could be transformed into mechanical work without energy being lost. This concept was basic to the development of thermodynamics, which had immediate relevance to industrial chemistry.

As scientists further refined the mathematical laws of thermodynamics in the later part of the century, it became possible not only to increase the efficiency of engines but also the utility for industrial purposes of alloys such as nickel-chromium steel.

Research on the relation of electricity and magnetism also yielded practical results almost immediately. Batteries furnishing a smooth current of electricity had been developed by the early part of the nineteenth century. Faraday patented an electric motor for which he later invented an electric generator, thus making its use on a wide scale possible. The existence of electromagnetic waves that traveled at the speed of light was demonstrated theoretically in the 1870s, and proved experimentally by Heinrich Hertz in 1884. Guglielmo Marconi put together equipment for the transmission and reception of these waves, and thus created the first radio.

Darwin's Theory of Evolution

The concept of biology as a separate field, and perhaps even the use of the word biology, was popularized by the French naturalist Jean Lamarck at the beginning of the nineteenth century. Working on invertebrate animals and on plants, Lamarck concluded that the view held by most biologists until the eighteenth century, that species were fixed and definite, was incorrect. To explain how species such as domesticated animals changed from an original form, Lamarck proposed an early version of the theory of evolution. Species acquire characteristics to meet a need created by their environment, he argued, and those acquired characteristics are passed on to their offspring. This process had been continuous throughout geologic time.

Meanwhile, advances in geology were challenging the concept taught in the Christian churches, that the earth had been created complete in its present form by God as described in the Book of Genesis in the Bible. The modern science of geology had been founded by James Hutton in 1785, with publication of his *Theory of the Earth,* in which he demonstrated systematically that rock strata, with the fossils embedded in them, could be studied to show the process of the formation of the earth. The French naturalist Georges Cuvier was even able to reconstruct the appearance of mammals from their fossilized remains, and thus prove the vast variations in life forms over the long periods of geologic change. The summation of contemporary geologic knowledge in Charles Lyell's *Principles of Geology* (1830–1833), with its assertation that the earth had not only changed in the past but was continually being transformed by earthquakes, volcanic action, and erosion, further weakened support for the literal interpretation of Biblical creation.

The discussion of the concept of evolution was thus widespread among biologists and naturalists by the 1830s when Charles Darwin, the grandson of one of the earliest proponents of a theory of evolution, accepted a position as naturalist on a surveying expedition to the South Atlantic and South Pacific. For five years, from 1831 to 1836, Darwin collected documentation on the fossils and living birds and animals he found, especially those on the Galapagos Islands 600 miles off the coast of Ecuador. There, he was able to show conclusively, birds, animals, and plants had developed differently from the same species on the mainland, and even differed from island to island.

After studying his evidence for twenty years, Darwin published in 1859 *On the Origin of Species by Means of Natural Selection or the Preservation of the Favoured Races in the Struggle for Life*. The book caused an immediate sensation, and earned the condemnation of most Christian ministers, because Darwin dismissed the idea of immutable species created by God, and demonstrated that in the struggle for existence those individuals of a species favored by some accident, with strength or protective coloring that gives them superiority, will survive and others will not. Worse, in the churches' view, he argued that all life was derived from a common ancestor, and he suggested that human beings were closely related to monkeys in the process of evolution. The battle over Darwin's theses was at its most vehement in England, where such leading scientific thinkers as Thomas Huxley debated evolution with leading clerics before impassioned audiences. The major part of Darwin's theories came to be accepted by the scientific community by the end of the century, especially after the Dutch botanist Hugo De Vries, drawing upon the work on heredity of an obscure Austrian monk, Gregor Mendel, showed that the variations within a species are caused by sudden mutations in germ cells, which can be passed on to descendants, unlike acquired characteristics, which could not.

Spencer and Social Darwinism

The theory of evolution was applied to the study of human society by the philosopher Herbert Spencer (1820–1903), who coined the phrase "survival of the fittest," which is frequently used to summarize Darwin's conclusions. Spencer argued in a wide-ranging series of books published between 1860 and 1896 that the process of evolution occurred not merely in living things but in ideas, customs, societies, and even solar systems, moving always from simplicity to complexity and thus continually progressing. In society, he argued that individualism, the individual's search for personal betterment by competition with others, was the instrument by which societies progressed. Interference by the state would only result in hampering this beneficial process.

Spencer thus prepared the way for the industrialists, militarists, and imperialists of the late nineteenth century to argue what came to be called Social

Darwinism—that competition of all kinds is beneficial to humanity as a whole, and ought to be won by the superior at the expense of the inferior. For industrialists, it could justify the wiping out of their competitors. For militarists it could justify war against smaller, weaker states. For imperialists, it proved the superiority of the white race and their right to rule racially inferior groups.

LITERATURE AND THE ARTS: FROM ROMANTICISM TO SYMBOLISM

Although not all forms of culture followed exactly the same pattern throughout the nineteenth century, we must identify a certain pattern of development before indicating ways in which specific types of creativity differed. From the late eighteenth century to about the middle of the nineteenth century, the prevailing style in literature and most of the arts was Romanticism, a style that rejected the classical, rational manner of the eighteenth century and focused instead on the expression of human emotions, the self-realization of the individual, and the revolt against authority.

From the middle of the nineteenth to the beginning of the twentieth century, many writers and artists were influenced by the industrial changes around them and attempted a more scientific approach to the everyday life they encountered, first in the style called Realism and, later, in an even more analytical form called Naturalism, in which all human action is seen as the product of such natural forces as environment or heredity.

Beginning in the 1870s, the Impressionist painters in France rejected the subjects' style and technique of academic painting, which tended to be frigid depictions of an imagined grandeur or sentimental renderings of domestic scenes. The Impressionists, by contrast, sought to depict the transitory visual impression of a scene as experienced by the artist both through sight and feeling. In effect, they softened the Realist approach to subject matter. The Impressionists were succeeded in the 1880s by the Post-Impressionist painters, who, though far less of a school, were linked by their common emphasis on design within painting, often deliberately distorting reality for this purpose, and on emotion as evoked by the use of color. In literature, the attack on the conventional styles of the day was led by the Symbolist poets in the 1880s, who proclaimed the affinity of poetry to music, the use of images or symbols that would free the imagination, and the need for constant innovation and experiment.

Romanticism in Literature

As we saw in Chapter 11, a reaction against the rationalism of the Enlightenment writers had been led in the late eighteenth century by Rousseau in France, by the *Sturm und Drang* writers in Germany, and by Wordsworth and Coleridge in England. Knowledge of the German literary revolution was brought back to France by Madame de Staël, whose book *On Germany* (1810) made unfavorable comparisons between the level of French culture and that of the Germany of Goethe, whom she had met in 1804 during a stay in Weimar. Nevertheless, an authentically French form of Romanticism was already being created by the exiled French aristocrat, the Vicomte de Chateaubriand, above all in his book *The Genius of Christianity* (1802), in which he established several of the lasting characteristics of French Romanticism—a reverence of the Middle Ages, an evocation of nature, and personal melancholia.

Romanticism did not, however, triumph in France until the 1820s and 1830s. Many of the themes developed by Chateaubriand resound in the poetry of Alphonse de Lamartine (1790–1869): the mystical appeal of religion, the worship of nature, and the sadness of human passion. Already in his *Poetic Meditations* (1820), Lamartine had created the image of the self-pitying, self-dramatizing hero that was the model for French youth in the years after the defeat of Napoleon:

> I have seen too much, felt too much, loved too much in my life;
> Alive, I have come to search for the calm of Lethe.
> Sweet place, become for me that river that brings forgetfullness.
> Forgetfullness is henceforth my only happiness.[1]

The same characteristics dominate the hero in the play, *Hernani* (1830), by Victor Hugo, whose long life and immensely varied output of plays, novels, and poems made him the giant of French Romanticism. *Hernani* so deliberately broke the established rules both of permissible verse forms and acceptable standards of plot that at its first presentation the theater erupted in a riot between classicists and romanticists, and left Hugo the darling of the iconoclastic young.

The freedom from social convention demanded by the Romantics became the principal theme of the life and works of the novelist George Sand (1804–1876), whose real name was Lucile-Aurore Dupin. Abandoning her husband, she moved to Paris with her two children, supported herself by writing 80 novels, and lived openly in disregard of public opinion with the poet Alfred de Musset, the pianist Frédéric Chopin, and others. Throughout her novels, as in her own life, she argued that women have the right to the social freedom and self-development that men take for granted.

In Britain in the early nineteenth century, a new generation of Romantic poets seemed in their own lives and their premature deaths to be themselves examples of the Romantic heroism proclaimed so often by the long-lived Victor Hugo. John Keats (1795–1821), after a long struggle with tuberculosis, died at the age of twenty-five. Percy Bysshe Shelley (1792–1822) was drowned while sailing off the Italian coast, at the age of thirty. George Gordon, Lord Byron (1788–1824), who had gone to aid the Greeks in their war of independence against the Turks, died of fever at the age of thirty-six.

[1] Alphonse de Lamartine, *Le Vallon*. Author's translation.

Keats shared the Romantic movement's love of the Middle Ages, its emphasis on spontaneity of feeling, and its belief in the role of the poet in helping humanity experience the joy of beauty. As did Shelley and Byron, he succeeded in distilling his vision into short lyrics of great power:

> A thing of beauty is a joy forever:
> Its loveliness increases; it will never
> Pass into nothingness; but still will keep
> A bower quiet for us, and a sleep
> Full of sweet dreams, and health, and quiet breathing.[2]

Shelley was the Romantic revolutionary *par excellence*. Expelled from Oxford University for atheism, he blasted the English ruling classes for their treatment of the poor in pamphlets and poems, and he also displayed the Romantics' willingness to experiment with form, as in his "Ode to the West Wind," which combines the rhyme scheme of Dante with the form of the English sonnet for each of the stanzas. His finest verses were those in which he displayed his generous feeling for others, especially the poem *Adonais*, in which he mourned the death of Keats.

Lord Byron was for the French Romantics the epitome of what a poet should be. Good-looking, flamboyant, passionate in love and politics, he was regarded as the "Bonaparte of poetry." While traveling throughout the Mediterranean, he wrote a great deal of verse, much of it very popular in his own day, as was *Childe Harold's Pilgrimage*, in which he used a travel poem to present his observations on history, politics, and morality. Byron's major work is an unfinished social satire called *Don Juan*.

Romanticism in Painting

Painters searched both past and present for suitably exotic or sentimental subject matter. In 1819, Théodore Géricault (1791–1824) startled the Parisian art world with his painting, *The Raft of the Medusa*. It depicted a real event, shipwrecked sailors off the African coast. To achieve a sense of shock, Géricault modeled the emaciated survivors on dying hospital patients and corpses, and even copied severed limbs. The public was outraged, and he never sold the picture in his lifetime.

Eugène Delacroix (1798–1863), the foremost of the French Romantic painters, was equally disturbing to the public for the extraordinary vividness with which he depicted wild scenes of carnage, such as Turks slaughtering Greeks during the war of independence (*Massacre at Chios*), or the Assyrian emperor Assurbanipal watching his wives and domestic animals being slaughtered before him (*Death of Sardanaplus*). The vitality of Delacroix's painting was, however, due not only to the drama of his subject matter but to the freshness of

---

[2] John Keats, *Endymion*, i.1.I.

***The Raft of the Medusa,* by Théodore Géricault (1791–1824)** *Géricault's brutal attack on the emotions in his graphic portrayal of the shipwrecked survivors was recognized as one of the first important paintings of the Romantic school.* (Giraudon/Art Resource.)

his color, which made him particularly successful in his later life as a painter of large-scale murals in the main public buildings of Paris.

The Romantic love of nature infused the landscape paintings of Camille Corot (1796–1875). In his early paintings especially, he sought a simple, direct presentation of scenes like the fishing towns of the French north coast, although later in life, perhaps influenced by the appearance of foliage in early photographs, he used fluffy, tinted grays in a new style that won him widespread popularity for the first time.

Romanticism did not completely triumph in French art, not least because the classical tradition was carried on by Jean-Auguste Ingres (1780–1867), who taught his pupils to avoid contemporary subjects and even landscape and to turn to classical mythology as a source for themes and classical sculpture as a lesson in style. Ingres himself won success, after initial disappointments, with a number of historical works, but he is best remembered for several paintings of female nudes, such as *La Grande Odalisque,* and for his portraits.

The early French Romantic painters acknowledged their debt to the contemporary painters in England. Delacroix had even repainted the *Massacre at*

The Lock, by John Constable (1776–1837) Constable, one of England's leading landscape painters, specialized in scenes of the English countryside, highlighting the play of sunshine on drifting clouds. (Philadelphia Museum of Art: The George W. Elikins Collection.)

Chios after becoming acquainted, during a visit to England, with the quiet, ruminating color of the landscape painter John Constable (1776–1837), as seen in his painting, *The Lock.* In fact, for perhaps the only time in the history of French painting, France's artists deliberately sought to learn from English models, not only from Constable but also from the mysterious exploration of the technique of presenting nature at its most dynamic, in storm or sunset, seen in the paintings of J. M. W. Turner (1775–1851).

Period Revivals in Architecture

Romanticism was probably a destructive force in architecture, since it persuaded the leading architects to disassociate themselves from the industrial revolution and the potential use of its new products, such as steel, but rather to attempt to reproduce the style of the Middle Ages and other past eras of architectural greatness. When the Houses of Parliament in London burned down in 1834, they were replaced by a massive neo-Gothic riverfront façade, decorated with intricately designed belltower and turrets. Even the new railroad stations, like that of Saint Pancras in London, were disguised with romantically conceived campaniles! But the architects, like the writers, felt free to pick from any period that appealed to their fancy. Some of the finest buildings in the new industrial cities of Britain and Germany were virtual reconstructions of the palaces of the Florentine patriciate, while in France many of the middle class favored contemporary versions of the sixteenth-century palaces that the king and nobles had built in the valley of the Loire.

Beethoven Between Classicism and Romanticism

By contrast, Romanticism proved a vitally enriching force in music, perhaps because it was Ludwig van Beethoven (1770–1827) who provided the transition from the classical style. Beethoven, supremely self-confident in his mastery of all that the classical style and the contemporary orchestra could offer, step by step drove music to achieve new dimensions of expression. He was a strongly intellectual composer, who worked out painstakingly the structure of his compositions; but he was also a man of driving passion who intended, as he said, to "take fate by the throat." The novelty in Beethoven, which prepared the way for the Romantics, was his demand on the orchestra for new forms of sound, his unorthodox use of keys, and above all his willingness to express emotions directly through the new music. When already recognized as one of the world's greatest composers, he suffered the great tragedy of slowly losing his hearing, and of knowing that he himself would never hear his own finest compositions. Fighting back, he emerged from desolation to master his own grief, and from his suffering produced the noblest of music, as in his celebration of heroism in the *Third Symphony,* popularly known as the *Eroica,* or of human brotherhood in the *Ninth Symphony,* often called the *Choral Symphony.*

Character of Romantic Music

Romantic music explored many new avenues of expression. In the songs of a composer such as Franz Schubert (1797–1826) or the waltzes of Johann Strauss, Jr. (1825–1899), the escapism of music became a high form of art. Nationalism was expressed by such composers as the Hungarian Franz Liszt, the Pole Frédéric Chopin, and the German Karl von Weber, all of whom used national or folk themes in their work. Theatricality appealed to composers like Hector Berlioz (1803–1869), not only in his enormous operas but also in such works as his *Fantastic Symphony.* With Berlioz, the Romantic composers became enamored of size, whether of orchestra or chorus, in the belief that a more direct assault on the emotions was made possible in this way.

Once Romanticism was well established in music, it did not lose its hold until the end of the century. Composers continued to experiment with the possibilities of new instruments, such as the saxophone, or new developments in symphony and opera. Johannes Brahms (1833–1896) prided himself with carrying on most directly the symphonic traditions of Beethoven, but another Viennese composer, Anton Bruckner (1824–1896), employed the orchestra more directly—to the annoyance of some patrons—to express the wind blowing through forests or even peasants dancing in hob-nailed boots. The nationalist movement was especially strong in Russia, in the works of Peter Tchaikovsky and Nicolai Rimsky-Korsakov, and in Eastern Europe, in the music of the Czech Antonin Dvořák.

Opera was perhaps the most persistently Romantic of musical forms, especially in the popular works of Giuseppe Verdi (1813–1901). It was, however, the German Richard Wagner (1813–1883) who attempted to make of opera the supreme instrument of synthesis, combining in one art form music, poetry, drama, and the visual arts, and using the new form, which he called a *Gesamtkunstwerk* ("Total Work of Art") to express nationalistic themes drawn from his own study of the ancient German epic poems. His most ambitious work was the cycle of four operas called *The Ring of the Nibelung,* in which, as in an ancient Greek drama, the gods quarrel among themselves as they seek to determine the destinies of the human beings struggling for the power that possession of the gold of the Rhine Maidens will bring.

Precursors of Realism

The reaction against the Romantic style was led by novelists who felt that, rather than ignore the new industrial, urban world, the writer should make sense of it. The forerunners of the new style had been Charles Dickens (1812–1870) in England and Honoré de Balzac (1799–1850) in France. Dickens' characters had been presented with the sentimentality of the true Romantic writer, with unabashed willingness to bring tears to his reader's eyes. But Dickens was unerringly realistic in his portrayal of social institutions, like the law courts or the debtors' prisons, or his depiction of the mean attics or cellars of the London slums or the clanking inferno of a Lancashire cotton mill.

Balzac set as his goal the depiction, in a wide-ranging series of novels known as *The Human Comedy,* of the whole French society of his time. Like Dickens, he intended to show what was wrong with his society. He loved Paris with the passion Dickens showed for London, and excelled in the portrayal of the poor whose sufferings, in his view, should not be tolerated in so great a city. To carry out his ambitious program, he chose to depict in minute detail the physical setting in which his characters lived; in this way, although his larger-than-life portrayals of his characters links him to the Romantic school, his accuracy of observation of concrete detail make him a precursor of the Realists.

The transition from Romanticism to Realism in painting was led by Honoré Daumier (1808–1879) and Jean-François Millet (1814–1874) in France. Daumier was a lithographer and painter who specialized in political and social satire. Daumier depicted the lawyers and politicians of contemporary French money-grubbing society with a savagery that drew inspiration from the terrifying paintings of the Spanish painter Francisco Goya, which depicted the brutality of the Napoleonic wars. One of the preoccupations of the coming Realist school, penetration into the emotions and suffering of the poor, is, however, seen in Daumier's *The Third Class Carriage.*

Peasant life preoccupied Millet, who presented life on the farm as heroic drudgery. His melancholy vision, derived from his own upbringing in a poor peasant family, was best expressed in *The Gleaners* and *Angelus,* both of which have been criticized for their excessively explicit moralizing and their sentimentality.

Realism and Naturalism

The leading French novelist of the Realist School was Gustave Flaubert (1821–1880). Flaubert was brought to trial for immorality (and exonerated) for his meticulous depiction of the love affairs of the wife of a pedantic provincial doctor in his *Madame Bovary;* but his exposure of the pretensions of the generation of youth carried away with the posturing of Romantic heroism, in *The Sentimental Education,* published in its final edition in 1870, proved a last blow to the Romantic ideal.

Russian novelists enthusiastically adopted the Realist style, as when Feodor Dostoevski (1821–1881) examined the motives of a murderer and the effects on him of his crime, in *Crime and Punishment,* or when Leo Tolstoy (1828–1910) examined the impact of war on each layer of Russian society in his *War and Peace.*

Drama too found Realist themes congenial, especially in presenting the problems of women both within marriage and within the strictures of middleclass society. The master of this form was the Norwegian Henrik Ibsen (1828–1906), whose play *A Doll's House* centered on a wife caught within the metaphorical doll's house of a marriage based on falsehood. The Russian playwright Anton Chekhov (1860–1904) also found a type of falsehood in the provincial life of the gentry whose social and intellectual pretentiousness he dramatizes.

Émile Zola (1840–1902) complained that Flaubert had not gone far enough toward achieving realism and became the theorist of the school called Naturalism. For the Naturalists, the novelist had to approach his subject matter like a scientist; and for that reason Zola wrote twenty novels examining different facts of one family, in a series he called the "Natural and Social History of a Family Under the Second Empire." In each of the novels Zola took apart one side of French life, often the seamier side, as in *Germinal,* which shows the misery of the French industrial worker, or *Nana,* which unglamorously examines prostitution in Paris.

In painting, Gustave Courbet (1819–1877) crusaded on behalf of painting "things as they are," and was in fact the person who coined the word Realism. His painting, *Funeral at Ornans,* grimly depicting a working-class family grouped around a burial in unrelieved gloom, made him famous as the protagonist of the forgotten poor, and he continued to attempt to shock by breaking all accepted conventions of subject matter. Although Courbet gained an unmerited reputation as a socialist radical, he did not restrict himself to paintings of the poor, but painted a wide variety of landscapes, seascapes, and figures on which his fame primarily rests.

Impressionism in Painting

A new technique of painting was launched by Edward Manet in his painting, *Luncheon on the Grass* (1863), which not only disturbed middle-class morality by depicting a nude woman and two clothed young men finishing a picnic but used what seemed broadly applied brush strokes to depict the forest scene instead of a highly polished style in which the strokes would be virtually invisible. Manet's lead was followed by a group of artists known as the Impressionists, a movement united by certain premises. One was that painting should represent the transient effect of light on objects. Another was that artists should paint out of doors. And a third was that painters should use a heightened palette or brighter colors than was traditional.

In one sense the Impressionists were the most realistic painters of all,

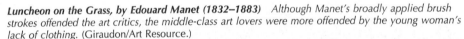

Luncheon on the Grass, by Edouard Manet (1832–1883) *Although Manet's broadly applied brush strokes offended the art critics, the middle-class art lovers were more offended by the young woman's lack of clothing. (Giraudon/Art Resource.)*

Five O'Clock Tea, by Mary Cassatt (1844–1926) The American Impressionist painter Cassatt lived most of her life in France, where she painted intimate scenes of her brother's family. (Museum of Fine Arts, Boston; Maria Hopkins Fund.)

because they showed that the brown-pigmented "realism" of the artist's schools and studios does not correspond to the experience of nature as seen in or out of doors. The Impressionists were interested first in the character of light, especially in scenes where it falls on water and land or shines through mist or steam. The leading Impressionist painter, Claude Monet (1840–1926), frequently painted the same scene several times to show how the changing light affects the appearance of such objects as haystacks, water lilies, cathedrals, or even railroad stations. At one point in his early career, Monet fitted up a studio on a barge so that he could paint river scenes. In painting light, the Impressionists used dabs of varying hues applied to the canvas, which from close up look utterly confusing but which from a distance fuse in the viewer's eye to make a rich, sparkling, unified color.

The second aspect of the Impressionists that showed their interest in reality was their choice of subject matter. Everyday life was to be celebrated. Hence, Edgar Degas roamed the ballet theaters for his subjects; Auguste Renoir painted lively dancers in open-air cafes; Henri de Toulouse-Lautrec immortalized the frowsy cabarets of the Montmartre district of Paris; Mary Cassatt, an American expatriate, painted intimate scenes of unaffected family life. Although they were at first ridiculed, many of the Impressionists lived long enough to experience triumph in the art world, see their work widely accepted in museums, and have their paintings purchased by the wealthy. Their rather extraordinary success was an important warning to art critics and to patrons that the unfamiliar was not necessarily the unworthy, and it encouraged other artists who wished to move on to even more startlingly novel experiments.

The Post-Impressionists

In the 1880s and 1890s, artists now known as the Post-Impressionists became disenchanted with Impressionism, which they felt was doing little more than capturing a fleeting version of reality. Without rejecting the subject matter of the Impressionists, such as landscapes or scenes of urban life, they set out to find new ways of perceiving and presenting those scenes so that they would have an eternal quality rather than the transitory character sought by the Impressionists.

For Paul Cézanne (1839–1906), who had begun his career as an Impressionist, the way to gain this eternal quality was to provide his paintings with a structure based on geometric shapes, such as the cylinder, sphere, and cone. He said that his goal was to do "Poussin over entirely from nature" and to

Mont Sainte-Victoire, by Paul Cézanne (1839–1906)   *Working in the rugged country of southern France, Cézanne sought geometric shapes, such as the cone or cylinder, in the outline of the mountains.* (National Gallery of Art, Washington, D.C.; gift of the W. Averell Harriman Foundation.)

Study for a Sunday Afternoon at La Grande Jatte, by Georges Seurat (1859–1891) Seurat used his *many preliminary studies, made both outside and inside the studio, as the basis for an overall de- sign before he would begin the final painting.* (The Metropolitan Museum of Art, Bequest of Sam A. Lewisohn, 1951.)

make his paintings from nature as solidly structured as those of the old masters. To realize his goal, Cézanne constructed his paintings around abstract forms, whether the subject was a group of apples on a table, a number of bathers in a wooded glen, or a mountain viewed from several angles.

Other Post-Impressionist painters believed color had symbolic value, in much the same way that Symbolist writers looked upon words (see pp. 492–493). Paul Gauguin (1848–1903), who is often considered a Symbolist painter, wished his forms, patterns, and flat contrasting areas of color to be suggestive rather than descriptive and thus affect the viewer much as music affects the listener. Gauguin achieved his finest work on the island of Tahiti where, influenced by the art of "primitive" peoples (those untutored in European styles of art), he worked in a flat, largely decorative manner on woodcuts and paintings in which the life and beliefs of the Tahitian Islanders were his subjects.

Vincent van Gogh (1853–1890) focused on color and the relationships among colors to carry symbolic import. He could, he said, portray two lovers by using two complementary colors and thereby show the vivacity of their feeling for each other. Complementary colors tend to vibrate when set next to each other. In his subject matter, too, he sought out symbols that revealed his own reaction to life. His early painting of *The Potato Eaters*, for example, which depicts a poverty-stricken group of workers eating a meager meal in semidarkness, focuses on the gnarled hands of the peasants as the symbols of the suffering of the poor. Later, when he moved to the bright landscapes of Provence, the natural features of the landscape, such as the roots of trees seeking a hold in the rocky soil, are themselves a symbol of the tension van Gogh himself felt in coming to terms with his own world.

Georges Seurat (1859–1891) also sought symbolic import in color, but, like Cézanne, he based the structure of his paintings on geometric form. Working from scientific theories of the nature of light and optics, Seurat developed a method of painting called "Pointillisme," in which very tiny dots of paint are juxtaposed so that they fuse in the eye of the beholder. In contrast to the Impressionists, he was extremely concerned to achieve a carefully planned, harmonious design. Seurat's method was to make a large number of oil studies from nature of the scene he wished to depict, such as the bank of the river Seine in *A Sunday Afternoon at La Grande Jatte*. Back in the studio, he then worked out on canvas the specific features and overall design of his conception before beginning the final painting. His method was immensely time-consuming, and he had completed less than forty paintings when he died of pneumonia at the age of thirty-one.

The Symbolists

In literature, the revolt against Realism and Naturalism was led by writers who called themselves Symbolists. They held that the concrete, precise use of words advocated by the Realists and Naturalists should be replaced by words that are suggestive and have a symbolic impact, very much as the Christian Church used the symbol of hell for the power of its emotional evocation. Rather than make clear statements, language should be evocative of what one Symbolist called the poet's "inner dream." So as to achieve what they thought of as pure poetry, Symbolists attempted to make poetry as much like music as possible.

The Symbolists believed that Charles Baudelaire (1821–1867) had shown in his slim volume of poems called *Fleurs du Mal* how images drawn from the senses, such as odors or colors, could correspond to each other symbolically. But of more immediate influence were the Tuesday evening receptions where Stéphane Mallarmé (1842–1898) expounded his views on poetry to a select gathering of artists and writers. Mallarmé's poem, *The Afternoon of a Faun*, which was set to music by Claude Debussy, was perhaps the first great Symbolist poem. But perhaps the best summation of the goals of the Symbolists was *The Art of Poetry* by Paul Verlaine (1844–1898), which begins, "Music before all else," and ends:

Let your verse be the great adventure
Flying high on the sharp wind of morning
Which floats scented with mint and with thyme
And the rest is literature.[3]

[3] Paul Verlaine, *Oeuvres poétiques complètes* (Paris: Bibliothèque de la Pléiade, 1951), pp. 206–207. Author's translation.

The original school of Symbolists were active from the 1880s to the end of the century, exercising considerable influence, as we have seen, not only on poetry but on painting and music as well. In drama, a particularly successful Symbolist work was Maurice Maeterlinck's play *Pelléas and Mélisande*, which Debussy turned into his only opera.

Toward the Twentieth Century

The writers, artists, and scientists of the late nineteenth century had brought Western culture to the verge of a revolutionary period of experimentation and discovery (see Chapter 20). The style of Cézanne led directly to the technique of Cubism. The use of color in the work of painters such as Gauguin and van Gogh was the starting point for the work of Henri Matisse and the Fauve painters. Symbolists deeply influenced the work of the most innovative writers of the early twentieth century, such as the poet T. S. Eliot and the novelists Marcel Proust and James Joyce. Debussy's experiments with harmony and dissonance and his use of the whole-tone scale pointed to the serial style or twelve-tone music by Arnold Schoenberg and his followers. Research on radioactivity was laying the foundations for the great advances in atomic physics that would be synthesized in the work of Albert Einstein. At the turn of the century, there was an exciting but also disturbing sense that the twentieth century would bring an extraordinary acceleration in the pace of change.

SUGGESTED READINGS

General Surveys

A solid overview of European economic history is David Landes, *The Unbound Prometheus: Technological Change and Industrial Development in Western Europe from 1750 to the Present* (1969). The working class is analyzed in Peter N. Stearns, *European Society in Upheaval: Social History Since 1800* (1967). Political philosophy is emphasized in both George L. Mosse, *The Culture of Western Europe: The Nineteenth and Twentieth Centuries* (1961), and Roland N. Stromberg, *European Intellectual History Since 1789* (1968).

The Second Industrial Revolution

The technological innovations, in steel and electricity in particular, are explained by S. J. Singer et al., eds., *A History of Technology*, vol. 5: *Late Nineteenth Century, 1850–1900* (1958). The resulting changes in business organization are the main subject of H. J. Habbakuk, *American and British Technology in the Nineteenth Century* (1962).

Demographic and Urban Growth

Adna F. Weber gives the startling statistics of urban expansion in *The Growth of Cities in the Nineteenth Century* (1963), but the human consequences are more evident in studies of individual cities such as Francis Sheppard, *London 1808–1870: The Infernal Wen* (1971), or Gerhard Masur, *Imperial Berlin* (1970). Demographic change is set in perspective in E. A. Wrigley, *Population and History* (1969).

Nineteenth-Century Science

Gertrude Himmelfarb assesses the impact of Darwin in *Darwin and the Darwinian Revolution* (1959). The shock caused by his ideas on evolution is described in W. Irvine, *Apes, Angels, and Victorians* (1959).

Literature and the Arts

The artistic revolutions of the nineteenth century are carefully analyzed in E. H. Gombrich, *The Story of Art* (1979), and G. H. Hamilton, *Nineteenth and Twentieth Century Art* (1972). On music, see D. J. Grout, *A History of Western Music* (1980); on architecture, see the short but extremely informative pages in Nikolaus Pevsner, *An Outline of European Architecture* (1970).

The lush self-indulgence of the Romantic movement is evident in art in M. Brion, *The Art of the Romantic Era* (1966); in music, in A. Einstein, *Music in the Romantic Era* (1947); and in architecture, in Kenneth Clark, *The Gothic Revival* (1950). Perhaps the best introduction to Romantic literature is to read the work of Victor Hugo, either his play *Hernani* or a novel such as *The Hunchback of Notre Dame.*

The French Realist writers can be approached through Harry Levin, *The Gates of Horn: A Study of Five French Realists* (1963). Angus Wilson shows how true to life were Dickens's descriptions of England in *The World of Charles Dickens* (1970), a fact only too obvious to anyone who reads *Oliver Twist* or *Bleak House.*

The Parisian intellectual world of the late nineteenth century is sparklingly portrayed in Roger Shattuck, *The Banquet Years* (1968), that of Vienna in Carl E. Schorske, *Fin-de-Siècle Vienna* (1980).

18

From the New Imperialism to the First World War

After the British defeat in the American war of independence in 1776–1783, the European powers became disillusioned with the mercantilist view that colonies were necessary to provide a nation-state with raw materials and captive markets. Most European leaders were inclined to agree with the French statesman Vergennes, who held that colonies were like fruit, which would fall from the mother bough when ripe. Some colonial expansion did, however, continue in the first part of the nineteenth century; the British took control of large parts of India, and the French annexed Algeria. But only after 1870 did a scramble among the Western powers for control of the underdeveloped parts of the world begin once more. Within thirty years, almost four-fifths of Africa, most of Southeast Asia, and all the territories in the South Pacific had been annexed, while South and Central America and the Chinese empire were subordinated to the political and economic influence of the Western powers.

In this new surge of imperialism, the Western powers were able, though barely, to avoid going to war among themselves for a share of the spoils. In 1914, however, rivalries in Europe, exacerbated by the imperial competition, brought the world to war. Two alliance systems—the German-dominated Triple Alliance created by Bismarck and the French-British-Russian alliance formed to counter it—faced each other with such mutual suspicion that the incompetent handling of any crisis, especially in the struggle of Austria and Russia for preeminence in the Balkans, could bring the sides into open conflict. That crisis occurred in June 1914 with the murder in Serajevo of the heir to the Austrian throne. By August, the alliances were at war.

This first "world war" shattered the autocratic empires of Eastern Europe, permitting minority national groups within the German, Austrian, Russian, and Turkish empires to form their own nation-states. It also provided the opportunity for the small Communist party in Russia to seize power in Europe's largest and most populous state in November 1917. And it so embittered national hatreds inside Europe, especially of the French for the Germans, that the principal goal of many of the participants in the Paris Peace Conference at the end of the war was to prevent Germany from ever again being able to make war on its neighbors.

THE NEW IMPERIALISM, 1870–1900

Motives of the New Imperialism

Imperialism became an important force in the late nineteenth century because it was supported by such a wide variety of groups within Western society, whose motives varied from charitable altruism to economic greed. Curiously enough, the missionary societies, and especially the antislavery groups, gave imperialism at least the façade and, some would argue, perhaps even a genuine underpinning of moral righteousness. As early as 1800, humanitarian groups in Europe and the European states were demanding the abolition of the slave trade and eventually of slavery itself; and their cause was aided by the fact that the sale of African slaves on the American continent was becoming less profitable as the natural increase of the slave population there supplied sufficient laborers.

One by one the European powers abolished the slave trade: first Denmark in 1805, then Britain in 1807, and shortly afterward most European powers except the Spanish and Portuguese. The British took the lead in using their navy to patrol the African coasts to seize slave-trading vessels, and they resettled many of the freed slaves in Sierra Leone on the coast of West Africa, which became a British colony. Slaves freed by the French were settled in Libreville, in what is now Gabon.

The desire to prevent the continuance of the slave trade provided an excuse for the British to annex Lagos on the coast of West Africa in 1861 and the island of Zanzibar on the east coast in 1890. Missionaries were sent into the interior of Africa by largely Protestant missionary societies in Britain and the United States and by Catholic societies in France and Belgium from the 1840s, both to Christianize the natives and to work against the slave trade; and their reports, such as the widely read book of the British missionary David Livingstone, *A Narrative of an Expedition to the Zambesi,* stimulated public demands for military intervention on the continent of Africa to stop the continuing slave trade.

The Meeting of Stanley and Livingstone, 1871 *The missionary explorer David Livingstone was "found" by the American journalist Henry Stanley after he took ill in central Africa, but refused to leave the African peoples with whom he was working.* (The Mansell Collection.)

Scientific curiosity led many explorers to Africa, and was the ostensible justification for government sponsorship of the many expeditions into the South Pacific that ultimately led to the annexation of the islands first visited for scientific purposes. The British were eager to discover the sources of the Nile, and the Royal Geographic Society of London sponsored many expeditions that brought knowledge of the great lake region of eastern Africa. Darwin had shown the biologist and zoologist the fascinating discoveries that could be made by getting away from the well-known regions of Europe, while anthropologists were avidly seeking knowledge of the unknown peoples with whom the explorers were coming into contact. More immediate gains were glimpsed as a result of the work of geologists, who were able to discover vast new sources of raw materials, such as the great copper deposits in the upper valley of the Congo.

As the potential of the newly explored regions of the world became evident, business groups in Europe and North America sought to gain their share. The expanding industries clearly needed new sources of raw materials, many of which were either becoming exhausted or did not exist at home. British expansion in southern Africa, for example, was motivated in part by the desire to exploit the diamond deposits of Kimberley and other mines. The Malayan peninsula attracted the British as a source of rubber. The French wished to develop West Africa as a source of coffee, palm nuts, and cocoa. King Leopold II (reigned 1865–1909) of Belgium made the Congo a private state under his personal control, to be able to sell for his own profit not only the copper but also the area's ivory and rubber.

497

The new colonies were also considered essential as captive markets for Western industry, especially as many new parts of Eastern Europe and North America became industrialized. Britain had demonstrated the value of controlling such a market, since by the 1880s one-fifth of all British exports were sent to India. Modern research has shown that these hopes were largely unrealized, and that the colonial territories acquired between 1870 and 1900 accounted for only a small percentage of the investment of the colonial powers and only a small part of their overseas trade. But the crucial factor is not the actual result of the acquisition of colonies but the expectation of the governing and industrial classes of the benefits they would receive. That expectation was the motive that drove them to support imperial expansion.

As it became obvious that a large number of powers were beginning to compete—among them Britain, France, Italy, Belgium, Portugal, Germany, Japan, and the United States—governments felt it imperative on military and strategic grounds to acquire territory simply to prevent their rivals from seizing it first. The British, for example, mounted a deliberate effort to annex Africa "from the Cape to Cairo," that is, to establish a continuous band of British territory from Egypt to Cape Colony in southern Africa, which would prevent the Portuguese from establishing a continuous strip of territory from their colony of Angola to their colony of Mozambique and would stop the French from controlling a band of territory from the West African coast to the Red Sea.

This motive was particularly strong in the rush to establish "spheres of influence" in the Chinese empire after 1895. Up to that point the British, French, and Americans had been content to take control by treaty of a small number of ports, such as Shanghai, from which they could gain access to the Chinese market, in addition to the British annexation of Hong Kong Island. But when Japan annexed Korea and the island of Taiwan, after defeating China in the war of 1894–1895, the European powers felt compelled to gain new centers of control for themselves. By 1914, spheres of influence had been taken by the Russians in Manchuria, by the Germans in Shantung, by the French in southeastern China, and by the British in the Yangtze and Pearl River valleys.

The Scramble for Africa

In 1870, only one-tenth of the vast continent of Africa was under colonial control; and the Dark Continent caught the imagination of the European public not least because it was the most obvious place in which the white races could, in the phrase of Rudyard Kipling, "take up the white man's burden." (When he wrote the phrase, Kipling was in fact urging the United States to annex the Philippines.) In 1870 Britain, France, Spain, and Portugal all possessed footholds along the coast, and they all sought to push their possessions inland, especially up the great river valleys that offered the only easy access to the interior.

Disraeli, in a diplomatic coup one weekend in 1875, gained control of the Suez Canal for Britain by purchasing the shares owned by the financially troubled Egyptian ruler; in 1882 Britain made Egypt a protectorate, and from there conquered the Sudan. In southern Africa, the British drove north from Cape Colony, which they had annexed from the Dutch in 1806, taking Bechuanaland in 1885, Rhodesia in 1889, and Nyasaland in 1893. After a savage war with the Boers, the descendants of the original Dutch settlers, in 1899–1902, they united the two independent Boer states of the Transvaal and the Orange Free State with the British-held territories to form the Union of South Africa in 1910. The British also extended their control inland from the eastern coast to form their colonies of British East Africa (Kenya) and Uganda, while on the west they vastly extended inland their possessions on the Gold Coast and Nigeria.

The French were not far behind the British. From Algeria, they were able to bring Tunisia under their rule in 1881 and Morocco in 1911, and they made the vast region of the Sahara and the grasslands to its south into French West Africa. Although the Spanish extended the area under their control only slightly, the Portuguese greatly increased the size of Angola and Mozambique. The Germans and Italians were latecomers into Africa. The Germans were, however, able to conquer the fertile lands of German East Africa, a section of the African rain forest that became the German Cameroons, and German Southwest Africa (Namibia). The Italians were humiliatingly defeated by the armies of Ethiopia in 1895–1896, but were able to retain hold of Eritrea and Italian Somaliland, on the Horn of Africa, and in 1911–1912 took Tripolitania and Cyrenaica (modern Libya).

An Attack of Zulu Warriors, 1879 In their final unsuccessful assault on the British troops subjugating southern Africa, the Zulus were armed not only with their short stabbing spears and cowhide shields but with modern rifles. Their lands were annexed by the British nine years later. (The Mansell Collection.)

All the European powers ran into desperate resistance from the African states they were attempting to annex. The states of sub-Saharan Africa were far from the benighted, primitive countries the popular European press represented them as being. Many, such as Benin, had long cultural traditions going back hundreds of years, and some, such as the Zulu kingdom, had well-organized armies that could even defeat Europeans armed with rifles and artillery. The Germans encountered especially desperate opposition. As many as two-thirds of the population of German Southwest Africa died in revolt, and resistance in German East Africa was subdued only after the Germans had killed up to 125,000 Africans. The French found great difficulty in suppressing the Tokolor empire in West Africa, because its ruler, Samori Touré, armed his troops with rifles copied from captured European guns. The British killed 20,000 Sudanese Muslims in one battle, Omdurman (1898), in the suppression of a religious uprising against their rule.

The degree of exploitation varied considerably. The most brutal regime was that of the Belgian King Leopold II in the Congo Free State, which he governed as a personal fief rather than as a Belgian colony, where almost half the population died either in the conquest or in labor gangs recruited to work the mines and build roads and railroads. So great was the outrage in Europe against Leopold's cruelties that he was finally forced to hand over control of the Congo to the Belgian government, thus converting his personal fief into a colony of the government. In all the African colonies, much of the best land was taken by white proprietors. The African population was forced to subsist on the poorer land, or to take up manual work on the European-owned farms, in the mines, or in the factories. They were not trained for technical work and educational levels often remained low. Only the British and French made serious efforts to provide university education, and even then the Africans were trained in British and French culture rather than in their own traditions. The provision of a basic infrastructure of roads, railroads, and power, the modernization of agriculture, and the beginnings of industry in Africa during the colonial period were inadequate compensation for the destruction of native African states and their culture or for almost a century of economic exploitation.

Colonialism in Asia and the South Pacific

Both the British and French were determined to expand their control in Southeast Asia. For the British, Southeast Asia offered both a threat to the eastern borders of India and a source of new wealth for Britain's industrial and financial classes. After skirmishes with the Burmese on the edge of Bengal, the British decided to punish their king, in the first Burmese war (1824–1826), by annexing part of the Burmese coast. From there, they saw the rich potential of exploiting the country's teak, rice, and tin. Provoking a second war in 1852, they took the capital of Rangoon and most of the south of the country. Finally, in 1885, to gain access to the Chinese silk trade from the south, they overthrew the king and took the rest of Burma. The country was immediately developed with British capital. The low-lying lands of the south became one of Asia's major rice-exporting regions, while teak production was developed in the northern forests. But little of the wealth filtered down to the Burmese peasants, and chronic unrest was common throughout British rule.

In the neighboring Malay peninsula, the British developed the tiny island of Singapore, which they annexed in 1819, into one of the world's great ports and trading centers. But the lure of profits from tin and rubber led them to force the inland sultans to cede power to Britain between 1874 and 1914; and large-scale immigration of Indian and Chinese workers for the mines and plantations led to growing racial antagonism with the native Malay population.

French missionaries first moved into Indochina (present-day Laos, Kampuchea, and Vietnam) at the beginning of the nineteenth century, and made considerable numbers of converts. Napoleon III sent French fleets to protect them from persecution, and between 1858 and 1867 seized the southern third of the country, including the port of Saigon. From there it was relatively easy for the French to take over the rest of Vietnam, Cambodia (Kampuchea), and Laos, which were linked together under a French governor-general as the Union of Indochina. Control of Indochina proved profitable for the French and for a small upper class of Vietnamese who cooperated with them, but not for the majority of the people. Good roads and railroads were built to carry off the country's exports of rice, rubber, coffee, and tea, grown on lands owned almost exclusively by the French and the very small number of wealthy collaborators.

The United States also succumbed to the lure of empire in the Pacific. By winning the right to trade from "treaty ports" in both China and Japan, it gained a foothold in those lucrative markets. In 1867, it took possession of the island of Midway and purchased Alaska from Russia. In 1893, after the overthrow of the last Hawaiian ruler, Queen Liliuokalani, by a group of Americans in alliance with missionary families, Congress was asked to annex the islands, which it finally did in 1898. In the same year, the United States annexed the Philippine Islands after the brief Spanish-American war. The United States thus became a major power in both the North and South Pacific. But the European powers were also seizing their share of the Pacific islands. The French had established a protectorate in Tahiti in 1843 and formally annexed it in 1880. The Germans took the Marianas and the Caroline Islands. The British took Fiji and shared the New Hebrides with France.

The balance sheet of this new imperialism is hard to establish. As early as 1902, John A. Hobson argued, in a widely read study called *Imperialism*, that the capitalists needed to find new outlets for investment and new markets for their growing production because they were failing, as a result of their payment of subsistence wages only to their workers in Europe, to create a consumer market at home. Lenin refined these views in his book *Imperialism: The Highest Stage of Capitalism* (1916). In the normal evolution of capitalism, he claimed, the capitalists grow fewer in number and richer, and engage in ever more desperate competition for markets and profits. The struggle for empire is the final confrontation within a capitalist system that is dying.

Scholars have recently calculated that the newly acquired colonies were far from being the sources of profit that both Hobson and Lenin believed. There was not a major shift of investment into the new colonies, and the cost of maintaining the military forces and administration necessary to keep them may have exceeded the economic benefits they offered as markets and even as sources of raw materials. Moreover, the colonies were not important as areas to which the surplus European population wished to emigrate, in comparison with the United States and the British Dominions. Perhaps for this reason, the European powers did not go to war with each other before 1914 in disputes over colonial territories; and the only war in which colonial expansion was a direct issue was the Spanish-American war of 1898.

THE ALLIANCE SYSTEMS

Formation of the Alliances

It was the existence in Europe of alliance systems intended to prevent war that eventually precipitated war. Bismarck had believed that he could create a single alliance system that would leave France isolated in Europe and permit the British to go their own way overseas. Even after forming the Triple Alliance with Austria-Hungary and Italy in 1882, he had attempted to keep good relations with Russia. In the 1880s and 1890s, however, Russia turned to France for the loans necessary for its industrialization and railroad construction; and, as its rivalry with Austria in the Balkans intensified, Russia decided in 1894 to conclude a military agreement with France. The two agreed to mobilize their forces in response to a mobilization by any member of the Triple Alliance and to unite against Germany if either should be attacked by a member of the Triple Alliance.

Britain was chary of joining in any pact that would entangle it in the rivalries of the European continent; but, once Germany had challenged its control of the seas by embarking on a massive program of naval construction and had begun to establish itself as a rival in Africa and the South Pacific, the British finally gave up their policy of "splendid isolation." In 1902, they concluded a defensive alliance with Japan. In 1904, they signed the Entente Cordiale with France, which, although not specifically a military alliance, promised cooperation in settlement of colonial disputes and implied British assistance in case of a future war in Europe. Finally, in 1907, the British signed a similar agreement with Russia, even though public opinion was opposed to the repressive nature of the tsarist regime.

Within the alliance systems, rearmament progressed rapidly, on the assumption that military strength would deter future aggression. The general staffs of the armies of the different countries, however, were far more realistic than the politicians, and prepared extremely detailed contingency plans for the defeat of their potential enemies. The politicians seemed to remain blithely unaware of the dangers they were courting, especially in view of the change in the nature of warfare itself that the industrial revolution had brought about. Indeed, the very speed of the Prussian victories in 1866 and 1870 may have misled them into thinking that future wars, rather than being longer and infinitely more destructive, would be over in a matter of weeks as a consequence of the advanced new weapons with which the armies had been equipped. If such were the case, it was more than ever essential that a country be prepared for immediate action upon the outbreak of war. Meanwhile, the politicians believed that their own diplomatic finesse would enable them to handle crises among them without ever passing the brink beyond which war between the alliance systems was inevitable.

The Moroccan and Balkan Crises

At first, their handling of the crises in Morocco and the Balkans appeared to prove them correct. In 1905, Emperor William II of Germany had announced during a visit to Tangier his support for the maintenance of the independence of the kingdom of Morocco, which the French were moving to take over. The resulting crisis was defused at the Conference of Algeciras (1906), in which, as a result of British support, the French were allowed to take over the Moroccan state bank and police. After the French occupied the Moroccan capital of Fez in 1911, the Germans sent a gunboat into the port of Agadir as a protest but were compelled, by international diplomatic pressure, to recognize French preeminence in Morocco. The two Moroccan crises had the result of embittering relations between Germany on one hand and Britain and France on the other, and had the direct effect of persuading the British to make detailed military agreements with the French.

The crises in the Balkans proved more difficult to handle, because Austria felt that the very existence of its empire was threatened by the desire of the independent state of Serbia to unite all South Slavs within its kingdom. The Austrian empire included not only the South Slav provinces of Croatia and Slovenia, but also Bosnia and Herzegovina, two provinces it had formally annexed from Turkey in 1908. The Russians had not backed the Serbs when they protested against this annexation, largely because Germany had supported Austria, but they had secretly promised aid in the future. In 1912, the Russians encouraged the Serbs, in alliance with the Bulgarians, Rumanians, and Greeks, to attack Turkey. Within months, the Turks had collapsed, and their opponents had seized all Turkish possessions in Europe except Constantinople. Austria, however, intervened at the peace conference to force Serbia to give up the Turkish province of Albania, which was made into an independent state. Serbia then demanded as compensation part of the territory that Bulgaria had taken; and, in alliance with Greece, Rumania, and Turkey, defeated Bulgaria in a second Balkan war. As a result of its gains in the two wars, Serbia doubled in size, and became even more determined to compel Austria to give up Bosnia and Herzegovina. In spite of the dangerously tense situation in the Balkans at the end of the wars, the statesmen of the great powers remained convinced that by careful diplomacy they could prevent the alliances from becoming embroiled in local wars.

The Serajevo Crisis

On June 28, while inspecting troops at Serajevo, the capital of Bosnia, the heir to the Austrian throne was assassinated by a Bosnian nationalist trained in Serbia. The ill-considered danger that the existence of the alliance systems would cause the escalation of a minor and isolated crisis into a general war was immediately realized. The Austrian military leaders persuaded the emperor to issue so strong an ultimatum to Serbia, which was believed to have planned the assassination, that it could not be accepted, thus giving Austria the excuse to carry out a preemptive attack on Serbia. The German emperor promised Austria his country's support. The Serbs rejected part of the ultimatum. Austria declared war on July 28, 1914, and immediately began bombarding the Serbian capital. Two days later, the tsar ordered full mobilization of the Russian armies; in response, Germany declared war on Russia on August 1. After the French

Archduke Francis Ferdinand and His Wife in Serajevo, June 28, 1914 *The couple was photographed one hour before they were assassinated by Bosnian terrorists trained in Serbia. Their death caused the Austrian ultimatum to Serbia, which brought about the First World War.* (The Bettmann Archive.)

refused a German ultimatum that they hand over their border fortresses, the Germans activated the Schlieffen plan, and on August 3 sent their troops into Belgium, which, to their surprise, resisted. On August 4, Britain declared war on Germany in defense of Belgium. In October, Turkey entered the war on the side of Germany, with whom it had developed close military and economic ties since the 1870s. Italy remained neutral until 1915, when it joined the war on the side of France. The United States entered the war only in 1917, when Germany began unrestricted submarine attacks on neutral shipping.

At the end of the war, the victorious allies were to blame Germany as the principal instigator of the war. But the blame should be far more widely shared. Serbian determination to annex Bosnia-Herzegovina, as well as the harboring of known terrorists in Serbia, provoked the Austrians to act. The Austrian ultimatum was deliberately framed to give the Austrians a justification for open hostilities. German support of Austria encouraged its action, and the German invasion of Belgium brought France and Britain into the war. British determination to maintain naval and colonial hegemony had prepared them for the possibility of a war with Germany, while French determination to retake Alsace-Lorraine had given the Germans a justification for drawing up the Schlieffen plan. Russia had encouraged Serbian ambitions in the Balkans, and its mobilization had made a war with Germany inevitable.

Volunteers Greeted by the Crowds, Berlin, August 2, 1914 *After the years of tension before 1914, crowds in the capitals of all the belligerents welcomed the coming of the war, in which 10 million people would be killed.* (Bildarchiv Preussischer Kulturbesitz.)

But there were far deeper causes for the conflict. The alliance system was basically unstable, and by its very existence made every crisis between the powers a potential cause for war. The governments had failed to grasp the nature of modern warfare, and hence were prepared to consider a conflict as a brief, relatively inexpensive settlement of disputes that diplomacy had failed to solve. The military, perhaps understanding better the power of destruction at their command, had argued that no country could afford the risk of letting its enemies strike first. Worst of all, there were many who believed that war was a good in itself, a necessary struggle in which nations, like the species described by Darwin, would engage in an essentially healthy struggle for the survival of the fittest. The crowds that demonstrated joyfully in the streets of all the European capitals in August 1914 were elated at the idea that this struggle had finally begun.

THE FIRST WORLD WAR, 1914–1918

The First Campaigns

Belgian resistance slowed up the German advance only a few days, and on August 27 the German armies entered France. By September 5 they were outside Paris. The French, however, threw in all their reinforcements, many of whom were driven to the front in Parisian taxis commandeered by the high command; and in the first Battle of the Marne, they ended the immediate threat to Paris. Meanwhile, in the east, the Russians, after drawing off German troops by invading East Prussia, were soundly defeated at the battle of Tannenberg (September 1914).

Both fronts settled down to a war of attrition. By November, the German army and the French and British forces had dug in, constructing long trench lines that eventually stretched all the way from the Channel coast to Switzerland. On this front, a totally different kind of warfare evolved than that which the statesmen and even the military leaders had expected. Unlike the rapid war of movement, as in the Franco-Prussian war, military strategy consisted of constantly pounding the enemy lines with heavy artillery and rifle fire, and mounting infantry assaults of hundred of thousands of men at frequent intervals.

The slaughter in these attacks was greater than any previously known in history. When in 1916 the Germans attempted to capture the fortress of Verdun, the pivotal point of the French lines, they lost 336,000 men. Poison gas, first used by the Germans in 1915, added to the horror, while the constant bombardment destroyed the landscape, leaving the soldiers in a featureless quagmire in which they could as easily drown in shellholes as be shot by the enemy.

The eastern front remained a little more mobile, largely because the vast numbers of Russian troops were so poorly supplied with weapons that they could not hold off major German attacks. But although Russian casualties were

Trench Warfare in the First World War
Chlorine gas was first used by the Germans on the western front in 1915. As the use of poison gas became widespread on both sides, soldiers were issued gas masks, but protection was poor. (Collection Viollet.)

extremely heavy—at least a million by the end of 1914—the vast Russian population provided a seemingly inexhaustible supply of recruits to replace those killed. In all, the Russians mobilized more than 16 million people in the armed forces.

The Home Fronts

The war quickly influenced the life of the civilian populations left behind on what was called the "home front." With the blockade of Germany by the British navy, the German government attempted to make up for the shortages of food and raw materials by increasing home production and by employing scientific research to find substitutes. Rationing of food and consumer goods was introduced; restrictions on female employment, which had been widespread in the nineteenth century, were lifted, and women took work on the farms, in the factories, and in the professions. All men between the ages of seventeen and seventy, who had not been drafted into the army, were compelled from 1916 on to take jobs of national importance.

France and Britain were slightly slower than Germany to impose state control over the economy, but by 1915 they too were compelled to take urgent steps to maintain production. As French losses mounted in the campaigns on the western front, women were called upon to drive buses, run the postal service, manufacture munitions, and work the farms. In 1916, the government even issued a list of jobs that men were forbidden to take because they could be filled by women. Only in 1916, when the British government finally imposed military conscription, were women in Britain recruited on a large scale into the work force to replace the men drafted into the army. By the end of the war, 3 million women were employed in industry, one-third of those in the munitions factories.

The war thus was an important influence in changing the status of women. Although many lost their jobs to returning veterans at the end of the war, a large number held on to their positions, especially if they were in services or in the professions. Moreover, a psychological change had been brought about, because women had proved to themselves and to male workers that they could compete not only in such jobs as teacher or shop assistant but even in such heavy employment as railroad construction or open-face mining. The symbolic recognition of the change of status came with the grant of the vote to women aged twenty-one and over in Germany in November 1918, in the United States in August 1920, and to women aged thirty and over in Britain in February 1918; women in France had to wait until 1944 before gaining the vote.

Government economic controls transformed the working of the capitalist system. All the belligerents set up boards or committees to control production and distribution of goods. The stock exchanges were strictly supervised. Industrial companies were regulated in part by government control of allocation of raw materials and of labor. Trade unions were persuaded not to strike. A number of countries took over administration of the railroads and the mines. Even in the United States, government controls over the life of the citizens increased greatly. Such bodies as the War Industries Board, the Food Administration, and the Fuel Administration proliferated in Washington, while military conscription, introduced in 1917, was presented as a method of training Americans in better citizenship.

Inevitably, governments backed up direct regulation with propaganda intended to elicit the enthusiastic cooperation of the population in acceptance of wartime hardships and in support of war goals. All countries embarked on massive campaigns to persuade people to help finance the war through purchase of war bonds, frequently by presenting their enemies as inhuman fiends. Posters advertising U.S. government bonds, for example, called on their purchasers to "Halt the Hun," who was shown brutalizing women and children. Government power was also used, however, to suppress discontent. More than 1000 people were tried in the United States under the Sedition Act of 1918 on charges of criticizing the government or the armed forces of the United States.

The War of Attrition

In 1916, both sides attempted to snatch victory by mounting vast new offensives. After the French had blunted the German attack on Verdun, the Russians succeeded in driving into Poland, although with terrible losses; and their victory was followed by the greatest Franco-British offensive of the war up to that point, an attack along the river Somme in which the British were to suffer 400,000 casualties, the French 200,000, and the Germans 500,000. The Italians, who had joined the war in 1915 on the side of the Entente in return for promises of territorial annexations from Austria, attacked the Austrians in the snows of the Alps, losing hundreds of thousands of lives. All these offensives failed to achieve any decisive victory, and in 1917 the morale of the soldiers on all the fronts began to collapse.

In April 1917, the French general Robert Nivelle, even though he knew the Germans had discovered his plan of campaign, sent his troops into battle, where they were massacred. Immediately mutiny spread throughout the French army. Soldiers seized trains to return home. Troops took control of their barracks and refused entry to their officers. Front-line regiments refused to leave the trenches in new offensives. The French high command ended the mutinies by a combination of force and concession. Some mutineers were arrested and executed, and harsh discipline was reimposed. But the new commander, Marshal Henri Pétain, also improved living conditions at the front and in rest areas, gave more leave, and rotated troops out of the front line more frequently. As a result, the mutiny was contained before the Germans realized the extent of French weakness.

Meanwhile, the Germans and Austrians were suffering greatly, both from reduced food supplies and shortages of raw materials as a result of the British naval blockade. The German government, under pressure from the military high command, therefore decided to counterattack by turning loose their submarines against neutral ships, primarily from the United States, that were supplying Britain and France. After the sinking of several American ships in early 1917, President Woodrow Wilson declared war on Germany in April 1917, and American troops began to arrive in Europe in large numbers at the beginning of 1918. At about the same time in 1918, the new Communist government in Russia, which had seized power in November 1917, had signed an armistice on the eastern front.

Once again both sides tried for a decisive breakthrough against the enemy lines. Both sides doubled the amount they were spending on the war, and both sides saw a doubling of their casualty rates. The Germans attacked first, using all their remaining resources in successive attacks on all parts of the western front between March and June 1918. Their drive once again brought them to the river Marne, where, as in 1914, the French again drove them back. The allied attacks that followed broke German resistance in the west. In September, Germany's allies began to desert it. Bulgaria, which had entered the war in 1915 to gain part of Serbia, overthrew its monarch and asked for peace. The Austrian empire fell apart, as each of its national minorities began to set up independent states. In October, the Turks stopped fighting. At the beginning of November, insurrection broke out in a number of German cities. The emperor abdicated on

November 9, and the new government, dominated by the Social Democrats, agreed to an armistice on November 11.

Results of the War

The costs of the four years of carnage had been enormous. Ten million people had been killed in the fighting, and another 20 million wounded. But there had been many other causes of loss of life. The Turks, for example, had massacred more than a million Armenians. Food shortages had caused vast numbers of civilian deaths, either from famine or inability to throw off disease. Influenza alone killed 20 million people in 1918.

The economic effects of the war were disastrous and long-lived. The war had cost the victorious Allies $156 billion and the defeated powers $63 billion. The devastation of France's eastern provinces, where most of the fighting on the western front had taken place, cost more to repair in the early 1920s than total income from taxation, and made the French determined to force the Germans to cover the cost of payment of reparations. In all the belligerents, agriculture was in decline because chemical fertilizer had been in short supply, herds had been slaughtered, and seed was lacking. Little capital had been available to renovate factory equipment. Wartime production had been primarily for military purposes, and there was a vast backlog of demand for consumer goods and housing.

Moreover, the war had seen the break-up of the great empires of Eastern Europe, with the result that long-established patterns of production and trade had been disturbed. The new nation-states of Eastern Europe were frequently at loggerheads with each other and with those states from which they had gained their independence, and made the revival of commerce more difficult by imposing trade sanctions on their neighbors. Thus, the victory that was celebrated so riotously in the streets of Paris, London, New York, and a thousand smaller cities as the culmination of the "war to end all wars" was hollow. Europe would live for a decade trying to recover from this war, only to spend the following decade preparing for the next world war.

Finally, because of the war, the center of economic power shifted from Europe to the United States. From this time onward, the European powers were to play a diminished part in shaping the patterns of world trade and finance, and indeed would later reluctantly come to accept the continually increasing role of the United States in their own internal and external affairs.

THE PARIS PEACE CONFERENCE

The Duel Between Wilson and Clemenceau

In January 1919, the diplomats of the victorious powers assembled in Paris, determined to write peace treaties that would make impossible the outbreak of another war like the Great War of 1914–1918. Two diametrically opposed conceptions of such a peace settlement were presented. The American President Woodrow Wilson, detesting the old European concept of power politics, sought a peace of reconciliation between the victors and the vanquished, following the grant throughout Central and Eastern Europe of the demands of liberals and nationalists. In a peace plan issued early in 1918, and at the conference itself, Wilson argued that, to make a fresh start, an international organization, the future League of Nations, was to mediate disputes among states; the peoples of Eastern Europe were to be allowed to form their own nation-states; and the defeated powers were not to be punished. The French prime minister, Georges Clemenceau, fearing above everything else the revival of German military power and yet another attack on France after those of 1870 and 1914, intended to prevent the revival of Germany by seizing parts of its territory and productive capacity, by compelling it to pay huge reparations, and by cutting its military forces and demilitarizing its border regions with France. In the long battles that took place in the inner council, where the major decisions of the conference were taken by Wilson, Clemenceau, British Prime Minister David Lloyd George, and Italian Premier Vittorio Orlando, Wilson ceded ground continually to Clemenceau, and the final treaties were far closer to Clemenceau's wishes than to Wilson's.

The Treaty of Versailles

The French were determined that signature of the Treaty of Versailles with Germany should give them symbolic revenge for the proclamation of the German Empire in the Palace of Versailles in 1871. For that reason, representatives of the new German republic were summoned to sign the treaty, which they had not been permitted to negotiate, in the Hall of Mirrors where Bismarck had orchestrated the earlier ceremony. The desire for revenge was equally evident in the clauses of the treaty. Germany was to return Alsace and Lorraine, which it had annexed from France in 1871, and to cede three small coal mining towns to Belgium. France was to take possession of the coal mining region of the Saar for fifteen years. The new Polish state was to be given a wide strip of territory, called the Polish Corridor, as an outlet to the sea. The port city of Danzig, which was ethnically German, was to become a free city under League of Nations supervision. After a plebiscite held in 1921, as required by the treaty, the Poles took part of the rich coal mining region of Silesia. Thus Germany was stripped of a number of its richest industrial areas in Europe and of its colonial empire in Africa and Asia.

Clemenceau had originally wanted Germany and its allies to pay the total cost of war expenses and damages of the victors, but was compelled by Wilson to agree that reparations should pay only for damage to civilian property. The treaty required payment of $5 billion at once by Germany, with the final sum to be settled later. The total was set at $31 billion in 1921, and Germany was to pay in gold and in goods.

Finally, to ensure the military weakness of Germany, its army was limited to 100,000 soldiers and its general staff was abolished. The left bank of the Rhine and a strip of territory 50 kilometers wide on the right bank were to be permanently demilitarized. Occupation troops, primarily French, were to take over important cities on the Rhine for fifteen years.

Punishing Germany's Allies

The treaties with Germany's allies, Austria, Hungary, Bulgaria and Turkey, were also harsh. The Austro-Hungarian empire was broken up. Czechoslovakia became an independent country, composed of the old Czech provinces of Bohemia and Moravia, Slovakia, the Ukrainian province of sub-Carpathian Ruthenia, and the largely German-speaking Sudetenland. Austria's Polish provinces became part of the new Polish state, while its Balkan provinces were linked with Serbia to form the new state of Yugoslavia (originally known as the Serb-Croat-Slovene state). The province of Transylvania was handed over to Rumania. Italy took the border regions of the South Tyrol and the Istrian peninsula. Finally, the Turkish empire was dismembered. It lost all its possessions in the Near East. Arabia became independent. Syria and Lebanon were placed under French mandate, and Palestine, Iraq, and Transjordan under British mandate.

Signature of the Treaty of Versailles in the Hall of Mirrors, June 28, 1919 The peace treaty with Germany was signed in Versailles to erase memories of the proclamation, in the same palace, of the creation of the Second German Empire in 1871. (The Bettmann Archive.)

Most of its remaining possessions in Europe were handed to Greece and Yugo-slavia.

Effects of the Paris Peace Conference

Debate over the effects of these harsh treaties and especially of the Treaty of Versailles, which the Germans had called a dictated peace, began almost immediately. British economist John Maynard Keynes, who had participated in the conference as a representative of the British foreign office, blasted the treaty in a widely read book published in 1919 and called *The Economic Consequences of the Peace*. Keynes argued that the treaty had destroyed not only the German economy but that of the other European powers as well, which were dependent on Germany for trade and capital, and he implied that political breakdown would follow the economic catastrophe caused by the peace. Later writers have criticized Keynes for overemphasizing the damage inflicted on the German economy, and blamed the weakness of the German economy in the 1920s on German political mismanagement and not on the treaty itself.

It is probable, however, that the psychological consequences of imposing this peace were more dangerous than the economic. Germany was presented as an international pariah, and compelled to accept the "war-guilt clause," which stated: "Germany accepts the responsibility of Germany and her allies for causing all the loss and damage to which the Allied and Associated Governments and their nationals have been subjected as a consequence of the war imposed upon them by the aggression of Germany and her Allies." The Germans never forgave the Allied peace makers for this humiliation, and Adolf Hitler was later able to turn this resentment against his democratic opponents in the new Weimar Republic who, after ousting the Kaiser in 1918, had found themselves forced by the Allied peace makers to accept a treaty they themselves regarded as unjust.

The psychological consequences in Britain and France were even more dangerous for the future. British and French statesmen, persuaded by writers such as Keynes that the economic problems of the 1920s and especially the Great Depression were in part the result of the decisions of the Paris Peace Conference, slowly came to believe that many of the clauses of the Treaty of Versailles were indefensible. Once in power, Adolf Hitler was able to count on British and French unwillingness to act to enforce the treaty when he deliberately violated its provisions.

SUGGESTED READINGS

Imperialism

Imperialism is seen in a world rather than a European perspective in two searching studies, Eric R. Wolf, *Europe and the People Without History* (1982), and Philip Curtin, *Cross-Cultural Trade in World History* (1984). D. K. Fieldhouse provides a comprehensive, reliable introduction to the acquisition of colonial empires from the eighteenth century on in *The Colonial Empires* (1966) and *Economics and Empire, 1830–1914* (1973). On the British empire see Ronald Hyam, *Britain's Imperial Century, 1815–1914: A Study of Empire and Expansion* (1976); on the French empire see Henri Brunschwig, *French Colonialism: Myths and Realities, 1871–1914* (1966). The intellectual causes of imperialism are analyzed in A. P. Thornton, *The Imperial Idea and Its Enemies: A Study in British Power* (1959).

An authoritative survey of imperialism in Africa is given by Robin Hallett, *Africa Since 1875: A Modern History* (1975). On Africa before the new imperialism, see Roland Oliver and Anthony Atmore, *Africa Since 1800* (1981). One should not, however, forget the brightest jewel in the British crown. Indian reaction to British rule is analyzed in Stanley Wolpert, *A New History of India* (1977), the lasting effects of imperial rule in Percival Griffiths, *The British Impact on India* (1965), and in Dharma Kumar, ed., *The Cambridge Economic History of India, Vol. 2: c. 1757–c. 1970* (1983).

The Alliance Systems and the First World War

The debate over the origins of the First World War is admirably summarized in Laurence Lafore, *The Long Fuse: An Interpretation of the Origins of World War I* (1965), and painstakingly dissected in Luigi Albertini, *The Origins of the War of 1914* (1952–1957). German motives are freshly exposed, and the blame shared equally among civilian as well as military leaders, in Fritz Fischer, *Germany's Aims in the First World War* (1967).

Barbara Tuchman, *The Guns of August* (1962), and Alexander Solzhenitsyn, *August 1914* (1974), are superb reconstructions of the opening campaigns on the western and eastern fronts, respectively. Alistair Horne, *The Price of Glory: Verdun, 1916* (1963), describes the worst of the butchery. Paul Fusell shows how the experience of trench warfare influenced the psychology of the postwar years, in *The Great War and Modern Memory* (1975).

For a short chronology of the fighting see Basil Liddell Hart, *The Real War, 1914–1918* (1964), or Cyril Falls, *The Great War* (1959).

A good comparative study of the impact of the war at home is John Williams, *The Home Fronts: Britain, France and Germany, 1914–1918* (1972).

Paris Peace Conference

The best study of the conference is Paul Birdsall, *Versailles Twenty Years After* (1941). Harold Nicolson, *Peacemaking, 1919* (1933) is the lively diary of a participant. John Maynard Keynes's sharp indictment of the peace, *The Economic Consequences of the Peace* (1919), should be compared with Etienne Mantoux's indictment of Keynes in *The Carthaginian Peace* (1946). Arno Mayer, *Politics and Diplomacy of Peacemaking* (1967), is a stimulating reappraisal.

part *VII*

The Contemporary Age

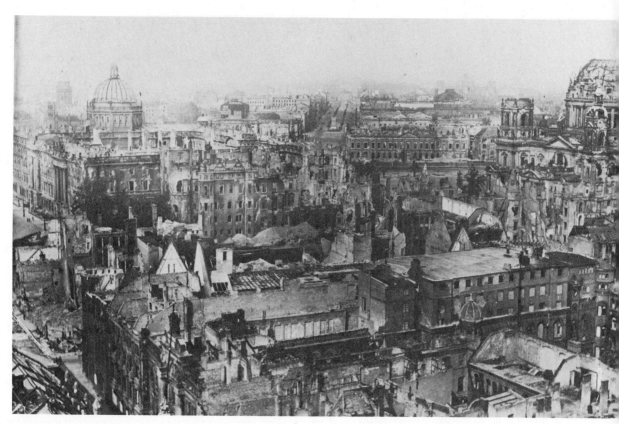

Berlin in 1945   *Bombing and streetfighting left Berlin's center in ruins when the Second World War ended.* (Ullstein Bilderdienst.)

THE CONTEMPORARY AGE

Dates	Political & Military Events	Social, Economic, & Demographic Events	Religion & Philosophy	Art, Architecture, Literature, & Music	Science & Technology
1900–1916				Fauves; Cubism Atonal Music Jazz (New Orleans, U.S.) Dadaism	Freudian psychology Planck's quantum theory Einstein's theory of relativity
1918				British War Poets	
1919	Paris Peace Conference	Red scare, U.S.			
1920				Bauhaus founded	First commercial radio station (U.S.)
1921		New economic policy, Russia			
1922	Mussolini in power, Italy			Joyce, *Ulysses* Eliot, *The Waste Land*	
1923	French occupy Ruhr	German inflation			
1924	d. Lenin; rise of Stalin, Russia	Dawes Plan		Forster, *Passage to India* Breton, *Surrealist Manifesto*	
1926		General Strike, Britain		Mann, *The Magic Mountain* Gide, *The Counterfeiters*	Television systems invented (1926–28)
1927			Heidegger, *Being and Time*	Proust, *Remembrance of Things Past*	Heisenberg's uncertainty principle First talking movie
1929		Wall Street Crash Great Depression (1929–1933) First 5-Year Plan, Russia	Mussolini's Lateran Treaty with Pope		
1933	Hitler takes power, Germany Roosevelt, President, U.S. (1933–45)				
1935	Italian invasion of Ethiopia				

1936	Spanish Civil War (1936–39) Popular Front, France	Great purges, Russia			
1939	Second World War (1939–45)				
1941	Germany invades Russia Japanese attack Pearl Harbor; U.S. enters war			Brecht, *Mother Courage*	
1943	Casablanca Conference		Sartre, *Being and Nothingness*		
1945	Yalta, Potsdam Conferences Atomic bomb, Hiroshima	Communization in Eastern Europe begins Welfare states in Western Europe		Orwell, *Animal Farm* Abstract Expressionism in art	Atomic bomb on Hiroshima
1947	British recognize Indian independence	Marshall Plan proposed		Camus, *The Plague*	
1950s		Civil Rights Movement, U.S.		Theatre of the Absurd	
1953	d. Stalin, Russia East Berlin uprising			"New Novel," France	
1956	Suez invasion Hungarian uprising	De-Stalinization, Russia			
1957					Sputnik, 1st artificial satellite in space (U.S.S.R.)
1958	De Gaulle in power, France (1958–69)	Common Market founded	John XXIII (1958–63)	van der Rohe's Seagram building, New York	
1960s		Women's Rights Movement, U.S.		Pop Art	
1962	Cuban Missile Crisis		Vatican II (1962–65)	Solzhenitsyn, *One Day in the Life of Ivan Denisovich*	
1964	Brezhnev in power, Russia (1964–82)				

(continued)

THE CONTEMPORARY AGE (continued)

Dates	Political & Military Events	Social, Economic, & Demographic Events	Religion & Philosophy	Art, Architecture, Literature, & Music	Science & Technology
1968	Student, worker riots, Paris Soviet invasion, Czechoslovakia		Catholic-Protestant conflict, N. Ireland		
1969	Pompidou, President, France (1969–75) Brandt, Chancellor, W. Germany (1969–74)				U.S. manned landing on moon
1973	Arab-Israeli Yom Kippur War	Oil embargo			
1978			John Paul II (1978–)		
1981	Reagan, President, U.S. Mitterand, President, France				
1985	Gorbachev in power, Russia				

19

The Age of the Dictators, 1919–1945

The French were largely responsible for the decisions of the Paris Peace Conference in 1919, even though they did not succeed in making it as punitive as they would have wished. For the remainder of the 1920s, France seemed to exercise hegemony in Europe, but its temporary dominance was due primarily to the fact that Germany, under the governments of the Weimar Republic, was making little effort to assert itself internationally and the United States and the Soviet Union were both deliberately isolating themselves from European affairs. From 1929 on, the mask of stability was shattered. The Great Depression of 1929–1933 ended the prosperity that most of Europe had enjoyed in the late 1920s, brought home to the Western democratic powers the essential fragility of their economic systems, and left them unwilling to make the sacrifices necessary to build up military strength to prevent international aggression.

Russia's isolation was due to the need to consolidate its Communist revolution in the face of both internal and external threats. After the Communist party seized power in November 1917, under the leadership of Vladimir Ilyich Lenin, its uprooting of the country's most basic economic and social institutions caused a civil war that left the country in economic chaos. After Lenin's death in 1924, a battle for political leadership followed, which was not finally resolved until Joseph Stalin consolidated his personal power in 1928. Stalin at once launched the country on a massive economic revolution, which absorbed Russia's energies during the 1930s. Thus, only when Stalin's political power was secure and the economic revolution successfully launched would Russia be able to act in international affairs from a position of strength.

Fascism in Italy from 1922 and National Socialism, or Nazism, in Germany after 1933 had offered to the failing societies of the states of Central and Eastern Europe a promise that right-wing totalitarian government could restore economic well-being and national strength; and by 1939 a majority of the governments of Europe were in the hands of some form of Fascist or Nazi regime. Thus, as Germany and Italy asserted their power in the late 1930s, they found themselves opposed only by democracies weakened by internal dissension and economic decline and willing to use any plausible excuse to "appease" the two aggressor countries. Only in 1939 did Britain and France finally decide that their own survival depended on their defense of Poland from German attack; and even then they were so little prepared for war that they could do nothing to prevent the collapse of Poland within a month. Most important of all, it required the German invasion of June 1941 to bring the Soviet Union into the war and the Japanese attack on Pearl Harbor in December 1941 to end American isolationism. These actions converted what had been essentially a European war up to that point into a second World War, and ensured the eventual defeat of the fascist coalition, but only after destruction even greater than that of the first World War.

THE FALTERING DEMOCRACIES

For France and Britain, the interwar years were a time of political incoherence and economic uncertainty, and as a result neither country proved capable of maintaining a firm direction in foreign policy.

Constitutional Weakness in France

The constitutional system of the Third French Republic was extremely shaky, and by the 1920s the bad political habits developed at the republic's foundation fifty years earlier had become deeply ingrained (see Chapter 16). The French had failed, or had not wished, to develop a two- or three-party system, in which groups of differing ideology could alternate in power in a relatively stable manner. Instead, the French electorate was presented with a choice of anywhere from six to eighteen different political parties, each of which claimed to hold a different political ideology, although many simply represented the personal ambitions of individual politicians. Even where ideological affinity might have been expected, the French parties quarreled. Communists battled with Socialists for the allegiance of the workers. The right was split between those favoring industry, those supporting the peasants, and those representing lower-middle-class civil servants and small business people. The party of the center, the Radicals, split in two on the issue of greater or lesser state intervention in the economy.

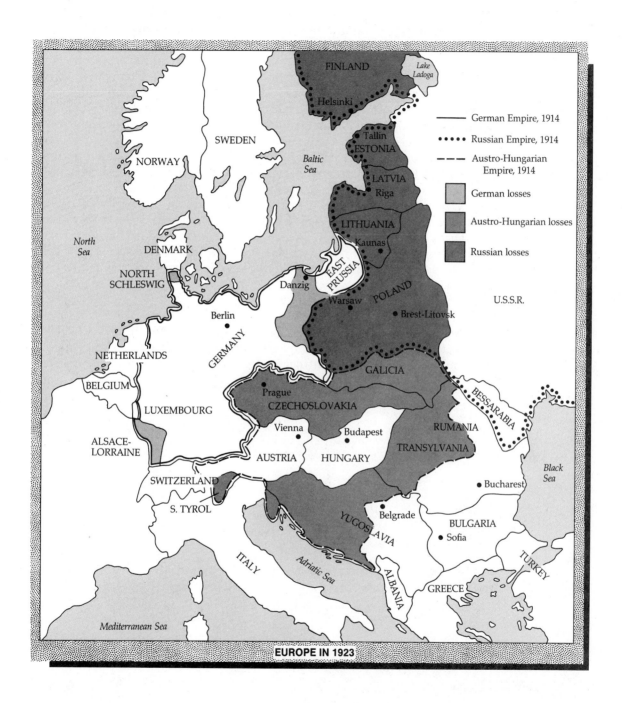

EUROPE IN 1923

German Empire, 1914
Russian Empire, 1914
Austro-Hungarian
Empire, 1914

German losses
Austro-Hungarian losses
Russian losses

FINLAND
Lake Ladoga
Helsinki
SWEDEN
NORWAY
Baltic Sea
Tallin
ESTONIA
LATVIA
Riga
LITHUANIA
Kaunas
North Sea
DENMARK
NORTH SCHLESWIG
Danzig
EAST PRUSSIA
Warsaw
POLAND
Brest-Litovsk
U.S.S.R.
Berlin
GERMANY
NETHERLANDS
BELGIUM
LUXEMBOURG
GALICIA
BESSARABIA
Prague
CZECHOSLOVAKIA
ALSACE-LORRAINE
Vienna
Budapest
RUMANIA
TRANSYLVANIA
SWITZERLAND
AUSTRIA
HUNGARY
S. TYROL
Bucharest
Black Sea
ITALY
Adriatic Sea
YUGOSLAVIA
Belgrade
BULGARIA
Sofia
ALBANIA
GREECE
TURKEY
Mediterranean Sea

As a result, all governments were coalitions of three or more parties and found it difficult to establish or maintain agreement on policy. Governments were constantly overthrown on votes of "no confidence" in the assembly, but only rarely was the collapse of a government followed by parliamentary elections. Instead, a new coalition was usually hammered out, often bringing back into power the very politicians who had just been defeated. Hence, the public developed considerable cynicism about the political process and about the motives of the politicians, especially since the electoral process seemed to have little affect on political behavior. Political cynicism was further magnified by the frequent revelation of financial scandals involving highly placed members of the government. The reaction of conservative groups was to look to a strong leader to save the system from the politicians, while on the extreme left the tendency was to work for direct action by the working classes under trade union leadership. The instability of the French political system would have been far worse had it not been for the effectiveness of the French bureaucracy, which continued to function regardless of the frequent changes of government.

Political Instability in the 1920s

The political infighting worsened in France during the 1920s. In 1920, Clemenceau, the architect of victory, was packed off into an embittered retirement, denied the position of president that he felt was his just reward. The dismal

The French Occupation of the Ruhr, 1923
In spite of a strike and passive resistance by German workers, the French troops occupying the Ruhr succeeded in shipping coal to France in payment of reparations. (Bilderdienst Süddeutscher Verlag.)

forming and re-forming of ministries began again. There were, however, two periods during the 1920s when a strong government was formed, in 1922–1924 and in 1926–1929, in each case under the direction of the right-wing politician Raymond Poincaré; but in each case the legislature withdrew its support when the immediate task for which he had been summoned was completed.

In the first of these ministries, Poincaré was called in to force Germany to meet its reparations payments, which the French claimed were badly in default. In January 1923 Poincaré sent the French army, with Belgian support, to occupy the industrial cities of the Ruhr. The Germans, however, responded with passive resistance; and the French were unable to break a general strike by the workers, even though they arrested hundreds of the leaders and used the army to maintain public services. Although the German government called off the resistance in September, after the total collapse of the German currency, the occupation had already caused severe budgetary difficulties in France; and Poincaré's governmental coalition lost the elections in 1924. The failure of the occupation of the Ruhr convinced the French that resorting to force was not a feasible solution to the German problem, and thus strengthened the position of the politicians who, in the 1930s, would argue that Hitler should be satisfied by appeasement rather than halted by force.

In 1926, Poincaré was called back to save the value of the French currency, which was threatened by huge transfers of business funds out of France after the election victory in 1924 of the Radical and Socialist parties. Poincaré, the darling of the business classes, reassured them by his very presence at the head of the government, and capital began quickly to flow back into the country. Poincaré was then able to stabilize the currency, although at only one-fifth of its prewar value.

The financial crisis that had brought Poincaré back into power emphasized for the French working class the political influence wielded by the business groups, with whom they were feuding. French financial and industrial interests possessed several organizations that enabled them to exert pressure on government policy. The Bank of France, the country's central bank, was controlled by an oligarchy of 200 directors, who were known as the "Two Hundred Families" and were regarded by the left-wing parties as a sinister cabal that dominated the French economy for their own benefit. The principal industrial leaders were represented in the General Confederation of French Production. The trade unions fought constantly against the owners throughout the interwar years, engaging in disruptive strikes that were rarely successful in winning their goals, and eventually throwing their support to the large Socialist party headed by Léon Blum or, increasingly, to the Communist party.

Solving the German Problem

France was thus a deeply divided country, whose own internal weakness made it essential to find a lasting solution to the German problem, in order to end its fear of invasion from its neighbor. Wilson and Lloyd George had both promised Clemenceau at the Paris conference that their countries would sign treaties with France, promising it their support in case of aggression; but neither country had acted on these promises. The French had then turned instead to forming their own alliance system with the states of Eastern Europe; but, although they signed mutual defense agreements with Poland, Rumania, Czechoslovakia, and Yugoslavia, the security the treaties offered was illusory because of the military weakness of the countries involved. France had even tried to cultivate a spirit of goodwill with Germany. At a meeting in the little Swiss lakeside town of Locarno in 1925, France, Germany, Belgium, Italy and Britain had signed a pact promising to respect the common frontiers of Germany with France and Belgium as established by the Treaty of Versailles; and Britain and Italy had agreed to act as guarantors that the pact would be kept.

In 1928, in a grandiose but essentially meaningless gesture, French Foreign Minister Aristide Briand and American Secretary of State Frank Kellogg had invited all the countries in the world to sign with each other a Kellogg-Briand peace pact, renouncing war as a means of settling disputes; and sixty-four countries signed the pact. But France showed how little confidence it had in the treaties when, in 1929, the government adopted the plan of the new minister of war, André Maginot, to construct a vast "Maginot line" of fortifications along France's border with Germany. The line proved to be as useless a solution to France's security problem as the diplomatic agreements. In 1940, the German tank columns out-flanked it from the north, and then attacked it from the rear!

British Economic and Social Problems

Britain's internal problems in the 1920s were similar to those of France. After the loss of 900,000 soldiers in the war, the country was war-weary; but the peace brought very little hope. The British economy, which had begun to flag in relation to the expansion of its international rivals, the United States and Germany, was entering a long decline. After two centuries of exploitation, Britain's mines were difficult to work and its miners increasingly rebellious because of the low wages and dangerous working conditions. Other long-established industries, such as textiles, were falling behind in technical efficiency and were vulnerable to declines in world demand during the recessions of 1919–1923 and 1929–1933. British unemployment never fell below 1 million even in the most prosperous of the interwar years. Moreover, industrial relations in Britain between labor and management and in a broader sense between the working class and the well-to-do classes were at least as bad in Britain as in France.

The deep class rift in Britain was dramatized during the general strike of 1926. When the miners struck for better pay and working conditions, the other trade unions went on strike in sympathy, paralyzing the country for nine days. But the Conservative government of Stanley Baldwin refused to compromise with the strikers. Armored cars brought food convoys into the cities. University students drove buses and trucks. Warships of the navy trained their guns on working-class areas of the port cities. Although bloodshed was avoided and the strikers returned to work in defeat, the handling of the general strike roused lasting resentment among the working classes of Britain, which was expressed in the elections of 1929 when they defeated the government of Baldwin and again, after the Second World War in 1945, when they turned out Winston Churchill in favor of a Labour government.

In the interwar years, however, the resort to political action proved a disappointment, just as it had in France. The Liberal Lloyd George had been chosen prime minister again after parliamentary elections in 1918, but only with Conservative backing; and his peacetime ministry proved disastrous. Demobilization of the army was at first too slow, and mutiny threatened. When it was speeded up, jobs were not available for the returning soldiers. Unemployment benefits were felt to be miserly, and strikes were put down harshly.

But Lloyd George's ministry was dominated by violence in Ireland, where the British government responded in kind to the attacks of the Irish Republican Army, which was fighting for the independence of the whole island. When peace finally came in Ireland in 1922 with the grant of Dominion status to the Catholic south, the retention of the Protestant north as part of the United Kingdom left the way open for new strife in the future.

The formation of the first Labour government in 1924, under the leadership of Ramsay MacDonald, deeply disappointed the working classes. Without previous experience in government and hampered by quarrels with its Liberal coalition partners, the Labour party proved ineffective in handling the economic disruption felt in Britain in the wake of the German inflation of 1923; and the government lasted only ten months. Baldwin's Conservative government (1924–1929), although administering Britain during years of improving economic conditions, was remembered chiefly for its handling of the general strike. The second Labour government of Ramsay MacDonald, formed after the defeat of Baldwin in the election of 1929, proved that it was as incapable as the other European governments of handling recession, especially one as deep as that provoked by the Wall Street Crash of October 1929.

The United States in the Roaring Twenties

President Woodrow Wilson returned from Paris to a Senate dominated by Henry Cabot Lodge, senator from Massachusetts, who was determined to block the president's program of international involvement. Wilson's stubbornness in rejecting any significant compromise played into Lodge's hands, and the United States neither ratified the Treaty of Versailles nor entered the League of Nations. Following the rejection of Wilson's program, America turned inward for the next decade.

The end of the war brought a speedy removal of wartime controls, a precipitate shift from military production to peacetime manufacturing, and a rapid demobilization of troops. This caused a twofold dislocation. The hasty and unplanned discharge of veterans in huge numbers caused a sharp rise in un-employment, while at the same time the uncontrolled changeover from a war-time economy accompanied by an abrupt lifting of price restrictions caused inflation. Almost 5 million workers were unemployed, as the cost of living rose to almost 77 percent above prewar levels. One result was an outburst of strikes, which were frequently suppressed by federal, state, or local troops. Neverthe-less, after an initial period of turmoil, the American economy lurched toward prosperity, although in an uneven fashion. Between 1919 and 1929, corporate profits increased by 60 percent and industrial productivity rose 43 percent, but workers' wages rose only 26 percent and farm prices declined as a result of overproduction.

The internal politics of the United States moved along a somewhat parallel course. Immediately after the war, in reaction to the labor turmoil, the federal government, during what has come to be called the "Red Scare," arrested thou-sands without charges being brought, deported aliens with no criminal records, and investigated large numbers of people for internal subversion. One outcome of this anticommunist activity was a resurgence of nativist hostility toward those of foreign birth, which led to the imposition of immigration quotas for the first time in American history. Most Americans, however, paid little attention to or supported these actions, seeking after the tension of the war years to go back to what President Warren G. Harding called "normalcy."

"Normalcy" in the 1920s meant for many the determination to get rich quickly. One example of this pursuit was the Teapot Dome scandal in which a Secretary of the Interior pocketed hundreds of thousands of dollars by illegally leasing government oil fields to private individuals. More pervasive, however, was the imprudent speculation on the stock market by millions of ordinary Americans of modest means. Small investors bought large amounts of stock on credit—on "margin" as this was called—and thus owed huge sums of money, far beyond their ability to pay if needed. In October 1929, the stocks tumbled in value in what became known as the Wall Street Crash, and within weeks the United States had led the world into the worst depression ever to hit the cap-italist system.

The Great Depression, 1929–1933

Between 1924 and 1929, most of Europe had known a prosperity that was real but that had, nevertheless, shaky foundations. First, currencies had been sta-bilized. After the great German inflation of 1923, the new German currency had been backed by loans provided under the Dawes plan, mostly by the United States, and its reparation payments had been scaled down. Several Eastern European countries had called in League of Nations' advisers to help them bring their budgets into balance. Britain had led the way in a return to the gold standard, promising convertibility of the pound into gold. Second, a constant flood of capital from the United States, Britain, and France to Germany and the countries of Eastern Europe enabled them to rebuild their economic base and to participate in the expansion of world trade. Third, important technological and managerial changes were introduced into European industry. New industries, such as the automobile, airplane, and electrical appliances industries, created employment opportunities for millions. Techniques borrowed from the United States included standardization of parts, time-and-motion studies, and wider use of the conveyor belt in production. Often the formation of cartels increased the profitability of production. Fourth, governments stimulated economic growth by large-scale investment in public works, such as new roads, harbors, and housing. Finally, the expansion of internal credit and a boost in real wages stimulated consumption.

Unfortunately, the system was fragile. Europe was dangerously dependent on the United States for capital and as a market for European exports, and the onset of a depression in the United States would be instantly felt in Europe. Governmental credit was overextended, with the result that the value of the currencies could easily be threatened in case of a decline in income from taxation. The cartels and trusts were unstable, and could bring down with them vast numbers of smaller companies at a time of sudden restriction of markets. Finally, agriculture remained depressed throughout the 1920s, and could not provide a stabilizing influence in time of industrial collapse.

Panic selling began on the Wall Street stock exchange on October 24, 1929, and within five weeks the value of American shares had fallen by half. Financiers were compelled to call in their loans, not only within the United States but from Europe also; and 5000 American banks failed. Demand for goods fell in the United States, and led to the unemployment within three years of 15 million American workers. The impact of the American crash was felt in Europe within weeks. Not only were old loans recalled, but new loans almost stopped. American demand for European goods sank drastically. European industries began to fail in 1930. In May 1931, one of Europe's greatest banks, the Creditanstalt of Austria, collapsed, causing chaos throughout the Austrian economy. Shortly after, several of Germany's largest banks also failed; and the great German companies laid off a large part of their workforce. A run on the British pound forced Britain to go off the gold standard, and Britain's unemployment reached 2.5 million by the end of 1932. The French seemed at first to have escaped the worst consequences of the depression, since their industry was still small in scale and their agriculture could absorb a flood of unemployed workers from the cities. But France too felt the effects of the decline of trade with the United States and Germany and of the worldwide fall in agricultural prices. In 1932–1933, just as Germany was beginning to recover from the depression, France plunged more deeply into it.

Britain and France in the 1930s

The most dramatic political consequence of the depression was to strengthen or to bring to power fascist governments throughout Central and Eastern Europe, as we shall see later in the chapter. But its effects on Britain and France were also profound. At a time when the future of democracy itself was dangerously challenged, Britain and France, reeling under the aftereffects of the depression, lost confidence in their own capacity to act from strength in international affairs.

The second Labour government in Britain, formed by Ramsay MacDonald in 1929, proved totally incapable of handling Britain's growing economic problems. Rather than resign as prime minister, however, MacDonald abandoned his own party and, with Conservative backing, became prime minister of a National Government composed of the Conservatives and his own faction of the Labour party, from 1931 to 1935. This act of political expediency further disgusted the working classes, especially when MacDonald cut unemployment benefits and reduced government spending. The slow recovery in Europe and the United States after 1933 benefited British trade. After MacDonald retired, Stanley Baldwin became prime minister in 1935–1937. His last term in office was, however, notable only for his insistence in 1936 that King Edward VII abdicate when he persisted in his wish to marry an American divorcée. Neville Chamberlain, who succeeded Baldwin as prime minister in 1937, was more skillful in handling economic than foreign affairs, but found himself totally occupied with a desperate attempt to postpone the war that Hitler's increasingly aggressive policy was making inevitable.

As the French economic situation worsened in 1932–1934, the assembly overthrew one government after another for its failure to come to grips with the crisis. In 1934, right-wing groups, many of them in favor of formation of an authoritarian government, formed armed militias that demonstrated in the streets of Paris against the government, whose reputation was tarnished by new revelations of financial scandal. For a brief time it seemed as though the government might be overthrown by force.

In reaction to the threat from the right, a coalition of Communists, Socialists, and Radicals called the Popular Front was formed, which won the elections in 1936. Once again, however, as in Britain with MacDonald's two Labour governments, the working classes were disappointed. The Popular Front had won 65 percent of the seats in the Chamber of Deputies. It had promised a long list of far-reaching reforms to bring "freedom, work, bread, and peace." In Léon Blum, it had a brilliant, trusted leader, who had shown his political skill by reconstructing the Socialist party after the defection of the Communists in 1920.

Yet the great expectations roused by this election victory were not realized. Capital was sent out of the country by the industrialists, causing a run on the gold reserves of the central bank. A campaign of anti-Semitism was launched by extreme right-wing groups against Blum himself. The Communists refused to join the new government, in order to avoid responsibility for the government's inability to keep its promises. Even the workers went out on nationwide strikes. As a result, only a few reforms including nationalization of the armaments industry and reduction of the work week from 48 to 40 hours were passed before Blum fell from office in 1937.

His successor, the Radical leader Edouard Daladier, was as ineffective as Chamberlain in facing up to the threat of Nazi Germany, especially as elements of the right were campaigning in favor of an agreement with Hitler and the implementation in France of parts of the Nazi internal program. Like the British, moreover, Daladier was convinced that France needed to win time, to increase its armed forces and to strengthen the Maginot line. Thus neither Britain nor France in the interwar years had the economic strength, social cohesion, or political will power necessary to face up to the threat of fascism and Nazism.

The United States in the 1930s

When the stock exchange crashed in 1929, the Republican president, Herbert Hoover, was convinced that the downward spiral of the economy could be reversed by a show of optimism. In addition to reassuring words, he recommended a large reduction in personal and corporate taxes in the mistaken belief that this would encourage investment in business. Since he did not believe that the federal government should provide relief for the poor, Hoover tried unsuccessfully to persuade local governments to take on this responsibility. He also proposed insufficiently funded public works projects to the Congress.

Dismayed by Hoover's posture and meager attempts to solve the crisis, in 1932 American voters overwhelmingly chose Franklin Delano Roosevelt, the Democratic candidate, for the first of his four terms as president. As a result of experiments in national planning, the economy slowly recovered during Roosevelt's first two terms. The gross national product (GNP) moved upward from $74 billion in 1933 to $111 billion in 1939, average weekly earnings of industrial workers rose from $17 to $24 during the same period, while unemployment declined from 25 percent of the work force to 17 percent.

As part of a "New Deal," the Roosevelt administration devised social programs that both restored the pride of working people and gave them some degree of security. For example, when individuals lost their jobs, they could find employment with the Works Progress Administration (WPA). At age 65, workers could retire from the labor market and receive Social Security benefits. The Social Security Act also provided help to mothers of dependent children and to permanently disabled individuals, thereby reducing the sense of desperation felt by large numbers of Americans.

Roosevelt did not, however, use his considerable persuasive powers to wean the American people away from isolationism until fairly late in the 1930s. Concerned primarily with gaining support for his domestic programs, he suppressed his internationalist inclinations and espoused a pacifist course until the aggressive actions of Germany, Italy, and Japan appeared too ominous to ignore. Referring to the expansionist behavior of what was to become the Axis Powers, Roosevelt warned that "the present reign of terror and international lawlessness [had gone so far that] the very foundations of civilization are seriously threatened," and if continued, he prophesied, "let no one imagine America will escape." Only in 1940, however, was he finally able to persuade a reluctant Congress to allow him to send military equipment to Great Britain as it fought on alone against Hitler after the defeat of France.

RUSSIA: FROM THE REVOLUTIONS OF 1917 TO THE DICTATORSHIP OF STALIN

The most significant of the political upheavals caused by the First World War were the March and November revolutions in Russia in 1917. In March, the autocratic tsarist system was overthrown and replaced by a provisional government dedicated to civil liberties and democratic government. As a result of crucial errors by the provisional government, it was overthrown in November in a revolution planned by the Communists of the Bolshevik party under the leadership of Lenin that made Russia the world's first communist state.

The March Revolution, 1917

During the early weeks of 1917, workers in Petrograd[1] began to riot to protest the lack of food, and factories went on strike. The local garrison joined the crowds, and almost spontaneously committees of workers, soldiers, and sailors called soviets were formed in Petrograd and other cities. They at first collaborated with the parliament, or *Duma,* in restoring order, and they approved the *Duma*'s decision to send a delegation to demand the abdication of the tsar, which Nicholas II signed on March 15. The administration of Russia was taken over by a provisional government appointed by the *Duma.*

The provisional government was determined to make Russia a constitutional democracy like Britain. It immediately guaranteed freedom of speech and assembly, and released all political and religious prisoners. It made preparations for a constituent assembly that would write a constitution, under which both men and women would have the suffrage. But under pressure from the British and French, the government decided not to seek peace, in spite of the disaffection in the army, and merely appointed a committee to study the question of giving more land to the peasantry. In that way it played into the hands of the Bolsheviks, whose leader Lenin was permitted to cross Germany from his exile in Switzerland in order to reach Russia and, so the German government hoped, at least disrupt the Russian war effort and at most bring Russia out of the war. From the moment of Lenin's return to Petrograd in April, Lenin set out to bring about the Communist revolution for which he had prepared his whole life.

Lenin was born in 1870, the younger son of a school inspector. His brother

---

[1] The name of Saint Petersburg was changed to Petrograd in 1914. It was renamed Leningrad in 1924, after the death of Lenin.

had been hanged for attempting to assassinate the tsar; and Lenin himself was expelled form the university for joining a terrorist group. He became a convert to Marxism, and was sent to Siberia in 1897 for attempting to convert the workers to its doctrines. In 1900, with his wife Nadezhda Krupskaya, whom he had married in Siberia, he was allowed to go into exile abroad. In 1902, in his book, *What Is to Be Done?*, he elaborated his theory that only a small, tightly disciplined band of professional revolutionaries could lead the working class into successful revolution. The following year, he split the Social Democratic party on this issue, his own followers who had won the vote calling themselves Bolsheviks (or Majority) and the others, who advocated a more moderate, widely based movement, being labeled the Mensheviks (or Minority). After years of impatient waiting in Europe, he realized that the war was destroying the power structure in Russia, and that the conflict might offer the opportunity for which he had been waiting.

In his first speech upon arriving in Russia, Lenin pinpointed the essential weakness of the position of the provisional government. "The people needs peace; the people needs bread; the people needs land. And they give you war, hunger, no bread—leave the landlords still on the land," he shouted to the crowd awaiting his arrival in front of the Finland Station. In November, he felt the situation was ripe for the Bolsheviks to move. Desertions were mounting. The food supply had again broken down. The navy was mutinous. Lenin ordered the seizure of Petrograd, according to the plan worked out by the brilliant Bolshevik strategist Leon Trotsky. In one night, the principal government buildings were taken and the provisional government arrested. On the morning of November 7, Lenin announced that Russia had a new government, a Council of People's Commissars with himself as chairman. The council immediately passed two decrees, a land decree taking possession of all land for the state but guaranteeing it to those who tilled it, and a peace decree, demanding an immediate armistice followed by a peace without indemnities or annexations. Most of the Russian cities accepted the new government within a few days, but in Moscow there was a week of savage fighting before the Bolsheviks triumphed.

First Communist Measures

Lenin was determined to change the whole character of Russian society in the shortest possible time. The factories were put under the administration of workers' committees. Banks were nationalized, apartment buildings and private homes were taken over and occupants compelled to share living space with homeless workers. Women were declared equal with men under the law; and divorce and abortion were made legal. The Church was separated from the state, and its possessions confiscated. A new secret police called the *Cheka* (Extraordinary Commission for Combating Counterrevolution and Speculation) was given powers of arrest and punishment. Finally, Lenin won a breathing space by accepting the Treaty of Brest-Litovsk with Germany and its allies in March 1918, gaining

Lenin Addressing a May Day Demonstration Moscow, 1918 *After making peace with Germany and its allies in March 1918, Lenin transferred the capital of Russia back from Petrograd to Moscow.* (Culver Pictures.)

peace in return for the recognition of the independence of Finland, the Ukraine, Russia's Polish territories, and the Baltic provinces of Estonia, Latvia, and Lithuania. Russia lost more than one-quarter of its territory and 60 million of its inhabitants. But the treaty left the Bolsheviks free to gather all their forces for survival in the civil war then beginning.

The Civil War and War Communism

By the end of 1918, the Communists were faced by three separate anti-Communist, or White armies in the Ukraine, Estonia, and Siberia. Their recruits were composed of middle- and upper-class people hurt by the economic and social changes, peasants who objected to the state confiscation of their produce from what they thought were their own lands, and minority nationalities such as the Ukrainians, who were resentful of the dominance of the Great Russians. The White armies were aided by intervention of the Allied powers. The British sent forces to the Arctic ports of Archangel and Murmansk. The Japanese and later the Americans established themselves in Vladivostok on the Pacific coast. The French supplied arms through the Black Sea port of Odessa.

The Whites appeared at first to have a good chance of victory. The Bolsheviks were disorganized, and only slowly were able, under the leadership of

Trotsky, to build up a new Red Army. The measures imposed during the war emergency, which came to be called War Communism, roused great opposition. All industry except small workshops was nationalized. Foreign and internal trade was taken over by the state. The labor force was "militarized," drafted into labor brigades, and issued passbooks in which their performance could be checked. Luxury goods such as paintings were confiscated. The peasantry were required to hand over their production to the state for distribution. The Whites, however, failed to profit from the opposition to these measures, because they themselves embarked upon a repressive policy in the areas they controlled. Not only Bolsheviks but socialists and liberals were executed. The land taken by the peasants was handed back to its former owners. And the very fact that they were helped by the Allies made the Whites appear unpatriotic.

Trotsky proved to be a brilliant general. He used the central geographic position of the Bolsheviks to good advantage, shifting his armies from front to front to strike in full force at each of the separate White armies. By 1920 the White forces had begun to disintegrate. The Allies withdrew their troops from the Russian ports. The Reds reconquered the Ukraine in 1919, the Caucasus in 1920, and Georgia in 1921. When the Red victory became clear, more than 2 million Russians fled from the country to find refuge in Europe and in China.

The New Economic Policy

The civil war left Russia in economic chaos. The opposition of the peasantry, combined with disastrous climatic conditions in 1920, had brought huge areas of the country to starvation, and as many as 5 million may have died in the famine of 1920–1921. Industrial production was down to one-seventh of prewar levels. Lenin realized that he would have to pull back, at least temporarily, from the extreme measures of Communism. In March 1921, he announced the New Economic Policy. Although the state would retain control of the banks, large factories, and foreign trade, the peasantry would be permitted to hire laborers and sell their produce freely. Internal trade was carried on by private traders, who brought the peasants' produce into the cities for sale to the workers. Once goods were available to buy, the workers themselves returned to their jobs; and production, both in agriculture and industry, slowly crept back to prewar levels by 1928.

Lenin himself did not live to see this achievement. He suffered a first paralytic stroke in 1922, which left him unable to speak and incapable of influencing the power struggle that began even before his death in January 1924. The obvious heir to Lenin was Trotsky, who had engineered the November revolution and taken the major role in winning the civil war. Trotsky was, however, a poor administrator in the daily work of government. As a result, the innumerable personnel decisions were taken by the party secretary, a Georgian named Joseph Djugashvili, whose pseudonym was Stalin, the Russian word for "steel." Only two weeks before his death, Lenin added a note to his political testament, begging the central committee not to appoint Stalin in his place and to remove him from his position as secretary general. "Stalin is too rude, and this fault, entirely supportable in relation to us Communists, becomes insupportable in the office of General Secretary. Therefore I propose to the comrades to find a way to remove Stalin from that position and appoint to it another man who in all respects differs from Stalin in one characteristic—namely, more patient, more loyal, more polite, and more attentive to comrades, less capricious, etc."[2] Although Lenin was embalmed and put on view in a mausoleum in Red Square in Moscow, his last wishes were ignored. The central committee voted to keep his testament secret, and Stalin was free to mount a successful campaign for the ouster of his rival Trotsky, who was first forced out from the Council of Commissars and then from the party. In 1928, he was sent into exile in Turkestan, and the following year ordered into exile abroad. (He was murdered in Mexico in 1940.)

The Significance of Lenin

It is still open to debate whether the Russian form of Communism was more influenced by Lenin, who controlled its formative years in 1917 to 1922, or by Stalin, whose power was unchallenged from at least 1928 to 1953. Lenin had established the rule of a single party whose numbers would rarely exceed more than 1 to $1\frac{1}{2}$ percent of the Russian population. He had endowed that party with absolute power, enforced by a vast secret police, and he had given the party leader virtually dictatorial rule. Ruthlessly, he had undertaken the destruction of the classes that he believed exploited Russian workers, and he had established a system in which he believed the rewards of labor would be shared equitably among those responsible for its production.

Lenin thought he had set in motion the process by which human beings would be remodeled and would lose the deeply ingrained characteristics of greed and self-aggrandizement that were the by-products of capitalism. At least until Lenin's death, the extraordinary social experiment conducted in Russia excited people throughout the world, and they flocked to Moscow to see how such a new society would be created. They had come to believe, as the American journalist John Reed wrote, that the November Revolution had been "ten days that shook the world." At the time, most were unaware of the full potential for repression that Lenin had created.

The Five-Year Plans

In 1928, Stalin ordered implementation of a Five-Year Plan so far-reaching in its effects on the Russian economy and society that it could be forced through only by dictatorial means. In the countryside, he ordered the incorporation of peasant farms into large "collective farms." These farms were owned by the

---

[2] *The Crimes of the Stalin Era: Special Report to the 20th Congress of the Soviet Union* by Nikita S. Khruschev. Edited by Boris I. Nicolaevsky (New York: The New Leader, 1956), p. 9.

state and managed by officials appointed by the Communist party. The workers received only what was left over of the produce of the farm after it had met delivery quotas assigned by the state and purchased at low prices. The peasants worked as a group, that is, "collectively," at tasks assigned by the farm managers, and were thus changed from owners to hired workers. Agricultural production was to be mechanized by use of tractors provided by the state from Machine Tractor Stations, where party members could check on the reliability of the collective's members. The well-to-do peasants, or *kulaks*, fought back, breaking their machinery and killing their animals rather than hand them over to the collectives; and Stalin employed the poorer peasants and the Red Army to seize their land and animals. Some *kulaks* were killed in the clashes, others were sent to labor camps. The collectivization caused a famine in 1932–1933, in which between 2 and 3 million peasants may have died. But, within one year, half of Russia's land was in collective farms; by 1939, 90 percent of the farmland had been collectivized.

The agricultural changes were intended to provide the food necessary for a vastly expanded industrial workforce. The first Five-Year Plan laid down detailed goals for the creation of heavy industry, based largely on the unused resources in raw materials of the Ural Mountains and Siberia, where huge new factory towns were to be built. Coal, iron ore, and oil were to be exploited. Vast dams were to be constructed for electric power. New roads, railroads, and canals, often built by prisoners from labor camps operated by the secret police, were to open up the underdeveloped regions of the country. Patriotic propaganda was widely used to persuade workers to meet the high production goals assigned them; and artists, novelists, and playwrights were compelled to extoll the virtues and happiness of a working class devoting itself to fulfilling the goals of the Five-Year Plans.

The program laid down in the first Five-Year Plan was continued in the second Five-Year Plan (1933–1938) and in the Third, which was interrupted by the German invasion of 1941. By then, although agricultural production was only slightly higher than in 1929, Russia had been forcibly converted into one of the world's great industrial powers. Coal production had increased more than 400 percent; steel production, 450 percent; and power production 800 percent. Moreover, the major part of the new production was from plants in the Urals and Siberia, beyond the furthest line of advance of Hitler's armies during the Second World War. Stalin had in fact made good on the demand he had proclaimed in 1931: "We are fifty or a hundred years behind the advanced countries. Either we close this gap within ten years, or they [the capitalist countries] crush us."

The Great Purges

To ensure total loyalty during the period of sacrifice demanded by the Five-Year Plans, Stalin embarked upon massive purges. In 1933, those accused of an insufficient commitment to Communist ideology were purged from the party.

The following year, after the assassination of Sergei Kirov, the party leader in Leningrad, the greatest and most violent purges ever undertaken in Russia began. Almost all the surviving colleagues and friends of Lenin, and even those who had worked with Stalin for the ouster of Trotsky, were arrested by the secret police. In 1936, a first public trial of these so-called Old Bolsheviks was held, in which most of them confessed, after torture, that they were guilty of treason. Other trials of leading Communist politicians followed. But in 1938 the purge took on a new dimension when several of the leading generals in the Red Army were publicly tried for espionage, found guilty, and executed. By then the purge had affected every level of Russian society. Citizens with no political background were denounced by their neighbors, and 8 million people were sent to labor camps. More than $1\frac{1}{2}$ million members and candidate members were dropped from the Communist party. More than four-fifths of the members and candidate members of the Central Committee were shot. The whole country was disoriented by the savagery and the capriciousness of the purge, not least the officer corps of the army, which saw its most experienced and loyal generals swept away.

It is hard to find a rational explanation for the purges. Nikita Khruschev, who had been an associate of Stalin and became the ruler of the Soviet Union himself between 1955 and 1964, told the Communist party in 1956 that it was mental sickness, or paranoia, that caused Stalin to act in this way. Yet Stalin did achieve the goal of wiping out all potential opposition to his own personal rule, by replacing the older generation of Communist leaders both in the party and in the army by a younger generation loyal to him for their advancement. He had removed those who could see the difference between his policies and those of Lenin. In the population as a whole, the ubiquitous fear had silenced opposition even if it had not stimulated support for him personally.

ITALY UNDER FASCISM

Weaknesses of Italian Democracy

Italy, for complex social, economic, and nationalistic reasons, was the first country in Europe to fall under the rule of the right-wing authoritarian regime known as Fascism. After unification in 1871, the new Italian state had remained fragmented by regional rivalries. Provincial xenophobia in regions that had previously been self-governing, such as Tuscany, remained strong. The south as a whole felt exploited by the economic policy imposed by northern politicians, who protected northern industry with tariffs but exposed southern agriculture to outside competition, and concentrated state investment on public works in the north. The pope multiplied the difficulties of the new political system by discouraging Catholics from participating in the political system. The advance of industrialization in the north created an industrial proletariat that felt itself aggrieved by the low wages and poor working conditions provided by the owners, while the southern peasantry continued to feel their age-old grievances against the semifeudal landowning class. Italian losses in the First World War, which exceeded 600,000 killed and 1 million wounded, brought social tension to a climax, especially when Italy received less compensation in territory from the Austrian empire, especially along the Adriatic coast, than it had expected.

In September 1919, the port city of Fiume, which was claimed by Yugoslavia, was seized by several thousand demobilized soldiers under the leadership of the poet and adventurer Gabriele D'Annunzio. D'Annunzio set the style for the Fascists in his little city-state, dressing his troops in black shirts and giving bombastic nationalistic speeches from a balcony to screaming crowds. He was overthrown in 1920 by troops sent by the Italian government, which in agreement with the Yugoslavs turned Fiume into a free state. (It was seized again by Italy in 1922, after the Fascists had come to power.) Meanwhile, in Italy itself, workers had begun to seize their factories to reinforce their demands for higher wages, and had locked out the owners and managers. Peasants followed their example, and began to seize land that was not being cultivated. To many, it looked as though Italy was on the verge of a Communist revolution.

Founding of the Fascist Movement

To the upper and middle classes, a former socialist agitator named Benito Mussolini offered salvation from what he called the "red plague." In March 1919 Mussolini had enlisted bands of demobilized soldiers in *fasci di combattimento* ("fighting bands"), which he promised to hurl against left-wing agitators; and in 1920 Mussolini turned the movement into a political party, which had 300,000 members by 1922, drawn mostly from the discontented middle classes.

Mussolini preached the basic themes that became the official ideology of Fascism. Human beings can find full satisfaction only within the nation-state, for which they must be prepared to work and if necessary to sacrifice themselves. Struggle is the essential condition of life, and the highest form of struggle is war, which ennobles those who take part in it. Each state must be governed by an elite, and that elite must have a single leader, a *Duce*. The leader's function is to embody within himself the highest ideals of the nation, and to express those ideals in action. In a philosophic sense, Mussolini asserted, "the leader is always right," since his will is the will of the nation. Finally, every nation must seek to expand; the role of the Italian nation was to revive the Roman Empire, by seeking Mediterranean hegemony and an African empire.

Fascist Internal Policy

The inability of the democratic governments to stop the seizures of the factories and the landed estates gave Mussolini his opportunity. In October 1922, he called for a March on Rome, in which every Fascist in Italy was to assemble in

Mussolini Addressing Mass Demonstration in Roman Forum, June 1, 1934 As chief commander of the Italian armed forces, Mussolini decided to speak to his Fascist supporters in front of Caesar's altar in the Forum. (Bildarchiv Preussischer Kulturbesitz.)

the capital on the same day to terrify the prime minister and his cabinet into resigning. Ten thousand Fascists eventually reached Rome, at which point the government collapsed and the king, Victor Emmanuel III (reigned 1900–1946), invited Mussolini to form a new government, which was confirmed by the legislature.

Although he had respected the constitutional forms in taking power, between 1922 and 1927 Mussolini turned Italy into a Fascist dictatorship. The Fascist party was declared the only legal political party. The state was divided into "corporations," similar to trade unions, composed of workers or of employers, with a single union for intellectuals; but industrial policy was set by the corporations dominated by large industrialists. Strikes were forbidden. A secret police was formed, which arrested opponents and sent them to exile on islands in the Mediterranean or in isolated villages in the south. Securely in power, Mussolini began to stimulate the economic development of Italy. Marshes were drained, and new roads and railroads constructed. Industrial companies were subsidized and granted large government contracts, especially for military preparation; companies in difficulty were taken over by the state. To encourage population growth, migrants were urged to return from abroad, and large families were subsidized.

Mussolini's Foreign Policy

But Mussolini's primary goal was Italian expansion abroad. During the 1920s he built up the armed forces and Italian heavy industry. Then, in 1935, profiting from the weakness of Britain and France, he invaded Ethiopia, which was conquered within a year. In 1936, he sent Italian troops and planes to aid the rightist forces of General Francisco Franco in the Spanish Civil War. Finally, in 1939, he seized Albania. Thus, Mussolini claimed, by 1939 his Fascist regime had restored the health of the Italian economy, brought political stability, and won a new empire and increased prestige. Undoubtedly his successes had been an important factor in encouraging many other European countries to opt for fascism in the interwar years.

GERMANY: THE WEIMAR REPUBLIC AND THE THIRD REICH

As in Italy, the totalitarian right-wing party of the National Socialists led by Adolf Hitler came to power in Germany as a result of manipulation of the political system. After a period of economic crisis in 1919–1923, it seemed as though the Weimar Republic, as the new state was called after its constitution had been adopted in the city of Weimar in 1919, might collapse. Attempted coups in 1923 by both Communists and National Socialists were easily defeated, however, and Germany enjoyed prosperity and political stability from 1924 to 1929. Hitler skillfully exploited the distress of the Great Depression, during which he presented the Nazis as the only party with the capacity to solve Germany's economic problems. His party won a temporary majority in the *Reichstag*, thus enabling him to outmaneuver his bickering rivals and legally become chancellor in January 1933.

Attacks on the Weimar Republic

The Weimar constitution was regarded as a model of democratic representation, and it was copied by several states in Eastern Europe. It guaranteed civil rights, and gave universal suffrage to men and women. Proportional representation was introduced to enable the expression of all varieties of political opinion. The president was chosen by universal suffrage for a term of seven years. The chancellor, who headed the executive, was chosen by the president but was responsible to the lower house, or *Reichstag*, and required the support of a majority of its members to remain in office. In times of national emergency, the chancellor could, with the president's approval, govern by decree. The greatest weakness of the system lay in the proliferation of parties which, as in France, made it difficult for any government to pursue a coherent policy. Chancellor after chancellor resigned rather than handle the crises that faced the governments between 1919 and 1923; and those who dared take unpopular decisions risked assassination by right-wing murder squads.

The worst crisis of the immediate postwar years was provoked by the French and Belgian occupation of the Ruhr in January 1923 for the purpose of enforcing reparations payments. When the German government ordered passive resistance by the Ruhr workers, the German economy ground to a standstill, and the value of the currency collapsed. The mark, which had been priced at 4.2 to the dollar in 1914, fell by September 1923 to 6 billion to the dollar, as the government recklessly printed paper money. Both extreme-left and extreme-right groups sought to profit from the chaos in the country. Communists seized a number of cities, including Hamburg, but were quickly defeated by the regular army. In Munich, Adolf Hitler made a first but badly prepared attempt, known as the Beerhall Putsch, to take power.

Rise of Hitler

Adolf Hitler (1889–1945), the son of middle-class Austrian parents, had spent his formative years in the slums of Vienna, where he had become obsessed with the danger to the Germanic race of the Jews who, he felt, dominated much of Austrian business life and helped pervert Austrian cultural standards. He even blamed his failure to enter the Academy of Fine Arts on Jewish prejudice. In Munich, to which he moved in 1913, he felt at home, and he volunteered for service in the First World War in a Bavarian regiment. Upon returning to Munich, he took over a small anti-Semitic political group, which he renamed the National Socialist German Workers' Party, and made himself its *Führer* (leader). Recruiting followers from among the demobilized soldiers, he formed a brown-shirted band of storm troopers, who were little more than street toughs. Working closely with his brilliant secretary, Rudolf Hess, and a former war ace, Hermann Göring, he elaborated new techniques of propaganda in which his movement was made to appear as an irresistible force capable of smashing all opposition, and especially of cleansing Germany of Jewish influence. Hitler felt that the disastrous situation in 1923 had made it possible for his storm troopers to take control of Bavaria as a preliminary to taking over all Germany. His storm troopers seized the Bavarian government at a political rally in a Munich beerhall, but were dispersed by police the next day when they marched on the city hall. Hitler himself was arrested, found guilty of treason, and spent eight months in jail. During his imprisonment, he wrote his autobiography, *Mein Kampf* (My Struggle), which was to become the sacred book of the Nazi movement.

Upon his release, Hitler found it difficult to revive his movement as prosperity returned. Gustav Stresemann as chancellor had ended the passive resistance in the Ruhr, and the following year the American-sponsored Dawes plan had guaranteed the stability of the currency. A great productive boom lasted until 1929. Germany too had returned to international respectability. After Locarno it had become a member of the League of Nations, and it had signed the Kellogg-Briand peace pact. The government was in the hands of the three parties most committed to maintenance of the democratic regime: the Social Democrats, the Catholic Center party, and the Democrats.

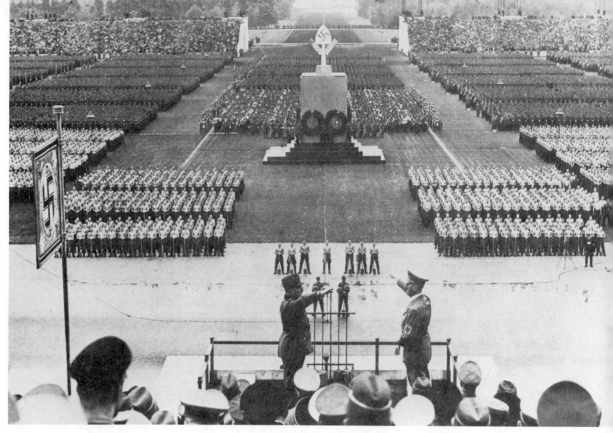

Hitler Addressing the Nuremberg Party Rally *The Nazis staged a dramatic rally of hundreds of thousands of party members at Nuremberg every year to stimulate popular enthusiasm for their programs.* (UPI/Bettmann Newsphotos.)

But there were signs of danger, even during the years when economic conditions were improving. The Communists commanded 3 million votes on the extreme left. Hitler's National Socialist party received 800,000 votes in the election of 1928, and other right-wing parties, such as the Nationalists, did even better. Most important, in the presidential election of 1925, the seventy-five-year-old Field Marshal Paul von Hindenburg, the candidate of the right-wing parties, defeated the candidate supported by the moderates. In the crisis years of depression in 1930–1933, Hindenburg was to be an easy prey to the backstairs intrigue of unprincipled politicians.

When the depression struck, Hitler was ready to move. He had formulated a simple ideology that could be repeated endlessly to crowds seeking an immediate panacea for their troubles. All nations were part of a hierarchy in which purity of blood denoted racial quality. The head of the hierarchy was the Aryan or Teutonic race, which had, however, been tainted by the impure blood of the Jews, which must be removed. All nations should possess their own fatherland; and, in particular, all Germans should live within the German fatherland. Those regions inhabited by Germans that were not part of the German state, such as Austria or the Sudetenland of Czechoslovakia, should be united with Germany. This German fatherland was too small, and needed *Lebensraum* ("living space"),

541

which it should find by expansion eastward into the lands of the Slavs. Germany itself was to be governed, like other fascist countries, by an elite composed of the Nazi party, which itself would have a *Führer* ("Leader"). To dramatize the appeal of the Nazi party, Hitler equipped the Nazis with uniforms, jackboots, flying banners, and military bands, and held vast parades throughout the country, often by torchlight, which would culminate in a long tirade by Hitler himself against the Versailles Treaty, the Weimar politicians, and the Jews.

Although many regarded him as a charlatan or an entertainer, the Nazi vote grew until, in July 1932, the party received 13 million votes, and became the largest party in the parliament. Hindenburg, however, regarded Hitler as an uncultivated upstart. When he fired the Center party chancellor, Heinrich Brüning, in May 1932, instead of Hitler he appointed as chancellor Franz von Papen, a conservative nobleman who was a member of the Center party. Then, in November 1932, following elections in which the Nazi vote dropped by 2 million, he replaced Papen with one of his own favorites, General Kurt von Schleicher. Hitler cunningly allied with Papen and the Nationalist party, and put together a coalition government with himself as chancellor, which Hindenburg reluctantly accepted in January 1933.

Consolidation of Nazi Power

Having come to power legally, Hitler set out to destroy every vestige of the democratic constitution. The Communists were accused of having burned down the *Reichstag* building, and banned. The Enabling Act of March 1933 gave Hitler the power to govern by decree for four years, during which he banned all political parties except the Nazi party. When Hindenburg died in 1934, he took the positions of both president and chancellor himself, and compelled the armed forces to swear loyalty to him personally. Special law courts were created to deal with criminal or political cases. A secret police (*Gestapo*) was created to search out opposition, and concentration camps were started where communists, socialists, Jews, and indeed many simply regarded as unreliable or unneeded in the new society were imprisoned. The army was placated by the decision in 1935 to rearm Germany. Hitler even tried to please the Catholics by signing a concordat with the pope in 1933, in which the Catholic Church recognized the Nazi regime.

At first it appeared that Hitler's intention was to force the Jews to emigrate from Germany. In 1935, the Nuremberg Laws took away German citizenship from anyone who had even one Jewish grandparent, and forbade the employment of Jews in government positions and in most cultural or intellectual posts. In November 1938, however, the Nazis organized a nationwide campaign of synagogue burning and pillage of Jewish shops, and Jews were ordered to wear a yellow star with *Jude* ("Jew") printed on it. By 1939, almost half of Germany's 600,000 Jews had emigrated, often after paying large fees to Nazi officials. (The massacre of the Jews reached its full enormity after the Nazi armies came into control of the far larger Jewish populations of Eastern Europe in 1939–1941. There, in camps such as Auschwitz, the Nazis killed the major part of the 6 million Jews who died at their hands by 1945. In all, Hitler was responsible for the annihilation of two-thirds of the prewar Jewish population of Europe.)

Most Germans, however, were more concerned with Nazi economic policy, which until 1939 seemed to be extremely successful. Unemployment had been wiped out within three years, as a result of Nazi programs of public works such as the construction of a freeway network, contracts to industry for rearmament, and conscription of the unemployed into labor batallions. Some Germans too had been able to take over the jobs from which Jews had been expelled, while farmers of "Aryan" race were given financial aid to enable them to keep possession of the ancestral lands. Inexpensive summer camps run by the "Strength Through Joy" program were used to win over worker support, while young people received indoctrination in the Hitler Youth. The German people were not, however, anxious to become involved in war once more, and foreign journalists reported that Hitler's popularity began to drop when it became obvious that he was risking war with Britain and France. By then, however, the Nazi totalitarian machine was able to cow all opposition.

THE ROAD TO WAR, 1933–1939

The Opening Moves

Hitler subtly profited from the economic troubles of Britain, France, and the United States, which made them reluctant to undertake new responsibilities abroad, and from Russia's absorption in its programs of industrialization and its purges. He was already convinced that the League of Nations, which had done nothing more than condemn verbally the Japanese invasion of Manchuria in 1931, could be ignored; and in 1933 he withdrew Germany from membership. He then undermined the French alliance system in Eastern Europe by establishing close ties with the conservative governments of Rumania, Bulgaria, and Hungary, and by concluding a nonaggression pact with Poland. To disarm the opposition of Britain and France, he played upon their feeling of guilt over the Treaty of Versailles. After the people of the Saar voted overwhelmingly in 1935 to return to Germany, he promised the French that no quarrel remained between them. He excused German rearmament in 1935 as a countermeasure to French rearmament just announced.

Mussolini had also become convinced that the democracies would do nothing to prevent Italian expansion in Africa. In October, he sent Italian tanks and troops armed with poison gas against the poorly armed troops of Emperor Haile Selassie in Ethiopia. His action was condemned in the League of Nations, and economic sanctions were ordered against Italy. The sanctions did not, however, include an embargo on oil, and thus in effect Italy was permitted the fuel necessary for its tanks, planes, and troop carriers. In March 1936, two months before Italian victory in Ethiopia, Hitler used the distraction of the British and French to carry out his most blatant infringement of the Treaty of Versailles, the movement of German troops into the Rhineland. When neither the French nor the British acted, he felt free to push on more openly with his plans in Eastern Europe.

The Spanish Civil War

Once again, the British and French found themselves distracted from Hitler's moves by a new international crisis—the revolt of the Spanish army under General Francisco Franco against the elected government of the Spanish Republic in July 1936. Mussolini, and shortly afterwards Hitler, promised military aid to Franco's forces, known as the Nationalists in what had become a savage civil war with the Republicans, who supported the elected government. In October, Stalin decided to come to the aid of the Republicans by sending military supplies and supporting the formation of International Brigades composed of volunteers while Britain and France were attempting to persuade other powers to remain neutral.

The Spanish Civil War served Hitler's interests perfectly. The war embroiled the Russians with the British and the French. The German air force was able to try out its new weapons and its strategy of terror bombing. During the war Mussolini moved closer to Hitler by signing a military agreement creating a "Rome-Berlin axis," or coalition, in October 1936. The victory of Franco in March 1939 brought to power another authoritarian ruler sympathetic to fascism. Finally, Hitler himself had been able to avoid international condemnation for the invasion of Austria that he ordered in March 1938 and its union, or *Anschluss*, with Gemany following a plebiscite carried out by the Nazis.

Appeasement

Both the British and French governments had persuaded themselves that Hitler was honest in his declaration that his only remaining goal was to unite the Germans still outside Germany into the fatherland. In September 1938, British Prime Minister Neville Chamberlain and French Premier Edouard Daladier met with Hitler and Mussolini at Munich, and agreed, without Czech consent, that Germany should be allowed to annex the Sudetenland from Czechoslovakia. Six months later, Hitler finally woke Chamberlain and Daladier to the worthlessness of his promises, by dismembering the rest of Czechoslovakia. Bohemia and Moravia became a German protectorate. Slovakia was recognized as an independent state. Hungary annexed Sub-Carpathian Ruthenia. When Hitler began to demand Danzig and the Polish Corridor from Poland, the British and French were finally prepared to oppose him.

Stalin, however, had become convinced that the British and French would permit Hitler to attack Russia, and he decided to gain time by concluding a

Nonaggression Pact with Germany in August 1939. In return for Stalin's promise to remain neutral when Hitler attacked Poland, the Soviet Union was promised, in secret clauses, the right to establish a "sphere of influence" in eastern Poland, Estonia, Latvia, and the Rumanian province of Bessarabia; and later Lithuania was added to the Russian sphere. On September 1, Germany invaded Poland, and after Hitler ignored British and French demands that he halt his aggression, they declared war on Germany on September 3. It was, declared Winston Churchill, a decision "taken at the worst possible moment and on the least satisfactory ground, which must surely lead to the slaughter of tens of millions of people." But it was, he felt, the only possible decision other than to wait for inevitable defeat in the future.

THE SECOND WORLD WAR

The First Campaigns, 1939–1941

By the end of September the German army had totally defeated the Polish forces and was in occupation of the western two-thirds of the country. The Russians, meeting little resistance, occupied the eastern third, and incorporated it into the Soviet Union. Russia then compelled Estonia, Latvia, and Lithuania to give it access to their military installations, and in November opened hostilities with Finland. By mid-1940, it had annexed Estonia, Latvia, Lithuania, and a large area of Finland.

The German invasion of Western Europe began in April 1940, with successful attacks on Denmark and Norway, which were followed in May by the long-awaited invasion of France. By June the German armies were in Paris; and the newly formed French government of Marshal Philippe Pétain signed an armistice that left it in control only of the southern third of France. Meanwhile, the Netherlands, Belgium, and Luxembourg had been occupied.

Only Britain continued to fight, bolstered by the rhetoric of its new prime minister, Winston Churchill, and by the shipment of military supplies from the United States. German bombers pounded British cities night after night for the rest of 1940, during the "Battle of Britain," but sustained heavy losses as a result of the superiority of British fighter planes and British use of radar; and in October Hitler decided to abandon the invasion of Britain in order to prepare his ground forces for an invasion of Russia in the spring of 1941.

Mussolini's impetuous attack on Greece in October 1940 delayed Hitler's plans, because Hitler was forced to send troops to the aid of the Italian armies fleeing under the unexpectedly ferocious resistance of the Greeks. Moreover, Hitler made a major miscalculation when he decided to invade Yugoslavia as well as Greece, as punishment for refusing German troops free passage across Yugoslav territory. Both Yugoslavia and Greece were under German control by April 1941, but Hitler had lost several crucial weeks in organizing his invasion of Russia.

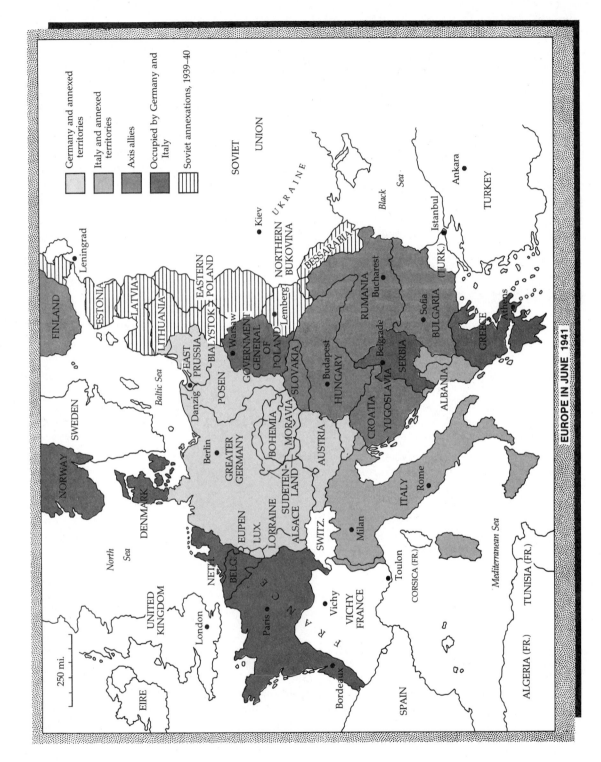

EUROPE IN JUNE 1941

Germany and annexed territories

Italy and annexed territories

Axis allies

Occupied by Germany and Italy

Soviet annexations, 1939–40

SOVIET UNION

U K R A I N E

Kiev

Leningrad

FINLAND

ESTONIA

LATVIA

LITHUANIA

EASTERN POLAND

BIALYSTOK

Warsaw

GOVERNMENT GENERAL OF POLAND

Lemberg

NORTHERN BUKOVINA

BESSARABIA

Black Sea

Ankara

TURKEY

Istanbul (TURK.)

Bucharest

RUMANIA

Sofia

BULGARIA

Belgrade

SERBIA

Athens

GREECE

ALBANIA

Budapest

HUNGARY

CROATIA

YUGOSLAVIA

EAST PRUSSIA

POSEN

Danzig

Baltic Sea

SWEDEN

NORWAY

DENMARK

North Sea

BERLIN

Berlin

GREATER GERMANY

BOHEMIA

MORAVIA

SUDETEN- LAND

AUSTRIA

SWITZ.

ALSACE

LORRAINE

LUX.

EUPEN

BELG.

NETH.

Milan

ITALY

Rome

SLOVAKIA

Toulon

CORSICA (FR.)

Mediterranean Sea

TUNISIA (FR.)

ALGERIA (FR.)

SPAIN

Vichy

VICHY FRANCE

Paris

F R A N C E

Bordeaux

UNITED KINGDOM

London

EIRE

250 mi.

546

On June 22, 1941, three vast German armies struck into Russia. The northern prong reached the edge of Leningrad by September. A central force reached within 65 miles of Moscow. A southern wing captured the wheatlands of the Ukraine and was approaching the oilfields of the Caucasus. Neither Leningrad nor Moscow had fallen, however, when in the winter snows Stalin's reequipped armies mounted a counteroffensive that drove the Germans back 200 miles. For the first time, the war had turned against the Nazis, who by then had lost 1 million men in the Russian invasion.

On December 7, 1941, Japanese bombers destroyed the major part of the American Pacific fleet at Pearl Harbor in the Hawaiian Islands, and Japanese forces began concerted attacks that, within six months, put them in control of almost all the European and American colonies in East and Southeast Asia and the southeastern Pacific. What had hitherto been a largely European war was thus transformed into a global war.

Counteroffensive in the West, 1942–1943

The American government decided to devote the major part of its war effort to the defeat of Germany and Italy before mounting a final attack on Japan, and to begin by joining the British in an invasion in November 1942 of the French colonies of Algeria and Morocco, which were placed under a committee headed by General Charles de Gaulle, leader of the Free French forces continuing the fight against Germany. By removing control of Algeria and Morocco from what was its legal government, that of Pétain, the Allies thus established the important principle that liberation would not necessarily be followed by a return to the political status quo of the prewar years.

In July 1943, the Allied forces invaded Sicily and southern Italy, where they were hailed as liberators. Mussolini was deposed by his own Fascist Grand Council on July 25, and arrested by the king the next day. Although Mussolini had fallen, Hitler flooded northern Italy with German troops, which resisted savagely at two defense lines, one south of Rome, which was broken in May 1944, and a line north of Florence, broken only in April 1945. However, in the south, the Allies supported the creation of a multiparty government, which at the end of the war was to create a workable democratic system. In this way, a second principle had been established: at liberation, the British and Americans would ensure that fascist governments would be replaced by constitutional systems in harmony with their own forms of parliamentary democracy (and, by implication, in contrast with the Soviet system).

In Russia, Hitler mounted new offensives in 1942 with the purpose of capturing the great port of Stalingrad on the Volga River and many of Russia's mines and oilfields. Stalin felt that his own prestige was involved in the defense of the town named after him. In September he launched a massive offensive that cut off the German army in Stalingrad, which suffered more than 300,000 casualties before surrendering. The defeat at Stalingrad marked the end of German expansion. In 1943, one Russian army pushed on from Stalingrad to recapture the cities of southern Russia, while other forces struck from Moscow and Leningrad to drive the Germans back toward Poland.

Disagreements Among the Allies

As victory came nearer, disagreements between the Americans and British and the Russians became sharper. Roosevelt was strongly opposed to Soviet annexation of Estonia, Latvia, Lithuania, and eastern Poland. Churchill wished to forestall the Communization of the other states of Eastern Europe by supporting non-Communist resistance forces there and by gaining a foothold for Anglo-American forces in the Balkans. Stalin believed that Russian security demanded the establishment of a line of friendly states along the Russian border in Eastern Europe. To ensure that the governments installed by the Red Army in those countries would be allies of the Soviet Union, he had trained and supported in Moscow native Communists who were prepared to crush the non-Communist forces in their own countries. He feared, however, that the British and Americans were allowing the Germans to direct major thrusts against Russia in order to destroy Soviet Communism. When Stalin, Roosevelt, and Churchill met in November 1943 at the Teheran Conference, Stalin quashed Churchill's proposal for an Anglo-American invasion of Yugoslavia and enthusiastically welcomed the assurance that their cross-Channel invasion of France would be mounted in the spring of 1944.

The Final Assault

The Allied cross-Channel invasion of France began on D Day, June 6, 1944, and by August Paris had been taken. By September, Allied forces had established a continuous line from the Channel coast to the Mediterranean. The Red Army launched an offensive to coincide with the D Day invasion that by August had brought them within a few miles of Warsaw, where the non-Communist resistance forces rose up against the Germans. Then, to the surprise and anger of the British and Americans, rather than continue the attack on Warsaw, the Red Army halted, and permitted the Germans to wipe out the Polish underground in an attack that devastated the heart of Warsaw. Meanwhile, other Russian forces swung southward into Rumania and Bulgaria, which were occupied by September, and into eastern Yugoslavia, where in October they joined up with Communist resistance forces under Josip Broz Tito to drive out the Germans. By December, the Red Army was in the suburbs of the Hungarian capital of Budapest. Only then did the Soviet army in Poland renew the attack on Warsaw, which fell in January 1945.

Roosevelt, Churchill, and Stalin met at Yalta in southern Russia in February

Sniper Fire in Paris, August 1944 *Even after French and American tanks entered Paris, sporadic shooting continued against celebrating crowds in the city center. (UPI/Bettmann Newsphotos.)*

1945, to coordinate their plans for the last campaigns and their postwar collaboration. Churchill and Roosevelt realized at once that they had little leverage on Soviet policy in Eastern Europe, where the Red Army had installed governments that were either Communist-dominated or in which Communists held vitally important ministries. Roosevelt, moreover, had come to Yalta to persuade Stalin to declare war on Japan, and to aid in the final assault against Japanese forces. Stalin agreed, in return for territorial concessions at the expense of Japan. Churchill's sole victory at Yalta was to get Stalin and Roosevelt to agree that France should become one of the occupying powers in Germany, and thus be restored to great-power status.

After February 1945, German defenses collapsed on every front. The Russian armies completed the conquest of Hungary, Austria, and most of Czechoslovakia, and surrounded Berlin. Meanwhile, the Allied armies in the west crossed the Rhine, captured the industrial area of the Ruhr, and made contact with the Russians at the Elbe River. Hitler himself, broken in health, took refuge in an underground concrete fortress. When the Russians finally fought their way into the center of the city, they found that Hitler had shot himself, and his body had been burned. Fighting stopped on May 8, and final surrender documents were signed on May 9.

The Defeat of Japan

In 1942, the Japanese Empire in East Asia consisted of eastern China, Burma, Malaya, French Indochina, the Dutch East Indies (Indonesia), the Philippine Islands, Wake Island, and Guam. The ease with which the Japanese had defeated the armies of the colonial powers had dispelled forever the carefully cultivated myth of white military supremacy, and the Japanese had made some efforts to persuade the colonial peoples to collaborate with them. Their economic exploitation was so blatant, however, that only in Indonesia were they able to channel anticolonial feeling to their support. The American counterattack in the Pacific was slow, and the tactic of attacking island by island was perhaps unnecessarily costly in lives. However, by June 1944, the United States possessed airbases from which Japan itself could be bombed, and the Philippines were recaptured in the spring of 1945.

Fearing stiff resistance from fanatical Japanese soldiers, American advisers warned Roosevelt that U.S. forces would suffer a million casualties if they invaded Japan. To avoid those losses, Harry S Truman, who had become president upon Roosevelt's death in April 1945, ordered the atomic bomb, which had been secretly developed during four years of research, to be dropped on Hiroshima. The bomb killed 70,000 people and laid the whole city in ruins. When the Japanese government, dominated by the military, still refused to surrender, a second bomb was dropped on Nagasaki and killed 36,000 people. At that point, the Japanese emperor ordered his government to accept the surrender terms, and fighting stopped on August 14, 1945.

The Significance of the Second World War

The Second World War had begun, in the worst tradition of European diplomacy, because ineffective statesmen had failed to deter the aggression of a large, well-armed power, Nazi Germany, against a smaller country, Poland, which it had chosen as its prey. Between 1939 and 1941, the war had been fought almost exclusively by European powers. But with Hitler's invasion of the Soviet Union in June 1941 and the Japanese attack on the United States at Pearl Harbor in December 1941, the struggle became worldwide, and thereby changed not only its scale but its possible effects on the evolution of Western civilization after the end of the fighting.

First, from 1941 on, the conflict was dominated by the entry of the Soviet Union and the United States, whose populations and resources dwarfed those of any European state. Whereas both powers had remained largely isolated from the international politics of Europe during the interwar years, they were to be the primary influences on the development of the European state system after the end of the war in 1945. Second, the entry of the Soviet Union into the war gave it the opportunity to increase its own security and advance Communist power by transforming the political and social structure of almost all the states of Eastern Europe on the model of the Soviet Union itself. Third, the several defeats of the Western European powers and the United States during the initial expansion of Japan into their colonies destroyed the myth of Western superiority, and marked the beginning of the movements for independence that, in the postwar years, were to influence almost all the peoples living under Western colonial rule.

SUGGESTED READINGS

General Surveys

R. J. Sontag emphasizes diplomatic relations in *A Broken World, 1919–1939* (1971). Economic problems are briefly analyzed in W. Arthur Lewis, *Economic Survey, 1919–1939* (1949), and more fully in Joseph S. Davis, *The World Between the Wars, 1919–1939* (1975). Two fine surveys of Eastern Europe are Hugh Seton-Watson, *Eastern Europe Between the Wars, 1918–1941* (1962), and C. A. MacCartney and A. W. Palmer, *Independent Eastern Europe* (1962).

The Faltering Democracies

C. L. Mowat, *Britain Between the Wars, 1918–1940* (1955), provides good political coverage, while Sean Glynn and John Oxborrow, *Interwar Britain: A Social and Economic History* (1976), explain Britain's debilitating social conflicts. David Thomson, *Democracy in France Since 1870* (1946), throws light on the confusion of French politics. The failures in foreign policy are explained in Keith Middlemass, *The Strategy of Appeasement* (1972), and denounced by Lewis Namier, *Diplomatic Prelude, 1938–1939* (1948). Good biographies include David Marquand, *Ramsay MacDonald* (1977); Keith Middlemass and J. Barnes, *Baldwin: A Biography* (1970); Keith G. Feiling, *The Life of Neville Chamberlain* (1946), which is, however, a little too appreciative. On the Great Depression, see Charles P. Kindleberger, *The World in Depression, 1929–1939* (1973).

On the United States in the interwar years, fine surveys are provided by John D. Hicks, *Republican Ascendancy, 1921–1933* (1960), and by William E. Leuchtenberg, *Franklin D. Roosevelt and the New Deal, 1932–1940* (1963). John Kenneth Galbraith gives a clear explanation of the Wall Street Crash in *The Great Crash, 1929* (3d ed., 1972). For a detailed discussion of the first Roosevelt administration, see Arthur M. Schlesinger, Jr., *The Coming of the New Deal* (1958) and *The Politics of Upheaval* (1960). American isolationism is impartially discussed by a fine French scholar in Jean-Baptiste Duroselle, *From Wilson to Roosevelt: Foreign Policy of the United States, 1913–1945* (1963).

The Russian Revolution

Theodore von Laue briefly examines the origins of the Russian revolution, in *Why Lenin? Why Stalin?* (1971). M. T. Florinsky ranges broadly over the failings of the tsarist system in *The End of the Russian Empire* (1961). For an eye-witness account of the November Revolution, see John Reed, *Ten Days That Shook the World* (1919), or N. N. Sukhanov, *The Russian Revolution, 1917: A Personal Record* (1955).

Two excellent biographies of Lenin are David Shub, *Lenin: A Biography* (1976), and Robert Payne, *The Life and Death of Lenin* (1964). The best biography of Trotsky is Isaac Deutscher, *The Prophet Armed, 1879–1921* (1954) and *The Prophet Unarmed, 1921–1929*

(1961). The immediate aftermath of Lenin's death is described in the fine biography of his wife by Robert H. McNeal, *Krupskaya and Lenin* (1972).

The Bolshevik transformation of Russia's institutions during the first years of the revolution is documented in E. H. Carr, *The Bolshevik Revolution* (1951–1953).

Soviet Union Under Stalin

Isaac Deutscher's standard biography, *Stalin* (1967), can be supplemented with the broad analysis of *Stalinism* (1977), edited by Robert C. Tucker, and with Adam B. Ulam, *Stalin: The Man and His Era* (1973). Ulam describes Stalin's foreign policy in *Expansion and Coexistence* (1974). Robert Conquest emphasizes the destructive effects of the purges in *The Great Terror* (1971). The results of the Five-Year Plans are calculated in Naum Jasny, *Soviet Industrialization, 1928–1952* (1961).

Fascism

Ernst Nolte, *Three Faces of Fascism* (1966), is a penetrating, philosophical discussion of fascist ideology in Germany, Italy, and France. The best biography of the *Duce* is Denis Mack Smith, *Mussolini: A Biography* (1982). His foreign policy is analyzed in Alan Cassels, *Mussolini's Early Diplomacy* (1970), and Mack Smith's *Mussolini's Roman Empire* (1976). The impact of Mussolini's economic and social policies is weighed by Edward R. Tannenbaum, *The Fascist Experience: Italian Society and Culture, 1922–1945* (1972).

Nazism

Erich Eyck gives a detailed political analysis of the Weimar Republic in *A History of the Weimar Republic* (1962). Alan Bullock's fine biography, *Hitler: A Study in Tyranny* (1952), is particularly good on the formation of the Nazi movement and on Hitler's personality. Karl D. Bracher, *The German Dictatorship* (1970), is a masterly synthesis, covering all aspects of Nazi rule. On the massacre of the Jews, see Gerald Reitlinger, *The Final Solution: The Attempt to Exterminate the Jews of Europe, 1939–1945* (1954).

The Coming of the Second World War

Mussolini's aggression before 1939 can be followed in George Baer, *The Coming of the Italian-Ethiopian War* (1967), and John F. Coverdale, *Italian Intervention in the Spanish Civil War* (1976). The mistakes of the Republican politicians that led to Franco's revolt are analyzed in Gabriel Jackson, *The Spanish Republic and the Civil War* (1965). Joachim Remak thoughtfully appraises responsibility in *The Origins of the Second World War* (1976).

The Second World War

Two excellent short surveys of the war are Basil Liddell-Hart, *The Second World War* (1972), and Cyril Falls, *The Second World War: A Short History* (1948). Gordon Wright, *The Ordeal of Total War, 1939–1945* (1968), emphasizes the economic and scientific aspects of the conflict. Economic planning is described in Alan S. Milward, *War, Economy, and Society, 1939–1945* (1977).

20

Twentieth-Century Culture

Between the end of the nineteenth century and the First World War, an intellectual revolution transformed Western culture. Advances in atomic physics led to the rejection of the certainties of the Newtonian explanation of the universe, with its concepts of absolute space, time, and motion. Sigmund Freud led psychology into an exploration of the subconscious and irrational in human behavior. Novelists sought to show the hidden motivations of their characters, and analyzed how memories of different periods of time coexist with one's experience of the present. Painters such as the Fauves and the Cubists abandoned representational art, at a time when composers such as Arnold Schoenberg were giving up traditional harmony and replacing it with a new method of musical composition known as atonality.

The fundamental ideas of this intellectual revolution were widely accepted in the years between the wars, with Paris, London, Berlin, and New York taking the lead in working out the potential for change in these ideas. But there was also a reaction during the interwar years to these ideas. First, authoritarian movements, most notably the Nazi-Fascist and the Communist, demanded that the culture of their societies should express and support only state-approved values. Second, many intellectuals, regardless of political considerations, embarked on a renewed search for certainty, through a new approach to religion or philosophy. Third, popular culture became more than ever divorced from the unpalatable or unintelligible "high" culture, turning to styles that were immediately appealing, hedonistic, or escapist.

Following the Second World War, writers attempted to come to terms with the experience of war and with the sense of guilt for having participated in, or merely witnessed, the inhumanity of the Nazi era. In the 1950s, perhaps in reaction to the return of material prosperity, a many-sided revolt was renewed, which has continued, taking ever new forms, until the present. The search for change, whether political, social, or cultural, had become the norm.

SCIENTIFIC AND CULTURAL REVOLUTIONS, 1900–1919

Development of Atomic Physics

In the late nineteenth and early twentieth centuries, advances in atomic physics proved even more sensational than Darwin's theories had been, since they attacked the very concept of the nature of matter, which seemed to have been so satisfactorily settled by Newton. As always, progress was the result of discoveries in several interrelated fields of science. The notion that the atom was not indivisible and solid was destroyed by the work of Wilhelm Roentgen and of Pierre and Marie Curie. In 1895, Roentgen discovered X-rays, which were shortly after shown to be negatively charged particles of electricity called electrons. The Curies, working on the energy, or radioactivity, emitted by radium, were able to show that matter can be transformed into energy.

The behavior of the electron was explained by applying the "quantum theory" that the German physicist Max Planck (1858–1947) had developed in 1901. Planck had discovered experimentally, by study of the radiant heat given off by the sun, that energy is not emitted in a continuous stream but rather in discontinuous bursts, which he called packages or *quanta*. Moreover, he showed that these quanta were moving so fast and were so small in size that it was impossible to state their location either in space or in time, but only the probability of their being in a specific position. The British scientist Ernest Rutherford (1871–1937) suggested in 1903 that radioactivity was caused by explosions of atoms and was able to show in 1910 that the atom was composed of a positively charged core, or nucleus, around which negatively charged electrons moved in a kind of solar system. (In 1932, scientists discovered the existence of other particles within the atom, called neutrons, which are neither positively nor negatively charged. By 1934, positively charged electrons, called positrons, had been found, and subsequent research found hundreds of so-called elementary particles, considered to be the ultimate building blocks of the universe.)

Einstein and Relativity

The contribution of the German-Jewish physicist Albert Einstein (1879–1955) was similar to that of Newton, in that his theories unified the scientific explanations of the nature of the physical world. Working first as a clerk in the Swiss patent office, later in the University of Berlin, and, after Hitler's takeover of power in Germany, at the Institute for Advanced Study in Princeton, New Jersey, Einstein was recognized as the supreme theorist of twentieth-century physics for his special theory of relativity of 1905 and his general theory of relativity of 1916.

Einstein rejected Newton's view that space, time, and motion are absolutes, and can therefore be measured "objectively." Time, space, and motion, he held, are relative. The speed at which an observer is traveling determines the observed speed of a moving object. Moreover, mass and velocity are also related. As the speed of an object increases, its mass also grows. Most important, he demonstrated that mass and energy are interconvertible, and their relationship is controlled by the mathematical formula $E = mc^2$ (energy equals mass times the square of the speed of light). He had in fact shown theoretically what experimental scientists were realizing from their work on the atom, that enormous quantities of energy could be realized once the process of changing the nucleus of an atom into energy had been achieved, a realization that led eventually to the development of the atomic bomb. Einstein's view of the universe finally caught public attention with his assertion that space is curved, and thus the universe is finite. Experiments in observation of a solar eclipse in 1919 upheld Einstein's prediction that light would bend when passing through a gravitational field, such as that of the sun, and thus seemed to confirm the correctness of his revision of the Newtonian explanation of the universe.

The scientists of the late nineteenth and early twentieth centuries had thus upset several of the basic concepts that had provided certainty since Newton and the Age of Reason. The vast confidence that the universe was governed by simple natural laws was upset, since even the concept of nature itself, with absolute concepts of space, time, energy, and speed, had been rejected.

Revolution in Psychology

While the scientists were rejecting the established notions of space, time, and energy, Sigmund Freud (1856–1939) transformed psychology with his exploration of the role of the unconscious in forming human behavior. During the nineteenth century, scientists had demonstrated the relationship between human physiology and psychology. The function of the front brain lobe in controlling speech, for example, had been proven by the French doctor Paul Broca. Freud took the understanding of human psychology a major step forward by demonstrating, in one of his most famous cases, that physical paralysis could be caused by suppressed fears, and could be cured through psychoanalysis, by releasing the suppressed knowledge of disturbing childhood events. Beginning with his *Interpretation of Dreams* in 1900, Freud went on to develop a whole theory of the human personality, in which he argued that each person undergoes a conflict between the *ego*, the reasoning part of one's self that enables one to adapt to one's environment, and the *id*, the profound instinct that pushes one toward aggression and eroticism. Within one's personality, Freud wrote,

"in relation to the id, [the ego] performs that task [of self-preservation] by gaining control over the demands of the instincts, by deciding whether they shall be allowed . . . satisfaction, by postponing satisfaction . . . or by suppressing their excitations completely."[1] To make this determination, the ego must act as a kind of arbitrator between the demands of the id, which are above all sexual, and the rules imposed by what he called the superego, which represents the moral expectations placed on each person by the society and the civilization in which he or she lives.

Freud did not argue that one should give in to the impulses of the id, but rather that one should use reason in discovering the motivation behind one's impulses and in learning how to handle those impulses in a given social situation. He thus in a sense continued the work of the Enlightenment. But his greatest influence was his demonstration that human action is motivated to a large extent by the unconscious rather than by reason, and in particular by sexuality.

The Birth of a New Literature

The writers who were seeking new forms of literary expression in this period were probably not influenced greatly by the theories of Freud and the growing

[1] Sigmund Freud, *An Outline of Psychoanalysis* (New York: Norton, 1949), p. 15.

number of his disciples, although they welcomed them in the 1920s as vindi-
cation of what they themselves were working out more empirically. While the
most popular writers of these years, such as H. G. Wells in England, were still
writing in the Realist style, a small number of writers were working out a new
approach to literature that would receive public acceptance after the end of the
First World War.

Influenced by the theories of the Symbolist poets, these writers sought to
find symbolic events or experiences that would open an understanding of the
hidden motivations of their characters. They were interested in the way in which
language, especially when used in the form of images like those in dreams, can
be juxtaposed to create a form of truth which is grasped intuitively rather than
by the rational examination of the detailed descriptions of place and event in
which the Realist novelists excelled. Above all they sought to show that behind
human action there often lies fear or desires that are hidden and that are the
true explanation of a person's actions or words.

One of the pioneers in the transformation of the novel into an instrument
of analysis of hidden human motivation was André Gide (1869–1951), a homosexual struggling with the problem of reconciling his own personal drives with
both social convention and a strict Calvinist morality. In 1902, he had analyzed
in his novel *The Immoralist* the process of self-discovery of a married man realizing his own homosexual tendencies. In spite of his publication of a large
number of essays, novels, and plays in the prewar years, Gide was not, however, well known. Only in 1926, with publication of his novel *The Counterfeiters*,
did he win a wide following as well as the admiration of the avant-garde literary
world.

Marcel Proust (1871–1922) retired from Parisian social life in 1907 to a cork-
lined room where he created one of the most complex and revolutionary works
of modern literature, his seven-volume novel, *Remembrance of Things Past*. The
appearance of the first volume in 1913 was little noticed, but the second volume,
published in 1918, caused a sensation. Proust's book was in one sense an attempt to recapture his own past experiences, following what appeared to be
the random, almost accidental pattern of the movements of his own "stream of
consciousness." In an early part of the novel, for example, he is reminded
suddenly of the memories of his childhood village by tasting tea and madeleine
cake. But the rich detail of his memories, the search for meaning and unity
among them, and the ultimate theme, which is the pursuit of personal salvation,
made Proust's novel one of the most powerful influences on twentieth-century
literature.

In Germany, Thomas Mann (1875–1955) took the lead in the move away
from the realistic novel. Even though his first popular success, *Buddenbrooks*,
appeared to be a conventional saga of the kind favored by nineteenth-century
novelists of the life of three generations of a north German middle-class family,
it was in reality a subtle explanation of the spiritual decadence of a whole social
class. In his short novel, *Death in Venice*, he delved further into individual psy-

chology in describing the breakdown, under the influence both of illicit love and the longing for death, of a famous novelist who mistakenly seeks relaxation in a Venice struck by pestilence.

Britain was less influenced by stylistic experimentation, perhaps because of the great popularity of writers such as John Galsworthy, who were continuing the Realistic tradition in the novel. One group, however, known as the Bloomsbury Group, after the area in London where they lived, was already attempting to make known in Britain the more innovative literature from the continent. In the prewar years its best-known member was the novelist E. M. Forster (1879–1970), who before 1914 had published four novels in which he had explored how sensitive and aesthetically aware people find satisfaction when faced by the materialism of bourgeois life. He had also begun his finest novel, *A Passage to India*, which he published in 1924, in which he showed how the already difficult problem of finding an understanding between individuals is worsened when they experience at the same time the clash of civilizations.

Painting: Fauves, Cubists, and Expressionists

The Post-Impressionists had prepared painting for rapid change, and the artists of the early 1900s were especially sensitive to the lessons to be learned from the work of Cézanne and Gauguin—in particular the emphasis on clarity of design and patterns of color.

In 1905, a group of young painters led by Henri Matisse (1869–1954) startled the art world by exhibiting works characterized by violence of color and disregard for the actual appearance of objects or people. A critic named them, derisively, *fauves*, or "wild beasts." Matisse later explained that the contrasting colors, especially the use of orange and green, and the careful attention paid to the empty spaces around the objects portrayed, were used in accordance with a new theory of artistic expression in which composition was the artist's way of expressing his own feelings rather than the portrayal of "passion mirrored upon a human face or betrayed by a violent gesture."

The critics were even more surprised in 1907 by the first exhibition of Cubist painting, in which Pablo Picasso (1881–1973) displayed *Les Demoiselles d'Avignon.* Although Picasso had reverted to the geometric patterning to which Cézanne had accustomed the art world, the violent distortion of the female figures in the painting was completely original. What Picasso and the other Cubists were attempting to do through the apparent distortion was based on the theory that two-dimensional representation is not a true presentation of reality. They believed that the artist can take apart a familiar object, such as a violin, and present all its facets simultaneously. In *Les Demoiselles* Picasso attempted to present all aspects of the human body at once, so that a representation on flat canvas would no longer be an illusion but would be a representation of the memories one would retain after having seen at separate times the appearance of a body from many angles.

In Germany, the artists known as Expressionists were also determined to develop a new form of art that would enable them to express their personal feelings about the subject matter they were depicting. The Expressionists felt that painters like the Impressionists were superficial, literally so in that they depicted only the outer surface of people or objects and failed to go deeper into the psychological reality. Instead, most Expressionists were determined to impose their own personality, and especially the state of mind or emotional condition in which they approached their subject. In Dresden in 1905, Ernst Ludovic Kirchner (1880–1938) and several architect friends founded *Die Brücke* ("The Bridge"). Their landscape painting is a particularly good illustration of their determination to impose their own feelings onto subjects frequently treated impersonally. Houses, for example, become threatening objects, especially because the Bridge painters used harsh, jagged edges to define their subjects. They also excelled in printmaking from woodcuts, since the form lent itself particularly well to their use of flat areas of color for the purpose of creating an emotional response.

One year before the Bridge group disbanded in 1912, a new Expressionist group of painters was formed around Russian-born Wassily Kandinsky in Munich. They were known as the *Blaue Reiter* ("Blue Rider") group, apparently after the name of one of Kandinsky's paintings. Although the group as a whole lacked stylistic unity, Kandinsky and a co-founder of the group, Franz Marc, were notable in that they moved toward the abandonment of objective, or so-

559

called figurative painting. In short, they initiated the move toward the abstract, nonrepresentational painting that is one of the major components of twentieth-century art.

Atonal Music

While the painters were mounting the most radical attack ever begun on the basic theories dominant in art, composers were abandoning the very basis of Western music, the seven-tone scale with its major and minor keys. The rethinking of the nature of music composition was led by a Viennese composer, Arnold Schoenberg (1874–1951) and his two younger disciples, Alban Berg and Anton Webern. Schoenberg had caused something of a musical sensation as early as 1899 with his string sextet, *Verklärte Nacht* ("Transfigured Night") because of its harmonic extremes, but in 1909, in his *Piano Piece* Opus 11, No. 1, he completely abandoned tonality. Tonality was based on the idea that certain notes, such as the tonic, should be given preference, and that notes in keys or in succession should have specific tonal relations to each other. In its place, Schoenberg proposed the twelve-tone scale, using all the notes of an octave. Notes were to be related to each other in a tone row, or "series." The twelve notes would be placed in a specific order, and could then be played in different forms of orchestration and in other manners such as backwards or upside-down. The result was music that to the untutored ear (or rather the ear accustomed to the harmonies of the tonality) sounds dissonant; and the extraordinary difficulty for the average listener to recognize the tone row that was being used made the music far more inaccessible than the paintings of the Fauves or the Cubists.

Igor Stravinsky was the composer who gave notice to the Parisian public that a new music had arrived. Working with the Ballets Russes of Saint Petersburg for their annual season in Paris, he had composed two popular ballet scores, *The Firebird* and *Petrouchka*. But for the 1913 season he wrote *The Rite of Spring*, a work so dissonant and so rhythmically complex that it was greeted with howls of derision from the audience.

To sum up, in roughly the fifteen years before the outbreak of the First World War in 1914, the extraordinary vitality of experimentation had brought many forms of culture to the point where they had become incomprehensible not only to the great mass of the population but even in many cases to the interested amateur. This incomprehension was to create a gulf between creative artists and intellectuals and their potential audiences that was to be one of the most troublesome features of twentieth-century culture.

CULTURAL INNOVATION, 1919–1939

In the years between the First and Second World Wars, the centers of innovation in Western culture were Paris, London, Berlin, and New York. Paris, after the interruption of the war years, resumed the leadership of European culture, the variety of its intellectual life enhanced by an influx of refugees from all parts of the Western world. London remained one of the West's principal literary centers, increasingly open to the avant-garde influences from the continent. Berlin returned to the literary and artistic experimentation of the prewar decades, unhampered by the stultifying influence of the Kaiser and his court. New York became a city of skyscrapers, a center of popular culture, and home to a new generation of innovative American writers.

Interwar Paris

If Parisians had scoffed at the paintings of Picasso or the ballets of Stravinsky before 1914, after the war many were ready to be converted. The style of the Impressionists and Post-Impressionists had finally been accepted, and their paintings were rapidly increasing in price. The war had brought so widespread a reaction against tradition that a whole generation was ready to applaud the innovative approaches that before 1914 had seemed outrageous. The original Fauve painters were gaining acceptance. Matisse continued his experiments with color in a series of paintings in grays and off-whites, such as his *Lady in*

Persistence of Memory, by Salvador Dali (born 1904) As a Surrealist, Dali often showed how in dreams real objects such as clocks lose their objectivity, as Freud had pointed out at the beginning of the century. (Collection, The Museum of Modern Art, New York.)

White. The possibilities offered by Cubism were still being explored by Georges Braque and others among the first-generation Cubists.

The first new artistic movement to invade Paris in the interwar years was, however, Dadaism. Like many of the movements of the interwar years, Dada was as much a literary as an artistic movement. It had been started in Zürich in 1916 by Tristan Tzara, a Rumanian expatriate, as a cult of nonsense. The very word Dada was chosen because it was nonsensical. In French, it meant a hobby horse; in German, childish prattle. The Dadaists called for the overthrow of all existing styles of literature and art, the rejection of reason, and the expression of immediate impulse. Dada swept into Paris at the end of the war as an attack on "Fine Art," led by Tzara himself and a close friend from wartime Zürich, the Alsatian-born painter Jean Arp. They were welcomed into the literary circle formed by the poets Paul Éluard and André Breton. But the enthusiasm for Dadaism lasted only a short while. By 1924, Breton was ready to launch a far more influential movement, Surrealism.

Breton, who was a professional psychoanalyst as well as a poet, was determined to bring the findings of psychology into literature. In 1924, he issued the *Surrealist Manifesto,* in which he called on artists and poets to examine the subconscious world that is evident in dreams and fantasies where the mind is freed from both convention and reason. Two basic types of painting resulted. In one, dreams were presented simply as they might occur, without receiving rational planning by the artist. In the second, the artists attempted to stimulate nonrational understanding by juxtaposing familiar and unfamiliar objects in a setting that appears dream-like. In the paintings of a Surrealist like Salvador Dali, for example, watches seem to melt in nightmare-like landscapes. Picasso, who in the early 1920s had worked in a Cubist style, before returning to a kind of figurative classical style based in part on Greek and Roman models, turned to Surrealism at the end of the 1920s. Unlike the brief-lived Dada movement, the Surrealists continually widened their numbers and their audience. In the 1930s, they were joined by such painters as the Belgian René Magritte, founded a new journal called *Minotaur* for which Picasso designed the first cover, and held successful exhibitions in Paris, London, and New York.

The Surrealist poets, like the painters, used psychological images in their attempt to rouse unconscious associations in the viewer's mind. For example, Paul Éluard's poem, "Woman in Love," opens with a startling image: "She is standing on my eyelids."[2] But they also experimented with vocabulary and syntax in their search for a new form of personal expression.

During the 1920s, Paris was home to a number of important writers in English. Perhaps the most inventive of all was the Irish writer James Joyce (1882–1941). Joyce had published in 1916 *A Portrait of the Artist as a Young Man,* a psychological novel of the formative experiences of his own youth. In *Ulysses,* which he wrote between 1914 and 1921 but had difficulty publishing until 1922

---

[2] Paul Éluard, *Selected Writings,* with translation by Lloyd Alexander (Norfolk, Conn.: A New Directions Book, n.d.), p. 4.

because it was believed to be obscene, Joyce created one of the great master-pieces of twentieth-century literature. Written largely in "stream-of-conscious-ness" style, the novel is a story of events in the life of three people in Dublin during one day. Joyce seeks to describe not only what happens to them but what they think and feel, consciously or unconsciously, by constantly inter-rupting the narrative with random thoughts, memories, puns, and even word games. At the same time, the book has the structure of Homer's *Odyssey*, and each character and scene has a direct parallel in Homer's epic. In *Finnegan's Wake* (1939), Joyce left behind even those who had applauded *Ulysses* because his use of language had become so consciously idiosyncratic in his effort to represent the unconscious mind that it was, without scholarly guidance, vir-tually incomprehensible.

Many American expatriates, as well as some of the leading artists of Paris, gathered in the salon of the writer Gertrude Stein, whose own writing was extremely experimental, especially in the use of verbal rhythms and sound patterns. She, and the poet Ezra Pound, another American expatriate, helped Ernest Hemingway form the deceptively simple style that became his distinctive trademark in such novels as *The Sun Also Rises* (1926), where he portrays the lives of the young American expatriates whom Gertrude Stein called "the lost generation."

During the 1930s in Paris, individual writers and artists continued to de-velop their own styles, although they were less concerned to form new move-ments for the purpose of advancing aesthetic positions. The economic and po-litical situation, as the sufferings of the Depression were followed by the advances of fascism, put an end to the intoxicating vivacity of the years following the First World War. Many of the American expatriates returned home. French literary and artistic figures became less interested in purely artistic experiment than in political expression. Picasso, for example, became increasingly absorbed in the portrayal of suffering, which reached its height when the destruction of the small Spanish village of Guernica by German bombers stimulated him to a searing denunciation of the inhumanity of war. The poet Louis Aragon, like Picasso, saw Communism as the only way to combat fascism. Others, however, such as the novelist André Malraux, who had originally supported the Com-munist cause and even fought for the Communists in China, became disillu-sioned because of Soviet actions in Spain during the Civil War and the purges in Russia. Whatever the viewpoint adopted, it was virtually impossible for a French intellectual in the 1930s to avoid involvement in the decade's ideological struggles.

Literary London

The shattering experience of fighting in the trenches of the First World War marked many of the younger poets whose work appeared in England during the war or immediately after. Although in the early months of the fighting, poets, especially those who stayed at home, glorified battlefield sacrifices as necessary for the preservation of a romanticized England of country churches and waving fields, the violence and pathos of the war are poignantly presented in the work of Siegfried Sasson (1886–1967) and of Wilfrid Owen (1893–1918), and a powerful protest is made against the insane sacrifice of youth by politicians and generals.

Owen, who died one week before the end of the war, was perhaps the greatest of the War Poets. In him, pity and anger combined, as in his "Anthem for Doomed Youth."

> What passing-bells for those who die as cattle?
> Only the monstrous anger of the guns. . . .
> The shrill, demented choirs of wailing shells;
> And bugles calling for them from sad shires.[3]

In the aftermath of the war, the elegiac romanticism that had been the most popular approach to poetry in Britain throughout the nineteenth century, from Wordsworth on, seemed no longer suitable for expressing the sense of spiritual desolation that many felt was the principal legacy of the war. For them a revolution in the use of poetic language was needed. They had been taught before the war by Ezra Pound that imprecision and effusiveness were major faults in poetry. From the French Symbolist poets they had learned that language can consist of layers of meaning requiring both emotional and intellectual understanding from the reader. In T. S. Eliot (1888–1965), the American-born poet who settled permanently in London in 1914, the revolutionary forces in English poetry found a leader. Eliot's poem, *The Waste Land* (1922), was regarded as the manifesto of the new poetry and became a model influencing all innovative poets of the next decade. The waste land in Eliot's mind was the spiritual destruction left by the war; and to portray it he turned to anthropology, myth, oriental religion, and Christianity, each of which furnished him with symbols of the breakdown of civilization and the attempt to find salvation. The poem was extraordinarily difficult to understand, and required not only frequent rereading but annotation; yet it was immediately powerful, in such images as:

> April is the cruellest month, breeding
> Lilacs out of the dead land, mixing
> Memory and desire, stirring
> Dull roots with spring rain.[4]

In the 1930s, a younger school of poets, whose principal members were W. H. Auden (1907–1973), Cecil Day Lewis (1904–1972), and Stephen Spender

---

[3] From Wilfrid Owen, "Anthem for Doomed Youth," in *The Collected Poems of Wilfrid Owen* (New York: New Directions, 1964), p. 44. Copyright © 1963 by Chatto & Windus, Ltd. Reprinted by permission of New Directions and Chatto & Windus, Ltd.

[4] From "The Waste Land" in *Collected Poems 1909–1962* by T. S. Eliot, copyright © 1936 by Harcourt Brace Javanovich, Inc.; copyright © 1963, 1964 by T. S. Eliot. Reprinted by permission of Harcourt Brace Jovanovich, Inc., and Faber and Faber Ltd.

Virginia Woolf (1882–1941) *A member of the Bloomsburry Group, Woolf was photographed in the early 1930s. She was widely admired for such novels as* Mrs. Dalloway *and* The Waves. (The Bettmann Archive.)

(1909–   ) showed mastery of the techniques developed by Eliot, but saw not spiritual but actual devastation in the England of the Great Depression. For them, the themes to be explored were economic distress, urban decay, and class struggle.

Meanwhile, W. B. Yeats (1865–1939), an Irish poet who maintained close ties with both the London and Dublin literary worlds, was continuing the independent evolution of style that made him, in the eyes of many critics, the greatest poet in English of the first half of the twentieth century. Beginning with an exotic romanticism, Yeats had progressed through the use of symbols as in the French Symbolist school to the pared-down vocabulary recommended by Pound. He had, like Eliot, brought philosophy into his verse. Perhaps his greatest poems were *The Tower* and *The Winding Stair,* which contain his exploration of how one can find in timeless art a refuge from the decrepitude of age.

Although many of the prewar novelists of the Realistic school remained popular in London during the interwar years, the more innovative novelists were deeply influenced by the intellectual revolution of the early years of the century.

Virginia Woolf (1882–1941), in whose home in London the Bloomsbury Group frequently met, set out to use the novel to explore the consciousness of her characters rather than to tell a chronological story. She saw time not as a continuous flow but as a series of moments of experience that coexist in the mind, as Proust had demonstrated. She also saw that the mind has different levels of consciousness and subconsciousness that the novelist must present. In *Mrs. Dalloway,* she relates one day in the life of a well-to-do woman planning a party, but describes not so much the conviviality or even the logistics of giving a party as the mental responses of Mrs. Dalloway to a day that poses to her the problems of achieving communication with others, of loneliness, and eventually of death.

The influence of Freudian thought was most evident in the novels of D. H. Lawrence (1885–1930), in his belief in subconscious motivation and in his emphasis on the effect of modern society in denying human beings the value of their own sexuality. Lawrence's novels are all autobiographical, none more so than his exploration of his relations with his mother in *Sons and Lovers* and of his relations with his wife in *Aaron's Rod*. But whether writing about classical American literature, the Etruscans, or Aztec Mexico, he applies the same tests to the society he is describing that he does in his fiction. He asks whether the society is life-sustaining or as life-stunting as the industrial England where he grew up.

Weimar Berlin

In Germany, the period of the Weimar Republic was one of great cultural vitality, and Berlin in some ways rivaled Paris as a magnet for Europe's intellectuals. The University of Berlin, with Planck and Einstein in physics and Friedrich Meinecke in history, was one of the leading institutions of Europe. Freud's psychoanalytical theories were being taught to Europe's future psychologists at the Berlin Psychoanalytical Institute. Berlin was home to most of the major German publishing houses. It had three opera houses and two important orchestras as well as forty theaters. Moreover, the innovative artists and writers, who had been rejected by the official academies before the war, were now in charge. The artist Käthe Kollwitz, for example, who had been denied, by the Kaiser himself, a gold medal she had won for an illustration depicting the suffering of the weavers of Silesia, became, in 1919, the first woman elected to the Prussian Academy of Arts, and was its director of graphic arts from 1928 to 1933.

Expressionism remained the predominant artistic school. Wassily Kandinsky, after returning to the Soviet Union to direct its artistic programs in the early 1920s, came back to Dessau, Germany, to teach at the school of architecture and art known as the Bauhaus, which had been founded in 1919 by the architect Walter Gropius to form a bridge between industry and the artist. Kandinsky and his fellow teacher at the Bauhaus, the Swiss-born painter Paul Klee, continued the movement toward nonfigurative or abstract painting. Klee, for example, developed his paintings by playing with designs, making small changes in color, shade, or form, until the design suggested some subject to him. Only then did he proceed to create a final pattern for his painting which, as a result, would be in a direct sense the product of his subconscious mind. Other Expressionist painters, however, were less interested in abstraction than in commenting through their art on the social realities of postwar Germany. Max Beckman

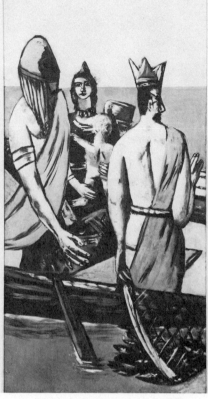

The Departure, by Max Beckman (1884–1950) *Beckman's savage triptych, painted in 1932–1933 as Hitler moved to take power in his native Germany, is a prescient glimpse of the horrors about to unfold. (Collection, The Museum of Modern Art, New York; given anonymously.)*

(1884–1950), who had served with the German Medical Corps during the war, sought to make his paintings into allegories of human self-destruction. He crowded his paintings with tormented figures, portrayed in harsh colors, based on scenes taken from the circus or the cabaret. George Grosz sketched a dream world in which the ugliness and brutality of the capitalist class becomes palpable, as grotesquely bloated bourgeois paw over painted women in subterranean night-clubs.

Social protest entered the theater most powerfully in the plays of Bertolt Brecht, who arrived in Berlin in 1925. A convinced Marxist, Bertolt Brecht did away with traditional staging and with conventional narrative. Working with Kurt Weill he turned the eighteenth-century English musical play, *The Beggar's Opera* by John Gay, into a savage satire on the capitalist class which he retitled *The Threepenny Opera*. In other works, such as *A Man's a Man*, he developed a new theatrical style, called "epic theater," in which the story is interrupted by argument or by superimposing related scenes to give the audience an intellectual understanding of the social themes being presented.

Comment by the leading novelists writing in German (though not necessarily in Germany) during this period in their society and indeed on the human conditions was equally acid. Weimar Germany became aware of the nightmarish world conjured up by the German-speaking Czech writer Franz Kafka only when his novels *The Trial* and *The Castle* were published after his death in 1924. Herman Hesse, who sought escape from the militarism of the Second Reich by moving to Switzerland, attacked the complacency of middle-class society and demanded a return to a rigorous individual morality in such penetrating psychological studies as his *Steppenwolf*. And Thomas Mann published in 1926 his most influential novel, *The Magic Mountain*, a brilliant narrative set in a tuberculosis hospital in the Alps where the patients, struggling daily with the imminence of suffering and death, engage in a series of debates that permit Mann to analyze not only all aspects of German class structure but the wide variety of human resilience in the face of calamity.

Finally, Weimar Germany, through the work of the Bauhaus and especially the teachings of Gropius himself, was the country most responsible for the development of the contemporary "Functional" or "International" style of architecture. Gropius emphasized that what was important for architecture was the function of a building, and that the new building materials, especially concrete, glass, and steel produced by modern industry, were ideally suited to providing the interior space required by such buildings as factories, hospitals, schools, or railroad stations, and indeed even to individual homes. Rather than hide the structure of the building with architectural motifs, such as Corinthian columns borrowed from earlier ages, Gropius held that a building in which the structure remained undisguised could be elegant in its own way. Although during the 1920s the style tended to consist almost entirely of cubes, in the 1930s it abandoned the excessively stark use of bare concrete façades and sought to humanize the appearance by creating a flow of space between the interior of the building and the outside and by creating a rhythm in the exterior by exposing the steel or concrete columns. After Hitler closed the Bauhaus in 1933, Gropius moved to Britain and then to the United States, where he found receptive students for his ideas.

New York, 1919–1939

During the years between the wars, New York City became the world's most dramatic example of the transformation brought about by modern technology. The great American companies vied with each other in the 1920s and 1930s to create the most impressive skyscraper, much as French bishops had competed in constructing their cathedrals in the thirteenth century. Following construction of the American Telephone and Telegraph building in 1924, the Chrysler Automobile Company building in 1929, and the McGraw Hill Publishing Company building in 1931, Rockefeller Center between 1931 and 1940 was constructed as a harmonious grouping of fourteen skyscrapers, a self-contained world such as the French Functionalist architect Le Corbusier had called for in his writings on urban planning. New York, wrote Le Corbusier, had become "the jewel in the crown of universal cities. . . . New York is a great diamond, hard and dry, sparkling, triumphant."[5]

For many of New York's writers in the 1920s and 1930s, the city was a refuge in which they could voice a protest against their society. Theodore Dreiser had criticized the city itself before 1914 in his indictments in such novels as *Sister Carrie*, and had continued his scathing attack after the war in *An American Tragedy*. The Midwestern businessman became the butt of Sinclair Lewis's satire in *Main Street* and *Babbit*, while John Dos Passos sprayed his shots more widely in the three volumes of *U.S.A.* Even F. Scott Fitzgerald, who at times came close to infatuation with the brittle brilliance of the wealthy he portrayed in *The Beautiful and the Damned* and *The Great Gatsby*, was conscious of the fragility of the society he portrayed and of the violence underlying its frivolities.

American art too had come of age, although there was no significant attempt to break away from the styles of painting dominant in Europe. Ben Shahn painted in both an abstract style and in a powerful figurative manner derived from his early experience as a lithographer. Among his most passionate works was a series of twenty-three paintings called *The Passion of Sacco and Vanzetti*, in which he bitterly attacked the execution of two immigrant Italians on charges of murder, which many Americans felt had been brought against them for being Anarchists rather than for being guilty of murder. Edward Hopper specialized in paintings of city streets, in which he was able to evoke a deep sense of loneliness or disquiet, in part by the coldness of the sunlight that falls on the buildings and often by the total absence of human figures. Many artists of this period were instructors in colleges and art schools, and thus were influential in shaping the artists of the 1940s and 1950s who were to make the United States a major center of innovation in post-World War II art. Thomas Hart Benton, for example, a mural painter specializing in presenting American themes, was the teacher of Jackson Pollock, who was one of the pioneers of the school of Abstract Expressionism.

American popular culture had already conquered the Western world, leading a war-weary generation into escapism and the pursuit of pleasure. The film industry of the interwar years was dominated by Hollywood, which drew talent from all over the world. Sound was added to the films in 1927 and technicolor in 1931. Audience response was so enthusiastic that palatial new theaters were built throughout the United States and Europe, and by 1938 the Hollywood studios were making more than 500 pictures a year. American jazz found an appreciative audience in Europe, and European visitors flocked to Harlem, in New York City, to hear such black artists as Count Basie and Duke Ellington. Broadway had, from the 1920s, challenged London as the home of musical comedy with such shows as the Ziegfeld Follies. Meanwhile, American play-

[5] Cited in Bayrd Still, ed., *Mirror for Gotham: New York as Seen by Contemporaries from Dutch Days to the Present* (New York: New York University Press, 1956), p. 335.

wrights wrote dramas of great subtlety and considerable psychological insight, especially in such plays as Eugene O'Neill's *Mourning Becomes Electra*. New York, with its speakeasies, its swing bands, its flaunting of wealth, and above all its frenetic pace of work and of pleasure seeking, had come to symbolize both the possibilities and the dangers of a society seemingly devoted to the creation and enjoyment of material wealth. A reaction was inevitable.

THE SEARCH FOR A NEW CERTAINTY

The sense of despair or at the very least of disorientation that permeated much of the culture of the interwar years led many to reaffirm the possibility of certainty in a world in which all traditional values and beliefs seemed to have been challenged.

Existentialism

A reaffirmation of the certainties of religion was the most traditional response, although the manner in which religion was conceived was often far from traditional. Beginning with a rejection of rationalism as it had influenced Western civilization since the Enlightenment of the eighteenth century, a number of theologians attempted to make Christianity adaptable to the new age. These writers found in the theories of the Danish theologian Sören Kierkegaard (1813–1855) an answer to how the individual could continue to believe in God when the rational or intellectual explanations fashionable in nineteenth-century theology have failed, and indeed when rationalist philosophers such as Immanuel Kant had shown logical flaws in the traditional proofs for the existence of God.

Kierkegaard was the forerunner of the twentieth-century philosophy called existentialism, and indeed was possibly the first to use the phrase "existence is prior to essence." He argued that the individual, after passing first through an aesthetic and then a moral phase, makes an intensely personal act of commitment to God, what later theologians called a "leap of faith." In this way the individual breaks away from the loss of self that is felt in absorption with the standards and activities of the "public," the impersonal society around one, and finds the value of individual loneliness in the relationship to God that is true "existence." These views became the starting point in the interwar years for the different forms of the philosophy of existentialism, a non-Christian form worked out primarily in Germany by Martin Heidegger and Karl Jaspers and a Christian existentialism worked out in a Catholic form in France by Jacques Maritain and in a Protestant form in Switzerland by Karl Barth.

One of the most influential statements of the views of non-Christian existentialism was Heidegger's *Being and Time* (1927), although Heidegger himself refused to be called an existentialist. Heidegger asked what it means to *be,* a problem he felt most people would rather not face. By asking what is the nature of our existence, he said, we deliberately take charge of that existence. We make choices that determine the character of our existence. Above all, when we consider death, which implies the end of our being, we understand better the nature of our existence, and we become determined to take control in forming the character of our life. In making these choices, he argued, we must understand the influence on us of time, or rather of the values and pressure developed over time within the society in which we live. But we must not accept these influences passively. Rather, by understanding them, we achieve the ability to regulate our own existence without regard to them.

In its Catholic form, Christian existentialism was expounded by the French theologian Jacques Maritain (1882–1973), who attempted to reconcile his reworking of the ideas of Saint Thomas Aquinas with those of the existentialist philosophers. In its Protestant form it was expounded by the Swiss Calvinist Karl Barth (1886–1968), who developed a "crisis theology" based on deep pessimism about the human condition and the individual's ability to improve without the intervention of God. Barth's certainty was that as life became blacker and social institutions disintegrated, a void would be created within the individual soul into which God could move. Reason, and indeed all the creations of society, were useless in throwing off the burden of original sin, but in the depth of the crisis the individual would reach out to a God who is known without being understood.

Christian existentialism was to be further developed after the Second World War, not only by Maritain and Barth themselves, but also by such influential writers as Paul Tillich. But when existentialism became the popular creed of Parisian intellectuals in the late 1940s, it was in the distinctly non-Christian form proclaimed by the philosopher Jean-Paul Sartre.

Logical Positivism

Some philosophers of the interwar years sought certainty by attempting to make the study of philosophy more scientific and by dismissing from the realm of philosophy all subjects that could not be scientifically and logically verified. The new approach was developed by a group of philosophers known as the Vienna Circle, led at the University of Vienna by Professor Moritz Schlick, who took their inspiration from the provocative *Tractatus Logico-Philosophicus* (1921) by Ludwig Wittgenstein. They began with the propositions that only data perceived by the senses can exist and that the data must be described in scientific statements of impeccably clear logic. Hence, their theories came to be called logical positivism or logical empiricism. They jettisoned such traditional aspects of philosophy as metaphysics, morality, and aesthetics as being unfit subjects for philosophy, since no scientific, objective knowledge of them was obtainable.

The field of philosophy within which they worked, the establishment of clear scientific method and concepts, became, almost by definition, the only one in which probability, if not absolute certainty, could be obtained.

The Appeal of Authoritarianism

A number of intellectuals in the interwar years sought certainty by converting to authoritarian political ideologies, whose very popularity was based on their determination to present themselves as possessors of the key, not only to social justice and economic prosperity, but also to intellectual reassurance. For a few, fascism seemed the solution. A number of Italy's leading artists and thinkers at first welcomed Mussolini, although most of them later regretted their enthusiasm. Large numbers of professors in the German universities welcomed Hitler. Outside Germany, isolated intellectuals, such as the American poet Ezra Pound, were also converts to the fascist creed.

But many more turned to the Soviet Union, idealizing the social experiment launched by Lenin and convincing themselves, on moral grounds, that they should support the great social experiment taking place there. Although a number of converts to Marxism, such as Pablo Picasso and Bertolt Brecht, remained faithful, most of those who were converted in the interwar years became disillusioned as a result of Stalin's repression of all freedoms and ruthless extermination of all political rivals. For example, Arthur Koestler, a Hungarian-born novelist who fled to Britain, became a Communist in 1931, but left the party during the Stalinist purge trials, and his evolution was typical of many who followed "the god that failed."

Nazi Culture

The authoritarian rulers, whether of the right or the left, in the interwar years regarded the idealistic intellectuals who followed them as easily dispensable aids in their propaganda. Their principal intellectual goal was to persuade the masses under their rule that their systems of government were intellectually unassailable; and they therefore brought all aspects of cultural and intellectual life under state control. Within days of taking power in Germany, Hitler had begun to crush the creative vitality that had distinguished the Weimar Republic. Regarding the Jews as responsible for most of the novelty in the art and literature of the 1920s, the Nazis imposed immediate controls over publishing, painting, and music. Grosz and Kandinsky went into exile, and Kollwitz lost her position in the Berlin Academy. The Bauhaus was closed in 1933, its Functionalist architectural style was banned, and Gropius and his followers left Germany. Even well-established novelists such as Thomas Mann felt compelled to leave as a protest against the new barbarism. But the Nazis were happy to be rid of these prophets of despair. The operas they favored, such as those of Wagner, extolled a mythical German past of national greatness. The Freudian writers, who used a stream-of-consciousness technique to churn up desires that the Nazis felt were better repressed, were supplanted by writers of straightforward narrative extolling the virtues of the new regime. Abstract art was forbidden. Hitler's personal interest was strongest in architecture, and he demanded that his architect, Albert Speer, produce plans that would transform Berlin into the world's finest city—avenues wider than those of Paris, bridges longer than those of San Francisco, a cathedral bigger than that in Rome.

Soviet Culture in the 1920s

Stalin was slower than Hitler in imposing his own standards on Soviet culture. The 1920s was a period of exciting experimentation in the Soviet Union, and writers and artists, finding few state restrictions on their style, flung themselves enthusiastically into extolling the revolution. The poet Vladimir Mayakovsky (1893–1930) attracted large crowds with his poetry readings, which included verses such as "I love the hugeness of our plans, the boldness of our mile-long strides," and even a splendid evocation of the Brooklyn Bridge, which begins:

> I clamber,
>   with pride,
>   on to Brooklyn Bridge.
> As a beauty-drunk artist
>   thrusts his eyes
> into a museum-madonna
>   love-gazing sharp-edged
> so I,
>   enveloped
>   in star-studded skies,
> look
>   at New York
>   through Brooklyn Bridge.[6]

Russian theater had been revitalized by the producer Vsevolod Meyerhold, who tried to democratize the theater by removing the curtain and changing the scenery in view of the audience. Individual actors were not permitted to dominate the play, which was written to give the appearance of a collective enterprise, usually involving mass demonstrations of large numbers of enthusiastic workers in which language was reduced to a minimum. Even more impressive spectacles were mounted by the film director Sergei Eisenstein, in such films as *Potemkin*, which relates the mutiny aboard the battleship Potemkin during the 1905 revolution, and especially in *October*, the brilliant recreation of the first

[6] Extracted from Vladimir Mayakovsky, "Brooklyn Bridge," translated and edited by Herbert Marshall. Durham, England: Dobson Books Ltd., 1965, p. 335. Reprinted by permission of the publisher.

days of the Bolshevik revolution of 1917. Russian novelists too were embroidering revolutionary themes in the style of the great nineteenth-century writers. Isaac Babel, a Jewish writer, drew on his own experiences in the Soviet army in his novel *Red Calvary*. Maxim Gorky, who had done much before the revolution to create sympathy and understanding for the sufferings of the Russian poor, in novels such as *Mother* and in his play *The Lower Depths*, was made head of the state publishing house, and used his influence with Lenin to allow a wide variety of writers to be published.

The heady atmosphere attracted many intellectuals from abroad. Le Corbusier designed a number of buildings for Moscow, including a steel-and-glass center for the cooperatives of the city. Soviet architects studied the work of the Bauhaus in Germany, and throughout the 1920s Soviet architecture stayed abreast of the most advanced buildings being erected by Gropius and his disciples.

Socialist Realism

About 1930, Stalin decided to put an end to the period of experimentation, which he considered to be influenced by the decadent bourgeois art of the capitalist West and to be making little contribution to the advance of a revolutionary consciousness inside Russia. Far from expounding the secure truths of the revolution, the intellectuals were breeding dissent. One by one over the next decade, the intellectual leaders of the 1920s were silenced. Mayakovsky committed suicide in 1930, after writing a last poem in which he declared in despair that he had been forced to plant "my foot on the throat of my song." The Central Committee, and on occasion Stalin himself, publicly denounced writers who failed to show sufficient enthusiasm for the Five-Year Plans, and many disappeared into the prisons and camps of the secret police during the purges. Isaac Babel was arrested in 1938, and died in one of the camps. Meyerhold was arrested, and his death never made public. Those who avoided arrest found their work suppressed. Even Eisenstein was forbidden to release part of his massive film trilogy, *Ivan the Terrible*.

The official style that Stalin required all intellectuals to follow was known as Socialist Realism. The title implied that in art or literature there must be realistic depiction not of the actual conditions of Soviet life, but of the way life would be as socialism was achieved. No form of experimentation was permitted, especially experiments inspired by the West. In architecture, the Bauhaus style was replaced by a kind of Russian Baroque favored by Stalin, highly decorated with pilasters, bas reliefs, and mosaics. Even the Moscow subway, constructed in the early 1930s, was in this luxuriant style, and was certainly the only subway in the world whose platforms were lighted by crystal candelabra. Stalin, however, proved eclectic in his architectural tastes, and permitted other period revivals, such as neo-Florentine or neo-Muscovite. Eventually, however, his architects satisfied his taste for the gigantic and the opulent by creating the "wedding cake" style, in which vast skyscrapers were embellished with traditional features

such as turrets and spires. Writers were told to dramatize the achievements of
the workers in the Five-Year Plans, and they responded with tedious novels
with titles like *The Big Assembly-Line*. Certainty, in short, had been achieved at
the expense of creativity.

COMING TO TERMS WITH DESTRUCTION

The Second World War brought a new sense of desolation that was not merely
material but was spiritual as well. There were many reasons for this feeling.
The destruction of the Second World War had been far more widely spread
than that of the First, carried by bombers to civilian targets far from the fighting
fronts. The war ended after the United States dropped two atomic bombs on
Japanese cities, actions that changed the character of war itself and opened the
possibility of annihilating civilization and even the human race itself. Human
beings had committed crimes against other human beings to a degree never
before seen in history, as the opening of the concentration camps showed. And
for Europeans, striving for bare sustenance amid the ruins of their civilization,
there was the added consciousness that they were no longer masters of the
postwar world. Their hold on their overseas empires was coming to an end,
and two great powers, the United States and the Soviet Union, dominated the
European continent.

War Experience as Literature

It was first necessary, as after the First World War, to come to terms with the
experience of the war itself; and many ex-soldiers were able to make the war a
living reality for those who had not experienced it personally. Novels such as
James Jones's *From Here to Eternity* and Norman Mailer's *The Naked and the Dead*
were popular in Europe as well as in the United States.

The suffering inflicted by the Nazis produced a powerful literature. In *The
Arms of Night*, the French Resistance fighter Vercors described how the Germans
had used the concentration camps not only to exterminate but to deprive the
inmates of their very sense of being human. Others saw the responsibility as
being more widely shared. The Soviet poet Yevgeny Yevtushenko, pondering
the murder of thousands of Jews by the Nazis on a hill near Kiev called Babiy
Yar, attacked the anti-Semites active in Russia itself, and declared that he, through
the common humanity that linked him with every Jew massacred, had suffered
with them:

> Today I am as old as the Jewish race.
> I seem to myself a Jew at this moment.
> I, wandering in Egypt.
> I, crucified. I perishing.
> Even today the mark of the nails . . .

I feel myself slowly going grey.
And I am one silent cry
over the many thousands of the buried;
am every old man killed here,
every child killed here.[7]

The Guilt Question

For Germans, there was the problem of the extent to which they as individuals were personally responsible for the inhumanity of the Nazi regime, a problem the philosopher Karl Jaspers posed in 1946 in the best-selling book, *The Guilt Question*. The answer of Jaspers, that the individual becomes dehumanized in a bureaucratic, mass society, seemed a little rarefied as an explanation of the Hitler regime. Bertolt Brecht, however, who returned to Communist-controlled East Berlin in 1948 to produce such plays as *Mother Courage*, written in 1941, reiterated the theme that the rottenness of bourgeois society is responsible for the loss of morality.

But it was only with the publication of Günter Grass's *The Tin Drum* in 1959 that the question of guilt was posed in down-to-earth terms. Grass looked at the corruption of society through the eyes of his hero, the dwarf Oskar, who has been committed to a mental asylum. "On days when an importunate feeling of guilt, which nothing can dispel, sits on the very pillows of my hospital bed," Oskar writes, "I tend, like everyone else, to make allowances for my ignorance—the ignorance which came into style in those years and which even today quite a few of our citizens wear like a jaunty and oh, so becoming little hat."[8] The same year, in *Billiards at Half-Past Nine*, Heinrich Böll brilliantly satirized the complacency of postwar Germany, showing how only a very few seemed capable of carrying into the prosperous times of German reconstruction a sense of their responsibility for the destruction itself. The exception is his hero, an introspective architect who, because of his knowledge of building construction, was given the task by the Nazis of commanding a demolition squad whose most important task was the destruction of a superb monastery built by his own father.

Writers in other European countries were prepared to shoulder much of the guilt for the crimes of the Second World War, and even for the very fact of the war, as their own failing as human beings. The French writer Albert Camus, in *The Plague*, described the isolation imposed on the town of Oran in Algeria when it was attacked by an outbreak of bubonic plague. After months of suffering, in which Camus is able to explore the reactions of individuals to a calamity for which they feel they have no responsibility, the plague finally recedes,

---

[7] Extracted from "Babiy Yar," in Yevgeny Yevtushenko, *Selected Poems*, translated by Robin Milner-Gulland and Peter Levi. London: Penguin Books, Ltd., 1962, pp. 82–83. Copyright © Robin Milner-Gulland and Peter Levi, 1962. Reprinted by permission of Penguin Books Ltd.
[8] Günter Grass, *The Tin Drum* (Greenwich, Conn.: Fawcett, 1962), p. 236.

and the survivors again move out into a world of freedom and sunshine. But for Camus the plague is a symbol for the curse of war. In a despairing ending to the book, he notes that the plague bacillus "never dies or disappears for good; that it can lie dormant for years and years in furniture and linen-chests; that it bides its time in bedrooms, cellars, trunks, and bookshelves; and that perhaps the day would come when, for the bane and the enlightenment of men, it would rouse up its rats again and send them forth in a happy city."[9] Camus's final message was not, however, of despair. He asserted the essential message of the postwar existentialists. A human being must stand witness against inhumanity, by commitment to purposeful action as an individual knowing one's own value and hence one's own dignity.

Postwar awareness of the horrors produced by the Nazi regime of Germany and the Communist regime of Russia led some writers to show that authoritarianism or the human desire for power over others leads to the corruption of all idealistic systems. The English novelist George Orwell, who had fought with the Republicans in the Spanish Civil War, in *Animal Farm,* in 1945, portrayed society as a farm in which men, the governors, are free to carry out unspeakable repression against the animals, their subjects, until the animals revolt; but once in power, the pigs who have led the revolt slowly begin again the round of repression. In 1948, Orwell wrote the even more horrifying *1984,* in which government mind control, through torture where necessary, has been brought

[9]Albert Camus, *The Plague,* translated by Stuart Gilbert (New York: Knopf, 1962), p. 278.

Simone de Beauvoir (1908–1986) and Jean-Paul Sartre (1908–1980) *Beauvoir and Sartre developed their views of existensialism in books of philosophy and showed its application to human conduct in their novels and plays.* (Ullstein Bilderdienst.)

to the point of perfection at which the citizens are not merely cowed but have been made to "love Big Brother," their oppressor.

Sartre's Existentialism

Many young Europeans in the immediate postwar years believed that they had found in Paris a new prophet for the age, Jean-Paul Sartre, with his clarion calls, such as "Invent yourself" and "Man is doomed to be free." Sartre had studied with the philosopher Martin Heidegger in the interwar years, and from him absorbed the central ideas of existentialism. Sartre's own principal philosophic contribution was his book *Being and Nothingness,* but he popularized his views in many novels and plays as well as by talking to those who sought him personally in the cafes of the Left Bank. Sartre taught that the world was absurd, without meaning, and that it was impossible for God to exist. Human beings naturally feel despair on realizing these facts. But hope springs again with the recognition that human beings exist and by their actions can give the universe— and their own lives—meaning and values. There is no guide to help one choose a course of action; but the final message of existentialism is basically optimistic. The ability to act gives back to the human being the ability to control one's own nature.

REVOLT RENEWED

New movements of revolt were provoked by the complacency that set in during the 1950s as a result of growing material prosperity and the apparent determination of Western governments to repeat the past mistake of fighting unwinnable and unjustifiable wars to hold on to ungovernable empires.

The Angry Young Men in Britain

In Britain, a new generation found that six years of socialist rule had done little to alter the privilege and power of a long-established upper class. The revolt of the "angry young men" was led by John Osborne in his play, *Look Back in Anger.* These writers, often of working-class origin, were determined to portray the grim life for which the working class had settled, in return for the hand-outs of the welfare state, in contrast to the self-righteous luxury of the well-to-do. Alan Sillitoe's *Saturday Night and Sunday Morning* mercilessly laid bare the empty pursuit of forgetfulness of a young worker in a weekend of drink and tame debauchery. The film *Room at the Top* taught the lesson that, no matter how well educated a man from the working class may be, he will find a place for himself at the top of the business world only by seducing the boss's daughter. The rage of most of these writers buried their sense of humor, but fortunately for comic writing, Kingsley Amis hilariously satirized in *Lucky Jim* the pursuit of success by a young man more accident-prone than angry.

A New Literature on the Continent

In France, the "new novel" (*nouveau roman*) or "antinovel" was invented by Alain Robbe-Grillet in the 1950s as a form of protest against the traditional novel with its standard narrative form and its choice of objects for symbolic purposes. The new style treated objects for their own sake; for their superficial meaning, rather than for any deeper one. The style was also successful when translated into film, as in *Last Year at Marienbad* produced in 1960, a daunting but deliberately mysterious evocation of an elegant aristocratic party at a mist-shrouded spa, for which Robbe-Grillet wrote the screenplay. The style of the new novel had much in common with the Theater of the Absurd in Paris in the 1950s and 1960s, of which the most popular plays were Eugène Ionesco's *The Bald Soprano* and *Rhinoceros* and Samuel Becket's *Waiting for Godot*. As Ionesco proclaimed it, this was to be a theater of the "absurd" because it was representing a life that had become devoid of purpose.

By the mid-1960s, the movements of revolt among students were developing political overtones, although it was unclear whether young people would support any of the established parties or ideologies. Marxism remained a vitally important influence in the West, but it was now a Marxism distanced by its exponents from the repressive Communism of the Soviet Union or from the conformist ideology of the Socialist and Communist parties of Western Europe.

One group of revisionist Marxists was the "Frankfurt school," a number of philosphers trained in sociology and psychology who had worked at Frankfurt in Germany in the early 1930s, moved to the United States to avoid Nazi persecution, and returned to Germany in 1950. These thinkers, who included Theodor Adorno and Max Horkheimer, had attempted to harmonize Marx with the findings of Freud and with the empirical methods of British and American philosophy. The writings of one of the original members of the school, Herbert Marcuse, rather unexpectedly were adopted by university students in the 1960s as a call to revolt. Marcuse, who had established his credentials as a far-left critic of the Soviet Union, went on to blast what he regarded as social, political, and sexual repression in America, and later extended his condemnation to all aspects of the consumer-oriented society.

A second influence on the student revolt was the liberation movements of the Third World. The Cuban revolutionary guerrilla, Che Guevara, became for a time a kind of cult hero, while the book *Wretched of the Earth*, by the West Indian Frantz Fanon, with its call for a black revolt against white domination, increased the indignation of the young against the injustices perpetrated by their own society.

Protest in the Soviet Union and Eastern Europe was dealt with harshly. Nevertheless, criticism of the Communist system was expressed in a number of works of high literary merit. In 1958, the poet Boris Pasternak had published abroad his remarkable semiautobiographical novel, *Doctor Zhivago*, but it was banned in Russia for its uncomplimentary picture of the Bolsheviks during the revolution as well as for its message of the heroism of individualism. However, in 1962, at a time when the Communist party leader Nikita Khruschev engaged in a campaign of "de-Stalinization," Alexander Solzhenitsyn was allowed to publish his exposé of life in Stalin's forced-labor camps, *One Day in the Life of Ivan Denisovich*. The "thaw," as the relaxation of censorship was called, soon ended. Solzhenitsyn was forced to circulate his later, even more scathing indictments of Soviet practices, the novels *Cancer Ward* and *The First Circle*, clandestinely in the Soviet Union. These works were published abroad. When he smuggled out to the West the manuscript of *The Gulag Archipelago*, his detailed reconstruction of Soviet political repression from Lenin on, he was arrested and sent abroad in 1973. Other writers were not so fortunate, many being sent to labor camps in Siberia, to prison, or to mental institutions.

Rights of Women and Minorities

The women's movement for greater rights, which became influential in the 1960s, was also stimulated by a number of significant works of fiction and nonfiction. Perhaps the original manifesto had been Simone de Beauvoir's *The Second Sex* (1949–1950), a profound dissection of the reasons for woman's inferior status. But with the publication in 1963 in the United States of Betty Friedan's *The Feminine Mystique*, a book that illuminated the pressures that society applies to women to force them to maintain a traditionally assigned role, the literature of protest became a call for action. In 1965, Tillie Olson, in *Silences*, explained the circumstances that prevent women (and others) from achieving their creative potential. In 1969, Kate Millet set out to demonstrate in *Sexual Politics* how works of literature can be analyzed to demonstrate the nature of male dominance, and concluded that patriarchy has been the normal relationship between men and women. Books such as Sue Kaufman's *Diary of a Mad Housewife* showed women taking for themselves a new role as a person independent of husband and family. Passing to Europe with the publication in Britain in 1970 of Germaine Greer's *The Female Eunuch*, the movement sparked demands for ease of divorce and the right to abortion as well as for more equitable access to positions of responsibility in government and business.

Demands for recognition of a distinctive black identity, as well as for equality, were voiced both in the United States and in Europe. In 1952, Ralph Ellison had shown American whites, in *Invisible Man*, that even in the presence of blacks they did not see them as people. The next year, James Baldwin's *Go Tell It on the Mountain* brought home the realities of growing up in a black community in the United States. Blacks from Africa and the West Indies educated in France developed both a poetry and a political theory of "négritude" (blackness). The leaders of the movement were the West Indian Léon Damas and Aimé Césaire, and the Senegalese Léopold Senghor, who later became president of the newly independent West African state of Senegal. In Europe too the reawakening nationalism of regional minorities such as the Basques and the Bretons stimulated a new literature, of which one fine example was the evocation of a Breton upbringing in Pierre-Jalsez Hélias, *The Horse of Pride*.

Autumn Rhythm, by Jackson Pollock (1912–1956) Pollock's "action paintings" achieved a sense of driving energy by his use of swirling lines of color, sometimes squeezed directly from a tube without the use of a brush. (The Metropolitan Museum of Art; George A. Hearn Fund, 1957.)

Architecture and Art: Innovation Triumphant

In no sphere was innovation so fully accepted after 1945 as in architecture and painting. (Composers continued to innovate, but their audience seemed to be growing smaller and smaller as they pursued not only the abandonment of the traditional tone scale but even the replacement of the traditional instruments with electronic instruments.) In painting, novelty had become the norm. In Paris, Picasso and Matisse were being treated as old masters and were showing that contemporary artists could become rich in their own time.

New York was, however, beginning to rival Paris as the fountainhead of Western painting. After the war, the predominant school was Abstract Expressionism, or "Action Painting," of which the most powerful exponent was Jackson Pollock (1912–1956). The aim of the school was to convey emotions and ideas without using any form of representation of real objects. Pollock would cover his canvases with swirling, energetic patterns of color as in *Autumn Rhythm*, often dripping color or applying it directly from the tube. Mark Rothko specialized in paintings consisting only of parallel bands and rectangles brilliantly varied in density and color.

Willem de Kooning, who had been one of the leaders of the Abstract Expressionist school, led the way back toward representational art in the 1950s with his savage series of representations called *Woman*, but returned later to abstract painting. Almost in reaction against the Abstract Expressionists, who were in their turn becoming wealthy as collectors learned to appreciate their style, a new group calling themselves "Pop Artists" decided to comment on the banality of everyday life by painting the most mundane objects around them, such as Coca-Cola bottles in the pictures of Andy Warhol or comic strips in the work of Roy Lichtenstein. George Segal brought the Pop Art movement into sculpture, by setting plaster casts of human beings in lifelike surroundings such as bedrooms or restaurant booths.

In architecture, innovation seemed primarily to be a continuation of the inventive use of glass, concrete, and steel pioneered in the United States by such architects as Frank Lloyd Wright and in Germany by the Bauhaus school. There was indeed continuity, because many of the innovators of the interwar years remained active. Wright, for example, who had always attempted to use natural forms in his buildings, turned to the shell of the nautilus as inspiration for the spiral ramp that dominates the interior of his Guggenheim Museum, built in 1956–1959 in New York City. In 1958, Mies van Der Rohe designed the Seagram Building, which many regard as the most perfect "curtain-wall" sky-scraper because the shimmering wall of bronze supports and amber glass creates a sense of space flowing through the building. Le Corbusier was invited to realize his plans for a "vertical city" in an apartment block complex outside Marseilles, and to create a whole new capital for Pakistan at Chandigarh. Per-haps the most inventive architect was the Italian Pier Luigi Nervi, who brought concrete construction to new heights. Nervi not only helped create some of the most elegant skyscrapers in Europe, such as the Pirelli building in Milan, he explored the potential of using reinforced concrete in vast domed ceilings for railroad stations or in shell domes for sports pavillions. At times, however, the architects failed to give a sense of humanity to their enormous office buildings and apartments, and by the 1970s a reaction against their "gigantism" had set in. Rather than tear down the narrow streets in the heart of Europe's older cities, an attempt was made to save them from the automobile, by turning them into the pedestrian malls and planting them with shrubs and flowers.

Thus, almost a century of experimentation that had begun at the end of the nineteenth century had made innovation acceptable as a permanent char-acter of intellectual and cultural creativity. Yet there were also clear signs that nostalgia for stability and tradition remained. Western civilization was once again faced with the task of synthesizing its traditional and its innovative ele-ments.

SUGGESTED READINGS

General Surveys

George L. Mosse emphasizes political philosophy in *The Culture of Western Europe: The Nineteenth and Twentieth Centuries. An Introduction* (1961). H. Stuart Hughes shows the late nineteenth-century foundations of European social thought in *Consciousness and Society: The Reorientation of European Social Thought, 1890–1930* (1960). Roland Stromberg struggles to make some sense of the short-lived intellectual and literary movements of the contemporary West in *After Everything: Western Intellectual History Since 1945* (1975).

The Interwar Years

The brilliant intellectual ferment of Paris and Berlin is brought alive in H. Stuart Hughes, *The Obstructed Path: French Social Thought in the Years of Desperation, 1930–1960* (1966), and Peter Gay, *Weimar Culture: The Outsider as Insider* (1968). The transition from Bauhaus to Nazi architecture can be followed in Barbara L. Lane, *Architecture and Politics in Germany, 1918–1945* (1968). Good specialized studies on painting include Hans Richter, *Dada: Art and Anti-Art* (1967), and Patric Waldberg, *Surrealism* (1965). American popular culture is amusingly described in Frederick Lewis Allen, *Only Yesterday* (1931). Le Corbusier's admiring comments on the New York skyscrapers appear in *When the Cathedrals Were White* (1947).

Scientific and Cultural Revolutions

The achievements of Albert Einstein are explained for the layman by Leopold Infeld, *Albert Einstein: His Work and Its Influence on Our World* (1950). The standard biography of Sigmund Freud is Ernest Jones, *The Life and Work of Sigmund Freud,* which is available in an abridged version by Lionel Trilling and Steven Marcus (1961). O. Mannoni, *Freud* (1971) is replete with quotations from Freud's writings. Stephen Kern's imaginative *The Culture of Time and Space, 1880–1918* (1983) shows how changing concepts of space and time affected not only science but art and even international relations. The persistence of symbolism in literature can be followed in Edmund Wilson, *Axel's Castle: A Study in the Imaginative Literature of 1870–1930* (1931) and in C. M. Bowra, *The Heritage of Symbolism* (1943). On the changes in art after 1900, see Herbert Read, *A Concise History of Modern Painting* (1968). For music, try Igor Stravinsky, *Autobiography* (1936).

The Search for a New Certainty

On existentialism, see Walter Kaufmann, ed., *Existentialism from Dostoevsky to Sartre* (1956), which includes helpful comments on a variety of readings. Morton White, ed., *The Age of Analysis* (1955) provides an even broader selection from the works of twentieth-century philosophers.

The standard work on Nazi intellectual life is George L. Mosse, *Nazi Culture* (1966). The excitement of Moscow in the 1920s is suggested in Robert C. Williams, *Artists in Revolution: Portraits of the Russian Avant-Garde, 1905–1925* (1978). Stalinist conformity is described in C. Vaughn James, *Soviet Socialist Realism: Origins and Theory* (1973).

Western Culture After the Second World War

Useful introductions to the postwar novel include Maurice Nadeau, *The French Novel Since the War* (1967); H. M. Waidson, *The Modern German Novel, 1945–1965* (1971); and F. R. Carl, *The Contemporary English Novel* (1963). On painting and sculpture, see the two fine books by Herbert Read, *A Concise History of Modern Painting* (1968), and *A Concise History of Modern Sculpture* (1964). The developments in existentialism, under the leadership of Sartre, are explained in Mary Warnock, *Existentialism* (1970). On the return to religion, see John Macquarrie, *Twentieth Century Religious Thought: The Frontiers of Philosophy and Theology 1900–1960* (1963).

To glimpse the many faces of revolt, see Frantz Fanon, *The Wretched of the Earth* (1966); Andrei Amalrik, *Will the Soviet Union Survive Until 1984?* (1970); Simone de Beauvoir, *The Second Sex* (1974); Malcolm X, *Autobiography* (1961); Piri Thomas, *Down These Mean Streets* (1971), on Spanish Harlem; and Carlos Casteneda, *The Teachings of Don Juan: A Yaqui Way of Knowledge* (1968).

21

The West in a New World Setting, 1945–Present

It seemed for a time at the war's end that the very extent of the destruction would bring home to the victorious powers the need to collaborate in the work of reconstruction. Losses in lives had been even greater than in the First World War. Perhaps 17 million troops died in combat and 35 to 40 million civilians perished from disease, starvation, military attack, and the Nazi extermination policy. Populations had been uprooted on a scale hitherto unknown. Eleven million prisoners of war and forced laborers had been moved into the Nazi empire. Between 6 and 9 million Germans had been driven out of the countries of Eastern Europe and forced penniless into occupied Germany. Total military expenditure in World War II amounted to more than $1 trillion, while total material costs of the war, including property destruction, may have been $3 trillion.

The physical destruction of the war was far more widely spread and more economically debilitating than that of the First World War. Large parts of European Russia had been laid waste both by Russian and German armies. Bombing attacks had reduced many of Europe's finest cities to rubble. Cities like Stalingrad, which had become battle grounds, had been annihilated block by block. As much as two-thirds of the railroad network was unusable. Canals and rivers were blocked by fallen bridges. Power lines were cut. Even where production had continued, efficiency was low because equipment was wearing out and workers were malnourished. In areas occupied by the Germans, the farms had been stripped of their livestock and machinery, and forests felled. Europe

Helsinki Security Conference, 1975 *The purpose of the conference, attended by 35 nations from Europe and North America, was to ease tension between the Communist and non-Communist blocs. (A. Nogues/Sygma.)*

in 1945 had sunk to its lowest level since the destruction of the Thirty Years War 300 years earlier.

Far from cooperating in the work of reconstruction, however, the former allies, whose collaboration had brought them victory, embarked upon a political and military confrontation that rapidly produced a situation in which they threatened not only each other but civilization itself with total destruction.

THE COLD WAR

The Goals of Russia

Stalin had hoped to obtain large-scale American aid for Russian reconstruction and was shocked when the wartime supplies were abruptly cut off by the American government. He had also hoped to receive from occupied Germany raw materials and industrial equipment, as had been agreed by Roosevelt and Churchill during the war. Delivery of German equipment from the U.S. zone of occupation in Germany was, however, cut off in 1946.

Revisionist historians of what has been called the "New Left" school have asserted that these actions by the American government were part of a pattern of anti-Communist actions in support of the goal of American world hegemony that forced Russia into a confrontation with the United States. Other writers,

585

Soviet acquisitions

Polish acquisitions

Bulgarian acquisitions

Yugoslav acquisitions

NORWAY

SWEDEN

FINLAND

North
Sea

Leningrad

ESTONIAN
S.S.R.

DENMARK

Baltic Sea

LATVIAN
S.S.R

LITHUANIAN
S.S.R.

SOVIET

UNION

NETH.

U.S.
ZONE

SOVIET
ZONE

EAST
PRUSSIA

BR. ZONE

Berlin

POLAND

BELG.

GERMANY

EASTERN
PRE-WAR
POLAND

LUX.

FR.
ZONE

CZECHOSLOVAKIA

FRANCE

U.S.
ZONE

FR.
ZONE

SOVIET
ZONE

Vienna

BESSARABIA

SWITZ.

FR.
ZONE

U.S.
ZONE

AUSTRIA

BR. ZONE

HUNGARY

N.
BUKOVINA

SUBCARPATHIAN
RUTHENIA

RUMANIA

YUGOSLAVIA

N.
DOBRUJA

ITALY

Adriatic Sea

BULGARIA

(TURK.)

ALBANIA

GREECE

TURKEY

300 mi.

DODECANESE IS. (GR.)

EUROPE IN 1950

586

however, have argued that the American actions in attempting to restrain Russia were a necessary reaction to the establishment by the Soviet Union of Communist governments throughout Eastern Europe. Wherever one places the blame for the opening of the conflict, by 1947 the Soviet Union and the Western powers were locked in an ideological confrontation that held the potential for bringing the world into an even more devastating conflict than the one from which it had barely emerged.

For Stalin, the first necessity was to rebuild the economy and military power of the Soviet Union, through completion of the Plan for National Reconstruction launched in 1946. Once again, as in 1929, Russia's heavy industry and armaments were to receive priority, and the shift of Soviet production to the Urals and Siberia was to continue. The Soviet people were to be disciplined to accept these new sacrifices by propaganda, often emphasizing the threat from the capitalist West, and by the action of the secret police, which may have sent 5 million people to labor camps in Siberia and the Arctic. This industrialization was to be aided by the integration of the economies of the East European countries with that of the Soviet Union, and initially by exploitation of the Soviet zone of occupation in Germany (now East Germany).

The second task was to complete the Communization of the countries of Eastern Europe. In Yugoslavia and Albania, where popular Communist leaders had carried out revolutions with wide public support, there seemed little need, or possibility, of tight Russian control. In most of the other East European countries, however, the Communists had been a small minority in the interwar years, and lacked the public backing given to the socialist and to the peasant or smallholder parties. It therefore became necessary to undermine or destroy these political rivals.

In Poland, a Communist-dominated government had been installed in Warsaw after its capture by the Red Army in 1945, and little attention had been paid to the pleas of the British and American governments that non-Communists should be given important government positions. By 1948, the non-Communist opposition had been broken, industry nationalized, and the great aristocratic estates taken over by the peasantry. Powerful Communist leaders closely allied with Moscow had taken control in Rumania and Bulgaria, and the opposition of the peasant parties was broken by the arrest of their leaders. For a time it appeared as though Hungary and Czechoslovakia would be able to maintain working coalitions of Communists and non-Communists, especially as both groups were collaborating on land reform. In 1947–1948, however, the Communists in Hungary broke the power of the smallholder party by arresting its leaders.

It was, however, the manner in which the coalition government in Czechoslovakia was overthrown in 1948 that galvanized the Western powers to form an anti-Communist military alliance. Czechoslovakia had been operating as a model of coexistence and cooperation of Communists and non-Communists. Its president, Eduard Beneš, was a confirmed democrat, its prime minister Klement

Gottwald a Communist, its foreign minister Jan Masaryk the son of the country's founder. In February 1948, most of the non-Communist ministers in the cabinet resigned in protest after the Communist minister of the interior replaced non-Communist police chiefs throughout Prague with Communists. The Communist party then organized huge demonstrations in order to pressure Beneš to agree to formation of a new, Communist-dominated government. Masaryk, who had remained foreign minister in the new government, was found a few days later in the courtyard below his office, with his spine broken. Beneš himself resigned in June, and his place was taken by Gottwald.

Formation of the Western Bloc

To the Western powers, and especially to the United States, events in Eastern Europe appeared to be a concerted attempt to use the tactic of Communization as an instrument for the extension of Russian hegemony; and by 1947 President Truman was determined to counter any further probing by the Soviet Union for weak spots around its periphery into which it could next expand. In March 1947, Truman announced that American financial and military aid would be given to Greece and Turkey, which were under Communist threat, and that the United States would "help free peoples to maintain their institutions and their national integrity against aggressive movements that seek to impose upon them totalitarian regimes." This Truman Doctrine was followed in June 1947 by Secretary of State George Marshall's offer of American aid to all countries in Europe for their economic reconstruction. Although the Soviet Union and the East European countries were specifically included in the invitation, it was accepted only by the non-Communist countries.

The Marshall Plan, which gave $13 billion in American aid to sixteen European countries in 1948–1952, established the first definitive break between a Western bloc and an Eastern bloc in Europe. Profiting from receipt of American food, raw materials, equipment, and technical assistance, and in the process becoming to some extent dependent on the United States, the countries of Western Europe experienced an economic boom that was to continue, without major interruption, until the 1970s. In only four years the West European gross national product rose 25 percent, and certain industries such as steel and chemicals showed even greater results. Nowhere was the contrast between the growing prosperity of Western Europe and the stagnation of the East European countries more evident than in Germany, where in 1949 the three Western zones had been united to form the Federal Republic (West Germany) and the Soviet zone had become the German Democratic Republic (East Germany).

The Communist coup in Czechoslovakia gave the West European countries a reason, or an excuse, to join an anti-Communist military alliance under American leadership. The Atlantic Pact, signed in Washington in April 1949 by the United States, Canada, and ten West European countries, set up a common military organization, known as the North Atlantic Treaty Organization

(NATO), for the purpose of repelling an attack against any one of its members. Thus, by 1949 a kind of stalemate had been reached in the Cold War in Europe. The spheres of influence of the two superpowers had been established on the continent. Western attempts to influence events in Eastern Europe had been held off, but Greece and Turkey had been declared outside the Soviet orbit, while prosperity had proved the most effective antidote to Communist advances within such West European countries as France and Italy.

The Arms Race

The stalemate reached in 1949 in Europe was believed by both blocs to depend on their possession of parity in military forces. The distrust between the two sides was so great, however, that even in periods of relaxation of tension between the two, each assumed, correctly, that the other was both building up its forces and conducting research into ever more destructive weapons. The result was a permanent arms race, which was intensified in times of tension when each bloc made determined efforts to gain an advantage over the other in military preparedness.

Both blocs continued to strengthen their military organizations. The North Atlantic Treaty Organization was broadened to include Greece and Turkey in 1952 and a rearmed West Germany in 1955. The withdrawal of France from the military operations of NATO in 1966 did not greatly weaken the alliance, since France remained within the planning structure and continued to coordinate its forces with those of NATO. The Soviet Union joined with the East European Communist powers in the formation of the Warsaw Treaty Organization in 1955, with a unified command in Moscow. While organized primarily as a direct counter to the presence of NATO forces in Europe, and especially to the rearmament of West Germany, the Warsaw Pact powers, as they are often called, were also prepared to take action against one of their own members whose internal policies deviated from what Moscow regarded as norms of Communist government behavior. (In 1968, four Warsaw pact countries invaded and occupied Czechoslovakia to put an end to a program of political liberalization undertaken by the government of Alexander Dubček.) The Warsaw Pact powers were believed to maintain a supremacy in conventional forces over those of NATO, and by 1980 to be maintaining over 150,000 more troops in Europe than NATO. As a result, NATO planners believed that the imbalance could be corrected only if NATO forces maintained a superiority in weapons.

Weapons research and deployment, particularly of nuclear armaments, was pressed, at enormous expense, by both blocs. In 1945, the United States was the only power to possess the atomic bomb. But in 1949 the Soviet Union exploded its first atomic bomb, followed in 1952 by Britain and in 1960 by France. The probability of world proliferation of atomic weapons became evident when China developed its own atomic bomb in 1964 and India its bomb in 1974. Meanwhile the United States and the Soviet Union were developing even more destructive atomic weapons. The United States exploded its first hydrogen bomb in 1952, and the Soviet Union followed only a year later. Moreover, a race was developing in the means for delivering these weapons against the other bloc. Bombers armed with atomic bombs were kept constantly in flight. Nuclear-powered submarines were developed to be able to launch an atomic attack, undetected, from any point of the world's seas. Land-launched delivery systems became ever more sophisticated. Intercontinental ballistic missiles were being constructed at such a pace that by 1984 the Soviet Union and the United States together possessed the capacity to launch 8000 nuclear warheads against each other. In other words, they were capable of exploding the equivalent of over 9000 megatons of TNT, that is, 9 billion tons, destroying the world's population many times over.

Realization that nuclear holocaust was a genuine possibility if the conflicting blocs ever employed these weapons finally brought the two blocs to open dis-armament discussions in the 1970s and 1980s for the purpose of slowing if not ending the arms race. Some gains were made, such as an agreement not to test nuclear weapons in the atmosphere. Slight progress was made in limiting the number of missile launchers. But so great was the level of mutual distrust that negotiations proved agonizingly slow.

A Period of Stalemate

In Europe after the death of Stalin in 1953, there was a recognition that neither bloc possessed the capacity to risk direct intervention in the internal affairs of the other. Even crises within the Eastern bloc such as the Soviet invasion of Hungary in 1956 and the Warsaw Pact occupation of Czechoslovakia in 1968 provoked little more than verbal condemnation in the West. Only one point of conflict in Europe threatened to revive the possibility of armed confrontation between the blocs—the isolated enclave of West Berlin, which in 1945 had been left under American, British, and French occupation. Throughout the 1950s, up to 230,000 East Germans a year crossed into West Berlin to find new lives there or in West Germany, draining East Germany of vitally needed skills and labor. On August 13, 1961, the East German government began constructing a wall cutting off West Berlin from East Berlin, which, within a few days, had almost entirely cut off the flight of refugees. The Western powers made no effort to destroy the wall, however, and, at the risk of appearing to the world as a prison state, East Germany had staunched the outflow of its lifeblood. Its success was crowned in the early 1970s when West German Chancellor Willy Brandt signed a treaty normalizing relations with East Germany, thus tacitly accepting the division of Germany, and treaties with the Soviet Union and Poland recognizing Germany's loss to Poland and the Soviet Union of the territories east of the Oder River that had been annexed by those countries in 1945.

Relations between the Western and Eastern blocs were so improved by 1975 that a Security Conference was held in Helsinki to establish amicable work-ing relations for the future. The thirty-five nations from Europe and North

America attending the conference recognized that European frontiers were to be inviolable, and promised easing of travel, migration, and cultural exchanges, and greater respect of human rights. Many observers considered that the treaties signed by West Germany and the agreements of the Security Conference were the equivalent of a peace treaty ending the Second World War.

A CHANGING WESTERN EUROPE

Decolonization in Asia and Africa

The opening of the Cold War brought home to West Europeans that the era when they dominated the world, politically and economically, was over. They would be compelled to adjust to new world realities. For many, the process of adjustment was most traumatic when they found themselves forced to relinquish control of their colonial empires. The ease with which decolonization was carried out by the colonial powers depended partly on the degree to which they were willing to collaborate with the peoples of their overseas possessions in granting independence; but decolonization was made infinitely more difficult in those areas, of which Indochina was the most significant, in which the struggle for independence became linked to the Cold War confrontation between the Communist and non-Communist blocs.

The Americans and British were prepared in 1945 to give independence to the majority of their colonies in Asia as rapidly as possible. The Philippines received its independence from the United States on July 4, 1946. In spite of growing violence between Muslims and Hindus, British forces were withdrawn precipitately from India in 1947, and the subcontinent was divided into a largely Muslim state of Pakistan and a mainly Hindu state of India. The unexpectedly rapid withdrawal of the British was followed by a bloodbath in which as many as a million people were killed, as Muslims left India and Hindus fled from Pakistan. Democratic rule took root in India under the leadership of Prime Minister Jawaharlal Nehru, from 1947 to 1964, but Pakistan turned almost at once to authoritarian rule under a series of generals. East Pakistan, separated from West Pakistan by more than a thousand miles of Indian territory, broke away to form the independent state of Bangladesh in 1971.

Britain withdrew from Ceylon in 1947 and from Burma in 1948, even though both countries faced severe problems integrating national minorities. In Malaya, the British first crushed Communist guerrillas operating in the jungle, before handing over power in 1957. Even though the predominantly Chinese island of Singapore seceded in 1965, the new country, which took the name of Malaysia in 1963 with the accession of the formerly British colonies of North Borneo and Sarawak, became one of the most prosperous in Southeast Asia. Britain, however, clung to its prosperous colony of Hong Kong, agreeing only in 1984 to return it to China in 1997.

By contrast with the British and Americans, the Dutch and French were determined not to be ousted from their colonies in Asia. The Dutch had sunk a quarter of their national capital in the islands of the Dutch East Indies, and a quarter of a million Dutch people had settled there. In 1945, however, the Indonesian Nationalist party, under Achmed Sukarno, declared the country independent. The Dutch fought back savagely for four years, managing to control the cities but suffering heavy losses from guerrilla attack in the countryside. When independence came in 1949, the government of the new state of Indonesia drove out most of the Dutch settlers and expropriated their properties.

The French were prepared to pay an even greater price than the Dutch had paid in Indonesia to retain control of their rich colonies in Indochina: Vietnam, Cambodia, and Laos. They faced a Communist-led independence movement headed by Ho Chi Minh and guerrilla forces organized by Vo Nguyen Giap.

The United States interpreted the French struggle to retain control of Indochina as part of the worldwide struggle to contain Communism. In spite of large-scale American aid, the Nationalist forces in China under Chiang Kai-shek had been defeated in 1949 by the Communists under Mao Tse-tung; and, at a time when the formation of NATO seemed to have halted Soviet expansionism in Europe, the Chinese, with Soviet backing, appeared to American policymakers to be ready to renew Communist expansion by probing for Western weakness in Asia. The United States therefore sent immediate military aid to the non-Communist government of South Korea when the Communist forces of North Korea invaded in June 1950, and fought, with token support from other non-Communist countries, for three years to force a stalemate peace in Korea in 1953.

At the same time, American financial support was given to the French in Indochina. Ho Chi Minh, however, used the techniques of "revolutionary war," including terrorism, propaganda, and guerrilla tactics, to bring the death toll of French soldiers to 100,000. In 1954, at an international conference in Geneva, the French agreed to give independence to all of Indochina, and to leave North Vietnam in the hands of the Communists. In the 1960s, the United States became the protector of the non-Communist state of South Vietnam, in spite of the incompetence and corruption of its leaders, and poured in money and troops to prevent a Communist takeover. When American troops were finally withdrawn in 1973 after negotiation of a face-saving cease-fire, the United States had lost more than 58,000 soldiers. In 1975, the forces of South Vietnam collapsed, and the country was reunited under Communist control. By then, Vietnamese military and civilian deaths were 1.5 million. The same year, Communist forces took over Cambodia and Laos as well.

In short, in Asia, where the colonial powers were prepared to grant independence amicably, the transition of power was relatively smooth, although vast internal problems plagued the newly independent countries. Where a colonial power was opposed to independence, as in the case of the Dutch, but was not faced by a significant Communist opposition, the transition was bloody but not prolonged. Where an independence struggle, as in Indochina, became part of the Cold War confrontation of Communist and non-Communist powers, the price of independence, both for the colonial power and its allies and for the people seeking independence, was devastatingly high.

Until the 1970s, the independence movement in Africa remained separate from the Cold War rivalries. The British were prepared to grant independence from the 1950s on to those colonies with few white settlers, but intended to resist black efforts to win control of those colonies, primarily in eastern Africa, where there were substantial numbers of whites.

The Gold Coast (Ghana) gained independence in 1957, followed by the huge state of Nigeria three years later, while in east Africa power passed fairly smoothly to the leaders of the independence movements in Tanzania, Zambia, and Malawi. In Kenya, however, where 50,000 white farmers owned the richest farmland from which Africans had been dispossessed, Africans fought a long guerrilla campaign in the 1950s to force out the British. The British finally withdrew in 1966, after order had been restored, handing control to the nationalist leader Jomo Kenyatta, who served as president of Kenya until his death in 1978. The white population of Southern Rhodesia, which numbered only 250,000 in contrast to a black population of 5 million, declared independence unilaterally from Britain in 1965. After fifteen years of civil war, both the whites and blacks of Rhodesia agreed to a compromise constitutional formula for independence, and in March 1980, a largely black government, under the former guerrilla leader Robert Mugabe, took over administration of the new country, renamed Zimbabwe.

In South Africa, which had gained its independence from Britain in 1910, a white population of only 4 million governed a mostly black population of 17 million, and appropriated for itself the major share of the country's wealth. *Apartheid* (separation of the races) was imposed increasingly from the late 1940s, and included creation of separate homelands for black Africans, controls over employment and movement within the country of blacks, and strict police supervision. Efforts to force the South African government to moderate its policies and to prepare for eventual majority rule by black South Africans were led by the newly independent states of southern Africa, and supported by many other countries both in black Africa and elsewhere.

The French, Belgians, and Portuguese were unwilling to give up their hold in Africa. Although the French gave independence to the Arab states of Tunisia and Morocco at the time they were extricating themselves from Indochina, their colony of Algeria, with a French population of 1 million, newly developed petroleum resources in the Sahara, and strategic importance for French security, had to fight for more than six years to gain its independence in 1962. In sub-Saharan Africa, however, President Charles de Gaulle permitted all French possessions to opt for independence in close association with France, and sixteen new states were created from the former French colonies.

The Belgians refused to consider independence for the Belgian Congo, and made no effort to prepare its inhabitants for self-government. In 1960, however, faced by a minor uprising, they suddenly withdrew all their administrators and troops. Civil war flared, and order had to be restored by the United Nations Organization. In 1965, power was seized by the army under General Sese Soko Mobutu, who became president.

Only with Portuguese withdrawal from its colonies of Angola and Mozambique in 1975 did Africa become a Cold War battleground. Mozambique was taken over without much difficulty by the Marxist Samora Machel, leader of the Mozambique Liberation Front. In Angola, however, three factions faced each other—one backed by the Soviet Union, one by Zaïre and China, and a third by the United States. Although the intervention of 21,000 Cuban troops brought the first faction to power, guerrilla opposition continued into the 1980s.

The process of decolonization in both Asia and Africa was, in most cases, carried out with tragic consequences. Destruction of lives and property in some of the poorest countries of the world was enormous. At independence, the average annual income per capita of the former African colonies was less than $100. Inadequate preparations were made for the handover of administrative responsibilities. Internal problems, especially of relations between antagonistic regional, tribal, or religious groups, remained strong. In the state of Chad, for example, northern Muslims had been linked with southern Christians and followers of traditional animistic religion. Civil war first broke out in 1965 and continued intermittently until the 1980s, with both France and Libya intervening on behalf of their own candidates for power. Bitter wars were fought by groups trying to secede from newly formed nations to form their own nation-states. The province of Biafra tried unsuccessfully to secede from Nigeria, the province of Katanga equally unsuccessfully from Zaïre. Boundaries, often the product of the colonial era and unrelated to ethnic or tribal groupings, were the cause of wars between the new nations. To complicate matters, the intrusion of Cold War rivalries had greatly increased the bloodshed of the wars of independence. Further, superpower rivalry made it more difficult for the new nations to establish policies independent of the blocs which had become their patrons. The manner in which decolonization was carried through must be held at least partly responsible for the fact that in 1986 there were more than 10 million refugees in the world, primarily in Africa and Asia.

The West European powers, which had feared calamitous consequences from the loss of empire, suffered almost no ill effects from decolonization. Although the thousands of settlers expelled from such countries as Indonesia and Algeria suffered the loss of their homes and part at least of their possessions, they were resettled in their home countries with generous government aid. Rather than lose economic contact with the former colonies, business companies in the West expanded their investments, often working through multinational corporations with greater ease than had been possible in the heyday of colonialism. The newly independent countries remained major markets for the exports of the West and important sources of the raw materials needed by the West. The former colonies also were often the source of inexpensive labor either in factories in their own countries or by migration to the former mother country. So great have these ties become that critics of this trend have described the process, both in the West's relations to its former colonies and to other developing countries of the Third World, as neo-colonialism.

Political and Social Change in Western Europe

For Western Europe, the period of détente between the Western and Communist blocs was marked by political stabilization and economic boom. Serious attempts had been made in the aftermath of the war to renovate the political structures of the nations of Western Europe. The Italians had replaced the Fascist organs of government with a democratic state, which very quickly came to be dominated by the Christian Democratic party. Although stubbornly refusing to collaborate with the large Italian Communist party until the 1970s, the Christian Democrats worked with most of the other parties to launch Italy on an "economic miracle" that for two decades gave it one of the highest growth rates in Europe. West Germany, permitted in 1949 by the Allied occupying powers to become self-governing, rapidly rebuilt its vast industrial base. Its booming economy enabled West Germany to absorb the refugees from East Germany without unemployment and with a stable currency.

France proved an exception in the pattern of successful political modernization. Although a new constitution establishing a Fourth Republic was approved in 1946, old political habits died hard. The Fourth Republic suffered from the same ills as the Third: too many political parties, constant changes of government, lack of coherent leadership. These weaknesses were exacerbated by France's colonial problems. Defeated in Vietnam in 1954, the French almost immediately became embroiled in the attempt to crush the independence movement in Algeria. In 1956, they attempted to overthrow Egypt's President Gamal Abdul Nasser, who was aiding the Algerian rebels, by joining with Britain and Israel in an attack on the Suez canal, which Nasser had nationalized. Under American and Soviet pressure, France and its allies were forced to withdraw ignominiously. By then, the French army had come to believe it was being betrayed by the civilian government, and in 1958 it seized control of Algeria and threatened to attack Paris itself. In despair, the politicians called in the one person acceptable to both them and the army, General Charles de Gaulle. De Gaulle, acting in 1958 as premier and then, in 1959–1969 as president of a new Fifth Republic, saw the impossibility of defeating the Algerians, and recognized that country's independence in 1962. He thereby finally gained the freedom to turn French efforts wholeheartedly to economic expansion, which he felt to be the necessary basis for a greater French role in world affairs.

In spite of ten years of steady economic progress, however, by 1968 several segments of French society had grown weary of the rigidity of Gaullist rule. Protest began with the university students, and spread rapidly to the workers. In May, students at a new campus on the edge of Paris began sit-ins to protest university rules and American policy in Vietnam. After the authorities closed that campus, the revolt broke out again at the Sorbonne in the center of the city, where the students seized the university buildings, and for several weeks ran a communal, revolutionary society there. Faced with a massive strike called by the unions to demand higher wages and better working conditions, the government was compelled to wait several weeks before finally clearing the protesters from the university. By then, the example of a society run by self-proclaimed anarchists had repelled the majority of the French people, and the temporary successes of the protest movement provoked a backlash of sympathy for the regime. De Gaulle himself, however, resigned the next year when the French turned down a referendum on decentralization that he had insisted they approve.

All the countries of Western Europe were determined to provide a more equitable and secure way of life for their citizens, by creating what came to be called a "welfare state." The pattern was set by the Labour government of Great Britain in 1945–1951. Many of Britain's basic industries, such as coal mining and steel, were nationalized. But what affected the average citizen's life most was the provision by the state of services "from the cradle to the grave." Payments were made by the state for old-age pensions, unemployment, maternity bene-fits, large families, and educational costs. In spite of great opposition from the medical profession, health care was nationalized. In return for a small, com-pulsory, weekly payment, everyone in Britain was to receive free medical and dental care. Although membership was voluntary, most British doctors joined the program; and in spite of many problems, the National Health Service be-came one of Britain's most important if much criticized institutions. Other re-forms included construction of public housing and the opening of higher edu-cation to everyone of ability, regardless of income or sex. Even though Conservative governments alternated in power with Labour governments after 1951, they accepted most of the basic institutions of the welfare state, and usually sought popularity by claiming to make them more efficient.

The continental countries varied in their methods of providing similar serv-ices. In Italy and France, government insurance programs were favored and worked through highly developed and costly social security systems. In the Scandinavian countries, where socialist parties had become powerful during the interwar years, more direct programs of state control were instituted. Social security payments accounted for as much as one-third of the Swedish national budget. In spite of the cost, the Scandinavian countries were exemplary in their control of factory conditions, working hours, paid vacations, and welfare benefits.

Welfare state programs were an important factor in demographic change. In some countries, the payment of family allowances was used as an incentive to promote population growth. In France, for example, state support for chil-dren began only with the birth of the second child, and increased for further children; and mothers were paid support to enable them to stay home with their children rather than to take paid employment. Other countries preferred to set up child-care centers to allow women to remain in the workforce. Improved health care for both mothers and infants greatly reduced the rate of infant mortality. In France, the infant mortality rate fell from 71 deaths per thousand in 1936 to 50 per thousand in 1950 to 10 per thousand in 1979.

The assurance that more children would survive increased the demand for access to the means of family planning and for the right to abortion, which became two of the central demands of many in the women's movement. In the North European countries and the United States, legal obstacles to the dissemination of birth control information and materials were struck down piecemeal, either by law or by court action. The Catholic countries followed more slowly. Contraception remained illegal in France until 1967. In both Protestant and Catholic countries, proponents and opponents of abortion clashed sharply. In 1973, the U.S. Supreme Court found that the right to an abortion was protected by the Constitution. It also determined that a woman could choose an abortion during the first three months of pregnancy without risk to the mother. Its action provoked an ongoing campaign by "right-to-life" groups to overturn this decision either by act of congress or by a Constitutional amendment. The British Parliament made abortion legal in 1967. The opposition of the Catholic Church was particularly effective in predominantly Catholic countries such as France and Italy; but even there the proponents of abortion finally triumphed. The French parliament sanctioned abortion in 1974. After the Italian parliament gave its sanction in 1978, opponents backed by the Catholic Church forced a nationwide referendum on the issue in 1981, but failed to overturn the law.

Women Demanding Right to Abortion, Rome, 1977 *The Italian parliament defeated a liberal abortion bill in 1977, but under popular pressure changed its stand the next year. (Ullstein Bilderdienst.)*

The family also began to change. The average age of marriage for women fell, partly because they wished to have their child or children while young, and to reenter the work force later. The majority of women in Western Europe had given up having children after the age of twenty-six. As a result the female workforce, which in 1900 had been largely single and young, had by the 1970s a majority of married women over the age of thirty-five. The size of the family was also shrinking. In France, where at the beginning of the century one woman in eight had six children or more, only one woman in a hundred had six by the 1970s. In 1978, the average number of children in a French family was 1.78, which implied that the population was not even reproducing itself.

Finally, the population was living longer. For women the phenomenon was even more marked than for men. A woman in the 1970s could expect to live between twenty-five and thirty years longer than a woman in the 1900s. But she could also expect to live up to eight years longer than a man, to about 77 compared with 69 for men. The number of widows in society was therefore growing as well. In France in 1978 there were 3 million widows compared with 670,000 widowers. In all Western societies, the presence of a large and growing elderly population poses both challenges and opportunities that have not yet been fully assessed or grappled with.

The Integration of Western Europe

Perhaps the greatest stimulus to Western Europe's progress was the decision to integrate the economy of the nation-states. Idealists at the end of the Second World War had called for the immediate end of the nation-state, which they felt had been responsible for the war, and for the creation of a united Europe. This revolutionary scheme was ignored by politicians jealous to retain their national power. But in 1950, under the guidance of the French economist Jean Monnet, six countries of Western Europe (France, West Germany, Italy, Belgium, the Netherlands, and Luxembourg) agreed to form the European Coal and Steel Community (ECSC). The coal and steel produced within the Community was to be traded freely, without imposition of customs duties; and capital and labor in the coal and steel industries were to be allowed to move from country to country without restriction. Perhaps even more important, the Community was to have a supranational governing body of nine members, a parliament, and a court of justice, as well as a committee of ministers representing the national states. In Monnet's view, the Community's constitution was to be the nucleus for a government of a United States of Europe.

The economic results of forming the ECSC were so good that it was decided to form a European Economic Community (EEC), or Common Market, which would cover all economic activity of its members, and would thus be a major step forward toward uniting Western Europe. The Common Market came into existence in 1958, with the same six members as the ECSC, and proved even more successful. Within ten years, all barriers to trade in industrial goods had been abolished within the Common Market, and complicated commodity markets had been created to permit agricultural goods to be traded freely within a system of EEC protection. Companies expanded rapidly to take advantage of the opening of a market of more than 200 million consumers, and production rose faster than at any other period in European history. Although President de Gaulle of France restrained the EEC administration's attempts to increase its independence of the member governments, the Common Market did develop habits of consultation for harmonizing foreign policies that promised well for the eventual achievement of some form of political unity in the future. Indeed, Western European countries that had at first refused to join the Common Market began to clamor for admittance. Britain, whose membership was blocked by de Gaulle, eventually was accepted in 1973, along with Ireland and Denmark. Greece was admitted in 1981. Spain and Portugal joined in 1986. Nevertheless, problems remained, not least uneven regional development and the high cost of protecting the agricultural producers from foreign competition.

The Tarnished Miracle: Western Europe After 1973

In November 1973, the Arab oil-producing countries placed a total embargo on oil sales to the United States and the Netherlands as punishment for their support of Israel in the Arab-Israeli Yom Kippur War, and then quadrupled oil prices. Although the embargo was soon lifted, oil prices continued to rise, reaching $32 a barrel in 1980 compared with less than $3 a barrel in 1972. The shock to the Western economies, although less damaging than to the poorer Third World countries, was great. In 1974 alone, the Western deficit in trade with the oil-producing countries was $60 billion. World trade slowed, and both inflation and unemployment remained dangerously high throughout the decade. In 1981, the average rate of inflation in Europe was 13 percent, and even countries like West Germany were facing an actual fall in real gross national product. Electorates became volatile, ousting established governments no matter whether conservative or liberal in philosophy. Only in 1985–1986, when conservation measures lowered demand in the West and competition developed among oil producers, causing oil prices to drop as low as $10 a barrel, did the West as a whole begin a faltering economic recovery.

Terrorism in the 1970s and 1980s

At a time when Western society was disillusioned by the collapse of its long economic boom, its sense of insecurity was dramatically increased by the escalation of terrorist attacks.

A large-scale terrorist movement began in the 1960s in reaction to a number of international problems. After the Israeli victories in the Six Day War of 1967, a number of Palestinians embarked upon terrorist tactics. One of the most dramatic was the seizure of a number of Israeli athletes during the Olympic Games of 1972 in Munich, Germany, who were all killed by the terrorists during a gun battle with the police. In Latin America, left-wing groups opposed to military regimes and to the dominance of restricted landed and industrial oligarchies turned to urban acts of terrorism, which included the kidnapping of prominent business people. The protest movement against American participation in the Vietnam war, which had enlisted much popular support in Western Europe, also gave birth to a small number of extremist groups prepared to use physical violence to achieve their goals. In West Germany, these extremists joined as the Baader-Meinhof group, which focused its attacks primarily against American military installations and personnel. In Italy, the Red Brigades turned their attacks after the end of the Vietnam war against Italian business and political leaders, carrying out as many as 1000 to 2000 terrorist bombings or shootings every year between 1977 and 1981. In 1978 they kidnapped the former Christian Democratic premier Aldo Moro, held him captive for two months, and then deposited his bullet-ridden body in the center of Rome.

The most favored targets for terrorists were airplanes, although buildings, trains, or even ships could also be seized. The original hijackings were carried out either by people trying to flee from the East European states or by individuals seeking to go to Cuba from the United States. But after 1970, when Palestinian terrorists seized, and later blew up, four airliners, the hijacking of planes and the seizure, and occasionally the murder, of their passengers became a frequently used method of applying pressure on governments to release prisoners. Occasionally, embassies were seized, embassy personnel held hostage, and barricades erected; or embassies were blown up by car bombs, as occurred at the American Embassy in Beirut, Lebanon, in 1983. Terrorists demanding independence from Indonesia for the Moluccan Islands, holding the Dutch partly responsible for the incorporation of the islands into Indonesia, even seized a train with their passengers as hostage in the Netherlands itself; and Palestinians took control of a cruise ship in the Mediterranean.

The causes for which terrorists acted were very numerous. A number of terrorist attacks, especially in Germany and Italy, were presented as efforts to disrupt the normal operation of capitalist society, as a step toward promoting its eventual collapse. Others were the work of "liberation fronts," seeking to take control of their homeland from what they regarded as an occupying power. Among these were the Palestinian groups; the Basque organization ETA in Spain; the Breton and Corsican fronts in France; and the Irish Republican Army, which was attempting to force the British government to agree to the union of Northern Ireland with the state of Eire. Religious differences often exacerbated or underlay acts that were primarily political in aim, or religious motives were cited as a justification for terrorist acts. Actions by terrorists against American forces in Lebanon, which included the car-bombing of a Marine barracks in Beirut, were presented as actions in a holy war, or *jihad*.

The number of deaths resulting from international terrorist actions between 1970 and 1980 was about 2000, a relatively small number in comparison with deaths by war or starvation during the same period; but their psychological impact and their disruption of the functioning of normal life was far out of proportion to the number of incidents that occurred.

EASTERN EUROPE AFTER STALIN

Russia from Malenkov to Khruschev

The death of Stalin in March 1953 brought to the Soviet Union and its East European satellites some relaxation from the pressure for political conformity and unremitting devotion to the goal of industrialization. In the Soviet Union, a group of leaders representing Communist party officials, industrial technocrats, the secret police, and the army formed a "collective leadership," with Georgi Malenkov (1902–   ) as their principal spokesman. Malenkov at once announced an increase in the production of consumer goods and foodstuffs, and the release of thousands who had been arrested in Stalin's last years. The power of the secret police was temporarily curbed with the arrest and execution of its leader, Lavrenti Beria, and greater respect for the constitutional rights of Soviet citizens was promised. Malenkov's power, which was based on the support of the industrial managers who ran the centralized Soviet economy from the ministries in Moscow, was very soon challenged by Nikita Khruschev (1894–1971) who had worked his way to prominence in the Communist party and in September 1953 became its First Secretary. Using the position to place his own supporters in prominent positions in the government and in the party hierarchy, Khruschev built a personal power base. In 1955, he forced Malenkov from his position as premier.

Khruschev dominated the Soviet government from 1955 to 1964, successfully foiling several attempts to oust him from power. He embarked upon ambitious attempts to make Soviet agriculture more productive. Millions of acres of undeveloped land in Soviet Asia was brought into cultivation. American farming methods and crops, especially corn, were introduced. Relations with the West were improved, with the signature of a peace treaty that gave Austria, which had been under occupation by Russia, the United States, Britain, and France, its independence.

Khruschev's most important shift in policy, however, was his denunciation of the "cult of personality" introduced by Stalin, and his attempt to "de-Stalinize" the Soviet Union by denouncing at the Twentieth Party Congress in 1956 the crimes committed by Stalin against Communist party members from the 1920s on. Stalin, Khruschev claimed, had created a despotism: "Possessing unlimited physical power, he indulged in great willfulness and choked a person morally and physically."

As Khruschev's own power increased, many of his rivals in the party leadership came to believe that he himself was indulging in a "cult of personality," which provoked a series of crises both within and outside the Soviet Union. His sudden shifts in industrial and agricultural policy weakened Soviet production. The policy of de-Stalinization was blamed for encouraging the East European states to demand greater freedom from Soviet direction. In 1964, while he was absent on vacation, his enemies, led by Leonid Brezhnev (1906–1982) removed him from his positions as premier and first party secretary, and sent him to retire to obscurity in his country villa.

The Brezhnev Era, 1964–1982

Brezhnev's first concern was to restore stability inside Russia after the uncertainty of Khruschev's whimsical changes of direction. He put an end to de-Stalinization, without, however, reviving the cult of Stalin. He restored centralized direction both of the party and of the economy. Dissent was harshly punished. Writers who refused to follow party directives were sent to labor camps or mental hospitals or, if internationally prominent like Alexander Solzhenitsyn, deported from the country. Although he revived the emphasis on heavy industry with the goal of overtaking the United States and continued the build-up of the military forces of the Soviet Union, he did permit a slow increase in the living standards of the Soviet people. The growth rate of the Soviet economy remained relatively slow, however, rarely exceeding 4 percent a year. Brezhnev's attempts to overcome the Soviet Union's lag behind the West by importing Western technology, with the aid of large loans from such countries as West Germany, made only slight progress in remedying the underlying Soviet economic problems of excessive bureaucratic controls, inefficient work habits, and agricultural backwardness.

Brezhnev was committed to achieving a relaxation of tension with the West. He welcomed West German efforts to normalize relations with the Soviet Union and the East European countries in the early 1970s. He was the principal advocate of the calling of the Helsinki Security Conference in 1975. He was concerned with the danger of an atomic war, and supported the negotiation of agreements to limit nuclear proliferation in the world and to limit the strategic arms possessed by the two superpowers. He was not, however, prepared to tolerate deviation from the Soviet-imposed pattern of Communism in Eastern Europe or any attempts to pull away from the Soviet alliance; and his conviction that the Soviet Union had superiority over the West in conventional forces and almost certainly had gained nuclear parity gave him the confidence to ignore Western protests at the Soviet invasion of Czechoslovakia in 1968 and the Soviet occupation of Afghanistan in 1979.

Russia After Brezhnev

On Brezhnev's death in November 1982, Yuri Andropov (1914–1984) who had been head of the Soviet secret police for a number of years, became secretary general of the Communist party and, shortly afterwards, president. During his

Leonid Brezhnev (1906–1982) *Brezhnev, the Communist party secretary, accompanied by Foreign Minister Andrei Gromyko, gave an impromptu press conference at Moscow airport in 1973, while waiting to greet the president of France.* (Henri Bureau-Sygma.)

eighteen months in office, he made attempts to enforce greater discipline on the industrial workers and even on the higher bureaucrats. Greater autonomy was promised to local managers, in an effort to stimulate production; and regional committees were given greater powers to improve marketing of food products. Andropov continued the sharp measures against dissidents within the Soviet Union, and took an uncompromising stand against the policies of the new United States president, Ronald Reagan (elected November 1980), who had embarked on a military build-up intended to balance that of the Soviet Union. When the United States continued to deploy intermediate-range missiles in Europe in reply to those already deployed by the Soviet Union, the Soviet negotiators broke off ongoing talks on strategic arms limitation, and it appeared that the era of détente was definitively over.

Andropov died in February 1984 after a long illness, and Konstantin Chernenko (1911–1985) an experienced party official, was appointed as his successor. At first Chernenko, who was seventy-two years old, seemed unwilling to change direction. The repression of Afghanistan was continued. The Soviet Union boycotted the Olympic Games in the United States, and compelled other Communist states to follow suit. More intermediate-range missiles were deployed in East Germany and Czechoslovakia. There was, however, a slight sign of thaw in the relations with the United States when it was agreed in 1985 to reopen talks on the limitation of strategic nuclear weapons.

During the last months before his death in March 1985, Chernenko also proved incapable of giving firm direction to Soviet policy; but with the appointment of 54-year-old Mikhail Gorbachev as general secretary of the Communist party, the Soviet Union once again received firm and confident leadership. Gorbachev had already impressed West European leaders on a visit to Britain in 1984 with his undogmatic approach and openness in negotiation. It was evident, however, in 1985 on his official visit to France and especially in November in his summit meeting with President Reagan that, in spite of his flexibility, he intended to maintain firmly the interests of the Soviet Union and of international Communism. Even though agreeing with Reagan to press on more rapidly with negotiations for the reduction of nuclear armaments, he ignored Western pleas for the withdrawal of Soviet troops from Afghanistan and for better respect for human rights within the Soviet Union. At home, he made clear that he intended to press on with the campaign for greater labor discipline and productivity that had been begun by Andropov. Nevertheless, the Western powers welcomed the restoration of a strong hand in the Soviet Union after the years of vacillation under Andropov and Chernenko.

Eastern Europe After Stalin

The East European countries reacted differently to the lightening of pressure from the Soviet Union after the death of Stalin, depending on the degree to which their leaders were convinced of the validity of Stalin's policies. The East German government, perhaps the most authoritarian in Eastern Europe, provoked massive riots in East Berlin and other cities in 1953 by raising work quotas at the very time that the Soviet Union was lowering them and making more consumer goods available; and peace was restored only after the intervention of Soviet occupation troops. Most of the other East European countries followed the Russian pattern, by releasing prisoners, modifying industrialization goals, and permitting slightly more freedom of expression.

Political ferment, however, soon got out of hand in Poland and Hungary, where students and workers became outspoken in their demands for further change. In 1956, factory workers rioted in Poznan, Poland, for higher wages, and up to a hundred were shot by the police. The violence, however, strengthened the hand of a liberal wing within the Communist party, led by Wladislaw Gomulka (1905–1982) who was chosen party secretary. Fearing that Gomulka was about to establish a distinctively Polish form of Communist state, similar to that of Marshal Tito in Yugoslavia, Khruschev for a time considered intervening militarily to overthrow him, but finally agreed to allow him time for moderate reforms. The same year in Hungary, however, the choice of Imre Nagy (1896–1958) as party leader, following an armed uprising against the Russians of workers and students, provoked a massive Soviet intervention. Nagy made the crucial error of threatening to pull Hungary out of the Warsaw Pact and of permitting the formation of non-Communist political parties. After ten heady days of freedom, the Hungarians were faced by the attack of hundreds of Soviet tanks, which were able to smash the resistance of the citizens of Budapest in a few days. Nagy was arrested and later executed. Janos Kádár, a more compliant Communist, was put in his place, and about 200,000 Hungarians took refuge in the West.

With the limits of deviance from the Soviet pattern of Communism thus clearly established, Eastern Europe embarked upon a fairly successful program of economic development for the next twelve years, although far from achieving the same progress as Western Europe. Rather surprisingly, the greatest successes were achieved in Hungary, where Kádár, after an initial period of repression, conciliated his opponents with an economic policy that rapidly raised the country's standard of living. Bulgaria, too, meticulously maintaining friendly relations with the Soviet Union, was able to build a sound industrial and agricultural base, while drawing on Western tourism for foreign currency. Rumania, which rejected the economic role of producer of oil and agricultural goods assigned to it by the East European Council for Mutual Economic Assistance (Comecon), embarked on a program of rapid industrialization funded by its oil revenues, while cultivating good relations with friendly Western countries such as France.

In Czechoslovakia and Poland, however, the Communist governments failed to achieve the improvement of living standards necessary to deflect the demands of their citizens for greater individual freedoms. In 1968, the liberal wing within the Czech Communist party was able to win the election of Alexander Dubček (1921–   ) as party secretary. Dubček immediately renounced the Soviet pattern of Communism. He decentralized industry, and encouraged production by giving bonuses for greater output. Freedom of internal trade was encouraged. Censorship of all forms of expression was virtually abolished, and open criticism of the Soviet Union was permitted. Like Nagy in 1956, he made the errors of permitting non-Communist political groups to operate and of implying that Czechoslovakia might become neutralist in the Cold War. Although Khruschev had been ousted from power in Russia in 1964, the new Soviet government of Leonid Brezhnev and Aleksei Kosygin could no more tolerate Dubček's heresy than Khruschev could allow Nagy's. In August 1968, Soviet tank columns, aided by forces from several other East European countries, invaded Czechoslovakia and halted the liberalization. Dubček was replaced in April 1969 by Gustav Husák, a more compliant Communist who hoped to gain for Czechoslovakia at least the economic privileges enjoyed by Kádár's Hungary. Brezhnev, however, intended to give warning that no further experiments in liberalization like Dubček's would be permitted; and in November 1968 he announced the so-called Brezhnev Doctrine, that attacks on "socialism" within any Communist country would invite intervention from all the other Communist states.

Poland appeared to be the country against which the doctrine was most likely to be evoked. Gomulka had betrayed the hopes of the liberal Communists

Soviet Tanks in Prague, Czechoslovakia, August 1968 *Unarmed students taunted the Soviet soldiers who invaded Czechoslovakia to end the liberalization begun by Party Secretary Alexander
Dubček. (Ullstein Bilderdienst.)*

who had supported him, by beginning a new policy of repression of freedom
of expression and by purging the Communist party. His industrial policy proved
disastrous, however, and in December 1970 workers rioted throughout Poland
for decent living standards. Gomulka resigned, and his successor Edward Gierek sought huge loans from the Western countries to push through a program
of industrial modernization. Poland, affected by the world recession, failed to
profit from the badly planned industrialization, and in 1980 workers again began
to riot both for better wages and for political reforms. Under the leadership of
Lech Walesa, a dockworker in Gdansk, strikers formed an independent trade
union movement called Solidarity, which succeeded in winning recognition
from the government. Gierek himself resigned, but the new leaders proved
unable to stem the demands of workers and farmers for a dismantling of the
powers of the Communist party. As in Czechoslovakia in 1968, Poles were
elated at their new freedom, even though aware of the danger of provoking
Soviet intervention. Such a move was forestalled by the Polish Communist party
secretary, General Wojcieck Jaruzelski, who imposed martial law in December
1981, and arrested hundreds of leaders of the trade union movement. Although
demonstrations broke out and an underground organization of trade unionists

survived, once again an attempt to liberalize an East European Communist regime from within had failed.

A NEW WORLD SETTING

In a challenging book entitled *Europe and the People Without History*, Eric R. Wolf has recently argued that "the world of humankind constitutes a manifold, a totality of interconnected processes," and that attempts to understand any one part of that world without reference to the other parts falsify reality. Our book, as we said in the introduction, although conceived as a study of only one of the great world civilizations, has kept Wolf's warning in mind. Wherever possible, we have attempted to show the connections that have existed between the West and the world in which its civilization was evolving, whether we were considering the influence of the Near East, the relations between Europe and America, the opening of the New World, or the rise and fall of Western imperialism. It is too easy to conclude a history of Western civilization by repeating the comforting pablum that the West has always faced and overcome challenges from without and will do so again. If, however, the West and the other civilizations that share this globe are to meet the challenges of the coming decades, they will need to collaborate in devising strategies and solutions of a totally new kind, because the challenges they face have no parallel in earlier times.

What distinguishes today's challenges from earlier ones is their magnitude. For the first time, they are global in scale. The "one world," which utopian thinkers have often seen as an ideal of human harmony, has become an ecological, a demographic, an economic, and a military reality; but it has not become a political reality. In short, while contemporary problems were becoming worldwide, the political machinery by which they must ultimately be met was becoming ever more fragmented.

The first challenge is ecological—the abuse and overuse of the world's resources. In the 1980s the urbanization of the world is well under way toward what the Greek city planner Constantinos Doxiadis has called Ecumenopolis, the formation of an uninterrupted urbanized band of settlement linking all the great metropolitan centers of the world. This urbanization is already presenting almost insuperable problems of organization for city governments charged with the health, safety, and employment of their citizens. The population of Mexico City, for example, rose from 3 million in 1950 to 17 million in 1984 and was predicted to rise to 26 million by the year 2000. In all cities faced with such rapid growth, the result is air and water pollution, epidemics of disease, massive unemployment, inadequate housing, and increasing crime.

City growth is not the only danger to the environmental conditions that support human life. Fertilizers and pesticides that are used to increase food supplies are dangerous to the land itself and to the consumers of the food grown with their use. The peaceful use of nuclear energy brings with it the danger of radiation. The burning of coal and petroleum products threatens not only the planet's air but the ozone layer that protects it from the sun's high-energy radiation.

Moreover, there is fear that the world's natural resources are being used up. The energy crisis of 1973–1974 brought home to the West's consumers that the world's oil reserves are becoming depleted and might well not last more than half a century more. Many other basic raw materials such as natural gas, copper, bauxite, zinc, and uranium are expected to grow scarce. Urbanization is absorbing large areas of productive farmland. Efforts to open new farmland, in such areas as the Amazon basin, are destroying the world's timber resources, as well as adversely affecting its climate.

Ecological, demographic, and economic challenges are directly related. The world faces a growing imbalance between its population, its arable land, and its food supply. Although the population of the industrialized countries of North America and Europe is expected to increase only slightly in the late twentieth century, the population of most of the rest of the world is likely to increase rapidly as birth rates remain high and medical advances ensure the survival of more children and longer life for the old. By the year 2000, the world's population is expected to reach more than 6 billion, compared with 4 billion in 1975. The situation in Africa in 1986 is an example of the dangers faced by large parts of the world's population. Population in Africa increased more than 3 percent each year from 1960, while food supplies increased only 2 percent a year. When drought struck in 1973, a million people died of starvation. In the 1980s, when prolonged drought combined with overgrazing caused enlargement of the desert land throughout the savanna region that runs across Africa immediately to the south of the Sahara, the situation became even more dangerous. Lacking reserves of food and already weakened by hunger, as many as 150 million people faced the possibility of starving to death unless massive outside aid was given. In Ethiopia alone, 2 million starving people were massed in camps awaiting the distribution of food.

The problem of the relationship between the industrialized countries of the North of the globe, whether Communist or non-Communist, with the underdeveloped countries of the South has become in some ways as significant as the political confrontation of East and West in the Cold War. Aid programs to the underdeveloped nations have proven to be of only temporary value. Only in rare cases have the economic growth rates of Third World countries exceeded population growth. Unless a massive transfer of resources from the North to the South, accompanied by well-designed programs of economic development, are implemented quickly, the probability is that between one-fifth and one-half of the world's population will be malnourished or actually starving by the end of the century.

Finally, there is the problem of peace. Preparation for war costs the world $500 billion or more each year. During the 1970s, when the world as a whole was ostensibly at peace, 6 million people were killed in war. The situation was exacerbated by the sale or gift of arms, often of the most sophisticated kind, by the great powers to those in the Third World. France, for example, the third largest exporter of arms after the United States and the Soviet Union, was selling almost $1 billion worth of arms each year during the 1970s. But, as we saw earlier in the chapter, the most immediate challenge is the possibility of a nuclear war between the Communist and non-Communist blocs, from which neither they nor the rest of the world's population would be likely to survive.

Perhaps from our study of our civilization we can draw a few simple lessons as we face these awesome challenges. The long struggle to safeguard and extend the rights of individual human beings should not be regarded as a Western monopoly but should be extended to all human beings in the world. Science and technology, which can be a danger to the human beings who have developed them, can also be instruments of human betterment if we exercise care in their management. The state is a mechanism that human beings must operate to benefit the human condition and not an organism for whose aggrandizement human beings exist. Finally, reason, which in the twentieth century has shown it can explain even the irrational, is humanity's most powerful tool in the great task the future imposes upon it.

SUGGESTED READINGS

General Surveys

Geoffrey Barraclough, *An Introduction to Contemporary History* (1975), is a subtle analysis of the principal trends in world history since the 1890s. More detailed narratives of contemporary European history include Wilfrid J. Knapp, *A History of War and Peace, 1939–1965* (1967); Walter Laqueur, *Europe Since Hitler: The Rebirth of Europe* (1982); and H. Stuart Hughes, *Contemporary Europe: A History* (5th ed., 1981).

The Origins of the Cold War

The American government is cast as villain in Gabriel Kolko, *The Politics of War* (1968). Stalin's motives are dissected in Adam Ulam, *Expansion and Coexistence: The History of Soviet Foreign Policy, 1917–1967* (1968), and William O. McCagg, *Stalin Embattled, 1943–1948* (1978). The Cold War is approached from a European viewpoint in André Fontaine, *A History of the Cold War* (1969). Roy Douglas, *From War to Cold War, 1942–48* (1981), thinks Churchill and Roosevelt succumbed to the charms of Stalin.

The Communist takeover of Eastern Europe is related to the internal problems of those states by Hugh Seton-Watson, *The East European Revolution* (1965), and to Soviet policy in Zbigniew Brzezinski, *The Soviet Bloc: Unity and Conflict* (1961). On Soviet intervention in Hungary in 1956, see Paul Zinner, *Revolution in Hungary* (1962); and in Czechoslovakia in 1968, see R. R. James, ed., *The Czechoslovak Crisis, 1968* (1968), and William Shawcross, *Dubček* (1970). On the failure of the Solidarity trade union movement in Poland, see Neil Ascherson's comprehensive, *The Polish August: The Self-Limiting Revolution* (1982).

Decolonization in Asia and Africa

Rupert Emerson, *From Empire to Nation: End of Colonialism in Asia and Africa* (1960), provides basic coverage of British decolonization. The quagmire of Vietnam is explained in Bernard Fall, *The Two Viet Nams* (1967), and American intervention is sharply criticized in David Halberstam, *The Best and the Brightest* (1972). On decolonization in Africa, see John Hatch, *A History of Postwar Africa* (1965).

The Two Europes

Jacques Freymond deals primarily with the integration movement in *Western Europe Since the War* (1964), M. M. Postan with the recovery from the wartime destruction in *An Economic History of Western Europe, 1945–1964* (1966). Good surveys of individual nations include John Ardagh, *The New France: A Society in Transition, 1945–1977* (1977), and his *France in the 1980s* (1982); Alfred Grosser, *Germany in Our Time* (1971); Norman Kogan, *A Political History of Postwar Italy* (1966; 1981); C. J. A. Bartlett, *A History of Postwar Britain* (1977); and Arthur Marwick, *British Society Since 1945* (1982). Harry G. Shaffer, *Women in the Two Germanies* (1981), compares the status of women under capitalism and Communism.

Eastern Europe since Stalin's death is comprehensively described by François Fejtö, *A History of the People's Democracies: Eastern Europe Since Stalin* (1971). The contrasts between the policies and manner of Khruschev and Brezhnev can be followed in Michel Tatu, *Power in the Kremlin: From Khruschev to Kosygin* (1969); and Robert Conquest, *Russia After Khruschev* (1965).

Ongoing Problems

The dangers of nuclear weapons are soberly laid out in Herbert York, *Race to Oblivion* (1970) and related to other world problems such as overpopulation in R. L. Heilbroner, *An Inquiry into the Human Prospect* (1974). The relations of the developed and underdeveloped parts of the world are wisely discussed in Barbara Ward, *The Rich Nations and the Poor Nations* (1962), and G. Borgstrom, *Hungry Planet* (1972). A few thinkers were still hopeful, however, such as Herman Kahn et al., *The Next Two Hundred Years* (1976).

Index